Praise for *Counseling the Culturally Diverse*

"This book is the one to read. It has invaluable information that is current, is extremely well written, and stands out from the other books in the field. The book touches the reader on multiple levels, bringing in personal stories, pushing one's thinking, and very clearly linking theory, history, policies, contemporary trends, and practice. Absolutely outstanding—don't miss it!"

—Fred Bemak, Ed.D.
Professor and Director of the Diversity Research and Action Center
Graduate School of Education
George Mason University

"Derald Sue and David Sue have achieved new heights with this most recent edition of their classic text, and they do not disappoint. Paralleling the evolving nature of multiculturalism itself, the book addresses the latest topics critical to the field, and generously expands the rest. The reader is given an opportunity to personally reflect, analyze, and apply material at every turn. Readers will find that this text more than lives up to its great expectations."

—Beth A. Durodoye, Ed.D.
Professor of Counseling
University of Texas at San Antonio

"With its most recent updates and revisions, Counseling the Culturally Diverse *remains as relevant today as its first edition. Sue and Sue have continued to maintain the integrity of the content and continue to expand and include progressing perspectives within the multicultural and social justice literature. Their inclusion of the most up-to-date topical areas in the field, with personal narratives and examples, makes this edition a "comprehensive guide" that provides critical foundational materials, with real-world examples and practical ideas for implementation in the counseling and psychotherapy contexts. I have no doubt this sixth edition will remain the most utilized book in classroom settings across the country."*

—Miguel E. Gallardo, Psy.D.
Associate Professor of Psychology
Graduate School of Education and Psychology
Pepperdine University

"Sue and Sue, through their text, have found a substantive way to encourage a meaningful dialogue about the role of culture and experience in the counseling process. Their treatment of the contextual uniqueness that clients bring to the counseling relationship will undoubtedly serve to help counseling students and practicing counselors alike to find their sense of self throughout their 'professional journey.'"

—Thomas J. Hernandez, Ed.D.
LMHC Associate Professor and Chair
Department of Counselor Education
The College at Brockport

SIXTH EDITION

COUNSELING THE CULTURALLY DIVERSE

Theory and Practice

Derald Wing Sue
David Sue

WILEY

JOHN WILEY & SONS, INC.

Library of Congress Cataloging-in-Publication Data:
Sue, Derald Wing.
  Counseling the culturally diverse: theory and practice/Derald Wing Sue, David Sue.—6th ed.
    p. cm.
  Includes bibliographical references and index.
  ISBN 978-1-118-02202-3 (cloth)
  ISBN 978-1-118-28383-7 (ebk)
  ISBN 978-1-118-28213-7 (ebk)
  ISBN 978-1-118-28513-8 (ebk)
  1. Cross-cultural counseling. I. Sue, David. II. Title.
  BF637.C6S85 2012
  158.3—dc23

                                        2011045565

Printed in the United States of America

10 9 8 7 6 5 4 3 2 1

Contents

v

Preface

Since its publication in 1981, *Counseling the Culturally Diverse: Theory and Practice (CCD)* has become a classic in the field, used in nearly 50% of graduate training programs in counseling, and now forms part of the multicultural knowledge base of licensing and certification exams. It continues to lead the field in the theory, research, and practice of multicultural counseling/therapy and upholds the highest standards of scholarship; it is the most frequently cited text in multicultural psychology and ethnic minority mental health. We believe that the success of *CCD* is related to its (a) integrated conceptual framework; (b) up-to-date coverage of research in the field; (c) ability to actively address clinical applications through translating research/concepts to practice; (d) use of numerous examples, vignettes, and case studies that add life and meaning to the material; (e) engaging writing style; and (f) passionate style of communication—hard hitting, intense, and challenging. Further, the chapters on specific populations continue to be hailed as among the best thumbnail sketches of how multicultural counseling relates to the various marginalized groups in our society. The sixth edition of *CCD* does not change the basic formula, which has made and continues to make it a success in the academic and clinical markets.

NEW CHAPTERS

The sixth edition has significant revisions, however, that reflect changes in the field and new frontiers of importance to the mental health professions. Four very important chapters have been added to Sections One and Two: In Section One, Chapter 3, *Multicultural Counseling Competence for Minority Group Counselors/Therapists*, and Chapter 9, *Multicultural Evidence-Based Practice*, break new ground in the multicultural field. With respect to the former, we discuss how cultural competence is not only important for majority group clinicians but also for people of color, women, and other minority group therapists. To illustrate this, we devote an entire chapter (Chapter 3) to discussing challenges related to interracial/interethnic counseling, minority counselor–majority client relationships, and the unique and common clinical situations and dilemmas likely to arise in such therapeutic encounters. This chapter makes it clear that multicultural counseling is composed of many dyadic combinations and not simply a majority-minority relationship.

In Chapter 9, we discuss how evidence-based practice (EBP) represents one of the visible aspects of the profession's use of research to determine the most effective forms of therapy for various disorders. Multicultural psychologists have cautioned, however, that most of the studies used to determine therapeutic effectiveness have been conducted on primarily White participants or clients and lack validity for clients of color and other marginalized groups. In response to this legitimate criticism, we review research on how EBP has begun to concentrate on specific populations, such as African Americans, Asian Americans, Latino/a Americans, and Native Americans. What types of treatments are most effective for which population, problem, and situation? We believe that an important subfield within MCT— multicultural evidence-based practice—will soon exert major influence on the profession.

In Section Two, Chapter 13, *Culturally Competent Assessment*, provides an overarching umbrella introduction to all the special population chapters. It provides guidelines of how to approach the use of the population-specific chapters from the perspective of open and flexible assessment to the avoidance of using the material in a rigid, stereotypical manner. It weaves together common threads that affect nearly all marginalized groups and balances them with group-specific issues. Chapter 25, *Poverty and Counseling*, is a very important addition to the special populations section. Our reviewers have constantly pointed out how important it was for mental health providers to understand the impact of poverty on their clients. We were very fortunate to have Dr. Laura Smith, an expert on poverty and social class, share her research and work with us on this chapter.

CHAPTER REVISIONS

Nearly all remaining chapters have undergone revisions; some have quite extensively updated references, introduce new research and concepts, and discuss future directions in counseling, therapy, and mental health. Chapter 1, *The Multicultural Journey to Cultural Competence: Personal Narratives*, continues to serve as an anchor to help students process the emotive nature of the material. Although the passionate nature of the text has proved strong in generating difficult dialogues on race, gender, sexual orientation, and other sociodemographic differences, it has also posed unique challenges to instructors. For some students, the strong passions and feelings aroused on these topics occasionally lead to defensiveness and require a skilled instructor to help students through the learning process. To aid instructors in processing the meaning of their emotional reactions, Chapter 1 presents three personal narratives by Drs. Mark Kiselica, Le Ondra Clark, and Derald Wing Sue of their racial/cultural awakening. Drs. Kiselica and Clark describe their reactions to reading *CCD* as students in their respective graduate programs, and Dr. Sue reflects upon how *CCD* came to be written.

Dr. Mark Kiselica, a White counseling psychologist, has written in several professional publications about how influential the book was for his personal awakening to multicultural issues as a graduate student at Pennsylvania State University. Dr. Kiselica, a well-respected scholar and researcher in counseling psychology, describes his initial reactions of anger and disgust with the contents of the book and his eventual understanding of his strong emotional reactions. On the other hand, Dr. Le Ondra Clark, an African American psychologist, contrasts her reaction to that of Dr. Kiselica. She describes how her experiences in a primarily White, Western European graduate program served to assail her racial/cultural identity. She describes how, being one of the few students of color in the counseling psychology program at the University of Wisconsin, Madison, the content and views expressed in the book served as a source of "cultural nutrients" that nourished her through her graduate training and validated her racial identity. The inclusion of two brief personal narratives, back to back in the same chapter, illustrates lessons related to topical areas of the text. It is hoped that students will be able to obtain insights into how *CCD* was developed from the senior author's perspective and also understand Kiselica's initial defensiveness and anger and Clark's feelings of liberation and validation to the contents of the book. Instructors will find these narratives helpful in discussing the personal reactions of their students to the material and allowing for an exploration of differences in worldviews exhibited by Drs. Kiselica and Clark.

Because social justice plays such an important role in the counseling profession, the contents from the social justice chapter (formerly Chapter 12) have been moved and integrated with Chapter 4, *The Politics of Counseling and Psychotherapy: Social Justice in Counseling*, and Chapter 5, *Systemic Oppression: Trust, Mistrust, Credibility, and Worldviews*, to give the issue front-and-center coverage. One of the most ground-breaking chapters in the fifth edition was our inclusion of microaggressions as an important topic in the mental health professions. Chapter 6, *Microaggressions in Counseling and Psychotherapy*, has been completely revised with the most updated research and scholarly works in the field. We are very appreciative of Dr. Christina M. Capodilupo's major contribution to this chapter. Rather than discussing racial microaggressions only, we broaden the concept to cover gender and sexual orientation microaggressions as well. Research and study on the manifestation, dynamics, and impact of microaggressions is one of the most exciting developments in the field of mental health.

Another major change in the practice dimension of multicultural counseling and therapy has been our reworking of two chapters considered core content of the fifth edition. We have chosen to combine a discussion of the generic characteristics of counseling/therapy as it applies to both individual counseling and family counseling in Chapter 7, *Barriers to Multicultural Counseling and Therapy: Individual and Family Perspectives*. Feedback from instructors suggested that the interplay of the generic characteristics of counseling were equally applicable to group definitions of individual and family functioning and that they were more appropriately combined. The two chapters on culturally appropriate intervention strategies and non-Western and indigenous methods of healing have been updated and revised. Chapter 10 has new examples of Native American healing rituals and a discussion of the role religion may play in the healing process. Chapters 11 and 12 on racial/cultural identity development for persons of color and White Americans have also been updated and include a focus on identity development and dyadic combinations in therapy.

We have maintained our two-part division of the book with 12 separate chapters in Section One, *The Multiple Dimensions of Multicultural Counseling and*

Therapy, and 13 specific population-related chapters in Section Two, *Multicultural Counseling and Specific Populations.* As mentioned earlier, new to this section are Chapters 13 and 25. Each population-specific chapter has been thoroughly updated using common topical headings that will allow for better cross-comparisons. We are very appreciative of Dr. Diane M. Sue's contributions to the special population chapters.

TEACHING AND LEARNING AIDS

For instructors using the text, we have included a new feature in each of the chapters in Section One. Each chapter opens with broad ***Chapter Focus Questions*** followed by more specific, and oftentimes controversial, ***Reflection and Discussion Questions*** interspersed throughout. In many respects, the Chapter Focus Questions serve as opening "course objectives" for the entire chapter, but these questions not only preview the content to be covered but also allow instructors and trainers to use them as discussion questions throughout the course or workshop. The specific Reflection and Discussion Questions allow for more concentrated and detailed discussion by students on identifiable topical areas. The questions not only were developed from the content of each chapter but also have been tested in our classes and workshops for their educational value. In many cases, we have divided students or participants into small discussion groups and used these questions to stimulate further exploration and learning. These questions have been found to effectively engage students with the content of the material, allow them to share their own perspectives, and allow them to point out alternative ways of viewing the world. As in the previous edition, we have retained the **"Implications for Clinical Practice"** sections in each major chapter. Instructors continue to comment on their helpfulness to students.

New auxiliary materials have also been developed to aid in teaching the concepts for students. We are grateful to Drs. Gina Torino and Christina Capodilupo for their work in developing materials (overheads, tests, resources, learning activities, role-plays, etc.) that correlate with specific chapters of *CCD.* Professors will find the *Instructor's Manual* a valuable tool in teaching the concepts of multicultural counseling and therapy.

To further aid instructors using the text, a series of videotapes or DVDs in lecture format sponsored by Microtraining, an imprint of Alexander Street Press, are available. Each tape/DVD was specifically developed to cover the content of specific chapters and/or to illustrate a topical area of the text. They can be used as stand-alone lectures on multicultural counseling for classes on counseling and therapy, minority mental health issues, or broader multicultural/diversity topics. Such use allows instructors to assign specific chapters of the text and show the tapes associated with the content. We are hopeful that such an approach will allow instructors greater freedom in developing their own class activities (see the *Instructor's Manual*) to supplement both chapter readings and taped lectures. Approximately a dozen DVDs can be used throughout the duration of the course. To purchase the DVDs, please visit Microtraining's website at www.emicrotraining.com.

APPRECIATION

There is an African American proverb that states, "We stand on the head and shoulders of many who have gone on before us." We would like to acknowledge all the dedicated multicultural pioneers in the field who have journeyed with us along the path of multiculturalism before it became fashionable. They are too numerous to name, but their knowledge and wisdom have guided the production of *CCD*. Certainly this book would not have been possible without their wisdom, commitment, and sacrifice. We thank them for their inspiration, courage, and dedication, and hope that they will look down on us and be pleased with our work. Special thanks go to Rachel Livsey, our editor, who supported the revision efforts and constantly encouraged the many new directions exemplified in the sixth edition. We also wish to thank the staff of John Wiley & Sons, especially Sweta Gupta, for the enormous time and effort placed in obtaining, evaluating, and providing us with the necessary data and feedback to produce this edition of *CCD*. Their help was no small undertaking, and we feel fortunate to have Wiley as our publisher.

We would also like to extend our gratitude to those who reviewed the fifth edition and the proposal for the sixth edition: Candia Elliott, Portland Community College; Leila A. Vaughn, EdD, NCC, formerly at Troy University; Alfred Bryant, Jr., PhD, University of North Carolina at Pembroke; Thomas J. Hernández, EdD, LMHC, The College at Brockport; Kelley Haynes, PsyD, Argosy University; Isabel S. Perez-Yanez, MPH, CHES, CATC, Principal at Isabel and Training Associates; Peter J. McKimmin, PhD, CPRP, Alliant International University; Beth A. Durodoye, EdD, NCC, The University of Texas at San Antonio; Leah M. Rouse Arndt, PhD, University of Wisconsin–Milwaukee.

Working on this sixth edition continues to be a labor of love. It would not have been possible, however, without the love and support of our families, who provided the patience and nourishment that sustained us throughout our work on the text. Derald Wing Sue wishes to express his love for his wife, Paulina, his son, Derald Paul, and his daughter, Marissa Catherine. David Sue wishes to express his love and appreciation to his wife and his children.

We hope that *Counseling the Culturally Diverse: Theory and Practice, Sixth Edition*, will stand on "the truth" and continue to be the standard bearer of multicultural counseling and therapy texts in the field.

Derald Wing Sue
David Sue

About the Authors

Derald Wing Sue is Professor of Psychology and Education in the Department of Counseling and Clinical Psychology at Teachers College, Columbia University. He served as president of the Society for the Psychological Study of Ethnic Minority Issues, the Society of Counseling Psychology, and the Asian American Psychological Association. Dr. Sue is an Associate Editor of *American Psychologist* and continues to be a consulting editor for numerous publications. He is author of over 150 publications, including 15 books, and is well known for his work on racism/antiracism, cultural competence, multicultural counseling and therapy, and social justice advocacy. Two of his books, *Counseling the Culturally Diverse: Theory and Practice* and *Overcoming our Racism: The Journey to Liberation* (John Wiley & Sons) are considered classics in the field. Dr. Sue's most recent research on racial, gender, and sexual orientation microaggressions has provided a major breakthrough in understanding how everyday slights, insults and invalidations toward marginalized groups create psychological harm to their mental and  physical health and create disparities for them in education, employment, and health care. His most recent book *Microaggressions in Everyday Life: Race, Gender, and Sexual Orientation* (John Wiley & Sons) won the 2010 National Diversity and Inclusion Book Prize from UnityFirst.com. A national survey has identified Derald Wing Sue as "the most influential multicultural scholar in the United States," and his works are among the most frequently cited.

David Sue is Professor Emeritus of Psychology at Western Washington University where he has served as the director of both the Psychology Counseling Clinic and the Mental Health Counseling Program. He is also an associate of the Center for Cross-Cultural Research at Western Washington University. He and his wife, Diane M. Sue, have co-authored the books *Foundations of Counseling and Psychotherapy: Evidence-Based Practices for a Diverse Society*, *Understanding Abnormal Psychology* (10th edition), and *Essentials of Abnormal Psychology*. He is co-author of *Counseling the Culturally Diverse: Theory and Practice*. He received his Ph.D. in Clinical Psychology from Washington State University. His writing and research interests revolve around multicultural issues in individual and group counseling and the integration of multicultural therapy with evidence-based practice. He enjoys hiking, snowshoeing, traveling, and spending time with his family.

The Multiple Dimensions of Multicultural Counseling and Therapy

Becoming culturally competent in working with diverse populations is a complex interaction of many dimensions that involve broad theoretical, conceptual, research, and practice issues. This section is divided into four parts (each part contains a number of chapters) that describe, explain, and analyze necessary conditions that mental health practitioners must address on issues related to multicultural counseling/therapy, cultural competence, and sociopolitical influences that cut across specific populations.

- Part I: *The Affective and Conceptual Dimensions of Multicultural Counseling and Therapy* makes clear that the journey to cultural competence requires an emotional awakening related to one's knowledge, beliefs, attitudes, and behaviors related to race, culture, ethnicity, gender, and other diverse groups. To become culturally competent means developing a broad conceptual framework in viewing diversity and multiculturalism. It also means an understanding that multicultural counseling competence applies equally to majority and minority trainees and to helping professionals.

- Part II: *The Political Dimensions of Mental Health Practice* discusses (a) the need to acknowledge the political bases of western European approaches, (b) the need to recognize that counseling and psychotherapy may represent a microcosm of race relations, gender relations, and other majority-minority relations in our larger society, and (c) how modern forms of bias (microaggressions) may affect both the psychological health of socially marginalized groups in our and their standard of living.

- Part III: *The Practice Dimensions of Multicultural Counseling/Therapy* integrates multicultural premises developed from the first two parts into the domain of clinical work. It reviews, analyzes, and points to best practices in working with diverse populations at the individual, familial, group, institutional, and societal levels. The theme of social justice counseling is carried over from Part II but is uniquely balanced with two major new developments in the field: multicultural evidence-based practice and the contributions of non-Western indigenous methods of healing.

- Part IV: *Racial/Cultural Identity Development in Multicultural Counseling and Therapy* has always been a challenging journey for both persons of color and White people. The most recent and up-to-date findings of racial identity development are contained in two chapters. Who clinicians and clients are as racial/cultural beings and its impact on the dyadic combinations in therapy can either enhance or negate the therapeutic outcome. Questions such as "Who are you as a racial/cultural being?," "What does it mean to be a person of color?," and "What does it mean to be White?" must be adequately addressed in the journey to cultural competence.

PART I

The Affective and Conceptual Dimensions of Multicultural Counseling/Therapy

The Multicultural Journey to Cultural Competence: Personal Narratives

CHAPTER FOCUS QUESTIONS

1. In what ways do our personal reactions to topics of race, gender, sexual orientation, and oppression have to do with counseling diverse clients?
2. Why do many majority group members react so differently from marginalized group members (people of color, women, and lesbian/gay/bisexual/transgender (LGBT) populations) when issues of racism, sexism, or heterosexism are discussed?
3. Who are you as a racial/cultural being? How often have you thought about yourself as a man/woman, White individual/person of color, or straight/gay?
4. How well can you understand the worldviews of majority and/or socially devalued group members in this society? Why are the perspectives so different from one another?
5. What implications for multicultural counseling do your worldviews have for your ability to understand, empathize, and work effectively with diverse clients?
6. Using racial identity as an example, can you construct your own personal/historical narrative as to when you became aware of race, how it has developed, and where it now fits into your life?
7. Why are these questions important for your development as a culturally competent mental health professional?

Reading *Counseling the Culturally Diverse: Theory and Practice* (*CCD*) is very likely to elicit strong emotions among readers. Not only may the content of the book challenge your racial, gender, and sexual orientation realities, but its passionate, direct, and hard-hitting nature is likely to arouse deep feelings of guilt, defensiveness, anger, sadness, hopelessness, and anxiety in some of you. Some readers, however, will find solace in the book; they will experience a sense of validation, comfort, and even feelings of liberation as they read the text. In most cases, these individuals will come from socially devalued groups in our society. What accounts for these two very different reactions? For practicing professionals and trainees in the helping professions, understanding the differing worldviews of our culturally diverse clients is tantamount to effective multicultural counseling. But understanding our own reactions to issues of diversity, multiculturalism, oppression, race, gender, and sexual orientation is equally important to our development as counselors/therapists (Todd & Abrams, 2011). The adage "counselor or therapist, know thyself" is the basic building block to cultural competence in the helping professions.

Becoming culturally competent in mental health practice demands that nested or embedded emotions associated with race, culture, gender, and other sociodemographic differences be openly experienced and discussed. It is these intense feelings that often block our ability to hear the voices of those most oppressed and disempowered (D. W. Sue, 2011). How we, as helping professionals, deal with these strong feelings can either enhance or negate a deeper understanding of ourselves as racial/cultural beings and our understanding of the worldviews of culturally diverse clients. Using racism as an example, Sara Winter (1977, p. 24), a White female psychologist, powerfully enumerates the reactions that many Whites experience when topics of race or racism are openly discussed. These disturbing feelings, she contends, serve to protect us from having to examine our own prejudices and biases.

> When someone pushes racism into my awareness, I feel **guilty** (that I could be doing so much more); **angry** (I don't like to feel like I'm wrong); **defensive** (I already have two Black friends . . . I worry more about racism than most whites do—isn't that enough); **turned off** (I have other priorities in my life with guilt about that thought); **helpless** (the problem is so big—what can I do?). I HATE TO FEEL THIS WAY. That is why I minimize race issues and let them fade from my awareness whenever possible.

On the other hand, many marginalized groups react equally strongly when issues of oppression are raised, especially when their stories of discrimination and pain are minimized or neglected. Their reality of racism, sexism, and homophobia, they contend, is relatively unknown or ignored by those in power because of the discomfort that pervades such topics. Worse yet, many well-intentioned majority persons seem disinclined to hear the personal stories of suffering, humiliation, and pain that accrue to persons of color and other marginalized groups in our society. As Winters says, it is just easier to minimize race issues and not think about them. The following quote gives some idea of what it is like for a Black man to live his life day in and day out in a society filled with both covert and overt racist acts that often are invisible to well-intentioned White Americans.

I don't think white people, generally, understand the full meaning of racist discriminatory behaviors directed toward Americans of African descent. They seem to see each act of discrimination or any act of violence as an "isolated" event. As a result, most white Americans cannot understand the strong reaction manifested by blacks when such events occur. . . . They forget that in most cases, we live lives of quiet desperation generated by a litany of daily large and small events that, whether or not by design, remind us of our "place" in American society. [Whites] ignore the personal context of the stimulus. That is, they deny the historical impact that a negative act may have on an individual. "Nigger" to a white may simply be an epithet that should be ignored. To most blacks, the term brings into sharp and current focus all kinds of acts of racism—murder, rape, torture, denial of constitutional rights, insults, limited opportunity structure, economic problems, unequal justice under the law and a myriad of . . . other racist and discriminatory acts that occur daily in the lives of most Americans of African descent. (Feagin & Sikes, 1994, pp. 23–24)

REFLECTION AND DISCUSSION QUESTIONS

1. Look at the two quotes provided in this section. From a White perspective and a Black one, what worldviews are being reflected in each?
2. As a White counselor working with a Black client, would you be able to truly relate to the worldview being expressed? As a Black counselor working with a White client, what challenges do you anticipate in the therapeutic relationship?

Our opening chapter is meant to be a reflective and emotional one. Although the entire volume is filled with the knowledge base of multicultural counseling and therapy derived from research findings, it is important to realize that cognitive understanding and intellectual competence are not enough. Concepts of multiculturalism, diversity, race, culture, ethnicity, and so forth, are more than intellectual concepts. Multiculturalism deals with real human experiences, and as a result, understanding your emotional reactions is equally important in the journey to cultural competence. To aid you in your journey, we present several personal narratives concerning the text you are about to read. Try to identify the (a) emotive reactions being expressed by the writer, (b) reasons that provoked the feelings, and (c) effects they had on their definitions of counseling/therapy. We hope that you will carefully monitor your own emotional reactions throughout this course, not allow them to interfere with your journey to cultural competence, and try to understand them as they relate to your own racial/cultural awakening and identity.

MY PERSONAL AND PROFESSIONAL JOURNEY AS A WHITE PERSON: REACTIONS TO *COUNSELING THE CULTURALLY DIVERSE: THEORY AND PRACTICE*

by Mark S. Kiselica

I was shaken to my core the first time I read *Counseling the Culturally Different* (now *Counseling the Culturally Diverse*) by Derald Wing Sue (1981). At the time, I was a doctoral candidate at The Pennsylvania State University's counseling psychology program, and I had been reading Sue's book in preparation for my comprehensive examinations, which I was scheduled to take toward the end of the spring semester of 1985.

Mark S. Kiselica

I wish I could tell you that I had acquired Sue's book because I was genuinely interested in learning about multicultural counseling, or, as it was labeled back then, "cross-cultural counseling." I am embarrassed to say, however, that that was not the case. I had purchased Sue's book purely out of necessity, figuring out that I had better read the book because I was likely to be asked a major question about cross-cultural counseling on the comps. During the early and middle 1980s, taking a course in multicultural counseling was not a requirement in many graduate counseling programs, including mine, and I had decided not to take my department's pertinent course as an elective. I saw myself as a culturally sensitive person, and I concluded that the course wouldn't have much to offer me. Nevertheless, I understood that Dr. Harold Cheatham, the professor who taught the course, would likely submit a question to the pool of materials being used to construct the comps. So, I prudently went to the university bookstore and purchased a copy of *Counseling the Culturally Different (CCD)* because that was the text Dr. Cheatham used for his course. I had decided that reading and studying the book would prepare me for whatever question Dr. Cheatham might devise, so I read it carefully, making sure to take detailed notes on everything Sue had to say.

I didn't get very far with my highlighting and note-taking before I started to react to Sue's book with great anger and disgust. Early on in the text, Sue blasted the mental health system for its historical mistreatment of people who were considered to be ethnic minorities in the United States. He especially took on White mental health professionals, charging them with a legacy of ethnocentric and racist beliefs and practices that had harmed people of color and made them leery of counselors, psychologists, and psychiatrists. It seemed that Sue didn't have a single good thing to say about White America. I was ticked off at him, and I resented that I had to read his book. However, I knew I had better complete his text and know the subject matter covered in it if I wanted to succeed on the examinations. So, out of necessity, I read on and struggled with the feelings that Sue's words stirred in me.

I was very upset as I read and reread Sue's book. I felt that Sue had an axe to grind with White America and that he was using his book to do so. I believed that his accusations were grossly exaggerated and, at least to some extent, unfair. And I felt defensive because I am White and my ancestors had not perpetrated any of the offenses against ethnic minorities that Sue had charged. I looked forward to the day when I would be relieved of him and his writings.

Yet for reasons I didn't fully understand at the time, my anger, defensiveness, and resentment began to fade, and I found myself reading Sue's book again and again. Something was happening to me, and I couldn't put my finger on it. Surprisingly, once I had reached the point where I understood the content and theory provided in Sue's book and, hence, had achieved my purposes for reading the text, I kept opening it up again. And strangely, with each fresh reading, I experienced new waves of emotions. Instead of reacting with bitterness, I was now feeling sadness—mild sadness at first, but later, a profound sense of sadness, and even grief. At times, my eyes filled with tears, and I found myself now wanting to absorb the message that Sue was trying to convey. *What was happening to me?*

I tried to make sense of my emotions—to ascertain why I was drawn back to Sue's book again and again in spite of my initial rejection of it. I know it may sound crazy, but I read certain sections of Sue's book repeatedly and then reflected on what was happening inside of me. I spent quite a bit of time alone with Sue's book, sometimes in my office. A couple of other times, I went for long walks in the woods, trying to understand why this book was becoming so important to me. *My life was changing and I needed to know why.*

I began to discover important lessons about myself, significant insights prompted by reading Sue's book that would shape the direction of my future. I gradually realized that my entire life I had identified with oppressed peoples because my ancestors and my immediate family had encountered so many hardships throughout our history. My mother's family was from Ireland, and throughout the ages, they had suffered severe poverty and political and cultural domination by the British. Their language, Gaelic, had been taken from them. They were forced to change the spelling of their last name. They left Ireland for a better life in America, realizing that they would never be able to return to their homeland, and their hearts were ripped apart by such a heart-wrenching departure. Yet they arrived in America with the hope of providing something better for their children, and they stood up to the terrible stereotypes about and maltreatment of the Irish by the American establishment. My maternal grandfather worked as a railroad laborer until it killed him, and my grandmother cleaned the homes of wealthy Americans until she could work no longer, still poor and living in a ghetto at the time of her death. All of these images came back to me as I read Sue's book.

More images entered my mind, this time regarding my father's family from Slovakia. They, too, had been poor. They, too, suffered through years of external domination and persecution, including the destruction of their homes and villages by invading armies, and the desecration of their churches and their political institutions. My paternal grandparents fled to the United States, and my father was raised in a poor, immigrant neighborhood where English was his second language. My father had a learning disability and was lame from a horrific leg injury for which he received inadequate medical care. For decades, he labored in factories under deplorable conditions that would eventually disable him. Yet all he ever dreamed about was giving my brothers and sisters and me a better life. Sue's book reminded me of my father and all that he and his family went through, and their pain surged through me, leaving me teary-eyed.

These memories helped me to look at Sue's book from a different point of view. It caused me to realize more fully that the historical experiences of other racial and ethnic groups were similar in some respects to those of my family. And with that particular realization, more tears swelled in my eyes—tears of empathy and tears of shame. I began to feel—*really feel*—for what people of color had experienced in this country, and I was ashamed of the fact that it had taken me so long to develop that level of empathic understanding. "How could I have been so clueless?" I wondered to myself at the time.

My head began to spin as a vortex of thoughts swirled in my mind. I now realized that Sue was right! The system *had* been destructive toward people of color, and although my ancestors and I had not directly been a part of that oppressive system, I had unknowingly contributed to it. I began to think about how I had viewed people of color throughout my life, and I had to admit to myself that I had unconsciously bought into the racist stereotypes about African Americans and Latinos. Yes, I had laughed at and told racist jokes. Yes, I had used the "N" word when referring to African Americans. *Yes, I had been a racist.*

Admitting that I have been racist is not an easy thing for me to do. It isn't easy now, and it certainly wasn't easy in 1985, when I naively thought I was such a culturally sensitive person. I had good reasons to conclude, albeit erroneously, that I was *not* a racist. I had never been a member of the Ku Klux Klan. When I was a boy, I had had a handful of Cuban American and African American friends. My family and I had always supported the Democratic Party and liberal legislative initiatives. Yes, I was one of the good guys, so the word *racist* couldn't apply to me. But I was wrong, blinded by the insular world in which I had been raised, a world of well-meaning Whites in an era of racial segregation that dictated little substantive contact with people who were different from me: a world that socialized American Whites, including me, to become racist.

Sue's book forced me to remove my blinders. He helped me to see that I was both a product and an

> Admitting that I have been racist is not an easy thing for me to do. It isn't easy now, and it certainly wasn't easy in 1985, when I naively thought I was such a culturally sensitive person. . . . Yes, I was one of the good guys, so the word *racist* couldn't apply to me. But I was wrong, blinded by the insular world in which I had been raised, a world of well-meaning Whites in an era of racial segregation that dictated little substantive contact with people who were different from me: a world that socialized American Whites, including me, to become racist.

architect of a racist culture. Initially, I didn't want to admit this to myself. That is part of the reason I got so angry at Sue for his book. "His accusations don't apply to *me*!" was the predominant, initial thought that went through my mind. But Sue's words were too powerful to let me escape my denial of my racism. It was as though I was in a deep sleep and someone had dumped a bucket of ice-cold water onto me, shocking me into a state of sudden wakefulness: The sleep was the denial of my racism; the water was Sue's provocative words; and the wakefulness was the painful recognition that I was a racist.

It was very unsettling to achieve this recognition, and I faced a tough dilemma afterward: Should I continue to confront my ethnocentrism and racism and experience all of the discomfort that goes with that process, or should I retreat from that process and go on living my life of comfort in my White-dominated world? What else would I discover about myself if I continued with the process of exploring my cultural biases? Where would it take me?

As I wrestled with this dilemma, two considerations helped me to move beyond my anxiety about fully committing myself to becoming a more culturally sensitive person. I realized I had an obligation to my ancestors to confront my fears and cultural biases, for without further growth on my part, I would continue to do to others what had been done to my ancestors. I also was deeply moved by the historical experiences of people of color in the United States. Sue and the contributing authors who wrote some of the chapters in the first edition of his book did a nice job of summarizing these experiences. Their work inspired me to learn more about the history and experiences of people who were culturally different from me.

As I look back on this period of soul-searching, I now realize that the reading of *CCD* sparked a period of important White racial identity development for me. Prior to reading Sue's book, I had neither thought of myself as a racial being nor considered my role as a White person in a racist society. Reading *CCD* pushed me to have a greater awareness of racial issues. My decision to explore racial matters further led me to make an important professional decision that would have a lasting impact on me and move me to yet deeper levels of understanding about my Whiteness: I decided to apply for and accept a predoctoral internship in clinical child and adolescent psychology on the outpatient unit of the Community Mental Health Center of the University of Medicine and Dentistry of New Jersey (UMDNJ), which was located in the heart of Newark, New Jersey. Because the center at UMDNJ served primarily African American and Latino families, the internship provided me with extensive contact with people who are culturally different from me. So when I left Penn State in the summer of 1986 to begin my internship in Newark, I was about to immerse myself in a cross-cultural experience.

The year I spent in Newark changed me forever. Developing everyday relationships with African American and Latino colleagues at UMDNJ; studying about the history and traditions of African Americans and Latinos; and counseling children, adolescents, and families from these two racial/ethnic groups gave me a real-world feel for the material I had first read about in *CCD*. By immersing myself in the cultures of these two populations, I acquired an affective understanding about racism and oppression, which is a form of understanding Sue said is necessary for true multicultural growth. I also became acutely aware of my Whiteness. Being one of the few White, non-Latino people at UMDNJ, I was now the minority, and I stood out as a White person. I enjoyed many conversations with my colleagues and clients about our respective roots. I learned that we shared distinct, yet overlapping, historical experiences. I understood for the first time the advantages I had enjoyed by being White in America, of how the system is open to people who look like me but is often closed and dangerous for people of color. To put it in a different way, I recognized that my White skin and blond hair and blue eyes afforded me White privilege in a racist society. Best of all, I experienced the joy that comes with crossing cultural boundaries and discovering the beauty of different cultures and people.

When my year in Newark was over, I felt compelled to write an account of these experiences that had been prompted by reading *CCD*. I had a week off between the completion of my internship and the start of a new job at the Piscataway campus of UMDNJ. Rather than go on vacation, I sequestered myself in the bedroom of our apartment in Bordentown, New Jersey, where my wife and I lived at the time, pouring my heart into writing about my cross-cultural experiences. When that week was over, I had completed the first draft of a manuscript titled "Reflections of a Multicultural Internship Experience." I sent the manuscript to Dr. Harold Cheatham, who was still a professor at Penn State, and asked him to critique my paper, even though I had never enrolled in his course. In a gesture of kindness and generosity I will always appreciate, Harold not only reviewed the manuscript but encouraged me to try to publish it. Shortly afterward, I noticed a call for manuscripts for a special issue of the *Journal of Counseling and Development* (*JCD*) on multiculturalism as a fourth force in counseling, which was to be edited by Paul Pederson, a well-known multicultural scholar who was a professor of counseling at Syracuse University at the time. I considered sending my manuscript to Dr. Pedersen but hesitated due to several doubts I had about the paper. I had little experience as a writer and feared that my paper was too personal and heartfelt for a professional journal. I also felt vulnerable knowing that I was about to allow others to read my intensely personal experiences. I nevertheless submitted the manuscript to Dr. Pedersen. Much to my surprise, the manuscript was accepted for publication after the reviewers who read it commented that it was a very special article representing a unique voice in the field.

I was now on my way to complementing my clinical experiences counseling the culturally different with extensive scholarship on the subject. In 1990, I took a position as an assistant professor of counseling psychology at Ball State University in Muncie, Indiana, and my article about my multicultural internship appeared in *JCD* during the following year. Over the course of the next 21 years, I would focus many of my more than 130 publications on the subjects of multicultural counseling and education, and the process of confronting prejudice and racism. I owe much of my productivity in multicultural counseling to Dr. Derald Wing Sue, not only for the influence *Counseling the Culturally Diverse* had on me, but also for the personal manner in which Dr. Sue has mentored me. That he and I would become friends is yet another reason why I am grateful that I read his book.

On January 30, 1995, approximately 10 years after I had read *CCD* for the first time, I decided to write a letter to Dr. Sue. By this point in my career, I was an assistant professor of counselor education at Trenton State College, which has since been given its current name, The College of New Jersey. I had just published my first book, *Multicultural Counseling with Teenage Fathers*, the seventh volume in the Sage Series on Multicultural Aspects of Counseling. I wanted to mark the publication of my book by expressing my gratitude to Dr. Sue for the profound impact he had had on me. So, once again, I poured my heart into words, composing a three-page letter and mailing it to Dr. Sue at his office at The California State University–Hayward, where Dr. Sue was employed at the time. In my letter, I told him the entire story about my comprehensive exams, my initial and later reactions to his book, and the racial identity development his words had prompted in me. I also described the impact of some of his subsequent publications on me, and I thanked him for the role he had played in my life.

A few weeks later, the phone in my office rang, and Dr. Sue was on the other end of the line. He introduced himself to me and then reported that, although he had received many letters from people about his book over the years, he had never read any commentary about his book that was as moving and honest as mine. So he was calling to thank me for my thoughtfulness.

I will cherish that phone call for the rest of my life. It was a fantasy come true to talk with a man who had become one of my idols. We talked for a while about our lives and our interests. When I hung up the phone at the conclusion of our conversation, I was in a state of disbelief. Derald Wing Sue had just taken the time to call and thank *me*.

This thoughtful gesture was just one of many acts of kindness by people like Derald who understood the importance of affirming multicultural allies, people like Harold Cheatham, Cheryl Thompson, Joe Ponterotto, Paul Pedersen, Don Locke, MaryLou Ramsey, Roger Herring, Allen Ivey, Michael D'Andrea, Judy Daniels, Larry Gerstein, and Leo Hendricks—all accomplished respected scholars who have supported and affirmed my efforts to be a positive contributor to the multicultural movement. This support was crucial to me because the emotionally laden process of developing multicultural sensitivity did not stop with the completion of my internship in 1986. On the contrary, my cultural immersion experience in Newark was only one phase of my White racial identity development, and I would need the understanding and counsel of these and other friends as I struggled with the ups and downs of my never-ending multicultural journey.

What were these struggles? For one, I went through a period of overidentifying with people of color, which is a common reaction of Whites who experience guilt after they have an awakening about themselves as racial beings. For a while, I acted as though I were one of the saved, a former racist who was now on a mission to save other, fellow Whites from their racism. At times, I became a judgmental nuisance to my White friends. I sought the approval of friends who were people of color for my conversion, annoying them in the process. I got slammed a few times for this behavior, and at other times, as I continued to cross cultural boundaries, I encountered the stinging resentment of me by people of color who drew conclusions about my character based simply on that fact that I am White. As I became more involved in intercultural forums and organizations, I grew weary of the tensions that had to be negotiated about racial matters. These were painful times, so I retreated from substantive interracial contact for about a year, feeling that the price I had to pay for my cross-cultural involvement just wasn't worth it. During this hiatus, I did a lot of soul-searching, and I confided in people I trusted about the feelings I was having, emerging with some new perspectives about racial matters and relations. I realized that we will never make progress with the racial problems that have plagued our country unless Whites like me are willing to accept and manage the pain and discomfort associated with negotiating racial issues. I recognized more fully the complicated nature of racial issues and was less prone to judge others for their racism, even though I stood ready to confront racism when it reared its ugly head. I gradually reengaged myself in the work to promote cultural harmony, joining national organizations, such as the Southern Poverty Law Center, and local movements, such as the Newtown Township No Place for Hate Campaign, to combat prejudice in all its forms. Through my work with these organizations and my continued interchanges with others about racial issues, I have realized that a variety of different tactics are necessary in the battle to eliminate hate. Virulent racism must be confronted with strong systemic policies and community-wide stands communicating that hatred will not be tolerated. More subtle forms of racism can be addressed by taking a less ardent approach, one that involves the tricky challenge of balancing discomforting confrontation with empathic understanding. I have learned that the language we use to promote multiculturalism can be problematic and that we must replace such terminology as "teaching tolerance" with the words "fostering appreciation." You see, people who sense that they are being "tolerated" don't feel welcome, but people who know that they are being "appreciated" feel that they have an honored place at the table.

As I have made these discoveries and moved toward higher stages of White racial identity development, Derald Wing Sue has repeatedly influenced me along the way, affirming me and promoting my growth through his continued writings and encouragement. For example, in one especially cogent article, Derald criticized the professions of counseling and psychology for sometimes lacking a soul (D. W. Sue, 1993), thereby affirming that there must be a place in the professional literature for publications like mine, which tend to be written from both the head *and* the heart. Bolstered by his words, I have published several influential manuscripts in which I have merged material from counseling theory and research with narratives about my own highly personal reflections regarding racism, anti-Semitism, and multicultural education (Kiselica, 1998, 1999a, 1999b, 2003). Derald has also reinforced my belief that people from different backgrounds must work together in order to address interracial difficulties when he wrote, "If we are to move forward, both minority and majority researchers must make a genuine effort to reach out to one another for mutual understanding and respect" (D. W. Sue, 1993, p. 245). In addition, Derald has welcomed Whites like me to the multicultural movement by expressing his belief, "We should view them [White multicultural scholars] as allies because the future of multiculturalism depends on the positive alliances we form with our White brothers and sisters" (p. 248). Finally, like me, Derald emphasized the importance of empathic understanding regarding racial matters when he offered this compassionate statement regarding White racism:

> I do not believe that any of us were born wanting to be biased, prejudiced, racist, or sexist. These statements are not meant to absolve White people from the guilt of bias and discrimination (although guilt is counter-productive), but to indicate that some White researchers are engaged in a different battle: overcoming negative aspects of their cultural condition-ing. (D. W. Sue, 1993, pp. 247–248)

Derald's influence on me has not been limited to these writings or that one unforgettable phone call he made to me in 1995. On two occasions, he and I served on the same panels at conference symposiums pertaining to multicultural counseling and education (Iwamasa, 1995; McCree & Bromley, 2002). In addi-tion, I played a key role in convincing the administration of The College of New Jersey to bring Derald to our campus one year to give an address for our Multi-cultural Lecture Series, during which he shared his keen observations about the status of racial relations in our country. Every time we see each other at confer-ences of the American Psychological Association, the American Counseling Asso-ciation, and other professional organizations, we enjoy a warm exchange, updating each other about our families and our work. From time to time, we talk via the phone or e-mail, discussing both professional issues and personal matters that are important to us.

Throughout all of these contacts, Derald Wing Sue has welcomed me to the multicultural movement and made me feel that I am his respected colleague. To think that he and I have reached this stage in our relationship in spite of my initial, unfair reactions to the first edition of *CCD* is a remarkable accomplishment, for which we both deserve credit and about which I am once again moved to tears. As for me, I feel proud of the fact that I worked through my strong, harsh reactions to Derald's book and saw the truth and wisdom in his observations. I am grateful to Derald for writing that book because it was the catalyst for so much growth in me. I know that his words will echo in my mind for years to come as I continue on my multicultural journey. I also have no doubt that this, the sixth edition of *Counseling the Culturally Diverse*, will have a positive influence on a new generation of coun-seling students, just as it did with me more than 25 years ago. To those students, I send my warmest regards and my wish that you will embrace this book and the soul-searching that it will stimulate in you. And if you struggle with unsettling feelings as you read Dr. Sue's latest edition, please know that I will be there to help you during your multicultural journey, just as Derald Wing Sue was there to support me with mine.

In closing, to Derald Wing Sue, I say this: Thank you for being my brother!

REFLECTION AND DISCUSSION QUESTIONS

1. Can you identify all the emotions and feelings experienced by Mark Kiselica from reading *CCD*? Where did these feelings come from and why do you think they occurred?
2. What accounts for his journey from seeing himself as a good, moral, and decent human being to admitting his own racist thoughts and behaviors? Does this mean that Mark is a bad person?
3. Can you list the forces in Mark's life that helped him overcome the resistance to admitting his own biases and prejudices?
4. As a White person, what reactions do you have to Mark's personal story? As a person of color, what reactions do you have to Mark's personal story? In what ways might the reactions be similar and different? Why?
5. What implications does this narrative have for multicultural counseling and therapy?

MY PERSONAL AND PROFESSIONAL JOURNEY AS A RACIAL AND ETHNIC MINORITY INDIVIDUAL: REACTIONS TO *COUNSELING THE CULTURALLY DIVERSE: THEORY AND PRACTICE*

by Le Ondra Clark

An Invitation to Contribute

Le Ondra Clark

In 2009, I was contacted by Dr. Thomas Parham and asked to contribute to an article in The Legacies and Traditions forum in *The Counseling Psychologist* journal (Parham, 2011). The Legacies and Traditions forum recognizes the accomplishments of acclaimed psychologists. This particular article would honor the impact of Dr. Derald Wing Sue's work on the field of psychology, and I was asked to share about how Dr. Sue's work influenced my educational journey. I must admit I experienced initial trepidation, as I was not sure that I was qualified enough to comment on such a great contributor to the field of psychology. This feeling quickly dissipated as I reflected on my educational journey and realized much of my matriculation through higher education had been shaped by the work of individuals such as Dr. Sue. After the Legacies and Traditions article was published, I was pleasantly surprised to receive an e-mail from Dr. Sue thanking me for sharing my story. I was moved that such a prominent figure was interested in reaching out to me. I was even more surprised when Dr. Sue invited me to contribute to the sixth edition of *Counseling the Culturally Diverse: Theory and Practice (CCD)*. This invitation caused me to reflect on the beginnings of my educational journey, including what initially attracted me to the field of psychology and what factors helped sustain me along the way.

First Impressions: Psychology for the Privileged?

It was at a very young age that I made my first career decision. I decided that the one profession I would *not* pursue was psychology. This decision was influenced by an early observation. My mother was a mental health therapist, and she had a private practice. She saw clients who did not reflect my reality. Her clients were adults who were financially stable and did not represent the racial diversity that existed in the Southern California community that we resided in. This early portrait led me to believe that seeing a therapist was a luxury that could not be afforded by the young, the poor, or the racially and ethnically diverse. My assumption was that therapy was intended for White middle-class individuals. I viewed the practice of therapy as a privilege for those who could afford services versus an important healing element for all people regardless of race, ethnicity, or social class. These early misconceptions influenced my attitude toward the mental health profession and, ironically, later helped me to understand the perspective of many of my racial and ethnic minority clients who held stigmatizing beliefs about mental health treatment.

During my undergraduate years at California State Polytechnic University, Pomona, I worked at residential treatment facilities for adolescent males. Being exposed to this population challenged my previous beliefs about therapy. I saw racial and ethnic minority youth greatly benefit from the services they received from mental health professionals. This exposure led me to declare psychology as my major field of study.

As a result of my academic scholarship, I was accepted into the McNair Scholars Program. My participation in this program was salient, as it introduced me to the idea of obtaining a doctoral degree in psychology. Through the program, I gained research experience and presented my research across the nation. Importantly, the preparation I received enabled me to obtain the Advanced Opportunity Fellowship at the University of Wisconsin, Madison's Counseling Psychology Program that helped to fund my graduate studies.

Constructing the Puzzle: My Journey Through Graduate School

During my six years in graduate school, many pivotal moments shaped me as a clinician, scholar, and advocate for social justice. I describe each of these moments as puzzle pieces that would eventually fit together to create a complete picture representing my matriculation through higher education.

Similar to a myriad of other graduate students, my first exposure to Dr. Sue's work was during my master's program. I, a native of Southern California, arrived at the University of Wisconsin, Madison, and was eager to learn. I remember the harsh reality I experienced as I confronted the Midwest culture. I felt like I stood out, and I learned quickly that I did. As I walked around the campus and surrounding area, I remember counting on one hand the number of racial and ethnic minorities I saw. I was not completely surprised about this, as I had done some research and was aware that there would be a lack of racial and ethnic diversity on and around campus. However, I was baffled by the paucity of exposure that the 25 members of my master's cohort had to racial and ethnic minority individuals. I assumed that because I was traveling across the country to attend this top-ranked program focused on social justice, everyone else must have been as well. I was wrong.

The majority of my cohort was from the Midwest, and their experiences varied greatly from mine. For example, I remember sitting in my Theories of Counseling course during the first week of the semester. The instructor asked each of us to share about our first exposure to individuals who were racially and ethnically different from ourselves. I thought this was a strange question. I could not even remember an initial encounter with another person who was different from me. I was quite surprised as I listened to what my cohort members shared. I listened to several members share that their first exposure to someone different from them had not occurred until high school and, for some, college. When it came time for me to share, I remember stating that, as a racial and ethnic minority, I had never been in a situation where there was not some type of racial and ethnic diversity. Just sharing this made me feel distant from my cohort, as our different cultural experiences were now plainly highlighted. I remember thinking to myself, "Where am I?" For the first time in my life, I felt as if I was a foreigner, and I badly needed something or someone to relate to.

I did not begin to feel comfortable until I attended the Multicultural Counseling course later that week. Students were assigned a number of textbooks as part of this course, including *CCD*. Little did I realize that reading *CCD* would be the first piece of the puzzle. I never imagined a textbook would bring me so much comfort. I vividly remember reading each chapter and vigorously taking notes in the margins. I also remember the energy I felt as I wrote about my reactions to the readings each week. I felt like the book legitimized the experiences of racial and ethnic minorities and helped me understand what I was encountering in my Midwest surroundings. It became a platform from which I could explain my own experience as a racial and ethnic minority from Southern California who was transplanted to the Midwest. The personal stories, concepts, and theories illustrated in *CCD* resonated with me and ultimately helped me overcome my feelings of isolation. *CCD* provided me with the language to engage in intellectual discourse about race, ethnicity, social class, privilege, and disparities. I remember the awareness that swept over the class as we progressed

> I never imagined a textbook would bring me so much comfort. I vividly remember reading each chapter and vigorously taking notes in the margins. . . . I felt like the book legitimized the experiences of racial and ethnic minorities and helped me understand what I was encountering in my Midwest surroundings. . . . The personal stories, concepts, and theories illustrated in *CCD* resonated with me and ultimately helped me overcome my feelings of isolation. *CCD* provided me with the language to engage in intellectual discourse about race, ethnicity, social class, privilege, and disparities.

through the textbook. I began to see a positive change in my classmates. Our conversations shifted. We were no longer discussing differences that were limited to racial and ethnic differences between groups, but rather we were extending the conversation to discuss the depths of the politics of privilege. This was a salient experience for me, as the distance I initially felt between members of my cohort and me began to shrink. I felt that they were beginning to view things through my cultural lens, and I through theirs. We were gaining greater understanding of how our differing cultural realities had shaped us and would impact the work we conducted as therapists.

After graduation, I decided to remain at the University of Wisconsin, Madison, and pursue a doctoral degree in the Counseling Psychology Department. While the experiences I had within my department continued to be enriching and growth promoting, those that I had outside of the university setting were not congruent with the safety of the microcosm that existed in the department. It was around this time that I was first exposed to Dr. Sue's writings about microaggressions. The concept of microaggressions resonated with me as I reflected on many of the experiences I had had since my arrival in Madison. For example, subtle comments were made about how "different" I was from other Black people in the community. I remember a White woman approaching me in a grocery store and touching the braids in my hair. She remarked "It's beautiful . . . I've never seen hair like that." Her intended compliment and her touching me without asking actually made me feel marginalized and uncomfortable. Another woman in the community asked me, "You're not from here, are you?" When I asked why she would ask me such a thing, her response was, "You go to the university . . . you are articulate . . . you dress really nice." Was she communicating that Black people in Madison were not educated, articulate, or dressed well? Even more disturbing were the blatant experiences that confirmed the racism that existed in the community around me. I can recall going to a dinner party at a cohort member's home and her husband getting drunk and telling me that I only got into the graduate program because of affirmative action. As painful as they were, these experiences fueled my passion to focus my clinical work and research on providing culturally sensitive services to racial and ethnic minorities.

I remember reflecting on the readings from *CCD* several times during my first practicum placement. As I worked with different individuals and families, I revisited the readings about culturally appropriate intervention strategies and counseling techniques. Fortunately, my clinical supervisors noticed my ability to glean information from *CCD* and translate this knowledge to practice, as well as my long-standing passion to serve the underserved. Following completion of my practicum, I was hired as a clinician at the agency. While pursuing my doctoral degree, I continued working at the agency and became licensed as a professional counselor. I did not realize it then, but my experiences at the agency would shape my trajectory as a clinician and scholar and would become the second piece of my puzzle.

I was one of the only Black clinicians at the mental health agency. This was not abnormal for me, as I had grown used to being one of the only racial and ethnic minorities in myriad settings since grade school. However, the paucity of racial and ethnically diverse staff illustrated to me that there was a significant dearth of Black mental health professionals in the Madison community, despite the fact that 90% of the clients were Black, Latino, or Hmong. This reality made me even more determined to reach these communities and provide culturally sensitive services. Many of my clients lived in poor communities and were impacted by the harsh disparities that plagued their communities. Although I valued my experiences as a clinician, I also found myself becoming angry inside. I was angry about the poverty, the racism, the foster care system, the prison system, and the education system that affected my clients' lives. I desired to change these systemic barriers that prevented my clients from engaging in or matriculating through therapy. I was in the trenches, and I was restless.

One day, I received a call from former Wisconsin Lieutenant Governor Barbara Lawton's office. A colleague of mine was invited to speak as part of a national webcast and had recommended that I speak in her absence. I was humbled and honored by the invitation. I was asked to speak about my work with African American women as part of the Wisconsin United for Mental Health campaign. I discussed the specific strategies that I utilized with African American women who were participants in a group I facilitated. The group was composed of Black women and held in the community in order to reduce stigma; a large portion of our work included discussions about the historical injustices, such as slavery and institutional racism, that impact African American families. This was the first time I had presented about my clinical work to an audience of nonacademics and non–mental health professionals. This experience piqued my interest about ways the public could become more informed about the prevalence of mental illness and treatment options for racial and ethnic minorities.

In 2007, I wrote about my experiences as a clinician and my desire to impact systemic barriers in my application to the American Psychological Association's Minority Fellowship Program (APA MFP). The third puzzle piece fell into place when I was chosen as an APA MFP fellow. The APA MFP provided me with the support necessary to conduct research about the barriers that were impacting my clients. I decided to examine these barriers in my dissertation entitled *Seeing Through Our Clients' Eyes: An Assessment of Cultural Competence in a Community Mental Health Agency* (Clark, 2010).

In 2008, another critical piece of the puzzle was added. I was selected to attend the APA MFP's Psychology Summer Institute (PSI). PSI provided me with the opportunity to receive intensive mentorship on my dissertation project. However, what most impacted me was the advocacy day that I participated in. Each participant was tasked with going to Capitol Hill to advocate for the continued federal funding of the APA MFP. While I met with my state representative, I shared how the APA MFP had supported me financially during graduate school, allowing me the opportunity to focus on clinical work and scholarship. I also shared about the clients I was working with and the barriers that impacted their recovery. These barriers were economic, social, and systemic in nature. Madison is a very segregated community, and the state of Wisconsin has the highest incarceration rate for Black males and the largest White-Black graduation gap for school-aged youth in the nation. These bleak statistics were apparent as I worked with clients. My clients could not afford bus fare to make it to therapy appointments or money for rent. They were disproportionately represented in the special education system, and they were overwhelmed by the multiple demands of the many professionals that were involved in their personal lives (e.g., parole officers, social workers). My frustration about the aforementioned inequities in my clients' lives and my passion about changing systemic barriers came tumbling out. I was tearful as I spoke, and I realized something very significant was happening. Things began to connect for me. *This* was the forum where decisions were made about the systems that were prevalent forces in my clients' lives. *This* was the type of place where I needed to be!

I returned to Madison with new energy. My experience on Capitol Hill clarified so much for me, but I was unsure as to what my next steps would be. I began to share with others about my passion for advocacy and my hope to someday work in the policy arena. A mentor of mine, Dr. Joseph White, suggested I connect with a colleague of his, Dr. Vivian Ota Wang, a counseling psychologist and program director at the National Human Genome Research Institute at the National Institutes of Health. Vivian, a brilliant researcher and scholar, understood how to utilize psychological science to affect policy. She believed in my vision and in me. Her confidence in my passion and ability was fervent, and my relationship with Vivian would prove to be another salient puzzle piece in my journey.

I had many other impactful experiences while in Madison, and, importantly, I had support. There were key individuals who nourished my growth and bolstered me as I collected puzzle pieces and began to put them together. From my first reading of *CCD* to my participation in advocacy at the nation's capitol five years later, I was never alone on my journey. From the beginning, professors at the University of Wisconsin, Madison, including Drs. Hardin L. K. Coleman, Angela Byars-Winston, Alberta M. Gloria, Earlise Ward, Bruce Wampold, Carmen Valdez, and Corissa Lotta, supported me. My supervisors at the mental health center—Jennie McCann, Jim Van den Brandt, and Drs. Rebecca Ramirez and Armando Hernandez-Morales—provided me with opportunities to work with racial and ethnic minority clients and to provide culturally specific services. These supervisors were the people I cried with, celebrated with, and learned from. I also involved myself extensively in professional organizations. My membership in the Association of Black Psychologists exposed me to crucial supporters, such as Drs. Joseph White, Halford Fairchild, Thomas Parham, Nancy Boyd Franklin, Kevin Cokley, Derek Wilson, Gayle Hamlett, Mawiyah Kambon, Paris Finner Williams, Wade Nobles, Leon Caldwell, Daryl Rowe, Cheryl Grills, Adisa Ajamu, and Linda James Myers. These individuals encouraged me with their words, through their scholarly and clinical work, and, most importantly, by example. Their genius, strength, and undying support helped me successfully complete my graduate school journey and continue to sustain me as an early career professional.

From Clinical Practice to Public Policy

At the end of my time in Madison, I felt eager to return to the urban Southern California setting that I had left six years prior. Over the next two years, I would complete my predoctoral internship at the University of Southern California's Childrens Hospital Los Angeles and my postdoctoral fellowship at UCLA's Mattell Children's Hospital. I also moved to San Francisco the summer between these positions and worked as the Lisa Kernan Social Justice Fellow at the Center for Policy Analysis. My project was to analyze the Affordable Care Act and present information to providers of mental health services and to client's who received services. This experience represented a puzzle piece that would aid in opening the doors for the policy position I now assume at the California state capital. In 2011, I was accepted as the first social scientist to participate in the California Science and Technology Policy Fellowship. This opportunity represents so much for me and for the clients I have worked with and researched about for the past seven years. The culmination of my prior experiences has well prepared me to advise legislators about policies that affect the mental health of racial and ethnic minority populations. And it all began with the information I first learned, and later applied, from the *CCD* textbook.

The Journey Continues

It is clear that my personal path has been influenced by the scholarly work of Dr. Sue and, specifically, the *CCD* textbook. However, Dr. Sue's influence reaches far beyond myself and continues to touch students and professionals across the world. Dr. Sue's writings have impacted the way students conceptualize their own presence in the field of psychology, their contributions to their communities, and the multicultural psychology canon. It is in part from his pioneering efforts that I am able to sit here today, a successful leader, clinician, scholar, and advocate for individuals who represent disenfranchised populations. I am able to picture myself and others who look like me as prominent forces advancing the field of psychological science for years to come. Importantly, the information contained in *CCD* is translational in nature, making it relevant to various individuals as they pursue clinical work with and research about racial and ethnic minority populations. In my estimation, this is the hallmark of exemplary scholarship.

As you read *CCD*, reflect on your journey. I encourage you to begin to construct your own puzzle. Begin by examining why you are here, how you arrived here, who influenced you, and where you hope to go. Then, think about how you will use your education to better the lives of those you will serve. It is my hope that *CCD* becomes a valuable piece of your puzzle, just as it has been a valuable piece of mine.

REFLECTION AND DISCUSSION QUESTIONS

1. What must it be like for a person of color, such as Le Ondra Clark, to be one of the few African American students in a predominantly White, Western-European graduate program in psychology? What do you think Le Ondra means when she describes feeling like a foreigner in graduate school?
2. Unlike Mark Kiselica's initial reaction, Le Ondra immediately found the book validating and affirming. Why do you think this is so?
3. Le Ondra indicates that the textbook provided her with a platform from which she could explain her own experiences. What does she mean by this statement, and why is this so important to people of color?
4. In what ways are Le Ondra Clark's definitions of counseling similar to those of Mark Kiselica? Why the convergence?
5. What implications does this narrative have for multicultural counseling and therapy?

MY PERSONAL AND PROFESSIONAL JOURNEY AS A PERSON OF COLOR: THE HEART AND SOUL OF *COUNSELING THE CULTURALLY DIVERSE**

by Derald Wing Sue

Derald Wing Sue

I am grateful to Mark Kiselica and Le Ondra Clark for their willingness to share such deep personal reflections with all of us.

Mark's honesty in confronting his own racism is refreshing, and his insights are invaluable to those who wish to become allies in the struggle for equal rights. He is a rarity in academic circles, even rarer because he was willing to put his words on paper for the whole world to read as a means to help others understand the meaning of racism on a human level. Mark Kiselica's courageous and open exploration of his initial reactions to *CCD* indicates what I have come to learn is a common, intensely emotional experience from many readers. Because *CCD* deals openly, honestly, and passionately with issues of racism, sexism, and homophobia and challenges our belief that we are free of biases, it is likely to evoke defensiveness, resentment, and anger in readers. In Mark's case, he did not allow these reactions to sabotage his own self-exploration and journey to cultural competence. And we hope you will not allow your emotional "hot buttons" to detract you from your journey to cultural competence as well.

---

*Adapted from D. W. Sue (2005a), The continuing journey to multicultural competence. In R. K. Conyne & F. Bemak (Eds.), *Journeys to professional excellence: Lessons from leading counselor educators and practitioners* (pp. 73–84). Alexandria, VA: American Counseling Association. Reprinted with permission.

Likewise, Le Ondra's story voices a continuing saga of how persons of color and many marginalized individuals must function in an ethnocentric society that unintentionally invalidates their experiences and enforces silence upon them. She talks about how the text provided a language for her to explain her experiences and how she resonated with its content and meaning. To her, the content of the book tapped into her experiential reality and expressed a worldview that is too often not acknowledged or discussed in graduate-level programs. Le Ondra found comfort and solace in the book, and she found significant others in her life who validated her thoughts, feelings, and aspirations and allowed her to pursue a social justice direction in counseling. Le Ondra is also a rarity in her own right; she has been able to overcome great odds and to obtain her doctorate in the field without losing her sense of integrity or racial/cultural identity. I am pleased and flattered that both Mark and Le Ondra believe that *CCD* has been instrumental in their personal and professional developments.

Counseling the Culturally Diverse: Theory and Practice represents a labor of love and is written from my heart and soul. It is filled with all the passion, frustration, and anger concerning the detrimental nature and harm our society and its helping professions have wrought on many marginalized groups, albeit unintentionally. Its goals are to enlighten you about how counseling and psychotherapy may represent cultural oppression and to provide a vision of change that is rooted in social justice. As a person of color, I can say at the onset that my anger is not directed at White Americans nor at our country. The anger *is* directed, however, at White supremacy, sexism, heterosexism, and the many manifestations of bigotry and discrimination that accompany it. As someone once said about racism, "White people are not the enemies, but White supremacy is!"

We are all products of our cultural conditioning and thus inherit the racial, gender, and heterosexual biases of our society. In many respects we have all been victimized by a socialization process that has instilled in everyone the biases and prejudices of our forebears. It does not matter whether you are White or a person of color, straight or gay, a man or woman. Everyone (regardless of race, gender, or sexual orientation) possesses biased beliefs, attitudes, and stereotypes toward others.

When first written in 1981, I knew my words and assertions would come across as provocative and accusatory and would make many in the field defensive and angry, despite the fact that it was based heavily on research findings. Upon publication, that was what happened. I received calls from colleagues who criticized the book and claimed that it was a prime example of White bashing. Strangely enough, while many colleagues and students found the book distressful and disturbing, it became a success that surprised even my publisher. Much of this was fueled by scholars and students of color who embraced it and claimed it was one of the few texts that spoke to their experiential reality. Since its publication, *Counseling the Culturally Diverse* has gone through five revisions, and I am proud to say it is now the most frequently used text on multicultural counseling; further, it forms the knowledge base of many items on counseling and psychology licensing exams. Many have credited the text as the forerunner of the cultural competence movement, but in actuality, the product was the result of many pioneers of color whose important contributions have been overlooked, ignored, or neglected.

Many professors and students have written to me about their reactions to *CCD*. Some assert that it is too political and too emotional. I have also discovered that my writings are often seen by people in the profession as too filled with emotions and not consistent with the objective style so prevalent in academia. That has been one of my pet peeves regarding so-called scholarly writings in the field. Many of my colleagues operate from a mistaken notion that rational thought can come from only objective discourse, devoid of emotions. To me, speaking from the heart and with passion is not antagonistic to reason. Further, it is difficult for many of my colleagues and students to hear others speaking the truth, especially pointing out how counseling and therapy have oppressed, harmed, and damaged marginalized groups (often unintentionally). They are likely to react negatively, making it difficult for them to accept challenges to their concept of mental health practice and perhaps to their own complicity in perpetuating unjust treatment of clients of color and other socially devalued groups in our society. I suppose they view my writings as accusatory and off-putting. Yet, how does one nicely and objectively speak about stereotyping, prejudice, and discrimination in the helping professions and the helping professional? Should I soften the message and not speak about the unspeakable?

Being Chinese American in a Monocultural Society

To help you understand the passion of *CCD*, it may be helpful if I share some of my life experiences as a minority in this society. The lessons I have learned as a Chinese American, born and raised in a predominantly White, Western society, have played a central role in the content and context of this text. Some of these lessons form the basic building blocks of *CCD*. Let me try to enumerate some of them.

I was born and raised in Portland, Oregon, to proud parents who believed strongly in the primacy of the family and extolled the virtues of hard work and achievement. My father emigrated from China; indeed, he stowed away on a ship to the United States at the age of 14. Not knowing how to speak English and unfamiliar with this country, my father survived. And that has been the story of our family, surviving in the face of great odds. For the brief period we were on welfare, I could sense the shame and humiliation my parents felt. Everyone in the family worked to contribute until my parents could again stand with their heads held high. People who have never seriously lacked the necessities of life will never truly understand the experience of being poor, constantly worrying about how to pay even the most inexpensive bills, facing the catastrophic event a broken appliance represents, not being able to pay for school trips, walking miles every day to save bus fare, working after school till midnight to help the family, having to completely support ourselves through college and graduate school, and knowing that others seemed to shun us because we were poor. Watching my mother and father deal with our early experiences of poverty and discrimination has taught us to struggle and fight against social injustice. **I attribute my work on social justice, multiculturalism, and diversity that is strongly reflected in *CCD* to these early experiences.**

In graduate school I recall how my classmates in counseling psychology often spoke about the desire to help those less fortunate than them, actively spoke against inequality in our society, and spoke of their desire to work on behalf of social justice. I never doubted their sincerity, but I often doubted their ability to understand what they spoke so passionately about. To me, the many social injustices they talked about were purely an intellectual exercise for them. Although well intentioned, they seemed much more interested in private practice, opening an office, and hanging out their shingles. Perhaps I am being harsh on them, but that was how it struck me then. **These experiences led me to conclude that helping others required understanding worldviews influenced by socioeconomic status, race, ethnicity, gender, and so forth, on both cognitive and emotional levels.**

When I was in fourth grade, my father wanted better housing for his family, so he moved us outside of Chinatown. The new neighborhood, which was primarily White, was not receptive to a family of color, and we were objects not only of curiosity but of ridicule and scorn as well. **As I reflect upon it now, this was the beginning of my racial/cultural awakening and my experience with racial prejudice and discrimination. And although I did not know it then, it was the beginning of my journey to understanding the meaning of racism and the many social injustices that infect our society.** But in those early days, I allowed the reactions of my classmates to make me feel ashamed of being Chinese.

I vividly recall one incident that was to forever change my perception of being Chinese American. A large group of White students, who had been antagonistic to us for the better part of our early school years, chased my two other brothers and me to our front yard. There they circled us, chanting unmentionable names, and told us to leave the neighborhood. I was truly frightened, but I stood shoulder to shoulder with my older brother Dave and younger brother Stan to confront the large group. All three of us were much smaller than our White peers, and I kept glancing to our house porch, trying to get my brothers to break for it. Dave, however, kept inching toward the group, and I could see he had somehow turned his fear to anger. I realized later that for us to start running would reinforce the stereotype that Asians were weaklings and were afraid to fight.

Just as it appeared a fight was imminent, my mother burst through the door of the house, strode to the edge of the porch, and, in a voice filled with anger, asked what was going on. When no one responded, she said if a fight was to happen, it should be fair. She identified one of the ringleaders in the group and asked my brother Dave to fight him. This not only shocked us, but the entire group of boys. To make a long story short, Dave gave the other boy a bloody nose due to a series of lucky blows. The fight ended as fast as it had begun. At times, I have often wondered what would have happened if he had lost. It was a gamble that my mother was willing to take, because she believed that despite the outcome, pride and integrity could not be lost.

I will never forget that incident. It taught me several important lessons in life that have remained with me to this day and form the basis of much of my professional work. **First, we live in a society that has low tolerance for racial/cultural differences.** Our unconscious social conditioning makes it easy for us to associate differences with deviance, pathology, and lesser value in society. **Second, stereotypes held by society can also do great harm to racial/ethnic minorities.** Not only are they held by the majority culture, but they can become deeply ingrained in minorities as well. When facing the wrath of the band of boys, I never imagined Dave would stand his ground and fight as he did. More astonishing, however, was to witness a tiny Asian woman—my mother—take charge of the situation and encourage a fight. Any thought on my part that Asians were weak and unable to fight back disappeared that day.

Third, I felt a sense of pride in being a member of the Sue family and of being Chinese, something my Dad had always stressed. No group, I realized, should be made to feel ashamed of themselves.

College and Graduate School Years

In my college and graduate school years, I continued to feel like an outsider. Perhaps that was the reason I chose to go into the field of psychology. Not only was I always trying to understand people as an observer, but I became attuned to myself as a racial/cultural being. Although my classmates were friendly and accepting, I felt that the curriculum often lacked validity and did not seem to match my experiential reality. I found psychology fascinating, but the theories of human behavior seemed culture bound and limited in their ability to explain my own personal journey as an Asian American. This was especially true when I entered the counseling psychology program at the University of Oregon.

Despite being enthused and motivated by graduate work, my education continued to be monocultural. Indeed, the terms *multicultural, diversity, cultural competence*, and *racial identity*, common in psychology curricula today, were non-existent during my graduate school years. Although issues relating to minority groups were occasionally raised in my courses, the focus was always on the uniqueness of the individual or the universal aspects of the human condition. My professors operated with the certainty that similarities could bridge all differences, that stressing differences was potentially divisive, and that we were all the same under the skin. It was only later that I realized why I was so alienated from these concepts, although they had a degree of legitimacy. **First, for me as an Asian American, the avoidance of discussing racial differences negated an important aspect of my racial identity. Second, I realized that my professors knew little about racial groups and felt uncomfortable talking about group differences.**

First Job—A Counseling Psychologist

I guess you would say that it was no coincidence that my first job was as a counseling psychologist at the University of California, Berkeley, Counseling Center. Throughout my doctoral studies, I always believed that I wanted to practice and work with clients. Although I interviewed at places that offered me a larger salary, the allure of Berkeley and its social activism was too much to resist. **My Berkeley years represented a racial and cultural awakening for me unsurpassed in any other period of my life.** In Oregon, there were few Asian Americans, but at Berkeley, the student body was greatly represented by Asian Pacific Islanders.

While I was working at Berkeley, I had the good fortune to meet my future wife, Paulina. She was in her last year of obtaining her teaching credentials and was a resident assistant at one of the dormitories on campus. I marveled at her racial/ethnic pride. Contrary to my early feelings of inferiority associated with being Asian, she had never experienced such feelings; another important seed was planted in my journey to cultural awareness and pride. We eventually married and raised two children, a son and a daughter, whom I hope will always feel pride in their ethnic heritage.

At the counseling center, I saw many Asian American clients, many of them expressing personal and social problems that were similar to mine. Like me, they were made to believe that their differences were the problem. It was at that period in my life that I came to the realization that being different was not the problem. It was society's perception of being different that lay at the heart of problems encountered by many racial/ethnic minorities. Although I like to think that I helped them in their adjustment to societal intolerance, I confess that they helped me more. **They validated my thinking, made me see how counseling/therapy attempted to adjust them to an intolerant system, demonstrated how the practices of clinical work were antagonistic to their cultural and life experiences, and showed the importance of realizing that many of the problems encountered by minorities lay in the social system.**

Going Into Academia

Although I enjoyed working with clients, I was not satisfied with the slow pace of therapy and the knowledge that the problems encountered by many clients were due to external circumstances. **I discovered that many of the problems encountered, for example, by Asian Americans and other people of color were due to systemic forces, such as discrimination, prejudice, and injustice.** Having access to data at the Berkeley Counseling Center on Asian American students led me to conduct a series of studies on Chinese and Japanese students. The results reaffirmed my belief that sociopolitical forces were important considerations in the lives of people of color. The results of my early research instilled a hunger in me to contribute to the knowledge base of psychology. At that time, getting research published in top-notch psychology journals was difficult. Editors and editorial boards did not consider ethnic research of importance or of major relevance to the profession. It was a difficult time to get multicultural research published.

Work on Multicultural Counseling and Therapy

Throughout the 1970s, my clinical experience and research on minority mental health led me to conclude that traditional counseling and psychotherapy were Western European constructions that were oftentimes inappropriately applied to racial/ethnic minorities. Indeed, I began to realize that although mental health providers could be well intentioned in their desire to help clients of color, the goals and process of counseling and psychotherapy were often antagonistic to the life experiences and cultural values of their clients. Without awareness and knowledge of race, culture, and ethnicity, counselors and other helping professionals could unwittingly engage in cultural oppression. Studying the culture-bound nature of counseling led me to study other racial groups as well. What I found were similar concerns among African American, Latino/Hispanic American, and Native American colleagues. All felt that traditional mental health concepts and practices were inappropriate and sometimes detrimental to the life experiences of the very clients they hoped to help.

Expanding Social Justice Horizons

In 1997 I was invited to address President Clinton's Race Advisory Board on what the average American could do to help eradicate racism. That experience had a major impact on my current work and my burgeoning belief that social therapy or work toward social justice is also a part of what helping professionals should be doing. I do not mean to minimize the importance of counseling and therapy (it will always be needed), but such an approach tends toward remediation rather than prevention. **If injustice in the form of racism, sexism, homophobia, and other forms of social oppression forms the basis of the many individual and social ills of society, do not we as helping professionals also have a moral and ethical responsibility to address those systemic forces responsible for psychological problems?** If depression, anxiety, and feelings of low self-esteem are the result of unhealthy societal forces (stereotyping, limited opportunities, prejudice, and discrimination), shouldn't our efforts be directed at eradicating societal policies, practices, and structures that oppress, rather than simply changing the individual? While all of us must make choices about where to place our efforts, it is now clear to me that multiculturalism and the eradication of racism are about social justice. And this current edition of *CCD* is filled with these beliefs. Social justice is about equal access and opportunity and about building a healthy, validating society for all groups. That is why it is so important that psychology, and especially counseling, move toward cultural competence and multiculturalism.

In closing, I want to emphasize that understanding the worldview of diverse populations means not only acquiring knowledge of cultural values and differences but being aware of the sociopolitical experiences of culturally diverse groups in a monocultural society. This perspective means the ability to empathize with the pain, anguish, mistrust, and sense of betrayal suffered by persons of color, women, gays, and other marginalized groups. **Sad to say, this empathic ability is blocked when readers react with defensiveness and anger upon hearing the life stories of those most disempowered in our society.** I implore you not to allow your initial negative feelings to interfere with your ultimate aim of learning from this text as you journey toward cultural competence. I have always believed that our worth as human beings is derived from the collective relationships we hold with all people; that we are people of emotions, intuitions, and spirituality; and that the lifeblood of people can be understood only through lived realities. Although I believe strongly in the value of science and the importance psychology places on empiricism, *Counseling the Culturally Diverse* is based on the premise that a profession that fails to recognize the heart and soul of the human condition is a discipline that is spiritually and emotionally bankrupt. **In many respects, *CCD* is the story of my life journey as a person of color.** As such, the book not only touches on the theory and practice of multicultural counseling and psychotherapy but also reveals the hearts and souls of our diverse clientele.

REFLECTION AND DISCUSSION QUESTIONS

1. What reactions, thoughts, and feelings are you experiencing as you read the passage by Derald Wing Sue? What do you think your reactions mean? What do these thoughts and feelings say about you as a person?

2. How have Derald's experiences shaped or influenced his beliefs about multicultural counseling and therapy? List as many of these life events as possible, and discuss how they relate to the helping professions.

3. What does Derald mean when he suggests that traditional counseling and therapy may represent forms of cultural oppression? How do social justice and sociopolitical issues enter into his definition of *multicultural counseling and therapy*?

4. Can you construct your own life story of when you became aware of race issues, gender issues, and sexual orientation issues? What emotions or reactions initially accompanied your awareness? Have they changed over time? What meaning do you attribute to your awareness? As a helping professional, why is it important to address these questions?

Implications for Clinical Practice

1. Listen and be open to the stories of those most disempowered in this society. Counseling has always been about listening to our clients. Don't allow your emotional reactions to negate their voices because you become defensive. Know that although you were not born wanting to be racist, sexist, or heterosexist or to be prejudiced against any other group, your cultural conditioning has imbued certain biases and prejudices in you. No person or group is free from inheriting the biases of this society. It does not matter whether you are gay or straight, White or a person of color, or male or female. All of us have inherited biases. Rather than deny them and allow them to unintentionally control our lives and actions, we should openly acknowledge them so that their detrimental effects can be minimized. The ability to understand the worldview of clients means listening in an open and nondefensive way.

2. Understanding groups different from you requires more than book learning. In your journey to cultural competence, it is necessary to supplement your intellectual development with experiential reality. Socialize with, work with, and get to know culturally diverse groups by interacting with them on personal and intimate levels. You must actively reach out to understand their worldviews. After all, if you want to learn about sexism, do you ask men or women? If you want to learn about racism, do you ask Whites or persons of color? If you want to understand homophobia, do you ask straights or gays?

3. Don't be afraid to explore yourself as a racial/cultural being. An overwhelming number of mental health practitioners believe they are decent, good, and moral people. They believe

strongly in the basic tenets of the Declaration of Independence, the U.S. Constitution, and the Bill of Rights. Concepts of democracy and fairness are present throughout these important and historic documents. Because most of us would not intentionally discriminate, we often find great difficulty in realizing that our belief systems and actions may have oppressed others. As long as we deny these aspects of our upbringing and heritage, we will continue to be oblivious to our roles in perpetuating injustice to others. As mentioned in this chapter, multiculturalism is about social justice.

4. When you experience intense emotions, acknowledge them and try to understand what they mean for you. For example, *CCD* speaks about unfairness, racism, sexism, and prejudice, making some feel accused and blamed. The "isms" of our society are not pleasant topics, and we often feel unfairly blamed. However, blame is not the intent of multicultural training; rather, accepting responsibility for rectifying past injustices and creating a community that is more inclusive and equitable in its treatment of racial/ethnic minorities are central to its mission. We realize that it is unfair and counterproductive to attribute blame to counselors for past injustices. However, it is important that helping professionals realize how they may still benefit from the past actions of their predecessors and continue to reap the benefits of the present social/educational arrangements. When these arrangements are unfair to some and benefit others, we must all accept the responsibility for making changes that will allow for equal access and opportunity. Further, our concerns are directed at the present and the future, not the past. Although history is important in many ways, there are certainly enough issues in the here and now that require our attention. Prejudice and discrimination in society are not just things of the past.

5. Don't be afraid of or squelch dissent and disagreements. Open dialogue—to discuss and work through differences in thoughts, beliefs, and values—is crucial to becoming culturally competent. It is healthy when we are allowed to engage in free dialogue with one another. Many people of color believe that dialogues on race, gender, and sexual orientation turn into monologues in order to prevent dissenting voices. The intense expressions of affect often produce discomfort in all of us. It is always easier to avoid talking or thinking about race and racism, for example, than it is to enter into a searching dialogue about the topics. The academic protocol and, to some extent, the politeness protocol serve as barriers to open and honest dialogue about the pain of discrimination and how each and every one of us perpetuates bias through our silence or obliviousness.

6. Last, continue to use these suggestions in reading throughout the text. Although every chapter ends with a section titled "Implications for Clinical Practice," we encourage you to apply these five suggestions at the end of every reading: What emotions or feelings are you experiencing? Where are they coming from? Are they blocking your understanding of the material? What do they mean for you personally and as a helping professional? Take an active role in exploring yourself as a racial cultural being, as Mark Kiselica and Le Ondra Clark did.

The Superordinate Nature of Multicultural Counseling and Therapy

Professor Jonathon Murphy felt annoyed at one of his Latina social work graduate students. Partway through a lecture on family systems theory, the student had interrupted him with a question. Dr. Murphy had just finished an analysis of a case study on a Latino family in which the 32-year-old daughter was still living at home and could not obtain her father's approval for her upcoming marriage. The caseworker's report suggested excessive dependency, as well as "pathological enmeshment" on the part of the daughter. As more and more minority students entered the program and took Dr. Murphy's classes on social work and family therapy, questions such as the following began to come up more frequently and usually in a challenging manner.

STUDENT: Aren't these theories culture bound? It seems to me that counseling strategies aimed at helping family members to individuate or become autonomous units would not be received favorably by many Latino families. I've been told that Asian Americans would also find great discomfort in the value orientation of the White social worker.

PROFESSOR: Of course, we need to consider the race and cultural background of our clients and their families. But it's clear that healthy development of family members must move toward the goal of maturity, and that means being able to make decisions on their own without being dependent or enmeshed in the family network.

STUDENT: But isn't that a value judgment based on seeing a group's value system as pathological? I'm just wondering whether the social worker might be culturally insensitive to the Latino family. She doesn't appear culturally competent. To describe a Latino family member as "excessively dependent" fails to note the value placed on the importance of the family. The social worker seems to have hidden racial biases, as well as difficulty relating to cultural differences.

PROFESSOR: I think you need to be careful about calling someone incompetent and racist. You don't need to be a member of a racial minority group to understand the experience of discrimination. All counseling and therapy is to some extent multicultural. What we need to realize is that race and ethnicity are only one set of differences. For example, class, gender, and sexual orientation are all legitimate group markers.

STUDENT: I wasn't calling the social worker a racist. I was reading a study that indicated the need for social workers to become culturally competent and move toward the development of culture-specific strategies in working with racial minorities. Being a White person, she seems out of touch with the family's experience of discrimination and prejudice. I was only trying to point out that racial issues appear more salient and problematic in our society and that . . .

PROFESSOR [INTERRUPTING AND RAISING HIS VOICE]:

I want all of you [class members] to understand what I'm about to say. First, our standards of practice and codes of ethics have been developed over time to apply equally to all groups. Race is important, but our similarities far exceed differences. After all, there is only one race, the human race! Second, just because a group might value one way of doing things does not make it healthy or right. Culture does not always justify a practice! Third, I don't care whether the family is red, black, brown, yellow, or even white: Good counseling is good counseling! Further, it's important for us not to become myopic in our understanding of cultural differences. To deny the importance of other human dimensions, such as sexual orientation, gender, disability, religious orientation, and so forth, is not to see the whole person. Finally, everyone has experienced bias, discrimination, and stereotyping. You don't have to be a racial minority to understand the detrimental consequences of oppression. As an Irish descendant, I've heard many demeaning Irish jokes, and my ancestors certainly encountered severe discrimination when they first immigrated to this country. Part of our task, as therapists, is to help all our clients deal with their experiences of being different.

In one form or another, difficult dialogues such as these are occurring throughout our training institutions, halls of ivy, governmental agencies, corporate boardrooms, and community meeting places (D. W. Sue, Lin, Torino, Capodilupo, & Rivera, 2009). Participants in such dialogues come with different perspectives and strong convictions that operate from culturally conditioned assumptions outside their levels of awareness. These assumptions are important to clarify because they define different realities and determine our actions. In the helping professions, insensitive counseling and therapy can result in cultural oppression rather than liberation (Lum, 2011; Parham, Ajamu, & White, 2011). Let us explore more thoroughly the dialogue between professor and student to understand the important multicultural themes being raised.

THEME 1: CULTURAL UNIVERSALITY VERSUS CULTURAL RELATIVISM

One of the primary issues raised by the student and the professor relates to the *etic* (culturally universal) versus *emic* (culturally specific) perspectives. The professor operates from the etic position. He believes, for example, that good counseling is good counseling; that disorders such as depression, schizophrenia, and sociopathic behaviors appear in all cultures and societies; that minimal modification in their diagnosis and treatment is required; and that Western concepts of normality and abnormality can be considered universal and equally applicable across cultures (Arnett, 2009; Howard, 1992; Suzuki, Kugler, & Aguiar, 2005).

The student, however, operates from an emic position and challenges these assumptions. She tries to make the point that lifestyles, cultural values, and worldviews affect the expression and determination of deviant behavior. She argues that all theories of human development arise from a cultural context and that using the Euro-American value of independence as healthy development—especially on collectivistic cultures such as Latinos or Asian Americans—may constitute bias (Ivey, Ivey, Myers, & Sweeney, 2005; Kail & Cavanaugh, 2013; D. Sue, D. W. Sue, D. M. Sue, & S. Sue, in press).

This is one of the most important issues currently confronting the helping professions. There is little doubt that to a large degree the code of ethics and standards of practice in counseling, psychotherapy, social work, and other mental health specialties assumes universality. Thus, if the assumption is correct that the origin, process, and manifestation of disorders are similar across cultures, then guidelines and strategies for treatment would appear to be appropriate in application to all groups.

In the other camp, however, are mental health professionals who give great weight to how culture and life experiences affect the expression of deviant behavior and who propose the use of culture-specific strategies in counseling and therapy (Moodley & West, 2005; Parham, Ajamu, & White, 2011; D. W. Sue & Constantine, 2005). Such professionals point out that current guidelines and standards of clinical practice are culture bound and often inappropriate for racial/ethnic minority groups.

Which view is correct? Should treatment be based on cultural universality or cultural relativism? Few mental health professionals today embrace the extremes of either position, although most gravitate toward one or the other. Proponents of cultural universality focus on disorders and their consequent treatments and minimize cultural factors, whereas proponents of cultural relativism focus on the culture and on how the disorder is manifested and treated within it. Both views have validity.

It is naive to believe that no disorders cut across different cultures/societies or share universal characteristics. In addition, one could make the case that even though hallucinating may be viewed as normal in some cultures (cultural relativism), proponents of cultural universality argue that it still represents a breakdown in "normal" biological-cognitive processes. Likewise, it is equally naive to believe that the relative frequencies and manners of symptom formation for various disorders do not reflect the dominant cultural values and lifestyles of a society. Nor would it be beyond our scope to entertain the notion that various diverse groups may respond better to culture-specific therapeutic strategies. A more fruitful approach to these opposing views might be to address the following two questions: (a) What is universal in human behavior that is also relevant to counseling and therapy? and (b) What is the relationship between cultural norms, values, and attitudes, on the one hand, and the manifestation of behavior disorders and their treatments, on the other?

THEME 2: THE EMOTIONAL CONSEQUENCES OF RACE

A tug-of-war appears to be occurring between the professor and the student concerning the importance of race in the therapeutic process. Disagreements of this type are usually related not only to differences in definitions but also to hot buttons being pushed in the participants. We will address the former shortly but here concentrate on the latter because the interaction between the professor and the student appears to be related more to the emotive qualities of the topic, as discussed in Chapter 1. What motivates the professor, for example, to make the unwarranted assumption that the Latina was accusing the social worker of being a racist? What leads the professor, whether consciously or unconsciously, to minimize or avoid considering race as a powerful variable in the therapeutic process? He seemingly does this by two means:(a) diluting the importance of race by using an abstract and universal statement ("There is only one race, the human race") and (b) shifting the dialogue to discussions of other group differences (gender, sexual orientation, disability, and class) and equating race as only one of these many variables.

We are not dismissing the importance of other group differences in affecting human behavior, nor the fact that we share many commonalities regardless of our race or gender. These are very legitimate points. We submit, however, that like many others, the professor is uncomfortable with open discussions of race because of the embedded or nested emotions that he has been culturally conditioned to hold (D. W. Sue, Torino, Capodilupo, Rivera, & Lin, 2009). For example, discussions of race often evoke strong passions associated with racism, discrimination, prejudice, personal blame, political correctness, anti-White attitudes, quotas, and many other emotion-arousing concepts. At times, the deep reactions that many people have about discussions on race interfere with their ability to communicate freely and honestly and to listen to others. Feelings of guilt, blame, anger, and defensiveness (as in the case of the professor) are unpleasant (Todd & Abrams, 2011). No wonder it is easier to avoid dealing with such a hot potato. Yet it is precisely these emotionally laden feelings that must be expressed and explored before productive change will occur. In Chapter 11 we devote considerable space to this issue. Until mental health providers work through these intense feelings, which are often associated with their own biases and preconceived notions, they will continue to be ineffective in working with a culturally diverse population.

> Feelings of guilt, blame, anger, and defensiveness (as in the case of the professor) are unpleasant. . . . It is precisely these emotionally laden feelings that must be expressed and explored before productive change will occur.

THEME 3: THE INCLUSIVE OR EXCLUSIVE NATURE OF MULTICULTURALISM

Although the professor may be avoiding the topic of race by using other group differences to shift the dialogue, he raises a very legitimate content issue about the inclusiveness or exclusiveness of multicultural dialogues. Are definitions of multiculturalism based only on race, or does multiculturalism encompass gender, sexual orientation, disability, and other significant marginalized groups? Isn't the professor correct in observing that almost all counseling is multicultural? We believe that resistance to including other groups in the multicultural dialogue is related to three factors: (a) Many racial minorities believe that including other groups (as in the previous example) in the multicultural dialogue will enable people who are uncomfortable with confronting their own biases to avoid dealing with the hard issues related to race and racism; (b) taken to the extreme, saying that all counseling is multicultural makes the concept meaningless because the ultimate extension equates all differences with individual differences; and (c) there are philosophical disagreements among professionals over whether gender and sexual orientation, for example, constitute distinct overall cultures.

We believe that each of us is born into a cultural context of existing beliefs, values, rules, and practices. Individuals who share the same cultural matrix with us exhibit similar values and belief systems. The process of socialization is generally the function of the family and occurs through participation in many cultural groups. Reference groups related to race, ethnicity, sexual orientation, gender, age, and socioeconomic status exert a powerful influence over us and affect our worldviews.

Whether you are a man or a woman, Black or White, gay or straight, disabled or able-bodied, married or single, and whether you live in Appalachia or New York all result in sharing similar experiences and characteristics. Although this text is focused more on racial/ethnic minorities, we also believe in the inclusive definition of multiculturalism; it does include gender, sexual orientation, disability, socioeconomic class, and other marginalized groups in our society.

THEME 4: THE SOCIOPOLITICAL NATURE OF COUNSELING/THERAPY

The dialogue between professor and student illustrates nicely the symbolic meanings of power imbalance and power oppression. Undeniably, the relationship between the professor and the student is not an equal one: The professor occupies a higher-status role and is clearly in a position of authority and control. He determines the content of the course and the textbooks to read; he determines right or wrong answers on an exam, and he evaluates the learning progress of students. Not only is he in a position to define reality (standards of helping can be universally applied; normality is equated with individualism; and one form of discrimination is similar to another), but he can enforce this reality through grading students as well. As we usually accept the fact that educators have knowledge, wisdom, and experience beyond that of their students, this differential power relationship does not evoke surprise or great concern, especially if we hold values and beliefs similar to those of our teachers. However, what if the upbringing, beliefs, and assumptions of minority students render the curriculum less relevant to their experiential reality? More important, what if minority students' worldviews are a more accurate reflection of reality than are those of professors?

Many racial/ethnic minorities, gays and lesbians, and women have accused those who hold power and influence of imposing their views of reality upon them. The professor, for example, equates maturity with autonomy and independence. The Latina student points out that among Latinos, collectivism and group identity may be more desirable than individualism. Unfortunately, Dr. Murphy fails to consider this legitimate point and dismisses the observation by simply stating, "Culture does not always justify a practice." In the mental health fields, the standards used to judge normality and abnormality come from a predominantly Euro-American perspective (Arnett, 2009; Brammer, 2012). As such, they are culture bound and may be inappropriate in application to culturally diverse groups. When mental health practitioners unwittingly impose these standards without regard for differences in race, culture, gender, and sexual orientation, they may be engaging in cultural oppression (Neville, Worthington, & Spanierman, 2001). As a result, counseling and psychotherapy become a sociopolitical act. Indeed, a major thesis of this book is that counseling and psychotherapy have done great harm to culturally diverse groups by invalidating their life experiences, by defining their cultural values or differences as deviant and pathological, by denying them culturally appropriate care, and by imposing the values of a dominant culture upon them.

THEME 5: THE NATURE OF MULTICULTURAL COUNSELING COMPETENCE

The Latina student seems to question the social worker's clinical or cultural competence in treating a family of color. In light of the professor's response to his student, one might question his cultural sensitivity as a teacher as well. If counseling, psychotherapy, and education can be viewed as sociopolitical acts, and if we accept the fact that our theories of counseling are culture bound, then is it possible that mental health providers trained in traditional Euro-American programs may be guilty of cultural oppression in working with clients of color? The question our profession must ask is this: Is counseling/clinical competence the same as multicultural counseling competence? Dr. Murphy seems to believe that "good counseling" subsumes cultural competence, or that it is a subset of good clinical skills. Our contention, however, is that cultural competence is superordinate to counseling competence. Let us briefly explore the rationale for our position.

> Although there are disagreements over the definition of cultural competence, many of us know clinical incompetence when we see it; we recognize it by its horrendous outcomes or by the human toll it takes on our minority clients.

Although there are disagreements over the definition of cultural competence, many of us know clinical incompetence when we see it; we recognize it by its horrendous outcomes or by the human toll it takes on our minority clients. For example, for some time the profession and mental health professionals themselves have been described in very unflattering terms by multicultural specialists: (a) They are insensitive to the needs of their culturally diverse clients; do not accept, respect, and understand cultural differences; are arrogant and contemptuous; and have little understanding of their prejudices (Ridley, 2005; Thomas & Sillen, 1972); (b) clients of color, women, and gays and lesbians frequently complain that they feel abused, intimidated, and harassed by nonminority personnel (Atkinson, Morten, & Sue, 1998; President's Commission on Mental Health, 1978); (c) discriminatory practices in mental health delivery systems are deeply embedded in the ways in which the services are organized and in how they are delivered to minority populations and are reflected in biased diagnoses and treatment, in indicators of dangerousness, and in the type of personnel occupying decision-making roles (Parham et al., 2011; T. L. Cross, Bazron, Dennis, & Isaacs, 1989; and (d) mental health professionals continue to be trained in programs in which the issues of ethnicity, gender, and sexual orientation are ignored, regarded as deficiencies, portrayed in stereotypic ways, or included as an afterthought (Laird & Green, 1996; Ponterotto, Utsey, & Pedersen, 2006; U.S. Public Health Service, 2001).

From our perspective, mental health professionals have difficulty functioning in a culturally competent manner. Rather, they have functioned in a monoculturally competent manner with only a limited segment of the population (White, male, and straight Euro-Americans), but even that has become a topic of debate (Ridley & Mollen, 2011). We submit that much of the current therapeutic practice taught in graduate programs derives mainly from clinical experience and research with middle- to upper-class Whites (Constantine, 2007). Even though our profession has advocated moving into the realm of evidence-based practice (EBP), little evidence exists that they are applicable to racial/ethnic minorities (Atkinson, Bui, & Mori, 2001). A review of studies on EBP reveals few, if any, on racial minority populations, which renders assumptions of external validity questionable when applied to people of color

(Atkinson, Morten, et al., 1998; Hall, 2001; S. Sue, 1999). If we are honest with ourselves, we can conclude only that many of our standards of professional competence are derived primarily from the values, belief systems, cultural assumptions, and traditions of the larger (Eurocentric) society. We will, however, in Chapter 9 attempt to summarize multicultural evidence-based practices that have recently begun to work their way into the scientific literature.

Thus, values of individualism and psychological mindedness and using rational approaches to solve problems have much to do with how competence is defined. Yet many of our colleagues continue to hold firmly to the belief that good counseling is good counseling, thereby dismissing the centrality of culture in their definitions. The problem with traditional definitions of counseling, therapy, and mental health practice is that they arose from monocultural and ethnocentric norms that excluded other cultural groups. Mental health professionals must realize that "good counseling" uses White Euro-American norms that exclude most of the world's population. In a hard-hitting article, Arnett (2009) indicates that psychological research, which forms the knowledge base of our profession, focuses on Americans that constitute only 5% of the world's population. He concludes that the knowledge of human behavior neglects 95% of the world's population and is an inadequate representation of humanity. Thus, it is clear to us that the more superordinate and inclusive concept is that of multicultural counseling competence, not clinical/counseling competence. Standards of helping derived from such a philosophy and framework are inclusive and offer the broadest and most accurate view of cultural competence.

A TRIPARTITE FRAMEWORK FOR UNDERSTANDING THE MULTIPLE DIMENSIONS OF IDENTITY

All too often, counseling and psychotherapy seem to ignore the group dimension of human existence. For example, a White counselor who works with an African American client might intentionally or unintentionally avoid acknowledging the racial or cultural background of the person by stating, "We are all the same under the skin" or "Apart from your racial background, we are all unique." We have already indicated possible reasons why this happens, but such avoidance tends to negate an intimate aspect of the client's group identity (Apfelbaum, Sommers, & Norton, 2008). These forms of microinvalidations will be discussed more fully in Chapter 6. As a result, the African American client might feel misunderstood and resentful toward the helping professional, hindering the effectiveness of multicultural counseling. Besides unresolved personal issues arising from the counselor, the assumptions embedded in Western forms of therapy exaggerate the chasm between therapist and minority client.

First, the concepts of counseling and psychotherapy are uniquely Euro-American in origin, as they are based on certain philosophical assumptions and values that are strongly endorsed by Western civilizations. On the one side are beliefs that people are unique and that the psychosocial unit of operation is the individual; on the other side are beliefs that clients are the same and that the goals and techniques of counseling and therapy are equally applicable across all groups. Taken to its extreme, this latter approach nearly assumes that persons of color, for example, are White and that race and culture are insignificant variables in counseling and psychotherapy. Statements such as "There is only one race, the human race" and "Apart from your racial/cultural background, you are no different from me" are indicative of the tendency to avoid acknowledging how race, culture, and other group dimensions may influence identity, values, beliefs, behaviors, and the perception of reality (Carter, 2005; D. Lum, 2011; D. W. Sue, 2001). Indeed, in an excellent conceptual/analytical article proposing a new and distinct definition of *counseling competence*, Ridley, Mollen, and Kelly (2011) conclude that "counseling competence is multicultural counseling competence" and that "competent counselors consistently incorporate cultural data into counseling, and they must be careful never to relegate cultural diversity to the status of a sidebar" (p. 841).

Related to the negation of race, we have indicated that a most problematic issue deals with the inclusive or exclusive nature of multiculturalism. A number of psychologists have indicated that an inclusive definition of *multiculturalism* (one that includes gender, ability/disability, sexual orientation, etc.) can obscure the understanding and study of race as a powerful dimension of human existence (Carter, 2005; Helms & Richardson, 1997). This stance is not intended to minimize the importance of the many cultural dimensions of human identity but rather emphasizes the greater discomfort that many psychologists experience in dealing with issues of race rather than with other sociodemographic differences (D. W. Sue, Lin, Torino, et al., 2009; D. W. Sue, Torino, Capodilupo, et al., 2009). As a result, race becomes less salient and allows us to avoid addressing problems of racial prejudice, racial discrimination, and systemic racial oppression. This concern appears to have great legitimacy. We have noted, for example, that when issues of race are discussed in the classroom, a mental health agency, or some other public forum, it is not uncommon for participants to refocus the dialogue on differences related to gender, socioeconomic status, or religious orientation (à la Dr. Murphy).

On the other hand, many groups often rightly feel excluded from the multicultural debate and find themselves in opposition to one another. Thus, enhancing multicultural understanding and sensitivity means balancing our understanding of the sociopolitical forces that dilute the importance of race, on the one hand, and our need to acknowledge the existence of other group identities related to social class, gender, ability/disability, age, religious affiliation, and sexual orientation, on the other (Anderson & Middleton, 2011; D. W. Sue, 2010a).

There is an old Asian saying that goes something like this: "All individuals, in many respects, are (a) like no other individuals, (b) like some individuals, and (c) like all other individuals." Although this statement might sound confusing and contradictory, Asians believe these words to have great wisdom and to be entirely true with respect to human development and identity. We have found the tripartite framework shown in Figure 2.1 (D. W. Sue, 2001) to be useful in exploring and understanding the formation of personal identity. The three

> "All individuals, in many respects, are (a) like no other individuals, (b) like some individuals, and (c) like all other individuals."

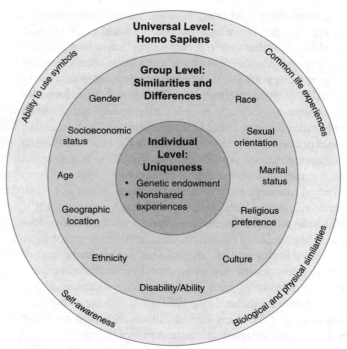

Figure 2.1   Tripartite Development of Personal Identity

concentric circles illustrated in Figure 2.1 denote individual, group, and universal levels of personal identity.

Individual Level: "All Individuals Are, in Some Respects, Like No Other Individuals"

There is much truth in the saying that no two individuals are identical. We are all unique biologically, and recent breakthroughs in mapping the human genome have provided some startling findings. Biologists, anthropologists, and evolutionary psychologists had looked to the Human Genome Project as potentially providing answers to comparative and evolutionary biology that would allow us to find the secrets to life. Although the project has provided valuable answers to many questions, scientists have discovered even more complex questions. For example, they had expected to find 100,000 genes in the human genome, but approximately 20,000 were initially found, with the possible existence of another 5,000—only two or three times more than are found in a fruit fly or a nematode worm. Of those 25,000 genes, only 300 unique genes distinguish us from the mouse. In other words, human and mouse genomes are about 85% identical! Although it may be a blow to human dignity, the more important question is how so relatively few genes can account for our humanness.

Likewise, if so few genes can determine such great differences between species, what about within the species? Human inheritance almost guarantees differences because no two individuals ever share the same genetic endowment. Further, no two of us share the exact same experiences in our society. Even identical twins, who theoretically share the same gene pool and are raised in the same family, are exposed to both shared and nonshared experiences. Different experiences in school and with peers, as well as qualitative differences in how parents treat them, will contribute to individual uniqueness. Research indicates that psychological characteristics, behavior, and mental disorders are more affected by experiences specific to a child than are shared experiences (Bale et al., 2010; Foster & MacQueen, 2008).

Group Level: "All Individuals Are, in Some Respects, Like Some Other Individuals"

As mentioned earlier, each of us is born into a cultural matrix of beliefs, values, rules, and social practices. By virtue of social, cultural, and political distinctions made in our society, perceived group membership exerts a powerful influence over how society views sociodemographic groups and over how its members view themselves and others (Atkinson, Morten, et al., 1998; Szymanski & Gupta, 2009). Group markers such as race and gender are relatively stable and less subject to change. Some markers, such as education, socioeconomic status, marital status, and geographic location, are more fluid and changeable. Although ethnicity is fairly stable, some argue that it can also be fluid. Likewise, debate and controversy surround the discussions about whether sexual orientation is determined at birth and whether we should be speaking of sexuality or sexualities (D. Sue, D. W. Sue, D. M. Sue, & S. Sue, 2013). Nevertheless, membership in these groups may result in shared experiences and characteristics. Group identities may serve as powerful reference groups in the formation of worldviews. On the group level of identity, Figure 2.1 reveals that people may belong to more than one cultural group (e.g., an Asian American female with a disability), that some group identities may be more salient than others (e.g., race over religious orientation), and that the salience of cultural group identity may shift from one to the other depending on the situation. For example, a gay man with a disability may find that his disability identity is more salient among the able-bodied but that his sexual orientation is more salient among those with disabilities.

Universal Level: "All Individuals Are, in Some Respects, Like All Other Individuals"

Because we are members of the human race and belong to the species *Homo sapiens*, we share many similarities. Universal to our commonalties are (a) biological and physical similarities, (b) common life experiences (birth, death, love, sadness, etc.), (c) self-awareness, and (d) the ability to use symbols, such as language. In Shakespeare's *Merchant of Venice*, Shylock attempts to acknowledge the universal nature of the human condition by asking, "When you prick us, do we not bleed?" Again, although the Human Genome Project indicates that a few genes may cause major differences between and within species, it is startling

---

REFLECTION AND DISCUSSION QUESTIONS

1. Select three group identities you possess related to race, gender, sexual orientation, disability, religion, socioeconomic status, and so forth. Of the three you have chosen, which one is more salient to you? Why? Does it shift or change? How aware are you of other sociodemographic identities?

2. Using the tripartite framework just discussed, can you outline ways in which you are unique, share characteristics with only certain groups, and share similarities with everyone?

3. Can someone truly be color-blind? What makes seeing and acknowledging differences so difficult? In what ways does a color-blind approach hinder the counseling relationship when working with diverse clients?

---

how similar the genetic material within our chromosomes is and how much we share in common.

INDIVIDUAL AND UNIVERSAL BIASES IN PSYCHOLOGY AND MENTAL HEALTH

Psychology—and mental health professionals in particular—has generally focused on either the individual or the universal levels of identity, placing less importance on the group level. There are several reasons for this orientation. First, our society arose from the concept of rugged individualism, and we have traditionally valued autonomy, independence, and uniqueness. Our culture assumes that individuals are the basic building blocks of our society. Sayings such as "Be your own person," "Stand on your own two feet," and "Don't depend on anyone but yourself" reflect this value. Psychology and education represent the carriers of this value, and the study of individual differences is most exemplified in the individual intelligence testing movement that pays homage to individual uniqueness (Suzuki et al., 2005).

Second, the universal level is consistent with the tradition and history of psychology, which has historically sought universal facts, principles, and laws in explaining human behavior. Although an important quest, the nature of scientific inquiry has often meant studying phenomena independently of the context in which human behavior originates. Thus, therapeutic interventions from which research findings are derived may lack external validity (Chang & S. Sue, 2005).

Third, we have historically neglected the study of identity at the group level for sociopolitical and normative reasons. As we have seen, issues of race, gender, sexual orientation, and disability seem to touch hot buttons in all of us because they bring to light issues of oppression and the unpleasantness of personal biases (Lo, 2011; Zetzer, 2011). In addition, racial/ethnic differences have frequently been interpreted from a deficit perspective and have been equated with being abnormal or pathological (Guthrie, 1997; Parham et al., 2011). We have more to say about this in Chapter 4.

Nevertheless, disciplines that hope to understand the human condition cannot neglect any level of our identity. For example, psychological explanations that acknowledge the importance of group influences, such as gender, race, culture, sexual orientation, socioeconomic class, and religious affiliation, lead to more accurate understanding of human psychology. Failure to acknowledge these influences may skew research findings and lead to biased conclusions about human behavior that are culture bound, class bound, and gender bound.

Thus, it is possible to conclude that all people possess individual, group, and universal levels of identity. A holistic approach to understanding personal identity demands that we recognize all three levels: individual (uniqueness), group (shared cultural values and beliefs), and universal (common features of being human). Because of the historical scientific neglect of the group level of identity, this text focuses primarily on this category.

Before closing this portion of our discussion, however, we would like to add a caution. Although the concentric circles in Figure 2.1 might unintentionally suggest a clear boundary, each level of identity must be viewed as permeable and ever-changing in salience. In counseling and psychotherapy, for example, a client might view his or her uniqueness as important at one point in the session and stress commonalities of the human condition at another. Even within the group level of identity, multiple forces may be operative. As mentioned earlier, the group level of identity reveals many reference groups, both fixed and nonfixed, that might impact our lives. Being an elderly, gay, Latino male, for example, represents four potential reference groups operating on the person. The culturally competent helping professional must be willing and able to touch all dimensions of human existence without negating any of the others.

THE IMPACT OF GROUP IDENTITIES ON COUNSELING AND PSYCHOTHERAPY

Accepting the premise that race, ethnicity, and culture are powerful variables in influencing how people think, make decisions, behave, and define events, it is not far-fetched to conclude that such forces may also affect how different groups define a helping relationship (Fraga, Atkinson, & Wampold, 2002; D. W. Sue, 2001). Multicultural psychologists have long noted, for example, that theories of counseling and psychotherapy represent different worldviews, each with its own values, biases, and assumptions about human behavior (Katz, 1985). Given that schools of counseling and psychotherapy arise from Western European contexts, the worldview that they espouse as reality may not be shared by racial/ethnic minority groups in the United States, nor by those who reside in different countries (Parham et al., 2011). Each cultural/racial group may have its own distinct interpretation of reality and offer a different perspective on the nature of people, the origin of disorders, standards for judging normality and abnormality, and therapeutic approaches.

Among many Asian Americans, for example, a self orientation is considered undesirable, whereas a group orientation is highly valued (Kim, 2011). The Japanese have a saying that goes like this: "The nail that stands up should be pounded back down." The meaning seems clear: Healthy development is considering the needs of the entire group, whereas unhealthy development is thinking only of oneself. Likewise, relative to their Euro-American counterparts, many African Americans value the emotive and affective quality of interpersonal interactions as qualities of sincerity and authenticity (West-Olatunji & Conwill, 2011). Euro-Americans often view the passionate expression of affect as irrational, impulsive, immature, and lacking objectivity on the part of the communicator. Thus, the autonomy-oriented goal of counseling and psychotherapy and the objective focus of the therapeutic process might prove antagonistic to the worldviews of Asian Americans and African Americans, respectively.

It is therefore highly probable that different racial/ethnic minority groups perceive the competence of the helping professional differently than do mainstream client groups. Further, if race/ethnicity affects perception, what about other group differences, such as gender and sexual orientation? Minority clients may see a clinician who exhibits therapeutic skills that are associated primarily with mainstream therapies as having lower credibility. The important question to ask is, "Do such groups as racial/ethnic minorities define cultural competence differently than do their Euro-American counterparts?" Anecdotal observations, clinical case studies, conceptual analytical writings, and some empirical studies seem to suggest an affirmative response to the question (Constantine et al., 2007; Fraga et al., 2002; Guzman & Carrasco, 2011; Garrett & Portman, 2011; McGoldrick, Giordano, & Garcia-Preto, 2005; Nwachuku & Ivey, 1991).

WHAT IS MULTICULTURAL COUNSELING/THERAPY?

In light of the previous analysis, let us define *multicultural counseling/therapy (MCT)* as it relates to the therapy process and the roles of the mental health practitioner:

> Multicultural counseling and therapy can be defined as both a helping role and a process that uses modalities and defines goals consistent with the life experiences and cultural values of clients; recognizes client identities to include individual, group, and universal dimensions; advocates the use of universal and culture-specific strategies and roles in the healing process; and balances the importance of individualism and collectivism in the assessment, diagnosis, and treatment of client and client systems. (D. W. Sue & Torino, 2005)

This definition often contrasts markedly with traditional views of counseling and psychotherapy. A more thorough analysis of these characteristics is described in Chapter 7. For now, let us extract the key phrases in our definition and expand their implications for clinical practice.

1. *Helping role and process:* MCT involves broadening the roles that counselors play and expands the repertoire of therapy skills considered helpful and appropriate in counseling. The more passive and objective stance taken by therapists in clinical work is seen as only one method of helping. Likewise, teaching, consulting, and advocacy can supplement the conventional counselor or therapist role.

2. *Consistent with life experiences and cultural values:* Effective MCT means using modalities and defining goals for culturally diverse clients that are consistent with their racial, cultural, ethnic, gender, and sexual orientation backgrounds. Advice and suggestions, for example, may be effectively used for some client populations.

3. *Individual, group, and universal dimensions of existence:* As we have already seen, MCT acknowledges that our existence and identity are composed of individual (uniqueness), group, and universal dimensions. Any form of helping that fails to recognize the totality of these dimensions negates important aspects of a person's identity.

4. *Universal and culture-specific strategies:* Related to the second point, MCT believes that different racial/ethnic minority groups might respond best to culture-specific strategies of helping. For example, research seems to support the belief that Asian Americans and Latino/a Americans are more responsive to directive/active approaches (Guzman & Carrasco, 2011; Kim, 2011) and that African Americans appreciate helpers who are authentic in their self-disclosures (Parham et al., 2011). Likewise, it is clear that common features in helping relationships cut across cultures and societies as well.

5. *Individualism and collectivism:* MCT broadens the perspective of the helping relationship by balancing the individualistic approach with a collectivistic reality that acknowledges our embeddedness in families, significant others, communities, and cultures. A client is perceived not just as an individual, but as an individual who is a product of his or her social and cultural context.

6. *Client and client systems:* MCT assumes a dual role in helping clients. In many cases, for example, it is important to focus on individual clients and to encourage them to achieve insights and learn new behaviors. However, when problems of clients of color reside in prejudice, discrimination, and racism of employers, educators, and neighbors or in organizational policies or practices in schools, mental health agencies, government, business, and society, the traditional therapeutic role appears ineffective and inappropriate. The focus for change must shift to altering client systems rather than individual clients.

WHAT IS CULTURAL COMPETENCE?

Consistent with the definition of MCT, it becomes clear that a culturally competent healer is working toward several primary goals (American Psychological Association, 2003; D. W. Sue et al., 1982; D. W. Sue, Arredondo, & McDavis, 1992; D. W. Sue et al., 1998). First, a culturally competent helping professional is one who is actively in the process of becoming aware of his or her own assumptions about human behavior, values, biases, preconceived notions, personal limitations, and so forth. Second, a culturally competent helping professional is one who actively attempts to understand the worldview of his or her culturally different client. In other words, what are the client's values and assumptions about human behavior, biases, and so on? Third, a culturally competent helping professional is one who is in the process of actively developing and practicing appropriate, relevant, and sensitive intervention strategies and skills in working with his or her culturally different client. These three attributes make it clear that cultural competence is an active, developmental, and ongoing process and that it is aspirational rather than achieved. Let us more carefully explore these attributes of cultural competence.

Competency 1: Therapist Awareness of One's Own Assumptions, Values, and Biases

In almost all human service programs, counselors, therapists, and social workers are familiar with the phrase, "Counselor, know thyself." Programs stress the importance of not allowing our own biases, values, or hang-ups to interfere with our ability to work with clients. In most cases, such a warning stays primarily on an intellectual level, and very little training is directed at having trainees get in touch with their own values and biases about human behavior. In other words, it appears to be easier to deal with trainees' cognitive understanding about their own cultural heritage, the values they hold about human behavior, their standards for judging normality and abnormality, and the culture-bound goals toward which they strive.

What makes examination of the self difficult is the emotional impact of attitudes, beliefs, and feelings associated with cultural differences, such as racism, sexism, heterosexism, able-body-ism, and ageism. For example, as a member of a White Euro-American group, what responsibility do you hold for the racist, oppressive, and discriminating manner by which you personally and professionally deal with persons of color? This is a threatening question for many White people. However, to be effective in MCT means that one has adequately dealt with this question and worked through the biases, feelings, fears, and guilt associated with it. A similar question can be asked of men with respect to women and of straights with respect to gays.

Competency 2: Understanding the Worldview of Culturally Diverse Clients

It is crucial that counselors and therapists understand and can share the worldview of their culturally diverse clients. This statement does not mean that providers must hold these worldviews as their own, but rather that they can see and accept other worldviews in a nonjudgmental manner. Some have referred to the process as cultural role taking: Therapists acknowledge that they may not have lived a lifetime as a person of color, as a woman, or as a lesbian, gay, bisexual, or transgendered person (LGBT). With respect to race, for example, it is almost impossible for a White therapist to think, feel, and react as a racial minority individual. Nonetheless, cognitive empathy, as distinct from affective empathy, may be possible. In cultural role taking, the therapist acquires practical knowledge concerning the scope and nature of the client's cultural background, daily living experience, hopes, fears, and aspirations. Inherent in cognitive empathy is the understanding of how therapy relates to the wider sociopolitical system with which minorities contend every day of their lives.

Competency 3: Developing Appropriate Intervention Strategies and Techniques

Effectiveness is most likely enhanced when the therapist uses therapeutic modalities and defines goals that are consistent with the life experiences and cultural values of the client. This basic premise will be emphasized throughout future chapters. Studies have consistently revealed that (a) economically and educationally marginalized clients may not be oriented toward "talk therapy"; (b) self-disclosure may be incompatible with the cultural values of Asian Americans, Hispanic Americans, and American Indians; (c) the sociopolitical atmosphere may dictate against self-disclosure from racial minorities and gays and lesbians; (d) the ambiguous nature of counseling may be antagonistic to life values of certain diverse groups; and (e) many minority clients prefer an active/directive approach over an inactive/nondirective one in treatment. Therapy has too long assumed that clients share a similar background and cultural heritage and that the same approaches are equally effective with all clients. This erroneous assumption needs to be challenged.

Because groups and individuals differ from one another, the blind application of techniques to all situations and all populations seems ludicrous. The interpersonal transactions between the counselor and the client require different approaches that are consistent with the person's life experiences (Choudhuri, Santiago-Rivera, & Garrett, 2012). It is ironic that equal treatment in therapy may be discriminatory treatment! Therapists need to understand this. As a means to prove discriminatory mental health practices, racial/ethnic minority groups have in the past pointed to studies revealing that minority clients are given less preferential forms of treatment (medication, electroconvulsive therapy, etc.). Somewhere, confusion has occurred, and it was believed that to be treated differently is akin to discrimination. The confusion centered on the distinction between equal access and opportunities versus equal treatment. Racial/ethnic minority groups may not be asking for equal treatment so much as they are asking for equal access and opportunities. This dictates a differential approach that is truly nondiscriminatory. Thus, to be an effective multicultural helper requires cultural competence. In light of the previous analysis, we define *cultural competence* in the following manner:

> Cultural competence is the ability to engage in actions or create conditions that maximize the optimal development of client and client systems. Multicultural counseling competence is defined as the counselor's acquisition of awareness, knowledge, and skills needed to function effectively in a pluralistic democratic society (ability to communicate, interact, negotiate, and intervene on behalf of clients from diverse backgrounds), and on an organizational/societal level, advocating effectively to develop new theories, practices, policies, and organizational structures that are more responsive to all groups. (D. W. Sue & Torino, 2005)

This definition of cultural competence in the helping professions makes it clear that the conventional one-to-one, in-the-office, objective form of treatment aimed at remediation of existing problems may be at odds with the sociopolitical and cultural experiences of their clients. Like the complementary definition of MCT, it addresses not only clients (individuals, families, and groups) but also client systems (institutions, policies, and practices that may be unhealthy or problematic for healthy development). Addressing client systems is especially important if problems reside outside rather than inside the client. For example, prejudice and discrimination such as racism, sexism, and homophobia may impede the healthy functioning of individuals and groups in our society.

Second, cultural competence can be seen as residing in three major domains: (a) attitudes/beliefs component—an understanding of one's own cultural conditioning, which affects the personal beliefs, values, and attitudes of a culturally diverse population; (b) knowledge component—understanding and knowledge of the worldviews of culturally diverse individuals and groups; and (c) skills component—an ability to determine and use culturally appropriate intervention strategies when working with different groups in our society. Box 2.1 provides an outline of cultural competencies related to these three domains.

Third, in a broad sense, this definition is directed toward two levels of cultural competence: the person/individual and the organizational/system levels. The work on cultural competence has generally focused on the micro level, the individual. In the education and training of psychologists, for example, the goals have been to increase the level of self-awareness of trainees (potential biases, values, and assumptions about human behavior); to acquire knowledge of the history, culture, and life experiences of various minority groups; and to aid in developing culturally appropriate and adaptive interpersonal skills (clinical work, management, conflict resolution, etc.). Less emphasis is placed on the macro level: the profession of psychology, organizations, and the society in general (Lum, 2011; D. W. Sue, 2001). We suggest that it does little good to train culturally competent helping professionals when the very organizations that employ them are monocultural and discourage or even punish psychologists for using their culturally competent knowledge and skills. If our profession is interested in the development of cultural competence, then it must become involved in impacting systemic and societal levels as well.

Box 2.1 Multicultural Counseling Competencies

I. Cultural Competence: Awareness
   1. Moved from being culturally unaware to being aware and sensitive to own cultural heritage and to valuing and respecting differences.
   2. Aware of own values and biases and of how they may affect diverse clients.
   3. Comfortable with differences that exist between themselves and their clients in terms of race, gender, sexual orientation, and other sociodemographic variables. Differences are not seen as deviant.

    4. Sensitive to circumstances (personal biases; stage of racial, gender, and sexual orientation identity; sociopolitical influences; etc.) that may dictate referral of clients to members of their own sociodemographic group or to different therapists in general.

    5. Aware of their own racist, sexist, heterosexist, or other detrimental attitudes, beliefs, and feelings.

II. Cultural Competence: Knowledge

    1. Knowledgeable and informed on a number of culturally diverse groups, especially groups that therapists work with.

    2. Knowledgeable about the sociopolitical system's operation in the United States with respect to its treatment of marginalized groups in society.

    3. Possess specific knowledge and understanding of the generic characteristics of counseling and therapy.

    4. Knowledgeable of institutional barriers that prevent some diverse clients from using mental health services.

III. Cultural Competence: Skills

    1. Able to generate a wide variety of verbal and nonverbal helping responses.

    2. Able to communicate (send and receive both verbal and nonverbal messages) accurately and appropriately.

    3. Able to exercise institutional intervention skills on behalf of their client when appropriate.

    4. Able to anticipate impact of their helping styles and limitations they possess on culturally diverse clients.

    5. Able to play helping roles characterized by an active systemic focus, which leads to environmental interventions. Not restricted by the conventional counselor/therapist mode of operation.

Source: D. W. Sue et al. (1992) and D. W. Sue et al. (1998). Readers are encouraged to review the original 34 multicultural competencies, which are fully elaborated in both publications.

Last, our definition of cultural competence speaks strongly to the development of alternative helping roles. Much of this comes from recasting healing as involving more than one-to-one therapy. If part of cultural competence involves systemic intervention, then such roles as consultant, change agent, teacher, and advocate supplement the conventional role of therapy. In contrast to this role, alternatives are characterized by the following:

- Having a more active helping style
- Working outside the office (home, institution, or community)
- Being focused on changing environmental conditions, as opposed to changing the client
- Viewing the client as encountering problems rather than having a problem
- Being oriented toward prevention rather than remediation
- Shouldering increased responsibility for determining the course and the outcome of the helping process

It is clear that these alternative roles and their underlying assumptions and practices have not been perceived as activities consistent with counseling and psychotherapy.

REFLECTION AND DISCUSSION QUESTIONS

1. If the basic building blocks of cultural competence in clinical practice are awareness, knowledge, and skills, how do you hope to fulfill competency one, two, and three? Can you list the various educational and training activities you would need to work effectively with a client who differs from you in terms of race, gender, or sexual orientation?

2. Look at the six characteristics that define alternative roles for helping culturally diverse clients. Which of these roles are you most comfortable playing? Why? Which of these activities would make you uncomfortable? Why?

MULTIDIMENSIONAL MODEL OF CULTURAL COMPETENCE IN COUNSELING

Elsewhere, one of the authors (D. W. Sue, 2001) has proposed a *multidimensional model of cultural competence (MDCC)* in counseling/therapy. This was an attempt to integrate three important features associated with effective multicultural counseling: (a) the need to consider specific cultural group worldviews associated with race, gender, sexual orientation, and so on; (b) components of cultural competence (awareness, knowledge, and skills); and (c) foci of cultural competence. These dimensions are illustrated in Figure 2.2. This model is used throughout the text to guide our discussion because it allows for the systematic identification of where interventions should potentially be directed.

Dimension 1: Group-Specific Worldviews

In keeping with our all-encompassing definition of multiculturalism, we include the human differences associated with race, gender, sexual orientation, physical ability, age, and other significant reference groups. Figure 2.2 reveals how the model would apply to a number of socially devalued groups in our society. Additionally, Figure 2.3 reveals how group identities can be further broken down into specific categories along the lines of race/ethnicity (African Americans, Asian Americans, Latino Americans, Native Americans, and European Americans), sexual orientation (straights, gays, lesbians, and bisexuals), gender (men and women), and so forth.

Dimension 2: Components of Cultural Competence

As we have already stated, most multicultural specialists have used the divisions of awareness, knowledge, and skills to define cultural competence. To be effective

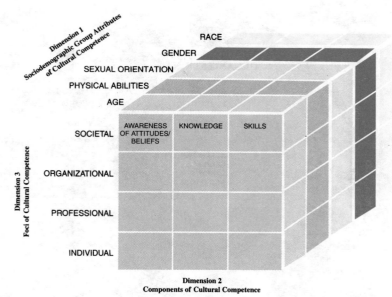

Figure 2.2 Multidimensional Model for Developing Cultural Competence—Various Marginalized Groups

multicultural therapists, specialists must be aware of their own biases and assumptions about human behavior, must acquire and have knowledge of the particular groups they are working with, and must be able to use culturally appropriate intervention strategies in working with different groups.

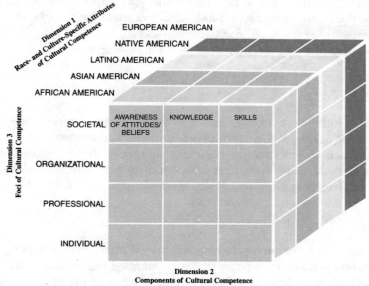

Figure 2.3 Multidimensional Model for Developing Cultural Competence—Race/Ethnicity

Figure 2.4 The Foci of Cultural Competence: Individual, Professional, Organizational, and Societal

Dimension 3: Foci of Therapeutic Interventions

A basic premise of MCT is that culturally competent helping professionals must not confine their perspectives to just individual treatment but must be able to intervene effectively at the professional, organizational, and societal levels as well. Figure 2.4 reveals the four foci of intervention and development.

Focus 1: Individual

To provide culturally effective and sensitive mental health services, helping professionals must deal with their own biases, prejudices, discrimination, and misinformation/lack of information regarding culturally diverse groups in our society. In this case, positive changes must occur in their attitudes, beliefs, emotions, and behaviors regarding multicultural populations.

Focus 2: Professional

It is clear that our profession has developed from a Western European perspective. As a result, how we define *psychology* (the study of mind and behavior) may be biased and at odds with different cultural groups. Further, if the professional standards and codes of ethics in mental health practice are culture bound, then they must be changed to reflect a multicultural worldview.

Focus 3: Organizational

Since we all work for or are influenced by organizations, it is important to realize that institutional practices, policies, programs, and structures may be oppressive to certain groups, especially if they are monocultural. If organizational policies and practices deny equal access and opportunity for different groups or oppress them (redlining in home mortgages, laws against domestic partners, inequitable mental health care, etc.), then those policies and practices should become the targets for change.

Focus 4: Societal

If social policies (racial profiling, misinformation in educational materials, inequities in health care, etc.) are detrimental to the mental and physical health of minority groups, for example, does not the mental health professional have a responsibility to advocate for change? Our answer, of course, is affirmative.

Often, psychologists treat individuals who are the victims of failed systemic processes. Intervention at the individual level is primarily remedial when a strong need exists for preventive measures. Because psychology concentrates primarily on the individual, it has been deficient in developing more systemic and large-scale change strategies.

Implications for Clinical Practice

Using our tripartite levels of identity model (Figure 2.1), the multidimensional model of cultural competence (Figures 2.2 and 2.3), and the foci of cultural competence (Figure 2.4), we can discern several guiding principles for effective MCT.

1. Understand the terms *sociodemographic* and *diverse backgrounds* in the MCT definition to be inclusive and to encompass race, culture, gender, religious affiliation, sexual orientation, age, disability, and so on.
2. Realize that you are a product of cultural conditioning and that you are not immune from inheriting biases associated with culturally diverse groups in our society. As such, you must be vigilant for emotional reactions that may lead to a negation of other group values and lifestyles.
3. When working with different cultural groups, attempt to identify culture-specific and culture-universal domains of helping. Do not neglect the ways in which American Indians, Latinos/Hispanics, and African Americans, for example, may define normality/abnormality, the nature of helping, and what constitutes a helping relationship.
4. Be aware that persons of color, gays/lesbians, women, and other groups may perceive mental illness/health and the healing process differently than do Euro-Americans. To disregard differences and impose the conventional helping role and process on culturally diverse groups may constitute cultural oppression.

(continued)

(continued)

5. Be aware that Euro-American healing standards originate from a cultural context and represent only one form of helping that exists on an equal plane with others. As a helping professional, you must begin the task of recognizing the invisible veil of Euro-American cultural standards that influence your definitions of a helping relationship. As long as counselors and therapists continue to view Euro-American standards as normative, they will unwittingly set up a hierarchy among the groups.

6. Realize that the concept of *cultural competence* is more inclusive and superordinate than is the traditional definition of *clinical competence*. Do not fall into the trap of thinking "good counseling is good counseling." Know that cultural competence must replace clinical competence. The latter is culture bound, ethnocentric, and exclusive. It does not acknowledge racial, cultural, and gender differences sufficiently to be helpful. To assume universality of application to all groups is to make an unwarranted inferential leap.

7. If you are planning to work with the diversity of clients in our world, you must play roles other than that of the conventional counselor. Simply concentrating on the traditional clinical role ignores the importance of interventions at other levels. New helping roles, such as consultant, advisor, change agent, facilitator of indigenous healing systems, and so on, have been suggested as equally valuable.

8. Realize that organizational/societal policies, practices, and structures may represent oppressive obstacles that prevent equal access and opportunity. If that is the case, systems intervention is most appropriate.

9. Use modalities that are consistent with the lifestyles and cultural systems of clients. In many cases, psychoeducational approaches, working outside of the office, and engaging in practices that violate traditional Euro-American standards (e.g., advice giving and self-disclosure) may be dictated.

10. Finally, but most important, realize that MCT (and cultural competence) is inclusive because it includes all groups (including Whites, males, and heterosexuals). Conventional counseling and therapy are exclusive and narrow and are based on Euro-American norms. As such, cultural competence is superordinate to clinical competence.

Multicultural Counseling Competence for Minority Group Counselors/Therapists

CHAPTER FOCUS QUESTIONS

1. Is multicultural counseling for majority group members only?
2. Does being a member of a marginalized group mean the person is automatically culturally competent? If so, in what ways?
3. Do African Americans, Asian Americans, Latino/a Americans, and American Indians hold stereotypes about one another? Can they interfere with working in interracial/interethnic counseling?
4. What barriers are likely to arise between a minority group counselor and a majority group client?
5. Does being a member of an oppressed or marginalized group make the person more understanding of issues related to oppression and bigotry? In other words, is a White woman better able to work with a racial minority group member than a White man?
6. What can students of color, women, and lesbian, gay, bisexual, or transgendered persons (LGBT) learn about multicultural counseling and cultural competence?
7. What role does the racial, gender, and sexual orientation identity of counselors play in working with a member of their own group?

As a professor of color who has taught many courses on multicultural counseling/-therapy and conducted numerous workshops on race relations, I [senior author] have always been aware that my teaching and training were more directed at educating White trainees and counselors to their own biases and assumptions about human behavior. I operated from the assumption that people of color knew much of the material on oppression, discrimination, and stereotyping. After all, I reasoned, we were members of the oppressed group and had experiential knowledge of how racism harmed us. Yet in the back of my mind, I knew that I was short-changing my students of color by making this supposition. I knew that they also had biases and prejudices toward one another and that oftentimes their strong negative reactions toward fellow White students (albeit often justified) could prevent their development toward cultural competence. I knew that much of my trepidation in addressing interracial and interethnic relations had to do with presenting a united front among people of color, and I erroneously operated from a "common enemy" perspective. I knew that by taking this stance, I was perpetuating the belief that only Whites needed to change. I also knew that avoiding broader discussions of interethnic relations blocked the ability of people of color to more deeply explore their own biased beliefs about one another.

Increasingly, however, I have realized that it was an educational disservice to avoid such discussions, as it became more apparent that cultural competence was not just for majority group members. With this realization, I became more active in addressing these issues in my classes and workshops, often pushing emotional hot buttons in some of my students and participants of color. The following journal entry made by a former African American student makes clear some of these issues.

I've been angry at Professor Sue for this whole semester. I wish that they would have had a Black professor teach the class. How could he possibly have given me a B− in the midterm [racial counseling lab course]? I'll bet the White students got better grades. As a Black woman I know racism firsthand. They [White students] don't get it and still get better grades. And then we have to keep this stupid journal so he [professor] can have the TA help us process our feelings. I don't care if you read this stupid journal or not. . . . I know what I feel and why. . . . Well, I'm angry and furious that you gave me a low grade. . . . I'm angry at the White students who hide their racism and just say the right things in class. They are phonies. They are scared to death of me. . . . I just won't put up with their lies and I don't care if I make them cry. . . . I'm sure they think I'm just an angry Black woman. . . .

Why am I not getting an A in the course? I know why. It has to do with our role-play last week. The class thought I should have been more empathetic with Sandy [Asian American female who played the role of a client]. They said I couldn't relate to her and didn't explore her feelings of discrimination as an Asian. Well, I did. But you can't tell me that she suffers like Blacks do. I felt like saying . . . good, now you know what it feels like!!!! . . .

Then, Dr. Sue had to stop us from continuing and made process observations. He said I seemed to have difficulty being empathic with the client and believing her. What does he know? How does he know what's going on inside my head? But truth be told, Sandy doesn't have anything to complain or whine about. She doesn't understand what discrimination really is . . . maybe she has been treated poorly . . . but . . . but . . . well, I don't consider Asians people of color anyway. How can they claim to be oppressed when they are so successful? On this campus, they are every-where, taking slots away from us. Sometimes I think they are whiter than Whites. I'll probably get an even worst grade because of what I'm saying, but who cares.

It took much class time and several individual meetings to finally get the stu-dent to begin examining her reactions to fellow White students and her images and prejudices toward Asians and Asian Americans. I [senior author] tried to focus the discussion on the meaning of her extreme reactions to majority group mem-bers and to other minorities and on what significance it would have if they were her clients. Although the student did not change significantly because of her class-room experience, the lessons that came out from that role-play provided an oppor-tunity for the entire class to enter a discussion of interracial/interethnic counseling topics. Some important themes are the following.

First, we must not blame the victim (African American student) for the strong and emotive feelings of anger, resentment, and bitterness emanating from her. It is important to understand and be empathic to the fact that these reactions are most likely the result of cumulative years of prejudice and discrimination directed toward her as a member of a socially devalued group member (Parham, Ajamu, & White, 2011; Ridley, 2005). Is she justified in her anger? The answer is probably "yes." But is her anger and bitterness misdirected and likely to cause her difficulty in working with Asian American and White clients? Again, the answer is probably "yes." In working with White clients, minority group counselors might (a) be un-able to contain their anger and rage toward majority group clients as they are viewed as the oppressor, (b) have difficulty understanding the worldview of their clients, (c) be hindered in their ability to establish rapport, (d) be pulled between opposing tendencies of helping and harming their clients, and (d) be guilty of im-posing their racial realities upon clients. Such a conflict can be manifested in al-most any relationship involving a minority counselor and a majority or other minority client. The following quote indicates that this type of dilemma can occur in any minority-majority therapeutic relationship. In this case, the female therapist echoes this challenging dilemma in working with a male client.

> My challenge has been in my work with men. I have always felt somewhat constrained with my male clients and did not like the impact it had on our therapy. I had talked to other women therapists about my difficulties and found that they had similar experiences. My problems became most evi-dent to me when issues related to privilege, gender, and power needed to be discussed. I found myself caught between being too adversarial and challenging on one hand and the "all-giving" protector trained to soothe pain on the other. (Kort, 1997, p. 97)

Second, it is obvious that the African American student possesses many ster-eotypes and inaccurate beliefs about Asian Americans. The student seems to operate from the assumptions that Asian Americans "are not people of color," that they know little about racism and discrimination, and that they are like Whites. These statements and her desire that a Black professor should teach the course rather than an Asian American reflect these beliefs. As you will see shortly in Chapter 16, "Counseling Asian American and Pacific Islanders," headlines in the national press such as "Asian Americans: Outwhiting Whites" and "Asian Americans: The Model Minority" have perpetuated the success myth and belief that Asians are a "model minority" and somehow immune to prejudice and racism (D. W. Sue, 2010b). However, a critical analysis of the success myth reveals truths that are at odds with these conclusions (Kim, 2011). These false stereotypes of Asian Americans have often played into major misunderstandings and conflicts between the Black American and the Asian American communities. The issue here is the stereotypes that various racial/ethnic minority groups hold toward one another. For example, in one study, it was found that greater than 40% of African Americans and Hispanics believe that Asian Americans are unscrupulous, crafty, and devious in business (National Conference of Christians and Jews, 1994). How do these beliefs affect interethnic relations, and how do they affect the counseling/therapy process? No racial/ethnic group is immune from inheriting the biased beliefs, misinformation, and stereotypes of one another. This is a reality often not discussed in courses on diversity and multiculturalism.

Third, we have some flavor of the "who's more oppressed?" trap being played out in the mind of the African American student. She believes that the Asian American student can in no way equate her experiences of discrimination and prejudice with that of Black Americans. And, perhaps she is right! There is little doubt that a racial hierarchy exists in our society in which various groups can be ordered along a continuum. The fact that African Americans have historically been and continue to be in the national forefront of the civil rights debate must be acknowledged and appreciated by all. There is also, however, little doubt that each group—whether Native American, African American, Latino/a American, or Asian American—can claim that it has suffered immensely from racism. But what we need to realize is that all oppression is damaging and serves to separate rather than unify. Playing the "who is more oppressed?" game is destructive to group unity and counterproductive to combating racism. If we understand our own group's oppression, shouldn't it be easier to recognize the oppression of another? To use one group's oppression to negate that of another group is to diminish, dismiss, or negate the claims of another. This leads to separation rather than mutual understanding.

MINORITY GROUP COUNSELORS WORKING WITH MAJORITY AND MINORITY GROUP CLIENTS

Counseling the Culturally Diverse has never shied away from tackling controversial issues and topics, especially when they are central to the education and training of culturally competent mental health professionals. Persons of color, for example, have major hesitations and concerns about publicly airing interracial/interethnic conflicts, differences, and misunderstandings because of the possible political ramifications for group unity. But it appears that cultural competency objectives are equally applicable to therapists of color and other minority group clinicians. There is legitimacy, however, as to why greater emphasis has been placed on the education of White trainees: (a) the majority of mental health providers are White or members of the majority group; (b) the theories and practices of counseling/therapy arise from a predominantly White, Western perspective and form the educational foundations of our graduate programs; and (c) White, male, and straight Euro-Americans continue to control and hold power in being able to determine normality/abnormality and to define mental health reality for marginalized groups. Even if counselors/therapists of color work with other culturally diverse groups, they are generally educated in White, Western ways of describing, explaining, diagnosing, and treating mental disorders. Thus, there is great justification for continuing to focus primarily upon the education and training of those who control the gateways to the delivery of mental health services to socially devalued client populations.

In reality, however, it is clear that all groups can benefit from learning to work with one another. Being a therapist or trainee of color does not automatically denote cultural competence in working with other clients of color or even with White clients. Being a member of an oppressed or marginalized group (e.g., a gay and/or a woman therapist) does not mean you are more effective in treating other culturally diverse clients than if you were a straight or male therapist. It is important to recognize that in the area of racial interactions, multicultural counseling and therapy is more than White-Black, White-Asian, or White-Latino/a. To be a truly multicultural discipline, we must also recognize that MCT involves multiple combinations such as Asian-Black, Latino/a-Native American, Black-Latino/a, and so on. Further, we have not emphasized strongly enough the unique challenges encountered by counselors of color, for example, when counseling White clients and fellow minority clients. Some of these challenges are seen in the reflection questions that follow.

REFLECTION AND DISCUSSION QUESTIONS

1. How does a counselor of color work with a White client who expresses racist thoughts and feelings in the therapeutic session? Should he or she confront the client about these biased attitudes? Is this therapeutic?
2. What biases and prejudices do people of color have toward one another? How do you think they interfere in work with clients?
3. Do people of color hold stereotypes and biases toward each other? What are they?

We address these issues from a number of perspectives: sociopolitical group relationships, cultural differences, racial identity development, and practice implications. We are aware that addressing potential biases held by people of color toward one another or toward other marginalized groups may prove very controversial among our brothers and sisters of color. However, it is important for providers of all groups to confront these issues realistically and to open up an avenue for dialogue. Because the number of specific groups is so great, we will concentrate primarily on the challenges confronting counselors of color but point to how principles and practices have implications for dyadic counseling that may involve nonracial minority-majority combinations as well.

We start with the assumption that people in the United States, regardless of race and ethnicity, are exposed to the racial, gender, and sexual orientation socialization processes of this society and also inherit racial, gender, and sexual orientation biases about various populations. With regard to racial/ethnic minorities, sociopolitical histories between specific groups of color in this country have caused racial tension and stereotypes to evolve. Multicultural competence models emphasize that racial/ethnic groups have different sociopolitical histories, hold different cultural values, and develop racial/cultural identities in such a way as to impact group/individual relations in the wider society. As counseling and therapy is a microcosm of race relations in the United States, these dynamics are likely to be manifest in the counseling relationship.

THE POLITICS OF INTERETHNIC AND INTERRACIAL BIAS AND DISCRIMINATION

People of color generally become very wary about discussing interethnic and interracial misunderstandings and conflicts between various groups for fear that such problems may be used by those in power to (a) assuage their own guilt feelings and excuse their own racism—"People of color are equally racist, so why should I change when they can't even get along with one another?" (b) divide and conquer—"As long as people of color fight among themselves, they can't form alliances to confront the establishment," and (c) divert attention away from the injustices of society by defining problems as residing between various racial minority groups. Further, readers must understand that minority prejudice toward other groups (e.g., people of color or Whites) occurs under an umbrella of White racial superiority and supremacy; although minority groups may discriminate, they do not have the systemic power to oppress on a large-scale basis (Spradlin & Parsons, 2008; Sue, 2003). In other words, although they may be able to hurt one another on an individual basis and to individually discriminate against White Americans, they possess little power to cause systemic harm, especially to White Americans. Some people of color have even suggested that interethnic prejudice among minorities serves to benefit only those in power.

As a result, people of color are sometimes cautioned not to "air dirty laundry in public." These concerns are certainly legitimate, and we would be remiss in not alerting readers to how society has historically used conflicts between racial groups as a justification for continued oppression and avoidance in dealing with White racism. But the admonition not to "air dirty laundry in public" speaks realistically to the existence of miscommunications, disagreements, misunderstandings, and potential conflicts between and among ethnic/racial minority groups. When people of color constituted a small percentage of the population, it was to their advantage to become allies in a united front against the sources of injustice. Avoiding or minimizing interethnic group differences and conflicts served a functional purpose: to allow them to form coalitions of political, economic, and social power to effect changes in society. Although historically beneficial on a political and systemic level, the downside has been neglect in dealing with interracial differences that have proven to become problematic. This issue is even more pressing when one considers that people of color, for example, will become a numerical majority in the next several decades.

We believe that the time has long passed when not openly addressing these issues continues to hold unquestioned merit. People of color have always known that they, too, harbor prejudicial and detrimental beliefs about one another and about majority group members. Feminists have acknowledged difficulty in relating to men who hold traditional beliefs about appropriate female gender roles.

> I know that I'm a good therapist, but it galls me to have to work with men that are so dense about their own sexism. Last week I was doing marital counseling, and the husband kept interrupting his wife and berating her for not having his dinner on time when he returned from work, not having the home tidy, and keeping the kids quiet. He said she did not appreciate how hard he worked to keep food on the table. Well, I thought, what a chauvinistic attitude. What about his poor wife? Doesn't he have any idea of what it's like for her to raise the three kids? Does he think she has been lying on the couch and eating bon bons all day? I nearly blew up at him when he dismissed my observations about his behavior. He was treating me like his wife. I was furious at him. [His wife] would be better off getting a divorce. (female therapist)

GLBT groups describe negative reactions to straights who voice beliefs that gay sex is immoral, that marriage should be between a man and a woman, or that their religion condemns such a lifestyle.

> My greatest difficulty is working with patients who are strongly homophobic. You see, I am gay, an invisible minority. People assume I'm heterosexual, so in therapy they give voice to many anti-gay beliefs. I'm often conflicted about what to say or do. By ignoring the comments or allowing them to go unchallenged, am I perpetuating such beliefs? Is it my role to challenge them? (gay male therapist)

If we look at the relationships between groups of color, for example, misunderstandings and mistrust become very obvious. In the early 1990s, the racial discourse in urban America was dominated by African American boycotts of Korean mom-and-pop grocery stores, which was followed by looting, firebombing, and mayhem that engulfed Los Angeles (Chang, 2001). Many in the Black community felt that Koreans were exploiting their communities as had White businesses. Reports of Hispanic and Black conflicts in the inner cities have also been reported throughout the country. As Latinos have surpassed Blacks in numbers, they have increasingly demanded a greater voice in communities and in the political process. Since Latinos and Blacks tend to gravitate toward the same inner-city areas and compete for the same jobs, great resentment has grown between the groups (D. B. Wood, 2006).

The immigration issue has also sparked fierce debate within the Latino and Black communities, as some Blacks believe jobs are being lost to the huge influx of Latinos (Behnken, 2011). In essence, the discourse of race that once was confined to Black-White relations has become increasingly multiethnic and multiracial. These differences are reflected in the perceptions that groups of color have toward one another. One major national survey (National Conference of Christians and Jews, 1994) found the following:

1. More than 40% of African Americans and Hispanics and one of every four Whites believe that Asian Americans are "unscrupulous, crafty, and devious in business."
2. Nearly half the Hispanic Americans surveyed and 40% of African Americans and Whites believe Muslims "belong to a religion that condones or supports terrorism."
3. Blacks think they are treated far worse than Whites and worse than other minority groups when it comes to getting equal treatment in applying for mortgages, in the media, and in job promotions.
4. Only 10% of African Americans—a staggeringly low number—believe the police treat them as fairly as other groups.
5. African Americans believe that everyone else is treated with more equality and especially that Asian Americans are doing better.
6. There is tremendous resentment of Whites by all minority groups.
7. Two-thirds of minorities think Whites "believe they are superior and can boss people around," "are insensitive to other people," "control power and wealth in America," and "do not want to share it with non-Whites."

Two primary conclusions are noteworthy here: First, racial/ethnic groups experience considerable mistrust, envy, and misunderstandings toward one another as well. Surprisingly, African Americans and Latinos held stronger negative beliefs about Asian Americans than did White Americans (40% versus 25%)! Second, and not surprisingly, people of color continue to hold beliefs and attitudes toward Whites that are very negative and filled with resentments, anger, and strong mistrust.

Some might argue, however, that a therapist of color working with a White client may be different from a therapist of color working with a client of color because power differentials still exist on a systemic level for White clients. Little in the way of research or conceptual scholarly contributions has addressed these issues or questions.

REFLECTION AND DISCUSSION QUESTIONS

1. What effect does interethnic bias on the part of therapists of color have upon their culturally diverse clients?
2. If an African American therapist works with an Asian American client or vice versa, what therapeutic issues are likely to arise?
3. Likewise, in light of the strong negative feelings expressed by all groups of color against Whites, how might a therapist of color react intentionally and unintentionally toward a White client?

It may not be far-fetched, however, to surmise that these racial combinations may share some similar dynamics and clinical issues to White therapist/client-of-color dyads. Some increased understanding of these issues, however, may come from a brief review of the historical analysis of interracial/interethnic relationships between groups of color in other venues of their lives.

THE HISTORICAL AND POLITICAL RELATIONSHIPS BETWEEN GROUPS OF COLOR

Most articles in the field of psychology that focus on interracial interactions between Asian, Black, Native, and Latino/a Americans concentrate mainly on interracial romantic relationships (e.g., Yancey, 2002), interracial friendships (e.g., Way, Becker, & Greene, 2006), interracial interactions on college campuses (e.g., Cowen, 2005; Halualani, Chitgopekar, Morrison, & Dodge, 2004; Mack et al., 1997), or historical interracial conflict (e.g., Black/Korean conflict after the LA Riots of 1992; Myers, 2001). There is a paucity of literature that focuses specifically on interracial interactions between counselors and clients of different racial/ethnic minority groups (e.g., Asian, Black, Latino/a, or Native Americans). This may falsely convey that there is limited tension between groups of color and that discrimination and stereotyping does not occur between these groups. However, given the history of the United States, it is apparent that discrimination and stereotyping does occur between all racial groups. It is important to recognize that the biases of a counselor of color could be detrimental in a therapeutic relationship with culturally diverse clients. An important distinction to make is the difference between biases toward groups of color held by a White counselor and those held by a counselor of color. Although both are potentially detrimental and can create barriers to effective therapeutic treatment, White counselors have greater power to oppress people on systemic and societal levels than do counselors of color, who can do so only on the individual level (Ponterotto, Utsey, & Pedersen, 2006).

> . . . Given the history of the United States, it is apparent that discrimination and stereotyping does occur between all racial groups. It is important to recognize that the biases of a counselor of color could be detrimental in a therapeutic relationship with culturally diverse clients.

One might wonder why scholars and researchers have avoided discussing the types of discrimination that may occur between different groups of color. During the civil rights movement, people of color banded together to combat economic and social injustices that were against them. Because of their small numbers, recognizing and/or publicizing interracial group dynamics or conflicts would be a barrier to the movement. As a result, people of color have avoided public dialogue (on both individual and group levels) about historical and existing tensions between their groups. Furthermore, people of color may have difficulty admitting to their biases or stereotypes about other groups because of their unwillingness to admit to their own prejudices (D. W. Sue, 2003). Because individuals of color have experienced racism throughout their lives, it may prove difficult for them to understand the biases they hold toward other groups. Some people of color believe that they would not be able to discriminate, stereotype, or pass judgment on others because they themselves have been racially victimized. Other people of color may recognize their biases but may believe that because they do not have any systemic power, their biases are acceptable or nonthreatening. Regardless of these perspectives, through examining the history of the United States, it must be understood that both interracial alliances and tension may occur between all racial groups. These unique histories and experiences may lead to several dynamics in our personal, professional, and therapeutic relationships.

Historical Stereotypes and Tension Between Groups

Given the aforementioned sociopolitical histories between and among groups of color in the United States and given that therapy is often seen as a microcosm of race relations in society, it seems that interracial tension in the counseling relationship is a real possibility. The history of race relations in the United States usually outlines the history between people of color and Whites. Literature concentrating on institutional racial discrimination (e.g., voting rights, segregation from public schools) has traditionally focused on discrimination of Native Americans by Whites (Jaimes, 1992), discrimination of Black Americans by Whites (Fireside, 2004), discrimination of Asians by Whites (Takaki, 1998), or discrimination of Latinos by Whites (Haney-Lopez, 2003). However, a closer look at the history of race relations between these four groups reveals biases, stereotypes, misunderstandings, and often bitterness between the groups.

African American and Asian American Relationships

The conflicting relationships between African Americans and Asian Americans remained relatively unspoken until the Los Angeles Riots in 1992, in which some Black Americans looted Asian American businesses. The riot occurred when African Americans were outraged at the acquittal of four White officers from the Los Angeles Police Department in the beating of Rodney King, a Black motorist. Of the 4,500 stores that were looted and burned, 2,300 were Korean-owned (Yoon, 1997). Although this tension existed prior to the riots, this experience led to overt tension between the groups throughout the United States (Kim, 1999). In interviews with several Korean American business owners, it was clear that they stereotyped Black American customers as likely to steal or become violent; likewise, some Black Americans who acted out against Korean businesses stereotyped Asian Americans as being racist and hostile toward them and thought that they took economic advantage of their communities. This may have even led to overt racist behaviors toward one another, in which Asian American store owners would blatantly refuse business from Black American patrons or follow them around stores and Black Americans might blatantly use racial slurs such as "Chinaman" or "chink" when speaking to Korean workers (Myers, 2001).

These feelings and beliefs, if held firmly, might indeed infect the therapeutic relationship between the two groups. In our opening case vignette, for example, the African American student dismissed and negated the feelings of discrimination expressed by the Asian American client as not real discrimination. She saw Asian Americans like Whites and believed in the success myth of Asian Americans in our society. On the other hand, Asians and Asian Americans may harbor images of Blacks as criminals, prone to violence, and dangerous. Despite the fact that both of these groups may have unique oppressive experiences (e.g., African Americans being seen as untrustworthy or inferior and Asian Americans being seen as foreigners in their own country), individuals from both groups may have the inability to empathize with the other group's experiences.

Asian and Latino/a Americans

The historical relationship between Asian Americans and Latino/a Americans is not discussed and is usually invisible in discussions of race (De Genova, 2006). However, there are several ways in which these two groups may share a sense of camaraderie with one another and may experience divisive tension. Both groups share the experience of immigration; the majority of Asian Americans and Latino/a Americans are first- or second-generation Americans (De Genova, 2006; Kim, 2011). This shared history may lead to similar experiences of biculturalism (maintaining Asian or Latino/a and American values), culture conflicts, similar linguistic concerns (bilingualism), and experiences of pursuing the American dream. One of the dominant similarities of both groups is their shared experience of being treated like a foreigner in one's own country (particularly when an individual was born and raised in the United States), as well as a solidarity in that both groups are often left out of the Black-White racial paradigm debate. When issues or matters of race are discussed in the news media, for example, the dialogue is usually Black-White and seldom includes Asian Americans or Latino/a Americans. The invisibility as groups of color in the racial debate has often created hard feelings in these two groups toward African Americans as well.

Although this experience may be shared, it can also lead to competition between the groups. Because these groups may feel invisible, they may compete with each other in order to have their voices heard. Historically, this was present during the Chicano-Filipino United Farm Workers Movement in the 1930s, in which Mexican and Filipino Americans worked cohesively for farm workers' rights in California, yet disbanded when the groups could not agree upon common interests (Scharlin & Villanueva, 1994). Currently, this may be exemplified with U.S. politics in which Asian and Latino Americans may run against each other in local elections instead of working harmoniously to form a unified alliance.

Latino/a Americans and Black Americans

The history between Latino/a Americans and Black Americans also has both solidarity and discord. Historically, there has been solidarity between the two groups, particularly in their quest for equality during the civil rights era (Behnken, 2011). Traditionally, both groups recognized each other as oppressed minority groups, understanding that the other may experience racism, be subjected to stereotyping, and be denied equal access and opportunities given to White people. However, there are also points of contention between these two groups.

First, similar to the relationships between Asians and Latinos, there may be tension between Latinos and Blacks, as a result of fighting for the sociopolitical issues and needs for one's own group. In recent years, Latino/a Americans have overwhelmingly exceeded Black Americans in regard to population; this has led to Latinos gaining more visibility in politics and education (D. B. Wood, 2006). The rise of Latino/a demands has also created tension amongst Latinos and Blacks because they now find themselves competing for jobs, which has forced some Black Americans to oppose many Latino/a Americans in the immigration debate (Behnken, 2011). This has often resulted in problems related to a lack of alliance between the two groups, particularly when it comes to advocacy in government, education, and community organizing (Samad et al., 2006).

Second, it is important to recognize that racism within the Latino/a community has historical roots as a result of Spanish colonialism in Latin America. It is important to note that the term *Latino/a* is an ethnic designator and not a racial one. Thus, Latinos may be members of any racial grouping. As a result, they may range from phenotypically appearing Black to White, with many appearing to be somewhere in between (Bautista, 2003). However, because of colonial mentality, *mestizos*, or light-skinned Latinos, are valued more highly than darker-skinned Latinos, who may be viewed as inferior, unintelligent, or unattractive (Patrinos, 2000). This may lead to a hierarchy within the Latino/a community, in which light-skinned groups, such as Argentineans, Colombians, or Cubans, may view themselves as superior to darker-skinned groups, such as Dominicans or Mexicans. This colonial mentality may transcend a Latino/a individual's view of a Black American; this is supported by studies that have shown that Latinos hold negative stereotypes of Black Americans as being lazy and untrustworthy, whereas Black Americans do not feel the same way about Latinos (McClain et al., 2006).

Native Americans and Black, Latino/a, and Asian Americans

The relationship between Native Americans and Black, Latino/a, and Asian Americans may not be discussed or known, due to the small numbers of Native Americans in the United States. Black Americans, Latinos, and Asians may have little interaction with Native Americans, which may lead to less obvious tension or dynamics between Native Americans and another racial group. Concurrently, because 40% of the Native American population may be of another race (U.S. Census Bureau, 2005), many Native Americans may physically look like members of other racial groups, causing others to perceive them and treat them in different ways. However, a Native American interacting with members of these racial groups may share similarities or experience tensions with individuals of other races, perhaps empathizing with a Black American's experiences of oppression or bonding with a Latino/a's or an Asian's feelings of being an invisible minority. At the same time, a Black, a Latino/a, or an Asian individual who does not recognize the Native American's racial identity, realities, history, or experiences may cause the Native American to feel dismissed, ignored, or invalidated.

CULTURAL DIFFERENCES IN VALUES AND PERSPECTIVES BETWEEN RACIAL/ETHNIC GROUPS

To further understand interracial/interethnic dynamics, it is important to recognize that different groups of color hold values, beliefs, and behaviors unique to their culture, which may conflict with those of other groups. Many of these differences in cultural values are addressed in Chapter 7. Specifically, previous literature has found that racial/ethnic groups have differences in worldviews and communication styles. Additionally, these groups may have different views of therapy, based on cultural stigma and the group's historical experiences with mental health institutions. By highlighting these cultural differences, mental health practitioners can better understand the types of dynamics that may occur in a therapeutic relationship. Let us explore a few of these differences.

Cultural Values

Because we give thorough coverage throughout the text about differences in cultural values, we will discuss only a few here. Shared and nonshared values held by groups of color may lead to an experience of camaraderie or to one of tension and antagonism. For example, although many White Americans typically believe that people have mastery and control over the environment, persons of color typically believe that people and nature are harmonious with one another (C. P. Chen, 2005; McCormick, 2005). Additionally, whereas Whites adhere to the value of individualism, Asian, Native, Black, and Latino/a Americans may maintain the values of collectivism, in which the needs of the group/family/community are paramount. Within collectivism, emphasis is placed on the family, what Latinos call *familialism* or *familismo;* a high valuation is placed on family loyalty and unity (Guzman & Carrasco, 2011; Santiago-Rivera, Arredondo, & Gallardo-Cooper, 2002). If a Latino/a counselor ascribes to familismo and works with a client of color who does not place the same central importance on the family, the counselor may inadvertently interpret this person to be emotionally disconnected and isolated.

Although sharing a cultural value may lead to a therapeutic working relationship between two different individuals of color, its expression may potentially cause a misunderstanding in therapy as well. For example, respect for elders is a value traditionally held by both Asian Americans (Kim, 2011) and African Americans (West-Olatunji & Conwill, 2011). However, expression of this value may differ among members of each racial group. In some Asian American cultures, respect is shown by not talking unless spoken to and by averting one's eyes and thus not making direct eye contact with the elder or respected person (Nadal, 2011). An African American counselor may misinterpret an avoidance of eye contact by an Asian American client to be a sign of disrespect, avoidance, or even deceitfulness. In fact, during the Los Angeles riots, this major cultural difference created much animosity between Black patrons and Korean American shop owners; the former saw Koreans as unable to be truthful about prices in the store because they wouldn't "look you in the eye." Conversely, the Korean shop owner saw the African American customer as rude, demanding, and aggressive.

Communication Styles

The previous examples lead to our discussion of differences in communication styles between various racial/ethnic groups. Communication style differences (see Chapter 8), which may be displayed by ethnic minorities or therapists, can impact the expectations or responsiveness of clients from different backgrounds. Native Americans for example, are more likely to speak softly, use an indirect gaze, and interject less frequently, whereas White Americans are more likely to speak loudly, have direct eye contact, and show a direct approach (Duran, 2006). These same characteristics may be displayed by therapists when they interact with clients. Ethnic minority therapists need to be aware of their verbal and nonverbal styles and to determine how they may either facilitate or act as a barrier to the formation of a therapeutic alliance. In a study of nonverbal communication (B. S. K. Kim, Liang, & Li, 2003), Asian American and European American female therapists were observed conducting one session of career counseling with Asian American volunteer clients. During the session, European American therapists smiled more frequently and had more postural shifts than did Asian American therapists. In terms of client ratings, frequency of smiles was correlated with positive feelings about the session. The results lend some support to the view that cultural differences in verbal and nonverbal styles of communicating feelings may affect the therapist-client relationship.

How clients and counselors communicate with one another is often dictated by cultural imperatives that determine what is appropriate and inappropriate. Communication is important in understanding the dynamics that may occur between racial groups. Communication styles may include overt verbal communication that may occur between two people (content of what is said) but may also include nonverbal communication (body language, tone of voice, volume of speech, what is not said, and the directness of speech), which is equally as important as the spoken word. African American communication style tends to be direct, passionate, and forthright (an indication of sincerity and truthfulness) (Kochman, 1981; Parham et al., 2011). However, Asian culture highly prizes a person's subtlety and indirectness in communication, as it is considered a sign of respect to the other person (B. S. K. Kim, 2011a). Even when disagreements are present, differences are discussed tactfully, avoiding direct confrontation.

Native Americans and Latino/a Americans may be nonconfrontational like Asian Americans, but their communication styles may change depending on the varying levels of authority between two people (Garrett & Portman, 2011). For example, Latino/a children are expected to respect their parents, to speak only when spoken to, to have younger siblings defer to older ones, and to yield to the wishes of someone with higher status and authority. Latino/a students, thus, may feel uncomfortable challenging or speaking directly to their teachers (Santiago-Rivera et al., 2002). This value may also conflict with the White American value of egalitarianism, where children are encouraged to freely express their thoughts and feelings. Although African American communication styles may be egalitarian as well, it is likely to be more animated and interpersonal, generating much emotion, affect, and feelings (Hecht, Jackson, & Ribeau, 2002; Weber, 1985). Given this, if an African American counselor communicates in a more animated and passionate fashion, it may negatively impact Latino/a or Asian American clients.

Issues Regarding Stage of Ethnic Identity

> Kavita, a clinician of South Asian descent, is unsure of her ethnic identity and has trouble balancing being American with being South Asian. Seeing South Asian clients only makes this conflict more important to her. Will this affect her attitudes toward treating minority clients? (Gurung & Mehta, 2001, p. 139)

The processes of assimilation and acculturation for various racial/ethnic minority groups in the United States are powerful forces in the development of identity. Studies continue to indicate that as groups of color are exposed to the values, beliefs, and standards of the larger society, many become increasingly westernized. This process is described more fully in Chapter 11, so we will only briefly acknowledge it here. People of color who are born and raised in the United States may continue to cling to their traditional racial/ethnic group heritage, actively reject it in favor of an "American identity," or form an integrated new identity. Depending on where they may fall on this continuum, their reactions to other people of color (both within and outside their own group) and to majority individuals may differ considerably. The stage of identity of ethnic minority therapists is likely to affect their work with clients. Kavita reveals a struggle in identity between being either South Asian or American. This conflict may be unconscious but is displayed by minority therapists during therapy, especially with clients of the same ethnicity.

In a study of 150 students of Indian descent, for example, those who were more westernized expressed less interest in serving minority clients. It was found that some individuals rejected their own ethnic group, preferring to have the majority culture as their standard. In other words, they tended to identify with Western values and Western standards of behavior and to seek validation from fellow White Americans. In general, they revealed a preference for working with White clients rather than members of their own race. In such situations, ethnic minority therapists may have to acknowledge and resolve identity issues, since it may affect their reactions to a client from the same ethnicity or in dealing with clients from the majority culture (Gurung & Mehta, 2001).

> Mikki, a 27-year-old social worker, who immigrated to Israel from Ethiopia at the age of 10, worked in a municipal unit for adolescents in distress. . . . Recognizing the huge gap between his family's traditional lifestyle and the modernity of the Israelis, he soon began to feel ashamed of his parents . . . he rejected the boys who represented his traditional Ethiopian self and favored those who represented the Israeli part of him. (Yedidia, 2005, pp. 165–166)

> Ethnic and racial identity and cultural affiliation are also strong factors affecting a client of color's experiences with and perceptions of a counselor of color.

During supervision, Mikki came to realize that his hostility to Ethiopian boys was a result of countertransference and that it reflected the inner conflict he was having between his identification as an Ethiopian and that of an Israeli. Mikki's reaction was not unusual: Yedidia (2005) found this same type of identity conflict among other immigrant therapists from Ethiopia and Russia. Immigrant and ethnic minority therapists need to consider possible identity conflicts in their work with culturally or ethnically similar clients. It is highly possible that ethnic minority therapists at the conformity stage of identity development (see Chapter 11) may either respond defensively or negatively to an ethnically similar client who is struggling with identity issues.

Ethnic and racial identity and cultural affiliation are also strong factors affecting a client of color's experiences with and perceptions of a counselor of color. Asian American clients with strong traditional values rate their Asian American therapists as more empathetic and credible than more westernized clients (B. S. K. Kim & Atkinson, 2002). Conversely, Western-oriented Asian American clients judged European American counselors to be more empathetic than did clients with high adherence to Asian cultural values. Thus, in ethnically similar therapist-client matches, potential matches or mismatches in cultural identity may need to be explored. Nevertheless, it is clear that the more divergent the cultural attitudes, beliefs, and behaviors are between client and counselor, the more conflict may exist in the therapeutic relationship. In fact, it appears that for African Americans, the more salient a participant's racial identity is to him or her, the more important it is to be matched with a Black American counselor (Ward, 2005). In the same study, however, participants who placed less importance and salience on their own Black identity believed their counselor's ideology (e.g., beliefs about parenting, past drug and alcohol use, religious beliefs) and not race similarity was more important in counseling effectiveness. This study supports the notion that within-group differences affect ratings of counselor effectiveness; for some Black American clients, the race of the counselor was very important, and for others it was not important at all.

COUNSELORS OF COLOR AND DYADIC COMBINATIONS WITH WHITE CLIENTS AND CLIENTS OF COLOR: SITUATIONAL EXAMPLES

The analysis in this chapter indicates how important sociopolitical factors, historical relationships between racial/ethnic minority groups, differences in cultural values, and racial identity of counselors and clients can serve to enhance or negate the counseling process. Little actual research has been conducted on the challenges and difficulties that counselors of color face when working with other culturally diverse groups. Less yet has been done on the subject of cultural competence as it relates to therapists of color. Nevertheless, the foregoing analysis would imply several situational challenges that therapists and trainees of color might expect on their journey to cultural competence.

Challenges Associated With Counseling White Clients

When working with White clients, a counselor of color is likely to operate in a situation of power reversal (Comas-Diaz & Jacobsen, 1995). When the counselor is White and the client is a person of color, the power relationship is congruent with historical and sociopolitical racial roles and structures in our society. The roles of colonizer-colonized and master-slave have defined relationships of who are leaders and followers, who is superior and inferior, and who is given higher or lower status. When the counselor is a person of color, however, it fosters a role reversal because the status of therapist denotes a person who possesses a set of expertise that surpasses that of the White client. In this case, the White client is in need of help, and the counselor of color is in a position to provide it (to diagnose, treat, advise, teach, and guide). Many White clients may find this dependent role very disturbing and manifest it in various ways. Some may, however, find the new relationship exotic or even a positive development. Counselors of color may also misuse the power reversal to harm or to deny appropriate help to their White clients.

> When working with White clients, a counselor of color is likely to operate in a situation of power reversal . . . When the counselor is White and the client is a person of color, the power relationship is congruent with historical and sociopolitical racial roles and structures in our society. . . . When the counselor is a person of color, however, it fosters a role reversal because the status of therapist denotes a person who possesses a set of expertise that surpasses that of the White client.

Situation 1: Having the Competency of the Therapist of Color Challenged

Whether White clients are conscious of it or not, they may directly or indirectly engage in maneuvers that challenge the credibility of the therapist of color, question the therapist's competence, negate the therapist's insights and advice, and undermine the therapeutic process. Such challenges are not necessarily conscious to the client nor expressed overtly. They may be manifested through an excessive interest in seeking greater information about the counselor's training and background, type of degrees received, place of training, and number of years in clinical practice. Or, they may be expressed through a tendency to be hypercritical of even the smallest omissions, oversights, and mistakes of the counselor. Behind these resistant behaviors is a presumption that therapists of color are less qualified than White ones—that therapists of color achieved their positions not through their own internal attributes (intelligence and abilities) or efforts (motivation) but through external circumstance, such as attending lesser qualified schools or being recipients of affirmative action programs. A study exploring both White and African American therapists' experiences in working with White clients supports these observations. Ethnic minority therapists consistently reported being the recipient of greater hostility, resistance, and mistrust in cross-racial practice than their White counterparts (Davis & Gelsomino, 1994).

For the therapist of color, there are no easy answers or solutions to dealing with challenges to a counselor's credibility. A decision to explore or confront White client resistant to the counselor of color depends on many internal and contextual factors: (a) the counselor of color's comfort with his or her racial/cultural identity, (b) clinical significance of the behavior, (c) timeliness of the intervention, (d) strength of the relationship, and (e) the form in which the intervention would take place. Regardless, several overarching guidelines might prove helpful here. First and foremost, a challenge to one's competence is not a pleasant thing, especially if it is tinged with racial overtones. Although the counselor may become upset with the client, becoming defensive and allowing it to dictate one's actions in the therapeutic session is counterproductive to helping the client. Second, before an effective intervention can take place, a counselor must recognize the resistance for what it is. This means an accurate diagnosis separating out behaviors such as questioning one's qualifications from other clinical motivations. Third, a decision to intervene must be dictated by timeliness in that it should occur at an opportune time that would maximize enlightenment of the client. Last, as the therapist of color will need to address racial issues, he or she must feel comfortable with engaging in a difficult dialogue on race.

Situation 2: Needing to Prove Competence

The fact that some Whites may consciously and unconsciously harbor beliefs that persons of color are less capable than Whites may affect people of color in two ways: (a) they may internalize these beliefs and stereotypes about themselves and their own group, or (b) they can become victims of stereotype threat, despite not believing in their own inferiority (Steele, 1997). With respect to the former, this may be especially true for therapists who have not resolved issues surrounding their racial identity and have accepted and adopted the standards and beliefs of mainstream society (Comas-Diaz & Jacobsen, 1995). In these cases, counselors of color may be trapped in the need to prove their competence and capabilities; unfortunately, this proof must come from White society, other White helping professionals, and even from White clients. In the therapy session, this type of conflict may be played out in seeking affirmation from White clients and abdicating their roles as experts in the relationship. They may also have a disinclination to see clients of color because it may bring to mind their own internalized racism that creates discomfort for them. In such cases, counselors of color may be paralyzed in discussing racial dynamics, experience extreme anxiety when racial issues arise, and allow their clients to take the lead in the sessions.

Even if a therapist of color has a healthy racial identity and does not believe in stereotypes of his or her own group's inferiority, that therapist may experience stereotype threat (Steele, 2003; Steele, Spencer, & Aronson, 2002). Research on stereotype threat suggests that persons of color are oftentimes placed in a position in which they fear confirming a mistaken notion about themselves. For example, Black students taking a math test and being told that it was a measure of intelligence have been found to perform more poorly than their White counterparts, despite possessing equal skills and abilities. Yet when given the identical task but instructed that the test was not a measure of intelligence, the performance of Black students equaled that of Whites. These researchers concluded that the fear of confirming a stereotype (e.g., Blacks are less intelligent than Whites and lack higher-order abstract conceptual ability) created emotional threat and tension and Black students worked hard to disconfirm stereotypes, which drained energies away from the task at hand. The result was underperformance in problem solving.

It is not too far-fetched to imagine how stereotype threat might also affect a counselor of color's performance in therapy. He or she may repeatedly feel pressure to disconfirm stereotypes, to enhance credibility, and to prove to White clients and White mental health professionals that he or she is capable and competent.

> For example, an African-American woman found herself placing on her office wall every professional certificate that she had received during her working career. When a colleague commented to her that her office's walls were appearing cluttered, the therapist was able to identify this behavior with the onset of her working with White patients. (Comas-Diaz & Jacobsen, 1995, p. 102)

Situation 3: Transferring Racial Animosity Toward White Clients

This situation is likely to arise through a process of countertransference where the therapist of color transfers feelings of resentment, anger, and antagonism toward White society to the client. In general, the therapist of color is unable to separate out the experiences of racism, discrimination, and prejudice experienced through years of oppression from those of the client. The White client may become a symbol of the inherent mistrust that exists in majority-minority interpersonal relationships; thus, the therapist may harbor negative feelings that infect and distort the counseling relationship. In most cases these grudges do not operate at a conscious level, but they are likely to present themselves in various forms: (a) dismissing or diluting the pain and suffering of their White clients, (b) being unable to form a working alliance, (c) having difficulty in being empathetic to their plight, (d) being ultrasensitive to potential racial slights, (e) distorting or misinterpreting their actions to include a racial motivation, and (f) possessing an unconscious desire to harm rather than help White clients. This is potentially a toxic situation and is best resolved within therapists of color prior to clinical practice.

Situation 4: Unrealistically Viewing the Therapist of Color as a Super Minority Therapist

It may appear contradictory, but evidence exists in the form of counselor preference studies and clinical narratives that indicate some White clients actually prefer a therapist of color over a White one. It has been found, for example, that some White college students actually indicate a preference for seeing a Black helping professional. The reason behind such a preference flies in the face of traditional race relations and is difficult to explain. In our own work with White clients and in speaking to colleagues of color, however, several possibilities may be entertained.

First, many White clients may possess an exaggerated sense of the therapist of color's qualifications, reasoning that to have achieved the status of therapist would require a nearly superhuman effort against the forces of discrimination. His or her accomplishments could come only from high intelligence, outstanding abilities, and high motivation. Thus, the therapist of color is seen as immensely superior and likely to better help the client. Second, many clients, regardless of race, often feel rejected, invalidated, misunderstood, and put down and suffer from pangs of inferiority and feelings of worthlessness. White clients may possess a mistaken notion that a therapist of color (who himself or herself has suffered from racism and stigmatization) may be able to sympathize and empathize better with the client. Third, the therapist of color may be perceived as an expert on race relations, and some Whites may be consciously or unconsciously attempting to deal with their own racial attitudes. At times the White client may be coping either with a conscious interracial relationship (e. g., dating a person of another race) or with more subtle unconscious personal dilemmas (e.g., White guilt and issues of privilege).

There is certainly a seductive quality to being perceived in such a favorable light, to be viewed as an expert, and to be accorded such high respect. This challenge is particularly difficult for therapists of color who in their daily lives outside of therapy sessions are not easily accorded the respect and dignity given to others. Yet to allow the "super minority counselor" image to persist is to perpetuate the false illusion of White clients and to potentially harm therapeutic progress. In this situation, the White clients may abdicate responsibility for their own improvements and become overly dependent on the counselor for answers to their problems. Counselors of color need to have a good sense of themselves as racial/cultural beings and not fall into the all-omnipotent trap.

Situation 5: Dealing With Expressions of Racist Attitudes/Beliefs/Behaviors

It goes without saying that therapists of color often encounter racist, sexist, and heterosexist statements and reactions from their clients. Whereas many LGBT people may remain invisible, people of color represent a visible racial/ethnic minority with distinguishable physical features. Counselors of color, through appearance, speech, or other factors, generate reactions. These perceived differences may influence the development of a therapeutic relationship. As Asian American therapists, we've had clients make statements such as, "I like Chinese food" or "The Chinese are very smart and family-oriented," or they exhibit some discomfort when meeting us for the first time. In one study (Fuertes & Gelso, 2000), male Hispanic counselors who spoke with a Spanish accent were rated lower in expertise by Euro-American students than those counselors without an accent. This phenomenon may also exist for therapists with other accents and may need to be discussed in therapy to allay anxiety in both the therapist and the client. One graduate student from Bosnia would discuss her accent and would let clients know that English was her second language. Although her command of English was good, this explanation helped establish a more collaborative relationship.

Acknowledging differences or investigating the reasons for client reactions, is important since they may affect the therapeutic process. In one instance, an African American psychology intern working with a man in his 70s noticed that the client persisted in telling stories about the "Negro fellas" that he served with in the army. He made positive comments about his Black comrades and talked about their contributions to the unit. The intern responded by saying, "I guess you noticed I'm Black" (Hinrichsen, 2006, p. 31). This response led to a discussion of client concerns that he would say something that might be considered offensive. He also worried about whether the intern could understand the experience of an older White man.

White therapists facing an ethnic minority client often struggle with whether to ask, "How do you feel working with a White therapist?" Likewise, this situation is also faced by minority therapists working with White clients. When differences between therapist and client are apparent (e.g., ethnicity, gender, ability, age) or revealed (e.g., religion, sexual orientation), acknowledging them is important. Both African American and White American students revealed a stronger preference for openness and self-disclosure when asked to imagine a counselor of a different ethnicity (Cashwell, Shcherbakova, & Cashwell, 2003). Self-disclosure, or the acknowledgment of differences, may increase feelings of similarity between therapist and client and reduce concerns about differences. In this respect, the same might apply when both the therapist and the client are persons of color but are from a different racial/ethnic group.

Challenges Associated With Counseling Clients of Another Minority Group or Own Group

Many of the challenges facing therapists of color working with White clients can also make their appearance in the minority-minority counseling dyad. Like their White counterparts, people of color are socialized into the dominant values and beliefs of the larger society. As a result, they may inherit the perceptions and beliefs of other racial/ethnic minority groups as well. In this case, the biases and stereotypes held for other groups of color may not be all that different from that of White Americans. A Latino/a American client can harbor doubts about the qualifications of a Native American therapist; an Asian American client can act out racist attitudes toward an African American therapist; and an African American counselor may downplay the role that prejudice and discrimination play in the life of Asian Americans. Other interethnic/interracial specific challenges may also make their appearance in the counseling dyad.

Situation 6: Overidentification With the Client

Overidentification with clients of color, whether with ingroup or outgroup dyadic therapeutic racial relationships, is often manifested through countertransference. Although it is accepted that the transference of symbolic feelings, thoughts, and experiences of the client of color can occur to that of the therapist, an equally powerful countertransference can occur from therapist to client, especially in interracial and interethnic dyadic combinations.

Years ago, one of the authors was supervising a young African American male trainee in the college counseling center. He was meeting for the first time with an African American male student-athlete who came to the clinic complaining of "not being played enough" in the football games and spending more time warming the bench than most of his fellow White students. He described experiencing racial taunts from fans on the opposing teams and described how he felt isolated from his own teammates and believed his White coach and his staff were prejudiced. He was fearful of being dropped by the team and losing his scholarship. The experience of discrimination was so disturbing, according to the student, that he was unable to concentrate on his studies and was depressed. By the end of the first session, the African American trainee agreed to contact his professors to obtain an extension in taking further finals, speak to the coach about the many racist incidents he was being subjected to, and contact the ombudsperson about the plight of the student. In fact, the two even discussed possible legal action that could be taken on behalf of the student.

Although it would appear admirable that the African American trainee was willing to engage in all these advocacy actions, there was only one thing wrong: He accepted the story of the client without exploration or corroboration from other sources. As it turned out, the African American football player had equal, if not greater, playing time as his White teammates, his supposed isolation was due to his own disinclination to mix with other students, and his poor school performance was evident even prior to these supposed incidents. In fact, the coach stated that the student was an outstanding tight end and that it would be serious blow to the prospects of the team should he be unable to play. He emphatically emphasized that the student was in no danger of being dropped from the team, unless his academic performance made such a decision inevitable. In processing the situation with the African American counselor, it became apparent that he overidentified with the Black client. He too had been a football player in high school and experienced hearing racial epithets directed at him during games. When he heard the tale of the Black client, he experienced rage and anger. He was too quick to accept the story of the client and became immersed in the situation. Because emotional hot buttons were pushed in him, his own experiences were transferred to the student, producing tunnel vision that prevented him from entertaining other perspectives.

It is said that people of color share a sense of peoplehood in that, despite cultural differences, they know what it is like to live and deal with a monocultural society. They have firsthand experience with prejudice, discrimination, stereotyping, and oppression. It is a constant reality in their lives. They know what it is like to be "the only one," to have their thoughts and feelings invalidated, to have their sons and daughters teased because of their differences, to be constantly seen as inferior or lesser human beings, and to be denied equal access and opportunity. For these reasons, countertransference among counselors of color working with clients of color is a real possibility. Thus, although therapists of color must work hard not to dismiss the stated experiences of their clients, they must work equally hard to separate out their own experiences from those of their clients.

Situation 7: Encountering Clashes in Cultural Values

As we have mentioned earlier, cultural differences can impact the way we perceive events. This was clearly seen in a study involving Chinese American and White American psychiatrists (Li-Repac, 1980). Both groups of therapists viewed and rated recorded interviews with Chinese and White patients. When rating White patients, White therapists were more likely to use terms such as *affectionate, adventurous,* and *capable,* whereas Chinese therapists used terms such as *active, aggressive,* and *rebellious* to describe the same patients. Similarly, White psychiatrists described Chinese patients as *anxious, awkward, nervous,* and *quiet,* whereas Chinese psychiatrists were more likely to use the terms *adaptable, alert, dependable,* and *friendly.* It is clear that both majority and minority therapists are influenced by their ethnocentric beliefs and values.

Many cultural value differences between groups of color are as equally great and prone to misinterpretations and conflicts as are those among groups of color and White Americans. Using the previous study, it was clear that the Chinese psychiatrists made such evaluations based upon a number of cultural values. They saw the more active and direct expressions of feelings as aggressive, hostile, and rebellious and the more controlled, sedate, and indirect expressions of emotions as indicative of dependable and healthy responding. A prime example of how different cultural dictates affect interpersonal behavior and interpretation is seen in how emotions are expressed among Asian Americans, Latino/a Americans, and African Americans. Restraint of strong feelings is considered a sign of maturity, wisdom, and control among many Asian cultures. The wise and mature "man" is considered able to control feelings (both positive and negative). Thus, Asian Americans may avoid overtly displaying emotions and even discussing them with others (Kim, 2011). This is in marked contrast to many Latinos, who value emotional and physical closeness when communicating with each other (Guzman & Carrasco, 2011; Santiago-Rivera et al., 2002). Likewise, African Americans operate from a cultural context in which the presence of affect and passion in interpersonal interactions are signs of sincerity, authenticity, and humanness (Parham et al., 2011).

Therapists of color who operate from their own worldview without awareness of the different worldviews held by other clients of color may be guilty of cultural oppression, imposing their values and standards upon culturally diverse clients. The outcome can be quite devastating and harmful to clients of color. Let us use the example of a potential misunderstanding likely to occur between an African American counselor and an Asian American client (both holding the values described earlier). As the African American counselor encounters an Asian American client who values restraint of strong feelings, several potential culture-clash scenarios are likely to occur in a situation where the expression of feelings seem called for: First, the Asian American client's reluctance to express feelings in an emotional situation (loss of a job, death of a loved one, etc.) might be perceived as denial, emotionally inappropriate, or unfeeling. Second, in a situation where the feelings are being discussed and the client does not desire to or appears unable to express them, the counselor may potentially interpret the behavior of the client as resistant, unable to access emotions, repressed, or inhibited. These potentially negative misinterpretations have major consequences for the client, who may be misdiagnosed and treated inappropriately. It is clear that counselors of color, when working with clients of color, must be aware of their own worldviews and those of their diverse clients.

Situation 8: Experiencing Clashes in Communication and Therapeutic Styles

An example of a clash in communication styles relates to how groups use personal space when speaking to one another. Africans, Black Americans, and Latinos, as a rule, have a much closer conversing distance with one another than either White Americans or Asian Americans (Jensen, 1985; Nydell, 1996). How culture dictates conversation distances is pronounced and varies according to many sociodemographic differences, including race, ethnicity, and gender. Whereas a Black therapist may value close proximity to an Asian American client in therapy (e.g., sitting closer or learning forward), the latter may feel quite uncomfortable and find such close conversing distances to be an intrusion of personal space. Worse yet, the client may interpret the counselor as excessively aggressive, rude, or disrespectful. The Black therapist, on the other hand, may view the Asian American client as cold, unfeeling, and evasive. Further, major differences may be exaggerated by the manner of communication. Blacks tend to be more direct in their communication styles (thoughts and feelings), whereas Asian Americans tend to be more indirect and subtle in communication; an Asian American client may feel uncomfortable with a Black American who expresses himself or herself in such a forthright and open manner.

Therapy is a context in which communication is paramount, and there are many ways that these differences in communication styles across races and cultures manifest in the therapeutic relationship. First, because Asian Americans, Latino/a Americans, and Native Americans may be indirect in their communication styles and may avoid eye contact when listening and speaking, they are often pathologized as being resistant to therapy (D. W. Sue, 2010a). At the same time, because Black Americans are stereotyped as being quick to anger and prone to violence and crime, they are often viewed as threatening and can trigger fear in people (D. W. Sue, 2010a). The combination of these two contrary types of communication can lead to various tensions in a therapeutic relationship. Again, counselors of color must (a) understand their communication and therapeutic styles and the potential impact they have on other clients of color, (b) be aware of and knowledgeable about the communication styles of other groups of color, and (c) be willing to modify their intervention styles to be consistent with the cultural values and life experiences of their culturally diverse clients.

Situation 9: Receiving and Expressing Racial Animosity

A counselor of color may be the object of racial animosity from clients of color simply because he or she is associated with the mental health system. Many people of color have viewed mental health practice and therapy as a White middle-class activity with values that are often antagonistic to the ones held by groups of color. African Americans, for example, may have a negative view of therapy, often holding a "historical hostility" response because of the history of oppression of Blacks in the United States (Ridley, 2005). Therapy is highly stigmatizing among many in the Asian American community, who often view it as a source of shame and disgrace (Kim, 2011). Latino/a Americans may react similarly, believing that therapy is not only stigmatizing but that "talk therapies" are less appropriate and helpful than concrete advice and suggestions (de las Fuentes, 2007). Native Americans may vary in their views of therapy, depending on their level of assimilation; traditional Native Americans may view westernized institutions and practices as not trustworthy or as ineffective, in comparison to spiritual healing or indigenous practices (Duran, 2006). Given these different views of therapy and mental health practices, there are several dynamics that can occur between racial groups. Black American clients may view therapy as a symbol of political oppression and may perceive a Latino/a American therapist or even a Black counselor as a sellout to the broader society. Or because traditional forms of therapy oftentimes emphasize insight through the medium of verbal self-exploration, many Asian and Latino/a clients may view the process as inappropriate and question the qualifications of the therapist. Native American clients who value nontraditional counseling or spiritual healing may not seek or continue therapy, especially if a counselor of any race does not recognize alternatives to Western practices. All of these factors may influence the dynamics in a counseling relationship in which the therapist of color is responded to as a symbol of oppression and as someone who cannot relate to the client's problems. Their credibility and trustworthiness are suspect, and they will be frequently tested in the session. These tests may vary from overt hostility to other forms of resistance.

We have already spent considerable time discussing the racial animosity that has historically existed between racial groups and how they may continue to affect the race relations between groups of color. Like Situations 3 and 5 (therapists of color working with White clients), similar dynamics can occur between racial/ethnic minority individuals in the therapy sessions. Therapists of color may be targets or perpetrators of racial animosity in therapy sessions. This is often exaggerated by differences in cultural values and communication styles that often trigger stereotypes about counselors and clients of color toward one another. Thus, if Latino/a clients hold stereotypes (consciously or unconsciously) toward Black counselors (e.g., believing them violent, dangerous, and aggressive), these beliefs may reinforce the hostility they feel toward Black Americans. Clinically, like Situation 3, counselors of color may transfer their animosity toward minority clients; or, like Situation 5, they may receive racial animosity. Our clinical analysis and suggestions in those situations would be similar for counselors of color working with clients of color.

Situation 10: Dealing With the Stage of Racial Identity of Counselors and Clients

We have already stressed the importance of considering the racial/cultural identity stage of both therapists of color and clients of color. We explore this issue in detail in Chapter 11, "Racial/Cultural Identity Development in People of Color: Therapeutic Implications." How it affects within-group and between-group racial/ethnic minority counseling is extremely important for cultural competence. Thus, we will defer our discussion for now, until we reach that point. Suffice it to say that the degree of assimilation/acculturation and racial identity of both the counselor and the client of color can result in dyadic combinations that create major conflicts.

REFLECTION AND DISCUSSION QUESTIONS

1. What are some of the therapeutic issues that face counselors of color working with members of their own group or with another minority group member?
2. As a counselor of color, which other minority group member do you anticipate would be most difficult to work with? Why?
3. If you were a client of color and had to choose the race of the counselor, who would you choose? Why?
4. As a White person, would working with a minority group counselor bother you? What reactions or thoughts do you have about this question?

CONCLUSIONS

It appears that in nearly all these situations, addressing race is extremely important in overcoming racial animosity and cultural differences that impede effective therapeutic relationships. How comfortable therapists of color feel about difficult dialogues on race and how skilled they are in addressing this topic is a major determinant of therapeutic outcome. In our society, we have major hang-ups about speaking to issues of race and racism. Although studies show that race is a difficult topic for White therapists to address, people of color seem more comfortable and likely to discuss issues related to race and cultural differences (D. W. Sue, 2010b). In one study, African American therapists, for example, were more likely to routinely address race with ethnic minority clients or when race seemed to be part of the presenting problem than White therapists were (Knox, Burkard, Johnson, Suzuki, & Ponterotto, 2003). Most believed that addressing race had a positive impact on the therapeutic alliance and in the outcome of therapy. Therapists who are responsive to cultural issues are perceived by clients, especially those from ethnic minorities, as more credible and culturally competent. We believe that all therapists should be willing to discuss differences with clients but also should be aware of situations where this might not be beneficial.

In summary, it is clear that cultural competence goals do not apply only to White helping professionals. All therapists and counselors, regardless of race, culture, gender, and sexual orientation need to (a) become aware of their own worldviews, their biases, values, and assumptions about human behavior; (b) understand the worldviews of their culturally diverse clients; and (c) develop culturally appropriate intervention strategies in working with culturally diverse clients. Race, culture, ethnicity, gender, and sexual orientation are functions of everyone.

Implications for Clinical Practice

Multicultural counseling and therapy is not for White helping professionals only! Persons of color, women, LGBT populations, and other marginalized group members in our society are not immune from inheriting the racial, gender, and sexual orientation issues of our forebears. Working toward cultural competence is a function of everyone, regardless of race, gender, sexual orientation, religious preference, and so on. In this chapter we have tried to use counselors of color as an example to identify the unique challenges that all minority group counselors face in their journey to cultural competence. For helping professionals of color (and to White colleagues who need to understand), these recommendations may prove helpful.

1. People of color are not immune from having biases and prejudices. Most of this book will be or has been directed at the biases and prejudices of White Americans. However, people of color also inherit the biases and stereotypes of the larger society. Thus, while we address White supremacy and White racism, people of color need to "confess their sins" as well.

(continued)

(continued)

We have met Asian Americans who possess strong stereotypes and prejudices against not only Whites but other racial minorities as well. Likewise, we have encountered brothers and sisters of color who expressed negativism toward our racial group.

2. Avoid the "who's more oppressed" trap. Because all oppression is damaging and serves to separate rather than unify, playing the "I'm more oppressed" game is destructive to group unity and counterproductive to combating racism. There is little doubt that each group, whether Native American, African American, Latino/Hispanic American, or Asian American, can claim that it has suffered immensely from racism. If we understand our own group's oppression, we should find it easier to recognize the oppression of another. But to use one group's oppression to negate that of another group is to diminish, dismiss, or negate the claims of another. It leads to separation rather than mutual understanding.

3. Don't let interethnic/interracial conflicts destroy intergroup unity. We must face the fact that there is also much misunderstanding and bias among and between groups of color. It goes without saying, for example, that in some parts of the country, friction between Asian Americans and African Americans is greater than that between Blacks and Whites. People of color must learn to validate one another's experiences and to credit and appreciate how each group has struggled to survive in a racist and oppressive environment. In some respects, we have avoided dealing with one another for political reasons. We have functioned under the "common enemy" dictum in dealing with White society. We have submerged our differences with one another, avoided airing out our "dirty laundry" in the eyes of White society, and been wary of the divide-and-conquer ploy used against us. Although a source of strength in dealing with racism, this approach also belies the need to work on our group misunderstandings and differences. It is time for us to truly have a dialogue with one another and to build bridges of mutual understanding.

4. Not all bad things that happen to people of color are the results of racism. Although we need to trust our intuitive or experiential reality, it is equally important that we do not externalize everything. While blaming the victim is detrimental to our psychological well-being, it is equally destructive to attribute all negative events in our lives to racism! We have borne witness to brothers and sisters who tend to find fault in everything but themselves. Sometimes it is easier to blame others and to attribute negative outcomes to external forces in our lives than it is accept responsibility for our own actions. Regardless of race, all of us have faults, limitations, and weaknesses. Owning up to them is a source of strength.

5. Know that understanding your own worldview (values, biases, and assumptions about human behavior) and how your worldview may potentially clash with that of clients of color is important. Despite sharing similar experiences of oppression, cultural differences may infect the therapeutic process and render your attempts to help the client ineffective. Worse yet, you may be guilty of cultural oppression when you are unaware of the cultural differences that exist between you and the client; you may be prone to misinterpret the behavior of the client.

6. Realize how your communication style (direct versus subtle, passionate versus controlled) and nonverbal differences may impact the client. Awareness of communication style differences between the therapist and the client is important. Being able to anticipate your social impact on others and modify your responses so as to relate better to clients is all important. Know that intervention styles (confrontation, for example) may work better for some cultural groups than others.

7. It is important to realize that your awareness of yourself as a racial/cultural being is paramount to effectively working with other clients of color. Likewise, clients' racial identities may differ with respect to assimilation and acculturation influences. Therapists must evaluate their own and the client's stage of identity and determine how they might impact work with clients of the same or different ethnicity.

8. Be comfortable in addressing topics such as race, gender, and sexual orientation. Research consistently reveals that most people find it anxiety provoking and uncomfortable to engage in dialogue about race and race differences. Addressing ethnic or other differences between the therapist and the client can be helpful. In terms of therapists of color, clients are aware of the ethnic difference, and bringing it up in a routine manner deals with the "elephant in the room." However, therapists need to use their clinical judgment to determine when it might be contraindicated.

9. White people can be valuable allies. We need to acknowledge and appreciate the fact that many White Americans are eager to help and represent powerful allies. It is important for us to realize that our enemy is not White Americans, but White supremacy. As a group, Euro-Americans are decent and fair-minded. Once they begin to understand themselves as racial/cultural beings, take responsibility for their roles in the perpetuation of racism, and connect back with their humanity, they become eager allies with people of color. Some of the greatest friends of people of color have been Whites.

10. Don't write off people's racially insensitive remarks without a chance for rectification. Realize that we all need an opportunity to learn and grow (i.e., making insensitive remarks or racial blunders cannot be the sole test of a person's value). There have been times in which our comments or actions reflected bias or insensitivity to another group. And although our immediate reaction was one of defensiveness, we very much appreciated the opportunity afforded us by others to be educated about our offensive remarks. All of us are born and raised in a highly racist and sexist culture. As such, many of us have taken on many of the biases of our society. Helping one another understand the meaning of our words and actions must also be one of our primary responsibilities.

11. We must form multicultural alliances. Recognize that we also need to reach out to each other to form multicultural alliances and to realize that race, culture, and ethnicity are functions of each and every one of us. Race is not just an Asian American thing, an African American thing, a Latino American thing, or a minority thing. Whites must begin to see that they are also racial/cultural beings and have an equal investment in racial/ethnic matters. We must allow them to enter into our world if we are to build bridges of mutual understanding. Any one group, alone, cannot achieve the struggle for equal rights.

12. Being bicultural or multicultural is not selling out. We cannot confuse our bicultural assets with the myth of the melting pot. Being able to function in White society is different from "acting White." We need to realize that there are acceptable and unacceptable things in all cultures, and it is important for us to be able to examine and accept or reject aspects of cultures based upon their merits, not just because they come from the dominant group. We need to own and accept those aspects of U.S. culture that are seen as healthy and to stand against those that are toxic (racism, sexism, and oppression). There is a major difference between our reactions related to forced compliance (cultural oppression via assimilation and acculturation) and freedom of choice in adopting functional values in all cultures. The issue before us is not whether to maintain one way of life, but how we can function in a bicultural manner without losing our sense of integrity.

PART II

The Political Dimensions of Mental Health Practice

The Politics of Counseling and Psychotherapy: Social Justice in Counseling

CHAPTER FOCUS QUESTIONS

1. What role does the sociopolitical climate play in the manifestation, etiology, diagnosis, and treatment of psychological disturbances in socially devalued groups in our society?
2. In what ways may traditional mental health practice represent cultural oppression?
3. How has the field of mental health historically viewed the psychological development of persons of color?
4. In what ways are the racial realities (worldviews) of people of color different from those of White Americans? How does this pose problems in race relations and multicultural counseling/therapy?
5. What role do systemic factors (institutional policies, practices, and regulations) play in mental health and mental health practices?
6. What is social justice counseling and what role does it play in the mental health professions?

Multicultural counseling/therapy means understanding the worldviews and life experiences of diverse groups in our nation. To be culturally competent means to understand the history of oppression experienced by marginalized groups in our society. The stories of discrimination and pain of the oppressed are often minimized and neglected. Many, for example, contend that the reality of racism, sexism, and homophobia is relatively unknown or ignored by those in power because of the discomfort that pervades such topics. Vernon E. Jordan, Jr., an African American attorney and former confidant of President Bill Clinton, made this point about racism in startling terms. In making an analogy between the terrorist attacks of September 11, 2001, and the racism directed at African Americans, Jordan stated:

> None of this is new to Black people. War, hunger, disease, unemployment, deprivation, dehumanization, and terrorism define our existence.

They are not new to us. Slavery was terrorism, segregation was terrorism, and the bombing of the four little girls in Sunday school in Birmingham was terrorism. The violent deaths of Medgar, Martin, Malcolm, Vernon Dahmer, Chaney, Shwerner, and Goodman were terrorism. And the difference between September 11 and the terror visited upon Black people is that on September 11, the terrorists were foreigners. When we were terrorized, it was by our neighbors. The terrorists were Americans. (excerpted from a speech by Vernon E. Jordan, June 2002)

Likewise, in speaking about the history of psychological research conducted on ethnic minority communities by White social scientists, Charles W. Thomas (1970), a respected African American psychologist, voiced his concerns even more strongly:

White psychologists have raped Black communities all over the country. Yes, raped. They have used Black people as the human equivalent of rats run through Ph.D. experiments and as helpless clients for programs that serve middle-class White administrators better than they do the poor. They have used research on Black people as green stamps to trade for research grants. They have been vultures. (p. 52)

To many people of color, the "Tuskegee experiment" represents a prime example of the allegation by Thomas. The Tuskegee experiment was carried out from 1932 to 1972 by the U.S. Public Health Service; more than 600 Alabama Black men were used as guinea pigs in the study of what damage would occur to the body if syphilis were left untreated. Approximately 399 were allowed to go untreated, even when medication was available. Records indicate that 7 died as a result of syphilis, and an additional 154 died of heart disease that may have been caused by the untreated syphilis! In a moving ceremony in 1997, President Clinton officially expressed regret for the experiment to the few survivors and apologized to Black America.

Likewise, in August 2011, a White House bioethics panel heard about American-run venereal disease experiments conducted on Guatemalan prisoners, soldiers, and mental patients from 1946 to 1948: The United States paid for syphilis-infected Guatemalan prostitutes to have sex with prisoners. Approximately 5,500 Guatemalans were enrolled, 1,300 were deliberately infected, and 83 died (McNeil, 2011). The aim of the study was to see whether penicillin could prevent infection after exposure. When these experiments came to light, President Obama apologized to President Alvaro Colom of Guatemala. Dr. Amy Gutman, the chairwoman of the bioethics panel and president of the University of Pennsylvania, described the incident as a dark chapter in the history of medical research. Experiments of this type are ghastly and give rise to suspicions that people of color are being used as guinea pigs in other medical and social experiments as well.

Are these beliefs by people of color accurate? Aren't they simply exaggerations from overly mistrustful individuals? Aren't people of color making a mountain out of a molehill? What has all this to do with counseling and psychotherapy? Because the worldviews of culturally diverse clients are often linked to the historical and current experiences of oppression in the United States (Ponterotto, Utsey, & Pedersen, 2006), it is a necessity to understand the worldview of culturally diverse clients from both a cultural and a political perspective (Ridley, 2005). Clients of color, for example, are likely to approach counseling and therapy with a great deal of healthy skepticism regarding the institutions from which therapists work and even the conscious and unconscious motives of the helping professional.

The main thesis of this book is that counseling and psychotherapy do not take place in a vacuum, isolated from the larger sociopolitical influences of our societal climate (Constantine, 2006; Katz, 1985; W. M. Liu, Hernandez, Mahmood, & Stinson, 2006). Counseling people of color, for example, often mirrors the nature of race relations in the wider society as well as the dominant-subordinate relationships of other marginalized groups (lesbian, gay, bisexual, and transgendered [LGBT] people; women; and the physically challenged). It serves as a microcosm, reflecting Black-White, Asian-White, Hispanic-White, and American Indian–White relations. But as we saw in Chapter 3, it also mirrors interethnic/interracial relations as well.

We will explore the many ways in which counseling and psychotherapy have failed with respect to providing culturally appropriate mental health services to disempowered groups in our society. We do this by using racial minorities as an example of the damaging majority-minority relationships that historically characterize many other marginalized groups. Many readers may have a very powerful negative reaction to the following material. However, only by honestly confronting these unpleasant social realities and accepting responsibility for changing them will our profession be able to advance and grow (D. W. Sue, 2010a). For racial/ethnic minorities, these failures can be seen in three primary areas:(a) the education and training of mental health professionals, (b) biased and inaccurate therapeutic and mental health literature, and (c) the need to treat social problems (social justice counseling).

THE EDUCATION AND TRAINING OF MENTAL HEALTH PROFESSIONALS

While national interest in the mental health needs of ethnic minorities has increased, the human service professions have historically neglected this population. Evidence reveals that the populations of color, in addition to the common stresses experienced by everyone else, are more likely to encounter problems such as immigrant status, poverty, cultural racism, prejudice, and discrimination (Choudhuri, Santiago-Rivera, & Garrett, 2012; West-Olatunji & Conwill, 2011). Yet studies continue to reveal that American Indians, Asian Americans, African Americans, and Latino/Hispanic Americans tend to underutilize traditional mental health services in a variety of contexts (Cheung & Snowden, 1990; Kearney, Draper, & Baron, 2005; S. Wang & Kim, 2010). Some years back, S. Sue and associates found that clients tended to terminate counseling/therapy at a rate of more than 50% after only one contact with the therapist. This was in marked contrast to the less than 30% termination rate among White clients (S. Sue, Allen, & Conaway, 1975; S. Sue, Fujino, Hu, Takeuchi, & Zane, 1991; S. Sue & McKinney, 1974; S. Sue, McKinney, Allen, & Hall, 1974). Although utilization data for groups of color are changing, these early findings led many to search for enlightened explanations.

For example, some researchers hypothesized that minority-group individuals underutilize and prematurely terminate counseling/therapy because of the biased nature of the services themselves (Kearney et al., 2005). The services offered are frequently antagonistic or inappropriate to the life experiences of the culturally different client; they lack sensitivity and understanding, and they are oppressive and discriminating toward minority clients (Cokley, 2006). Many believed that the presence of ill-prepared mental health professionals was the direct result of a culture-bound and biased training system (Mio, 2005; Utsey, Grange, & Allyne, 2006). Although directors of training programs report that multicultural coursework has increased significantly in mental health education (Bernal & Castro, 1994; Hills & Strozier, 1992), it is interesting to note that graduate students in mental health programs and multicultural psychologists have a different view. They report few courses offered in multicultural psychology and inadequate coverage of work with diverse populations within required core courses (Allison, Crawford, Echemendia, Robinson, & Knepp, 1994; Mintz, Bartels, & Rideout, 1995).

It is our contention that reports of increased multicultural coverage (while gaining a degree of prominence) are inflated or are superficially developed. Most graduate programs continue to give inadequate treatment to the mental health issues of ethnic minorities (Ponterotto & Austin, 2005; Utsey, Grange & Allyne, 2006). Cultural influences affecting personality formation, career choice, educational development, and the manifestation of behavior disorders are infrequently part of mental health training or are treated in a tangential manner (Parham, Ajamu, & White, 2011; Vazquez & Garcia-Vazquez, 2003). When minority-group experiences are discussed, they are generally seen and analyzed from the White, Euro-American, middle-class perspective. In programs where minority experiences have been discussed, the focus tends to be on their pathological lifestyles and/or maintenance of false stereotypes. The result is twofold: (a) Professionals who deal with mental health problems of ethnic minorities lack understanding and knowledge about ethnic values and their consequent interaction with a racist society, and (b) mental health practitioners are graduated from our programs believing that minorities are inherently pathological and that therapy involves a simple modification of traditional White models.

This ethnocentric bias has been highly destructive to the natural help-giving networks of minority communities (Duran, 2006). Oftentimes mental health professionals operate under the assumption that racial and ethnic minorities never had such a thing as "counseling" and "psychotherapy" until it was "invented" and institutionalized in Western cultures. For the benefit of those people, the mental health movement has delegitimized natural help-giving networks that have operated for thousands of years by labeling them as unscientific, supernatural, mystical, and not consistent with "professional standards of practice." Mental health professionals are then surprised to find that there is a high incidence of psychological distress in the minority community, that their treatment techniques do not work, and that some culturally diverse groups do not utilize their services.

Contrary to this ethnocentric orientation, we need to expand our perception of what constitutes valid mental health practices. Equally legitimate methods of treatment are nonformal or natural support systems (e.g., family, friends, community self-help programs, and occupational networks), folk-healing methods, and indigenous formal systems of therapy (Gone, 2010; Moodley & West, 2005). Instead of attempting to destroy these practices, we should be actively trying to find out why they may work better than Western forms of counseling and therapy (Trimble, 2010). We cover indigenous healing in Chapter 10.

DEFINITIONS OF MENTAL HEALTH

Counseling and psychotherapy tend to assume universal *(etic)* applications of their concepts and goals to the exclusion of culture-specific *(emic)* views (Choudhuri, Santago-Rivera, & Garrett, 2012; Draguns, 2002). Likewise, graduate programs have often been accused of fostering *cultural encapsulation*, a term first coined by Wrenn (1962). The term refers specifically to (a) the substitution of modal stereotypes for the real world, (b) the disregarding of cultural variations in a dogmatic adherence to some universal notion of truth, and (c) the use of a technique-oriented definition of the counseling process. The results are that counselor roles are rigidly defined, implanting an implicit belief in a universal concept of "healthy" and "normal."

If we look at criteria used by the mental health profession to judge normality and abnormality, this ethnocentricity becomes glaring. Several fundamental approaches that have particular relevance to our discussion have been identified (D. Sue, D. W. Sue, D. M. Sue, & S. Sue, 2013): (a) normality as a statistical concept, (b) normality as ideal mental health, and (c) abnormality as the presence of certain behaviors (research criteria).

First, statistical criteria equate normality with those behaviors that occur most frequently in the population. *Abnormality* is defined in terms of those behaviors that occur least frequently. Despite the word *statistical*, however, these criteria need not be quantitative in nature: Individuals who talk to themselves, disrobe in public, or laugh uncontrollably for no apparent reason are considered abnormal according to these criteria simply because most people do not behave in that way. Statistical criteria undergird our notion of a normal probability curve, so often used in IQ tests, achievement tests, and personality inventories. Statistical criteria may seem adequate in specific instances, but they are fraught with hazards and problems. For one thing, they fail to take into account differences in time, community standards, and cultural values. If deviations from the majority are considered abnormal, then many ethnic and racial minorities that exhibit strong cultural differences from the majority have to be so classified. When we resort to a statistical definition, it is generally the group in power that determines what constitutes normality and abnormality. For example, if a group of African Americans were to be administered a personality test and it was found that they were more suspicious than their White counterparts, what would this mean?

Some psychologists and educators have used such findings to label African Americans as paranoid. Statements by Blacks that "The Man" is out to get them may be perceived as supporting a paranoid delusion. This interpretation, however, has been challenged by many Black psychologists as being inaccurate (Grier & Cobbs, 1968, 1971; Guthrie, 1997; Parham, Ajamu, & White, 2011). In response to their heritage of slavery and a history of White discrimination against them, African Americans have adopted various behaviors (in particular, behaviors toward Whites) that have proved important for survival in a racist society. "Playing it cool" has been identified as one means by which Blacks, as well as members of other minority groups, may conceal their true thoughts and feelings. A Black person who is experiencing conflict, anger, or even rage may be skillful at appearing serene and composed. This tactic is a survival mechanism aimed at reducing one's vulnerability to harm and to exploitation in a hostile environment.

> Personality tests that reveal Blacks as being suspicious, mistrustful, and paranoid need to be understood from a larger sociopolitical perspective. Minority groups who have consistently been victims of discrimination and oppression in a culture that is full of racism have good reason to be suspicious and mistrustful of White society.

Personality tests that reveal Blacks as being suspicious, mistrustful, and paranoid need to be understood from a larger sociopolitical perspective. Minority groups who have consistently been victims of discrimination and oppression in a culture that is full of racism have good reason to be suspicious and mistrustful of White society. In their classic book *Black Rage*, Grier and Cobbs (1968) point out how Blacks, in order to survive in a White racist society, have developed a highly functional survival mechanism to protect them against possible physical and psychological harm. The authors perceive this "cultural paranoia" as adaptive and healthy rather than dysfunctional and pathological. Indeed, some psychologists of color have indicated that the absence of a *paranorm* among minorities may be more indicative of pathology than its presence. The absence of a paranorm may indicate either poor reality testing (denial of oppression/racism in our society) or naiveté in understanding the operation of racism.

Second, humanistic psychologists have proposed the concept of ideal mental health as the criteria of normality (Cain, 2010). Such criteria stress the importance of attaining some positive goal. For example, the consciousness-balance of psychic forces (Freud, 1960; Jung, 1960); self-actualization/creativity (Maslow, 1968; Rogers, 1961); competence, autonomy, and resistance to stress (Allport, 1961; White, 1963); or self-disclosure (Jourard, 1964) have all been historically proposed. The discriminatory nature of such approaches is grounded in the belief in a universal application (all populations in all situations) and reveals a failure to recognize the value base from which the criteria are derived. The particular goal or ideal used is intimately linked with the theoretical frame of reference and values held by the practitioner. For example, the psychoanalytic emphasis on *insight* as a determinant of mental health is a value in itself (London, 1988).

It is important for the mental health professional to be aware, however, that certain socioeconomic groups and ethnic minorities do not particularly value insight. Furthermore, the use of self-disclosure as a measure of mental health tends to neglect the earlier discussion presented on the paranorm. One characteristic often linked to the healthy personality is the ability to talk about the deepest and most intimate aspects of one's life: to self-disclose. This orientation is very characteristic of our counseling and therapy process, in which clients are expected to talk about themselves in a very personal manner. The fact that many minorities are initially reluctant to self-disclose can place them in a situation where they are judged to be mentally unhealthy and, in this case, paranoid (Parham, 2002).

Definitions of mental health such as competence, autonomy, and resistance to stress are related to White middle-class notions of individual maturity (Ahuvia, 2001; Triandis, 2000). The mental health professions originated from the ideological milieu of individualism (Ivey, D'Andrea, Ivey, & Simek-Morgan, 2007). Individuals make their lot in life. Those who succeed in society do so because of their *own* efforts and abilities. Successful people are seen as mature, independent, and possessing great ego strength. Apart from the potential bias in defining what constitutes competence, autonomy, and resistance to stress, the use of such a person-focused definition of maturity places the responsibility on the individual. When people fail in life, it is because of their own lack of ability, interest, maturity, or some inherent weakness of the ego. If, on the other hand, we see minorities as being subjected to higher stress factors in society and placed in a one-down position by virtue of racism, then it becomes quite clear that the definition will tend to portray the lifestyle of minorities as inferior, underdeveloped, and deficient. Ryan (1971) was the first to coin the phrase "blaming the victim" to refer to this process. Yet a broader system analysis would show that the economic, social, and psychological conditions of minorities are related to their oppressed status in America.

Third, an alternative to the previous two definitions of *abnormality* is a research one. For example, in determining rates of mental illness in different ethnic groups, "psychiatric diagnosis," "presence in mental hospitals," and scores on "objective psychological inventories" are frequently used (D. Sue, D. W. Sue, D. M. Sue, & S. Sue, 2013). Diagnosis and hospitalization present a circular problem. The definition of normality/abnormality depends on what mental health practitioners say it is! In this case, the race or ethnicity of mental health professionals is likely to be different from that of minority clients. Bias on the part of the practitioner with respect to diagnosis and treatment is likely to occur (Constantine, Myers, Kindaichi, & Moore, 2004). The inescapable conclusion is that minority clients tend to be diagnosed differently and to receive less preferred modes of treatment (Paniagua, 2005).

Furthermore, the political and societal implications of psychiatric diagnosis and hospitalization were forcefully pointed out nearly 40 years ago by Laing (1967, 1969) and Szasz (1970, 1971). Although it appears that minorities under-utilize outpatient services, they appear to face greater levels of involuntary hospital commitments (Snowden & Cheung, 1990). Laing believes that individual madness is but a reflection of the madness of society. He describes schizophrenic breakdowns as desperate strategies by people to liberate themselves from a "false self" used to maintain behavioral normality in our society. Attempts to adjust the person back to the original normality (sick society) are unethical. Szasz states this opinion even more strongly:

> In my opinion, mental illness is a myth. People we label "mentally ill" are not sick, and involuntary mental hospitalization is not treatment. It is punishment. . . . The fact that mental illness designates a deviation from an ethnical rule of conduct, and that such rules vary widely, explains why upper-middle-class psychiatrists can so easily find evidence of "mental illness" in lower-class individuals and why so many prominent persons in the past fifty years or so have been diagnosed by their enemies as suffering from some types of insanity. Barry Goldwater was called a paranoid schizophrenic. . . . Woodrow Wilson, a neurotic. . . . Jesus Christ, according to two psychiatrists . . . was a born degenerate with a fixed delusion system. (Szasz, 1970, pp. 167–168)

Szasz (1987, 1999) views the mental health professional as an inquisitor, an agent of society exerting social control over those individuals who deviate in thought and behavior from the accepted norms of society. Psychiatric hospitalization is believed to be a form of social control for persons who annoy or disturb us. The label *mental illness* may be seen as a political ploy used to control those who are different, and therapy is used to control, brainwash, or reorient the identified victims to fit into society. It is exactly this concept that many people of color find frightening. For example, many Asian Americans, American Indians, African Americans, and Hispanic/Latino Americans are increasingly challenging the concepts of normality and abnormality. They believe that their values and lifestyles are often seen by society as pathological and thus are unfairly discriminated against by the mental health professions (Constantine, 2006).

In addition, the use of "objective" psychological inventories as indicators of maladjustment may also place people of color at a disadvantage. Many are aware that the test instruments used on them have been constructed and standardized according to White middle-class norms. The lack of culturally unbiased instruments makes many feel that the results obtained are invalid. Indeed, in a landmark decision in the State of California (*Larry P. v. California*, 1986), a judge ruled in favor of the Association of Black Psychologists' claim that individual intelligence tests, such as versions of the WISC, WAIS, and Stanford Binet, could not be used in the public schools on Black students. The improper use of such instruments can lead to an exclusion of minorities from jobs and promotion, to discriminatory educational decisions, and to biased determination of what constitutes pathology and cure in counseling/therapy (Samuda, 1998). Further, when a diagnosis becomes a label, it can have serious consequences. First, a label can cause people to interpret all activities of the affected individual as pathological. No matter what African Americans may do or say that breaks a stereotype, their behaviors will seem to reflect the fact that they are less intelligent than others around them. Second, the label may cause others to treat individuals differently, even when they are perfectly normal. Third, a label may cause those who are labeled to believe that they do indeed possess such characteristics (Rosenthal & Jacobson, 1968) or that the threats of being perceived as less capable can seriously impair their performance (Steele, 2003).

Curriculum and Training Deficiencies

It appears that many of the universal definitions of mental health that have pervaded the profession have primarily been due to severe deficiencies in training programs. Educators (C. P. Chen, 2005; Mio & Morris, 1990; D. W. Sue, 2010b) have asserted that the major reason for ineffectiveness in working with culturally different populations is the lack of culturally sensitive material taught in the curricula. It has been ethnocentrically assumed that the material taught in traditional mental health programs is equally applicable to all groups. Even now, when there is high recognition of the need for multicultural curricula, it has become a battle to infuse such concepts into course content (Vera, Buhin, & Shin, 2006). As a result, course offerings continue to lack a non-White perspective, to treat cultural issues as an adjunct or add-on, to portray cultural groups in stereotypic ways, and to create an academic environment that does not support minority concerns, needs, and issues (Turner, Gonzalez, & Wood, 2008). Further, a major criticism has been that training programs purposely leave out antiracism, antisexism, and antihomophobia curricula for fear they require students to explore their own biases and prejudices (Carter, 2005; Vera, Buhin, & Shin, 2006). Because multicultural competence cannot occur without students or trainees confronting these harmful and detrimental attitudes about race, gender, and sexual orientation, the education and training of psychologists remain at the cognitive and objective domain, preventing self-exploration (D. W. Sue, Torino, Capodilupo, Rivera, & Lin, 2009). It allows students to study the material from their positions of safety. The curriculum must also enable students to understand feelings of helplessness and powerlessness, low self-esteem, and poor self-concept and how they contribute to low motivation, frustration, hate, ambivalence, and apathy. Each course should contain (a) a *consciousness-raising* component, (b) an *affective/experiential* component, (c) a *knowledge* component, and (d) a *skills* component. Importantly, the American Psychological Association (2004) recommended that psychology training programs at all levels provide information on the political nature of the practice of psychology and that professionals need to "own" their value positions.

COUNSELING AND MENTAL HEALTH LITERATURE

Many psychologists have noted how the social science literature, and specifically research, has failed to create a realistic understanding of various ethnic groups in America (Cokley, 2006; Guthrie, 1997; Samuda, 1998; Thomas & Sillen, 1972). In fact, certain practices are felt to have done great harm to minorities by ignoring them, maintaining false stereotypes, and/or distorting their lifestyles. Mental health practice may be viewed as encompassing the use of social power and functioning as a handmaiden of the status quo (Halleck, 1971; Katz, 1985). Social sciences are part of a culture-bound social system, from which researchers are usually drawn; moreover, organized social science is often dependent on the status quo for financial support. Ethnic minorities frequently see the mental health profession in a similar way—as a discipline concerned with maintaining the status quo (Ponterotto,

Utsey, & Pedersen, 2006). As a result, the person collecting and reporting data is often perceived as possessing the social bias of his or her society (Ridley, 2005).

Social sciences, for example, have historically ignored the study of Asians in America (Hong & Domokos-Cheng Ham, 2001; Nadal, 2011). This deficit has contributed to the perpetuation of false stereotypes, which has angered many younger Asians concerned with raising consciousness and group esteem. When studies have been conducted on minorities, research has been appallingly unbalanced. Many social scientists (Cokley, 2006; Jones, 1997) have pointed out how "White social science" has tended to reinforce a negative view of African Americans among the public by concentrating on unstable Black families instead of on the many stable ones. Such unfair treatment has also been the case in studies on Latinos that have focused on the psychopathological problems encountered by Mexican Americans (Falicov, 2005). Other ethnic groups, such as Native Americans (Sutton & Broken Nose, 2005) and Puerto Ricans (Garcia-Preto, 2005), have fared no better. Even more disturbing is the assumption that the problems encountered by minorities are due to intrinsic factors (racial inferiority, incompatible value systems, etc.) rather than to the failure of society (D. W. Sue, 2003). Although there are many aspects of how minorities are portrayed in social science literature, two seem crucial for us to explore: (a) minorities and pathology and (b) the role of scientific racism in research.

Minorities and Pathology

When we seriously study the "scientific" literature of the past relating to people of color, we are immediately impressed with how an implicit equation of minorities and pathology is a common theme. The historical use of science in the investigation of racial differences seems to be linked with White supremacist notions (J. M. Jones, 1997; Samuda, 1998). The classic work of Thomas and Sillen (1972) refers to this as *scientific racism* and cites several historical examples to support their contention:

1. Census figures (fabricated) from 1840 were used to support the notion that Blacks living under unnatural conditions of freedom were prone to anxiety.
2. Mental health for Blacks was contentment with subservience.
3. Psychologically normal Blacks were faithful and happy-go-lucky.
4. Influential medical journals presented fantasies as facts, supporting the belief that anatomical, neurological, or endocrinological aspects of Blacks were always inferior to those of Whites.
5. Black persons' brains are smaller and less developed.
6. Blacks were less prone to mental illness because their minds were so simple.
7. The dreams of Blacks are juvenile in character and not as complex as those of Whites.

More frightening, perhaps, is a survey that found that many of these stereotypes continue to be accepted by White Americans: 20% publicly expressed a belief that African Americans are innately inferior in thinking ability, 19% believe that Blacks have thicker craniums, 23.5% believe they have longer arms than Whites, 50% believe Blacks have achieved equality, and 30% believe problems of Blacks reside in their own group (Astor, 1997; Babbington; 2008; Pew Research Center, 2007; Plous & Williams, 1995). One wonders how many White Americans hold similar beliefs privately but because of social pressures do not publicly voice them.

Furthermore, the belief that various human groups exist at different stages of biological evolution was accepted by G. Stanley Hall. He stated explicitly in 1904 that Africans, Indians, and Chinese were members of adolescent races and in a stage of incomplete development. In most cases, the evidence used to support these conclusions was either fabricated, extremely flimsy, or distorted to fit the belief in non-White inferiority (Thomas & Sillen, 1972). For example, Gossett (1963) reports that when one particular study in 1895 revealed that the sensory perception of Native Americans was superior to that of Blacks and that of Blacks was superior to that of Whites, the results were used to support a belief in the mental superiority of Whites: "Their reactions were slower because they belonged to a more deliberate and reflective race than did the members of the other two groups" (p. 364). The belief that Blacks are "born athletes," as opposed to scientists or statesmen, derives from this tradition. The fact that Hall was a well-respected psychologist, often referred to as "the father of child psychology," and first president of the American Psychological Association did not prevent him from inheriting the racial biases of the times.

The Genetically Deficient Model

The portrayal of people of color in literature has generally taken the form of stereotyping them as deficient in certain desirable attributes. For example, de Gobineau's (1915) *Essay on the Inequality of the Human Races* and Darwin's (1859) *The Origin of Species by Means of Natural Selection* were used to support the genetic intellectual superiority of Whites and the genetic inferiority of the "lower races." Galton (1869) wrote explicitly that African "Negroes" were "half-witted men" who made "childish, stupid, and simpleton-like mistakes," while Jews were inferior physically and mentally and only designed for a parasitical existence on other nations of people. Terman (1916), using the Binet scales in testing Black, Mexican American, and Spanish Indian families, concluded that they were uneducable.

The genetically deficient model is present in the writings of educational psychologists and academicians. In 1989, Professor Rushton of the University of Western Ontario claimed that human intelligence and behavior were largely determined by race, that Whites have bigger brains than Blacks, and that Blacks are more aggressive (Samuda, 1998). Shockley (1972) has expressed fears that the accumulation of weak or low intelligence genes in the Black population will seriously affect overall intelligence. Thus, he advocates that people with low IQs should not be allowed to bear children—they should be sterilized. Allegations of scientific racism can also be seen in the work of the late Cyril Burt, eminent British psychologist, who fabricated data to support his contention that intelligence is inherited and that Blacks have inherited inferior brains. Such an accusation is immensely important when one considers that Burt is a major influence in American and British psychology, is considered by many to be the father of educational psychology, was the first psychologist to be knighted, and was awarded the

American Psychological Association's Thorndike Prize and that his research findings form the foundation for the belief that intelligence is inherited.

A belief that race and gender dictate intelligence continues to be expressed in modern times and even by our most educated populace. In 2005, then–Harvard President Larry Summers (former director of President Obama's National Economic Council) suggested that innate differences between the sexes might help explain why relatively few women become professional scientists or engineers. His comments set off a furor, with demands that he be fired. Women academicians were reported to have stormed out of the conference in disgust as Summers used "innate ability" as a possible explanation for sex differences in test scores. Ironically, Summers was lecturing to a room of the most accomplished women scholars in engineering and science in the nation.

The publication of *The Bell Curve* (Herrnstein & Murray, 1994) continues to echo the controversy in both the public and the academic domains. The two authors assert that intelligence is inherited to a large degree, that race is correlated with intellect, and that programs such as Head Start and Affirmative Action should be banished because they do no good. Instead, resources and funding should be reallocated to those who can profit from it (meaning White Americans). Samuda (1998) concludes about the authors: "Simply stated, they essentially recommend that those of lower intelligence should serve those of higher intelligence" (p. 175). He further concludes: "*The Bell Curve* remains astonishingly antiquated and immune to evidence from the physiological and neurobiological sciences, quantitative genetics, and statistical theory, and it overlooks the significance of environmental factors that research has uncovered" (p. 176).

The questions about whether there are differences in intelligence between races are both complex and emotional. The difficulty in clarifying these questions is compounded by many factors. Besides the difficulty in defining *race*, questionable assumptions exist regarding whether research on the intelligence of Whites can be generalized to other groups, whether middle-class and lower-class ethnic minorities grow up in environments similar to those of middle- and lower-class Whites, and whether test instruments are valid for both minority and White subjects. More important, we should recognize that the average values of different populations tell us nothing about any one individual. Heritability is a function of the population, *not* a trait. Ethnic groups all have individuals in the full range of intelligence, and to think of any racial group in terms of a single stereotype goes against all we know about the mechanics of heredity. Yet much of social science literature continues to portray ethnic minorities as being genetically deficient in one sense or another. Those interested in both the issues and consequences of testing American minorities and the technical and sociopolitical analyses of *The Bell Curve* are directed to the excellent rebuttal by Samuda (1998).

The Culturally Deficient Model

Well-meaning social scientists who challenged the genetic deficit model by placing heavy reliance on environmental factors nevertheless tended to perpetuate a view that saw minorities as culturally disadvantaged, deficient, or deprived. Instead of a biological condition that caused differences, the blame now shifted to the lifestyles or values of various ethnic groups. The term *cultural deprivation* was first popularized by Riessman's widely read book, *The Culturally Deprived Child* (1962). It was used to indicate that many groups perform poorly on tests or exhibit deviant characteristics because they lack many of the advantages of middle-class culture (education, books, toys, formal language, etc.). In essence, these groups were culturally impoverished!

While Riessman introduced such a concept so as to add balance to working with minorities and ultimately to improve their condition in America, some educators strenuously objected to the term. First, the term *culturally deprived* means to lack a cultural background (e.g., enslaved Blacks arrived in America culturally naked), which is contradictory, because everyone inherits a culture. Second, such terms cause conceptual and theoretical confusions that may adversely affect social planning, educational policy, and research; for example, the oft-quoted Moynihan Report (Moynihan, 1965) asserts that "at the heart of deterioration of the Negro society is the deterioration of the Black family. It is the fundamental source of the weakness in the Negro community" (p. 5). Action was thus directed toward infusing White concepts of the family into those of Blacks. Third, cultural deprivation is used synonymously with deviation from and superiority of White middle-class values. Fourth, these deviations in values become equated with pathology, in which a group's cultural values, families, or lifestyles transmit the pathology. Thus, it provides a convenient rationalization and alibi for the perpetuation of racism and the inequities of the socioeconomic system.

The Culturally Diverse Model

Many now maintain that the culturally deficient model serves only to perpetuate the myth of minority inferiority. The focus tends to be one of blaming the person, with an emphasis on minority pathology and a use of White middle-class

REFLECTION AND DISCUSSION QUESTIONS

1. What reactions are you experiencing in learning that the history of the mental health movement was filled with racist formulations? As a White trainee, what thoughts and feelings are you experiencing? As a trainee of color (or a member of a marginalized group), what thoughts and feelings do you have?
2. Go back to Chapter 1 and reread the reactions to this book by Mark Kiselica and Le Ondra Clark. Do their reactions provide you insights about your own thoughts and feelings?
3. Given the preceding discussion, in what ways may counseling and psychotherapy represent instruments of cultural oppression? How is this possibly reflected in definitions of normality and abnormality, the goals you have for therapy, and the way you practice your trade with marginalized groups in our society?

definitions of desirable and undesirable behavior. The social science use of a common, standard assumption implies that to be different is to be deviant, pathological, or sick. Is it possible that intelligence and personality scores for minority children really measure how Anglicized a person has become? Therefore, minorities should no longer be viewed as deficient, but rather as *culturally diverse*. The goal of society should be to recognize the legitimacy of alternative lifestyles, the advantages of being bicultural (capable of functioning in two different cultural environments), and the value of differences.

NEED TO TREAT SOCIAL PROBLEMS—SOCIAL JUSTICE COUNSELING

Case Study: Daryl

Daryl Cokely (a pseudonym) is a 12-year-old African American student attending a predominantly White grade school in Santa Barbara, California. He was referred for counseling by his homeroom teacher because of "constant fighting" on the school grounds, inability to control his anger, and exhibiting "a potential to seriously injure others." In addition, his teachers reported that Daryl was doing poorly in class and was inattentive, argumentative toward authority figures, and disrespectful. He appeared withdrawn in his classroom and seldom participated, but when Daryl spoke, he was "loud and aggressive." Teachers would often admonish Daryl "to calm down."

The most recent problematic incident, an especially violent one, required the assistant principal to physically pull Daryl away to prevent him from seriously injuring a fellow student. He was suspended from school for 3 days and subsequently referred to the school psychologist, who conducted a psychological evaluation. Daryl was diagnosed with a conduct disorder, and the psychologist recommended immediate counseling to prevent the untreated disorder from leading to more serious antisocial behaviors. He worried that Daryl was on his way to developing an antisocial personality disorder. The recommended course of treatment consisted of medication and therapy aimed at eliminating Daryl's aggressive behaviors and "controlling his underlying hostility and anger."

Daryl's parents, however, objected strenuously to the school psychologist's diagnosis and treatment recommendations. They described their son as a "normal child" when at home and not a behavior problem before moving from Los Angeles to Santa Barbara. They described him as feeling isolated, having few friends, being rejected by classmates, feeling invalidated by teachers, and feeling "removed" from the content of his classes. They also noted that all of the "fights" were generally instigated through "baiting" and "name-calling" by his White classmates, that the school climate was hostile toward their son, that the curriculum was very Eurocentric, and that school personnel and teachers seemed naive about racial or multicultural issues. They hinted strongly that racism was at work in the school district and enlisted the aid of the only Black counselor in the school, Ms. Jones. Although Ms. Jones seemed to be understanding and empathic toward Daryl's plight, she seemed reluctant to intercede on behalf of the parents. Being a recent graduate from the local college, Ms. Jones feared being ostracized by other school personnel.

The concerns of Daryl's parents were quickly dismissed by school officials as having little validity. In fact, the principal was quite incensed by these "accusatory statements of possible racism." He indicated to the parents that "your people" do not have a history of academic pursuit and that discipline in the home was usually the culprit. School officials contended that Daryl needed to be more accommodating, to reach out and make friends rather than isolating himself, to take a more active interest in his schoolwork, and to become a good citizen. Further, they asserted that it was not the school climate that was hostile, but that Daryl needed to "learn to fit in." "We treat everyone the same, regardless of race. This school doesn't discriminate." stated the principal. He went on to say, "Perhaps it was a mistake to move to Santa Barbara. For the sake of your son, you should consider returning to L.A. so he can better fit in with his people." These statements greatly angered Daryl's parents.

Adapted from D. W. Sue & Constantine, 2003, pp. 214-215.

If you were a mental health professional, how would you address this case? Where would you focus your energies? Traditional clinical approaches would direct their attention to what they perceive as the locus of the problem—Daryl and his aggressive behavior with classmates, his inattentiveness in class, and his disrespect of authority figures. This approach, however, makes several assumptions: (a) that the locus of the problem resides in the person, (b) that behaviors that violate socially accepted norms are considered maladaptive or disordered, (c) that remediation or elimination of problem behaviors is the goal, (d) that the social context or status quo guides the determination of normal versus abnormal and healthy versus unhealthy behaviors, and (e) that the appropriate role for the counselor is to help the client "fit in" and become "a good citizen."

But as we have just seen, mental health assumptions and practices are strongly influenced by sociopolitical factors. An enlightened approach that acknowledges potential oppression in the manifestation, diagnosis, etiology, and treatment is best accomplished by taking a social justice approach (Toporek, Lewis, & Crethar, 2009). Such an approach might mean challenging the traditional assumptions of therapy and even reversing them as follows:

1. The locus of the problem may reside in the social system (other students, hostile campus environment, alienating curriculum, lack of minority teachers/staff/students, etc.) rather than in the individual.
2. Behaviors that violate social norms may not be disordered or unhealthy.
3. The social norms, prevailing beliefs, and institutional policies and practices that maintain the status quo may need to be challenged and changed.
4. Although remediation is important, the more effective long-term solution is prevention.
5. Organizational change requires a macrosystems approach involving other roles and skills beyond the traditional clinical one.

These five assumptions illustrate several basic principles related to social change and especially social justice counseling. Using Daryl as an example, let us illustrate our points.

Principle 1: A Failure to Develop a Balanced Perspective Between Person and System Focus Can Result in False Attribution of the Problem

It is apparent that school officials have attributed the locus of the problem—that he is impulsive, angry, inattentive, unmotivated, disrespectful, and a poor student—to reside in Daryl. He is labeled as possessing a conduct disorder with potential antisocial personality traits. Diagnosis of the problem is internal; that is, it resides in Daryl. When the focus of therapy is primarily on the individual, there is a strong tendency to see the locus of the problem as residing solely in the person (Cosgrove, 2006) rather than in the school system, curriculum, or wider campus community. As a result, well-intentioned counselors may mistakenly blame the victim (e.g., by seeing the problem as a deficiency of the person) when, in actuality, the problem may reside in the environment (prejudice, discrimination, racial/cultural invalidation, etc.). We would submit that it is highly probable that Daryl is the victim of (a) a monocultural educational environment that alienates and denigrates him (Davidson, Waldo, & Adams, 2006); (b) curricula that does not deal with the contributions of African Americans or portrays them in a demeaning fashion; (c) teaching styles that may be culturally biased (Cokley, 2006); (d) a campus climate that is hostile to minority students (perceives them as less qualified) (D. W. Sue, Rivera, Watkins, N. L. Kim, R. H. Kim, & Williams, 2011); (e) support services (counseling, study skills, etc.) that fail to understand the minority student experience; and (f) the lack of role models (presence of only one Black teacher in the school) (Alexander & Moore, 2008). For example, would it change your analysis and focus of intervention if Daryl gets into fights because he is teased mercilessly by fellow students who use racial slurs (nigger, jungle bunny, burr head, etc.)? In other words, suppose there is good reason for why this 12-year-old feels isolated, rejected, devalued, and misunderstood.

Principle 2: A Failure to Develop a Balanced Perspective Between *Person* and *System* Focus Can Result in an Ineffective and Inaccurate Treatment Plan Potentially Harmful Toward the Client

Failure to understand how systemic factors contribute to individual behavior can result in an ineffective and inaccurate treatment plan; the treatment itself may be potentially harmful. A basic premise of a broad ecological approach is the assumption that person-environment interactions are crucial to diagnosing and treating problems (J. Goodman, 2009; L. A. Goodman et al., 2004). Clients, for example, are not viewed as isolated units but as embedded in their families, social groups, communities, institutions, cultures, and in major systems of our society

(Vera & Speight, 2003). Behavior is always a function of the interactions or trans-actions that occur between and among the many systems that comprise the life of the person. For example, a *micro* level of analysis (the individual) may lead to one treatment plan, whereas a *macro* analysis (the social system) would lead to another. In other words, how a helping professional defines the problem affects the treat-ment focus and plan. If Daryl's problems are due to internal and intrapsychic dynamics, then it makes sense that therapy be directed toward changing the individual. The fighting behavior is perceived as dysfunctional and should be eliminated through Daryl learning to control his anger or through medication that may correct his internal biological dysfunction.

But what if the problem is external? Will having Daryl stop his fighting behavior result in the elimination of teasing from White classmates? Will it make him more connected to the campus? Will it make him feel more valued and accepted? Will he relate more to the content of courses that denigrate the contri-butions of African Americans? Treating the symptoms or eliminating fighting behavior may actually make Daryl more vulnerable to racism.

Principle 3: When the Client Is an Organization or a Larger System and Not an individual, a Major Paradigm Shift Is Required to Attain a True Understanding of Problem and Solution Identification

Let us assume that Daryl is getting into fights because of the hostile school climate and the invalidating nature of his educational experience. Given this assumption, we ask the question "Who is the client?" Is it Daryl or the school? Where should our therapeutic interventions be directed? In his analysis of schizophrenia, R. D. Laing (1969), an existential psychiatrist, once asked the following question: "Is schizophrenia a sick response to a healthy situation, or is it a healthy response to a sick situation?" In other words, if it is the school system that is dysfunctional (sick) and not the individual client, do we or should we adjust that person to a sick situa-tion? In this case, do we focus on stopping the fighting behavior? Or if we view the fighting behavior as a healthy response to a sick situation, then eliminating the unhealthy situation (teasing, insensitive administrators and teachers, monocultural curriculum, etc.) should receive top priority for change (Lee, 2007). In other words, rather than individual therapy, social therapy may be the most appropriate and effective means of intervention. Yet mental health professionals are ill-equipped and untrained as social change agents (Lopez-Baez & Paylo, 2009).

Principle 4: Organizations Are Microcosms of the Wider Society From Which They Originate. As a Result, They Are Likely to Be Reflections of the Monocultural Values and Practices of the Larger Culture

As we have repeatedly emphasized, we are all products of our cultural conditioning and inherit the biases of the larger society. Likewise, organizations are microcosms of the wider society from which they originate. As a result, they are likely to be reflections of the monocultural values and practices of the larger culture. In this case, it is not far-fetched to assume that White students, helping professionals, and educators may have inherited the racial biases of their forebears. Further, multicultural education specialists have decried the biased nature of the traditional curriculum. Although education is supposed to liberate and convey truth and knowledge, we have seen how it has oftentimes been the culprit in perpetuating false stereotypes and misinformation about various groups in our society. It has done this, perhaps not intentionally, but through omission, fabrication, distortion, or selective emphasis of information designed to enhance the contributions of certain groups over others. The result is that institutions of learning become sites that perpetuate myths and inaccuracies about certain groups in society, with devastating consequences to students of color. Further, policies and practices that claim to "treat everyone the same" may themselves be culturally biased. If this is the institutional context from which Daryl is receiving his education, little wonder that he exhibits so-called problem behaviors. Again, the focus of change must be directed at the institutional level.

Principle 5: Organizations Are Powerful Entities That Inevitably Resist Change and Possess Many Ways to Force Compliance Among Workers. To Go Against the Policies, Practices, and Procedures of the Institution, for Example, Can Bring About Major Punitive Actions

Let us look at the situation of the Black teacher, Ms. Jones. There are indications in this case that she understands that Daryl may be the victim of racism and a monocultural education that invalidates him. If she is aware of this factor, why is she so reluctant to act on behalf of Daryl and his parents? First, it is highly probable that, even if she is aware of the true problem, she lacks the knowledge, expertise, and skill to intervene on a systemic level. Second, institutions have many avenues open to them, which can be used to force compliance on the part of employees. Voicing an alternative opinion against prevailing beliefs can result in ostracism by fellow workers, a poor job performance rating, denial of a promotion, or even an eventual firing (D. W. Sue, Rivera, Watkins, et al., 2011). This creates a very strong ethical dilemma for mental health workers or educators when the needs of their clients differ from those of the organization or employer. The fact that counselors' livelihoods depend on the employing agency (school district) creates additional pressures to conform. How do counselors handle such conflicts? Organizational knowledge and skills become a necessity if the therapist is to be truly effective (Toporek, Lewis, & Crethar, 2009). So even the most enlightened educators and counselors may find their good intentions thwarted by their lack of systems intervention skills and fears of punitive actions.

Principle 6: When Multicultural Organizational Development Is Required, Alternative Helping Roles That Emphasize Systems Intervention and Advocacy Skills Must Be Part of the Repertoire of the Mental Health Professional

Alternative helping roles that emphasize systems intervention must be part of the repertoire of the mental health professional. Because the traditional counseling/therapy roles focus on one-to-one or small-group relationships, they may not be productive when dealing with larger ecological and systemic issues. Competence in changing organizational policies, practices, procedures, and structures within institutions requires a different set of knowledge and skills that are more action oriented. Among them, consultation and advocacy become crucial in helping institutions move from a monocultural to a multicultural institution (Davidson et al., 2006). Daryl's school and the school district need a thorough cultural audit, institutional change in the campus climate, sensitivity training for all school personnel, increased racial/ethnic personnel at all levels of the school, revamping of the curriculum to be more multicultural, and so on. This is a major task that requires multicultural awareness, knowledge, and skills on the part of the mental health professional.

Principle 7: Although Remediation Will Always Be Needed, Prevention Is Better

Conventional practice at the micro level continues to be oriented toward remediation rather than prevention. Although no one would deny the important effects of biological and internal psychological factors on personal problems, more research now acknowledges the importance of sociocultural factors (inadequate or biased education, poor socialization practices, biased values, and discriminatory institutional policies) in creating many of the difficulties encountered by individuals. As therapists, we are frequently placed in a position of treating clients who represent the aftermath of failed and oppressive. policies and practices. We have been trapped in the role of remediation (attempting to help clients once they have been damaged by sociocultural biases). Although treating troubled clients (remediation) is a necessity, our task would be an endless and losing venture unless the true sources of the problem (stereotypes, prejudice, discrimination, and oppression) are changed. Would it not make more sense to take a proactive and preventative approach by attacking the cultural and institutional bases of the problem?

REFLECTION AND DISCUSSION QUESTIONS

1. Exactly how do organizational policies and practices oppress?
2. What do you need to know in order to effectively be a social-change agent?
3. Is organizational change difficult?
4. If individual counseling/therapy is ineffective in systems intervention, what alternative roles would you need to play?

SOCIAL JUSTICE COUNSELING

The case of Daryl demonstrates strongly the need for a social justice orientation to counseling and therapy. Indeed, multicultural counseling/therapy competence is intimately linked to the values of social justice (Hage, 2005; D. W. Sue, 2001; Warren & Constantine, 2007). If mental health practice is concerned with bettering the life circumstances of individuals, families, groups, and communities in our society, then social justice is the overarching umbrella that guides our profession. The welfare of a democratic society very much depends on equal access and opportunity, fair distribution of power and resources, and empowering individuals and groups with a right to determine their own lives (Ratts & Hutchins, 2009). J. M. Smith (2003) defines a socially just world as having access to

> adequate food, sleep, wages, education, safety, opportunity, institutional support, health care, child care, and loving relationships. "Adequate" means enough to allow [participation] in the world . . . without starving, or feeling economically trapped or uncompensated, continually exploited, terrorized, devalued, battered, chronically exhausted, or virtually enslaved (and for some reason, still, actually enslaved). (p. 167)

Bell (1997) states that the goal of social justice is

> full and equal participation of all groups in a society that is mutually shaped to meet their needs. Social justice includes a vision of society in which the distribution of resources is equitable and all members are physically and psychologically safe and secure. (p. 3)

Given these broad descriptions, we propose a working definition of social justice counseling/therapy:

Social justice counseling/therapy is an active philosophy and approach aimed at producing conditions that allow for equal access and opportunity; reducing or eliminating disparities in education, health care, employment, and other areas that lower the quality of life for affected populations; encouraging mental health professionals to consider micro, meso, and macro levels in the assessment, diagnosis, and treatment of client and client systems; and broadening the role of the helping professional to include not only counselor/therapist but advocate, consultant, psychoeducator, change agent, community worker, and so on.

It is clear that systems forces can be powerful and oppressive; Daryl is a prime example of how a failure to understand systemic dynamics may derail productive change. Becoming culturally competent requires not only changes at an individual practice level but also changes associated with how we define our helping role. Unfortunately, an overwhelming majority of mental health practitioners desire to enter direct clinical service, especially counseling and psychotherapy (Shullman, Celeste, & Strickland, 2006). The mental health profession has implicitly or

Social justice counseling/therapy:

1. Aims to produce conditions that allow for equal access and opportunity;
2. Reduces or eliminates disparities in education, health care, employment, and other areas that lower the quality of life for affected populations;
3. Encourages mental health professionals to consider micro, meso, and macro levels in the assessment, diagnosis, and treatment of client and client systems;
4. Broadens the role of the helping professional to include not only counselor/therapist but advocate, consultant, psychoeducator, change agent, community worker, and so on.

explicitly glamorized and defined clinicians as ones who conduct their trade—working with individuals—in an office environment. While the development of individual intervention skills has been the main focus in many graduate training programs, little emphasis is given to other roles, activities, or settings (Pieterse, Evans, Risner-Butner, Collins, & Mason, 2009; Toporek & McNally, 2006).

Thus, not only might therapists be lacking in systems intervention knowledge and skills, but they may also become unaccustomed to, and uncomfortable about, leaving their offices. Yet work with racial/ethnic minority groups and immigrant populations suggests that out-of-office sites (client homes, churches, volunteer organizations, etc.), activities, and alternative helping roles (ombudsperson, advocate, consultant, organizational change agent, facilitator of indigenous healing systems, etc.) may prove more therapeutic and effective (Atkinson & Wampold, 1993; Warren & Constantine, 2007). Social justice counseling with marginalized groups in our society is most enhanced (a) when mental health professionals can understand how individual and systemic worldviews shape clinical practice and (b) when they are equipped with organizational and systemic knowledge, expertise, and skills.

Institutional Dynamics, Advocacy, and Change

All helping professionals need to understand two things about mental health practice: (a) They often work within organizations that may be monocultural in policies and practices, and (b) the problems encountered by clients are often due to organizational or systemic factors. This is a key component of the ecological or person-in-environment perspective (Fouad, Gerstein, & Toporek, 2006). In the first case, the policies and practices of an institution may thwart the ability of counselors to provide culturally appropriate help for their diverse clientele. In the second case, the structures and operations of an organization may unfairly deny equal access and opportunity (access to health care, employment, and education) for certain groups in our society. It is possible that many problems of mental health are truly systemic problems caused by racism, sexism, and homophobia. Thus, understanding organizational dynamics and possessing multicultural institutional intervention skills are part of the social justice framework (Pieterse et al., 2009). Making organizations responsive to a diverse population ultimately means being able to help them become more multicultural in outlook, philosophy, and practice.

Social justice counseling (a) takes a social change perspective that focuses on ending oppression and discrimination in our society (e.g., within organizations, communities, municipalities, governmental entities); (b) believes that inequities that arise within our society are due not necessarily to misunderstandings, poor communication, lack of knowledge, and so on, but to monopolies of power; and (c) assumes that conflict is inevitable and not necessarily unhealthy. Diversity trainers, consultants, and many industrial-organizational (I/O) psychologists increasingly ascribe to multicultural change, which is based on the premise that organizations vary in their awareness of how racial, cultural, ethnic, sexual orientation, and gender issues impact their clients or workers. Increasingly, leaders in the field of counseling psychology have indicated that the profession should promote the general welfare of society; be concerned with the development of people, their communities, and their environment; and should promote social, economic, and political equity consistent with the goals of social justice (Toporek, Gerstein, et al., 2006).

Thus, social justice counseling includes social and political action that seeks to ensure that all people have equal access to the resources, employment, services, and opportunities they require to meet their basic human needs and to develop fully (Goodman et al., 2004). If mental health professionals are concerned with the welfare of society and if society's purpose is to enhance the quality of life for all persons, then they must ultimately be concerned with the injustices and obstacles that oppress, denigrate, and harm those in our society (Warren & Constantine, 2007). They must be concerned with issues of classicism, racism, sexism, homophobia, and all the other "isms" that deny equal rights to everyone. As mentioned previously, counselors/therapists practice at three levels: micro—where the focus is on individuals, families, and small groups; meso—where the focus is on communities and organizations; and macro—where the focus is on the larger society (e.g., statutes and social policies).

Conventional clinical work operates primarily from the micro level, is aimed primarily at helping individuals, and is not adequate in dealing with these wider social issues. It is too time-consuming, is aimed at remediation, and does not recognize the fact that many problems that clients encounter may actually reside in the social system. Let us use the example of racism to illustrate some of the basic tenets of antiracism work that are consistent with a social justice approach. We use racism as an example, but social justice work extends to all forms of cultural oppression (poverty, inadequate health care, immigrant rights, educational inequities, etc.) that deny equal access and opportunity (Smith, 2010).

Antiracism as a Social Justice Agenda

It is not enough for psychologists to simply work with those victimized by stereotyping, prejudice, and discrimination at the micro level. It is not enough for psychologists, on an individual basis, to become bias free and culturally sensitive when the very institutions that educate, employ, and govern are themselves biased in policy, practice, assumption, and structure. In using race and racism as an example of the need to combat social issues on a systemic level, psychologists need to realize that racial attitudes and beliefs are formed from three main sources: (a) schooling and education, (b) mass media, and (c) peers and social groups (D. W. Sue, 2003). Just as these channels can present a biased social construction of knowledge regarding race and race relations, they also offer hope as vehicles to overcome intergroup hostility, misunderstanding, and the development of norms associated with equity and social justice.

In essence, psychologists can be helpful in working for a multicultural curriculum in society that stresses social justice (equity and antiracism). This work must be done in the schools, in all media outlets, and in the many groups and organizations that touch the lives of our citizens. Yet to use these tools of socialization to combat racism and to reconstruct a nonbiased racial reality means that psychologists must impact social policy. Work at the local, state, and federal levels involves psychologists in political advocacy and social change.

Gordon Allport, a social psychologist well known for his classic book, *The Nature of Prejudice* (1954), proposed conditions that offer a guide to antiracism work. Since its publication, others have conducted revealing and important work on reducing prejudice through creating conditions found to lower intergroup hostility. It has been found that racism is most likely to diminish under the following conditions: (a) having intimate contact with people of color, (b) experiencing a cooperative rather than competitive environment, (c) working toward mutually shared goals as opposed to individual ones, (d) exchanging accurate information rather than stereotypes or misinformation, (e) interacting on equal footing with others rather than an unequal or imbalanced one, (f) viewing leadership or authority as supportive of intergroup harmony, and (g) feeling a sense of unity or interconnectedness with all humanity (Jones, 1997; D. W. Sue, 2003). Further, it appears that no single condition alone is sufficient to overcome bigotry. To be successful in combating racism, all conditions must coexist in varying degrees to reduce prejudice.

Social Justice Requires Counseling Advocacy Roles

To achieve these conditions is truly an uphill battle. But, just as the history of the United States is the history of racism, it is the history of antiracism as well. There have always been people and movements directed toward the eradication of racism, including abolitionists, civil rights workers, private organizations (Southern Poverty Law Center, NAACP, and B'nai Brith), political leaders, and especially people of color. Racism, like sexism, homophobia, and all forms of oppression, must be on the forefront of social justice work. Efforts must be directed at social change in order to eradicate bigotry and prejudice. In this respect, psychologists must use their knowledge and skills to (a) impact the channels of socialization (e.g., education, media, groups, organizations) to spread a curriculum of multiculturalism and (b) aid in the passage of legislation and social policy (e.g., affirmative action, civil rights voting protections, sexual harassment laws) (Goodman, 2009; Lopez-Baez & Paylo, 2009; Ratts, 2010). To accomplish these goals, we need to openly embrace systems intervention roles identified by Atkinson et al. (1993): advocate, change agent, consultant, adviser, facilitator of indigenous support systems, and facilitator of indigenous healing methods. In closing, we include the words of Toporek (2006, p. 496) about the social justice agenda and its implications for psychologists:

> The vastness of social challenges facing humanity requires large-scale intervention. Although the expertise of counseling psychologists is well suited to individual empowerment and local community involvement, likewise, much of this expertise can, and should, be applied on a broad scale. Public policy decisions such as welfare reform, gender equity, same-sex marriage and adoption, and homelessness must be informed by knowledge that comes from the communities most affected. Counseling psychologists, with expertise in consulting, communicating, researching, and direct service, are in a unique position to serve as that bridge.

Implications for Clinical Practice

If the mental health profession and its practitioners are to receive acceptance from marginalized groups in our society and be of help, they must demonstrate in no uncertain terms their good faith and their ability to contribute to the betterment of a group's quality of life. This demonstration can take several directions.

1. The mental health profession must take the initiative in confronting the potential political nature of mental health practice. For too long we have deceived ourselves into believing that the practice of counseling/therapy and the database that underlie the profession are morally, ethically, and politically neutral. The results have been (a) subjugation of minority groups, (b) perpetuation of the view that they are inherently pathological, (c) perpetuation of racist practices in treatment, and (d) provision of an excuse to the profession for not taking social action to rectify inequities in the system.

2. Mental health professionals must move quickly to challenge certain assumptions that permeate our training programs. We must critically reexamine our concepts of what constitutes normality and abnormality, begin mandatory training programs that deal with these issues,

critically examine and reinterpret past and continuing literature dealing with socially marginalized groups in society, and use research in such a manner as to improve the life conditions of the researched populations.

3. We must make sure that educational programs no longer present a predominantly White Anglo-Saxon Protestant (WASP) orientation. The study of minority group cultures must receive equal treatment and fair portrayal at all levels of education. Courses dealing with minority group experiences and fieldwork and internship practices must become a required part of the training programs.

4. The education and training of psychologists have, at times, created the impression that its theories and practices are apolitical and value free. Yet we are often impressed by the fact that the actual practice of therapy can result in cultural oppression; that what happens in the therapist's office may represent a microcosm of race relations in the larger society; that the so-called psychological problems of minority groups may reside not within but outside of our clients; and that no matter how well intentioned the helping professionals, they are not immune from inheriting the racial biases of their forebears.

5. Social scientists must realize that many so-called pathological socioemotional characteristics of ethnic minorities can be directly attributed to unfair practices in society. Research and practice must shift from focusing on the poor and culturally diverse to focusing on the groups and institutions that have perpetuated racism and obstructed needed changes.

6. We need to balance our study by also focusing on the positive attributes and characteristics of ethnic minorities. Social scientists have had a tendency to look for pathology and problems among minorities. Too much research has concentrated on the mental health problems and cultural conflict of minorities, while little has been done to determine the advantages of being bicultural and the strengths and assets of these groups. Such an orientation will do much to present a more balanced picture of different minority groups.

7. Psychological disturbances and problems in living are not necessarily caused by internal attributes (low intelligence, lack of motivation, character flaws, etc.) but may result from external circumstances, such as prejudice, discrimination, and disparities in education, employment, and health care. When these inequities result in a denial of equal access and opportunities for our culturally diverse client, systems intervention may be required of the mental health provider.

8. Cultural competence and multicultural counseling and therapy are about social justice. Social justice counseling may dictate social and political actions that seek to ensure that all people have equal access to the resources, employment, services, and opportunities they require to meet their basic human needs.

9. Social justice advocacy is quite different from the traditional clinical role in which students are trained. In many respects it dictates playing roles that involve advocating on behalf of clients who are victimized by the social system that creates disparities in health care, education, and employment.

Systemic Oppression: Trust, Mistrust, Credibility, and Worldviews

CHAPTER FOCUS QUESTIONS

1. In what ways may traditional counseling and therapy conflict or be antagonistic to the lifestyles, cultural values, and sociopolitical experiences of marginalized clients?
2. What role does historical oppression play in how people of color react to counselors and therapists? How might it be played out in the counseling session between a client of color and a White therapist?
3. What is ethnocentric monoculturalism? Does it differ from ethnocentrism? How may it be manifested in our theories of counseling and psychotherapy?
4. Why are trust and mistrust so important in multicultural counseling? What makes counselors credible to clients? What are the special challenges that White helping professionals may encounter as to their credibility (expertness and trustworthiness) when working with clients of color?
5. How are worldviews formed? Why is understanding the concepts of *locus of control* and *locus of responsibility* important to multicultural counseling? In what ways may the worldviews of therapists clash with those of culturally diverse clients?

Case Study: Malachi

I have worked with very few African American clients during my internship at the clinic, but one particular incident left me with very negative feelings. A Black client named Malachi was given an appointment with me. Even though I'm White, I tried not to let his being Black get in the way of our sessions. I treated him like everyone else, a human being who needed help.

(continued)

(continued)

At the onset, Malachi was obviously guarded, mistrustful, and frustrated when talking about his reasons for coming. While his intake form listed depression as the problem, he seemed more concerned about nonclinical matters. He spoke about his inability to find a job, about the need to obtain help with job-hunting skills, and about advice in how best to write his résumé. He was quite demanding in asking for advice and information. It was almost as if Malachi wanted everything handed to him on a silver platter without putting any work into our sessions. Not only did he appear reluctant to take responsibility to change his own life, but left he needed to go elsewhere for help. After all, this was mental health clinic, not an employment agency.

Confronting him about his avoidance of responsibility would probably prove counter-productive, so I chose to focus on his feelings. Using a humanistic-existential approach, I reflected his feelings, paraphrased his thoughts, and summarized his dilemmas. This did not seem to help immediately, as I sensed an increase in the tension level, and he seemed antagonistic toward me.

After several attempts by Malachi to obtain direct advice from me, I stated, "You're getting frustrated at me because I'm not giving you the answers you want." It was clear that this angered Malachi. Getting up in a very menacing manner, he stood over me and angrily shouted, "Forget it, man! I don't have time to play your silly games. " For one brief moment, I felt in danger of being physically assaulted before he stormed out of the office. This incident occurred several years ago, and I must admit that I was left with a very unfavorable impression of Blacks. I see myself as basically a good person who truly wants to help others less fortunate than myself. I know it sounds recist, but Malachi's behavior only reinforces my belief that Blacks have trouble controlling their anger, like to take the easy way out, and find it difficult to be open and trusting of others. If I am wrong in this belief, I hope this workshop [multicultural counseling/therapy] will help me better understand the Black personality.

REFLECTION AND DISCUSSION QUESTIONS

1. Is it possible that Malachi has a legitimate reason for being angry?
2. Is it possible that the therapist and the therapeutic process are contributing to Malachi's frustration and anger?
3. Is it possible that the therapist was never in physical danger but that his own affectively based stereotype of the dangerous Black male caused his unreasonable fear?
4. Might not this potential misinterpretation be a clash of different communication styles, which triggers unrealistic racial fears and apprehensions?
5. Is giving advice and suggestions, helping clients prepare a résumé, or helping them find a job part of therapy?

A variation of the preceding incident was supplied at an in-service training workshop by a White male therapist and is used here to illustrate some of the major issues addressed in this chapter. In Chapter 4 we asserted that mental health practice is strongly influenced by historical and current sociopolitical forces that impinge on issues of race, culture, and ethnicity. Specifically, we made a point that (a) the therapeutic session is often a microcosm of race relations in our larger society, (b) therapists often inherit the biases of their forebears, (c) therapy represents a primarily Euro-American activity that may clash with the worldviews of culturally diverse clients, and (d) social justice counseling requires counselors to play alternative helping roles that have not traditionally been considered therapy. In this case, we question neither the sincerity of the White therapist nor his desire to help the African American client. However, it is obvious to us that the therapist is part of the problem and not the solution. The male therapist's preconceived notions and stereotypes about African Americans appear to have affected his definition of the problem, assessment of the situation, and therapeutic intervention. Let us analyze this case in greater detail to illustrate our contention.

First, statements about Malachi's wanting things handed to him on a "silver platter," his "avoidance of responsibility," and his "wanting to take the easy way out" are symbolic of social stereotypes that Blacks are lazy and unmotivated. The therapist's statements that African Americans have difficulty "controlling their anger," that Malachi was "menacing," and that the therapist was in fear of being assaulted seem to paint the picture of the hostile, angry, and violent Black male—again an image of African Americans to which many in this society consciously and unconsciously subscribe. Although it is always possible that the client was unmotivated and prone to violence, studies suggest that White Americans continue to cling to the image of the dangerous, violence-prone, and antisocial image of Black men (Babbington, 2008; J. M. Jones, 1997).

Second, mental health practice has been characterized as primarily a White middle-class activity that values rugged individualism, individual responsibility, and autonomy (Parham, Ajamu, & White, 2011). Because people are seen as being responsible for their own actions and predicaments, clients are expected to make decisions on their own and to be primarily responsible for their fate in life. The traditional therapist's role should be to encourage self-exploration so that the client can act on his or her own behalf (Lum, 2011). The individual-centered approach tends to view the problem as residing within the person. If something goes wrong, it is the client's fault. In Chapter 4 we pointed out how many problems encountered by minority clients reside externally to them (bias, discrimination, prejudice, etc.) and that they should not be faulted for the obstacles they encounter. To do so is to engage in victim blaming (Ridley, 2005; Ryan, 1971).

Third, therapists are expected to avoid giving advice or suggestions and disclosing their thoughts and feelings not only because they may unduly influence their clients and block individual development, but also because they may become emotionally involved, lose their objectivity, and blur the boundaries of the helping relationship (Pack-Brown & Williams, 2003). Parham (1997) states, however, that a fundamental African principle is that human beings realize themselves only in moral relations to others (collectivity, not individuality): "Consequently, application of an African-centered worldview will cause one to question the need for objectivity absent emotions, the need for distance rather than connectedness, and the need for dichotomous relationships rather than multiple roles" (p. 110). In other words, from an African American perspective, the helper and the helpee are not separated from one another but are bound together both emotionally and spiritually. The Euro-American style of objectivity encourages separation that may be interpreted by Malachi as uninvolved, uncaring, insincere, and dishonest—that is, "playing silly games."

Fourth, the more active and involved role demanded by Malachi goes against what the helping profession considers therapy. Studies seem to indicate that clients of color prefer a therapeutic relationship in which the helper is more active, self-disclosing, and not adverse to giving advice and suggestions when appropriate (Choudhuri, Santiago-Rivera, & Garrett, 2012; D. W. Sue, Ivey, & Pedersen, 1996). The therapist in this scenario fails to entertain the possibility that requests for advice, information, and suggestions may be legitimate and not indicative of pathological responding. The therapist has been trained to believe that his role as a therapist is to be primarily nondirective; therapists do therapy, not provide job-hunting information. This has always been the conventional counseling and psychotherapy role, one whose emphasis is a one-to-one, in-the-office, remedial relationship aimed at self-exploration and the achievement of insight (Atkinson, Thompson, & Grant, 1993). We will have more to say about how these generic characteristics of counseling and psychotherapy may act as barriers to effective multicultural counseling/therapy in Chapter 7.

Fifth, if the male therapist is truly operating from unconscious biases, stereotypes, and preconceived notions with his culturally different client, then much of the problem seems to reside within him and not with Malachi. In almost every introductory text on counseling and psychotherapy, lip service is paid to the axiom, "Counselor, know thyself." In other words, therapeutic wisdom endorses the notion that we become better therapists the more we understand our own motives, biases, values, and assumptions about human behavior. Unfortunately, as indicated in Chapter 4, most training programs are weak in having their students explore their values, biases, and preconceived notions in the area of racist/sexist/homophobic attitudes, beliefs, and behaviors. We are taught to look at our clients, to analyze them, and to note their weaknesses, limitations, and pathological trends; less often do we either look for positive healthy characteristics in our clients or question our conclusions. Questioning our own values and assumptions, the standards that we use to judge normality and abnormality, and our therapeutic approach are infrequently done. As mental health professionals, we may find it difficult and unpleasant to explore our racism, sexism, and homophobia, and our training often allows us the means to avoid it (Choudhuri, Santiago-Rivera, & Garrett, 2012).

When the therapist ends his story by stating that he hopes the workshop will "help me better understand the Black personality," his worldview is clearly evident. The assumption is that multicultural counseling/therapy simply requires the acquisition of knowledge and that good intentions are all that is needed. This statement represents one of the major obstacles to self-awareness and dealing with one's own biases and prejudices. Although we tend to view prejudice, discrimination, racism, and sexism as overt and intentional acts of unfairness and violence, unintentional and covert forms of bias may be the greater enemy because they are unseen and more pervasive (Boysen & Vogel, 2008). Like this therapist, well-intentioned individuals experience themselves as moral, just, fair-minded, and decent. Thus, it is difficult for many mental health professionals to realize that what they do or say may cause harm to their minority clients.

Sixth, the therapist states that he tried to not let Malachi's "being Black get in the way" of the session and that he treated him like any other "human being." This is a very typical statement made by Whites who unconsciously subscribe to the belief that being Black, Asian American, Latino/a American, or a person of color is the problem. In reality, color is not the problem. It is society's perception of color that is the problem! In other words, the locus of the problem (racism, sexism, and homophobia) resides not in marginalized groups but in the society at large. Often this view of race is manifested in the myth of color blindness: If color is the problem, let's pretend not to see it (Apfelbaum, Sommers, & Norton, 2008). Our contention, however, is that it is nearly impossible to overlook the fact that a client is Black, Asian American, Hispanic, and so forth. When operating in this manner, color-blind therapists may actually be obscuring their understandings of who their clients really are. To overlook one's racial group membership is to deny an intimate and important aspect of one's identity. Those who advocate a color-blind approach seem to operate under the assumption that Black is bad and that to be different is to be deviant.

Last, and central to the thesis of this chapter, is the statement by the counselor that Malachi appears guarded and mistrustful and has difficulty being open (self-disclosing). We have mentioned several times that a counselor's inability to establish rapport and a relationship of trust with culturally diverse clients is a major therapeutic barrier. When the emotional climate is negative, and when little trust or understanding exists between the therapist and the client, therapy can be both ineffective and destructive. Yet if the emotional climate is realistically positive and if trust and understanding exist between the parties, the two-way communication of thoughts and feelings can proceed with optimism. This latter condition is often referred to as *rapport* and sets the stage on which other essential conditions can become effective. One of these, self-disclosure, is particularly crucial to the process and goals of counseling because it is the most direct means by which individuals make themselves known to others.

This chapter attempts to discuss trust-mistrust, credibility, and worldviews as they relate to minority clients. Our discussion does not deal with cultural variables among certain groups (Asian Americans, American Indians, etc.) that dictate against self-disclosure to strangers. This topic is presented in Chapter 7. First, we present a brief discussion of the sociopolitical situation as it affects the trust-mistrust dimension of certain culturally diverse populations. The operation of ethnocentric monoculturalism is especially important in this respect. Second, we look at factors that enhance or negate the therapist's cultural effectiveness and how counseling relates to the theory of social influence. Third, we systematically examine how therapist credibility and similarity affect a client's willingness to work with a therapist from another race/culture. Last, we discuss the concepts of *locus of control* and *locus of responsibility* and how they are important dimensions of worldviews.

EFFECTS OF HISTORICAL AND CURRENT OPPRESSION

Mental health practitioners must realize that racial/ethnic minorities and other marginalized groups (women, gays/lesbians, and the disabled) in our society live under an umbrella of individual, institutional, and cultural forces that often demean them, disadvantage them, and deny them equal access and opportunity (Croteau, Lark, Lidderdale, & Chung, 2005; Ponterotto, Utsey, & Pedersen, 2006; Ridley, 2005). Experiences of prejudice and discrimination are a social reality for many marginalized groups and affect their worldviews of the helping professional who attempts to work in the multicultural arena. Thus, mental health practitioners must become aware of the sociopolitical dynamics that form not only their clients' worldviews, but their own as well. As in the clinical case presented earlier, racial/cultural dynamics may intrude into the helping process and cause misdiagnosis, confusion, pain, and a reinforcement of the biases and stereotypes that both groups have of one another. It is important for the therapist to realize that the history of race relations in the United States has influenced us to the point where we are extremely cautious about revealing to strangers our feelings and attitudes about race. In an interracial encounter with a stranger (i.e., therapy), each party will attempt to discern gross or subtle racial attitudes of the other while minimizing vulnerability. For minorities in the United States, this lesson has been learned well. While White Americans may also exhibit caution similar to that of their minority counterparts, the structure of society places more power to injure and damage in the hands of the majority culture. In most self-disclosing situations, White Americans are less vulnerable than their minority counterparts.

As the individual chapters on American Indians, Asian Americans, Blacks, Hispanics, and other culturally diverse groups (gays/lesbians, women, persons with disabilities, those in poverty, and the elderly) will reveal, the histories and experiences of these groups have been fraught with oppression, discrimination, and racism. Institutional racism has created psychological barriers among minorities and White Americans that are likely to interfere with the therapy process. Understanding how the invisibility of ethnocentric monoculturalism has affected race, gender, and sexual orientation relationships is vital to successful multicultural competence.

Ethnocentric Monoculturalism

It is becoming increasingly clear that the values, assumptions, beliefs, and practices of our society are structured in such a manner as to serve only one narrow segment of the population (D. W. Sue, 2001). Most mental health professionals, for example, have not been trained to work with anyone other than mainstream individuals or groups. This is understandable in light of the historical origins of education, counseling/guidance, and our mental health systems, which have their roots in

Euro-American or Western cultures (E. Duran, 2006; Lum, 2011; McGoldrick, Giordano, & Garcia-Preto, 2005). As a result, American (U.S.) psychology has been severely criticized as being ethnocentric, monocultural, and inherently biased against racial/ethnic minorities, women, gays/lesbians, and other culturally diverse groups (Arnett, 2009; Chin, 2009; Constantine & Sue, 2006; Ridley, 2005). As voiced by many multicultural specialists, our educational system and counseling/-psychotherapy have often done great harm to our minority citizens. Rather than educate or heal, rather than offer enlightenment and freedom, and rather than allow for equal access and opportunities, historical and current practices have restricted, stereotyped, damaged, and oppressed the culturally different in our society.

In light of the increasing diversity of our society, mental health professionals will inevitably encounter client populations that differ from themselves in terms of race, culture, and ethnicity. Such differences, however, are believed to pose no problems as long as psychologists adhere to the notion of an unyielding, universal psychology that is applicable across all populations. Although few mental health professionals would voice such a belief, in reality the very policies and practices of mental health delivery systems do reflect such an ethnocentric orientation. The theories of counseling and psychotherapy, the standards used to judge normality-abnormality, and the actual process of mental health practice are culture bound and reflect a monocultural perspective of the helping professions (Highlen, 1994; Katz, 1985; D. Sue, 1990). As such, they are often culturally inappropriate and antagonistic to the lifestyles and values of minority groups in our society. Indeed, some mental health professionals assert that counseling and psychotherapy may be handmaidens of the status quo, instruments of oppression, and transmitters of society's values (Halleck, 1971; D. W. Sue & D. Sue, 1990; A. Thomas & Sillen, 1972).

We believe that ethnocentric monoculturalism is dysfunctional in a pluralistic society such as the United States. It is a powerful force, however, in forming, influencing, and determining the goals and processes of mental health delivery systems. As such, it is very important for mental health professionals to unmask or deconstruct the values, biases, and assumptions that reside in it. Ethnocentric monoculturalism combines what Wrenn (1962, 1985) calls *cultural encapsulation* and what J. M. Jones (1972, 1997) refers to as *cultural racism*. Five components of ethnocentric monoculturalism have been identified (D. W. Sue, 2004; D. W. Sue et al., 1998).

Belief in Superiority

First, there is a strong belief in the superiority of one group's cultural heritage (history, values, language, traditions, arts/crafts, etc.). The group norms and values are seen positively, and descriptors may include such phrases as "more advanced" and "more civilized." Members of the society may possess conscious and unconscious feelings of superiority and feel that their way of doing things is the best way. In our society, White Euro-American cultures are seen as not only desirable but normative as well. Physical characteristics such as light complexion, blond hair, and blue eyes; cultural characteristics such as a belief in Christianity (or monotheism), individualism, Protestant work ethic, and capitalism; and linguistic characteristics such as standard English, control of emotions, and the written tradition are highly valued components of Euro-American culture (Anderson & Middleton, 2011; Katz, 1985). People possessing these traits are perceived more favorably and often are allowed easier access to the privileges and rewards of the larger society (Furman, 2011). McIntosh (1989), a White woman, refers to this condition as *White privilege*, an invisible knapsack of unearned assets that can be used to cash in each day for advantages not given to those who do not fit this mold. Among some of the advantages that she enumerates are the following (paraphrased):

- I can, if I wish, arrange to be in the company of people of my race most of the time.
- I can turn on the television or open to the front page of the newspaper and see people of my race widely represented.
- When I am told about our national heritage or about civilization, I am shown that people of my color made it what it is.
- I can be sure that my children will be given curricular materials that testify to the existence of their race.

Belief in the Inferiority of Others

Second, there is a belief in the inferiority of the entire cultural heritage of racial/ethnic minorities, which extends to their customs, values, traditions, and language (Jones, 1997). Other societies or groups may be perceived as less developed, uncivilized, primitive, or even pathological. The groups' lifestyles or ways of doing things are considered inferior. Physical characteristics such as dark complexion, black hair, and brown eyes; cultural characteristics such as belief in non-Christian religions (Islam, Confucianism, polytheism, etc.), collectivism, present-time orientation, and the importance of shared wealth; and linguistic characteristics such as bilingualism, nonstandard English, speaking with an accent, use of nonverbal and contextual communication, and reliance on the oral tradition are usually seen as less desirable by the society (Katz, 1985; D. W. Sue, 2010b). Studies consistently reveal that individuals who are physically different, who speak with an accent, and who adhere to different cultural beliefs and practices are more likely to be evaluated more negatively in our schools and workplaces. Culturally diverse groups may be seen as less intelligent, less qualified, and less popular, and as possessing more undesirable traits.

Power to Impose Standards

Third, the dominant group possesses the power to impose their standards and beliefs on the less powerful group (Jones, 1997; D. W. Sue, 2010a). This third component of ethnocentric monoculturalism is very important. All groups are to some extent ethnocentric; that is, they feel positive about their cultural heritage and way of life. Minorities can be biased, can hold stereotypes, and can strongly believe that their way is the best way. Yet if they do not possess the power to impose their values on others, then hypothetically they cannot oppress. It is power or the unequal status relationship between groups that defines ethnocentric monoculturalism. The issue here is not to place blame but to speak realistically about how our society operates. Ethnocentric monoculturalism is the individual, institutional, and cultural expression of the superiority of one group's cultural heritage over another, combined with the possession of power to impose those standards broadly on the less powerful group. Since minorities generally do not possess a share of economic, social, and political power equal to that of Whites in our society, they are generally unable to discriminate on a large-scale basis (Ponterotto et al., 2006). The damage and harm of oppression is likely to be one-sided, from majority to minority group.

Manifestation in Institutions

Fourth, the ethnocentric values and beliefs are manifested in the programs, policies, practices, structures, and institutions of the society. For example, chain-of-command systems, training and educational systems, communications systems, management systems, and performance-appraisal systems often dictate and control our lives. Ethnocentric values attain untouchable and godfather-like status in an organization. Because most systems are monocultural in nature and demand compliance, racial/ethnic minorities and women may be oppressed. J. M. Jones (1997) labels *institutional racism* as a set of policies, priorities, and accepted normative patterns designed to subjugate, oppress, and force dependence of individuals and groups on a larger society. It does this by sanctioning unequal goals, unequal status, and unequal access to goods and services. Institutional racism has fostered the enactment of discriminatory statutes, the selective enforcement of laws, the blocking of economic opportunities and outcomes, and the imposition of forced assimilation/acculturation on the culturally different. The sociopolitical system thus attempts to define the prescribed role occupied by minorities. Feelings of powerlessness, inferiority, subordination, deprivation, anger and rage, and overt/covert resistance to factors in interracial relationships are likely to result.

The Invisible Veil

Fifth, since people are all products of cultural conditioning, their values and beliefs (worldviews) represent an *invisible veil* that operates outside the level of conscious awareness. As a result, people assume universality: that regardless of race, culture, ethnicity, or gender, everyone shares the nature of reality and truth. This assumption is erroneous but is seldom questioned because it is firmly ingrained in our worldview. Racism, sexism, and homophobia may be both conscious (intentional) and unconscious (unintentional). Neo-Nazis, skinheads, and the Ku Klux Klan would definitely fall into the first category. Although conscious and intentional racism as exemplified by these individuals, for example, may cause great harm to culturally different groups, it is the latter form that may ultimately be the most insidious and dangerous. As mentioned earlier, it is the well-intentioned individuals who consider themselves moral, decent, and fair-minded who may have the

> Perhaps the greatest obstacle to a meaningful movement toward a multicultural society is our failure to understand our unconscious and unintentional complicity in perpetuating bias and discrimination via our personal values/beliefs and our institutions.

greatest difficulty in understanding how their belief systems and actions may be biased and prejudiced. It is clear that no one is born wanting to be racist, sexist, or homophobic. Misinformation related to culturally diverse groups is not acquired by our free choice but rather is imposed through a painful process of social conditioning; all of us were taught to hate and fear others who are different in some way (D. W. Sue, 2003). Likewise, because all of us live, play, and work within organizations, those policies, practices, and structures that may be less than fair to minority groups are invisible in controlling our lives. Perhaps the greatest obstacle to a meaningful movement toward a multicultural society is our failure to understand our unconscious and unintentional complicity in perpetuating bias and discrimination via our personal values/beliefs and our institutions. The power of racism, sexism, and homophobia is related to the invisibility of the powerful forces that control and dictate our lives. In a strange sort of way, we are all victims. Minority groups are victims of oppression. Majority group members are victims who are unwittingly socialized into the role of oppressor.

Historical Manifestations of Ethnocentric Monoculturalism

The European American worldview can be described as possessing the following values and beliefs: rugged individualism, competition, mastery and control over nature, a unitary and static conception of time, religion based on Christianity, separation of science and religion, and competition (Katz, 1985). It is important to note that worldviews are neither right or wrong, nor good or bad. They become problematic, however, when they are expressed through the process of ethnocentric monoculturalism. In the United States, the historical manifestations of this process are quite clear. First, the European colonization efforts toward the Americas operated from the assumption that the enculturation of indigenous peoples was justified because European culture was superior. Forcing the colonized to adopt European beliefs and customs was seen as civilizing them. In the United States, this practice was clearly evident in the treatment of Native Americans, whose lifestyles, customs, and practices were seen as backward and uncivilized, and attempts were made to make over the "heathens" (E. Duran, 2006; Gone, 2010). Such a belief is reflected in Euro-American culture and has been manifested also in attitudes toward other racial/ethnic minority groups in the United States. A common belief is that racial/ethnic minorities would not encounter problems if they would assimilate and acculturate.

Monocultural ethnocentric bias has a long history in the United States and is even reflected as early as the uneven application of the Bill of Rights, which favored White immigrants/descendants over minority populations (Barongan et al., 1997). More than 200 years ago, Britain's King George III accepted a

Declaration of Independence from former subjects who moved to this country. This proclamation was destined to shape and reshape the geopolitical and socio-cultural landscape of the world many times over. The lofty language penned by its principal architect, Thomas Jefferson, and signed by those present was indeed inspiring: *"We hold these truths to be self evident, that all men are created equal."*

Yet as we now view the historic actions of that time, we cannot help but be struck by the paradox inherent in those events. First, all 56 of the signatories were White males of European descent, hardly a representation of the current racial and gender composition of the population. Second, the language of the declaration suggests that only men were created equal; what about women? Third, many of the founding fathers were slave owners who seemed not to recognize the hypocritical personal standards that they used because they considered Blacks to be subhuman. Fourth, the history of this land did not start with the Declaration of Independence or the formation of the United States of America. Nevertheless, our textbooks continue to teach us an ethnocentric perspective ("Western Civilization") that ignores over two thirds of the world's population. Last, it is important to note that those early Europeans who came to this country were immigrants attempting to escape persecution (oppression), who in the process did not recognize their own role in the oppression of indigenous peoples (American Indians) who had already resided in this country for centuries. As Barongan et al. (1997, p. 654) described,

> . . . the natural and inalienable rights of individuals valued by European and European American societies generally appear to have been intended for European Americans only. How else can European colonization and exploitation of Third World countries be explained? How else can the forced removal of Native Americans from their lands, centuries of enslavement and segregation of African Americans, immigration restrictions on persons of color through history, incarceration of Japanese Americans during World War II, and current English-only language requirements in the United States be explained? These acts have not been perpetrated by a few racist individuals, but by no less than the governments of the North Atlantic cultures. . . . If Euro-American ideals include a philosophical or moral opposition to racism, this has often not been reflected in policies and behaviors.

We do not take issue with the good intentions of the early founders. Nor do we infer in them evil and conscious motivations to oppress and dominate others. Yet the history of the United States has been the history of oppression and discrimination against racial/ethnic minorities and women. The Western European cultures that formed the fabric of the United States of America are relatively homogeneous compared not only to the rest of the world but also to the increasing diversity in this country. This Euro-American worldview continues to form the foundations of our educational, social, economic, cultural, and political systems.

As more and more White immigrants came to the North American continent, the guiding principle of blending the many cultures became codified into such concepts as *the melting pot* and *assimilation/acculturation*. The most desirable outcome of this process was a uniform and homogeneous consolidation of cultures—in essence, becoming monocultural. Many psychologists of color, however, have referred to this process as *cultural genocide*, an outcome of colonial thought (Guthrie, 1997; Parham et al., 2011; Samuda, 1998; A. Thomas & Sillen, 1972). Wehrly (1995, p. 24) states, "Cultural assimilation, as practiced in the United States, is the expectation by the people in power that all immigrants and people outside the dominant group will give up their ethnic and cultural values and will adopt the values and norms of the dominant society—the White, male Euro-Americans."

While ethnocentric monoculturalism is much broader than the concept of race, it is race and color that have been used to determine the social order (Carter, 1995). The White race has been seen as superior and White culture as normative. Thus, a study of U.S. history must include a study of racism and racist practices directed at people of color. The oppression of the indigenous people of this country (Native Americans), enslavement of African Americans, widespread segregation of Hispanic Americans, passage of exclusionary laws against the Chinese, and the forced internment of Japanese Americans are social realities. Thus it should be of no surprise that our racial/ethnic minority citizens may view Euro-Americans and our very institutions with considerable mistrust and suspicion. In health care delivery systems and especially in counseling and psychotherapy, which demand a certain degree of trust among therapist and client groups, an interracial encounter may be fraught with historical and current psychological baggage related to issues of discrimination, prejudice, and oppression. Carter (1995, p. 27) draws the following conclusion related to mental health delivery systems: "Because any institution in a society is shaped by social and cultural forces, it is reasonable to assume that racist notions have been incorporated into the mental health systems."

Therapeutic Impact of Ethnocentric Monoculturalism

Many multicultural specialists (Parham et al., 2011; Ponterotto et al., 2006; A. Thomas & Sillen, 1972) have pointed out how African Americans, in responding to their forced enslavement, history of discrimination, and America's reaction to their skin color, have adopted toward Whites behavior patterns that are important for survival in a racist society. These behavior patterns may include indirect expressions of hostility, aggression, and fear. During slavery, to rear children who would fit into a segregated system and who could physically survive, African American mothers were forced to teach them (a) to express aggression indirectly, (b) to read the thoughts of others while hiding their own, and (c) to engage in ritualized accommodating/subordinating behaviors designed to create as few waves as possible. This process involves a "mild dissociation" whereby African Americans may separate their true selves from their roles as "Negroes" (Boyd-Franklin, 2003, 2010; Jones, 1997). In this dual identity the true self is revealed to fellow Blacks, while the dissociated self is revealed to meet the expectations of prejudiced Whites. From the analysis of African American history, the dissociative process may be manifested in two major ways.

First, "playing it cool" has been identified as one means by which African Americans or other minorities may conceal their true feelings (Boyd-Franklin, 2003; W. E. Cross, Smith, & Payne, 2002; Grier & Cobbs, 1971; A. C. Jones, 1985). This behavior is intended to prevent Whites from knowing what the minority person is thinking or feeling and to express feelings and behaviors in such a way as to prevent offending or threatening Whites (C. Jones & Shorter-Gooden, 2003; Ridley, 2005). Thus, a person of color who is experiencing conflict, explosive anger, and suppressed feelings may appear serene and composed on the surface. This is a defense mechanism aimed at protecting minorities from harm and exploitation. Second, the *Uncle Tom syndrome* may be used by minorities to appear docile, nonassertive, and happy-go-lucky. Especially during slavery, Blacks learned that passivity is a necessary survival technique. To retain the most menial jobs, to minimize retaliation, and to maximize survival of the self and loved ones, many minorities have learned to deny their aggressive feelings toward their oppressors.

The overall result of the experiences of minorities in the United States has been to increase their vigilance and sensitivity to the thoughts and behaviors of Whites in society. We mentioned earlier that African Americans have been forced to read the thoughts of others accurately in order to survive (W. E. Cross, Smith, & Payne, 2002). It has been found that certain minority groups, such as African Americans, are better readers of nonverbal communication than their White counterparts (Kochman, 1981; D. W. Sue, 1990). This will be discussed in greater detail in Chapter 8. Many African Americans have often stated that Whites say one thing but mean another. This better understanding and sensitivity to nonverbal communication has enhanced Black people's survival in a highly dangerous society. As we will see later, it is important for the minority individual to read nonverbal messages accurately—not only for physical survival, but for psychological reasons as well.

In summary, it becomes all too clear that past and present discrimination against certain culturally diverse groups is a tangible basis for minority distrust of the majority society (Ponterotto et al., 2006). White people are perceived as potential oppressors unless proved otherwise. Under such a sociopolitical atmosphere, minorities may use several adaptive devices to prevent Whites from knowing their true feelings. Because multicultural counseling may mirror the sentiments of the larger society, these modes of behavior and their detrimental effects may be reenacted in the sessions. The fact that many minority clients are suspicious, mistrustful, and guarded in their interactions with White therapists is certainly understandable in light of the foregoing analysis. Despite their conscious desires to help, White therapists are not immune from inheriting racist attitudes, beliefs, myths, and stereotypes about Asian American, African American, Latino/ Hispanic American, and American Indian clients (D. W. Sue, 2005). For example, White counselors often believe that Blacks are nonverbal, paranoid, and angry and that they are most likely to have character disorders (Carter, 1995; A. C. Jones, 1985) or to be schizophrenic (Pavkov, Lewis, & Lyons, 1989). As a result, they view African Americans as unsuitable for counseling and psychotherapy. Mental health practitioners and social scientists who hold to this belief fail to understand the following facts:

1. As a group, African Americans tend to communicate nonverbally more than their White counterparts and to assume that nonverbal communication is a more accurate barometer of one's true thoughts and feelings. E. T. Hall (1976) observed that African Americans are better able to read nonverbal messages (high context) than are their White counterparts and that they rely less on verbalizations than on nonverbal communication to make a point. Whites, on the other hand, tune in more to verbal messages than to nonverbal messages (low context). Because they rely less on nonverbal cues, Whites need greater verbal elaborations to get a point across (D. W. Sue et al., 1996). Being unaware of and insensitive to these differences, White therapists are prone to feel that African Americans are unable to communicate in complex ways. This judgment is based on the high value that therapy places on intellectual/verbal activity.

2. Rightfully or not, White therapists are often perceived as symbols of the Establishment, who have inherited the racial biases of their forebears. Thus, the culturally diverse client is likely to impute all the negative experiences of oppression to them. This may prevent the minority client from responding to the helping professional as an individual. While the therapist may be possessed of the most admirable motives, the client may reject the helping professional simply because he or she is White. Thus, communication may be directly or indirectly shut off.

3. Some culturally diverse clients may lack confidence in the counseling and therapy process because the White counselor often proposes White solutions to their concerns (Atkinson et al., 1998). Many pressures are placed on minority clients to accept an alien value system and reject their own. We have already indicated how counseling and psychotherapy may be perceived as instruments of oppression whose function is to force assimilation and acculturation. As some racial/ethnic minority clients have asked, "Why do I have to become White in order to be considered healthy?"

4. The "playing it cool" and Uncle Tom responses of many minorities are present also in the therapy sessions. As pointed out earlier, these mechanisms are attempts to conceal true feelings, to hinder self-disclosure, and to prevent the therapist from getting to know the client. These adaptive survival mechanisms have been acquired through generations of experience with a hostile and invalidating society. The therapeutic dilemma encountered by the helping professional in working with a client of color is how to gain trust and break through this maze. What the therapist ultimately does in the sessions will determine his or her trustworthiness.

To summarize, culturally diverse clients entering counseling or therapy are likely to experience considerable anxiety about ethnic/racial/cultural differences. Suspicion, apprehension, verbal constriction, unnatural reactions, open resentment and hostility, and passive or cool behavior may all be expressed. Self-disclosure and the possible establishment of a working relationship can be seriously delayed or prevented from occurring. In all cases, the therapist's trustworthiness may be put to severe tests. Culturally effective therapists are ones who (a) can view these behaviors in a nonjudgmental manner (i.e., they are not necessarily indicative of pathology but are a manifestation of adaptive survival mechanisms), (b) can avoid personalizing any potential hostility expressed toward them, and (c) can adequately resolve challenges to their credibility. Thus, it becomes important for us to understand those dimensions that may enhance or diminish the culturally different client's receptivity to self-disclosure.

CREDIBILITY AND ATTRACTIVENESS IN MULTICULTURAL COUNSELING

Theories of counseling and psychotherapy attempt to outline an approach designed to make them effective (Corey, 2012; Wampold, 2010). It is our contention that multicultural helping cannot be approached through any one theory of counseling (D. W. Sue et al., 1996). There are several reasons for such a statement. First, theories of counseling are composed of philosophical assumptions regarding the nature of humans and a theory of personality (Stricker, 2010; Wampold, 2010). As pointed out earlier, these characteristics are highly culture bound (Katz, 1985; D. W. Sue, 1995a, 1995b). The true nature of people is a philosophical question. What constitutes the healthy and unhealthy personality is also debatable and varies from culture to culture and from class to class.

Second, theories of counseling and psychotherapy are composed also of a body of therapeutic techniques and strategies. These techniques are applied to clients with the hope of effecting change in behaviors, perceptions, or attitudes. A theory dictates what techniques are to be used and, implicitly, in what proportions (Corey, 2012; D. W. Sue et al., 1996). For example, it is clear that humanistic-existential therapists (Cain, 2010) behave differently than do rational-emotive ones (A. Ellis & D. J. Ellis, 2011). The fact that one school of counseling/therapy can be distinguished from another has implications: It suggests a certain degree of rigidity in working with culturally diverse clients who might find such techniques offensive or inappropriate. The implicit assumption is that these techniques are imposed according to the theory and not based on client needs and values.

Third, theories of counseling and psychotherapy have often failed to agree among themselves about what constitutes desirable outcomes. This makes it extremely difficult to determine the effectiveness of counseling and therapy. For example, the psychoanalytically oriented therapist uses "insight"; the behaviorist uses "behavior change"; the client-centered person uses "self-actualization"; and the rational-emotive person uses "rational cognitive content/processes." The potential for disagreement over appropriate outcome variables is increased even further when the therapist and the client come from different cultures.

Counseling as Interpersonal Influence

Counselors who are perceived by their clients as credible (expert and trustworthy) and attractive are able to exert greater social influence over their clients than are those perceived as lacking in credibility and attractiveness (Heesacker

& Carroll, 1997). Regardless of the counseling orientation (person-centered, psychoanalytic, behavioral, transactional analysis, etc.), the therapist's effectiveness tends to depend on the client's perception of his or her expertness, trustworthiness, and attractiveness. Stanley Strong (1969) is probably the person most credited with providing a conceptual framework for understanding parallels between the role of the therapist and that of social influence theory. Most studies on social influence and counseling, however, have dealt exclusively with a White population (Heesacker, Conner, & Pritchard, 1995). Thus, findings that certain attributes contribute to a counselor's credibility and attractiveness may not be so perceived by culturally diverse clients. It is entirely possible that credibility, as defined by credentials indicating specialized training (e.g., LMHC, MFCC, MSW, PsyD, PhD, MD), might only indicate to a Latino/a client that the White therapist has no knowledge or expertise in working with Latinos. It seems important, therefore, for helping professionals to understand what factors/conditions may enhance or negate counselor credibility and attractiveness when working with clients of color.

Psychological Sets of Clients

The therapist's credibility and attractiveness depend very much on the mind-set or frame of reference for culturally diverse clients. We all know individuals who tend to value rational approaches to solving problems and others who value a more affective (e.g., attractiveness) approach. It would seem reasonable that a client who values rationality might be more receptive to a rational counseling approach as a means to enhance counselor credibility. Understanding a client's psychological mind-set may facilitate the therapist's ability to exert social influence in counseling. In a very useful model, Collins (1970) proposed a set of conceptual categories that can be used to understand people's perception of communicator (counselor) credibility and receptiveness to influence. We apply those categories here with respect to the therapy situation. Note that race, ethnicity, and the experience of discrimination often affect the type of set that will be operative in a minority client.

1. *The problem-solving set: Information orientation.* In the problem-solving set, the client is concerned about obtaining correct information (solutions, outlooks, and skills) that has adaptive value in the real world. The client accepts or rejects information from the therapist on the basis of its perceived truth or falsity: Is it an accurate representation of reality? The processes that are used tend to be rational and logical in analyzing and attacking the problem. First, the client may apply a consistency test and compare the new facts with earlier information. For example, a White male therapist might try to reassure an African American client that he is not against interracial marriage but might hesitate in speech and tense up whenever the topic is broached (Utsey, Gernat, & Hammar, 2005). In this case, the verbal or content message is inconsistent with nonverbal cues, and the credibility and social influence of the therapist are likely to decline. Second, the Black client may apply a corroboration test by actively

seeking information from others for comparison purposes. If he or she hears from a friend that the therapist has racial hang-ups, then the therapist's effectiveness is again likely to be severely diminished. The former test makes use of information that the individual already has (understanding of nonverbal meanings), while the latter requires him or her to seek out new information (asking a trusted African American friend). Through their experiences, clients of color may have learned that many Whites have little expertise when it comes to their lifestyles and that the information or suggestions that they give are White solutions or labels.

2. *The consistency set.* People are operating under the consistency set whenever they change an opinion, belief, or behavior in such a way as to make it consistent with other opinions, beliefs, or behaviors. For example, since therapists are supposed to help, we naturally believe that they would do nothing to harm us. A therapist who is not in touch with personal prejudices or biases may send out conflicting messages to a minority client. The counselor may verbally state, "I am here to help you," but at the same time indicate racist attitudes and feelings nonverbally. This can destroy the counselor's credibility very quickly, for example, in the case of a minority client who accurately applies a consistency set such as, "White people say one thing, but do another. You can't believe what they tell you." Culturally different clients will actively seek out disclosures on the part of the therapist to compare them with the information they have about the world. Should the therapist pass the test, new information may be more readily accepted and assimilated.

3. *The identity set.* An individual who strongly identifies with a particular group is likely to accept the group's beliefs and to conform to behaviors dictated by the group. If race or ethnicity constitute a strong reference group for a client, then a counselor of the same race/ethnicity is likely to be more influential than one who is not. It is believed that racial/ethnic similarity may actually increase willingness to return for therapy and facilitate effectiveness. The studies on this are quite mixed, as there is considerable evidence that membership group similarity may not be as effective as belief or attitude similarity. It has also been found that the stage of cultural or racial identity affects which dimensions of similarities will be preferred by the racial/ethnic minority client (W. E. Cross, Smith, & Payne, 2002). We have much more to say about cultural identity development later in Chapter 11. It is obvious, however, that racial differences between counselor and client make bridging this gap a major challenge.

4. *The economic set.* In the economic set, the person is influenced because of the perceived rewards and punishments that the source is able to deliver. In this set, a person performs a behavior or states a belief in order to gain rewards and avoid punishments. In the counseling setting, this means that the therapist controls important resources that may affect the client. For example, a therapist may decide to recommend expulsion of a student from school or deny a positive parole recommendation to a client who is in prison. In less subtle ways, the therapist may ridicule or praise a client during a group counseling session. In these cases, the client may decide to alter his or her behavior because the therapist holds greater power. The major problem with the use of rewards and punishments to induce

change is that although it may assure *behavioral compliance*, it does not guarantee *private acceptance*. For culturally diverse clients, therapy that operates primarily on the economic set is more likely to prevent the development of trust, rapport, and self-disclosure.

5. *The authority set.* Under this set, some individuals are thought to have a particular position that gives them a legitimate right to prescribe attitudes or behaviors. In our society, we have been conditioned to believe that certain authorities (police officers, chairpersons, designated leaders, etc.) have the right to demand compliance. This occurs via training in role behavior and group norms. Mental health professionals, such as counselors, are thought to have a legitimate right to recommend and provide psychological treatment to disturbed or troubled clients. This psychological set legitimizes the counselor's role as a helping professional. Yet for many minorities, these roles in society are exactly the ones that are perceived as instruments of institutional oppression and racism.

It should be clear at this point that characteristics of the influencing source (therapist) are of the utmost importance in eliciting types of changes. In addition, the type of mental or psychological set placed in operation often dictates the permanency and degree of attitude/belief change. While these sets operate similarly for majority and minority clients, their manifestations may be quite different. Obviously, a minority client may have great difficulty identifying with a counselor from another race or culture (identification set). Also, what constitutes credibility to minority clients may be far different from what constitutes credibility to a majority client.

Therapist Credibility

Credibility (which elicits the problem-solving, consistency, and identification sets) may be defined as the constellation of characteristics that makes certain individuals appear worthy of belief, capable, entitled to confidence, reliable, and trustworthy. Expertness is an *ability variable*, whereas trustworthiness is a *motivation variable*. Expertness depends on how well informed, capable, or intelligent others perceive the communicator (counselor/therapist) to be. Trustworthiness is dependent on the degree to which people perceive the communicator as motivated to make valid or invalid assertions. The weight of evidence supports our commonsense beliefs that the helping professional who is perceived as expert and trustworthy can influence clients more than can one who is perceived to be lower on these traits.

> *Credibility* may be defined as the constellation of characteristics that makes certain individuals appear worthy of belief, capable, entitled to confidence, reliable, and trustworthy.

Expertness

Clients often go to a therapist not only because they are in distress and in need of relief but also because they believe the counselor is an expert, that is, that he or she has the necessary knowledge, skills, experience, training, and tools to help (problem-solving set). Perceived expertness is typically a function of (a) reputation, (b) evidence of specialized training, and (c) behavioral evidence of proficiency/competency. For culturally diverse clients, the issue of therapist expertness seems to be raised more often than when clients go to a therapist of their own culture and race. The fact that therapists have degrees and certificates from prestigious institutions (authority set) may not enhance perceived expertness. This is especially true of clients who are culturally different and are aware that institutional bias exists in training programs. Indeed, it may have the opposite effect, by reducing credibility! Additionally, reputation-expertness (authority set) is unlikely to impress a minority client unless the favorable testimony comes from someone of his or her own group.

Thus, behavior-expertness, or demonstrating the ability to help a client, becomes the critical form of expertness in effective multicultural counseling (problem-solving set). It appears that using counseling skills and strategies appropriate to the life values of the culturally diverse client is crucial. We have already mentioned evidence that certain minority groups prefer a much more active approach to counseling. A counselor playing a relatively inactive role may be perceived as being incompetent and unhelpful. The following example shows how the therapist's approach lowers perceived expertness.

ASIAN AMERICAN MALE CLIENT:	It's hard for me to talk about these issues. My parents and friends . . . they wouldn't understand . . . if they ever found out I was coming here for help . . .
WHITE MALE THERAPIST:	I sense it's difficult to talk about personal things. How are you feeling right now?
ASIAN AMERICAN CLIENT:	Oh, all right.
WHITE THERAPIST:	That's not a feeling. Sit back and get in touch with your feelings. [pause] Now tell me, how are you feeling right now?
ASIAN AMERICAN CLIENT:	Somewhat nervous.
WHITE THERAPIST:	When you talked about your parents and friends not understanding and the way you said it made me think you felt ashamed and disgraced at having to come. Was that what you felt?

Although this exchange appears to indicate that the therapist could (a) see the client's discomfort and (b) interpret his feelings correctly, it also points out the therapist's lack of understanding and knowledge of Asian cultural values. Although we do not want to be guilty of stereotyping Asian Americans, many believe that publicly expressing feelings to a stranger is inappropriate. The therapist's persistent attempts to focus on feelings and his direct and blunt interpretation of them may indicate to the Asian American client that the therapist lacks the more subtle skills of dealing with a sensitive topic or that the therapist is shaming the client.

Furthermore, it is possible that the Asian American client in this case is much more used to discussing feelings in an indirect or subtle manner. A direct response from the therapist addressed to a feeling may not be as effective as one that deals with it indirectly. In many traditional Asian groups, subtlety is a highly prized art, and the traditional Asian client may feel much more comfortable when dealing with feelings in an indirect manner.

Many educators claim that specific therapy skills are not as important as the attitude one brings into the therapeutic situation. Behind this statement is the belief that universal attributes of genuineness, love, unconditional acceptance, and positive regard are the only things needed. Yet the question remains: How does a therapist communicate these things to culturally diverse clients? While a therapist might have the best of intentions, it is possible that his or her intentions might be misunderstood. Let us use another example with the same Asian American client.

ASIAN AMERICAN CLIENT: I'm even nervous about others seeing me come in here. It's so difficult for me to talk about this.

WHITE THERAPIST: We all find some things difficult to talk about. It's important that you do.

ASIAN AMERICAN CLIENT: It's easy to say that. But do you really understand how awful I feel, talking about my parents?

WHITE THERAPIST: I've worked with many Asian Americans, and many have similar problems.

Here we find a distinction between the therapist's intentions and the effects of his comments. The therapist's intentions were to reassure the client that he understood his feelings, to imply that he had worked with similar cases, and to make the client feel less isolated (i.e., that others have the same problems). The effects, however, were to dilute and dismiss the client's feelings and concerns and to take the uniqueness out of the situation.

Trustworthiness

Perceived trustworthiness encompasses such factors as sincerity, openness, honesty, and perceived lack of motivation for personal gain. A therapist who is perceived as trustworthy is likely to exert more influence over a client than one who is not. In our society, many people assume that certain roles, such as ministers, doctors, psychiatrists, and counselors, exist to help people. With respect to minorities, self-disclosure is very much dependent on this attribute of perceived trustworthiness. Because mental health professionals are often perceived by minorities to be agents of the Establishment, trust is something that does not come with the role (authority set). Indeed, many minorities may perceive that therapists cannot be trusted unless otherwise demonstrated. Again, the role and reputation that the therapist has as being trustworthy must be evidenced in behavioral terms. More than anything, challenges to the therapist's trustworthiness will be a frequent theme blocking further exploration and movement until it is resolved to the satisfaction of the client. These verbatim transcripts illustrate the trust issue.

WHITE MALE THERAPIST:	I sense some major hesitations . . . It's difficult for you to discuss your concerns with me.
BLACK MALE CLIENT:	You're damn right! If I really told you how I felt about my [White] coach, what's to prevent you from telling him? You Whities are all of the same mind.
WHITE THERAPIST [ANGRY]:	Look, it would be a lie for me to say I don't know your coach. He's an acquaintance but not a personal friend. Don't put me in the same bag with all Whites! Anyway, even if he were a close friend, I hold our discussion in strictest confidence. Let me ask you this question: What would I need to do that would make it easier for you to trust me?
BLACK CLIENT:	You're on your way, man!

This verbal exchange illustrates several issues related to trustworthiness. First, the minority client is likely to test the therapist constantly regarding issues of confidentiality. Second, the onus of responsibility for proving trustworthiness falls on the therapist. Third, to prove that one is trustworthy requires, at times, self-disclosure on the part of the mental health professional. That the therapist did not hide the fact that he knew the coach (openness), became angry about being lumped with all Whites (sincerity), assured the client that he would not tell the coach or anyone else about their sessions (confidentiality), and asked the client how he could work to prove he was trustworthy (genuineness) were all elements that enhanced his trustworthiness.

Handling the "prove to me that you can be trusted" ploy is very difficult for many therapists. It is difficult because it demands self-disclosure on the part of the helping professional, something that graduate training programs have taught us to avoid. It places the focus on the therapist rather than on the client and makes many uncomfortable. In addition, it is likely to evoke defensiveness on the part of many mental health practitioners. Here is another verbatim exchange in which defensiveness is evoked, destroying the helping professional's trustworthiness.

BLACK FEMALE CLIENT:	Students in my drama class expect me to laugh when they do "steppin' fetchit" routines and tell Black jokes. . . . I'm wondering whether you've ever laughed at any of those jokes.
WHITE MALE THERAPIST:	[long pause] Yes, I'm sure I have. Have you ever laughed at any White jokes?
BLACK CLIENT:	What's a White joke?

| WHITE MALE THERAPIST: | I don't know [nervous laughter]; I suppose one making fun of Whites. Look, I'm Irish. Have you ever laughed at Irish jokes? |
| BLACK CLIENT: | People tell me many jokes, but I don't laugh at racial jokes. I feel we're all minorities and should respect each other. |

Again, the client tested the therapist indirectly by asking him if he ever laughed at racial jokes. Since most of us probably have, to say "no" would be a blatant lie. The client's motivation for asking this question was to find out (a) how sincere and open the therapist was and (b) whether the therapist could recognize his racist attitudes without letting it interfere with therapy. While the therapist admitted to having laughed at such jokes, he proceeded to destroy his trustworthiness by becoming defensive. Rather than simply stopping with his statement of "Yes, I'm sure I have" or making some other similar remark, he defends himself by trying to get the client to admit to similar actions. Thus the therapist's trustworthiness is seriously impaired. He is perceived as motivated to defend himself rather than to help the client.

The therapist's obvious defensiveness in this case has prevented him from understanding the intent and motive of the question. Is the African American female client really asking the therapist whether he has actually laughed at Black jokes before? Or is the client asking the therapist if he is a racist? Both of these speculations have a certain amount of validity, but it is our belief that the Black female client is actually asking the following important question of the therapist: "How open and honest are you about your own racism, and will it interfere with our session here?" Again, the test is one of trustworthiness, a motivational variable that the White male therapist has obviously failed.

REFLECTION AND DISCUSSION QUESTIONS

1. Think about yourself, your characteristics, and your interaction style. Think about your daily interactions with friends, coworkers, colleagues, or fellow students. How influential are you with them? What makes you influential?
2. As a counselor or therapist, what makes you credible with your clients? Using the psychological sets outlined earlier, how do you convey expertness and trustworthiness?
3. What do you believe would stand in the way of your trustworthiness with clients of color? How would you overcome it?

Understanding Individual and Systemic Worldviews

The dimensions of trust-mistrust and credibility in the helping professions are strongly influenced by worldviews. Worldviews determine how people perceive their relationship to the world (nature, institutions, other people, etc.), and they are highly correlated with a person's cultural upbringing and life experiences (Koltko-Rivera, 2004). Put in a much more practical way, not only are worldviews composed of our attitudes, values, opinions, and concepts, but they also affect how we think, define events, make decisions, and behave. For marginalized groups in America, a strong determinant of worldviews is very much related to the subordinate position assigned to them in society. Helping professionals who hold a worldview different from that of their clients and who are unaware of the basis for this difference are most likely to impute negative traits to clients and to engage in cultural oppression. To understand this assertion, we discuss two different psychological orientations considered important in the formation of worldviews: (a) locus of control and (b) locus of responsibility.

Locus of Control

Rotter's (1966) historic work in the formulation of the concepts of internal and external (I-E) control has contributed greatly to our understanding of human behavior. *Internal control* (IC) refers to people's beliefs that reinforcements are contingent on their own actions and that they can shape their own fate. *External control* (EC) refers to people's beliefs that reinforcing events occur independently of their actions and that the future is determined more by chance and luck. Early researchers (Lefcourt, 1966; Rotter, 1966, 1975) have found that high internality is associated with (a) greater attempts at mastering the environment, (b) superior coping strategies, (c) better cognitive processing of information, (d) lower predisposition to anxiety, (e) higher achievement motivation, (f) greater social action involvement, and (g) greater value on skill-determined rewards. These attributes are highly valued by U.S. society and seem to constitute the core features of Western mental health.

It has been found that socially devalued groups (people of color, women, and people from low socioeconomic status [SES]) score significantly higher on the external end of the locus-of-control continuum (D. W. Sue, 1978; Koltko-Rivera, 2004). Using the I-E dimension as a criterion of mental health would mean that minority, poor, and female clients would be viewed as possessing less desirable attributes. Thus, a clinician who encounters a minority client with a high external orientation ("It's no use trying," "There's nothing I can do about it," and "You shouldn't rock the boat") may interpret the client as being inherently apathetic, procrastinating, lazy, depressed, or anxious about trying. The problem with an unqualified application of the I-E dimension is that it fails to take into consideration different cultural and social experiences of the individual. This failure may lead to highly inappropriate and destructive applications in therapy. It seems plausible that different cultural groups, women, and people from a lower SES have learned that control in their lives operates differently from how it operates for society at large (American Psychological Association, 2007a; Ridley, 2005). For example, externality related to impersonal forces (chance and luck) is different from that ascribed to cultural forces and from that ascribed to powerful others.

Chance and luck operate equally across situations for everyone. However, the forces that determine locus of control from a cultural perspective may be viewed by the particular ethnic group as acceptable and benevolent. In this case, externality is viewed positively. American culture, for example, values the uniqueness, independence, and self-reliance of each individual. It places a high premium on self-reliance, individualism, and status achieved through one's own efforts. In contrast, the situation-centered Chinese culture places importance on the group, on tradition, social roles expectations, and harmony with the universe (Kim, 2011; Uba, 1994). Thus, the cultural orientation of the more traditional Chinese tends to elevate the external scores. In contrast to U.S. society, Chinese society highly values externality.

Likewise, high externality may constitute a realistic sociopolitical presence of influence from powerful others. A major force in the literature dealing with locus of control is that of powerlessness. *Powerlessness* may be defined as the expectancy that a person's behavior cannot determine the outcomes or reinforcements that he or she seeks. There is a strong possibility that externality may be a function of a person's opinions about prevailing social institutions. For example, low SES individuals and Blacks are not given an equal opportunity to obtain the material rewards of Western culture. Because of racism, African Americans may perceive, in a realistic fashion, a discrepancy between their ability and attainment. In this case, externality may be seen as a malevolent force to be distinguished from the benevolent cultural ones just discussed. It can be concluded that although people with high externality are less effectively motivated, perform poorly in achievement situations, and evidence greater psychological distress, this does not necessarily hold for minorities and low-income persons. Focusing on external forces may be motivationally healthy if it results from assessing one's chances for success against real systematic and external obstacles rather than unpredictable fate. The I-E continuum is useful for therapists only if they make clear distinctions about the meaning of the external control dimension. High externality may be due to (a) chance/luck, (b) cultural dictates that are viewed as benevolent, and (c) a political force (racism and discrimination) that represents malevolent but realistic obstacles. In each case, it is a mistake to assume that pathological interpretations of externality is operative for culturally diverse clients.

Locus of Responsibility

Another important dimension in world outlooks was formulated from attribution theory (E. E. Jones, Kanouse, Kelley, Nisbett, Valins, & Weiner, 1972; J. M. Jones, 1997) and can be legitimately referred to as *locus of responsibility*. In essence, this dimension measures the degree of responsibility or blame placed on the individual or system. In the case of African Americans, their lower standard of living may be attributed to their personal inadequacies and shortcomings, or the responsibility for their plight may be attributed to racial discrimination and lack of opportunities. The former orientation blames the individual, while the latter explanation blames the system.

The degree of emphasis placed on the individual as opposed to the system in affecting a person's behavior is important in the formation of life orientations. Those who hold a person-centered orientation (a) emphasize the understanding of a person's motivations, values, feelings, and goals; (b) believe that success or failure is attributable to the individual's skills or personal in-adequacies; and (c) believe that there is a strong relationship between ability, effort, and success in society. In essence, these people adhere strongly to the Protestant ethic that idealizes rugged individualism. On the other hand, situation-centered or system-blame people view the sociocultural and sociopolitical environment as more potent than the individual. Social, economic, and political forces are powerful; success or failure is generally dependent on the social forces and not necessarily on personal attributes. Defining the problem as residing in the person enables society to ignore situationally relevant factors and to protect and preserve social institutions and belief systems. Thus, the individual/system blame continuum may need to be viewed differentially for minority groups. An internal response (acceptance of blame for one's failure) might be considered normal for the White middle class, but for minorities it may be extreme and intropunitive.

For example, an African American male client who has been unable to find a job because of prejudice and discrimination may blame himself ("What's wrong with me?" "Why can't I find a job?" "Am I worthless?"). An external response may be more realistic, healthy, and appropriate ("Institutional racism prevented my getting the job"). In fact, early research indicates that African Americans with high external orientation appeared healthier in outlook: They (a) more often aspired to nontraditional occupations, (b) were more in favor of group rather than individual action for dealing with discrimination, (c) engaged in more civil rights activities, and (d) exhibited more innovative coping behavior (Gurin, Gurin, Lao, & Beattie, 1969). It is important to note that the personal control dimension discussed in the previous section was correlated with traditional measures of motivation and achievement (grades), whereas individual/system blame was a better predictor of innovative social action behavior.

FORMATION OF WORLDVIEWS

The two psychological orientations, locus of control (personal control) and locus of responsibility, are independent of one another. As shown in Figure 5.1, both may be placed on the continuum in such a manner that they intersect, forming four quadrants: internal locus of control–internal locus of responsibility (IC-IR), external locus of control–internal locus of responsibility (EC-IR), internal locus of control–external locus of responsibility (IC-ER), and external locus of control–external locus of responsibility (EC-ER). Each quadrant represents a different worldview or orientation to life. Theoretically, then, if we know the individual's degree of internality or externality on the two loci, we can plot them on the figure. We would speculate that various ethnic and racial groups are not randomly distributed throughout the four quadrants. The previous discussion concerning cultural and societal influences on these two dimensions would seem to support this speculation. Because our discussion focuses on the political ramifications of the two dimensions, there is an evaluative desirable-undesirable quality to each worldview.

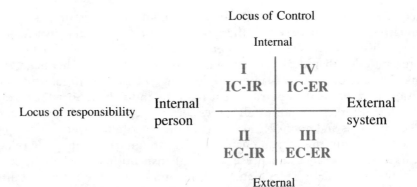

Figure 5.1 Graphic Representation of Worldviews

Source: D. W. Sue (1978), "Eliminating Cultural Oppression in Counseling: Toward a General Theory," *Journal of Counseling Psychology, 25,* p. 422. Copyright © 1978 by the *Journal of Counseling Psychology.* Reprinted by permission.

Internal Locus of Control (IC)–Internal Locus of Responsibility (IR)

As mentioned earlier, individuals high in internal personal control (IC) believe that they are masters of their fate and that their actions do affect the outcomes. Likewise, people high in internal locus of responsibility (IR) attribute their current status and life conditions to their own unique attributes; success is due to one's own efforts, and lack of success is attributed to one's shortcomings or inadequacies. Perhaps the greatest exemplification of the IC-IR philosophy is U.S. society. American culture can be described as the epitome of the individual-centered approach that emphasizes uniqueness, independence, and self-reliance. A high value is placed on personal resources for solving all problems; self-reliance; pragmatism; individualism; status achievement through one's own effort; and power or control over others, things, animals, and forces of nature. Democratic ideals such as "equal access to opportunity," "liberty and justice for all," "God helps those who help themselves," and "fulfillment of personal destiny" all reflect this worldview. The individual is held accountable for all that transpires. Constant and prolonged failure or the inability to attain goals leads to symptoms of self-blame (depression, guilt, and feelings of inadequacy). Most members of the White middle class would fall within this quadrant.

Therapeutic Implications

Western approaches to clinical practice occupy the quadrant represented by IC-IR characteristics. Most therapists are of the opinion that people must take major responsibility for their own actions and that they can improve their lot in life by their own efforts. The epitome of this line of thought is represented by the numerous self-help approaches currently in vogue in our field. Clients who occupy this quadrant tend to be White middle-class clients, and for these clients such approaches might be entirely appropriate. In working with clients from different cultures, however, such an approach might be inappropriate. Cultural oppression in therapy becomes an ever-present danger.

External Locus of Control (EC)–Internal Locus of Responsibility (IR)

Individuals who fall into this quadrant are most likely to accept the dominant culture's definition for self-responsibility but to have very little real control over how they are defined by others. The term *marginal man* (person) was first coined by Stonequist (1937) to describe a person living on the margins of two cultures and not fully accommodated to either. Although there is nothing inherently pathological about bicultural membership, J. M. Jones (1997) feels that Western society has practiced a form of cultural racism by imposing its standards, beliefs, and ways of behaving onto minority groups. Marginal individuals deny the existence of racism; believe that the plight of their own people is due to laziness, stupidity, and a clinging to outdated traditions; reject their own cultural heritage and believe that their ethnicity represents a handicap in Western society; evidence racial self-hatred; accept White social, cultural, and institutional standards; perceive physical features of White men and women as an exemplification of beauty; and are powerless to control their sense of self-worth because approval must come from an external source. As a result, they are high in person-focus and external control.

It is quite clear that marginal persons are oppressed, have little choice, and are powerless in the face of the dominant-subordinate relationship between the middle-class Euro-American culture and their own minority culture. According to Freire (1970), if this dominant-subordinate relationship in society were eliminated, the phenomenon of marginality would also disappear. For if two cultures exist on the basis of total equality (an ideal for biculturalism), then the conflicts of marginality simply do not occur in the person.

Therapeutic Implications

The psychological dynamics for the EC-IR minority client are likely to reflect his or her marginal status and self-hate. For example, White therapists might be perceived as more competent and preferred than are therapists of the client's own race. To EC-IR minority clients, focusing on feelings may be very threatening because it ultimately may reveal the presence of self-hate and the realization that clients cannot escape from their own racial and cultural heritage. A culturally encapsulated White counselor or therapist who does not understand the sociopolitical dynamics of the client's concerns may unwittingly perpetuate the conflict. For example, the client's preference for a White therapist, coupled with the therapist's implicit belief in the values of U.S. culture, becomes a barrier to effective counseling. A culturally sensitive helping professional needs to help the client (a) understand the particular dominant-subordinate political forces that have created this dilemma and (b) distinguish between positive attempts to acculturate and a negative rejection of one's own cultural values.

External Locus of Control (EC)–External Locus of Responsibility (ER)

The inequities and injustices of racism seen in the standard of living tend to be highly damaging to minorities. Discrimination may be seen in the areas of housing, employment, income, and education. A person high in system blame and external control feels that there is very little one can do in the face of such severe external obstacles as prejudice and discrimination. In essence, the EC response might be a manifestation of (a) having given up or (b) attempting to placate those in power. In the former, individuals internalize their impotence even though they are aware of the external basis of their plight. In its extreme form, oppression may result in a form of learned helplessness (Seligman, 1982). When minorities learn that their responses have minimal effects on the environment, the resulting phenomenon can best be described as an expectation of helplessness. People's susceptibility to helplessness depends on their experience with controlling the environment. In the face of continued racism, many may simply give up in their attempts to achieve personal goals.

The dynamics of the placater, however, are not related to the response of giving up. Rather, social forces in the form of prejudice and discrimination are seen as too powerful to combat at that particular time. The best one can hope to do is to suffer the inequities in silence for fear of retaliation. The phrases that most describe this mode of adjustment include, "Don't rock the boat," "Keep a low profile," and "Survival at all costs." Life is viewed as relatively fixed, and there is little that the individual can do. Passivity in the face of oppression is the primary reaction of the placater. Slavery was one of the most important factors shaping the sociopsychological functioning of African Americans. Interpersonal relations between Whites and Blacks were highly structured and placed African Americans in a subservient and inferior role. Those Blacks who broke the rules or did not show proper deferential behavior were severely punished. The spirits of most African Americans, however, were not broken. Conformance to White Euro-American rules and regulations was dictated by the need to survive in an oppressive environment. Direct expressions of anger and resentment were dangerous, but indirect expressions were frequent.

Therapeutic Implications

EC-ER African Americans are very likely to see the White therapist as symbolic of any other Black-White relations. They are likely to show "proper" deferential behavior and not to take seriously admonitions by the therapist that they are the masters of their own fate. As a result, an IC-IR therapist may perceive the culturally different client as lacking in courage and ego strength and as being passive. A culturally effective therapist, however, would realize the basis of these adaptations. Unlike EC-IR clients, EC-ER individuals do understand the political forces that have subjugated their existence. The most helpful approach on the part of the therapist would be (a) to teach the clients new coping strategies, (b) to have them experience successes, and (c) to validate who and what they represent.

Internal Locus of Control (IC)–External Locus of Responsibility (ER)

Individuals who score high in internal control and system-focus believe that they are able to shape events in their own life if given a chance. They do not accept the fact that their present state is due to their own inherent weakness. However, they also realistically perceive that external barriers of discrimination, prejudice, and exploitation block their paths to the successful attainment of goals. There is a considerable body of evidence to support this contention. Recall that the IC dimension was correlated with greater feelings of personal efficacy, higher aspirations, and so forth, and that ER was related to collective action in the social arena. If so, we would expect that IC-ER people would be more likely to participate in civil rights activities and to stress racial identity and militancy. Pride in one's racial and cultural identity is most likely to be accepted by an IC-ER person. The low self-esteem engendered by widespread prejudice and racism is actively challenged by these people. There is an attempt to redefine a group's existence by stressing consciousness and pride in their own racial and cultural heritage. Such phrases as "Black is beautiful" represent a symbolic relabeling of identity from *Negro* and colored to Black or African American. To many African Americans, *Negro* and *colored* are White labels symbolic of a warped and degrading identity given them by a racist society. As a means of throwing off these burdensome shackles, the Black individual and African Americans as a group are redefined in a positive light.

Therapeutic Implications

Much evidence indicates that minority groups are becoming increasingly conscious of their own racial and cultural identities as they relate to oppression in U.S. society. If the evidence is correct, it is also probable that more and more minorities are likely to hold an IC-ER worldview. Thus, therapists who work with the culturally different will increasingly be exposed to clients with an IC-ER worldview. In many respects, these clients pose the most difficult problems for the White IC-IR therapist. These clients are likely to raise challenges to the therapist's credibility and trustworthiness. The helping professional is likely to be seen as a part of the Establishment that has oppressed minorities. Self-disclosure on the part of the client is not likely to come quickly; more than any other worldview, an IC-ER orientation means that clients are likely to play a much more active part in the therapy process and to demand action from the therapist.

An interesting transactional analysis of the mind-sets of all four quadrants can be found in Figure 5.2.

IC-IR	IC-ER
I. (Assertive/Passive) I'm okay and have control over myself. Society is okay, and I can make it in the system.	*IV. (Assertive/Assertive)* I'm okay and have control, but need a chance. Society is not okay, and I know what's wrong and seek to change it.
EC-IR	**EC-ER**
II. (Marginal/Passive) I'm okay but my control comes best when I define myself according to the definition of the dominant culture. Society is okay the way it is; it's up to me.	*III. (Passive/Aggresive)* I'm not okay and don't have much control; I might as well give up or please everyone. Society is not okay and is the reason for my plight; the bad system is all to blame.

Figure 5.2 Transactional Analysis of Cultural Identity Quadrants

Source: J. A. Axelson (1993), *Counseling and Development in a Multicultural Society* (p. 399), Copyright © 1993 by Wadsworth, Inc. Reprinted by permission of Brooks/Cole Publishing Company, Pacific Grove, California 93950, a division of Wadsworth, Inc.

Implications for Clinical Practice

It is clear that counseling and psychotherapy, in both process and goals, contain a powerful sociopolitical dimension. How minority clients relate to therapists different from themselves often mirrors the state of interracial relationships in the wider society. Several guidelines suggested from this chapter can aid us in our journey toward cultural competence.

1. Be able to understand and apply the concepts of ethnocentric monoculturalism to the wider society and to marginalized groups and understand how it may manifest and affect the dynamics in an interracial counseling relationship.
2. In working with diverse clients, it is important to distinguish between behaviors indicative of a true mental disorder and those that result from oppression and survival. A client of color may not readily self-disclose to you and may engage in specific behaviors for self-protection. These represent functional survival skills rather than pathology.
3. Do not personalize the suspicions a client may have of your motives. If you become defensive, insulted, or angry with the client, your effectiveness will be seriously diminished.
4. Monitor your own reactions and question your beliefs. All of us are victims of our social conditioning and have unintentionally inherited the racial biases of our forebears. Be willing to understand and overcome your stereotypes, biases, and assumptions about other cultural groups.
5. Know that expertness and trustworthiness are important components of any therapeutic relationship. In multicultural counseling/therapy, however, the counselor or therapist may not be presumed to possess either. The therapist working with a minority client is likely to experience

severe tests of his or her expertness and trustworthiness before serious therapy can proceed. The responsibility for proving to the client that you are a credible therapist is likely to be greater when working with a minority client than with a majority client. How you meet the challenge is important in determining your effectiveness as a multicultural helping professional.

6. Be aware that clients of color or other marginalized groups may consider your professional credentials insufficient. Know that your credibility and trustworthiness will be tested. Evidence of specialized training is less impressive than such factors as authenticity, sincerity, and openness. Tests of credibility may occur frequently in the therapy session, and the onus of responsibility for proving expertness and trustworthiness lies with the therapist.

7. In multicultural counseling/therapy you may be unable to use the client's identification set (membership group similarity) to induce change. At times, racial dissimilarity may prove to be so much of a hindrance as to render therapy ineffective. In this situation, referring out should not be viewed negatively or as a defeat. One could argue that a counselor or therapist who is aware of limitations and is nondefensive enough to refer out is evidencing cultural competence.

8. Be aware that difficulties in multicultural counseling may not stem from race factors per se, but from the implications of being a minority in the United States and thus having secondary status. In any case, a broad statement on this matter is overly simplistic. By virtue of its definition, multicultural therapy implies major differences between the client and the helper. How these differences can be bridged and under what conditions a therapist is able to work effectively with culturally diverse clients are key questions.

9. Understanding the worldviews of culturally diverse clients means understanding how they are formed. Of special importance is the ability to analyze how locus of control and locus of responsibility may influence not only the client's perspectives but your own as well. Know that traditional counseling and therapy operates from the assumption of high internal locus of control and responsibility. Be able to apply and understand how Western therapeutic characteristics may detrimentally interact with other worldviews.

Microaggressions in Counseling and Psychotherapy

Christina M. Capodilupo and
Derald Wing Sue

CHAPTER FOCUS QUESTIONS

1. What are microaggressions, and what do they look like?
2. Aren't microaggressions just small slights with minimal harm? Why make such a big thing out of them?
3. What types of psychological impact do they have on marginalized groups?
4. How can people who commit microaggressions be so unaware of their actions?
5. What lessons can we learn from a better understanding of the psychological dynamics of microaggressions?
6. In what ways do microaggressions cause problems in the therapeutic process and relationship?

Case Study: Michael

Michael is a 23-year-old Dominican American gay male. He is dark-skinned and often perceived by others to be African American though he self-identifies as Latino. He was born and raised in a large metropolitan city in the Northeast. Both of Michael's parents emigrated from the

(continued)

(continued)

Dominican Republic when they were children. Michael attended a prestigious university to obtain his graduate degree and currently teaches math at a private secondary school. Recently, Michael has been feeling hopeless about various aspects of his life, including his career and future. He feels "beaten down" and "emotionally exhausted" and has visited a community mental health counseling center to address these concerns. He was assigned to work with Kate, a 28-year-old white therapist.

In the first therapy session, Michael described his experiences interviewing for teaching positions. He had been thrilled at the response his résumé had generated: Nearly every school offered him an interview! However, Michael was disturbed by the many similar responses he received upon first meeting the interviewers. He described "a look of shock or surprise on their faces" when met in the waiting room, and on more than one occasion, interviewers even repeated his first and last name to make sure he was the applicant. When Michael talked about his experience being raised by immigrant parents, he sensed discomfort from the interviewers, and he was asked more than once about his interest in teaching Spanish instead of mathematics. Michael tried to "shake the experience off" but noticed that he was spending considerable time revisiting the experiences and trying to understand how much of it was related to his race. For example, one interviewer seemed to think she was complimenting him when she remarked on how proficient his English was. Michael's response was instant and sarcastic: "I should hope so." He felt himself regretting this statement on his way home that day, sure that he had cost himself the potential job. On the other hand, he would have felt wrong to accept her compliment.

When exploring the topic in counseling, Kate suggested that Michael may have been "nervous" and "reading too much" into the interviewer's reactions. For example, she noted that she detected a slight accent in Michael that the interviewer who complimented his English may have also picked up on. Michael then explained to Kate that it was not the first time his English proficiency or American citizenship had been questioned. He talked about how it caused him to feel like a perpetual foreigner, despite being born and raised in this country. Kate stayed largely silent and then offered that Michael's sensitivity may have been a "defense" to his fears of rejection.

Michael also relayed to Kate that he did not "feel free to be himself" at his current place of work. He mentioned several incidents that depressed and frustrated him. When asked to explain, he described how in faculty meetings, he would often hold back from sharing a strong opinion or viewpoint for fear of being taken as an "angry Black man. " He felt that his White coworkers could express themselves in a passionate fashion without facing the consequence of this label. Kate seemed to be doing her best to understand Michael, but her questions implied to him that she doubted his perceptions. For example, she asked him about the tone of voice he was using in these meetings and what evidence he had that colleagues were receiving him as angry. The questions frustrated Michael, and he noticed himself feeling reluctant to share other experiences with Kate that he felt were race-related.

During their intake interview, Kate asked Michael if he was currently seeing anyone romantically. When he replied that he was, Kate asked how long he had been seeing her. Michael responded that he been with his male partner for the past 4 years. Kate's facial features expressed surprise, and she apologized and fumbled over her words as she asked if the two men lived together. Michael felt the need to make Kate more comfortable by assuring her that her mistake was okay and a common one. He went on to tell Kate that in the school he worked at, students often used the word *gay* to refer to things that were stupid or weird. He wanted to talk to the students about the hurtful language but did not always want to disclose his sexuality. Kate empathized and stated that she imagined it would be very difficult to work with teenagers as a gay male. She also stated that Michael "comes off as very masculine" and imagines that the students are unaware that he is gay. Feeling discouraged and invalidated from their discussions, Michael failed to return for future sessions.

There is clearly misunderstanding and miscommunication between Michael and his therapist. His attempts to explain his interactions with others and his reactions to them are being unknowingly invalidated, negated, and dismissed by the therapist. This anecdote illustrates how racial, gender, and sexual orientation microaggressions can have a detrimental impact upon marginalized groups and also undermine the therapeutic process. Let us briefly review Michael's interactions with others from his perspective.

First, in interviewing for jobs, Michael has a nagging suspicion that nearly all the White interviewers were surprised or taken off guard to find a Latino or Black male applicant with such sterling credentials on his résumé and application. Yet he is placed in an unenviable position of not being absolutely certain that interviewers were reacting to his race. Second, he finds that his competence in mathematics is doubted and he is instead encouraged to teach Spanish. The interviewers are not only doubting his intelligence but assuming he has fluency in Spanish (and interest in teaching it!) because he is Latino. Third and related to the previous point, Michael finds his English being complimented, again an assumption that as a Latino, he is not an American citizen. Fourth, Michael feels he has to monitor the way he delivers his point of view for fear of being taken as the stereotypical "angry Black male."

Although the therapist may be attempting to help Michael by asking for "evidence" of this fear (a common intervention used in cognitive-behavioral therapy for working through irrational beliefs), she actually undermines and invalidates Michael's experiential reality. Kate also makes a heteronormative assumption about Michael's sexuality and then has difficulty owning up to her lack of awareness. She goes on to further alienate her client (and perhaps justify her assumption) by implying that Michael's masculinity is incongruent with being a gay male. As a Latino male, the expression of masculinity is actually very important to Michael, and the therapist has enacted the idea that he cannot be both gay and masculine, something he struggles with in his culture on a daily basis.

The incidents experienced by Michael are examples of microaggressions. The term *racial microaggressions* was originally coined by Chester Pierce to describe the subtle and often automatic put-downs that African Americans face (Pierce, Carew, Pierce-Gonzalez, & Willis, 1978). Since then, the definition has expanded to apply to any marginalized group. *Microaggressions* can be defined as brief, everyday exchanges that send denigrating messages to a target group, such as people of color; religious minorities; women; people with disabilities; and gay, lesbian, bisexual, and transgendered individuals (D. W. Sue, Capodilupo, et al., 2007; D. W. Sue, 2010a). These microaggressions are often subtle in nature and can be manifested in the verbal, nonverbal, visual, or behavioral realm. They are often enacted automatically and unconsciously (Pierce et al., 1978; Solórzano, Ceja, & Yosso, 2000), although the person who delivers the microaggression can do so intentionally or unintentionally (D. W. Sue, Capodilupo, et al., 2007).

The interviewers were shocked to see a person of color with Michael's credentials and communicated this nonverbally (facial expression) and verbally (repeating his name to make sure it was him). While seemingly innocuous, the hidden message conveyed from the interviewers was that Black and Latino people are less qualified, less competent, and less educated. This proved to be very distressing for Michael. As we shall see, microaggressions may seem innocent and innocuous, but their cumulative nature can be extremely harmful to the victim's physical and mental health. In addition, they create inequities such as not being offered a job because of unconscious biases and beliefs held by the interviewers.

To help in understanding the effects of microaggressions on marginalized groups, we will be (a) reviewing related literature on contemporary forms of oppression (e.g., racism, sexism, heterosexism, ableism, and religious discrimination); (b) presenting a framework for classifying and understanding the hidden and damaging messages of microaggressions; and (c) presenting findings from studies that have explored people's lived experiences of microaggressions.

CONTEMPORARY FORMS OF OPPRESSION

Most people associate racism with blatant and overt acts of discrimination that are epitomized by White supremacy and hate crimes. Studies suggest, however, that what has been called old-fashioned racism has seemingly declined (Dovidio & Gaertner, 2000). However, the nature and expression of racism (see Chapter 4) has evolved into a more subtle and ambiguous form, perhaps reflecting people's belief that overt and blatant acts of racism are unjust and politically incorrect (Dovidio, Gaertner, Kawakami, & Hodson, 2002). In a sense, racism has gone underground, become more disguised, and is more likely to be covert. A similar process seems to have occurred with sexism as well. Three types of sexism have been identified: overt, covert, and subtle (Swim & Cohen, 1997). *Overt sexism* is blatant unequal and unfair treatment of women. *Covert sexism* refers to unequal and harmful treatment of women that is conducted in a hidden manner (Swim & Cohen, 1997); for example, a person may endorse a belief in gender equality but engage in hiring practices that are gender biased. The third type, *subtle sexism*, represents "unequal and unfair treatment of women that is not recognized by many people because it is perceived to be normative, and therefore does not appear unusual" (Swim, Mallett, & Stangor, 2004, p. 117). Whereas overt and covert sexism are intentional, subtle sexism is not deliberate or conscious. An example of subtle sexism is sexist language, such as the use of the pronoun *he* to convey universal human experience.

In many ways, subtle sexism contains many of the features that define aversive racism, a form of subtle and unintentional racism (Dovidio & Gaertner, 2000). Aversive racism is manifested in individuals who consciously assert egalitarian values but unconsciously hold antiminority feelings; therefore, "aversive racists consciously sympathize with victims of past injustice, support the principles of racial equality, and regard themselves as nonprejudiced. At the same time, however, they possess negative feelings and beliefs about historically disadvantaged groups, which may be unconscious" (Gaertner & Dovidio, 2006, p. 618). Inheriting such negative feelings and beliefs about members of marginalized groups (e.g., people of color, women, and lesbian, gay, bisexual, or transgendered person [LGBT] populations) is unavoidable and inevitable due to the socialization process in the United States (D. W. Sue, 2004), where biased attitudes and stereotypes reinforce group hierarchy (Gaertner & Dovidio, 2006).

Subtle sexism is very similar to aversive racism in that individuals support and actively condone gender equality, yet unknowingly engage in behaviors that contribute to the unequal treatment of women (Swim & Cohen, 1997). For example, it has been found that people who endorsed egalitarian beliefs rated male and female leaders equally, but their nonverbal behaviors reflected greater negativity toward female than male leaders (Butler & Geis, 1990). In one study, participants were asked to pronounce 72 familiar and 72 unfamiliar famous and nonfamous names of men and women. Participants assigned more male names to fame than females and used a lower criterion to judge fame of familiar male than female names; however, these same participants did not explicitly endorse stereotypes or sexism (Banaji & Greenwald, 1995). Much like aversive racism, subtle sexism devalues women, dismisses their accomplishments, and limits their effectiveness in a variety of social and professional settings (Benokraitis, 1997).

Researchers have used the templates of modern forms of racism and sexism to better understand the various forms of modern heterosexism (Walls, 2008) and modern homonegativity (M. A. Morrison & T. G. Morrison, 2002). Heterosexism and antigay harassment has a long history and is currently prevalent in the United States, with as many as 94% of LGB (lesbian, gay, and bisexual) adults reporting hate crime victimization (Herek, Cogan, & Gillis, 2002). *Antigay harassment* can be defined as "verbal or physical behavior that injures, interferes with, or intimidates lesbian women, gay men, and bisexual individuals" (Burn, Kadlec, & Rexler, 2005, p. 24). Although antigay harassment includes comments and jokes that convey that LGB individuals are pathological, abnormal, or unwelcome, authors identify subtle heterosexism by the indirect nature of such remarks (Burn et al., 2005). For example, blatant heterosexism would be calling a lesbian a dyke, whereas subtle heterosexism would be referring to something as gay to convey that it is stupid. As in the case of Michael, hearing this remark may result in a vicarious experience of insult and invalidation (Burn et al., 2005). It may also encourage individuals to remain closeted, as the environment can be perceived as hostile. Subtle heterosexism is related to both aversive racism and subtle sexism in that those who engage in it may not intend to display prejudice toward LGB individuals, particularly in the case of making comments or jokes related to LGB persons (Plummer, 2001). Evidence suggests that heterosexuals do not associate homophobic language with sexual orientation (Thurlow, 2001). Further, studies that have measured the use of heterosexist language and antigay and homophobic attitudes have found that participants who use this language were not strongly antigay or biased against LGB individuals (Burn, 2000; Plummer, 2001).

The discriminatory experiences of transgendered people have been very rarely studied in psychology (Nadal, Rivera, & Corpus, 2010a). One term used to define prejudice against transgendered individuals is *transphobia*, "an emotional disgust toward individuals who do not conform to society's gender expectations" (Hill & Willoughby, 2005, p. 533). Although it is increasingly considered politically incorrect to hold racist, sexist, and, to some extent, heterosexist beliefs, gender roles and expectations tend to be rigid in the United States, and people may feel more justified in adhering to their transphobic views (Nadal et al., 2010a). Another area that has received limited attention in the psychological literature is religious discrimination, despite a high prevalence of religious-based hate crimes in the United States (Nadal, Issa, Griffin, Hamit, & Lyons, 2010b). The largest percentage of religious harassment and civil rights violations in the United States are committed against Jewish and Muslim individuals (Nadal et al., 2010b). Some commonly held anti-Semitic beliefs are that Jews (a) are more loyal to Israel than to the United States, (b) hold too much power in the United States, and (c) are responsible for the death of Jesus Christ (Nadal et al., 2010b).

The prejudice experienced by Muslim individuals is often referred to as Islamaphobia and has been well documented in Western European countries both before and after the September 11, 2001, terrorist attacks (Nadal et al., 2010b). The media tends to depict Muslims as religious fanatics and terrorists (James, 2008), and one study reveals that Americans hold both implicit and explicit negative attitudes toward this group (Rowatt, Franklin, & Cotton, 2005). Finally, though discriminatory practices toward people with disabilities (PWD) is long-standing in the United States and even believed to be increasing in frequency and intensity (Leadership Conference on Civil Rights Education Fund [LCCREF], 2009, as cited in Keller & Galgay, 2010) ableism is rarely included in discussions about modern forms of oppression (Keller & Galgay, 2010). The expression of ableism "favors people without disabilities and maintains that disability in and of itself is a negative concept, state, and experience" (Keller & Galgay, 2010).

Researchers have used the templates of modern racism and sexism to understand other contemporary forms of oppression, such as homonegativity (M. A. Morrison & T. G. Morrison, 2002), religious discrimination (Nadal et al., 2010b), and ableism (Keller & Galgay, 2010). As opposed to old-fashioned homonegativity, which refers to an antigay sentiment that is based on religious or moral condemnation (i.e., "Male homosexuality is a sin"), modern homonegativity reflects the belief that prejudice against LGB persons no longer exists and that this group contributes to its own marginalization by overemphasizing sexual orientation (T. G. Morrison, Kenny, & Harrington, 2005). Although empirical research on modern forms of religious discrimination and ableism are in nascent stages, there is considerable evidence to support the notion that old-fashioned and modern homonegativity are distinct concepts (M. A. Morrison & T. G. Morrison, 2002). Researchers simulated a movie theater situation and created two conditions: covert and overt. In both conditions, there was a confederate wearing a T-shirt that implied a gay sexual orientation. In the covert condition, there were two movies playing to choose from, which enabled participants who chose not to sit next to the confederate to do so on grounds of movie preference. In the overt condition, this justification of movie choice was removed, and participants were told that due to a technical glitch, the same movie would be shown in both theaters. The researchers found that those who scored highest on modern homonegativity were more likely to avoid sitting next to the confederate, but only in the covert condition. Those who scored high on old-fashioned homonegativity elected not to sit next to the confederate regardless of condition (M. A. Morrison & T. G. Morrison, 2002).

This research is very similar to the foundational research of aversive racism, which found that well-intentioned White liberals who endorsed racial equality were less likely to help a Black confederate (e.g., simulated car breaking down) when the situation was ambiguous and they were not sure their help was needed (Gaertner, 1973). In other words, when the situation is ambiguous and the individual is able to justify his or her actions based on some criteria other than the target's identity, he or she will act in a discriminatory and biased manner. What makes this phenomenon particularly complex is that such ambiguity and alternative explanations obscure the true meaning of the event not only for the person who engages in this behavior, but also for the person on the receiving end of the action. This is the central dilemma created by microaggressions, which are manifestations of these subtle forms of oppression.

The Evolution of the "Isms": Microaggressions

Microaggressions are "brief and commonplace daily verbal or behavioral indignities, whether intentional or unintentional, that communicate hostile, derogatory, or negative racial slights and insults that potentially have a harmful or unpleasant psychological impact on the target person or group" (D. W. Sue, Bucceri, Lin, Nadal, & Torino, 2007). Microaggressions can also be delivered environmentally through the physical surroundings of target groups, where they are made to feel unwelcome, isolated, unsafe, and alienated. For example, a prestigious Eastern university conducts new faculty orientations in their main conference room, which

Microaggressions are "brief and commonplace daily verbal or behavioral indignities, whether intentional or unintentional, that communicate hostile, derogatory, or negative racial slights and insults that potentially have a harmful or unpleasant psychological impact on the target person or group."

displays portraits of all past presidents of the university. One new female faculty of color mentioned that during the orientation she noticed that every single portrait was that of a White male. She described feelings of unease, alienation, and a strong desire to quickly leave the room. To her, the all-White-male portraits sent powerful messages: "Your kind does not belong here," "You will not be comfortable here," and "If you stay, there is only so far you can rise at this university!" Environmental microaggressions can occur when there is an absence of students or faculty of color on college campuses, few women in the upper echelons of the workplace, and limited or no access for disabled persons in buildings (e.g., only stairs and no ramp; no Braille in elevators).

Research suggests that the socialization process culturally conditions racist, sexist, and heterosexist attitudes and behaviors in well-intentioned individuals and that these biases are often automatically enacted without conscious awareness, particularly for those who endorse egalitarian values (Dovidio & Gaertner, 2000). Based on the literature on subtle forms of oppression, one might conclude the following about microaggressions: They (a) tend to be subtle, unintentional, and indirect; (b) often occur in situations where there are alternative explanations; (c) represent unconscious and ingrained biased beliefs and attitudes; and (d) are more likely to occur when people pretend not to notice differences, thereby denying that race, sex, sexual orientation, religion, or ability had anything to do with their actions (Sue et al., 2007). Three types of microaggressions have been identified: microassault, microinsult, and microinvalidation.

Microassault

The term *microassault* refers to a blatant verbal, nonverbal, or environmental attack intended to convey discriminatory and biased sentiments. This notion is related to overt racism, sexism, heterosexism, ableism, and religious discrimination in which individuals deliberately convey derogatory messages to target groups.

A *microassault* is a blatant verbal, nonverbal, or environmental attack intended to convey discriminatory and biased sentiments.

Using epithets like *spic, faggot,* or *kyke;* hiring only men for managerial positions; requesting not to sit next to a Muslim on an airplane; and deliberately serving disabled patrons last are examples. Unless we are talking about White supremacists, most perpetrators with conscious biases will engage in overt discrimination only under three conditions: (a) when some degree of anonymity can be insured, (b) when they are in the presence of others who share or tolerate their biased beliefs and actions, or (c) when they lose control of their feelings and actions.

Two past high-profile examples exemplify the latter: (a) Actor Mel Gibson made highly inflammatory anti-Semitic public statements to police officers when he was arrested for driving while intoxicated, and (b) comedian Michael Richards, who played Kramer on *Seinfeld*, went on an out-of-control rant at a comedy club and publicly insulted African Americans by hurling racial epithets at them and by demeaning their race. Gibson and Richards denied being anti-Semitic or racist and issued immediate apologies, but it was obvious both had lost control. Because microassaults are most similar to old-fashioned racism, no guessing game is likely to occur as to their intent: to hurt or injure the recipient. Both the perpetrator and the recipient are clear about what has transpired. We submit that microassaults are in many respects easier to deal with than those that are unintentional and outside the perpetrator's level of awareness (microinsults and microinvalidations).

Microinsult

Microinsults are unintentional behaviors or verbal comments that convey rudeness or insensitivity or demean a person's racial heritage/identity, gender identity, religion, ability, or sexual orientation identity. Despite being outside the level of conscious awareness, these subtle snubs are characterized by an insulting hidden message. For example, when a person frantically rushes to help a person with a disability onto public transportation, the underlying message is that disabled people are in constant need of help and dependent on others. When the interviewers in the case study at the beginning of this chapter expressed surprise (nonverbally and verbally) that a Black and Latino male (Michael) could possess such outstanding credentials on his résumé, they were conveying a hidden message: Blacks and Latinos are less capable intellectually. African Americans consistently report that intellectual inferiority is a common communication they receive from Whites in their everyday experiences (D. W. Sue, Capodilupo, & Holder, 2008). Latinos also report a variety of incidences in which their academic success is questioned or they are assumed to be less qualified (Rivera, Forquer, & Rangel, 2010). Similarly, when teachers in a classroom consistently call on male students rather than females to answer questions, the hidden message is that men are brighter and more capable than women. When California Governor Arnold Schwarzenegger referred to Democrats as "girly men," he meant to ridicule his political opponents, but what he insinuated is that women and men who possess feminine traits are weak and ineffective.

> Microinsults are unintentional behaviors or verbal comments that convey rudeness or insensitivity or demean a person's racial heritage/identity, gender identity, religion, ability, or sexual orientation identity.

Microinvalidation

Microinvalidations are verbal comments or behaviors that exclude, negate, or dismiss the psychological thoughts, feelings, or experiential reality of the target group. Like microinsults, they are unintentional and usually outside the

> Microinvalidations are verbal comments or behaviors that exclude, negate, or dismiss the psychological thoughts, feelings, or experiential reality of the target group.

perpetrator's awareness. When Kate dismissed Michael's belief that race played a role in his interviews and suggested that it was due to his personal insecurities, she negated the client's thoughts and feelings. The hidden message delivered to Michael is that he is overly sensitive and paranoid. Because Kate is in a position of power as a White therapist, she is able to define Michael's experiential reality, thereby engaging in microinvalidation. When a male interviewer informs a woman applicant that he believes the most qualified person should get the job, he is potentially conveying a message that women are not qualified and that his decision will have nothing to do with the applicant's gender. When gay male students are always selected last by fellow classmates for sports teams and share their feelings of discrimination with gym teachers, they are likely to be told that they are misreading the situation (thus invalidating their experiences of discrimination). When individuals claim that they do not see religion or color but instead see only the human being, they are negating the lived experiences of religious and ethnic minorities in the United States.

To further illustrate the concepts of microinsults and microinvalidations, Table 6.1 provides examples of comments, actions, and situations, as well as accompanying hidden messages and assumptions. There are sixteen distinct categories represented in this table: alien in one's own land, ascription of intelligence, assumption of abnormality, color blindness, criminality/assumption of criminal status, denial of individual racism/sexism/heterosexism/religious prejudice, myth

Table 6.1	Examples of Microaggressions	
Themes	**Microaggression**	**Message**
Alien in Own Land When Asian Americans and Latino Americans are assumed to be foreign-born	"Where are you from?" "Where were you born?"	You are not American.
	"You speak good English."	
	A person asking an Asian American to teach them words in their native language.	You are a foreigner.
Ascription of Intelligence Assigning intelligence to a person of color or a woman based on his or her race/gender	"You are a credit to your race."	People of color are generally not as intelligent as Whites
	"Wow! How did you become so good in math?"	It is unusual for a woman to be smart in math.
	Asking an Asian person to help with a math or science problem	All Asians are intelligent and good in math/sciences.

Table 6.1		
Themes	**Microaggression**	**Message**
	"You only got into college because of affirmative action."	You are not smart enough on your own to get into college.
Color Blindness Statements that indicate that a White person does not want to acknowledge race	"When I look at you, I don't see color."	Denying a person of color's racial/ethnic experiences.
	"America is a Melting Pot."	Assimilate/acculturate to dominant culture.
	"There is only one race, the human race."	Denying the individual as a racial/cultural being.
Criminality/Assumption of Criminal status A person of color is presumed to be dangerous, criminal, or deviant based on their race	A White man or woman clutching their purse or checking their wallet as a Black or Latino approaches or passes.	You are a criminal.
	A store owner following a customer of color around the store.	You are going to steal/You are poor/You do not belong.
	A White person waits to ride the next elevator when a person of color is on it.	You are dangerous.
Use of Sexist/Heterosexist Language Terms that exclude or degrade women and LGB persons	Use of the pronoun "he" to refer to all people.	Male experience is universal. Female experience is meaningless.
	Though a male-to-female transgendered employee has consistently referred to herself as "she," coworkers continue to refer to "he."	Our language does not need to change to reflect your identity; your identity is meaningless.
	Two options for Relationship Status: Married or Single.	LGB partnerships do not matter/are meaningless.
	An assertive woman is labeled a "bitch."	Women should be passive.
	A heterosexual man who often hangs out with his female friends more than his male friends is labeled a "faggot."	Men who act like women are inferior (women are inferior)/gay men are inferior.
Denial of Individual Racism/ Sexism/Heterosexism/Religious Discrimination A statement made when bias is denied	"I'm not racist. I have several Black friends."	I am immune to racism because I have friends of color.
	"I am not prejudiced against Muslims. I am just fearful of Muslims who are religious fanatics."	I can separate Islamaphobic social conditioning from my feelings about Muslim people in general.

(continued)

Table 6.1 (*continued*)

Themes	Microaggression	Message
	"As an employer, I always treat men and women equally."	I am incapable of sexism.
Myth of Meritocracy Statements that assert that race or gender does not play a role in life successes	"I believe the most qualified person should get the job."	People of color are given extra unfair benefits because of their race.
	"Men and women have equal opportunities for achievement."	The playing field is even; so if women cannot make it, the problem is with them.
Pathologizing Cultural Values/ Communication Styles The notion that the values and communication styles of the dominant/White culture are ideal	Asking a Black person: "Why do you have to be so loud/animated? Just calm down."	Assimilate to dominant culture.
	To an Asian or Latino person: "Why are you so quiet? We want to know what you think. Be more verbal." "Speak up more."	
	Dismissing an individual who brings up race/culture in work/school setting	Leave your cultural baggage outside.
Second-Class Citizen Occurs when a target group member receives differential treatment from the power group	Person of color mistaken for a service worker	People of color are servants to Whites. They couldn't possibly occupy high status positions.
	Female doctor mistaken for a nurse	Women occupy nurturing roles.
	Having a taxi cab pass a person of color and pick up a White passenger	You are likely to cause trouble and/or travel to a dangerous neighborhood.
	Being ignored at a store counter as attention is given to the White customer behind you	Whites are more valued customers than people of color.
	A lesbian woman is not invited out with a group of girlfriends because they thought she would be bored if they were talking to men.	You don't belong.
Traditional Gender Role Prejudicing and Stereotyping Occurs when expectations of traditional roles or stereotypes are conveyed	When a female student asked a male professor for extra help on a chemistry assignment, he asks, "What do you need to work on this for anyway?"	Women are less capable in math and science.

Table 6.1

Themes	Microaggression	Message
	A person asks a woman her age and, upon hearing she is 31, looks quickly at her ring finger.	Women should be married during child-bearing ages because that is their primary purpose.
	A woman is assumed to be a lesbian because she does not put a lot of effort into her appearance.	Lesbians do not care about being attractive to others.
Sexual Objectification Occurs when women are treated like objects at men's disposal.	A male stranger puts his hands on a woman's hips or on the swell of her back to pass by her.	Your body is not yours.
	Whistles and catcalls as a woman walks down the street	Your body/appearance is for men's enjoyment and pleasure.
	Students use the term *gay* to describe a fellow student who is socially ostracized at school.	People who are weird and different are "gay."
Assumption of Abnormality Occurs when it is implied that there is something wrong with being LGBT.	Two men holding hands in public receiving stares from strangers.	You should keep your displays of affection private because they are offensive.
	"Did something terrible happen to you in your childhood?" to a transgendered person.	Your choices must be the result of a trauma and not your authentic identity.
Helplessness* Occurs when people frantically try to help people with disabilities (PWDs).	Someone helps you onto a bus or train, even when you need no help.	You can't do anything by yourself because you have a disability.
	People feel they need to rescue you from your disability.	Having a disability is a catastrophe.
Denial of Personal Identity* Occurs when any aspect of a person's identity other than disability is ignored or denied.	"I can't believe you are married?"	Your life is not normal or like mine. The only thing I see when I look at you is your disability.
Exoticization Occurs when an LGBT, women of color, or a religious minority is treated as a foreign object for the pleasure/entertainment of others.	"I've always wanted an Asian girlfriend! They wait hand and foot on their men."	Asian American women are submissive and meant to serve the physical needs of men.
	"Tell me some of your wild sex stories!" to an LGBT person.	Your privacy is not valued; you should entertain with stories.

(continued)

Table 6.1 (continued)		
Themes	**Microaggression**	**Message**
	Asking a Muslim person incessant questions about his/her diet, dress, and relationships.	Your privacy is not valued; you should educate me about your cultural practices, which are strange and different.
Assumption of One's Own Religion as Normal**	Saying "Merry Christmas" as a universal greeting.	Your religious beliefs are not important; everyone should celebrate Christmas.
	The sole acknowledgment of Christian holidays in work and school.	Your religious holidays need to be celebrated on your time; they are unimportant.

Adapted from D. W. Sue, Bucceri et al., 2007.
*Themes and examples are taken from Keller & Galgay, 2010.
**Themes and examples are taken from Nadal et al., 2010b.

of meritocracy, pathologizing cultural values/communication styles, second-class status, sexual objectification, use of sexist/heterosexist language, traditional gender role prejudice and stereotyping, helplessness, denial of personal identity, and assumption of one's own religion as normal. Some of these categories are more applicable to certain forms of microaggressions (racial, gender, religion, ability, or sexual orientation), but they all seem to share commonalities.

REFLECTION AND DISCUSSION QUESTIONS

1. If microaggressions represent unintentional slights and insults, have you been guilty of committing microaggressive acts?
2. In looking at Table 6.1, can you identify how you may have committed microaggressions related to race, gender, and sexual orientation?
3. Compile a list of possible microaggressions you may have committed. Can you explore the potential hidden messages they communicate to the recipients?
4. It is often said that microaggressions are reflections of a worldview of inclusion-exclusion, superiority-inferiority, and so forth. What do your microaggressions tell you about your unconscious perception of marginalized groups?
5. If microaggressions are mostly outside the level of conscious awareness, what must you do to make them visible? What steps must you take to personally stop microaggressions?
6. What solutions can you offer that would be directed at individual change, institutional change, and societal change?

The Dynamics and Dilemmas of Microaggressions

Let us use the case of Michael to illustrate some of the dynamics and dilemmas presented by microaggressions. Research on subtle forms of racism (Dovidio et al., 2002; Ridley, 2005), sexism (Swim et al., 2004), and heterosexism (M. A. Morrison & T. G. Morrison, 2002) provide evidence that they operate in individuals who endorse egalitarian beliefs, adamantly deny that they are biased, and consider themselves to be moral, just, and fair. What people consciously believe or say (e.g., "I have no gay bias"), however, is oftentimes at odds with what they actually do (e.g., avoiding sitting next to an ostensibly gay man). Proving that one's actions or comments stem from an unconsciously held set of negative beliefs toward the target group is virtually impossible when alternative explanations exist. Because Whites who engage in microaggressions truly believe they acted without racial bias toward persons of color, for example, they will disclaim any racist meaning. Not only is the subtle and insidious nature of racial microaggressions outside the level of awareness of perpetrators, but recipients also find their ambiguity difficult to handle. Victims are placed in an unenviable position of questioning not only perpetrators, but themselves as well (e.g., "Did I misread what happened?") As we saw with Michael questioning the intention of the woman who complimented his English, victims often replay the incident over and over again to try to understand its meaning.

A study of Black undergraduates summarizes the energy that can go into the interpretation of microaggressions: "Participants also typically reported trying to balance responding to or educating others about racism, while not 'overthinking' these incidents or placing too much energy on [these] encounters" (Watkins, Labarrie, & Appio, 2010, p. 35). Similarly, when microaggressions occur in the classroom, students of color report feelings of anger, anxiety, and exhaustion (Sue, Lin, Torino, et al., 2009). In the face of microaggressions, many members of historically marginalized groups describe feeling a vague unease that something is not right and that they were insulted or disrespected. In this respect, overt acts of racism, sexism, or heterosexism may be easier to handle than microaggressions because the intent and meaning of the event are clear and indisputable (Solórzano et al., 2000; D. W. Sue, 2004). In support of this, recent studies found that racial microaggressions were more impactful, harmful, and distressing to African Americans and Asian Americans than everyday hassles (Utsey, Giesbrecht, Hook, & Stanard, 2008; Wang, Leu, & Shoda, 2011). Microaggressions toward marginalized groups, however, pose special problems. Four psychological dilemmas have been identified when microaggressions occur (Sue et al., 2007).

Dilemma 1: Clash of Sociodemographic Realities

For Michael, one major question was, "Were interviewers reacting to his race, or did he misinterpret their verbal and nonverbal behavior?" Although lived experience tells him that many Whites believe Blacks to be less capable and competent, chances are the White interviewers would be offended at such a suggestion. They would likely deny they possessed any stereotypes and even point to the number of people of color they have hired. In other words, they would emphasize that they and their organizations do not discriminate on the basis of color, sex, sexual orientation, or creed. The question becomes, "Whose reality is the true reality?" Oftentimes the perceptions held by the dominant group differ significantly from those of marginalized groups in our society. For example, studies show that many Whites believe that racism is no longer prevalent in society and not important in the lives of people of color (D. W. Sue, 2010a), that heterosexuals believe that homophobia is a "thing of the past" and that antigay harassment is on the decline (M. A. Morrison & T. G. Morrison, 2002), and that men (and women) assert that women have achieved equal status and are no longer discriminated against (Swim & Cohen, 1997). Most importantly, individuals in power positions do not consider themselves capable of discrimination based on race, gender, or sexual orientation because they are free of bias.

On the other hand, people of color perceive Whites to be racially insensitive, enjoy holding power over others, and think they are superior (Sue et al., 2007). LGB individuals consider homonegativity and antigay harassment to be a crucial aspect of their everyday existence (Burn et al., 2005), and women contend that sexism is alive and well in social and professional settings. Although research supports the fact that those most disempowered are more likely to have a more accurate perception of reality, it is groups in power that have the ability to define reality. Thus, people of color, women, and LGB individuals are likely to experience their perceptions and interpretations being negated or dismissed. This becomes particularly salient in the therapeutic encounter, which represents an unequal power dynamic.

For Michael, who has had countless experiences of being taken as an "angry Black man" when he expresses a strong opinion, he is clear that he needs to monitor and edit his point of view at work. Kate, however, has not experienced this racial reality and tries to "objectively" reason that Michael may be reading too much into the situation or even contributing to others' perceptions of him as angry by raising his voice. A recent study of lesbian, gay, bisexual, and transgendered clients revealed that "clients were left feeling doubtful about the effectiveness of therapy, the therapists' abilities, and the therapists' investment in the therapeutic process when therapists minimized their sexual reality" (Shelton & Delgado-Romero, 2011, p. 217).

Dilemma 2: The Invisibility of Unintentional Expressions of Bias

Although Michael did not ask the interviewer about the meaning behind her comment about his English proficiency, one can imagine that she might feel stunned and surprised to learn that Michael felt offended. She would likely explain that she was only complimenting his speech and found him articulate. She may even state that after hearing him talk about his parents' immigration experiences, she thought English might be a second language for him. To Michael, however, her statement reflected a common experience for him of people seeming surprised that he is articulate, well educated, and an American citizen. The message being conveyed to Michael was that Latinos are usually not intelligent, not proficient in English, and not American citizens. How could Michael "prove" that the interviewer was doubting his intelligence or citizenship? His only evidence is his felt experience and interpretation, which are easily explained away and disregarded by interviewers with alternative explanations.

Further compounding the situation is the idea that the interviewer is in a position to make hiring decisions that impact Michael's life. We saw Michael instinctively respond with sarcasm to the interviewer, a response that he ultimately regretted and worried might have cost him the job. On the other hand, if he were to thank the interviewer or act like her comment was acceptable, he would be negating his own experience at a cost to his self-concept. That the microaggression is essentially invisible to the perpetrator creates a psychological dilemma for victims that can leave them frustrated, feeling powerless, and even questioning their own sanity (D. W. Sue et al., 2008; Watkins et al., 2010).

Dilemma 3: Perceived Minimal Harm of Microaggressions

Oftentimes, when perpetrators are confronted about microaggressions, they accuse the victim of overreacting or being hypersensitive or touchy. Because the microaggressions are often invisible to the perpetrators, they cannot understand how the events could cause any significant harm to the victims. They see the events as innocent and innocuous and often tell victims to just let it go. Trivializing the impact of racial microaggressions by some White people can be an automatic, defensive reaction to avoid feeling blamed and guilty (D. W. Sue, Capodilupo, Nadal, & Torino, 2008). Visible and overt forms of discrimination, however, are more readily acknowledged as being dangerous and harmful (D. W. Sue, 2004, 2010a). It has been found that chronic experiences of discrimination and exclusion create levels of stress that are traumatic for target groups (Bloom, 1997; Pierce, 1995).

Racism and racial/ethnic discrimination cause significant psychological distress (Fang & Meyers, 2001; Krieger & Sidney, 1996; D. W. Sue et al., 2008; Watkins et al., 2010), depression (Kim, 2002; Comas-Diaz & Greene, 1994), and negative health outcomes (Harrell, Hall, & Taliaferro, 2003). Researchers have even coined the term *racism-related stress* (Harrell, 2000). With regard to sexism, studies have found that 94% of women reported experiencing sexual harassment, 92% being disrespected because of their gender, and 87% having experienced sexism by strangers (Berg, 2006). Researchers have long contended that the sociopolitical climate of the United States serves to subjugate, degrade, and objectify women (Root, 1992a). Similarly, research has found a host of negative effects related to stigmatization based on sexual orientation (American Psychological Association, Division 44, 2000). This stress has been linked to depression (D'Augelli, 1989), substance abuse, running away, and prostitution (American Psychological Association, Division 44, 2000).

Despite the perpetrator's perception that microaggressions result in minimal harm, more recent research has suggested that subtle forms of racism, sexism, and heterosexism cause significant distress and negatively impact well-being. One study that looked at racial microaggressions in the lived experience of African Americans found that the cumulative effect of these events was feelings of self-doubt, frustration, and isolation (Solórzano et al., 2000). Another study found that consequences of microaggressions for African Americans included feelings of powerlessness, invisibility, and loss of integrity (D. W. Sue, Capodilupo, & Holder, 2008). In a similar study, Asian Americans reported feeling belittled, angry, invalidated, invisible, and trapped by their experiences of racial microaggressions (Sue, Bucceri, Lin, Nadal, & Torino, 2007). Microaggressions have been found to cause anger, frustration, low self-esteem, and emotional turmoil (Brondolo et al., 2008); to saturate society with a devaluing of various social group identities (Purdie-Vaughns, Davis, Steele, & Ditlmann, 2008); and even to lower problem-solving abilities (Salvatore & Shelton, 2007).

With regard to subtle sexism, researchers have discovered that everyday sexist events, such as sexist language, gender role stereotyping, and objectifying commentaries, lead to feelings of anger, anxiety, and depression in women (Swim, Hyers, Cohen, & Ferguson, 2001). In this same study, female participants who recorded daily incidents in diaries reported an average of one or two experiences of subtle sexism a week (in the study they were to record daily "hassles" and then judge how prejudicial they felt they were). A recent study found that "the impact of daily, personal sexist interaction has an incremental effect that may result in the disturbing PTSD [posttraumatic stress disorder] symptomology" (Berg, 2006, p. 984).

There is very little research on the effects of subtle heterosexism on LGB persons. However, it has been argued that internalized homophobia is even more psychologically damaging and destructive than overt incidents of homophobia (Speight, 2007). One study provided LGB participants with subtle heterosexism scenarios (e.g., "A heterosexual assumes two unmarried men who spend a lot of time together are gay") to first assess if the participants found such scenarios to be offensive and prejudicial (due to the indirect nature of the scenario). Not only were participants offended by the scenarios and felt they were prejudicial against LGB persons, but they were also less likely to come out as a consequence of feeling offended (Burn, Kadlec, & Rexer, 2005). When one assumes that people of color, women, and LGB individuals are constantly exposed to multiple microaggressions, it becomes clear that the cumulative nature takes a huge psychological toll on their lives. Thus, microaggressions cause significant harm and psychological distress to victims. That perpetrators tend to deny their existence (because they are invisible) only serves to compound their detrimental effects.

Dilemma 4: The Catch-22 of Responding to Microaggressions

When a microaggression occurs, the recipient is often placed in an unenviable position of deciding what to do. This is compounded with numerous questions likely to go through the mind of the recipient: Did what I think happen really happen? If it did, how can I possibly prove it? How should I respond? Will it do any good if I bring it to the attention of the perpetrator? If I do, will it affect my relationship with coworkers, friends, or acquaintances? In Michael's case, would it jeopardize his chances of being hired if he confronted the interviewers? Many well-intentioned perpetrators are unaware of the exhausting nature of these internal questions as they sap the spiritual and psychic energy of victims. Michael was obviously caught in a conflict, asking himself: Should I respond by asking what interviewers or the students meant by their comments, or should I bother to respond at all? As a Black and Latino male, Michael has probably experienced many microaggressions throughout his lifetime, and so microaggressive comments from coworkers do not feel random (Ridley, 2005). On the other hand, White teachers who have not faced similar experiences are unable to see a pattern running throughout incidents encountered by people of color—hidden bias associated with race. People of color, for example, use context and experiential reality to interpret the meaning of micro-aggressions. The common thread operating in multiple situations is that of "race." Whites, however, see such situations as "isolated incidents," so the pattern of racism experienced by persons of color is invisible to them.

The fundamental issue is that responding to a microaggression can have detrimental consequences for the victim. In Michael's case, hiring decisions hang in the balance. Sometimes consequences of responding to microaggressions are relational. Consider when Kate assumed Michael was heterosexual and asked how long he had been with his female partner. Michael explained he had a male partner and continued talking to fill the awkward silence and to help Kate feel more comfortable. Lesbian, gay, and bisexual clients in a recent study describe a similar feeling: "Clients were left feeling pulled to minimize or rationalize microaggressions in hopes of rectifying therapeutic failures or rescuing therapists from uncomfortable feelings triggered by sexual orientation microaggressions" (Shelton & Delgado-Romero, 2011, pp. 218–219). If Michael responds to Kate with frustration or anger over her assumption, he risks being perceived as the "angry Black man" and potentially jeopardizing their therapeutic relationship. Michael might feel compelled to avoid this label and to simply forgo the hassles. Unfortunately, it has been found that such a reaction takes a psychological toll on the recipient because it requires Michael to suppress and obscure his authentic thoughts and feelings in order to avoid further discrimination (Franklin, 2004).

Confronting sexual orientation microaggressions is further complicated by LGB individuals who may not necessarily be out of the closet. In one study, half of lesbian and gay participants were uncomfortable disclosing their sexual orientation, and two thirds occasionally feared for their public safety (D'Augelli, 1989). The reality of looming antigay harassment and differential (unequal) treatment may prevent LGB persons from coming out in a variety of settings, especially when there is evidence to suggest that the environment is heterosexist. For example, Michael hears students at schools using the term *gay* in a derogatory fashion in public areas and observes that teachers never object or take issue with its use. The message he receives from colleagues is that they are complicit through their silence. As he mentions to Kate, confronting students on their use of the word *gay* may "out" him or cause the other teachers to wonder about his sexual orientation. He might also fear that the teachers will tell him he is "hypersensitive" and overly emotional—both microaggressions themselves!

Let us look at the meaning of these two terms. The first, *hypersensitive*, conveys that Michael is sensitive about his sexual orientation, as if there is no valid reason he should be; therefore his experiential reality of being a gay person who always feels marginalized is invalidated. The second, *overly emotional*, is a gender role stereotype about women that often gets applied to gay men by extension. Women and gay men are often seen as more nurturing, caring, and sensitive and so, therefore, emotional (and by association irrational) when it comes to making "sense" of "real issues." The intersections of Michael's identity further complicate this issue for him, as the expression of his masculinity is very important to him as a Latino male (Glassgold, 2009). Michael runs the risk of hearing any one of these things and facing these stereotypes if he confronts the microaggressions he experiences.

On the flip side, by not confronting these experiences, he is forced to shoulder the burden himself with detrimental mental health consequences. In one study, African American participants revealed some strategies for dealing with this catch-22: (a) empowering and validating the self and (b) sanity check. *Empowering and validating the self* refers to a process of interrupting the racism by "calling it what it is" and staying true to one's thoughts and feelings that the incident is related to one's race. *Sanity check* refers to a process of checking in with like-minded and same-race people about microaggressive incidents. Talking about the incident with someone who has faced similar discrimination helps participants to feel validated in their experience that the incident is racially motivated (Sue, Capodilupo, & Holder, 2008). In another study, Black undergraduates identified support systems, such as family, friends, religious faith, club involvement, journal writing, and academic leadership positions, as being factors that promote resilience in the face of racial microaggressions (Watkins et al., 2010).

Therapeutic Implications

We have repeatedly emphasized that clients of color tend to prematurely terminate counseling and therapy at a 50% rate after only the first initial contact with a mental health provider (à la Michael). We submit that racial microaggressions may lie at the core of the problem. There is growing evidence to suggest that gender and sexual orientation microaggressions have a detrimental effect on the therapeutic alliance for women (Owen, Tao, & Rodolfa, 2010) and LGBT individuals (Shelton & Delgado-Romero, 2011). The result is that clients of color, women, and gays may not receive the help they need. In counseling and psychotherapy, the credibility of the therapist is paramount in determining whether clients stay or leave sessions (Strong, 1969). As we have seen in Chapter 5, credibility is composed of two dimensions: expertness and trustworthiness. *Expertness* is a function of how much knowledge, training, experience, and skills clinicians possess with respect to the population being treated; it is an *ability component*. *Trustworthiness*, however, is a *motivational component* that encompasses trust, honesty, and genuineness. Although expertness is always important, trustworthiness becomes central in multicultural counseling and therapy.

Effective counseling is likely to occur when both therapists and clients are able to form a working relationship, therapeutic alliance, or some form of positive coalition. In mental health practice there is a near universal belief that effective and beneficial counseling requires that clients trust their counselors (Corey, 2012; Day, 2004). Essentially the therapist works to build rapport and establish a connection with the client through verbal and nonverbal interventions. Research supports the idea that the therapeutic alliance is a key component in therapy work and is correlated with successful outcomes (Lui & Pope-Davis, 2005). When clients do not feel heard or understood or when they are not sure they can trust the therapist, they often fail to return. A comprehensive report on the role of culture, race, and ethnicity in mental health care suggests that racism plays a major role in creating inequities that result in inferior and biased treatments for diverse clients (United States Department of Health and Human Services, 2001).

Because all people inherit bias about various identity groups through cultural conditioning in the United States, no one, including helping professionals, is free from these biases (Ridley, 2005). Therefore, racial, gender, and sexual orientation dynamics that exist in society are often recreated and reenacted between the therapist and the client in the therapy room. This fact poses a unique dilemma in therapy for several reasons: Helping professionals are supposed to work for the welfare of all groups, be trained to be "objective" and inclined to see problems as internally situated, and are usually in positions of power over the client. Mental health professionals who enter the field usually have a strong desire to help clients regardless of race, creed, gender, and so forth. They operate under the dictum of "liberating clients from their distress and doing no harm" whenever possible. Because helping professionals view themselves as just, fair, and nondiscriminating, they find it difficult to believe that they commit microaggressions and may be unhelpful and even oppressive. The fact that therapists possess unconscious biases and prejudices is problematic, especially when they sincerely believe they are capable of preventing them from entering sessions. Rather than heal or help, however, well-intentioned therapists may contribute to the oppressive experiences of culturally diverse clients. Although there have certainly been movements to understand the sociopolitical context of clients, less attention is given to the social context of the therapeutic relationship, which may reflect a microcosm of negative race relations in the larger society. Last, counselors often find themselves in positions of power in their ability to define their client's experiential reality (i.e., interpretation), which may prove harmful, especially if counselors adamantly deny the presence of microaggressions both inside and outside of the therapy situation. Recent research suggests that prejudice and bias continue to be manifested in the therapeutic process, despite the good intentions of mental health professionals (Owen et al., 2010; Shelton & Delgado-Romero, 2011; Utsey, Gernat, & Hammar, 2005).

Manifestations of Microaggressions in Counseling/Therapy

The importance of understanding how microaggressions manifest in the therapeutic relationship cannot be understated, especially as this phenomenon may underlie the high prevalence of drop-out rates among people of color and other marginalized groups. Let us use the case of Michael to illustrate how microaggressions may operate in the counseling process.

1. Michael revealed to Kate his experiences of racial, gender, and sexual orientation microaggressions, using therapy as a space for deeper exploration of a meaningful issue. Because Kate and Michael are not the same race, they do not share similar racial realities (Dilemma 1: clash of sociodemographic realities) or worldviews. The therapist has minimal understanding of what constitutes racial microaggressions, how they make their appearance in everyday interactions, how she herself may be guilty of microaggressive behaviors, the psychological toll it takes on persons of color, and the negative effects they have on the therapeutic relationship. We have emphasized earlier that cultural competence requires helping professionals to understand the worldviews of their culturally diverse clients.

2. The therapist tends to minimize the importance of the "shocked reactions" of interviewers to Michael's résumé, believe the event is trivial, and cannot relate to the negative impact these microaggressions have on her client. Even if the reactions do have some racial overtones, the therapist concludes they are insignificant ("small matter") and Michael should simply ignore them or "shrug it off" (Dilemma 3: minimal harm). For Michael, on the other hand, the looks of surprise represent one of many cumulative messages of intellectual inferiority about his race. He is placed in a constant state of vigilance in maintaining his sense of integrity in the face of constant invalidations and insults. Racial, gender, and sexual microaggressions are a constant reality for people of color as they assail group identities and experiences. White people seldom understand how much time, energy, and effort are expended by people of color to retain some semblance of worth and self-esteem. No wonder Michael is emotionally exhausted, frustrated, and occasionally doubts his own interpretations.

3. Another major detrimental event in the first session is that the therapist locates the source of problems within Michael by insinuating insecurities about his own abilities. While there may be some legitimacy to this interpretation, Kate is unaware that she has engaged in person-blame and that she has invalidated Michael's experiential reality by dismissing race as an important factor. As a mental health professional, Kate probably considers herself unbiased and objective. When discussing Michael's fears of being taken as "angry" in faculty meetings, Kate attempts to collect "evidence" for his feelings, failing to consider the sociocultural reality of being a Black male in U.S. society. This reaction represents a colorblind reaction and only reinforces Michael's feelings of invalidation by removing the salience of his race from the conversation (Dilemma 2: invisibility).

4. As a client, Michael is caught in a catch-22 of a "damned if you do and damned if you don't" conflict (Dilemma 4: catch-22). Both inside and outside of therapy, Michael is probably internally wrestling with a series of questions: Did

what I think happen really happen? Was this a deliberate act or an unintentional slight? How should I respond: Sit and stew on it or confront the person? What are the consequences if I do? If I bring the topic up, how do I prove it? Is it really worth the effort? Should I just drop the matter? These questions take a tremendous psychological toll on many people of color. If Michael chooses to do nothing, he may suffer emotionally by having to deny his own experiential reality or allow his sense of integrity to be assailed. Feelings of powerlessness, alienation, and frustration may take not only a psychological toll but also a physical toll on him. If he chooses to raise issues with the interviewers, students, or fellow teachers, he risks being isolated by others, seen as a troublemaker, oversensitive, and even paranoid. Worse yet, if he raises these issues in therapy, his reality is invalidated and his reactions are pathologized by the therapist.

Table 6.2 provides several more therapy-specific examples of microaggressions, using the same organizing themes presented in Table 6.1. We ask that you study these themes and ask if you have ever engaged in these or similar actions. If so, how can you prevent your own personal microaggressions from impairing the therapy process?

Table 6.2 Examples of Microaggressions in Therapeutic Practice		
Themes	**Microaggression**	**Message**
Alien in Own Land When Asian Americans and Latino Americans are assumed to be foreign-born	A White client does not want to work with an Asian American therapist because she "will not understand my problem."	You are not American.
	A White therapist tells an American-born Latino client that he/she should seek a Spanish-speaking therapist.	
Ascription of Intelligence Assigning a degree of intelligence to a person of color or a woman based on race or gender	A school counselor reacts with surprise when an Asian American student had trouble on the math portion of a standardized test.	All Asians are smart and good at math.
	A career counselor asking a Black or Latino student, "Do you think you're ready for college?"	It is unusual for people of color to succeed.
	A school counselor reacts with surprise that a female student scored high on a math portion of a standardized test.	It is unusual for women to be smart and good in math.

(continued)

Table 6.2 (*continued*)

Themes	Microaggression	Message
Color Blindness Statements that indicate that a White person does not want to acknowledge race	A therapist says, "I think you are being too paranoid. We should emphasize similarities, not people's differences," when a client of color attempts to discuss her feelings about being the only person of color at her job and feeling alienated and dismissed by her coworkers.	Race and culture are not important variables that affect people's lives.
	A client of color expresses concern in discussing racial issues with her therapist. Her therapist replies, "When I see you, I don't see color."	Your racial experiences are not valid.
Criminality/Assumption of Criminal Status A person of color is presumed to be dangerous, criminal, or deviant based on their race.	When a Black client shares that she was accused of stealing from work, the therapist encourages the client to explore how she might have contributed to her employer's mistrust of her.	You are a criminal.
	A therapist takes great care to ask all substance-abuse questions in an intake with a Native American client and is suspicious of the client's nonexistent history with substances.	You are deviant.
Use of Sexist/Heterosexist Language Terms that exclude or degrade women and LGB groups	During the intake session, a female client discloses that she has been in her current relationship for one year. The therapist asks how long the client has known her boyfriend.	Heterosexuality is the norm.
	When an adult female client explains she is feeling isolated at work, her male therapist asks, "Aren't there any girls you can gossip with there?"	Application of language that implies to adolescent females or to adult females "your problems are trivial."
Denial of Individual Racism/Sexism/Heterosexism A statement made when a member of the power group renounces their biases.	A client of color asks his/her therapist about how race affects their working relationship. The therapist replies, "Race does not affect the way I treat you."	Your racial/ethnic experience is not important.

Table 6.2

Themes	Microaggression	Message
	A client of color expresses hesitancy in discussing racial issues with his White female therapist. She replies, "I understand. As a woman, I face discrimination also."	Your racial oppression is no different than my gender oppression.
	A therapist's nonverbal behavior conveys discomfort when a bisexual male client is describing a recent sexual experience with a man. When he asks her about it, she insists she has "no negative feelings toward gay people" and says it is important to keep the conversation on him.	I am incapable of homonegativity, yet I am unwilling to explore this.
Myth of Meritocracy Statements that assert that race or gender does not play a role in succeeding in career advancement or education	A school counselor tells a Black student that "if you work hard, you can succeed like everyone else."	People of color/women are lazy and/or incompetent and need to work harder. If you don't succeed, you have only yourself to blame (blaming the victim).
	A female client visits a career counselor to share her concerns that a male coworker was chosen for a managerial position over her, despite that she was better qualified and in the job longer. The counselor responds that "he must have been better suited for some of the job requirements."	
Pathologizing Cultural Values/ Communication Styles The notion that the values and communication styles of the dominant/White culture are ideal	A Black client is loud, emotional, and confrontational in a counseling session. The therapist diagnoses her with borderline personality disorder.	Assimilate to dominant culture.
	A client of Asian or Native American descent has trouble maintaining eye contact with his therapist. The therapist diagnoses him with a social anxiety disorder.	
	Advising a client, "Do you really think your problem stems from racism?"	Leave your cultural baggage outside.

(continued)

Table 6.2 (*continued*)

Themes	Microaggression	Message
Second-Class Citizen Occurs when a member of the power group is given preferential treatment over a target group member	A male client calls and requests a session time that is currently taken by a female client. The therapist grants the male client the appointment without calling the female client to see if she can change times.	Males are more valued than women.
	Clients of color are not welcomed or acknowledged by receptionists.	White clients are more valued than clients of color.
Traditional Gender Role Prejudicing and Stereotyping Occurs when expectations of traditional roles or stereotypes are conveyed	A therapist continually asks the middle-aged female client about dating and "putting herself out there" despite that the client has not expressed interest in exploring this area.	Women should be married, and dating should be an important topic/part of your life.
	A gay male client has been with his partner for 5 years. His therapist continually probes his desires to meet other men and be unfaithful.	Gay men are promiscuous. Gay men cannot have monogamous relationships.
	A therapist raises her eyebrows when a female client mentions that she has had a one-night stand.	Women should not be sexually adventurous.
Sexual Objectification Occurs when women are treated like objects at men's disposal	A male therapist puts his hands on a female client's back as she walks out of the session.	Your body is not yours.
	A male therapist is looking at his female client's breasts while she is talking.	Your body/appearance is for men's enjoyment and pleasure.
Assumption of Abnormality Occurs when it is implied that there is something wrong with being LGBT	When discussing the client's bisexuality, the therapist continues to imply that there is a "crisis of identity."	Bisexuality represents a confusion about sexual orientation.
	A lesbian comes in for career counseling, but the therapist continually insists that she needs to discuss her sexuality.	Your sexual orientation represents pathology.
	The therapist of a 20-year-old lesbian inadvertently refers to sexuality as a "phase."	Your sexuality is something that is not stable.

Adapted from D. W. Sue, Bucceri, et al., 2007.

Implications for Clinical Practice

Clients trust mental health professionals to take an intimate and deeply personal journey of self-exploration with them through the process of therapy. They grant these professionals the opportunity to look into their inner world and also invite them to walk where they live in their everyday lives. Therapists and counselors have an obligation to their clients, especially when their clients differ from them in terms of race, gender, ability, religion, and/or sexual orientation, to work to understand their experiential reality. There is evidence to suggest that microaggressions are everyday experiences too innumerable to count. These experiences impact clients in ways that researchers are only beginning to understand. There is much work to be done to better understand the nuances and processes involved in this very complex phenomenon. Therapists and counselors are in a position to learn from their clients about microaggressions and their relationship to their presenting concerns and developmental issues. It is imperative to encourage clients to explore their feelings about incidents that involve their race, gender, and sexual orientation so that the status quo of silence and invisibility can be destroyed.

1. Be aware that racial, gender, and sexual orientation microaggressions are a constant reality in the lives of culturally diverse groups. They take a major psychological toll on people of color, people with disabilities, women, religious minorities, and GLBT individuals. The socioemotional problems brought to therapy often reside in the effects of microaggressions rather than in an attribute of the individual.
2. Be aware that everyone has and continues to engage in unintentional microaggressions. For helping professionals, these microaggressions may serve as impediments to effective multicultural counseling and therapy. All therapists have a major responsibility to make the invisible "visible." What biases, prejudices, and stereotypes do you hold that may result in microaggressions? What must you do to minimize allowing them to impact your client in the therapy sessions?
3. Do not invalidate the experiential reality of culturally diverse groups. Entertain the notion that they may have a more accurate perception of reality than you do, especially when it comes to issues of racism, sexism, or heterosexism. Reach out to culturally diverse clients, try to understand their worldviews, and don't be quick to dismiss or negate racial, gender, or sexual orientation issues.
4. Don't get defensive if your culturally different client implies that you have engaged in a microaggressive remark or behavior. Try to clarify the situation by showing you are open and receptive to conversations on race, gender, or sexual orientation. Remember, we all commit microaggressive blunders. In some cases, a simple "I'm sorry" and encouragement to the client to feel free in raising similar issues will do wonders for the therapeutic relationship. Remember, it's how the therapist "recovers" not how he/she "covers up" that is important.

PART III

The Practice Dimensions of Multicultural Counseling/Therapy

Barriers to Multicultural Counseling and Therapy: Individual and Family Perspectives

CHAPTER FOCUS QUESTIONS

1. What are the basic values, beliefs, and assumptions that characterize U.S. society? How are these manifested in the practice of counseling?
2. What are the generic characteristics of counseling and psychotherapy, and how may they act as barriers to the helping process?
3. In what way may the cultural values of diverse populations affect the counseling process? Can you give some examples?
4. What role may socioeconomic class issues play in the effective delivery of mental health services?
5. What are issues that a mental health provider faces when working with clients whose first language is not English?
6. How may Western values orientation affect definitions of the family, and how may they make their appearance in family counseling and therapy?
7. In understanding your therapeutic assumptions, values, and approach, with which population (Asian American, African American, Latino/a American, or Native American) do you anticipate having the greatest difficulty working? Can you give reasons why this would be so?

Case Study: Fernando and the M. Family

One of the most difficult cases I have ever treated was that of a Mexican American family in southern California. Fernando M. was a 56-year-old recent immigrant to the United States. He had been married some 35 years to Refugio, his wife, and had fathered 10 children. Only four of his children, three sons and one daughter, resided with him. Fernando was born in a small village in Mexico and resided there until 3 years ago, when he moved to California. He was not unfamiliar with California, having worked as a bracero for most of his adult life. he made frequent visits to the United States during annual harvest seasons.

The M. family resided in a small, old, unpainted rental house that sat on the back of a dirt lot and was sparsely furnished with their belongings. The family did not own a car, and public transportation was not available in their neighborhood. Although their standard of living was far below U.S. poverty levels, the family appeared quite pleased at their relative affluence when compared to their life in Mexico.

The presenting complaints concerned Fernando. He heard threatening voices, was often disoriented, and stated that someone was planning to kill him and that something evil was about to happen. He became afraid to leave his home, was in poor physical health, and possessed a decrepit appearance that made him essentially unemployable.

When the M. family entered the clinic, I was asked to see them because the bilingual therapist scheduled that day had called in sick. I was hoping that either Fernando or Refugio could speak enough English to understand the situation. Unfortunately, neither could understand me, nor I them. As luck would have it, however, it became apparent that the two older children could understand English. Since the younger one seemed more fluent, I called on him to act as a translator during our first session. I noticed that the parents seemed reluctant to participate with the younger son, and for some time the discussion between the family members was quite animated. Sensing something wrong and desiring to get the session underway, I interrupted the family and asked the son who spoke English best what was wrong. He hesitated for a second but assured me that everything was fine.

During the course of our first session, it became obvious to me that Fernando was seriously disturbed. He appeared frightened and tense, and if the interpretations from his son were correct, he was also hallucinating. I suggested to Refugio that she consider hospitalizing her husband, but she was adamant against this course. I could sense her nevousness and fear that I would initiate action to have her husband committed. I reassured her that no action would be taken without a follow-up evaluation and suggested that she return later in the week with Fernando. Refugio said that it would be difficult since Fernando was afraid to leave his home. She had to coerce him into coming this time and did not feel she could do it again. I looked at Fernando directly and stated, "Fernando, I know how hard it is for you to come here, but we really want to help you. Do you think you could possibly come one more time? Dr. Escobedo [the bilingual therapist] will be here with me, and he can communicate with you directly. "The youngest son interpreted.

The M. family never returned for another session, and their failure to show up has greatly bothered me. Since that time I have talked with several Latino/a psychologists who have pointed out multicultural issues that I was not aware of then. Now realize how uninformed and naive I was about working with Latinos, and I only hope the M. family has found the needed help elsewhere.

Whereas the previous three chapters dealt with the sociopolitical dynamics affecting multicultural counseling/therapy, this chapter discusses the cultural barriers that may render the helping professional ineffective, thereby denying help to culturally diverse clients. This case study illustrates important multicultural issues that are presented in the following questions.

REFLECTION AND DISCUSSION QUESTIONS

1. Was it a serious blunder for the therapist to see the M. family, or to continue to see them in the session, when he could not speak Spanish and the parents could not speak English? Should he have waited until Dr. Escobedo returned?

2. Although it may seem like a good idea to have one of the children interpret for the therapist and the family, what possible cultural implications might this have in a Mexican American family? Can one obtain an accurate translation through family interpreters? What are some of the pitfalls?

3. The therapist tried to be informal with the family in order to put them at ease. Yet some of his colleagues have stated that how he addresses clients (last names or first names) may be important. When the therapist used the first names of both husband and wife, what possible cultural interpretation from the family may have resulted?

4. The therapist saw Mr. M.'s symptoms as indications of serious pathology. What other explanations should he have entertained? Should he have so blatantly suggested hospitalization? How do Latinos perceive mental health issues?

5. Knowing that Mr. M. had difficulty leaving home, should the therapist have considered some other treatment avenues? If so, what might they have been?

The interplay of cultural differences and therapeutic approaches exemplified in the reflection questions is both complex and difficult to resolve. They challenge mental health professionals to (a) reach out and understand the worldviews, cultural values, and life circumstances of their culturally diverse clients; (b) free themselves from the cultural conditioning of what they believe is correct therapeutic practice; (c) develop new but culturally sensitive methods of working with clients; and (d) play new roles in the helping process outside of conventional psychotherapy. Three major potential barriers to effective individual and family counseling are illustrated in this case: class-bound values, linguistic issues, and culture-bound values.

First, Fernando's "paranoid reactions and suspicions" and his hallucinations may have had many causes. An enlightened mental health professional must consider whether there are sociopolitical, cultural, or biological reasons for his symptoms. Can his fears, for example, symbolize realistic concerns (e.g., fear of deportation, creditors, police)? How do Latino cultures view hallucinations? Some studies indicate that cultural factors make it more acceptable for some Spanish-speaking populations to admit to hearing voices or seeing visions. Indeed, Appendix I of the American Psychiatric Association's *Diagnostic and Statistical Manual of Mental Disorders* (2000) now recognizes a large group of *culture-bound syndromes*, or disorders that seem to appear only in specific cultures and societies. Another consideration is the life circumstances of Fernando's work. Could his agricultural work and years of exposure to pesticides and other dangerous agricultural chemicals be contributing to his mental state? Counselors and psychotherapists often focus so much on the internal dynamics of clients that there is a failure to consider external sources as causes. It is important for therapists to consider these explanations.

In addition, mental health practice has been described as a White, middle-class activity that often fails to recognize the economic implications in the delivery of mental health services. Class-bound factors related to socioeconomic status may place those suffering from poverty at a disadvantage and deny them the necessary help that they need. For example, Fernando's family is obviously poor, they do not own an automobile, and public transportation is not available in the rural area where they reside. Poor clients have difficulties traveling to mental health facilities for treatment. Not only is attending sessions a great inconvenience, but it can also be costly to arrange private transportation for the family. It seems that meeting the needs of the M. family might have entailed home visits or some other form of outreach. If the M. family was unable to travel to the therapist's office for treatment, what blocked the therapist from considering a home visit or a meeting point between the destinations? Many therapists feel disinclined, fearful, or uncomfortable doing the former. Their training dictates that they should practice in their offices and that clients should come to them. When mental health services are located away from the communities that they purport to serve, outreach programs are not available, and economic considerations are not addressed by mental health services, institutional bias is clearly evident.

Second, language barriers often place culturally diverse clients at a disadvantage. The primary medium by which mental health professionals do their work is through verbalization (talk therapies). Ever since Freud developed the *talking cure*, psychotherapy has meant that clients must be able to verbalize their thoughts and feelings to a practitioner in order to receive the necessary help. In addition, because of linguistic bias and monolingualism, the typical form of talk is via Standard English. Clients who do not speak Standard English, possess a pronounced accent, or have limited command of English (such as the M. family) may be victimized. The need to understand the meaning of linguistic differences and language barriers in counseling and psychotherapy has never been greater. As we mentioned previously, the result of changing demographics is that many of our clients are born outside of the United States and speak English as their second language. Although the use of interpreters might seem like a solution, such a practice may suffer from certain limitations. For example, can interpreters really give an accurate translation? Cultural differences in mental health concepts are not equivalent in various cultures. In addition, many concepts in English and Spanish do not have equivalent meanings. Likewise, the good intentions of the therapist to communicate with the M. family via the son, who seemed to speak English fluently, might result in a cultural family violation. It may undermine the authority of the father by disturbing the patriarchal role, relationships considered sacred in traditional Latino families. There is no doubt that the need for bilingual therapists is great. Yet the lack of bilingual mental health professionals does not bode well for linguistic minorities.

Third, a number of culture-bound issues seemed to be played out in the delivery of services to the M. family. The therapist's attempt to be informal and to put the family at ease resulted in greeting Mr. M. by using his first name (Fernando), as opposed to a more formal title (Mr. M.). In traditional Latino and Asian families, such informality or familiarity may be considered a lack of respect for the man's role as head of the household. Another cultural barrier might be operative in asking the son whether something was wrong. It is highly probable that the animated family discussion was based on objections to the son's interpreting because it placed the father and mother in a dependency position. Yet as you recall, the son denied that anything was wrong. Many traditional Latinos do not feel comfortable airing family issues in public and might consider it impolite to turn down the therapist's suggestion to have the younger son interpret.

CHARACTERISTICS OF COUNSELING/THERAPY

As we have described in Chapter 5, counseling and psychotherapy may be viewed legitimately as a process of interpersonal interaction, communication, and social influence (Lui & Pope-Davis, 2005). For effective therapy to occur, the therapist and the client must be able to *send and receive both verbal and nonverbal messages appropriately and accurately*. Although breakdowns in communication often happen between people who share the same culture, the problem becomes exacerbated between people of different racial or ethnic backgrounds. Many mental health professionals have noted that racial or ethnic factors may act as impediments to therapy by lowering social influence (Locke, 1998; Paniagua, 1998; D. W. Sue, 2001). Misunderstandings that arise from cultural variations in communication may lead to alienation or an inability to develop trust and rapport. Culture clashes can often occur between the values of counseling and psychotherapy and the values of culturally diverse groups.

GENERIC CHARACTERISTICS OF COUNSELING/THERAPY

All theories of counseling and psychotherapy are influenced by assumptions that theorists make regarding the goals for therapy, the methodology used to invoke change, and the definition of mental health and mental illness (Corey, 2012). Counseling and psychotherapy have traditionally been conceptualized in Western individualistic terms (Ivey, Ivey, Myers, & Sweeny, 2005). Whether the particular theory is psychodynamic, existential-humanistic, or cognitive behavioral in orientation, a number of multicultural specialists (Ponterotto, Utsey, & Pedersen, 2006; Ridley, 2005; D. Sue & D. M. Sue, 2008) indicate that they share certain common components of White culture in their values and beliefs. Katz (1985) has described these components of White culture (see Table 7.1) that are reflected in the goals and processes of clinical work.

Table 7.1   Components of White Culture: Values and Beliefs

Rugged Individualism
Individual is primary unit
Individual has primary responsibility
Independence and autonomy highly
   valued and rewarded
Individual can control environment

Competition
Winning is everything
Win/lose dichotomy

Action Orientation
Must master and control nature
Must always do something about a
   situation
Pragmatic/utilitarian view of life

Communication
Standard English
Written tradition
Direct eye contact
Limited physical contact
Control of emotions

Time
Adherence to rigid time
Time is viewed as a commodity

Holidays
Based on Christian religion
Based on White history and male leaders

History
Based on European immigrants'
   experience in the United States
Romanticize war

Protestant Work Ethic
Working hard brings success

Progress & Future Orientation
Plan for future
Delayed gratification
Value continual improvement and
   progress

Emphasis on Scientific Method
Objective, rational, linear thinking
Cause-and-effect relationships
Quantitative emphasis

Status and Power
Measured by economic possessions
Credentials, titles, and positions
Believe "own" system
Believe better than other systems
Owning goods, space, property

Family Structure
Nuclear family is the ideal social unit
Male is breadwinner and the head of the
   household
Female is homemaker and subordinate to
   the husband
Patriarchal structure

Aesthetics
Music and art based on European cultures
Women's beauty based on blonde, blue-
   eyed, thin, young
Men's attractiveness based on athletic
   ability, power, economic status

Religion
Belief in Christianity
No tolerance for deviation from single
   god concept

Source: From *The Counseling Psychologist* (p. 618) by Katz, 1985, Beverly Hills, CA: Sage. Copyright 1985 by Sage Publications, Inc. Reprinted by permission.

Table 7.2   Generic Characteristics of Counseling

Culture	Middle Class	Language
Standard English Verbal communication	Standard English Verbal communication	Standard English Verbal communication
Individual centered	Adherence to time schedules (50-minute sessions)	
Verbal/emotional/behavioral expressiveness	Long-range goals	
Client-counselor communication	Ambiguity	
Openness and intimacy		
Cause-effect orientation		
Clear distinction between physical and mental well-being		
Nuclear family		

In the United States and in many other countries as well, psychotherapy and counseling are used mainly with middle- and upper-class segments of the population (L. Smith, 2010). As a result, culturally diverse clients do not share many of the values and characteristics seen in both the goals and the processes of therapy (APA Task Force on Socioeconomic Status, 2007). Schofield (1964) has noted that therapists tend to prefer clients who exhibit the YAVIS syndrome: young, attractive, verbal, intelligent, and successful. This preference tends to discriminate against people from different minority groups or those from lower socioeconomic classes. This led Sundberg (1981) to sarcastically point out that therapy is not for QUOID people (quiet, ugly, old, indigent, and dissimilar culturally). Three major characteristics of counseling and psychotherapy may act as impediments to effective counseling.

- *Culture-bound values:* Individual-centered, verbal/emotional/behavioral expressiveness, communication patterns from client to counselor, openness and intimacy, analytic/linear/verbal (cause-effect) approach, and clear distinctions between mental and physical well-being.
- *Class-bound values:* Strict adherence to time schedules (50-minute, once- or twice-a-week meetings), ambiguous or unstructured approach to problems, and seeking long-range goals or solutions.
- *Language variables:* Use of Standard English and emphasis on verbal communication.

Table 7.3 summarizes these generic characteristics and compares them to four racial/ethnic minority groups. As mentioned earlier, such a comparison can also be done for other groups that vary in gender, age, sexual orientation, ability/disability, and so on.

Although an attempt has been made to clearly delineate three major variables that influence effective therapy, these are often inseparable from one another. For example, use of Standard English in counseling and therapy definitely places those

Table 7.3   Racial/Ethnic Minority Group Variables

Culture	Lower Class	Language
Asian Americans		
Asian language	Nonstandard English	Bilingual background
Family centered	Action oriented	
Restraint of feelings	Different time perspective	
One-way communication from authority figure to person	Immediate, short-range goals	
Silence is respect		
Advice seeking		
Well-defined patterns of interaction (concrete structured)		
Private versus public display (shame/disgrace/pride)		
Physical and mental well-being defined differently		
Extended family		
African Americans		
Black language	Nonstandard English	Black language
Sense of "people-hood"	Action oriented	
Action oriented	Different time perspective	
Paranorm due to oppression	Immediate, short-range goals	
Importance placed on nonverbal behavior	Concrete, tangible, structured approach	
Extended family		
Latino/Hispanic Americans		
Spanish-speaking	Nonstandard English	Bilingual background
Group centered	Action oriented	
Temporal difference	Different time perspective	
Family orientation	Extended family	
Different pattern of communication	Immediate short-range goals	
Religious distinction between mind/body	Concrete, tangible, structured approach	
American Indians		
Tribal dialects	Nonstandard English	Bilingual background
Cooperative, not competitive individualism	Action oriented	
Present-time orientation	Different time perspective	
Creative/experimental/intuitive/ nonverbal	Immediate, short-range goals	
Satisfy present needs	Concrete, tangible, structured approach	
Use of folk or supernatural explanations		
Extended family		

individuals who do not speak English fluently at a disadvantage (Ngo-Metzger et al., 2003). However, cultural and class values that govern conversation conventions can also operate via language to cause serious misunderstandings. Furthermore, the fact that many African Americans, Latino/Hispanic Americans, and American Indians come from less affluent backgrounds often compounds class and culture variables. Thus, it is often difficult to tell which variables are the sole impediments in therapy. Nevertheless, this distinction is valuable in conceptualizing barriers to effective multicultural counseling/therapy.

CULTURE-BOUND VALUES

Culture consists of all those things that people have learned to do, believe, value, and enjoy. It is the totality of the ideals, beliefs, skills, tools, customs, and institutions into which each member of society is born. Although being bicultural is a source of strength, the process of negotiating dual group membership may cause problems for many minorities. The term *marginal person* was first coined by Stonequist (1937) and refers to a person's inability to form dual ethnic identification because of bicultural membership. Racial and ethnic minorities are placed under strong pressures to adopt the ways of the dominant culture. The cultural-deficit models tend to view culturally diverse groups as possessing dysfunctional values and belief systems that are often handicaps to be overcome and a source of shame. In essence, racial and ethnic minorities may be taught that to be different is to be deviant, pathological, or sick.

Many social scientists (Boyd-Franklin, 2003; Duran, 2006; Guthrie, 1997; Halleck, 1971) believe that psychology and therapy may be viewed as encompassing the use of social power and that therapy is a handmaiden of the status quo. The therapist may be seen as a societal agent transmitting and functioning under Western values. An early outspoken critic, Szasz (1970) believes that psychiatrists are like slave masters, using therapy as a powerful political ploy against people whose ideas, beliefs, and behaviors differ from the dominant society. Several culture-bound characteristics of therapy may be responsible for these negative beliefs.

Focus on the Individual

Most forms of counseling and psychotherapy tend to be individual-centered (i.e., they emphasize the "I-thou" relationship). Pedersen and Pope (2010) note that U.S. culture and society are based on the concept of individualism and that competition between individuals for status, recognition, achievement, and so forth, forms the basis for Western tradition. Individualism, autonomy, and the ability to become your own person are perceived as healthy and desirable goals. If we look at most Euro-American theories of human development (e.g., Piaget, Erickson), we are struck by how they emphasize individuation as normal and healthy development (D. Sue & D. M. Sue, 2008). Pedersen and Pope (2010) note that not all cultures view individualism as a positive orientation; rather, it may be perceived in some cultures as a handicap to attaining enlightenment, one that may divert us from important spiritual goals. In many non-Western cultures, identity is not seen apart from the group orientation (collectivism). The notion of *atman* in India

> Many societies do not define the psychosocial unit of operation as the individual. In many cultures and subgroups, the psychosocial unit of operation tends to be the family, group, or collective society.

defines itself as participating in unity with all things and not being limited by the temporal world.

Many societies do not define the psychosocial unit of operation as the individual. In many cultures and subgroups, the psychosocial unit of operation tends to be the family, group, or collective society. In traditional Asian American culture, one's identity is defined within the family constellation. The greatest punitive measure to be taken out on an individual by the family is to be disowned. What this means, in essence, is that the person no longer has an identity. Although being disowned by a family in Western European culture is equally negative and punitive, it does not have the same connotations as in traditional Asian society. Although they may be disowned by a family, Westerners are always told that they have an individual identity as well. Likewise, many Hispanic individuals tend to see the unit of operation as residing within the family. African American psychologists (Parham, Ajamu, & White, 2011) also point out how the African view of the world encompasses the concept of "groupness."

Our contention is that racial/ethnic minorities often use a different psychosocial unit of operation, in that collectivism is valued over individualism. This worldview is reflected in all aspects of behavior. For example, many traditional Asian American and Hispanic elders tend to greet one another with the question, "How is your family today?" Contrast this with how most Americans tend to greet each other: "How are you today?" One emphasizes the family (group) perspective, while the other emphasizes the individual perspective.

Affective expressions in therapy can also be strongly influenced by the particular orientation one takes. When individuals engage in wrongful behaviors in the United States, they are most likely to experience feelings of guilt. In societies that emphasize collectivism, however, the most dominant affective element to follow a wrongful behavior is shame, not guilt. Guilt is an individual affect, whereas shame appears to be a group one (it reflects on the family or group).

Counselors and therapists who fail to recognize the importance of defining this difference between individualism and collectivism will create difficulties in therapy. Often we are impressed by the number of our colleagues who describe traditional Asian clients as being "dependent," "unable to make decisions on their own," and "lacking in maturity." Many of these judgments are based on the fact that many Asian clients do not see a decision-making process as an individual one. When an Asian client states to a counselor or therapist, "I can't make that decision on my own; I need to consult with my parents or family," he or she is seen as being quite immature. After all, therapy is aimed at helping individuals make decisions on their own in a "mature" and "responsible" manner.

Verbal/Emotional/Behavioral Expressiveness

Many counselors and therapists tend to emphasize the fact that verbal/emotional/behavioral expressiveness is important in individuals. For example, we like our clients to be verbal, articulate, and able to express their thoughts and feelings clearly. Indeed, therapy is often referred to as talk therapy, indicating the importance placed on Standard English as the medium of expression. Emotional expressiveness is also valued, as we like individuals to be in touch with their feelings and to be able to verbalize their emotional reactions. In some forms of counseling and psychotherapy, it is often stated that if a feeling is not verbalized and expressed by the client, it may not exist. We tend to value behavioral expressiveness and believe that it is important as well. We like individuals to be assertive, to stand up for their own rights, and to engage in activities that indicate they are not passive beings.

All these characteristics of therapy can place culturally diverse clients at a disadvantage. For example, many cultural minorities tend not to value verbalizations in the same way that Americans do. In traditional Chinese culture, children have been taught not to speak until spoken to. Patterns of communication tend to be vertical, flowing from those of higher prestige and status to those of lower prestige and status. In a therapy situation, many Chinese clients, to show respect for a therapist who is older and wiser and who occupies a position of higher status, may respond with silence. Unfortunately, an unenlightened counselor or therapist may perceive this client as being inarticulate and less intelligent.

Emotional expressiveness in counseling and psychotherapy is frequently a highly desired goal. Yet many cultural groups value restraint of strong feelings. For example, traditional Hispanic and Asian cultures emphasize that maturity and wisdom are associated with one's ability to control emotions and feelings. This applies not only to public expressions of anger and frustration but also to public expressions of love and affection. Unfortunately, therapists unfamiliar with these cultural ramifications may perceive their clients in a very negative psychiatric light. Indeed, these clients are often described as inhibited, lacking in spontaneity, or repressed.

In therapy it has become increasingly popular to emphasize expressiveness in a behavioral sense. For example, one need only note the proliferation of cognitive-behavioral assertiveness training programs throughout the United States (Craske, 2010) and the number of self-help books that are being published in the popular mental health literature. This orientation fails to realize that there are cultural groups in which subtlety is a highly prized art. Yet doing things indirectly can be perceived by the mental health professional as evidence of passivity and a need for an individual to learn assertiveness skills.

Therapists who value verbal, emotional, and behavioral expressiveness as goals in therapy may be unaware that they are transmitting their own cultural values. These generic characteristics of counseling are antagonistic not only to lower-class values but to different cultural ones as well. In their excellent review of assertiveness training, Wood and Mallinckrodt (1990) warn that therapists need to make certain that gaining such skills is a value shared by the minority client, and not imposed by therapists. For example, statements by some mental health professionals that Japanese Americans are the most repressed of all clients indicate that they expect their clients to exhibit openness, psychological-mindedness, and assertiveness. Such a statement may indicate the therapist's failure to understand the background and cultural upbringing of many Asian American clients. Traditional Chinese and Japanese cultures may value restraint of strong feelings and subtleness in approaching problems.

Insight

Another generic characteristic of counseling is the use of insight in both counseling and psychotherapy. This approach assumes that it is mentally beneficial for individuals to obtain insight or understanding into their underlying dynamics and causes (Levenson, 2010). Educated in the tradition of psychoanalytic theory, many theorists tend to believe that clients who obtain better insight into themselves will be better adjusted. Although many behavioral schools of thought may not subscribe to this, most therapists use insight in their individual practice, either as a process of therapy or as an end product or goal (Antony & Roemer, 2011).

We need to realize that insight is not highly valued by many culturally diverse clients. There are major class differences as well (APA Task Force on Socioeconomic Status, 2007). People from lower socioeconomic classes frequently do not perceive insight as appropriate to their life situations and circumstances. Their concern may revolve around such questions as, "Where do I find a job?" "How do I feed my family?" and "How can I afford to take my sick daughter to a doctor?" When survival on a day-to-day basis is important, it seems inappropriate for the therapist to use insightful processes. After all, insight assumes that one has time to sit back, reflect, and contemplate motivations and behavior. For the individual who is concerned about making it through each day, this orientation proves counterproductive.

Likewise, many cultural groups do not value insight. In traditional Chinese society, psychology has little relevance. It must be noted, however, that a client who does not seem to work well in an insight approach may not be lacking in insight or psychological-mindedness. A person who does not value insight is not necessarily one who is incapable of insight. Thus, several major factors tend to affect insight.

First, many cultural groups do not value this method of self-exploration. It is interesting to note that many Asian elders believe that thinking too much about something can cause problems. In an early study of the Chinese in San Francisco's Chinatown, Lum (1982) found that many believe the road to mental health was to "avoid morbid thoughts." Advice from Asian elders to their children when they encountered feelings of frustration, anger, depression, or anxiety was simply, "Don't think about it." Indeed, it is often believed that the reason one experiences anger or depression is precisely that one is thinking about it *too much!* The traditional Asian way of handling these affective elements is to "keep busy and don't think about it." Granted, it is more complex than this, because in traditional Asian families the reason self-exploration is discouraged is precisely because it is an individual approach. "Think about the family and not about yourself" is advice given to many Asians as a way of dealing with negative affective elements. This is totally contradictory to Western notions of mental health, namely, that it is best to get things out in the open in order to deal with them.

Second, many racial/ethnic minority psychologists have felt that insight is a value in itself. For example, it was generally thought that insight led to behavior change. This was the old psychoanalytic assumption that when people understood their conflicts and underlying dynamics, the symptoms or behavior would change or disappear. The behavioral schools of thought have since cast doubt on this one-to-one connection. Although insight does lead to behavior change in some situations, it does not always seem to do so. Indeed, behavioral therapies have shown that changing the behavior first may lead to insight (cognitive restructuring and understanding) instead of vice versa.

Self-Disclosure (Openness and Intimacy)

Most forms of counseling and psychotherapy tend to value one's ability to self-disclose and to talk about the most intimate aspects of one's life. Indeed, self-disclosure has often been discussed as a primary characteristic of a healthy personality. The converse of this is that people who do not self-disclose readily in counseling and psychotherapy are seen to possess negative features, such as being guarded, mistrustful, or paranoid. There are two difficulties in this orientation toward self-disclosure. One of these is cultural, and the other is sociopolitical.

First, intimate revelations of personal or social problems may not be acceptable because such difficulties reflect not only on the individual but also on the whole family. Thus, the family may exert strong pressures on the Asian American client not to reveal personal matters to strangers or outsiders. Similar conflicts have been reported for Hispanics (Leong, Wagner, & Tata, 1995; Paniagua, 1998) and for American Indian clients (Herring, 1999; LaFromboise, 1998). A therapist who works with a client from a minority background may erroneously conclude that the person is repressed, inhibited, shy, or passive. Note that all these traits are seen as undesirable by Western standards.

Related to this example is many health practitioners' belief in the desirability of self-disclosure. Self-disclosure refers to the client's willingness to tell the therapist what he or she feels, believes, or thinks. Jourard (1964) suggests that mental health is related to one's openness in disclosing. Although this may be true, the parameters need clarification. Chapter 4 uses as an example the paranorm of Grier and Cobbs (1968). People of African descent are especially reluctant to disclose to White counselors because of hardships that they experienced via racism (Ridley, 2005). African Americans initially perceive a White therapist more often as an agent of society who may use information against them, rather than as a person of goodwill. From the African American perspective, noncritical self-disclosure to others is not healthy.

The actual structure of the therapy situation may also work against intimate revelations. Among many American Indians and Hispanics, intimate aspects of life are shared only with close friends. Relative to White middle-class standards, deep friendships are developed only after prolonged contacts. Once friendships are formed, they tend to be lifelong in nature. In contrast, White Americans form relationships quickly, but the relationships do not necessarily persist over long periods of time. Counseling and therapy also seem to reflect these values. Clients talk about the most intimate aspects of their lives with a relative stranger once every week for a 50-minute session. To many culturally different groups who stress friendship as a precondition to self-disclosure, the counseling process seems utterly inappropriate and absurd. After all, how is it possible to develop a friendship with brief contacts once a week?

Scientific Empiricism

Counseling and psychotherapy in Western culture and society have been described as being highly linear, analytic, and verbal in their attempt to mimic the physical sciences. As indicated by Table 7.1, Western society tends to emphasize the so-called scientific method, which involves objective, rational, linear thinking. Likewise, we often see descriptions of therapists as objective, neutral, rational, and logical (Utsey, Walker, & Kwate, 2005). Therapists rely heavily on the use of linear problem solving, as well as on quantitative evaluation that includes psychodiagnostic tests, intelligence tests, personality inventories, and so forth. This cause-effect orientation emphasizes left-brain functioning. That is, theories of counseling and therapy are distinctly analytical, rational, and verbal, and they strongly stress the discovery of cause-effect relationships.

The emphasis on symbolic logic contrasts markedly with the philosophies of many cultures that value a more nonlinear, holistic, and harmonious approach to the world (D. W. Sue & Constantine, 2003). For example, American Indian worldviews emphasize the harmonious aspects of the world, intuitive functioning, and a holistic approach—a worldview characterized by right-brain activities, minimizing analytical and reductionistic inquiries. Thus, when American Indians undergo therapy, the analytic approach may violate their basic philosophy of life (Garrett & Portman, 2011).

It appears that the most dominant way of asking and answering questions about the human condition in U.S. society tends to be the scientific method. The epitome of this approach is the *experiment*. In graduate schools we are often told that only through the experiment can we impute a cause-effect relationship. By identifying the independent and dependent variables and controlling for extraneous variables, we are able to test a cause-effect hypothesis. Although correlation studies, historical research, and other approaches may be of benefit, we are told that the experiment represents the epitome of our science (Seligman & Csikszentmihalyi, 2001). As indicated, other cultures may value different ways of asking and answering questions about the human condition.

Distinctions Between Mental and Physical Functioning

Many American Indians, Asian Americans, African Americans, and Latinos hold different concepts of what constitutes mental health, mental illness, and adjustment. Among the Chinese, the concept of mental health or psychological well-being is not understood in the same way as it is in the Western context. Latino/a Americans do not make the same Western distinction between mental and physical health as do their White counterparts (Guzman & Carrasco, 2011). Thus, nonphysical health problems are most likely to be referred to a physician, priest, or minister. Culturally diverse clients operating under this orientation may enter therapy expecting therapists to treat them in the same manner that doctors or priests do. Immediate solutions and concrete tangible forms of treatment (advice, confession, consolation, and medication) are expected.

Ambiguity

The ambiguous and unstructured aspect of the therapy situation may create discomfort in clients of color. Culturally diverse clients may not be familiar with therapy and may perceive it as an unknown and mystifying process. Some groups, such as Latinos, may have been reared in an environment that actively structures social relationships and patterns of interaction. Anxiety and confusion may be the outcome in an unstructured counseling setting.

Patterns of Communication

The cultural upbringing of many minorities dictates different patterns of communication that may place them at a disadvantage in therapy. Counseling, for example, initially demands that communication move from client to counselor. The client is expected to take the major responsibility for initiating conversation in the session, while the counselor plays a less active role.

However, American Indians, Asian Americans, and Latinos function under different cultural imperatives, which may make this difficult. These three groups may have been reared to respect elders and authority figures and not to speak until spoken to. Clearly defined roles of dominance and deference are established in the traditional family. Evidence indicates that Asians associate mental health with exercising will power, avoiding unpleasant thoughts, and occupying one's mind with positive thoughts. Therapy is seen as an authoritative process in which a good therapist is more direct and active and portrays a kind of father figure. A racial/ethnic minority client who is asked to initiate conversation may become uncomfortable and respond with only short phrases or statements. The therapist may be prone to interpret the behavior negatively, when in actuality it may be a sign of respect. We have much more to say about these communication style differences in the next chapter.

CLASS-BOUND VALUES

Social class and classism have been identified as two of the most overlooked topics in psychology and mental health practice (American Psychological Association, Task Force on Socioeconomic Status, 2007; W. M. Liu, Ali, Soleck, Hopps, Dunston, & Pickett, 2004; L. Smith, 2005, 2010). Although many believe that the gap in income is closing, statistics suggest the opposite—income inequality is increasing. Those in the top 5% of income have enjoyed huge increases, whereas those in the bottom 40% are stagnant (American Psychological Association, Task Force on Socioeconomic Status, 2007). In the United States, 32 million Americans live in poverty. Blacks are three times more likely to live in poverty than Whites; the rate of poverty for Latinos is 23%; for Asian/Pacific Islanders it is 11%; and for Whites it is 8% (W. M. Liu et al., 2004). These statistics clearly suggest that social class may be intimately linked to race because many racial/ethnic minority groups are disproportionately represented in the lower socioeconomic classes (L. Smith, 2010).

Research indicates that lower socioeconomic class is related to higher incidence of depression (Lorant, Deliege, Eaton, Robert, Philippot, & Ansseau, 2003), lower sense of control (E. Chen, Matthews, & Boyce, 2002), poorer physical health (Gallo & Matthews, 2003), and exclusion from the mainstream of society (L. Smith, 2010). Mental health professionals are often unaware of additional stressors likely to confront clients who lack financial resources, nor do they fully appreciate how those stressors affect their clients' daily lives. For the therapist who comes from a middle- to upper-class background, it is often difficult to relate to the circumstances and hardships affecting the client who lives in poverty. The phenomenon of poverty and its effects on individuals and institutions can be devastating (W. M. Liu, Hernandez, Mahmood, & Stinson, 2006). The individual's life is characterized by low wages, unemployment, underemployment, little property ownership, no savings, and lack of food reserves. Meeting even the most basic needs of food and shelter is in constant jeopardy. Pawning personal possessions and borrowing money at exorbitant interest rates leads only to greater debt. Feelings of helplessness, dependence, and inferiority develop easily under these circumstances. Therapists may unwittingly attribute attitudes that result from physical and environmental adversity to the cultural or individual traits of the person. For example, note the clinical description of a 12-year-old child written by a school counselor:

Jimmy Jones is a 12-year-old Black male student who was referred by Mrs. Peterson because of apathy, indifference, and inattentiveness to classroom activities. Other teachers have also reported that Jimmy does not pay attention, daydreams often, and frequently falls asleep during class. There is a strong possibility that Jimmy is harboring repressed rage that needs to be ventilated and dealt with. His inability to directly express his anger had led him to adopt passive-aggressive means of expressing hostility (i.e., inattentiveness, daydreaming, falling asleep). It is recommended that Jimmy be seen for intensive counseling to discover the basis of the anger.

After 6 months of counseling, the counselor finally realized the basis of Jimmy's problems. He came from a home life marked by extreme poverty; hunger, lack of sleep, and overcrowding served to severely diminish his energy level and motivation. The fatigue, passivity, and fatalism evidenced by Jimmy were more a result of poverty than of some innate group or individual trait. Likewise, poverty may cause many parents to encourage children to seek employment at an early age. Delivering groceries, shining shoes, and hustling other sources of income may sap the energy of the schoolchild, leading to truancy and poor performance. Teachers and counselors may view such students as unmotivated and potential juvenile delinquents.

Considerable bias against people who are poor has been well documented (American Psychological Association, Task Force on Socioeconomic Status, 2007; L. Smith, 2005). Although considerable controversy exists over whether classism is unidirectional (directed toward those in lower classes) or bidirectional (equally likely to occur between the classes; W. M. Lui et al., 2004; L. Smith, 2005), it is clear to us that those who occupy the lower rungs of our society are the most likely to be oppressed and harmed. For example, clinicians perceive lower-social-class clients more unfavorably than upper-social-class clients (as having less education, being dysfunctional, and making poor progress in therapy). Research concerning the inferior and biased quality of treatment of lower-class clients is historically legend (Atkinson et al., 1998; Pavkov, Lewis, & Lyons, 1989; Rouse, Carter, & Rodriguez-Andrew, 1995). In the area of diagnosis, it has been found that an attribution of mental illness was more likely to occur when the person's history suggested a lower rather than higher socioeconomic class origin (W. M. Liu et al., 2006). Many studies seem to demonstrate that clinicians given identical test protocols tend to make more negative prognostic statements and judgments of greater maladjustment when the individual was said to come from a lower- rather than a middle-class background.

Several conclusions can be drawn from these findings: (a) low socioeconomic class presents stressors to people, especially those in poverty, and may seriously undermine the mental and physical health of clients; (b) failure of helping professionals to understand the life circumstance of clients who lack financial resources and/or their unintentional class biases may affect their ability to delivery appropriate mental health services; and (c) classism and its discriminating nature can make its appearance in the assessment, diagnosis, and treatment of lower socioeconomic clients.

In addition, the class-bound nature of mental health practice emphasizes the importance of assisting the client in self-direction through the presentation of the results of assessment instruments and self-exploration via verbal interactions between client and therapist. However, the values underlying these activities are permeated by middle-class values that do not suffice for those living in poverty. We have already seen how this operates with respect to language. As early as the 1960s, B. Bernstein (1964) investigated the suitability of Standard English for the lower class in psychotherapy and concluded that it works to the detriment of those individuals. In an extensive historic research of services delivered to minorities and low socioeconomic clients, Lorion (1973) found that psychiatrists refer to therapy those persons who are most like themselves—White rather than non-White and from upper socioeconomic status. Lorion (1974) pointed out that the expectations of lower-class clients are often different from those of psychotherapists. For example, lower-class clients who are concerned with survival or making it through on a day-to-day basis expect advice and suggestions from the counselor. Appointments made weeks in advance with short, weekly, 50-minute contacts are not consistent with the need to seek immediate solutions. Additionally, many lower-class people, through multiple experiences with public agencies, operate under what is called *minority standard time* (Schindler-Rainman, 1967). This is the tendency of poor people to have a low regard for punctuality. Poor people have learned that endless waits are associated with medical clinics, police stations, and governmental agencies. One usually waits hours for a 10- to 15-minute appointment. Arriving promptly does little good and can be a waste of valuable time. Therapists, however, rarely understand this aspect of life and are prone to see this as a sign of indifference or hostility.

People from a lower socioeconomic status may also view insight and attempts to discover underlying intrapsychic problems as inappropriate. Many lower-class clients expect to receive advice or some form of concrete tangible treatment. When the therapist attempts to explore personality dynamics or to take a historical approach to the problem, the client often becomes confused, alienated, and frustrated. A harsh environment, where the future is uncertain and immediate needs must be met, makes long-range planning of little value. Many clients of lower socioeconomic status are unable to relate to the future orientation of therapy. To be able to sit and talk about things is perceived as a luxury of the middle and upper classes.

Because of the lower-class client's environment and past inexperience with therapy, the expectations of the minority individual may be quite different, or even negative. The client's unfamiliarity with the therapy process may hinder success and cause the therapist to blame the client for the failure. Thus, the minority client may be perceived as hostile and resistant. The results of this interaction may be a premature termination of therapy. Considerable evidence exists that clients from upper socioeconomic backgrounds have significantly more exploratory interviews with their therapists and that middle-class patients tend to remain in treatment longer than lower-class patients (Gottesfeld, 1995; Leong, Wagner, & Kim, 1995; Neighbors, Caldwell, Thompson, & Jackson, 1994). Furthermore, the now-classic study of Hollingshead and Redlich (1968) found that lower-class patients tend to have fewer ego-involving relationships and less intensive therapeutic relationships than do members of higher socioeconomic classes.

Poverty undoubtedly contributes to the mental health problems among racial/ethnic minority groups, and social class determines the type of treatment a minority client is likely to receive. In addition, as Atkinson, Morten, and Sue (1998, p. 64) conclude, "Ethnic minorities are less likely to earn incomes sufficient to pay for mental health treatment, less likely to have insurance, and more likely to qualify for public assistance than European Americans. Thus, ethnic minorities often have to rely on public (government-sponsored) or nonprofit mental health services to obtain help with their psychological problems."

Working effectively with clients who are poor requires several major conditions. First, the therapist must spend time understanding his or her own biases and prejudices (American Psychological Association, Task Force on Socioeconomic Status, 2007; W. M. Liu et al., 2004; Smith, 2010). Not confronting one's own classist attitudes can lead to a phenomenon called "White trashism." Manifestation of prejudicial or negative attitudes can be found in such descriptors as "trailer parkism," "hillbillyism," "uppity," "red-neck," and so on. These attitudes can affect the diagnosis and treatment of clients. Second, it becomes essential that counselors understand how poverty affects the lives of people who lack financial resources; behaviors associated with survival should not be pathologized. Third, counselors should consider that taboos against information-giving activities and a more active approach in treatment might be more appropriate than the passive, insight-oriented, and long-term models of therapy. Last, poverty and economic disparities that are root causes affecting the mental health and quality of life of people in our society demand a social justice approach.

LANGUAGE BARRIERS

Ker Moua, a Laotian refugee, suffered from a variety of ailments but was unable to communicate with her doctor. The medical staff enlisted the aid of 12-year-old Jue as the liaison between the doctor and the mother. Ker was diagnosed with a prolapsed uterus, the result of bearing 12 children. She took medication in the doses described by her son but became severely ill after two days. Fortunately, it was discovered that she was taking an incorrect dosage that could have caused lasting harm. The hospital staff realized that Jue had mistranslated the doctor's orders. When inquiries about the translation occurred, Jue said, "I don't know what a uterus is. The doctor tells me things I don't know how to say." (Burke, 2005, p. 5b)

Asking children to translate information concerning medical or legal problems is common in many communities with high immigrant and refugee populations but may have devastating consequences: (a) It can create stress and hurt the traditional parent-child relationship; (b) children lack the vocabulary and emotional maturity to serve as effective interpreters; (c) children may be placed in a situation where they are privy to confidential medical or psychiatric information about their relatives; and (d) they may be unfairly burdened with emotional responsibilities that only adults should carry (J. Coleman, 2003). In 2008, California Assembly Bill 775 was introduced to ban the use of children as interpreters. Further, the federal government has acknowledged that not providing adequate interpretation for client populations is a form of discrimination. As our opening case of the M. family suggests, the lack of bilingual therapists can result in both inferior and damaging services to linguistic minorities. Recently, the National Council on Interpreting in Health Care (2005) published national standards for interpreters of health care that address issues of cultural awareness and confidentiality.

These standards were based upon a number of important findings derived from focus groups of immigrants (Ngo-Metzger et al., 2003). First, nearly all immigrants interviewed expressed a preference for professional translators rather than family members. They wanted translators who were knowledgeable and respectful of their cultural customs. Second, using family members to interpret—especially children—was negatively received for fear of their inability to translate correctly. Third, discussing very personal or familial issues was often very uncomfortable (shame, guilt, other emotional reactions) when a family member acted as the interpreter. Last, there was great concern that interpretation by a family member could be affected by the family dynamics or vice versa. Some general guidelines in selecting and working with interpreters are the following:

- Make sure that professional interpreters speak the same dialect. Monitor carefully if the interpreter and client appear to have significant cultural or social differences.
- Establish a degree of familiarity with the interpreters; they should be understanding and comfortable with your therapeutic style. Use the same interpreter with the same client.

- Be aware that the interpreter is not just an empty box in the therapeutic relationship. Rather than a two-person interaction in counseling, it is most likely a three-person alliance. Clients may initially develop a stronger relationship with the interpreter than with the counselor.
- Provide plenty of extra time in the counseling session.
- Help the interpreter to realize the code of confidentiality.
- If you believe the interpreters are not fully translating and/or are interjecting their own beliefs, opinions, and assumptions, it is important to have a frank and open discussion about your observations.
- Be aware that interpreters may also experience intense emotions when traumatic events are discussed. Be alert for overidentification or countertransference. In many respects, the therapist may need to work closely in allowing interpreters periodic debriefing sessions.

Clearly, use of Standard English in health care delivery may unfairly discriminate against those from a bilingual or lower socioeconomic background and result in devastating consequences (Vedantam, 2005). This inequity occurs in our educational system and in the delivery of mental health services as well. The bilingual background of many Asian Americans, Latino/a and Hispanic Americans, and American Indians may lead to much misunderstanding. This is true even if a minority group member cannot speak his or her own native tongue. Early language studies (M. E. Smith, 1957; M. E. Smith & Kasdon, 1961) indicate that simply coming from a background where one or both parents have spoken their native tongue can impair proper acquisition of English. Even African Americans who come from a different cultural environment may use words and phrases (Black Language, or Ebonics) not entirely understandable to the therapist. Although considerable criticism was directed toward the Oakland Unified School District for their short-lived attempt to recognize Ebonics in 1996, the reality is that such a form of communication does exist in many African American communities. In therapy, however, African American clients are expected to communicate their feelings and thoughts to therapists in Standard English. For some African Americans, this is a difficult task, since the use of nonstandard English is their norm. Black language code involves a great deal of implicitness in communication, such as shorter sentences and less grammatical elaboration (but greater reliance on nonverbal cues). On the other hand, the language code of the middle and upper classes is much more elaborate, relies less on nonverbal cues, and entails greater knowledge of grammar and syntax.

Schwartz, Rodriguez, Santiago-Rivera, Arredondo, and Field (2010) indicate that psychologists are finding that they must interact with consumers who may have English as a second language or who may not speak English at all. The lack of bilingual therapists and the requirement that the client communicate in English may limit the person's ability to progress in counseling and therapy. If bilingual individuals do not use their native tongue in therapy, many aspects of their emotional experience may not be available for treatment. For example, because English may not be their primary language, they may have difficulty using the wide complexity of language to describe their particular thoughts, feelings, and unique situations. Clients who are limited in English tend to feel like they are speaking as a child and choosing simple words to explain complex thoughts and feelings. If they were able to use their native tongue, they could easily explain themselves without the huge loss of emotional complexity and experience.

In therapy, heavy reliance is placed on verbal interaction to build rapport. The presupposition is that participants in a therapeutic dialogue are capable of understanding each other. Therapists often fail to understand an African American client's language and its nuances for building rapport. Furthermore, those who have not been given the same educational or economic opportunities may lack the prerequisite verbal skills to benefit from talk therapy. A client's brief, different, or poor verbal responses may lead many therapists to impute inaccurate characteristics or motives. As a result, the client may be seen as uncooperative, sullen, negative, nonverbal, or repressed on the basis of language expression alone. Since Euro-American society places such a high premium on one's use of English, it is a short step to conclude that linguistic minorities are inferior, lack awareness, or lack conceptual thinking powers. Such misinterpretation can also be seen in the use and interpretation of psychological tests. So-called IQ and achievement tests are especially notorious for their language bias.

PATTERNS OF "AMERICAN" CULTURAL ASSUMPTIONS AND MULTICULTURAL FAMILY COUNSELING/THERAPY

As we have seen throughout the chapter, the generic characteristics of counseling and therapy clash not only with how we define a healthy individual but also with our perceptions of the healthy family. Family systems theory may be equally culture bound and may be manifested in marital or couple counseling, parent-child counseling, or work with more than one member of the family (Doherty & McDaniel, 2010; Nichols & Schwartz, 2002). Family systems therapy possesses several important characteristics (Corey, 2005; McGoldrick, Giordano, & Garcia-Preto, 2005):

- Highlight the importance of the family (versus the individual) as the unit of identity.
- Focus on resolving concrete issues.
- Be concerned with family structure and dynamics.
- Assume that these family structures and dynamics are historically passed on from one generation to another.
- Attempt to understand the communication and alliances via reframing.
- Place the therapist in an expert position.

Many of these qualities, as we have seen, would be consistent with the worldviews of racial/ethnic minorities. Many culturally different families favorably view its emphases on the family as the unit of identity and study, understanding the cultural norms and background of the family system, and the need to balance the system.

Table 7.4 Cultural Value Preferences of Middle-Class White Euro-Americans and Racial/Ethnic Minorities: A Comparative Summary

Area of Relationships	Middle-Class White Americans	Asian Americans	American Indians	Black Americans	Hispanic Americans
People to nature/ environment	Mastery over	Harmony with	Harmony with	Harmony with	Harmony with
Time orientation	Future	Past-present	Present	Present	Past-present
People relations	Individual	Collateral	Collateral	Collateral	Collateral
Preferred mode of activity	Doing	Doing	Being-in-becoming	Doing	Being-in-becoming
Nature of man	Good & bad	Good	Good	Good & bad	Good

Source: From *Family Therapy with Ethnic Minorities* (p. 232) by M. K. Ho, 1987, Newbury Park, CA: Sage. Copyright 1987 by Sage Publications. Reprinted by permission.

The problem arises, however, in how these goals and strategies are translated into concepts of "the family" or what constitutes the "healthy" family. Some of the characteristics of healthy families may pose problems in therapy with various culturally different groups. In many respects, they are part and parcel of the generic characteristics of counseling. They tend to be heavily loaded with value orientations that are incongruent with the value systems of many culturally different clients (McGoldrick et al., 2005):

- Allow and encourage expressing emotions freely and openly.
- View each member as having a right to be his or her own unique self (individuate from the emotional field of the family).
- Strive for an equal division of labor among members of the family.
- Consider egalitarian role relationships between spouses desirable.
- Hold the nuclear family as the standard.

These orientations were first described by Kluckhohn and Strodtbeck (1961) as patterns of "American" values. This model allows us to understand the worldviews of culturally diverse families by contrasting the value orientations of the four main groups we are studying (as illustrated in Table 7.4): Asian Americans, American Indians, Black Americans, and Hispanic Americans. Table 7.4 also outlines in a different way the components of White culture, its values and beliefs. It is important to note that these basic assumptions, values, and beliefs are also the building blocks of traditional counseling and psychotherapy.

People-Nature Relationship

Traditional Western thinking believes in mastery and control over nature. As a result, most therapists operate from a framework that subscribes to the belief that problems are solvable and that both therapist and client must take an active part in solving problems via manipulation and control. Active intervention is stressed in controlling or changing the environment. As seen in Table 7.4, the four other ethnic groups view people as harmonious with nature.

Confucian philosophy, for example, stresses a set of rules aimed at promoting loyalty, respect, and harmony among family members (Moodley & West, 2005). Harmony within the family and the environment leads to harmony within the self. Dependence on the family unit and acceptance of the environment seem to dictate differences in solving problems. Western culture advocates defining and attacking the problem directly. Asian cultures tend to accommodate or deal with problems through indirection. In child rearing, many Asians believe that it is better to avoid direct confrontation and to use deflection. A White family may deal with a child who has watched too many hours of TV by saying, "Why don't you turn the TV off and study?" To be more threatening, the parent might say, "You'll be grounded unless the TV goes off!" An Asian parent might respond by saying, "That looks like a boring program; I think your friend John must be doing his homework now" or "I think father wants to watch his favorite program." Such an approach stems from the need to avoid conflict and to achieve balance and harmony among members of the family and the wider environment.

In an excellent analysis of family therapy for Asian Americans, S. C. Kim (1985) points out how current therapeutic techniques of confrontation and of having clients express thoughts and feelings directly may be inappropriate and difficult to handle. For example, one of the basic tenets of family therapy is that the identified patient (IP) typically behaves in such a way as to reflect family influences or pathology. Often, an acting-out child is symbolic of deeper family problems. Yet most Asian American families come to counseling or therapy for the benefit of the IP, not the family! Attempts to directly focus in on the family dynamics as contributing to the IP will be met with negativism and possible termination. S. C. Kim (1985, p. 346) states,

> A recommended approach to engage the family would be to pace the family's cultural expectations and limitations by (1) asserting that the IP's problem (therefore not the IP by implication) is indeed the problem; (2) recognizing and reinforcing the family's concerns to help the IP to change the behavior; and (3) emphasizing that each family member's contribution in resolving the problem is vitally needed and that, without it, the problem will either remain or get worse, bringing on further difficulty in the family.

Thus, it is apparent that U.S. values that call for us to dominate nature (i.e., conquer space, tame the wilderness, or harness nuclear energy) through control and manipulation of the universe are reflected in family counseling. Family systems counseling theories attempt to describe, explain, predict, and control family dynamics. The therapist actively attempts to understand what is going on in the family system (structural alliances and communication patterns), identify the problems (dysfunctional aspects of the dynamics), and attack them directly or indirectly through manipulation and control (therapeutic interventions). Ethnic minorities or subgroups that view people as harmonious with nature or believe that nature may overwhelm people ("acts of God") may find the therapist's mastery-over-nature approach inconsistent or antagonistic to their worldview. Indeed, attempts to intervene actively in changing family patterns and relationships may be perceived as the problem because it may potentially unbalance that harmony that existed.

Time Dimension

How different societies, cultures, and people view time exerts a pervasive influence on their lives. U.S. society may be characterized as preoccupied with the future (Katz, 1985; Kluckhohn & Strodtbeck, 1961). Furthermore, our society seems very compulsive about time, in that we divide it into seconds, minutes, hours, days, weeks, months, and years. Time may be viewed as a commodity ("time is money" and "stop wasting time") in fixed and static categories rather than as a dynamic and flowing process. It has been pointed out that the United States' future orientation may be linked to other values as well: (a) stress on youth and achievement, in which the children are expected to "better their parents"; (b) controlling one's own destiny by future planning and saving for a rainy day; and (c) optimism and hope for a better future. The spirit of the nation may be embodied in an old General Electric slogan, "Progress is our most important product." This is not to deny that people are concerned about the past and the present as well, but rather to suggest that culture, groups, and people may place greater emphasis on one over the other. Nor do we deny the fact that age, gender, occupation, social class, and other important demographic factors may be linked to time perspective. However, our work with various racial/ethnic minority groups and much of the research conducted support the fact that race, culture, and ethnicity are powerful determinants of whether the group emphasizes the past, present, or future.

Table 7.4 reveals that both American Indians and Black Americans tend to value a present time orientation, whereas Asian Americans and Hispanic Americans have a combination past-present focus. Historically, Asian societies have valued the past as reflected in ancestor worship and the equating of age with wisdom and respectability. This contrasts with U.S. culture, in which youth is valued over the elderly and one's usefulness in life is believed to be over once one hits the retirement years. As compared to Euro-American middle-class norms, Latinos also exhibit a past-present time orientation. Strong hierarchical structures in the family, respect for elders and ancestors, and the value of *personalismo* all combine in this direction. American Indians also differ from their White counterparts in that they are very grounded in the here and now rather than the future. American Indian philosophy relies heavily on the belief that time is flowing, circular, and harmonious. Artificial division of time (schedules) is disruptive to the natural pattern. African Americans also value the present because of the spiritual quality of their existence and their history of racism. Several difficulties may occur when the counselor or therapist is unaware of the differences of time perspective (Hines & Boyd-Franklin, 2005).

First, if time differences exist between the minority family and the White Euro-American therapist, it will most likely be manifested in a difference in the pace of time: Both may sense things are going too slowly or too fast. An American Indian family who values being in the present and the immediate experiential reality of being may feel that the therapist lacks respect for them and is rushing them (Herring, 1997; Sutton & Broken Nose, 2005) while ignoring the quality of the personal relationship. On the other hand, the therapist may be dismayed by the "delays," "inefficiency," and lack of "commitment to change" among the family members. After all, time is precious, and the therapist has only limited time to impact upon the family. The result is frequently dissatisfaction among the parties, no establishment of rapport, misinterpretation of the behaviors or situations, and probably discontinuation of future sessions.

Second, Inclan (1985) pointed out how confusions and misinterpretations can arise because Hispanics, particularly Puerto Ricans, mark time differently than do their U.S. White counterparts. The language of clock time in counseling (50-minute hour, rigid time schedule, once-a-week sessions) can conflict with minority perceptions of time (Garcia-Preto, 1996). The following dialogue illustrates this point clearly:

"Mrs. Rivera, your next appointment is at 9:30 A.M. next Wednesday."

"Good, it's convenient for me to come after I drop off the children at school."

Or, "Mrs. Rivera, your next appointment is for the whole family at 3:00 P.M. on Tuesday."

"Very good. After the kids return from school we can come right in." (Inclan, 1985, p. 328)

Since school starts at 8 A.M., the client is bound to show up very early, whereas in the second example, the client will most likely be late (school ends at 3 P.M.). In both cases, the counselor is most likely to be inconvenienced, but worse yet is the negative interpretation that may be made of the client's motives (anxious, demanding, or pushy in the first case, while resistant, passive-aggressive, or irresponsible in the latter one). The counselor needs to be aware that many Hispanics may mark time by events rather than by the clock.

Third, many minorities who are present time–oriented overall would be more likely to seek immediate, concrete solutions than future-oriented, abstract goals. In earlier chapters we noted that goals or processes that are insight-oriented assume that the client has time to sit back and self-explore. Career/vocational counseling, in which clients explore their interests, values, work temperaments, skills, abilities, and the world of work, may be seen as highly future oriented. Although potentially beneficial to the client, these approaches may pose dilemmas for both the minority family and the counselor.

Relational Dimension

In general, the United States can be characterized as an achievement-oriented society, which is most strongly manifested in the prevailing Protestant work ethic.

Basic to the ethic is the concept of *individualism:* (1) The individual is the psychosocial unit of operation; (2) the individual has primary responsibility for his or her own actions; (3) independence and autonomy are highly valued and rewarded; and (4) one should be internally directed and controlled. In many societies and groups within the United States, however, this value is not necessarily shared. Relationships in Japan and China are often described as being lineal, and identification with others is both wide and linked to the past (ancestor worship). Obeying the wishes of ancestors or deceased parents and perceiving your existence and identity as linked to the historical past are inseparable. Almost all racial/ethnic minority groups in the United States tend to be more collateral in their relationships with people. In an individualistic orientation, the definition of the family tends to be linked to a biological necessity (nuclear family), whereas a collateral or lineal view encompasses various concepts of the extended family. Not understanding this distinction and the values inherent in these orientations may lead the family therapist to erroneous conclusions and decisions. Following is a case illustration of a young American Indian.

> A young probationer was under court supervision and had strict orders to remain with responsible adults. His counselor became concerned because the youth appeared to ignore this order. The client moved around frequently and, according to the counselor, stayed overnight with several different young women. The counselor presented this case at a formal staff meeting, and fellow professionals stated their suspicion that the client was either a pusher or a pimp. The frustrating element to the counselor was that the young women knew each other and appeared to enjoy each other's company. Moreover, they were not ashamed to be seen together in public with the client. This behavior prompted the counselor to initiate violation proceedings. (Red Horse, Lewis, Feit, & Decker, 1981, p. 56)

If an American Indian professional had not accidentally come upon this case, a revocation order initiated against the youngster would surely have caused irreparable alienation between the family and the social service agency. The counselor had failed to realize that the American Indian family network is structurally open and may include several households of relatives and friends along both vertical and horizontal lines. The young women were all first cousins to the client, and each was as a sister, with all the households representing different units of the family. Likewise, African Americans have strong kinship bonds that may encompass both blood relatives and friends. Traditional African culture values the collective orientation over individualism (J. H. Franklin, 1988; Hines & Boyd-Franklin, 2005). This group identity has also been reinforced by what many African Americans describe as the sense of "peoplehood" developed as a result of the common experience of racism and discrimination. In a society that has historically attempted to destroy the Black family, near and distant relatives, neighbors, friends, and acquaintances have arisen in an extended family support network (Black, 1996). Thus, the Black family may appear quite different from the ideal nuclear family. The danger is that certain assumptions made by a White therapist may be totally without merit or may be translated in such a way as to alienate or damage the self-esteem of African Americans.

For example, the absence of a father in the Black family does not necessarily mean that the children do not have a father figure. This function may be taken over by an uncle or male family friend. M. B. Thomas and Dansby (1985) provide an example of a group-counseling technique that was detrimental to several Black children. Clients in the group were asked to draw a picture of the family dinner table and place circles representing the mother, father, and children in their seating arrangement. They reported that even before the directions for the exercise were finished, a young Black girl ran from the room in tears. She had been raised by an aunt. Several other Black clients stated that they did not eat dinners together as a family except on special occasions or Sundays—according to Willie (1981), a typical routine in some affluent Black families.

We give one example here to illustrate that the moral evaluation of a behavior may depend on the value orientation of the cultural group. Because of their collective orientation, Puerto Ricans view obligations to the family as primary over all other relationships (Garcia-Preto, 2005). When a family member attains a position of power and influence, it is expected that he or she will favor the relatives over objective criteria. Businesses that are heavily weighted by family members, and appointments of family members in government positions are not unusual in many countries. Failure to hire a family member may result in moral condemnation and family sanctions (Inclan, 1985). This is in marked contrast to what we ideally believe in the United States. Appointment of family members over objective criteria of individual achievement is condemned. It would appear that differences in the relationship dimension between the mental health provider and the minority family receiving services can cause great conflict. Although family therapy may be the treatment of choice for many minorities (over individual therapy), its values may again be antagonistic and detrimental to minorities. Family approaches that place heavy emphasis on individualism and freedom from the emotional field of the family may cause great harm. Our approach should be to identify how we might capitalize on collaterality to the benefit of minority families.

> The moral evaluation of a behavior may depend on the value orientation of the cultural group.

Activity Dimension

One of the primary characteristics of White U.S. cultural values and beliefs is an action (doing) orientation: (a) We must master and control nature; (b) we must always do things about a situation; and (c) we should take a pragmatic and utilitarian view of life. In counseling, we expect clients to master and control their own lives and environment, to take action to resolve their own problems, and to fight against bias and inaction. The doing mode is evident everywhere and is reflected in how White Americans identify themselves by what they *do* (occupations), how children are asked what they want to do when they grow up, and how a higher value is given to inventors over poets and to doctors of medicine over doctors of philosophy. An essay topic commonly given to schoolchildren returning to school in the fall is "What I did on my summer vacation."

It appears that both American Indians and Latinos/Hispanics prefer a being or being-in-becoming mode of activity. The American Indian concepts of self-determination and noninterference are examples. Value is placed on the spiritual quality of being, as manifested in self-containment, poise, and harmony with the universe. Value is placed on the attainment of inner fulfillment and an essential serenity of one's place in the universe. Because each person is fulfilling a purpose, no one should have the power to interfere or impose values. Often, those unfamiliar with Indian values perceive the person as stoic, aloof, passive, noncompetitive, or inactive. In working with families, the counselor role of active manipulator may clash with American Indian concepts of being-in-becoming (noninterference).

Likewise, Latino/Hispanic culture may be said to have a more here-and-now or being-in-becoming orientation. Like their American Indian counterparts, Hispanics believe that people are born with *dignidad* (dignity) and must be given *respeto* (respect). They are born with innate worth and importance; the inner soul and spirit are more important than the body. People cannot be held accountable for their lot in life (status, roles, etc.) because they are born into this life state (Inclan, 1985). A certain degree of *fatalismo* (fatalism) is present, and life events may be viewed as inevitable (*Lo que Dios manda*, what God wills). Philosophically, it does not matter what people have in life or what position they occupy (farm laborer, public official, or attorney). Status is possessed by existing, and everyone is entitled to *respeto*.

Since this belief system deemphasizes material accomplishments as a measure of success, it is clearly at odds with Euro-American middle-class society. Although a doing-oriented family may define a family member's worth via achievement, a being orientation equates worth simply to belonging. Thus, when clients complain that someone is not an effective family member, what do they mean? This needs to be clarified by the therapist. Is it a complaint that the family member is not performing and achieving (doing), or does it mean that the person is not respectful and accommodating to family structures and values (being)?

Ho (1987) describes both Asian Americans and African Americans as operating from the doing orientation. However, it appears that "doing" in these two groups is manifested differently than in the White American lifestyle. The active dimension in Asians is related not to individual achievement, but to achievement via conformity to family values and demands. Controlling one's own feelings, impulses, desires, and needs to fulfill responsibility to the family is strongly ingrained in Asian children. The doing orientation tends to be more ritualized in the roles of and responsibilities toward members of the family. African Americans also exercise considerable control (endure the pain and suffering of racism) in the face of adversity to minimize discrimination and to maximize success.

Nature of People Dimension

Middle-class Euro-Americans generally perceive the nature of people as neutral. Environmental influences, such as conditioning, family upbringing, and socialization, are believed to be dominant forces in determining the nature of the person. People are neither good nor bad but are a product of their environment. Although several minority groups may share features of this belief with Whites, there is a qualitative and quantitative difference that may affect family structure and dynamics. For example, Asian Americans and American Indians tend to emphasize the inherent goodness of people. We have already discussed the Native American concept of noninterference, which is based on the belief that people have an innate capacity to advance and grow (self-fulfillment) and that problematic behaviors are the result of environmental influences that thwart the opportunity to develop. Goodness will always triumph over evil if the person is left alone. Likewise, Asian philosophy (Buddhism and Confucianism) believes in peoples' innate goodness and prescribes role relationships that manifest the "good way of life." Central to Asian belief is the fact that the best healing source lies within the family (Daya, 2005; Walsh & Shapiro, 2006) and that seeking help from the outside (e.g., counseling and therapy) is nonproductive and against the dictates of Asian philosophy.

Latinos may be described as holding the view that human nature is both good and bad (mixed). Concepts of *dignidad* and *respecto* undergird the belief that people are born with positive qualities. Yet some Hispanics, such as Puerto Ricans, spend a great deal of time appealing to supernatural forces so that children may be blessed with a good human nature (Inclan, 1985). Thus, a child's "badness" may be accepted as destiny, so parents may be less inclined to seek help from educators or mental health professionals for such problems. The preferred mode of help may be religious consultations and ventilation to neighbors and friends who sympathize and understand the dilemmas (change means reaching the supernatural forces).

African Americans may also be characterized as having a mixed concept of people but in general they believe, like their White counterparts, that people are basically neutral. Environmental factors have a great influence on how people develop. This orientation is consistent with African American beliefs that racism, discrimination, oppression, and other external factors create problems for the individual. Emotional disorders and antisocial acts are caused by external forces (system variables) rather than by internal, intrapsychic, psychological forces. For example, high crime rates, poverty, and the current structure of the African American family are the result of historical and current oppression of Black people. White Western concepts of genetic inferiority and pathology (African American people are born that way) hold little validity for the Black person.

GENERALIZATIONS AND STEREOTYPES: SOME CAUTIONS

White cultural values are reflected in the generic characteristics of counseling (Table 7.1 and Table 7.2). These characteristics are summarized and can be compared with the values of four racial/ethnic minority groups: American Indians,

Asian Americans, Blacks, and Hispanics. Although it is critical for therapists to have a basic understanding of the generic characteristics of counseling and psychotherapy and the culture-specific life values of different groups, overgeneralizing and stereotyping are ever-present dangers. For example, the listing of racial/ethnic minority group variables does not indicate that all persons coming from the same minority group will share all or even some of these traits. Furthermore, emerging trends such as short-term and crisis-intervention approaches and other less verbally oriented techniques differ from the generic traits listed. Yet it is highly improbable that any of us can enter a situation or encounter people without forming impressions consistent with our own experiences and values. Whether a client is dressed neatly in a suit or wears blue jeans, is a man or a woman, or is of a different race will likely affect our assumptions.

First impressions will be formed that fit our own interpretations and generalizations of human behavior. Generalizations are necessary for us; without them, we would become inefficient creatures. However, they are guidelines for our behaviors, to be tentatively applied in new situations, and they should be open to change and challenge. It is exactly at this stage that generalizations remain generalizations or become stereotypes. *Stereotypes* may be defined as rigid preconceptions we hold about *all* people who are members of a particular group, whether it be defined along racial, religious, sexual, or other lines. The belief in a perceived characteristic of the group is applied to all members without regard for individual variations. The danger of stereotypes is that they are impervious to logic or experience. All incoming information is distorted to fit our preconceived notions. For example, people who are strongly anti-Semitic will accuse Jews of being stingy and miserly and then, in the same breath, accuse them of flaunting their wealth by conspicuous spending.

The information provided in the chapter tables should act as guidelines rather than absolutes. These generalizations should serve as the background from which the figure emerges. For example, belonging to a particular group may mean sharing common values and experiences. Individuals within a group, however, also differ. The background offers a contrast for us to see individual differences more clearly. It should not submerge but rather increase the visibility of the figure. This is the figure-ground relationship that should aid us in recognizing the uniqueness of people more readily.

Implications for Clinical Practice

In general, it appears that Western forms of healing involve processes that may prove inappropriate and antagonistic to many culturally diverse groups. The mental health professional must be cognizant of the culture-bound, class-bound, and linguistic barriers that might place minority clients and their families at a disadvantage. Some suggestions to the clinician involve the following:

1. Become cognizant of the generic characteristics of counseling and psychotherapy. It is clear that mental health services arise from a particular cultural context and are imbued with assumptions and values that may not be applicable to all groups.

2. Know that we are increasingly becoming a multilingual nation and that the linguistic demands of clinical work may place minority populations at a disadvantage. Be sensitive and ready to provide or advocate for multilingual services.

3. Consider the need to provide community counseling services that reach out to the minority population. The traditional one-to-one, in-the-office delivery of services must be supplemented by methods that are more action oriented. In other words, effective multicultural counseling must involve roles and activities in the natural environment of the clients (e.g., schools, churches, neighborhoods, playgrounds) rather than just in mental health clinics.

4. Realize that the problems and concerns of many minority groups are related to systemic and external forces rather than to internal psychological problems. The effects of poverty, discrimination, prejudice, immigration stress, and so forth indicate that counselors might be most effective in aiding clients to deal with these forces rather than in pursuing self-exploration and insight approaches.

5. Know that our increasing diversity presents us with different cultural conceptions of the family. Whether groups value a lineal, collateral, or individualistic orientation has major implications for their and our definitions of the family. One definition cannot be seen as superior to another.

6. Realize that families cannot be understood apart from the cultural, social, and political dimensions of their functioning. The traditional definition of the nuclear family as consisting of heterosexual parents in a long-term marriage, raising their biological children, and having the father as sole wage earner is a statistical minority. Extended families, intermarriage, divorce, openly gay/lesbian relationships, commingling of races, single parents, and two parents working outside the home make the conventional "normal family" definition an anomaly.

7. Be careful not to overgeneralize or stereotype. Knowing general group characteristics and guidelines is different from rigidly holding on to preconceived notions. In other words, knowing that certain groups, such as African Americans and Asian Americans, may share common values and worldviews does not mean that all Asian Americans, for example, are the same. Nor does our discussion imply that Euro-American approaches to therapy are completely inapplicable to minority groups.

Culturally Appropriate Intervention Strategies

CHAPTER FOCUS QUESTIONS

1. What is communication style? How would you characterize your own style of communication? Are you a "fast talker?" Do you speak in a loud voice? Do you speak with your hands?

2. How aware are you about your nonverbal communications? Is what you say consistent with how you say it?

3. How may different styles of communication affect your interactions with culturally diverse clients? Do African Americans communicate differently? Do Asian Americans have different styles of communication?

4. What possible misunderstandings can occur when the counselor/therapist is unaware of these differences?

5. In what ways may nonverbal communications (a) trigger off racial biases and fears and (b) be a more accurate barometer of one's own beliefs and assumptions about human behavior?

6. Can different theories of counseling and psychotherapy be distinguished by their communication or helping styles? If so, how?

7. What implication do communication styles have for therapeutic intervention techniques?

Case Study: Betty

As an Asian American trainee, I always thought I could use my dual heritage and experience to help Chinese immigrants cope with issues they experienced in the United States. It was with that thought in mind that I entered my first counseling experience with a Chinese immigrant while serving an externship in New York's Chinatown. My client was Betty Lau, a 30-year-old woman, living with her parents, who presented with depression, somatic symptoms, and conflicts related to parental wishes versus her own desires. Betty felt guilty and at fault for her family's tension and

(continued)

(continued)

unspoken conflicts; both parents disapproved of her new male friend, who occupied her time on the weekends. Her father was unemployed depressed most of the time, and seemed removed from the family; her mother felt overburdened and ineffective and did little of the housework. Being the oldest sibling, Betty felt obligated to help economically and was increasingly assuming most of the household duties. She harbored strong, unexpressed resentments toward her parents and seemed to feel trapped. Betty believed that if she was a better daughter, was more understanding, and worked harder, her family problems would diminish greatly. She often wondered aloud why she could not be more grateful toward her parents, as they sacrificed much to bring the family to a new country. Over the past year, her unhappiness grew so intense that she could not sleep nor eat well. She began to lose weight rapidly and sought help at the clinic.

Betty was a very difficult client to work with. She refused to involve her parents in family counseling and made me promise not to tell them about her use of our services. She was relatively quiet in the sessions, spoke in a barely audible voice, seemed unresponsive to questions, and volunteered little in the way of information. She seldom made eye contact, a sign of her shyness or depression. Her responses were polite, but very brief, and she avoided " feeling" statements. Instead, she talked about her fatigue, loss of appetite, headaches, inability to sleep, and other physical ailments. Talking with Betty was like "pulling teeth," as our sessions were punctuated by long silences. It was clear to me that Betty was too submissive and that part of her depression was putting family interests above her own. I saw two therapeutic goals for her: (a) encourage Betty to think of her own needs first, leave her family, live alone, and not let her parents override her wishes or (b) if Betty chose to stay at home, encourage her to be more forceful in setting limits for her parents.

Betty was obviously dependent and enmeshed in the pathology of the family. She had to rid herself of her guilt feelings, learn to stand up for her own rights, and not be a doormat to the world. At 30 years of age she needed to make a life of her own, get married and start her own family. My clinical goals at that time were to have Betty be more independent, assert herself appropriately (via assertiveness training), and express her feelings openly and honestly toward her parents. In the sessions, however, Betty had considerable difficulty with role playing and talking about her feelings. Although she indirectly acknowledged harboring feelings of resentment, she could never directly bring herself to verbally express them. Role-plays and behavioral rehearsal techniques failed miserably. When I tried the "Gestalt Empty Chair" technique and encouraged her to speak to her parents in the empty chair, she seemed to "freeze up" and would not cooperate. After her third appointment with me, Betty failed to return for any future sessions.

This case illustrates nicely how a Western European approach to counseling may lead to mistaken assessment, diagnosis, and treatment of culturally diverse clients. Even though the therapist is an Asian American trainee, he or she is still trained in a Western tradition that unintentionally pathologizes cultural values. The therapist seems not to consider how culture influences help-seeking behaviors, the manner of symptom formation, and what constitutes culturally relevant helping among different diverse groups. Let us briefly analyze the case to illustrate these points.

First, it is very clear that the therapist is using Western European standards to judge normality-abnormality and desirable-undesirable goals. Part of the problem resides in the implicit assumption that individuality is healthier, that people should be their "own person," and that individuation from the family (especially at age 30) is both desirable and healthy. In an individual-centered approach, there is a tendency to locate the problem as residing in the client. Change, therefore, starts with getting the client to take responsibility for his or her own life situation. A collectivistic orientation, however, may lead to a completely different view of Betty's dilemma. This contrast in cultural values and worldviews is most explicitly stated by a Chinese counselor from China commenting on a very similar case.

> I just cannot understand why putting the family's interest before one's own is not correct or "normal" in the dominant American culture. I believe a morally responsible son or daughter has the duty to take care of his or her parents, whether it means sacrifice on his or her own part or not. . . . What is wrong with this interdependence? To me, it would be extremely selfish for the client to leave her family when the family is in such need of her. . . . In contemporary China, submergence of self for the good of the family, community, and country is still valued, and individualism condemned. Western mental health practice could fail should we adopt American counseling theories and skills without considerable alteration. . . . Although I do not think the client has a significant psychological problem, I do believe that the parents have to become more sensitive to their daughter's needs. It is not very nice and considerate for the parents to think only of themselves at the cost of their daughter's well-being. If I were the counselor of this client, I would do everything in my power to try to help change the parents, rather than the client. I feel strongly that it is the selfish person who needs to change, not the selfless person. (Zhang, 1994, pp. 79–80)

Second, culture has been found to influence help-seeking behaviors and how psychological distress is expressed in counseling. It is entirely possible that Betty's reluctance to talk about her feelings toward her parents and her focus on somatic complaints is a manifestation of cultural dynamics. Restraint of strong feelings as a cultural dictate in Asian cultures is widely acknowledged, and an unenlightened therapist might perceive the client as repressed, inhibited, or avoiding feelings. The therapist might unwittingly not realize that asking Betty to express resentments toward her parents might violate a cultural dictate of filial piety. Further, among traditional groups, going for psychological help may bring shame and disgrace to the family, and there are strong cultural sanctions against disclosure of family problems for fear that it would bring dishonor to everyone. Studies reveal that Asians and Asian Americans tend to underutilize counseling services, especially those associated with psychiatric problems. When Chinese do seek help, they are likely to present with more severe psychological disorders and with a preponderance of somatic complaints. Some suggest that the former finding is related to a Chinese disinclination to seek psychiatric help unless it is a last resort to overwhelming problems. As a result, the disorders that are presented are more severe.

These factors may account for Betty's reluctance to involve the parents in counseling, her concern that they not be told, and her use of somatic complaints as an entree to discussing her problems. For Betty and many Asian clients, physical complaints are viewed as less stigmatic than psychological ones and are a condition more acceptable to seek help for.

Third, the actual process of counseling and psychotherapy may be antagonistic to the values held by culturally diverse clients. Betty's perceived resistance to counseling (short but polite responses, "unresponsiveness to questions," "avoidance of feeling statements," and lack of eye contact) and the therapist's use of potentially inappropriate counseling techniques (getting client to express feelings, role-plays, and behavioral rehearsal) may prove to be an oppressive and humiliating experience for the client. The therapist seems not to be aware of differences in communication style influenced by culture. For example, Chinese culture values restraint of strong feelings, and eye contact is avoided in the presence of higher-status individuals. The therapist may be prone to interpret avoidance of eye contact and speaking in a softer voice as signs of "depression" or "unassertiveness." Further, we have stated that in many cultures, similar to the Chinese, subtlety and indirectness in discussing delicate matters are highly valued attributes of communication. Discussion of personal and private matters is done indirectly rather than directly. In this case, Betty may be communicating her psychological and familial conflicts by talking about somatic complaints as a means to an end. Many Asian helpers are aware of this fact and would allow the client to "save face" by appearing to speak about physical/medical problems, but in actuality be discussing family matters. The relationship of communication style to helping style is intimately bound to one another. The counselor's use of role-plays, behavioral rehearsal, and the confrontive "Gestalt Empty Chair" technique may be placing clients in an awkward position because it asks them to violate basic cultural values.

The case of Betty illustrates the major focus of this chapter: understanding the need for culturally appropriate intervention strategies. Some 40 years ago, the importance of cultural flexibility in counseling and the need to approach counseling with culture-specific techniques was voiced by Draguns (1976):

> Be prepared to adapt your techniques (e.g., general activity level, mode of verbal intervention, content of remarks, tone of voice) to the cultural background of the client; communicate acceptance of and respect for the client in terms that are intelligible and meaningful within his or her cultural frame of reference; and be open to the possibility of more direct intervention in the life of the client than the traditional ethos of the counseling profession would dictate or permit. (p. 4)

It is ironic that this statement continues to hold and that despite the large accumulation of research in support of Draguns's conclusions, the profession of counseling and psychotherapy continues to operate from a universal perspective.

COMMUNICATION STYLES

Effective therapy depends on the therapist and the client being able to send and receive both verbal and nonverbal messages accurately and appropriately. It requires that the therapists not only *send* messages (make themselves understood) but also *receive* messages (attend to clients). The definition for effective therapy also includes *verbal* (content of what is said) and *nonverbal* (how something is said) elements. Most therapists seem more concerned with the *accuracy* of communication (getting to the heart of the matter) than with whether the communication is *appropriate*. The case of Betty illustrates how traditional Asian culture prizes a person's subtlety and indirectness in communication. The direct and confrontational techniques in therapy may be perceived by traditional Asian or Native American clients as lacking in respect for the client, a crude and rude form of communication, and a reflection of insensitivity (E. Duran, 2006; Garrett & Portman, 2011; B. S. K. Kim, 2011). In most cases, therapists have been trained to tune in to the content of what is said rather than to how something is said.

When we refer to communication style, we are addressing those factors that go beyond the content of what is said. Some communication specialists believe that only 30% to 40% of what is communicated conversationally is verbal (Condon & Yousef, 1975; Ramsey & Birk, 1983; Singelis, 1994). What people say and do is usually qualified by other things that they say and do. A gesture, tone, inflection, posture, or degree of eye contact may enhance or negate the content of a message. Communication styles have a tremendous impact on our face-to-face encounters with others. Whether our conversation proceeds with fits or starts, whether we interrupt one another continually or proceed smoothly, the topics we prefer to discuss or avoid, the depth of our involvement, the forms of interaction (e.g., ritual, repartee, argumentative, persuasive), and the channel we use to communicate (verbal-nonverbal versus nonverbal-verbal) are all aspects of communication style. Some refer to these factors as the *social rhythms* that underlie all our speech and actions. Communication styles are strongly correlated with race, culture, and ethnicity (Garrett & Portman, 2011; B. S. K. Kim, 2011). Gender has also been found to be a powerful determinant of communication style (Pearson, 1985; Robinson & Howard-Hamilton, 2000).

> When we refer to communication style, we are addressing those factors that go beyond the content of what is said. Some communication specialists believe that only 30% to 40% of what is communicated conversationally is verbal.

Reared in a Euro-American middle-class society, mental health professionals may assume that certain behaviors or rules of speaking are universal and possess the same meaning. This may create major problems for therapists and their culturally distinct clients. Since differences in communication style are most strongly manifested in nonverbal communication, this chapter concentrates on those aspects of communication that transcend the written or spoken word. First, we explore how race/culture may influence several areas of nonverbal behavior: (a) proxemics, (b) kinesics, (c) paralanguage, and (d) high-low context communication. Second, we briefly discuss the function and importance of nonverbal behavior as it relates to stereotypes and preconceived notions that we may have of diverse groups. Last, we propose a basic thesis that various racial minorities, such as Asian Americans, American Indians, African Americans, and Latino/Hispanic Americans, possess unique communication styles that may have major implications for mental health practice.

Nonverbal Communication

Although language, class, and cultural factors all interact to create problems in communication between the culturally diverse client and the therapist, an oft neglected area is nonverbal behavior (Duran, 2006; Singelis, 1994). What people say can be either enhanced or negated by their nonverbals. When a man raises his voice, tightens his facial muscles, pounds the table violently, and proclaims, "Goddamn it, I'm not angry!" he is clearly contradicting the content of the communication. If we all share the same cultural and social upbringing, we may all arrive at the same conclusion. Interpreting nonverbals, however, is difficult for several reasons. First, the same nonverbal behavior on the part of an American Indian client may mean something quite different than if it were made by a White person (Duran, 2006; Garrett & Portman, 2011). Second, nonverbals often occur outside our levels of awareness but influence our evaluations and behaviors. It is important to note that our discussion of nonverbal codes will not include all the possible areas, like olfaction (taste and smell), tactile cues, and artifactual communication (clothing, hairstyle, display of material things, etc.).

Proxemics

The study of *proxemics* refers to perception and use of personal and interpersonal space. Clear norms exist concerning the use of physical distance in social interactions. E. T. Hall (1969) identified four interpersonal distance zones characteristic of U.S. culture: intimate, from contact to 18 in.; personal, from 1.5 ft to 4 ft; social, from 4 ft to 12 ft; and public (lectures and speeches), greater than 12 ft.

In this society, individuals seem to grow more uncomfortable when others stand too close rather than too far away. This range of feelings and reactions associated with a violation of personal space includes flight, withdrawal, anger, and conflict (Pearson, 1985). On the other hand, we tend to allow closer proximity or to move closer to people whom we like or feel interpersonal attraction toward. Some evidence exists that personal space can be reframed in terms of dominance and status. Those with greater status, prestige, and power may occupy more space (larger homes, cars, or offices). However, different cultures dictate different distances in personal space. For Latin Americans, Africans, Black Americans, Indonesians, Arabs, South Americans, and French, conversing with a person dictates a much closer stance than is normally comfortable for Euro-Americans (Jensen, 1985; Nydell, 1996). A Latin American client's closeness may cause the therapist to back away. The client may interpret the therapist's behavior as indicative of aloofness, coldness, or a desire not to communicate. In some cross-cultural encounters, it may even be perceived as a sign of haughtiness and superiority. On the other hand, the therapist may misinterpret the client's behavior as an attempt to become inappropriately intimate, a sign of pushiness or aggressiveness. Both the therapist and the culturally different client may benefit from understanding that their reactions and behaviors are attempts to create the spatial dimension to which they are culturally conditioned.

Research on proxemics leads to the inevitable conclusion that conversational distances are a function of the racial and cultural background of the conversant (Mindess, 1999; Susman & Rosenfeld, 1982; Wolfgang, 1985). The factor of personal space has major implications for how furniture is arranged, where the seats are located, where you seat the client, and how far you sit from him or her. Latin Americans, for example, may not feel comfortable speaking to a person behind a desk. Euro-Americans, however, like to keep a desk between themselves and others. Some Eskimos may actually prefer to sit side by side rather than across from one another when talking about intimate aspects of their lives.

Kinesics

Whereas *proxemics* refers to personal space, *kinesics* is the term used to refer to bodily movements. It includes such things as facial expression, posture, characteristics of movement, gestures, and eye contact. Again, kinesics appears to be culturally conditioned (Mindess, 1999). Much of our counseling assessments are based upon expressions on people's faces (Pearson, 1985). We assume that facial cues express emotions and demonstrate the degree of responsiveness or involvement of the individual. For example, smiling is a type of expression in our society that is believed to indicate liking or positive affect. People attribute greater positive characteristics to others who smile; they are intelligent, have a good personality, and are pleasant (Singelis, 1994). However, when Japanese smile and laugh, it does not necessarily mean happiness but may convey other meanings (e.g., embarrassment, discomfort, shyness). Such nonverbal misinterpretations also fueled many of the conflicts in Los Angeles directly after the Rodney King verdict, when many African Americans and Korean grocery store owners became at odds with one another (Yoon, 1997). African Americans confronted their Korean American counterparts about exploitation of Black neighborhoods. African Americans became incensed when many Korean American store owners had a constant smile on their faces. They interpreted the facial expression as arrogance, taunting, and lack of compassion for the concerns of Blacks. Little did they realize that a smile in this situation more rightly indicated extreme embarrassment and apprehension.

On the other hand, some Asians believe that smiling may suggest weakness. Among some Japanese and Chinese, restraint of strong feelings (anger, irritation, sadness, and love or happiness) is considered to be a sign of maturity and wisdom. Children learn that outward emotional expressions (facial expressions, body movements, and verbal content) are discouraged except for extreme situations. Unenlightened therapists may assume that their Asian American client is lacking in feelings or is out of touch with them. More likely, the lack of facial expressions may be the basis of stereotypes, such as the statement that Asians are "inscrutable," "sneaky," "deceptive," and "backstabbing."

A number of gestures and bodily movements have been found to have different meanings when the cultural context is considered (LaBarre, 1985). In the Sung Dynasty in China, sticking out the tongue was a gesture of mock terror and meant as ridicule; to the Ovimbundu of Africa, it means "You're a fool" (when coupled with bending the head forward); a protruding tongue in the Mayan statues of gods signifies wisdom; and in our own culture, it is generally considered to be a juvenile, quasi-obscene gesture of defiance, mockery, or contempt.

Head movements also have different meanings (Eakins & Eakins, 1985; Jensen, 1985). An educated Englishman may consider the lifting of the chin when conversing as a poised and polite gesture, but to Euro-Americans it may connote snobbery and arrogance ("turning up one's nose"). Whereas we shake our head from side to side to indicate "no," Mayan tribe members say "no" by jerking the head to the right. In Sri Lanka, one signals agreement by moving the head from side to side like a metronome (Singelis, 1994).

Most Euro-Americans perceive squatting (often done by children) as improper and childish. In other parts of the world, people have learned to rest by taking a squatting position. On the other hand, when we put our feet up on a desk, it is believed to signify a relaxed and informal attitude. Yet Latin Americans and Asians may perceive it as rudeness and arrogance, especially if the bottoms of the feet are shown to them.

Shaking hands is another gesture that varies from culture to culture and may have strong cultural/historical significance. Latin Americans tend to shake hands more vigorously, frequently, and for a longer period of time. Interestingly, most cultures use the right hand when shaking. Since most of the population of the world is right-handed, this may not be surprising. However, some researchers believe that shaking with the right hand may be a symbolic act of peace, as in older times it was the right hand that generally held the weapons. In some Muslim and Asian countries, touching anyone with the left hand may be considered an obscenity (the left hand aids in the process of elimination and is "unclean," whereas the right one is used for the intake of food and is "clean"). Offering something with the left hand to a Muslim may be an insult of the most serious type.

Eye contact is, perhaps, the nonverbal behavior most likely to be addressed by mental health providers. It is not unusual for us to hear someone say, "Notice that the husband avoided eye contact with the wife," or "Notice how the client averted his eyes when. . . ." Behind these observations is the belief that eye contact or lack of eye contact has diagnostic significance. We would agree with that premise but in most cases, therapists attribute negative traits to the avoidance of eye contact: shy, unassertive, sneaky, or depressed.

This lack of understanding has been played out in many different situations when Black-White interactions have occurred. In many cases it is not necessary for Blacks to look one another in the eye at all times to communicate (E. J. Smith, 1981). An African American may be actively involved in doing other things when engaged in a conversation. Many White therapists are prone to view the African American client as being sullen, resistant, or uncooperative. E. J. Smith (1981, p. 155) provides an excellent example of such a clash in communication styles:

For instance, one Black female student was sent to the office by her gymnasium teacher because the student was said to display insolent behavior. When the student was asked to give her version of the incident, she replied, "Mrs. X asked all of us to come over to the side of the pool so that she could show us how to do the backstroke. I went over with the rest of the girls. Then Mrs. X started yelling at me and said I wasn't paying attention to her because I wasn't looking directly at her. I told her I was paying attention to her (throughout the conversation, the student kept her head down, avoiding the principal's eyes), and then she said that she wanted me to face her and look her squarely in the eye like the rest of the girls [who were all White]. So I did. The next thing I knew she was telling me to get out of the pool, that she didn't like the way I was looking at her. So that's why I'm here."

As this example illustrates, Black styles of communication not only may be different from that of their White counterparts but also may lead to misinterpretations. Many Blacks do not nod their heads or say "uh-huh" to indicate they are listening (E. T. Hall, 1976; Kochman, 1981; E. J. Smith, 1981). Going through the motions of looking at the person and nodding the head is not necessary for many African Americans to indicate that they are listening (E. T. Hall, 1974, 1976).

Statistics indicate that when White U.S. Americans listen to a speaker, they make eye contact with the speaker about 80% of the time. When speaking to others, however, they tend to look away (avoid eye contact) about 50% of the time. This is in marked contrast to many African Americans, who make greater eye contact when speaking and make infrequent eye contact when listening!

Paralanguage

The term *paralanguage* is used to refer to other vocal cues that individuals use to communicate. For example, loudness of voice, pauses, silences, hesitations, rate of speech, inflections, and the like all fall into this category. Paralanguage is very likely to be manifested forcefully in conversation conventions such as how we greet and address others and take turns in speaking. It can communicate a variety of different features about a person, such as age, gender, and emotional responses, as well as the race and sex of the speaker (Banks & Banks, 1993; Lass, Mertz, & Kimmel, 1978; Nydell, 1996).

There are complex rules regarding when to speak or to yield to another person. For example, U.S. Americans frequently feel uncomfortable with a pause or silent stretch in the conversation, feeling obligated to fill it in with more talk. Silence is not always a sign for the listener to take up the conversation. While it may be viewed negatively by many, other cultures interpret the use of silence differently. The British and Arabs use silence for privacy, while the Russians, French, and Spanish read it as agreement among the parties (E. T. Hall, 1969, 1976). In Asian culture, silence is traditionally a sign of respect for elders.

Paralanguage consists of vocal cues that individuals use to communicate, such as loudness of voice, pauses, silences, hesitations, rate of speech, and inflection.

Furthermore, silence by many Chinese and Japanese is not a floor-yielding signal inviting others to pick up the conversation. Rather, it may indicate a desire to continue speaking after making a particular point. Often silence is a sign of politeness and respect rather than a lack of desire to continue speaking.

The amount of verbal expressiveness in the United States, relative to other cultures, is quite high. Most Euro-Americans encourage their children to enter freely into conversations, and teachers encourage students to ask many questions and state their thoughts and opinions. This has led many from other countries to observe that Euro-American youngsters are brash, immodest, rude, and disrespectful (Irvine & York, 1995; Jensen, 1985). Likewise, teachers of minority children may see reticence in speaking out as a sign of ignorance, lack of motivation, or ineffective teaching (Banks & Banks, 1993), when in reality the students may be showing proper respect (to ask questions is disrespectful because it implies that the teacher was unclear). American Indians, for example, have been taught that to speak out, ask questions, or even raise one's hand in class is immodest.

A mental health professional who is uncomfortable with silence or who misinterprets it may fill in the conversation and prevent the client from elaborating further. An even greater danger is to impute incorrect motives to the minority client's silence. One can readily see how therapy, which emphasizes talking, may place many minorities at a disadvantage.

Volume and intensity of speech in conversation are also influenced by cultural values. The overall loudness of speech displayed by many Euro-American visitors to foreign countries has earned them the reputation of being boisterous and shameless. In Asian countries, people tend to speak more softly and would interpret the loud volume of a U.S. visitor to be aggressiveness, loss of self-control, or anger. When compared to Arabs, however, people in the United States are soft-spoken. Many Arabs like to be bathed in sound, and the volumes of their radios, DVDs, and televisions are quite loud. In some countries where such entertainment units are not plentiful, it is considered a polite and thoughtful act to allow neighbors to hear by keeping the volume high. We in the United States would view such behavior as being a thoughtless invasion of privacy.

A therapist or counselor working with clients would be well advised to be aware of possible cultural misinterpretations as a function of speech volume. Speaking loudly may not indicate anger and hostility, and speaking in a soft voice may not be a sign of weakness, shyness, or depression.

The directness of a conversation or the degree of frankness also varies considerably among various cultural groups. Observing the English in their parliamentary debates will drive this point home. The long heritage of open, direct, and frank confrontation leads to heckling of public speakers and quite blunt and sharp exchanges. Britons believe and feel that these are acceptable styles and may take no offense at being the object of such exchanges. However, U.S. citizens feel that such exchanges are impolite, abrasive, and irrational. Relative to Asians, Euro-Americans are seen as being too blunt and frank. Great care is taken by many Asians not to hurt the feelings of or embarrass the other person. As a result, use of euphemisms and ambiguity is the norm.

REFLECTION AND DISCUSSION QUESTIONS

1. How may proxemics affect conversation distances and the use of personal space with culturally diverse clients in therapy? Are you aware of your conversation distance with others around you?
2. How does kinesics affect your communication style with others? When conversing with others, how aware are you of using your hands to talk, making eye contact, smiling or frowning, and other bodily movements? How aware are you of how others converse? Why is awareness of kinesics important in therapy?
3. With respect to paralanguage, are you loud or soft-spoken? Do you speak quickly or slowly? When speaking to a person and a pause in the conversation occurs, are you comfortable or uncomfortable? Does silence bother you in counseling? How do you define a silent period: one second, two seconds, three seconds, or a minute? How may differences in paralanguage play out in the counseling session?

Since many minority groups may value indirectness, the U.S. emphasis on "getting to the point" and "not beating around the bush" may alienate others. Asian Americans, American Indians, and some Latino/Hispanic Americans may see this behavior as immature, rude, and lacking in finesse. On the other hand, clients from different cultures may be negatively labeled as evasive and afraid to confront the problem.

High-Low Context Communication

Edward T. Hall, author of such classics as *The Silent Language* (1959) and *The Hidden Dimension* (1969), is a well-known anthropologist who has proposed the concept of high-low context cultures (E. T. Hall, 1976). A high-context (HC) communication or message is one that is anchored in the physical context (situation) or internalized in the person. Less reliance is placed on the explicit code or message content. An HC communication relies heavily on nonverbals and the group identification/understanding shared by those communicating. For example, a normal-stressed "no" by a U.S. American may be interpreted by an Arab as "yes." A real negation in Arab culture would be stressed much more emphatically. A prime example of the contextual dimension in understanding communication is demonstrated in the following example:

> I was asked to consult with a hospital that was having a great deal of difficulty with their Filipino nurses. The hospital had a number of them on its staff, and the medical director was concerned about their competence in understanding and following directions from doctors. As luck would have it, when I came to the hospital, I was immediately confronted with a situation that threatened to blow up. Dr. K., a Euro-American physician, had brought charges against a Filipino American nurse for incompetence. He had observed her incorrectly using and monitoring life support systems on a critically ill patient. He relates

how he entered the patient's room and told the nurse that she was incorrectly using the equipment and that the patient could die if she didn't do it right. Dr. K. states that he spent some 10 minutes explaining how the equipment should be attached and used. Upon finishing his explanation, he asked the nurse if she understood. The Filipino nurse nodded her head slightly and hesitantly said, "Yes, yes, Doctor." Later that evening, Dr. K. observed the same nurse continuing to use the equipment incorrectly; he reported her to the head nurse and asked for her immediate dismissal. While it is possible that the nurse was not competent, further investigation revealed strong cultural forces affecting the hospital work situation. What the medical administration failed to understand was the cultural context of the situation. In the Philippines, it is considered impolite to say "no" in a number of situations. In this case, for the nurse to say "no" to the doctor (a respected figure of high status) when asked whether she understood would have implied that Dr. K. was a poor teacher. This would be considered insulting and impolite. Thus, the only option the Filipino nurse felt open to her was to tell the doctor "yes."

In Filipino culture, a mild, hesitant "yes" is interpreted by those who understand as a "no" or a polite refusal. In traditional Asian society, many interactions are understandable only in light of high-context cues and situations. For example, to extend an invitation only once for dinner would be considered an affront because it implies that you are not sincere. One must extend an invitation several times, encouraging the invitee to accept. Arabs may also refuse an offer of food several times before giving in. However, most Euro-Americans believe that a host's offer can be politely refused with just a "no, thank you."

If we pay attention to only the explicit coded part of the message, we are likely to misunderstand the communication. According to E. T. Hall (1976), low-context (LC) cultures place a greater reliance on the verbal part of the message. In addition, LC cultures have been associated with being more opportunistic, more individual oriented than group oriented, and as emphasizing rules of law and procedure.

It appears that the United States is an LC culture (although it is still higher than the Swiss, Germans, and Scandinavians in the amount of context required). China, perhaps, represents the other end of the continuum; its complex culture relies heavily on context. Asian Americans, African Americans, Hispanics, American Indians, and other minority groups in the United States also emphasize HC cues.

In contrast to LC communication, HC is faster, as well as more economical, efficient, and satisfying. Because it is so bound to the culture, it is slow to change and tends to be cohesive and unifying. LC communication does not unify but changes rapidly and easily.

Twins who have grown up together can and do communicate more economically (HC) than do two lawyers during a trial (LC). B. Bernstein's (1964) classic work in language analysis refers to restricted codes (HC) and elaborated codes (LC). Restricted codes are observed in families where words and sentences collapse and are shortened without loss of meaning. However, elaborated codes, where many words are used to communicate the same content, are seen in classrooms, diplomacy, and law.

African American culture has been described as HC. For example, it is clear that many Blacks require fewer words than their White counterparts to communicate the same content (Irvine & York, 1995; Jenkins, 1982; Stanback & Pearce, 1985; Weber, 1985). An African American male who enters a room and spots an attractive woman may stoop slightly in her direction, smile, and tap the table twice while vocalizing a long drawn out "uh huh." What he has communicated would require many words from his White brother! The fact that African Americans may communicate more by HC cues has led many to characterize them as nonverbal, inarticulate, unintelligent, and so forth.

SOCIOPOLITICAL FACETS OF NONVERBAL COMMUNICATION

There is a common saying among African Americans: "If you really want to know what White folks are thinking and feeling, don't listen to what they say, but how they say it." In most cases, such a statement refers to the biases, stereotypes, and racist attitudes that Whites are believed to possess but consciously or unconsciously conceal.

Rightly or wrongly, many minority individuals through years of personal experience operate from three assumptions: The first assumption is that all Whites in this society are racist. Through their own cultural conditioning, they have been socialized into a culture that espouses the superiority of White culture over all others (J. M. Jones, 1997; Ridley, 2005; D. W. Sue, 2003). The second assumption is that most Whites find such a concept disturbing and will go to great lengths to deny that they are racist or biased. Some of this is done deliberately and with awareness, but in most cases one's racism is largely unconscious (Todd & Abrams, 2011). The last of these assumptions is that nonverbal behaviors are more accurate reflections of what a White person is thinking or feeling than is what they say.

There is considerable evidence to suggest that these three assumptions held by various racial/ethnic minorities are indeed accurate (McIntosh, 1989; Ridley, 2006; D. W. Sue, 2010a). Counselors and mental health practitioners need to be very cognizant of nonverbal cues from a number of different perspectives. In the last section we discussed how nonverbal behavior is culture bound and how the counselor or therapist cannot make universal interpretations about it. Likewise, nonverbal cues are important because they often (a) unconsciously reflect our biases and (b) trigger off stereotypes we have of other people.

Nonverbals as Reflections of Bias

Some time ago, a TV program called *Candid Camera* was the rage in the United States. It operated from a unique premise, which involved creating very unusual situations for naive subjects who were then filmed as they reacted to them. One of these experiments involved interviewing housewives about their attitudes toward African American, Latino/Hispanic, and White teenagers. The intent was to select a group of women who by all standards appeared sincere in their beliefs that Blacks and Latinos were no more prone to violence than were their White counterparts. Unknown to them, they were filmed by a hidden camera as they left their homes to go shopping at the local supermarket.

The creator of the program had secretly arranged for an African American, a Latino, and a White youngster (dressed casually but nearly identically) to pass these women on the street. The experiment was counterbalanced; that is, the race of the youngster was randomly assigned as to which would approach the shopper first. What occurred was a powerful statement on unconscious racist attitudes and beliefs.

All the youngsters had been instructed to pass the shopper on the purse side of the street. If the woman was holding the purse in her right hand, the youngster would approach and pass on her right. If the purse was held with the left hand, the youngster would pass on her left. Studies of the film revealed consistent outcomes. Many women, when approached by the Black or the Latino youngster (approximately 15 feet away), would casually switch the purse from one arm to the other! This occurred infrequently with the White subject. Why?

The answer appears quite obvious to us. The women subjects who switched their purses were operating from biases, stereotypes, and preconceived notions about what minority youngsters are like: They are prone to crime, more likely to snatch a purse or rob, more likely to be juvenile delinquents, and more likely to engage in violence (Dovidio & Gaertner, 2000). The disturbing part of this experiment was that the selected subjects were, by all measures, sincere individuals who on a conscious level denied harboring racist attitudes or beliefs. They were not liars, nor were they deliberately deceiving the interviewer. They were normal, everyday people. They honestly believed that they did not possess these biases, yet when tested, their nonverbal behavior (purse switching) gave them away.

The power of nonverbal communication is that it tends to be least under conscious control. Studies support the conclusion that nonverbal cues operate primarily on an unawareness level (DePaulo, 1992; Singelis, 1994), that they tend to be more spontaneous and more difficult to censor or falsify (Mehrabian, 1972), and that they are more trusted than words. In our society, we have learned to use words (spoken or written) to mask or conceal our true thoughts and feelings. Note how our politicians and lawyers are able to address an issue without revealing much of what they think or believe.

Nonverbal behavior provides clues to conscious deceptions or unconscious bias (Utsey, Gernat, & Hammar, 2005). There is evidence that the accuracy of nonverbal communication varies with the part of the body used: Facial expression is more controllable than the hands, followed by the legs and the rest of the body (Hansen, Stevic, & Warner, 1982). The implications for multicultural counseling are obvious. A therapist who has not adequately dealt with his or her own biases and racist attitudes may unwittingly communicate them to a culturally different client. If counselors are unaware of their own biases, their nonverbals are most likely to reveal their true feelings. Studies suggest that women and minorities are better readers of nonverbal cues than are White males (E. T. Hall, 1976; Jenkins, 1982; Pearson, 1985; Weber, 1985). Much of this may be due to their HC orientation, but another reason may be *survival*. For an African American person to survive in a predominantly White society, he or she has to rely on nonverbal cues more often than verbal ones.

One of our male African American colleagues gives the example of how he must constantly be vigilant when traveling in an unknown part of the country. Just to stop at a roadside restaurant may be dangerous to his physical well-being. As a result, when entering a diner, he is quick to observe not only the reactions of the staff (waiter/waitress, cashier, cook, etc.) to his entrance but also the reactions of the patrons as well. Do they stare at him? What type of facial expressions do they have? Do they fall silent? Does he get served immediately, or is there an inordinate delay? These nonverbal cues reveal much about the environment around him. He may choose to be himself or to play the role of a "humble" Black person who leaves quickly if the situation poses danger.

Interestingly, this very same colleague talks about tuning in to nonverbal cues as a means of *psychological survival*. He believes it is important for minorities to accurately read where people are coming from in order to prevent invalidation of the self. For example, a minority person driving through an unfamiliar part of the country may find himself or herself forced to stay at a motel overnight. Seeing a vacancy light flashing, the person may stop and knock on the manager's door. Upon opening the door and seeing the Black person, the White manager may show hesitation, stumble around in his or her verbalizations, and then apologize for having forgotten to turn off the vacancy light. The Black person is faced with the dilemma of deciding whether the White manager was telling the truth or is simply not willing to rent to a Black person.

Some of you might ask, "Why is it important for you to know? Why don't you simply find someplace else? After all, would you stay at a place where you were unwelcome?" Finding another place to stay might not be as important as the psychological well-being of the minority person. Racial/ethnic minorities have encountered too many situations in which double messages are given to them (microaggressions). For the African American to accept the simple statement, "I forgot to turn off the vacancy light," may be to deny one's own true feelings at being the victim of discrimination. This is especially true when the nonverbals (facial expression, anxiety in voice, and stammering) may reveal other reasons.

Too often, culturally different individuals are placed in situations where they are asked to deny their true feelings in order to perpetuate *White deception*. Statements that minorities are oversensitive (paranoid?) may represent a form of denial. When a minority colleague makes a statement such as, "I get a strange feeling from John; I feel some bias against minorities coming out," White colleagues, friends, and others are sometimes too quick to dismiss it with statements like, "You're being oversensitive." Perhaps a better approach would be to say, "What makes you feel that way?" rather than to negate or invalidate what might be an accurate appraisal of nonverbal communication.

Thus, it is clear that racial/ethnic minorities are very tuned in to nonverbals. For the therapist who has not adequately dealt with his or her own racism, the minority client will be quick to assess such biases. In many cases, the minority client may believe that the biases are too great to be overcome and will simply not continue in therapy. This is despite the good intentions of the White counselor/therapist who is not in touch with his or her own biases and assumptions about human behavior.

> One of the major barriers to effective understanding is the common assumption that different cultural groups operate according to identical speech and communication conventions.

Nonverbals as Triggers to Biases and Fears

Often people assume that being an effective multicultural therapist is a straightforward process that involves the acquisition of knowledge about the various racial/ethnic groups. If we know that Asian Americans and African Americans have different patterns of eye contact and if we know that these patterns signify different things, then we should be able to eliminate biases and stereotypes that we possess. Were it so easy, we might have eradicated racism years ago. Although increasing our knowledge base about the lifestyles and experiences of minority groups is important, it is not a sufficient condition in itself. Our racist attitudes, beliefs, and feelings are deeply ingrained in our total being. Through years of conditioning they have acquired a strong irrational base, replete with emotional symbolism about each particular minority. Simply opening a text and reading about African Americans and Latinos/Hispanics will not deal with our deep-seated fears and biases.

One of the major barriers to effective understanding is the common assumption that different cultural groups operate according to identical speech and communication conventions. In the United States, it is often assumed that distinctive racial, cultural, and linguistic features are deviant, inferior, or embarrassing (Kochman, 1981; Singelis, 1994; Stanback & Pearce, 1985). These value judgments then become tinged with beliefs that we hold about Black people: racial inferiority, being prone to violence and crime, quick to anger, and a threat to White folks (Irvine & York, 1995; Weber, 1985). The communication style of Black people (manifested in nonverbals) can often trigger off these fears. We submit that the situation presented at the beginning of the chapter represents just such an example.

African American styles of communication are often high-key, animated, heated, interpersonal, and confrontational. Many emotions, affects, and feelings are generated (E. T. Hall, 1976; Shade & New, 1993; Weber, 1985). In a debate, African Americans tend to act as advocates of a position, and ideas are to be tested in the crucible of argument (Banks & Banks, 1993; Kochman, 1981). White middle-class styles, however, are characterized as being detached and objective, impersonal and nonchallenging. The person acts not as an *advocate* of the idea but as a *spokesperson* (truth resides in the idea). A discussion of issues should be devoid of affect because emotion and reason work against one another. One should talk things out in a logical fashion without getting personally involved. African Americans characterize their own style of communication as indicating that the person is sincere and honest, whereas Euro-Americans consider their own style to be reasoned and objective (Irvine & York, 1995). Many African Americans readily admit that they operate from a point of view and, as mentioned previously, are disinclined to believe that White folks do not. E. J. Smith (1981, p. 154) aptly describes the Black orientation in the following passage:

When one Black person talks privately with another, he or she might say: "Look, we don't have to jive each other or be like White folks; let's be

honest with one another." These statements reflect the familiar Black saying that "talk is cheap," that actions speak louder than words, and that
Whites beguile each other with words. . . . In contrast, the White mind
symbolizes to many Black people deceit, verbal chicanery, and sterile
intellectivity. For example, after long discourse with a White person, a
Black individual might say: "I've heard what you've said, but what do you
really mean?"

Although African Americans may misinterpret White communication styles,
it is more likely that Whites will misinterpret Black styles. The direction of the
misunderstanding is generally linked to the activating of unconscious triggers or
buttons about racist stereotypes and fears they harbor. As we have repeatedly
emphasized, one of the dominant stereotypes of African Americans in our society
is that of the hostile, angry, prone-to-violence Black male. The more animated
and affective communication style, closer conversing distance, prolonged eye contact when speaking, greater bodily movements, and tendency to test ideas in a con-
frontational/argumentative format lead many Whites to believe that their lives are
in danger. It is not unusual for White mental health practitioners to describe their
African Americans clients as being hostile and angry. We have also observed that
some White trainees who work with Black clients respond nonverbally in such a
manner as to indicate anxiety, discomfort, or fear (e.g., leaning away from their
African American clients, tipping their chairs back, crossing their legs or arms).
These are nonverbal distancing moves that may reflect the unconscious stereotypes that they hold of Black Americans. Although we would entertain the possibility that a Black client is angry, most occasions we have observed do not justify
such a descriptor.

It appears that many Euro-Americans operate from the assumption that when
an argument ensues, it may lead to a ventilation of anger with the outbreak of a
subsequent fight. What many Whites fail to realize is that African Americans distinguish between an argument used to debate a difference of opinion and one that
ventilates anger and hostility (DePaulo, 1992; Irvine & York, 1995; Kochman,
1981; Shade & New, 1993). In the former, the affect indicates sincerity and seri-
ousness; there is a positive attitude toward the material; and the validity of ideas is
challenged. In the latter, the affect is more passionate than sincere; there is a negative attitude toward the opponent; and the opponent is abused.

To understand African American styles of communication and to relate
adequately to Black communication would require much study in the origins,
functions, and manifestations of Black language (Jenkins, 1982). Weber (1985)
believes that the historical and philosophical foundations of Black language
have led to several verbal styles among Blacks. *Rapping* (not the White usage,
rap session) was originally a dialogue between a man and a woman in which
the intent was to win over the admiration of the woman. Imaginary statements, rhythmic speech, and creativity are aimed at getting the woman interested in hearing more of the rap. It has been likened to a mating call, an
introduction of the male to the female, and a ritual expected by some African
American women.

Another style of verbal banter is called *woofing*, which is an exchange of threats and challenges to fight. It may have derived from what African Americans refer to as *playing the dozens*, which is considered by many Blacks to be the highest form of verbal warfare and impromptu speaking (Kochman, 1981; Jenkins, 1982; Weber, 1985). To the outsider, it may appear cruel, harsh, and provocative. Yet to many in the Black community, it has historical and functional meanings.

The term *dozens* was used by slave owners to refer to Black people with disabilities. Because they were considered damaged goods, disabled Black people would often be sold at a discount rate with eleven (one dozen) other damaged slaves (Weber, 1985). It was primarily a selling ploy in which *dozens* referred to the negative physical features. Often played in jest, the game requires an audience to act as judge and jury over the originality, creativity, and humor of the combatants. Here are three examples:

Say man, your girlfriend so ugly, she had to sneak up on a glass to get a drink of water. . . . Man, you so ugly, yo mamma had to put a sheet over your head so sleep could sneak up on you. (Weber, 1985, p. 248)

A: Eat shit.
B: What should I do with your bones?
A: Build a cage for your mother.
B: At least I got one.
A: She is the least. (Labov, 1972, p. 321)

A: Got a match?
B: Yeah, my ass and your face or my farts and your breath. (Kochman, 1981, p. 54)

Woofing and playing the dozens seem to have very real functional value. First, they allow training in self-control about managing one's anger and hostility in the constant face of racism. In many situations, it would be considered dangerous by an African American to respond to taunts, threats, and insults. Second, woofing also allows a Black person to establish a hierarchy or pecking order without resorting to violence. Last, it can create an image of being fearless where one will gain respect.

This verbal and nonverbal style of communication can be a major aspect of Black interactions. Likewise, other minority groups have characteristic styles that may cause considerable difficulties for White counselors. One way of contrasting communication style differences may be in the overt activity dimension (the pacing/intensity) of nonverbal communication. Table 8.1 contrasts five different groups along this continuum. How these styles affect the therapist's perception and ability to work with culturally different clients is important for each and every one of us to consider.

Table 8.1 Communication Style Differences (Overt Activity Dimension—Nonverbal/Verbal)

American Indians	Asian Americans and Hispanics	Whites	Blacks
1. Speak softly/slower	1. Speak softly	1. Speak loud/fast to control listener	1. Speak with affect
2. Indirect gaze when listening or speaking	2. Avoidance of eye contact when listening or speaking to high-status persons	2. Greater eye contact when listening	2. Direct eye contact (prolonged) when speaking, but less when listening
3. Interject less; seldom offer encouraging communication	3. Similar rules	3. Head nods, nonverbal markers	3. Interrupt (turn taking) when can
4. Delayed auditory (silence)	4. Mild delay	4. Quick responding	4. Quicker responding
5. Manner of expression low-keyed, indirect	5. Low-keyed, indirect	5. Objective, task oriented	5. Affective, emotional, interpersonal

COUNSELING AND THERAPY AS COMMUNICATION STYLE

Throughout this text we have repeatedly emphasized that *different* theories of counseling and psychotherapy represent *different* communication styles. There is considerable early research support for this statement. The film series *Three Approaches to Psychotherapy* (Shostrom, 1966), which features Carl Rogers, Fritz Perls, and Albert Ellis, and the *Three Approaches to Psychotherapy: II* (Shostrom, 1977), which features Carl Rogers, Everett Shostrom, and Arnold Lazarus, have been the subject of much analysis. Some general conclusions may be tentatively drawn from all of these studies (Dolliver, Williams, & Gold, 1980; Weinrach, 1987). Each theoretical orientation (Rogers, person-centered therapy; Perls, existential therapy; Ellis, rational emotive therapy; Shostrom, actualizing therapy; and Lazarus, multimodal therapy) can be distinguished from one another, and the therapy styles/skills exhibited seem to be highly correlated with their theoretical orientations. For example, Rogers's style emphasizes attending skills (encouragement to talk: minimal encouragers, nonverbal markers, paraphrasing, and reflecting feelings); Shostrom relies on direct guidance, providing information, and so forth, whereas Lazarus takes an active, reeducative style.

Differential Skills in Multicultural Counseling/Therapy

Just as race, culture, ethnicity, and gender may affect communication styles, there is considerable evidence that theoretical orientations in counseling will influence helping styles as well. There is strong support for the belief that different cultural groups may be more receptive to certain counseling/communication styles because of cultural and sociopolitical factors (Choudhuri, Santiago-Rivera, &

Garrett, 2012; Diller, 2011; West-Olatunji & Conwill, 2011). Indeed, the literature on multicultural counseling/therapy strongly suggests that American Indians, Asian Americans, Black Americans, and Hispanic Americans tend to prefer more active-directive forms of helping than nondirective ones (Brammer, 2012; Ivey & Ivey, 2003). We briefly describe two of these group differences here to give the reader some idea of their implications.

Asian American clients who may value restraint of strong feelings and believe that intimate revelations are to be shared only with close friends may cause problems for the counselor who is oriented toward insight or feelings (as in the case of Betty). It is entirely possible that such techniques as reflection of feelings, asking questions of a deeply personal nature, and making in-depth interpretations may be perceived as lacking in respect for the client's integrity (B. S. K. Kim, 2011). Asian American clients may not value the process of insight into underlying processes. For example, some clients who come for vocational information may be perceived by counselors as needing help in finding out what motivates their actions and decisions. Requests for advice or information from the client are seen as indicative of deeper, more personal conflicts. Although this might be true in some cases, the blind application of techniques that clash with cultural values seriously places many Asian Americans in an uncomfortable and oppressed position.

Many years ago, Atkinson, Maruyama, and Matsui (1978) tested this hypothesis with a number of Asian American students. Two tape recordings of a contrived counseling session were prepared in which the client's responses were identical but the counselor's responses differed, being directive in one and nondirective in the other. Their findings indicated that counselors who use the directive approach were rated more credible and approachable than were those using the nondirective counseling approach. Asian Americans seem to prefer a logical, rational, structured counseling approach to an affective, reflective, and ambiguous one. Other researchers have drawn similar conclusions (Atkinson & Lowe, 1995; Leong, 1986; Y. Lin, 2001).

In a classic and groundbreaking study, Berman (1979) found similar results with a Black population. The weakness of the previous study was its failure to compare equal responses with a White population. Berman's study compared the use of counseling skills between Black and White, male and female counselors. A videotape of culturally varied client vignettes was viewed by Black and White counselor trainees. They responded to the question, "What would you say to this person?" The data were scored and coded according to a microcounseling taxonomy that divided counseling skills into attending and influencing ones. The hypothesis made by the investigator was that Black and White counselors would give significantly different patterns of responses to their clients.

Data supported the hypothesis. Black males and females tended to use the more active expressive skills (directions, expression of content, and interpretation) with greater frequency than did their White counterparts. White males and females tended to use a higher percentage of attending skills. Berman concluded that the person's race/culture appears to be a major factor in the counselor's choice of skills, that Black and White counselors appear to adhere to two distinctive styles of counseling. Berman also concluded that the more active styles of the

Black counselor tend to include practical advice and allow for the introjection of a counselor's values and opinions.

The implications for therapy become glaringly apparent. Mental health training programs tend to emphasize the more passive attending skills. Therapists so trained may be ill equipped to work with culturally different clients who might find the active approach more relevant to their own needs and values (Parham, Ajamu, & White, 2011).

Implications for Multicultural Counseling/Therapy

Ivey's continuing contributions (Ivey, 1981, 1986; Ivey, D'Andrea, & Ivey, 2011; Ivey & Ivey, 2003) in the field of microcounseling, multicultural counseling, and developmental counseling seem central to our understanding of counseling/ communication styles. He believes that different theories are concerned with generating different sentences and constructs and that different cultures may also be expected to generate different sentences and constructs. Counseling and psychotherapy may be viewed as special types of temporary cultures (Ivey et al., 2011). When the counseling style of the counselor does not match the communication style of his or her culturally diverse clients, many difficulties may arise: premature termination of the session, inability to establish rapport, or cultural oppression of the client. Thus, it becomes clear that effective multicultural counseling occurs when the counselor and the client are able to send and receive both verbal and nonverbal messages appropriately and accurately. When the counselor is able to engage in such activities, his or her credibility and attractiveness will be increased. Communication styles manifested in the clinical context may either enhance or negate the effectiveness of multicultural counseling. Several major implications for counseling can be discerned.

Therapeutic Practice

As practicing clinicians who work with a culturally diverse population, we need to move decisively in educating ourselves about the differential meanings of nonverbal behavior and the broader implications for communication styles. We need to realize that proxemics, kinesics, paralanguage, and high-low context factors are important elements of communication, that they may be highly culture bound, and that we should guard against possible misinterpretation in our assessment of clients. Likewise, it is important that we begin to become aware of and understand our own communication/helping style.

We believe that therapists must be able to shift their therapeutic styles to meet the developmental needs of clients. We contend further that effective mental health professionals are those who can also shift their helping styles to meet the cultural dimensions of their clients. Therapists of differing theoretical orientations will tend to use different skill patterns. These skill patterns may be antagonistic or inappropriate to the communication/helping styles of clients. In research cited earlier, it was clear that White counselors (by virtue of their cultural conditioning and training) tended to use the more passive attending and listening skills in

REFLECTION AND DISCUSSION QUESTIONS

1. What is your clinical/communication style?
2. What does it say about your values, biases, and assumptions about human behavior?
3. How do your nonverbals reflect stereotypes, fears, or preconceived notions about various racial groups?
4. What nonverbal messages might you be communicating unknowingly to your client?
5. In what way does your helping style hinder your ability to work effectively with a culturally different client?
6. What culturally/racially influenced communication styles cause you the greatest difficulty or discomfort? Why?

counseling/therapy, whereas racial/ethnic minority populations appear more oriented toward an active influencing approach. There are several reasons why this may be the case.

First, we contend that the use of more directive, active, and influencing skills is more likely to provide personal information about where the therapist is coming from (self-disclosure). Giving advice or suggestions, interpreting, and telling the client how you, the counselor or therapist, feel are really acts of counselor self-disclosure. Although the use of attending or more nondirective skills may also self-disclose, it tends to be minimal relative to using influencing skills. In multicultural counseling, the culturally diverse client is likely to approach the counselor with trepidation: "What makes you any different from all the Whites out there who have oppressed me?" "What makes you immune from inheriting the racial biases of your forebears?" "Before I open up to you [self-disclose], I want to know where you are coming from." "How open and honest are you about your own racism, and will it interfere with our relationship?" "Can you really understand what it's like to be Asian, Black, Hispanic, American Indian, or the like?" In other words, a culturally diverse client may not open up (self-disclose) until you, the helping professional, self-disclose first. Thus, to many minority clients, a therapist who expresses his or her thoughts and feelings may be better received in a counseling situation.

Second, the more positive response by people of color to the use of influencing skills appears to be related to diagnostic focus. Studies support the thesis that White therapists are more likely to focus their problem diagnosis in individual, rather than societal terms (Berman, 1979; Draguns, 2002; Nwachuku & Ivey, 1991; D. W. Sue et al., 1998). In a society where individualism prevails, it is not surprising to find that Euro-American counselors tend to view their client's problems as residing within the individual rather than society. Thus, the role of the therapist will be person-focused because the problem resides within the individual. Skills utilized will be individual-centered (attending), aimed at changing the person. Many minorities accept the importance of individual contributions to the problem, but they also give great weight to systemic or societal factors that may adversely impact their lives. Minorities who have been the victims of discrimination and oppression perceive that the problem resides externally to the person (societal forces). Active systems intervention is called for, and the most appropriate way to attack the environment (stressors) would be an active approach (Lewis, Lewis, Daniels, & D'Andrea, 1998). If the counselor shares this perception, he or she may take a more active role in the sessions, giving advice and suggestions, as well as teaching strategies (becoming a partner to the client).

Finally, although it would be ideal if we could effectively engage in the full range of therapeutic responses, such a wish may prove unrealistic. We cannot be all things to everyone; that is, there are personal limits to how much we can change our communication styles to match those of our clients. The difficulty in shifting styles may be a function of inadequate practice, inability to understand the other person's worldview, or personal biases or racist attitudes that have not been adequately resolved. In these cases, the counselor might consider several alternatives: (a) seek additional training/education, (b) seek consultation with a more experienced counselor, (c) refer the client to another therapist, and (d) become aware of personal communication style limitations and try to anticipate their possible impact on the culturally diverse client. Often, a therapist who recognizes the limitations of his or her helping style and knows how it will impact a culturally diverse client can take steps to minimize possible conflicts.

Interestingly, one study (Yao, Sue, & Hayden, 1992) found that once rapport and a working relationship are established with a minority client, the counselor may have greater freedom in using a helping style quite different from that of the client. The crucial element appears to be the counselor's ability to acknowledge limitations in his or her helping style and to anticipate the negative impact it may have on the culturally diverse client. In this way, the helping professional may be saying to the client, "I understand your worldview, and I know that what I do or say will appear very Western to you, but I'm limited in my communication style. I may or may not understand where you're coming from, but let's give it a try." For some minority clients, this form of communication may be enough to begin the process of bridging the communication-style gap.

Implications for Clinical Practice

This chapter has made it abundantly clear that communication styles are strongly influenced by such factors as race, culture, ethnicity, and gender. Most of the studies we have reviewed lend support to the notion that various racial groups do exhibit differences in communication styles. If counseling and therapy are seen as subsets of the communication process, then it may have significant implications for what constitutes helping. Some general suggestions gleaned from this chapter might prove helpful:

1. Recognize that no one style of counseling or therapy will be appropriate for all populations and situations. A counselor or therapist who is able to engage in a variety of helping styles and roles is most likely to be effective in working with a diverse population.

(continued)

(*continued*)

2. Become knowledgeable about how race, culture, and gender affect communication styles. It is especially important to study the literature on nonverbal communication and to test it out in a real-life situation by making a concerted and conscious effort to observe the ways in which people communicate and interact. Your clinical observation skills will be greatly enhanced if you sharpen your nonverbal powers of observation of clients.

3. Become aware of your own communication and helping styles. Know your social impact on others and anticipate how it affects your clients. How we behave often unconsciously reflects our own beliefs and values. It is important for us to realize what we communicate to others. Further, knowing how we affect people allows us to modify our behaviors should our impact be negative. To do this, we need to seek feedback from friends and colleagues about how we impact them.

4. Try to obtain additional training and education on a variety of theoretical orientations and approaches. Programs that are primarily psychoanalytically oriented, cognitively oriented, existentially oriented, person-centered oriented, or behaviorally oriented may be doing a great disservice to trainees. The goals and processes espoused by the theories may not be those held by culturally different groups. These theories tend to be not only culture bound but also narrow in how they conceptualize the human condition.

5. Know that each school of counseling and therapy has strengths, but they may be one-dimensional; they concentrate only on feelings, or only on cognitions, or only on behaviors. We need to realize that we are *feeling, thinking, behaving, social, cultural, spiritual*, and *political* beings. In other words, try to think holistically rather than in a reductionist manner when it comes to conceptualizing the human condition.

6. It is important for training programs to use an approach that calls for openness and flexibility both in conceptualizing the issues and in actual skill building. In many respects, it represents a metatheoretical and eclectic approach to helping. Rather than being random, haphazard, and inconsistent, the metatheoretical approach is an attempt to use helping strategies, techniques, and styles that consider not only individual characteristics, but cultural and racial factors as well.

Multicultural Evidence-Based Practice

1. Given so many differing perspectives in working with culturally diverse clients, how do you determine what therapy treatment is best suited for the client?
2. Although culture is very important, what role should science and research play in the selection of therapeutic approaches?
3. What are empirically supported therapies (ESTs)? Are ESTs culture bound, and do they apply to diverse populations?
4. What were the reasons for the development of empirically supported relationships (ESRs)? Can you describe the relationship variables that are considered to be research supported?
5. In what ways are evidence-based practice (EBP) and multicultural counseling converging?
6. What modifications might have to be made in the therapeutic alliance (empathy and relationship building) to work with different ethnic minorities?
7. What is EBP, and how does it differ from ESTs and ESRs? What are the advantages of focusing on client values and preferences? What do you see as similarities and differences between EBP and cultural competence?
8. What are the advantages and disadvantages of using "culturally adapted" forms of research-based psychotherapies?

Significant portions of this chapter are adapted from D. Sue & D. M. Sue (2008), *Evidence-based practices in a diverse society.*

Case Study: Hajimi Matsumoto

Hajimi was a first-generation, 18-year-old, Japanese American male who nevertheless lived most of his life in Japan before returning to the United States. He came to the university counseling center suffering from a severe social phobia. I was a White American female psychology intern being supervised by Dr. Katsumoto, a female Japanese American staff psychologist known for her work on multicultural psychology and cultural competence. I had seen the client, Hajimi, for approximately six sessions. Hajimi was an extremely shy young man who spoke in a barely audible voice, responded in short but polite statements, avoided eye contact, and sat facing my window rather than me. When I first met him, he would not shake my hand but simply nodded his head in acknowledgment. He fidgeted in his seat and seemed extremely uncomfortable in my presence. He described high anxiety in social or performance situations and was extremely nervous around women. He was afraid of being belittled by others, didn't know how to make "small talk," and constantly obsessed as to whether his personal hygiene (bad breath or body odor) might be offensive. Yet on none of his visits to my office did I detect any sort of strong or disagreeable odor.

Hajimi was referred to the counseling center by one of his professors after a particularly embarrassing and humiliating situation that occurred in the classroom: He "froze" in front of fellow students while doing a team oral presentation. Despite having detailed notes, he stammered, stuttered, and broke out in a profuse sweat that made it impossible to continue. When one of his female classmates on the team tried to offer support by placing her arm on his shoulder, Hajimi felt sure she could feel the perspiration on his shirt and panicked. He became embarrassed, broke away from her, quickly excused himself, and left the classroom. Apparently, these types of anxiety-provoking situations and encounters were very common in his life.

As all interns needed to take responsibility for making a client presentation at bimonthly case conference meetings, I chose to present my client, Hajimi. Case conferences are usually attended by staff psychologists, student interns, and the consulting psychiatrist. The psychiatrist, Dr. machovitch, a White male at the medical school, was known for his psychodynamic orientation, whereas most of the psychologists at the center had either a multicultural behavioral approach. After providing a detailed history of Hajimi, his symptoms, possible etiological factors, and proposed treatment plan, a clear difference of opinion began to emerge between Drs. Machovitch and Katsumoto and another psychologist, Dr. Barnard. The three had quite a heated exchange, and I felt caught in the middle because they each recommended a different approach. Further, they all differed in their analysis and diagnosis of the problem.

Their perspectives were based upon the following information I provided:

Hajimi was the only son of a traditional Japanese couple who had wanted many more children but for unknown reasons could not conceive any others. All their hopes for carrying on the family name resided in Hajimi. When Hajimi was first born, the parents were overjoyed to have a son, but as time wore on, the father became disappointed in his son's effeminate behavior, hypersensitivity, inability to control his emotions, and his social-outcast role among classmates. The father belittled him, seemed to be ashamed to introduce Hajimi to friends, and isolated him from family gatherings. Whenever Hajimi would do something wrong and show remorse by crying, his father would say in Japanese, "Leave me, you offend me. "The mother, who was more sympathetic to Hajimi's needs, nevertheless seldom intervened when her husband berated

Hajimi almost on a daily basis. On one particularly angry encounter in which his father severely criticized him, Hajimi wept openly in front of his mother. His mother tried to console him by placing her arms around his shoulder and reassuring him that one day his father would be proud of him. Rather than being comforted, however, her actions seemed to cause further distress as he quickly ran to his bedroom and slammed the door.

Although Hajimi had done well academically in his early years, his grades began to suffer in college. Much of this was due to his severe social phobia, which affected his ability to speak up in classes and isolated him from fellow students and teachers. He was awkward and inept in social situations, became anxious around people, and would seldom speak. In his physical education classes, which required dancing with girls, he would panic and perspire freely. He felt embarrassed to touch the hands of his partner or to have them touch him for fear they would find his wet hands and clothes offensive. Hajimi often expressed his belief that he was not perfact enough. In school, he became increasingly obsessed with avoiding failure, playing it safe, and not making mistakes. Unfortunately, this approach had a negative impact on his academic work, as he would often take incompletes and withdraw from classes for fear that he was not doing well. He would frequently choose a college course on the basis of whether it offered a pass/no pass option. Hajimi admitted to an intense fear of failure and was aware that these choices allowed him to temporarily avoid poor grades. He knew that failing grades generated only greater criticism form his father.

REFLECTION AND DISCUSSION QUESTIONS

1. Before you continue reading, reflect upon what you believe to be the source of Hajimi's problems. If you have time, break out into small groups in your class or workshop and brainstorm with others the following questions: What is causing him to be so anxious around people? What role do his parents play in the manifestation of his disorder?
2. How would you characterize your therapeutic orientation, and can you apply it to this case? Do your classmates and fellow peers offer different explanations? How would you work with Hajimi? Can you be specific in describing your treatment plan?
3. Are you knowledgeable about what research has shown about treating the type of disorder exhibited by Hajimi? How would you go about finding the information?
4. What role do you believe culture plays in Hajimi's problems?

The disagreement among the three therapists as to the diagnosis and treatment of Hajimi appeared tied to their theoretical orientations and/or their clinical experiences. Dr. Katsumoto stressed cultural factors, whereas Dr. Machovitch believed a psychodynamic approach was clearly indicated in work with Hajimi. The discussion was compounded by Dr. Barnard, a male psychologist with a strong cognitive-behavioral orientation who argued for a behavioral program of assertiveness training and systematic desensitization of his social phobia. The gist of their positions can be captured in the following snapshots of their arguments.

Dr. Katsumoto (Cultural Analysis):

"Sociodemographic factors such as race, culture, and ethnicity are important in understanding Hajimi's difficulties. Many of the behaviors exhibited by him may be cultural dictates rather than pathology. For example, his behavior in the counseling session (lack of eye contact, low tone of voice, short but polite responses, and social distance) with the counselor may not be considered pathological in Japanese culture. Although I do believe he suffers from psychological problems, the diagnosis of social phobia may be inaccurate and lead to an inappropriate treatment plan. Even *DSM-IV* recognizes the existence of culute-bound syndromes, which are locality-specific patterns of aberrant behavior not linked to a specific *DSM* diagnosis. For example, in Japan and Korea, there is a condition called 'taijin kyofusho' that resembles a social phobia, which is accompanied by an intense fear that the person's body, its parts, or its functions displease or are offensive to people. It is often manifested in a fear that one's body odor may prove interpersonally repulsive. This psychological problem is actually listed in the Japanese manual of mental disorders. My suggestion would be to explore the possible adaptation of indigenous methods of treatment found effective in Japan. Although he is an American citizen, I believe he is more Japanese than Japanese American."

Dr. Machovitch (Psychodynamic Analysis):

"Hajimi's social phobia is caused by a deep-seated underlying childhood conflict with his parents. The phobia is a symptom and symbolic of unresolved Oedipal feelings toward both parents that are reenacted in almost all his social relationships. His strong need for social approval from his father, his feelings of hostility toward him, and an intense fear of the father (fear of castration) make him uncomfortable and anxious around men and especially around authority figures. His unresolved oedipal relationship with his mother has impaired his ability to relate to members of the opposite sex and has contributed to his anxiety in developing intimacy with others. Note his intense feelings of anxiety around women and his overreaction to being touched by them. As a female therapist [reference to me as the intern], you probably evoke this conflicts as well. I believe that Hajimi, at crucial psychosexual stages, did not receive the love and care a child needs to develop into a healthy adult. He was neglected, rejected, and maternally/paternally isolated, a condition that symbolized all his social relationships. Because he left unloved and worthless, Hajimi reenacts his pathological relationship with his parents in other social situations. Note, for example, the symbolic relationship between the father's repetitive declarations that Hajimi is 'offensive, and Hajimi's fear that he will offend others; similar reactions to attempts by his mother and female classmate to comfort him; avoidance of being touched; and many other symboiic parallels. My suggestion is to deal with Hajimi's transference neurosis through an insight process so that he may be able to distinguish the pathological relationships of the past with the healthy ones he encounters now."

Dr. Barnard (Cognitive-Behavioral Analysis):

"All of these explanations appear well and good, but the ultimate test of therapeutic effectiveness must be guided by the research literature. Work on empirically supported treatments suggests that cognitive-behavioral approaches have shown to be most effective in the treatment of phobias. Although culture is important and a psychodynamic explanation seems appealing, we should be ethically obligated to select the treatment based upon what research has shown works. Describing the client's problems in measurable and specific terms rather than abstract concepts will ultimately lead to a better treatment plan. For example, the roots of Hajimi's problems can be traced to his behavioral repertoire. Many of the behaviors he has learned are inappropriate, and his repertoire lacks useful, productive social skills. He has little practice in social relationships, lacks good role models, and has difficulty distinguishing between appropriate and inappropriate behaviors. In addition, his constant belittlement by his father has probably created in his mind an irrational belief system that leads him to distort or misinterpret events: Others will reject him, he is worthless, and he will offend others. Much of this, no doubt, comes from the father's constant criticisms and belittlement. This leads Hajimi to believe that he is "worthless" and will always be worthless. I believe that a program of assertiveness training, systematic desensitization, and relaxation exercises will help him immensely to develop social skills and to combat his high performance and interpersonal anxieties. Further, I would supplement his behavioral program with a cognitive treatment plan that (a) identifies irrational thinking and beliefs, (b) teaches him cognitive restructuring methods to combat them, and (c) replaces them with positive and more realistic self-appraisals. If you look at the research literature on treating social phobias, you cannot deny their effectiveness in treating this type of disorder."

The case of Hajimi and the three differing treatment perspectives raises important therapeutic issues that have literally spawned the movement toward evidence-based practice (EBP). First, after careful assessment of the presenting problem and related factors, how does a counselor decide on the most appropriate treatment for an individual from an ethnic minority group? Indeed, this question is relevant to all groups regardless of race, culture, or ethnicity. Certainly, Drs. Katsumoto, Machovitch, and Barnard make important points, and their diagnosis, assessment, and treatment recommendations seem to make sense from their theoretical orientations. Because this text is about multicultural counseling, you might mistakenly assume that we will take the side of Dr. Katsumoto because she offers a perspective that we have emphasized throughout the text. As indicated in Chapter 2, however, it is entirely possible that all three perspectives may be right, but they may be limited in how they view the totality of the human condition. The cultural perspective views Hajimi as a cultural being, the psychodynamic perspective views him as a historical-developmental being, and the cognitive-behavioral approach views him as a behaving-and-thinking being. As we have emphasized throughout, we are all of these and more.

Second, historically therapeutic strategies used in treatment were often based on (a) the clinician's specific therapeutic orientation (à la Drs. Katsumoto, Machovitch, and Barnard), (b) ideas shared by "experts" in psychotherapy, or (c) "clinical intuition and experience" derived from years of work with clients. These approaches are problematic because there are countless "experts" and, at last count, some 400 schools of psychotherapy, each purporting that their techniques are valid (Corey, 2012); moreover, treatment is often implemented without questioning the relevance or appropriateness of a particular technique or approach for a specific client. Furthermore, reliance on clinical "intuition" to guide one's therapeutic approach can result in ineffective treatment. Thus, it appears that the choice of a treatment plan is dictated by one's theoretical orientation, expert opinion, and/or clinical intuition. In other words, different mental health professionals may differ significantly from one another in how they conceptualize and treat a problem of the client. Given these points, who are we to believe and how do we resolve this problem?

Third, this question has propelled the field of mental health practice, including multicultural counseling/therapy, to consider the role of science and research in the treatment of mental disorders. Of the three analyses given, Dr. Barnard brings up the issue of using the research literature to guide us in the choice of intervention techniques. Yet he offers a seemingly flawed culture-free or neutral interpretation of empirically supported treatments (ESTs), an issue we address shortly. Nevertheless, Dr. Barnard does raise very important questions for the field of multicultural counseling and therapy to consider. How important is it for counselors to be aware of and to utilize interventions that have research support? What interventions have been demonstrated in research to be effective for treating mental disorders? Has research on EBP been conducted on racial/ethnic minority groups, or is it simply for members of the majority culture? To help answer these questions, we consider the evolution of ESTs, empirically supported relationships (ESRs), and EBP as they apply to diverse populations.

EVIDENCE-BASED PRACTICE AND MULTICULTURALISM

The importance of EBP is becoming increasingly accepted in the field of multicultural counseling. Discussions of EBP originally focused on research-supported therapies for specific disorders, but the dialogue has now broadened to include clinical expertise, including "understanding the influence of individual and cultural differences on treatment" and the importance of considering client "characteristics, culture, and preferences" in assessment, treatment plans, and therapeutic outcome" (American Psychological Association, Presidential Task Force on Evidence-Based Practice, 2006). In an article titled "Evidence-Based Practices with Ethnic Minorities: Strange Bedfellows No More," Morales and Norcross (2010) describe how multiculturalism and evidence-based treatment (EBT), two forces that were "inexorable" and "separate," are now converging and how they can complement each other. According to the authors, "Multiculturalism without strong research risks becoming an empty political value, and EBT without cultural sensitivity risks irrelevancy" (p. 823).

Although the authors are optimistic about the convergence of these forces, there is still resistance to EBP among some individuals within the field of multicultural counseling (A. Ivey, personal communication, November 22, 2009). As BigFoot and Schmidt (2010) note, "Historically, government and social service organization utilization of nonadapted or poorly adapted mental health treatments with diverse populations has led to widespread distrust and reluctance in such populations to seek mental health services" (p. 849). Conflicts often exist between the values espoused in conventional psychotherapy and the cultural values and beliefs of ethnic minorities (Nagayama-Hall, 2001; J. S. Lau, Fung, & Yung, 2010). As we have discussed in previous chapters, Western approaches to psychological treatment are often based on individualistic value systems instead of on the interdependent values found in many ethnic minority communities. Additionally, conventional therapies often ignore cultural influences, disregard spiritual and other healing processes, and pathologize the behavior and values of ethnic minorities and other diverse groups (S. Sue, Zane, Nagayama-Hall, & Berger, 2009).

It is apparent that conventional delivery of Western-based therapies may not be meeting the needs of many individuals from ethnic and other cultural minorities. These groups tend to underutilize mental health services (Thurston & Phares, 2008) and are more likely to attend fewer sessions or drop out of therapy sooner, compared with their White counterparts (Fortuna, Alegria, & Gao, 2010; Lester, Resick, Young-Xu, & Artz, 2010; Triffleman & Pole, 2010). Unfortunately, research on the effectiveness of empirically supported therapies for ethnic minorities is limited, as these groups are often not included or specifically identified in research investigations of particular treatments.

Although questions remain regarding the validity of evidence-based approaches for ethnic minority populations and other diverse populations (Bernal & Sáez-Santiago, 2006), we believe that EBPs offer an opportunity for infusing multicultural and diversity sensitivity into psychotherapy. In addition, all mental health professions (psychiatry, social work, clinical psychology, and counseling) now espouse the view that treatment should have a research base. Evidence-based interventions are increasingly promoted in social work (Bledsoe et al., 2007; Gibbs & Gambrill, 2002), school psychology (Kratochwill, 2002), clinical psychology (Deegear & Lawson, 2003), counseling (American Counseling Association, 2005; Chwalisz, 2003), and psychiatry.

In this chapter, we will discuss the evolution of EBP, the integration of EST and ESR variables into multicultural counseling, and the relevance of enhancing cultural elements in therapy. We will also show how culturally sensitive strategies can become an important component of EBPs.

EMPIRICALLY SUPPORTED TREATMENT

The concept of ESTs was popularized when the American Psychological Association began promoting the use of "validated" or research-supported treatments—specific treatments confirmed as effective for specific disorders. Not only were ESTs seen as an effective response to concerns about the use of unsupported techniques and psychotherapies, but they also address the issue of unintended harm that can result from ineffective or hazardous treatments (Lilienfeld, 2007). ESTs typically involve a very specific treatment protocol for specific disorders. Because variability among therapists might produce error variance in research studies and because it is important for ESTs to be easily replicable as originally designed, ESTs are conducted using manuals.

According to the guidelines of the task force charged with defining and identifying ESTs (Chambless & Hollon, 1998), they must demonstrate (a) superiority to a placebo in two or more methodologically rigorous, controlled studies, (b) equivalence to a well-established treatment in several rigorous and independent controlled studies, usually randomized controlled trials, or (c) efficacy in a large series of single-case controlled designs (i.e., within-subjects designs that systematically compare the effects of a treatment with those of a control condition).

Table 9.1 Examples of Empirically Supported Treatments	
"Well-Established" Treatments	**"Probably Efficacious" Treatments**
Cognitive-behavioral therapy for panic disorder	Cognitive therapy for obsessive-compulsive disorder (OCD)
Exposure/guided mastery for specific phobias	Exposure treatment for posttraumatic stress disorder (PTSD)
Cognitive therapy for depression	Brief dynamic therapy for depression
Cognitive-behavioral therapy for bulimia	Brief dynamic therapy for opiate dependence
Cognitive-behavioral relapse prevention for cocaine dependence	Interpersonal therapy for bulimia
Behavior therapy for headache	Reminiscence therapy for geriatrics patients
Behavioral marital therapy	Emotionally focused couples therapy

Source: Chambless et al. (1998).

ESTs have been identified for anxiety, depressive and stress-related disorders, obesity and eating disorders, severe mental conditions such as schizophrenia and bipolar disorder, substance abuse and dependence, childhood disorders, and borderline personality disorder. Several hundred different manualized treatments are listed as empirically supported (Chambless & Ollendick, 2001; Society of Clinical Psychology, 2011). (See Table 9.1 for a few examples of empirically supported therapies.)

Additionally, the American Psychological Association has developed a list of ESTs and practice guidelines for ethnic minorities (American Psychological Association, 1993); women and girls (American Psychological Association, 2007a); older adults (American Psychological Association, 2009b); and lesbian, gay, and bisexual clients (American Psychological Association, 2012). These guidelines can be consulted and modified, if necessary, in working with clients from these groups.

The rationale behind the establishment of ESTs is admirable; we believe that decisions regarding treatment approaches for particular issues or disorders should be based on research findings rather than on idiosyncratic, personal beliefs or sketchy theories. We owe it to our clients to provide them with treatment that has demonstrated efficacy. However, it is our contention that relying only on manualized treatment methods, albeit research-supported approaches, is insufficient with many clients and many mental health problems. Additionally, most ESTs have not been specifically demonstrated to be effective with ethnic minorities or other diverse populations. The shortcomings of the EST approach are summarized here:

- Due to the focus on choosing treatment based on the specific disorder, contextual, cultural, and other environmental influences are not adequately considered.
- The validity of ESTs for minority group members is often questionable because these groups are not included in many clinical trials (Bernal & Sáez-Santiago; 2006; S. Sue et al., 2006).

- The importance of the therapist-client relationship is not adequately acknowledged. A number of studies have found that therapist effects contribute significantly to the outcome of psychotherapy. In many cases, these effects exceed those produced by specific techniques (Wampold, 2001).
- Too much emphasis is placed on randomized controlled trials versus other forms of research, such as qualitative research designs.
- When treating clients with specific disorders, multicultural therapists have had the choice of ignoring ESTs or adapting them. Increasing, there have been attempts to develop "cultural adaptations" of certain ESTs.

For example, Organista (2000) made the following modifications to empirically supported cognitive-behavioral strategies when working with low-income Latinos suffering from depression:

1. *Engagement strategies:* Recognizing the importance of *personalismo* (the value of personal relationships), initial sessions are devoted to relationship building. Time is allotted for *presentaciones* (introductions), during which personal information is exchanged between counselor and client and issues that may affect ethnic minorities, such as acculturation difficulties, culture shock, and discrimination, are discussed.
2. *Activity schedules:* In the treatment of depression, a common recommendation is for clients to take some time off for themselves. This idea may run counter to the Latino/a value of connectedness and putting the needs of the family ahead of oneself. Therefore, instead of solitary activities, clients can choose social activities they find enjoyable, such as visiting neighbors, family outings, or taking children to the park. In recognizing the income status of clients, activities discussed are generally free or affordable.
3. *Assertiveness training:* Assertiveness is discussed within the context of Latino values. Culturally acceptable ways of expressing assertiveness, such as prefacing statements with *con to do respect* (with all due respect) and *me permit e expresar missenti mientos?* (Is it okay if I express my feelings?) are discussed, as well as strategies for using assertion with spouses or higher status individuals.
4. *Cognitive restructuring:* Rather than labeling thoughts that can reduce or increase depression as rational or irrational, the terms "helpful thoughts" and "unhelpful thoughts" are used. Recognizing the religious nature of many Latinos, the saying *Ayundate, que Dios teayudara* (i.e., "God helps those who help themselves") is used to encourage follow-through with behavioral assignments.

This adapted approach, which maintains fidelity to both empirically supported techniques and cultural influences, has resulted in a lower dropout rate and better outcome for low-income Latino/a clients compared to nonmodified therapy. Cultural adaptations can include factors such as (a) matching language, racial or ethnic; (b) incorporating cultural values in the specific treatment strategies; (c) utilizing cultural sayings or metaphors in treatment; and (d) considering the impact of environmental variables, such as acculturation conflicts, discrimination, and income status.

Culturally adapted ESTs have been successfully used with Latino/a and Haitian American adolescents (Duarte-Velez, Guillermo, & Bonilla, 2010; Nicholas, Arntz, Hirsch, & Schjiedigen, 2011), Asian Americans experiencing phobias (Huey & Pan, 2006); Latino/a adults experiencing depression (Aguilera, Garza, & Munoz, 2010); American Indians suffering from trauma (BigFoot & Schmidt, 2010); African Americans recovering from substance abuse (Cunningham, Foster, & Warner, 2010); and Chinese immigrant families (A. S. Lau, Fung, & Yung, 2010).

Horrell (2008) reviewed 12 studies on the effectiveness of cognitive-behavioral therapy for African, Asian, and Hispanic Americans experiencing a variety of psychological disorders; the majority of these studies involved some type of cultural modification. Although the results for African American clients were mixed, Asian and Hispanic American clients demonstrated significant treatment gains over those in placebo or wait-list control conditions. Overall, evidence is increasing that ESTs can be effective with ethnic minorities, particularly when the approach includes cultural adaptation.

A meta-analysis of studies involving the adaptation of ESTs to clients' cultural background revealed that adapted treatments for clients of color are moderately more effective than nonadapted treatments and that the most effective therapies were those that had the most cultural adaptations (T. B. Smith, Rodriguez, & Bernal, 2011). In a review of both published and unpublished studies of culturally adapted therapies, it was found that culturally adapted psychotherapy is more effective than nonadapted psychotherapy for ethnic minorities (Benish, Quintana, & Wampold, 2011).

Interestingly, these researchers believe that cultural adaptations are effective because most adapted therapies in their review allowed the therapist to explore the "illness myth" of the client (i.e., the clients' explanation of their symptoms and beliefs about possible etiology, prognosis, and effective treatment). As the researchers conclude, "The superior outcomes resulting from myth adaptation indicate the importance of therapist inquiry and effort into understanding clients' beliefs about etiology, types of symptoms experienced, prediction of the course of illness, and consequences of the illness, as well as client opinion about what constitutes acceptable treatment"(p. 287). Even if a client's perspective regarding his or her symptoms is maladaptive, the process of listening and assessing client beliefs appears to enhance outcome.

ESTs are useful in providing clinicians with information regarding which therapies are most effective with specific disorders. We should always be aware of experimentally supported techniques when working with client problems. However, the identification of treatments is only one step in a complex process; it is vital that we also consider contextual and cultural influences and therapist-client relationship factors in treatment outcome. This view (i.e., that contextual and therapist factors are also important in therapy outcome) allows the field to move beyond the traditional clinical framework in which an "objective" illness can be diagnosed and a specific cure recommended, to a greater understanding of the complexities involved in mental health issues and psychological disorders.

Implications

The applicability of many ESTs for ethnic minorities has been insufficiently researched. Yet mental health practitioners are faced with the challenge of selecting effective interventions for their clients' mental health issues. For ethnic minority clients, we have the option of using a standard EST for the disorder, finding an EST (or adapted EST) with research demonstrating effectiveness for members of the client's ethnic group with the client's disorder (which is highly unlikely), or taking the time to develop and research a culture-specific EBT for the client's disorder. The latter would be inordinately difficult for most practitioners to accomplish. Additionally, culture-specific treatments may not be effective with ethnic minorities who are more acculturated. Thus, in choosing a treatment strategy, we believe that the best approach (given the current state of research) is for the counselor to select an intervention that is research based and subsequently adapt the approach for the individual client according to the client's individual characteristics, values, and preferences.

REFLECTION AND DISCUSSION QUESTIONS

1. What are your thoughts concerning the use of ESTs in your own practice? What reactions do you have about using research on therapeutic effectiveness to guide your work? Has your training exposed you to EBP? What challenges would you face trying to implement such an approach?

2. What would you need to know about ESTs and the cultural background of diverse clients in order to develop a culturally adapted therapeutic approach? Although it would be a massive undertaking, can you and your classmates discuss what specific steps need to be taken to culturally adapt an EST to African Americans, Asian Americans, and Latinos?

3. Do you believe that simply adapting ESTs to the cultural context of clients is sufficient in working with people of color?

EMPIRICALLY SUPPORTED RELATIONSHIPS

Not everyone believes that cultural adaptations of ESTs are sufficient to deal with cultural differences, and some express concern that such adaptations result in the imposition of Euro-American norms on ethnic minorities. As Gone (2009) argues, EBTs cannot be "adorned" with "a few beads here, some feathers there" (p. 760). Those critical of reliance on ESTs alone cite the multitude of other factors impacting treatment outcome, such as the therapeutic relationship, client values and beliefs, and the working alliance between client and therapist (H. Ahn & Wampold, 2001; DeAngelis, 2005). To remedy this shortcoming, the American Psychological Association Division 29 Psycho-therapy Task Force was formed to review research and identify characteristics responsible for effective therapeutic relationships and to determine means of tailoring therapy to individual clients.

This focus provided the first opportunity for the inclusion of multicultural concerns within the evidence-based movement. It is widely agreed that the quality of the working relationship between the therapist and the client (i.e., the therapeutic alliance) is consistently related to treatment outcome (Castonguay, Goldfried, Wiser, Raue, & Hayes, 1996; Weinberger, 2002). This relationship may assume even greater significance for clients from diverse backgrounds. In fact, difficulties in the therapeutic alliance may be a factor in the underutilization of mental health services and early termination of therapy seen with minority clients. After reviewing the research on therapist-client relationship variables as they relate to treatment outcome, the APA Division 29 Task Force reached these conclusions (Ackerman et al., 2001):

1. The therapeutic relationship makes substantial and consistent contributions to psychotherapy outcome, independent of the specific type of treatment.
2. The therapy relationship acts in concert with discrete interventions, client characteristics, and clinician qualities in determining treatment effectiveness.
3. Adapting or tailoring the therapy relationship to specific client needs and characteristics (in addition to diagnosis) enhances the effectiveness of treatment.
4. Practice and treatment guidelines should explicitly address therapist behaviors and qualities that promote a facilitative therapy relationship.

According to the APA Task Force, a number of relationship variables are considered "demonstratively effective" or "promising and probably effective" based on research findings (see Table 9.2). ESR variables include the development of a strong therapeutic alliance, a solid interpersonal bond (i.e., a collaborative, empathetic relationship based on positive regard, respect, warmth, and genuineness), and effective management of countertransference—all factors known to be critical for effective multicultural counseling.

Table 9.2 Empirically Supported Relationship Variables

Demonstrably Effective	Promising and Probably Effective
Therapeutic alliance	Positive regard
Cohesion in group therapy	Congruence/genuineness
Empathy	Feedback
Goal consensus and collaboration	Repair of alliance ruptures
Customizing therapy	Self-disclosure
Management of countertransference	

Source: From Ackerman et al. (2001).

The Therapeutic Alliance

Research on ESRs has consistently identified the importance of a strong therapeutic alliance, which includes the core conditions of effective treatment described by Rogers (1957): empathy, respect, genuineness, and warmth. These dynamics typify a therapeutic relationship in which a client feels understood, safe, and encouraged to disclose intimate material. These characteristics transcend the therapist's therapeutic orientation or approach to treatment. The therapeutic relationship, or working alliance, is an important factor in effective treatment. Clients specifically asked about what contributed to the success of treatment often point to a sense of connection with their therapist. *Connectedness* has been described as having feelings of closeness with the therapist, working together in an enabling atmosphere, receiving support for change, and being provided an equality of status within the working relationship (Ribner & Knei-Paz, 2002).

Similarly, clients report that therapist behaviors such as "openness to ideas, experiences, and feelings" or being "nonjudgmental and noncritical," "genuine," "warm," and "validating of experiences" are helpful in therapy (Curtis, Field, Knann-Kostmas, & Mannix, 2004). A counselor's relationship skills and ability to develop a therapeutic alliance contribute significantly to satisfaction among clients of color (Constantine, 2002). Mulvaney-Day, Earl, Diaz-Linhart, and Alegria (2011) found that relationship variables with the therapist were particularly important for African American and Latino/a clients and concluded that "the basic yearning for authentic connection with a provider transcends racial categories" (p. 36). Thus, the importance of feeling accepted by a therapist on an emotional and cognitive level seems to be a universal prerequisite for an effective therapeutic alliance.

Conceptualization of the therapeutic alliance often includes three elements: (a) an emotional or interpersonal bond between the therapist and the client; (b) mutual agreement on appropriate goals, with an emphasis on changes valued by the client; and (c) intervention strategies or tasks that are viewed as important and relevant by both the client and the therapist (Garber, 2004). Defined in this manner, the therapeutic alliance exerts positive influences on outcome across different treatment modalities, accounting for a substantial proportion of outcome variance (P. D. Brown & O'Leary, 2000; Conners, Carroll, DiClemente, Longabaugh, & Donovan, 1997; Hojat et al., 2011; Taber, Liebert, & Agaskar, 2011; Zuroff & Blatt, 2006). In fact, the therapist-client relationship contributes as much as 30% to the variance in therapeutic outcome (Lambert & Barley, 2001).

We believe that the therapeutic alliance is of critical importance in the outcome of therapy for ethnic minority clients and will describe possible modifications that may help clinicians enhance this relationship. It is important to remember that there is no set formula or response that will ensure the formation of strong therapeutic alliance with a particular client. In fact, counselors often need to demonstrate behavioral flexibility to achieve a good working relationship with clients; this may be particularly true when working with individuals from diverse populations.

In a qualitative study involving Black, Asian, Latino/a, and multiracial clients, most preferred an active counselor role, which was characterized by the counselor offering concrete suggestions, providing direct answers, challenging the client's

Table 9.3	Relational-Style Counselor Preferences of Ethnic Group Clients		
Themes	**African American Clients**	**Latino Clients**	**Non-Latino White Clients**
Listening	Listen to who the client really is; recognize that clients are experts on themselves.	Listen in a way that communicates "paying attention."	Listen so that the client is comfortable enough to talk and express feelings.
Understanding	Understand beyond immediate impressions; understand hidden aspects of the client.	Understand feelings of client.	Understand complexity of client choices and circumstances.
Counselor Qualities	Counselor should "lower" self to client's level; egalitarian relationship.	Be authoritative, but connect first, then offer concrete advice and solutions.	Not judge because of social distance; maintain professional distance but be human.
Spending Time	Not listed as factor	Take time to connect deeply.	Allow time for feelings to emerge at their own pace.

Source: Mulvaney-Day et al. (2011).

thinking with thought-provoking questions, and providing psychoeducation regarding the therapy (D. F. Chang & Berk, 2009). Mulvaney-Day and colleagues (2011) found variability in the counseling relational style preferred by ethnic minority clients. A summary of the preferred relationship styles reported by the African American, Latino/a, and non-Latino White clients in their sample is presented in Table 9.3.

Mental health practitioners need to be adaptable with their relationship skills in order to address the preferences and expectations of their clients. For example, many African American clients appear to value social interaction as opposed to problem-solving approaches, especially during initial sessions, whereas Latino/a clients seem to prefer a more interpersonal approach rather than clinical distance (Gloria & Peregoy, 1996; Kennedy, 2003). However, these are broad generalizations, and counselors must test out the effectiveness of different relational skills with a particular client, assessing the impact of their interactions with the client and asking themselves questions such as "Does the client seem to be responding positively to my relational style?" and "Have I succeeded in developing a collaborative and supportive relationship with this client?" and modifying the approach when necessary. Although it is important not to react to clients in a stereotypic manner, it is important to continually be aware of cultural and societal issues that may affect the client. Asian, Black, Latino/a, and multiracial clients who were dissatisfied in cross-racial therapy complained about their therapist's lack of knowledge about racial identity development; the dynamics of power and privilege; the effects of racism, discrimination, and oppression due to their minority status (or multiple minority statuses); and cultural stigma associated with seeking help (D. F. Chang & Berk, 2009).

Cultural information is useful in providing general guidelines regarding an ethnic minority client's counseling-style preference or issues that need to be addressed in therapy. However, as a counselor develops a comprehensive understanding of each client's background, values, strengths, and concerns, it is essential that the counselor determine if general cultural information "fits" the individual client. This ongoing "search for understanding" is important with respect to each of the following components of the therapeutic alliance.

Emotional or Interpersonal Bond

The formation of a bond between the therapist and the client is a very important aspect of the therapeutic relationship and is defined as a collaborative partnership based on empathy, positive regard, genuineness, respect, warmth, and self-disclosure. For an optimal outcome, the client must feel connected with, respected by, and understood by the therapist. In addition, the therapist must identify issues that may detract from the relationship, such as countertransference (i.e., reactions to the client based on the therapist's own personal issues). These qualities are described in detail below; their importance may vary according to the type of mental health issue being addressed and characteristics of the client (e.g., gender, socioeconomic status, ethnicity, cultural background).

The development of an emotional bond is enhanced by *collaboration*, a shared process in which a client's views are respected and his or her participation is encouraged in all phases of the therapy. An egalitarian stance and encouragement of sharing and self-disclosure facilitate the development of empathy (Dyche & Zayas, 2001) and reduce the power differential between therapist and client. The potential for a positive therapeutic outcome is increased when the client is "on board" regarding the definition of the problem, identification of goals, and choice of interventions. When differences exist between a client's view of a problem and the therapist's theoretical conceptualization, negative dynamics are likely to occur. Collaboration regarding definition of the problem reduces this possibility and is most effective when employed consistently throughout therapy.

Empathy

Empathy is known to significantly enhance the therapeutic bond. *Empathy* is defined as the ability to place oneself in the client's world, to feel or think from the client's perspective, or to be attuned to the client. Empathy allows therapists to form an emotional bond with clients, helping the clients to feel "understood." It is not enough for the therapist to simply communicate this understanding; the client must perceive the responses from the therapist as empathetic. This is why it is vital for therapists to be aware of client receptivity by evaluating both verbal and nonverbal responses from the client

> *Empathy* is the ability to place oneself in the client's world, to feel or think from the client's perspective, or to be attuned to the client. Empathy allows therapists to form an emotional bond with clients, helping the clients to feel "understood."

("How is the client responding to what I am saying?" "What are the client's verbal and bodily cues communicating?"). Empathy can be demonstrated in several different ways—having an emotional understanding or emotional connection with the client (emotional empathy) or understanding the client's predicament cognitively, whether on an individual, family, or societal level (cognitive empathy). Following is an illustration of emotional empathy:

> A white male therapist in his late 20s is beginning therapy with a recently immigrated, 39-year-old West Indian woman. The client expresses concern about her adolescent daughter who she describes as behaving in an angry, hostile way toward her fiancé. The woman is well dressed and is somewhat abrupt, seeming to be impatient with the therapist. Though not a parent himself, the therapist recognizes the distress behind his client's sternness, and thinking of the struggles he had with his own father, he responds to the woman's obvious discomfort saying, "I imagine that must hurt you." This intuitive response from the therapist reduced the woman's embarrassment, and she paused from the angry story of her daughter's ungratefulness to wipe a tear. (Dyche & Zayas, 2001, p. 249)

Many counselors are trained to be very direct with emotional responses, using statements such as "You feel hurt" or "You sound hurt" in an effort to demonstrate empathy. The response "I imagine that must hurt you" would be rated a more intermediate response. Statements that are even less direct might include "Some people might feel hurt by that" or "If I was in the same situation, I would feel hurt." We have found that people differ in their reaction to the directness of emotional empathy, depending on such factors as the gender, ethnicity, or cultural background of the counselor or the client, the degree of comfort and emotional bonding with the therapist, and the specific issue involved.

For example, when working with Asian international students, we have found that although there are individual differences in preference, many prefer a less direct style of emotional empathy. However, some Asian international students are fine with direct emotional empathy (this is why the counselor must be flexible and test out different forms of empathy with clients rather than prejudging them because of membership in a specific group). In general, recognition of emotional issues through either indirect or direct empathy increases the client's feeling of being understood. Effective therapists continually evaluate client responses and thus are able to determine if the degree and style of emotional empathy being used is enhancing (or detracting) from the emotional bond between therapist and client.

Cognitive empathy involves the therapist's ability to understand the issues facing the client. For example, in the case just described, the therapist might explore the possibility that the daughter's anger is related to her immigration experiences by saying, "Sometimes moving to a new country can be difficult." The degree of directness can vary by making the observation tentative by prefacing statements with "I wonder if . . . ?" or "Is it possible that . . . ?"

Cognitive empathy can also be demonstrated by communicating an understanding of the client's worldview, including the influences of family issues or discriminatory experiences, such as racism, heterosexism, ageism, or sexism. By exploring or including broader societal elements such as these, a therapist is able to incorporate diversity or cross-cultural perspectives and potentially enhance understanding of the client's concerns.

Communicating an understanding of different worldviews and acknowledging the possibility of cultural influences can increase the therapist's credibility with the client. When working with diverse clients, we believe that empathy must include the ability to accept and be open to multiple perspectives of personal, societal, and cultural realities. This can be achieved by exploring the impact of cultural differences or diversity issues on client problems, goals, and solutions (Dyche & Zayas, 2001; R. C. Chung & Bernak, 2002).

Empathy may be difficult in multicultural counseling if counselors are unable to identify personal cultural blinders or values they may hold. For example, among counselors working with African American clients, those with color-blind racial attitudes (i.e., a belief that race is not a significant factor in determining one's chances in society) showed lower levels of empathy than those who were aware of the significance of racial factors (Burkard & Knox, 2004). Some research suggests that counselors' multicultural counseling competence (awareness of issues of race, discrimination, and knowledge of their social impact on clients) accounts for a large proportion of the variance in ratings of counselor competence, expertise, and trustworthiness made by clients of color (Constantine, 2002; Fuertes & Brobst, 2002).

In a study of gay and bisexual clients, a counselor's *universal-diversity orientation* (i.e., interest in diversity, contact with diverse groups, comfort with similarities and differences) was positively related to client ratings of the therapeutic alliance, whereas, surprisingly, similarities in sexual orientation between therapist and client were not. Universal-diversity orientation may facilitate therapy through affirmation and understanding of the issues a culturally diverse client is facing (Stracuzzi, Mohr, & Fuertes, 2011).

In contrast, the therapeutic alliance can be adversely affected when ethnic minority clients perceive a therapist to be culturally insensitive or believe that the therapist is minimizing the importance of racial and cultural issues or pathologizing cultural values or communication styles (Constantine, 2007; Sue, Bucceri, Lin, Nadal, & Torino, 2007). This finding is likely true with other diverse groups who may endure heterosexism, ageism, religious intolerance, and/or prejudice against disability. Sensitivity to the possible impact of racial and societal issues can be made through statements such as the following:

- "Have experiences with discrimination or unfairness had an impact on the problems you are dealing with?"
- "Sometimes it's difficult to meet the societal demands of being a man (or a woman). Could this be related to your difficulty expressing your emotions?"
- "Some people believe that family members should be involved in making decisions for individuals in the family. Is this true in your family?"

- "Being or feeling different can be related to messages we receive from our family, society, or religious institutions. Have you considered whether your feelings of isolation are related to messages you are getting from others?"
- "Families change over time. What are some of the standards or values you learned as a young child? I wonder if the conflicts in your family are related to differences in expectations between you and your parents."

These examples are stated in a very tentative manner. If a counselor has sufficient information, more direct statements of cognitive empathy can be made. We believe that the perception of and response to empathy varies from individual to individual. There are no set responses that will convey empathy and understanding to all clients. In general, therapists must learn to evaluate their use of both cognitive and emotional empathy to determine whether it is improving the emotional bond with the client and to make modifications, if needed, to enhance the client's perception of empathy within the relationship.

Positive Regard, Respect, Warmth, and Genuineness

The characteristics of positive regard, respect, warmth, and genuineness are important qualities in establishing an emotional bond. *Positive regard* is the demonstration by the therapist that he or she sees the strengths and positive aspects of the client, including appreciation for the values and differences displayed by the client. Positive regard is demonstrated when the counselor identifies and focuses on the strengths and assets of the individual rather than attending only to deficits or problems. This is especially important for members of ethnic minorities and other diverse groups whose behaviors are often pathologized. *Respect* is shown by being attentive and by demonstrating that you view the client as an important person. Behaviors such as asking clients how they would like to be addressed, showing that their comments and insights are valuable, and tailoring your interaction according to their needs or values are all ways of communicating respect. *Warmth* is the emotional feeling received by the client when the therapist conveys verbal and nonverbal signs of appreciation and acceptance. Smiling, the use of humor, or showing interest in the client can convey this feeling. *Genuineness* can be displayed in many different ways. It generally means a therapist is responding to a client openly and in a "real" manner, rather than responding in accordance with expected roles. These interpersonal attributes can strengthen the therapist-client alliance and increase the client's trust, cooperation, and motivation to participate in therapy.

Self-Disclosure

Although self-disclosure is considered to be a "promising and probably effective" technique (Ackerman et al., 2001), the topic of a therapist revealing personal thoughts or personal information remains controversial. In one study, brief or limited therapist self-disclosure in response to comparable self-disclosure by the client was associated with reductions in symptom distress and greater liking for the therapist (Barrett & Berman, 2001).

Counselor disclosure in cross-cultural situations (e.g., sharing reactions to clients' experiences of racism or oppression) may also enhance the therapeutic alliance (Burkard, Knox, Groen, Perez, & Hess, 2006; Cashwell, Shcherbakova, & Cashwell, 2003). Self-disclosures may show the therapist's human qualities and lead to the development of closer ties with the client. Research to determine the impact of therapist self-disclosure is difficult since it depends on many variables, such as the type of disclosure, its timing and frequency, and client characteristics. Although many clients report that therapist self-disclosure enhances the therapeutic relationship, some self-disclosures by a therapist (e.g., being wealthy or politically conservative) can actually interfere with the therapist-client relationship (D. F. Chang & Berk, 2009).

Some therapists feel that self-disclosure is not appropriate in therapy, and they either will not answer personal questions or will bounce the question back to the client. However, some clients who ask, "Has this ever happened to you?" may be doing so in an attempt to normalize their experience. Bouncing the question back to the client by saying, "Let's find out why you want to know this," can be perceived as patronizing rather than helpful (Hays, 2001). Should you make self-disclosures to a client? The answer is, "It depends." Sharing experiences or reactions can strengthen the emotional bond between therapist and client. However, such self-disclosure should be limited and aimed at helping the client with his or her issues. If the requests for self-disclosure become frequent or too personal, the therapist should explore with the client the reason for the inquiries.

Management of Countertransference

Appropriate management of countertransference can enhance the therapeutic alliance, as well as minimize ruptures in the therapeutic relationship. *Countertransference* involves the therapist's emotional reaction to the client based on the therapist's own set of attitudes, beliefs, values, or experiences. These emotional reactions, whether negative or positive, can bias a therapist's judgment when working with a client. For example, a therapist might exhibit negative reactions to a client due to factors such as heterosexism, racism, or classism. Additionally, difficulty can occur when clients demonstrate values and perspectives similar to the therapist's own; such similarity may reduce therapist objectivity. Therapists sometimes overidentify with clients who are similar to them and subsequently underestimate the client's role in interpersonal difficulties. These "unconscious" reactions can interfere with the formation of a healthy therapeutic emotional bond with the client. Because of the negative impact of countertransference, clinicians should examine their experiences, values, and beliefs when experiencing an emotional reaction to a client that is beyond what is expected from the therapy session.

A scientific frame of mind necessitates the examination of one's own values and beliefs in order to anticipate the impact of possible differences and similarities in worldviews on the therapeutic alliance. Multicultural therapists have been in the forefront of stressing the importance of acknowledging the influence of values, preferences, and worldviews on psychotherapy and the psychotherapist. It is important to be self-aware and recognize when personal needs or values are being activated in the therapeutic relationship and to not project our reactions onto clients (Brems, 2000).

Goal Consensus

An agreement on goals between the therapist and the client (i.e., goal consensus) is another important relationship variable. Unless the client agrees on what the goals should be, little progress will be made. As therapists, we too easily envision what the appropriate outcome should be when working with a client and become dismayed or discouraged when a client does not feel the same way or seems satisfied with more limited solutions. Goals should be determined in a collaborative manner with input from both client and therapist. Although it is very important to get the client's response in regard to the problem and goals, the therapist has the important task of clarifying client statements and providing tentative suggestions.

Clients often identify global goals, such as "wanting to improve self-esteem." The therapist's job is to help the client define the goal more specifically and to foster alternative ways of interpreting situations (Hilsenroth & Cromer, 2007). Concrete goals enhance the ability to measure progress in therapy. To obtain more specificity regarding a global goal, therapists can ask such questions as: "What does your low self-esteem prevent you from doing?" "How would your life be different if you had high self-esteem?" "What would you be able to do if you had more self-esteem?" or "How would you know if you are improving in self-esteem?" The answer to these questions, such as "being able to hold a job or ask for a raise," "feeling more comfortable in group situations," or "standing up for myself," can help identify aspects of self-esteem that are more concrete. Each of these responses can be used to define sub-goals. A client might be asked, "What are small steps that you can make that will show you are moving in the direction of higher self-esteem?"

Once goals are identified, the client and the therapist can work together to identify which strategies and techniques will be employed to help the client achieve the stated goals. In order for interventions to be useful, they need to make sense to the client. For ethnic minority clients, interventions may require "cultural adaptation," such as the study by Huey and Pan (2006) in which the treatment of phobias was modified for Asian Americans by emphasizing the strategy of emotional control and maximizing a directive role for the therapist.

Although the selection of interventions depends upon the presenting problem and diagnosis, psychological interventions are most effective when they are consistent with client characteristics, including the client's culture and values (La Roche, Batista, & D'Angelo, 2011). It is also important that the client believe that the therapeutic approach will be helpful. In a study by Coombs, Coleman, and Jones (2002), clients who reported "understanding the therapy process" and "having positive expectations of the therapy" were more likely to improve.

Implications

The effectiveness of therapy is highly dependent on the quality of the relationship between the therapist and the client. This finding transcends racial and ethnic differences and contributes up to 30% of the variance in treatment outcome. It is evident that the relationship between the therapist and the client is critical. In many cases, when given a choice, clients would select a less effective treatment if it were provided by a caring, empathetic treatment. Ethnic minorities may differ in the relational styles preferences, so therapists should be flexible and evaluate the degree of fit between their relational style and that preferred by their client and should vary the approach, if necessary, to improve the therapeutic alliance. As mentioned by Benish, Quintana, and Wampold (2011), exploring the "illness myth" of the client in regard to his or her beliefs regarding etiology, course, and treatment is highly important in the therapeutic relationship and can enhance collaborative identification of goals and interventions.

REFLECTION AND DISCUSSION QUESTIONS

1. What was your therapy training in regard to the formation of the therapeutic alliance with a client? Indicate how the relationship skills were discussed in relation to cross-cultural competence.
2. What is your experience in working with ethnic minorities or other diverse populations? Did they appear to require different relationship skills? Did you evaluate the effectiveness of your responses?

EVIDENCE-BASED PRACTICE AND DIVERSITY ISSUES IN THERAPY

The American Psychological Association's focus on ESRs provided an opening for counselors to address multicultural concerns within an evidence-based framework. However, the broader and more recent focus on EBP has more formally introduced cultural sensitivity as an essential consideration in assessment, case conceptualization, and selection of interventions. Specifically, *EBP* refers to "the integration of the best available research with clinical expertise in the context of patient characteristics, culture, and preferences" (American Psychological Association, Presidential Task Force on Evidence-Based Practice, 2006, p. 273). (See Figure 9.1.)

Empirically based practice includes both evidence-based treatments and relationship variables but is broader and more comprehensive than their combination. How does EBP differ from the EST and ESR frameworks?

First, the assumption underlying EBP is that the search for the "best research evidence" *begins* with a comprehensive understanding of the client's background and problem and goes on to consider which therapeutic approach is most likely to provide the best outcome. In other words, the selection of intervention occurs *only after* individual characteristics, such as cultural background and values and preferences, are assessed. This allows for the individualizing of therapy with strong consideration given to client background and characteristics.

Second, unlike ESTs, which rely primarily on randomized controlled trials, EBP also accepts research evidence from qualitative studies, clinical observations, systematic case studies, and interventions delivered in naturalistic settings. This

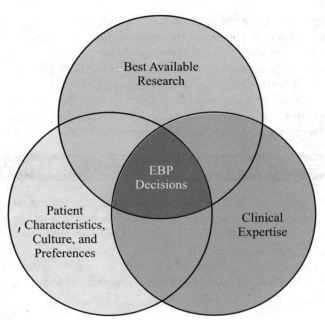

Figure 9.1 Three Pillars of Evidence-Based Practice
Source: Morales & Norcross (2010), p. 824.

broadening of the definition of research allows mental health professionals greater latitude in deciding which therapy may be the best match for a particular client. For example, the National Registry of Evidence-based Programs and Practices (NREPP) provides specific information regarding treatments for substance abuse that consider the race and ethnicity of the participants and treatments designed for certain ethnic groups, such as the American Indian Life Skills Development Program (Berke et al., 2011).

Third, the definition of clinical expertise within the EBP framework focuses not only on the quality of the therapeutic relationship and therapeutic alliance but also on skills essential for comprehensive assessment of the client's problem and client strengths. Additionally, EBP considers clinical expertise involving factors such as knowledge about cultural differences; best practices in assessment, diagnosis, and case conceptualization; strategies for evaluating and selecting appropriate research-based treatments; and adapting selected treatments in a manner that respects the client's worldview, values, and preferences.

Fourth, EBP is based on an ongoing emphasis on client characteristics, culture, and preferences and the importance of working collaboratively with the client to develop goals and treatment strategies that are mutually agreeable. Identification of client variables includes but is not limited to (a) age and life stage, (b) sociocultural factors (e.g., gender, sexual orientation, ethnicity, disability), (c) environmental stressors (e.g., unemployment, recent life events, racism, health disparities), and (d) personal treatment preferences (i.e., treatment expectations, goals, and beliefs).

Because the *focus* is on the client and the consideration of cultural variables, EBP sets the stages for a multiculturally sensitive counseling relationship. The following illustration of how EBP and multicultural sensitivity can be integrated is based on the case of Anna, an American Indian female who developed PTSD following a sexual assault.

Anna is a 14-year-old American Indian female who was sexually abused by a 22-year-old male in her small community. Anna disclosed the abuse to her school counselor, who then reported the incident to tribal law enforcement. After word of the incident spread through the community, several individuals accused Anna of lying and then harassed her in an attempt to recant her allegation. Anna began isolating herself at home and stopped attending school. Anna became increasingly depressed and demonstrated symptoms consistent with PTSD. (BigFoot & Schmidt, 2010, p. 854)

BigFoot and Schmidt (2010) were able to meld American Indian traditional healing processes and cultural teachings within an EBP framework. Aspects of this process included assessment of Anna's personal characteristics and preferences and the influence of culture on her reactions to the trauma. Following careful assessment, intervention strategies were selected based on assessment data, therapist expertise, research regarding effective treatments for posttraumatic stress, and cultural adaptation of the therapy selected. The steps involved the following:

- Research-supported treatments for childhood or adolescent trauma were identified. Trauma-focused cognitive-behavioral therapy (TF-CBT) was chosen because it was seen to complement many of the traditional healing practices used in Anna's tribe, including traditional beliefs about the relationship between emotions, beliefs, and behaviors. TF-CBT is a conjoint child and family psychotherapy that has been comprehensively evaluated and designated by the National Crime Victims Research and Treatment Center as having the highest level of research support as an "efficacious treatment" for childhood abuse and trauma. TF-CBT has been evaluated with Caucasian and African American children and adapted for American Indian/Alaska Native populations, Latinos, hearing-impaired individuals, immigrant Cambodians, and children of countries including Zambia, Uganda, South Africa, Pakistan, the Netherlands, Norway, Sweden, Germany, and Cambodia (National Childhood Traumatic Stress Network, 2008). The components of TF-CBT include a focus on reducing negative emotional and behavioral responses resulting from trauma and correcting trauma-related beliefs through gradual exposure to memories and emotional associations with the traumatic event. Relaxation training is used to reduce negative emotions. Parents are included in the treatment process as emotional support for the child; parents are provided with strategies for helping to manage their child's emotional reaction to the trauma.
- Client characteristics and values were identified through interviews with Anna and her family and by assessing their tribal and cultural identity. In Anna's case, both she and her family agreed that she had a strong American Indian identity

and valued traditional healing approaches. Thus, it was decided that a culturally adapted TF-CBT would be the most appropriate. (If Anna and her family had expressed minimal tribal or American Indian cultural identification, standard TF-CBT may have been the treatment of choice.)

• Cultural adaptations of TF-CBT were developed. Because of cultural beliefs that trauma can bring about disharmony and result in distorted beliefs and unhealthy behaviors, traditional healing efforts focus on returning the individual to a state of harmony through teachings, ceremonies, and tribal practices, including a ritual called Honoring Children, Mending the Circle (HC-MC). The Circle represents the interconnectedness of spirituality and healing and the belief that all things have a spiritual nature; prayers, tribal practices, and rituals connect the physical and the spiritual worlds, bringing wellness and harmony. Additionally, adaptation of the affect management, relaxation, cognitive coping, and enhancing the parent-child relationship aspects of TF-CBT incorporated spiritual (saying prayers), relational (support from friends and family), mental (hearing messages of love and support), and physical (helping Anna reacquire physical balance) supports, thus allowing Anna to increase feelings of safety and security. Further adaptation involved the TF-CBT goal of extinguishing the fear response using a "trauma narrative" during which the child "revisits" the traumatic incident and is gradually exposed to threatening cues. In the adaptation, culturally accepted methods for telling the trauma story—including use of a journey stick, tribal dances, and storytelling procedure—were used to facilitate exposure. Relaxation techniques were also adapted by having Anna breathe deeply while focused on culturally relevant images, such as the "sway of wind-swept grasses" or the movement of a "woman's shawl during a ceremonial dance."

As BigFoot and Schmidt concluded, "the adaption of TF-CBT within an American Indian/Alaskan Native well-being framework can enhance healing through the blending of science and indigenous cultures. . . . The HC-MC adaptation seeks to honor what makes American Indians and Alaska Natives culturally unique through respecting beliefs, practices, and traditions within their families, communities, tribes, and villages that are inherently healing" (p. 855).

REFLECTION AND DISCUSSION QUESTIONS

1. What is your reaction to EBP, especially as it applies to ethnic minorities and other diverse populations?
2. It is clear that using an EBP approach requires greater time and effort on the part of clinicians to develop a treatment plan. The implication is that counselors must do out-of-office education or consultation regarding what is available in the research literature that would help inform their practice. Is such an approach too time-consuming? Given that EBP research is exploding in the field, how would you keep current or informed as a practitioner?

Implications for Clinical Practice

We have seen that a focus on EBP in the counseling field began with the search for ESTs and relationship variables. However, both approaches inadequately addressed the needs of ethnic minority and other diverse populations. The standards used to determine ESTs and ESRs were often too rigid and ignored the cultural context in advocating for the role of science and research in the selection of therapeutic treatments and interventions. Since that time, most mental health professionals have moved to the concept of EBP, (a) allowing for a broader array of means to determine the selection, process, and outcome of effective treatments and (b) integrating cultural factors and/or modifying approaches to fit the needs of diverse clients. Given the movement to EBP, it is important for culturally competent mental health providers to be cognizant of the following implications for their practice.

1. Know that multicultural counseling and EBP are "strange bedfellows no more" and that these approaches need one another to provide legitimacy. Because of changing demographics and the vast range of cultural diversity among those who seek mental health treatment, it is obvious that traditional therapies need to incorporate cultural components. It is no longer adequate to devise a treatment plan solely on the basis of one's theoretical orientation, clinical intuition, or clinical expertise. The increasing accumulation of research on EBPs and its possible application to working with diverse clients provides another lens from which to view therapeutic strategies.

2. Be aware that EBP models focusing on client characteristics and evaluating the degree of fit between a therapeutic approach and an individual client have actually legitimized the outcry of those in the field of multicultural counseling—that it is essential to consider the cultural beliefs and values of the client and that relational counselor styles may need to vary according to an individual's cultural background.

3. Know that the integration of EBP and multiculturalism is resulting in an explosion of research. With the emphasis of the former on client characteristics, values, preference, and culture, EBP and multicultural therapy are becoming inextricably entwined, with each approach adding strengths to the other. Thus it is incumbent upon mental health professionals to spend time familiarizing themselves with the research literature and to take care in developing their culturally sensitive treatment plans.

4. Understand that identification of treatments is only one step in a complex process; it is vital that we also consider contextual and cultural influences and therapist-client relationship factors in treatment outcome. EBP can provide clinicians with information regarding which therapies are most effective with which specific disorders and which specific populations. We should always be aware of experimentally supported techniques when working with client problems. Thus, in choosing a treatment strategy, the best approach (given the current state of research) is for the counselor to select an intervention that is research based (if available) and subsequently adapt the approach for the individual client according to the client's individual characteristics, values, and preferences.

(continued)

(*continued*)

5. Know that culturally competent counseling and therapy is more than a technique-driven search for effective techniques and strategies. We now know that the therapeutic alliance or working relationship is crucial to therapeutic outcome. In fact, nearly one third of therapeutic effectiveness is attributable to the establishment of a good working relationship: (a) an emotional or interpersonal bond between therapist and client, (b) mutual agreement on appropriate goals between therapist and client, and (c) intervention strategies or activities considered relevant by both client and therapist. This relationship assumes greater significance for clients from diverse backgrounds. In fact, difficulties in the therapeutic alliance may be a factor in the underutilization of mental health services and early termination of therapy seen with minority clients.

6. Be prepared to modify your therapeutic style to be consistent with the cultural values, life styles, and needs of culturally diverse clients. Remember, respect, unconditional positive regard, warmth, and empathy are most effective in the therapeutic alliance when they are communicated in a culturally consistent manner. For example, it appears that Black, Asian, Latino/a, and multiracial clients prefer an active counselor role, which is characterized by the counselor offering concrete suggestions, providing direct answers, challenging the client's thinking with thought-provoking questions, and providing psychoeducation in the therapy.

7. Educate and enlighten yourselves in understanding the worldview of your clients and what it means for them to occupy a marginalized or socially devalued status in our society. As we have seen, Asian, Black, Latino/a, and multiracial clients who were dissatisfied in cross-racial therapy complained about their therapist's lack of knowledge about racial identity development; the dynamics of power and privilege; the effects of racism, discrimination, and oppression due to their minority status (or multiple minority statuses); and cultural stigma associated with seeking help. Some research suggests that a counselor's multicultural counseling competence (awareness of issues of race and discrimination and knowledge of their social impact on clients) accounts for a large proportion of the variance in ratings of counselor competence, expertise, and trustworthiness made by clients of color.

8. Lastly, it is important to note that most approaches to counseling and therapy attempt to adapt the research findings of EBP to fit the unique cultural characteristics and needs of diverse populations. But what if we approach the challenge to develop culturally appropriate therapeutic techniques and relationships from an indigenous perspective first? Rather than trying to adapt therapeutic techniques to persons of color, for example, what if we asked the following questions: "What indigenous healing approaches have proven effective in minority communities and in different societies?" "What if we start first from an indigenous healing perspective and then incorporate or merge EBP into the treatment plan?" "Would culturally competent care look any different?" These are questions we address in the next chapter (Chapter 10: *Non-Western and Indigenous Methods of Healing*).

Non-Western Indigenous Methods of Healing: Implications for Counseling and Therapy

CHAPTER FOCUS QUESTIONS

1. What is indigenous healing? What is shamanism?
2. How valid are shamanic explanations of illness? Are shamans therapists? In what ways do you believe they are the same? Can you identify commonalities between what therapists and shamans do?
3. What are the core features or characteristics of indigenous healing? Do you believe them to be valid or invalid?
4. What can we learn from indigenous forms of healing?
5. Isn't shamanism antagonistic to science? Are there dangers or downsides to shamanism as a belief system or form of treatment?
6. Do you believe in altered states of consciousness or different planes of existence?
7. In what ways do religion and spirituality affect your life?
8. Would you be uncomfortable talking to clients about religion and spirituality? Would you do it? Would you pray with a client?

Case Study: Vang Xiong

Vang Xiong is a former Hmong (Laotian) soldier who, with his wife and child, resettled in Chicago in 1980. The change from his familiar rural surroundings and farm life to an unfamiliar urban area must have produced a severe culture shock. In addition, Vang vividly remembers seeing people killed during his escape from Laos, and he expressed feeling of guilt about having to leave his brothers and sisters behind in that country. Five months after his arrival, the Xiong family moved into a conveniently located apartment, and that is when Vang's problems began.

Vang could not sleep the first night in the apartment, nor the second, nor the third. After three nights of very little sleep, Vang came to see his resettlement worker, a young bilingual Hmong man named Moua Lee. Vang told Moua that the first night he work suddenly, short of breath, from a dream in which a cat was sitting on his chest. The second night, the room suddenly grew darker, and a figure, like a large black dog, came to his bed and sat on his chest. He could not push the dog off, and he grew quickly and dangerously short of breath. The third night, a tall, white-skinned female spirit came into his bedroom from the kitchen and lay on top of him. Her weight made it increasingly difficult for him to breathe; as he grew frantic and tried to call out, he could manage nothing but a whisper. He attempted to turn onto his side but found he was pinned down. After 15 minutes, the spirit left him, and he awoke, screaming. He was afraid to return to the apartment at night, afraid to fall asleep, and afraid he would die during the night, or that the spirit would make it so that he and his wife could never have another child. He told Moua that once, when he was 15, he had a similar attack; that several times, back in Laos, his elder brother had been visited by a similar spirit; and that his brother was subsequently unable to father children due to his wife's miscarriages and infertility. (Tobin & Friedman, 1983, p. 440)

Moua Lee and mental health workers became very concerned in light of the high incidence of sudden death syndrome among Southeast Asian refugees. For some reason, the incidence of unexplained deaths, primarily among Hmong men, would occur within the first 2 years of residence in the United States. Autopsies produced no identifiable cause for the deaths. All the reports were the same: A person in apparently good health went to sleep and died without waking. Often the victim displayed labored breathing, screams, and frantic movements just before death. With this dire possibility evident for Vang, the mental health staff felt that they lacked the expertise for so complex and potentially dangerous a case. Conventional Western means of treatment for other Hmong clients had proved minimally effective. As a result, they decided to seek the services of Mrs. Thor, a 50-year-old Hmong woman who was widely respected in Chicago's Hmong community as a shaman. The description of the treatment follows.

Vang Xiong (*continued*)

That evening, Vang Xiong was visited in his apartment by Mrs. Thor, who began by asking Vang to tell her what was wrong. She listened to his story, asked a few questions, and then told him she thought she could help. She gathered the Xiong family around the dining room table, upon which she placed some candles alongside many plates of food that Vang's wife had prepared. Mrs. Thor lit the candles and then began a chant that Vang and his wife knew was an attempt to communicate with spirits. Ten minutes or so after Mrs. Thor had begun chanting, she was so intensely involved in her work that Vang and his family felt free to talk to each other and to walk about the room without fear of distracting her. Approximately 1 hour after she had begun, Mrs. Thor completed her chanting, announcing that she knew what was wrong. Vang said that she had learned from her spirit that the figures in Vang's dreams who lay on his chest and made it so difficult for him to breathe were the souls of the apartment's previous tenants, who had apparently moved out so abruptly they had left their souls behind. Mrs. Thor constructed a cloak out of newspaper for Vang to wear. She then cut hte cloak in two and burned the pieces, sending the spirits on their way with the smoke. She also had Vang crawl through a hoop, and then between two knives, telling him that these maneuvers would make it very hard for spirits to follow. Following these brief ceremonies, the food prepared by Vang's wife was enjoyed by all. The leftover meats were given in payment to Mrs. Thor, and she left, assuring Vang Xiong that his troubles with spirits were over. (Tobin & Friedman, 1983, p. 441)

Clinical knowledge regarding what is called the Hmong sudden death syndrome indicates that Vang was one of the lucky victims of the syndrome, in that he survived it. Indeed, since undergoing the healing ceremony that released the unhappy spirits, Vang has reported no more problems with nightmares or with his breathing during sleep. Such a story may appear unbelievable and akin to mysticism to many people. After all, most of us have been trained in a Western ontology that does not embrace indigenous or alternative healing approaches. Indeed, if anything, it actively rejects such approaches as unscientific and supernatural. Mental health professionals are encouraged to rely on sensory information, defined by the physical plane of existence rather than the spiritual plane (Pedersen & Pope, 2010; Walsh & Shapiro, 2006). Such a rigid stance is unfortunate and shortsighted because there is much that Western healing can learn from these age-old forms of treatment. Let us briefly analyze the case of Vang Xiong to illustrate what these valuable lessons might be and to draw parallels between non-Western and Western healing practices.

THE LEGITIMACY OF CULTURE-BOUND SYNDROMES: NIGHTMARE DEATHS AND THE HMONG SUDDEN DEATH PHENOMENON

The symptoms experienced by Vang and the frighteningly high number of early Hmong refugees who have died from these so-called nightmare deaths have baffled mental health workers for years. Indeed, researchers at the Federal Center for Disease Control and epidemiologists have studied it but remain mystified (D. Sue, D. W. Sue, D. M. Sue, & S. Sue, 2013; Tobin & Friedman, 1983). Such tales bring to mind anthropological literature describing voodoo deaths and *bangungut*, or Oriental nightmare death. What is clear, however, is that these deaths do not appear to have a primary biological basis and that psychological factors (primarily belief in the imminence of death, either by a curse, as in voodoo suggestion, or by some form of punishment and excessive stress) appear to be causative (Moodley,

2005). Beliefs in spirits and spirit possession are not uncommon among many cultures, especially in Southeast Asia (Eliade, 1972; Faiver, Ingersoll, O'Brien, & McNally, 2001). Such worldview differences pose problems for Western-trained mental health professionals who may quickly dismiss these belief systems and impose their own explanations and treatments on culturally diverse clients. Working outside of the belief system of such clients may not have the desired therapeutic effect, and the risk of unintentional harm (in this case the potential death of Vang) is great. That the sudden death phenomenon is a culture-bound reality is being increasingly recognized by Western science (Kamarck & Jennings, 1991). Most researchers now acknowledge that attitudes, beliefs, and emotional states are intertwined and can have a powerful effect on physiological responses and physical well-being. Death from bradycardia (slowing of the heartbeat) seems correlated with feelings of helplessness, as in the case of Vang (there was nothing he could do to get the cat, dog, or white-skinned spirit off his chest).

The text revision of the fourth edition of the American Psychiatric Association's *Diagnostic and Statistical Manual of Mental Disorders* (*DSM-IV-TR*, American Psychiatric Association, 2000) has made initial strides in recognizing the importance of ethnic and cultural factors related to psychiatric diagnosis. The manual warns that mental health professionals who work with immigrant and ethnic minorities must take into account (a) the predominant means of manifesting disorders (e.g., possessing spirits, nerves, fatalism, inexplicable misfortune), (b) the perceived causes or explanatory models, and (c) the preferences for professional and indigenous sources of care. Interestingly, the *DSM-IV-TR* now contains a glossary of culture-bound syndromes in Appendix I (see Table 10.1 for a listing of these disorders). They describe culture-bound syndromes as follows:

> Recurrent, locality-specific patterns of aberrant behavior and troubling experience that may or may not be linked to a particular *DSM-IV* diagnostic category. Many of these patterns are indigenously considered to be "illnesses," or at least afflictions, and most have local names. . . . Culture-bound syndromes are generally limited to specific societies or culture areas and are localized, folk, diagnostic categories that frame coherent meanings for certain repetitive, patterned, and troubling sets of experiences and observations. (American Psychiatric Association, 2000, p. 898)

Although *DSM-IV-TR* acknowledges the importance of culture in diagnosis, there is much controversy over current plans to eliminate culture-bound syndromes in the new *DSM-5* manual (due to be published in May 2013). Many multicultural psychologists believe such a move would be a major step backward. At this time, little is known about how the *DSM-5* Work Group plans to handle race, culture, ethnicity, and gender in the forthcoming classification system. In summary, it is very important for mental health professionals not only to become familiar with the cultural background of their clients but also to be knowledgeable about specific culture-bound syndromes. A primary danger from lack of cultural understanding is the tendency to overpathologize (overestimate the degree of

Table 10.1   Culture-Bound Syndromes from the *DSM-IV*

Culture-bound syndromes are disorders specific to a cultural group or society but not easily given a *DSM-IV-TR* diagnosis. These illnesses or afflictions have local names with distinct culturally sanctioned beliefs surrounding causation and treatment. Some of these are briefly described.

Amok
This disorder was first reported in Malaysia but is found also in Laos, the Philippines, Polynesia, Papua New Guinea, and Puerto Rico, as well as among the Navajo. It is a dissociative episode preceded by introspective brooding and then an outburst of violent, aggressive, or homicidal behavior toward people and objects. Persecutory ideas, amnesia, and exhaustion signal a return to the premorbid state.

Ataque de nervios
This disorder is most clearly reported among Latinos from the Caribbean but is recognized in Latin American and Latin Mediterranean groups as well. It involves uncontrollable shouting, attacks of crying, trembling, verbal or physical aggression, and dissociative or seizure-like fainting episodes. The onset is associated with a stressful life event relating to family (e.g., death of a loved one, divorce, conflicts with children).

Brain fag
This disorder is usually experienced by high-school or university students in West Africa in response to academic stress. Students state that their brains are fatigued and that they have difficulties in concentrating, remembering, and thinking.

Ghost sickness
Observed among members of American Indian tribes, this disorder is a preoccupation with death and the deceased. It is sometimes associated with witchcraft and includes bad dreams, weakness, feelings of danger, loss of appetite, fainting, dizziness, anxiety, and a sense of suffocation.

Koro
This Malaysian term describes an episode of sudden and intense anxiety that the penis of the male or the vulva and nipples of the female will recede into the body and cause death. It can occur in epidemic proportions in local areas and has been reported in China, Thailand, and other South and East Asian countries.

Mal de ojo
Found primarily in Mediterranean cultures, this term refers to a Spanish phrase that means "evil eye." Children are especially at risk, and symptoms include fitful sleep, crying without apparent cause, diarrhea, vomiting, and fever.

Nervios
This disorder includes a range of symptoms associated with distress, somatic disturbance, and inability to function. Common symptoms include headaches, brain aches, sleep difficulties, nervousness, easy tearfulness, dizziness, and tingling sensations. It is a common idiom of distress among Latinos in the United States and Latin America.

Rootwork
This refers to cultural interpretations of illness ascribed to hexing, witchcraft, sorcery, or the evil influence of another person. Symptoms include generalized anxiety, gastrointestinal complaints, and fear of being poisoned or killed (voodoo death). Roots, spells, or hexes can be placed on people. It is believed that a cure can be manifested via a root doctor who removes the root. Such a belief can be found in the southern United States among both African American and European American populations and in Caribbean societies.

Shen-k'uei (Taiwan); Shenkui (China)
This is a Chinese-described disorder that involves anxiety and panic symptoms with somatic complaints. There is no identifiable physical cause. Sexual dysfunctions are common (premature ejaculation and impotence). The physical symptoms are attributed to excessive semen loss from frequent intercourse, masturbation, nocturnal emission, or passing of "white turbid urine" believed to contain semen. Excessive semen loss is feared and can be life threatening because it represents one's vital essence.

Susto
This disorder is associated with fright or soul loss and is a prevalent folk illness among some Latinos in the United States as well as inhabitants of Mexico, Central America, and South America. Susto is attributed to a frightening event that causes the soul to leave the body.

(continued)

Table 10.1	(*continued*)
Zar	Sickness and death may result. Healing is associated with rituals that call the soul back to the body and restore spiritual balance.
	This term is used to describe spirits possessing an individual. Dissociative episodes, shouting, laughing, hitting the head against a wall, weeping, and other demonstrative symptoms are associated with it. It is found in Ethiopia, Somalia, Egypt, Sudan, Iran, and other North African and Middle Eastern societies. People may develop a long-term relationship with the spirit, and their behavior is not considered pathological.

pathology); the mental health professional would have been wrong in diagnosing Vang as a paranoid schizophrenic suffering from delusions and hallucinations. Most might have prescribed powerful antipsychotic medication or even institutionalization. The fact that he was cured so quickly indicates that such a diagnosis would have been erroneous. Interestingly, it is equally dangerous to underestimate the severity or complexity of a refugee's emotional condition.

Causation and Spirit Possession

Vang believed that his problems were related to an attack by undesirable spirits. His story in the following passage gives us some idea about beliefs associated with the fears.

Vang Xiong (*continued*)

The most recent attack in Chicago was not the first encounter my family and I have had with this type of spirit, a spirit we call Chia. My brother and I endured similar attacks about six years ago back in Laos. We are susceptible to such attacks because we didn't follow all of the mourning rituals we should have when our parents died. Because we didn't properly honor their memories, we have lost contact with their spirits, and thus we are left with no one to protect us from evil spirits. Without our parents' spirits to aid us, we will always be susceptible to spirit attacks. I had hoped flying so far in a plane to come to America would protect me, but it turns out spirits can follow even this far. (Tobin & Friedman, 1983, p. 444)

Western science remains skeptical of using supernatural explanations to explain phenomena and certainly does not consider the existence of spirits to be scientifically sound. Yet belief in spirits and its parallel relationship to religious, philosophic, and scientific worldviews have existed in every known culture, including the United States (e.g., the witch hunts of Salem, Massachusetts). Among many Southeast Asian groups, it is not uncommon to posit the existence of good and evil spirits, to assume that they are intelligent beings, and to believe that they are able to affect the life circumstances of the living (Fadiman, 1997; E. Lee, 1996). Vang, for example, believed strongly that his problems were due to spirits who were unhappy with him and were punishing him. Interestingly, among the Hmong, good spirits often serve a protective function against evil spirits. Because Vang's parental spirits had deserted him, he believed he was more susceptible to the workings of evil forces. Many cultures believe that a cure can come about only through the aid of a shaman or a healer who can reach and communicate with the spirit world via divination skills.

Although mental health professionals may not believe in spirits, therapists are similar to the Hmong in their need to explain the troubling phenomena experienced by Vang and to construe meaning from them. Vang's sleep disturbances, nightmares, and fears can be seen as the result of emotional distress. From a Western perspective, his war experiences, flight, relocation, and survivor stress (not to mention the adjustment to a new country) may all be attributed to combat fatigue (posttraumatic stress disorder, or PTSD) and survivor guilt (Mollica, Wyshak, & Lavelle, 1987; Tobin & Friedman, 1983). Studies on hundreds of thousands of refugees from Southeast Asia suggest that they were severely traumatized during their flight for freedom (Mollica et al., 1987). The most frequent diagnoses for this group were generally major affective disorder and PTSD. In addition to being a combat veteran, Vang is a disaster victim, a survivor of a holocaust that has seen perhaps 200,000 of the approximately 500,000 Hmong die. Vang's sleeplessness, breathing difficulties, paranoid belief that something attacked him in bed, and symptoms of anxiety and depression are the result of extreme trauma and stress. Tobin and Friedman (1983) believed that Vang also suffered from survivor's guilt and concluded:

> Applying some of the insights of the Holocaust literature to the plight of the Southeast Asian refugees, we can view Vang Xiong's emotional crisis (his breathing and sleeping disorder) as the result not so much of what he suffered as what he did not suffer, of what he was spared. . . . "Why should I live while others died?" So Vang Xiong, through his symptoms, seemed to be saying, "Why should I sleep comfortably here in America while the people I left behind suffer? How can I claim the right to breathe when so many of my relatives and countrymen breathe no more back in Laos?" (p. 443)

Even though we might be able to recast Vang's problems in more acceptable psychological terminology, the effective multicultural helping professional requires knowledge of cultural relativism and respect for the belief system of culturally different clients. Respecting another's worldview does not mean that the helping professional needs to subscribe to it. Yet the counselor or therapist must be willing and ready to learn from indigenous models of healing and to function as a facilitator of indigenous support systems or indigenous healing systems (Atkinson, Thompson, & Grant, 1993).

The Shaman as Therapist: Commonalities

It is probably safe to conclude that every society and culture has individuals or groups designated as healers—those who comfort the ailing. Their duties involve not only physical ailments but also those related to psychological distress or behavioral deviance (Harner, 1990). Although every culture has multiple healers, the shaman in non-Western cultures is perhaps the most powerful of all because only he or she possesses the ultimate magico-religious powers that go beyond the senses (Eliade, 1972). Mrs. Thor was a well-known and respected shaman in the Hmong community of the Chicago area. Although her approach to treating Vang (incense, candle burning, newspaper, trance-like chanting, spirit diagnosis, and even her home visit) on the surface might resemble mysticism, there is much in her behavior that is similar to Western psychotherapy. First, as we saw in Chapter 5, the healer's credibility is crucial to the effectiveness of therapy. In this case, Mrs. Thor had all the cultural credentials of a shaman; she was a specialist and professional with long years of training and experience dealing with similar cases. By reputation and behavior, she acted in a manner familiar to Vang and his family. More importantly, she shared their worldview as to the definition of the problem. Second, she showed compassion while maintaining a professional detachment, did not pity or make fun of Vang, avoided premature diagnosis or judgment, and listened to his story carefully. Third, like the Western therapist, she offered herself as the chief instrument of cure. She used her expertise and ability to get in touch with the hidden world of the spirits (in Western terms we might call it the unconscious) and helped Vang to understand (become conscious of) the mysterious power of the spirits (unconscious) to effect a cure.

Because Vang believed in spirits, Mrs. Thor's interpretation that the nightmares and breathing difficulties were spiritual problems was intelligible, desired, and ultimately curative. It is important to note, however, that Vang also continued to receive treatment from the local mental health clinic in coming to grips with the deaths of others (his parents, fellow soldiers, and other family members).

In the case of Vang Xiong, both non-Western and Western forms of healing were combined with one another for maximum effect. The presence of a mental health treatment facility that employed bilingual/bicultural practitioners, its vast experience with Southeast Asian immigrants, and its willingness to use indigenous healers provided Vang with a culturally appropriate form of treatment that probably saved his life. Not all immigrants, however, are so fortunate. Witness the following case of the Nguyen family.

Case Study: The Nguyen Family

Mr. and Mrs. Nguyen and their four children left Vietnam in a boat with 36 other people. Several days later, they were set upon by Thai pirates. The occupants were all robbed of their belongings; some were killed, including two of the Nguyens' children. Nearly all the women were raped repeatedly. The trauma of the event is still very much with the Nguyen family, who now reside in

St. Paul, Minnesota. The event was most disturbing to Mr. Nguyen, who had watched two of his children drown and his wife being raped. The pirates had beaten him severely and tied him to the boat railing during the rampage. As a result of his experiences, he continued to suffer feelings of guilt, suppressed rage, and nightmares.

The Nguyen family came to the attention of the school and social service agencies because of suspected child abuse. Their oldest child, 12-year-old Phuoc, came to school one day with noticeable bruises on his back and down his spinal column. In addition, obvious scars from past injuries were observed on the child's upper and lower torso. His gym teacher had seen the bruises and scars and immediately reported them to the school counselor. The school nurse was contacted about the possibility of child abuse, and a conference was held with Phuoc. He denied that he had been hit by his parents and refused to remove his garments when requested to do so. Indeed, he became quite frightened and hysterical about taking off his shirt. Since there was still considerable doubt about whether this was a case of child abuse, the counselor decided to let the matter drop for the moment. Nevertheless, school personnel were alerted to this possibility.

Several weeks later, after 4 days of absence, phuoc returned to school. The homeroom teacher noticed bruises on Phuoc's forehead and the bridge of his nose. When the incident was reported to the school office, the counselor immediately called Child Protective Services to report a suspected case of child abuse. Because of the heavy caseload experienced by Child Protective Services, a social worker was unable to visit the family until weeks later. The social worker, Mr. P., called the family and visited the home late on a Thursday afternoon. Mrs. Nguyen greeted Mr. P. upon his arrival. She appeared nervous, tense, and frightened. He English was poor, and it was difficult to communicate with her. Since Mr. P. had specifically requested to see Mr. Nguyen as well, he inquired about his whereabouts. Mrs. Nguyen answered that he was not feeling well and was in the room downstairs. She said he was having "a bad day," had not been able to sleep last night, and was having flashbacks. In his present condition, he would not be helpful.

When Mr. P. asked about Phuoc's bruises, Mrs. Nguyen did not seem to understand what he was referring to. The social worker explained in detail the reason for his visit. Mrs. Nguyen explained that the scars were due to the beating given to her children by the Thai pirates. She became very emotional about the topic and broke into tears. Although this had some credibility, Mr. P. explained that there were fresh bruises on Phouc's body as well. Mrs. Nguyen seemed confused, denied that there were new injuries, and denied that they would hurt Phuoc. The social worker pressed Mrs. Nguyen about the new injuries until she suddenly looked up and said, " Thùôc Nam." It was obvious that Mrs. Nguyen now understood what Mr. P. was referring to. When asked to clarify what she meant by the phrase, Mrs. Nguyen pointed at several thin bamboo sticks and a bag of coins wrapped tightly in a white cloth. It looked like a blackjack! She then pointed downstairs in the direction of the husband's room. It was obvious from Mrs. Nguyen's gestures that her husband had used these to beat her son.

A Case of Child Abuse?

There are many similarities between the case of the Nguyen family and that of Vang Xiong. One of the most common experiences of refugees forced to flee their country is the extreme stressors that they experience. Constantly staring into the face of death was, unfortunately, all too common an experience. Seeing loved ones killed, tortured, and raped; being helpless to change or control such situations; living in temporary refugee or resettlement camps; leaving familiar surroundings; and encountering a strange and alien culture can only be described as multiple severe traumas. It is highly likely that many Cambodian, Hmong/Laotian, and Vietnamese refugees suffer from serious PTSD and other forms of major affective disorders. Mr. and Mrs. Nguyen's behaviors (flashbacks, desire to isolate the self, emotional fluctuations, anxiety, and tenseness) might all be symptoms of PTSD. Accurate understanding of their life circumstances will prevent a tendency to overpathologize or underpathologize their symptoms (Mollica et al., 1987). These symptoms, along with a reluctance to disclose to strangers and discomfort with the social worker, should be placed in the context of the stressors that they experienced and their cultural background. More important, as in the case of the Nguyen family, behaviors should not be interpreted to indicate guilt or a desire not to disclose the truth about child abuse.

Second, mental health professionals must consider potential linguistic and cultural barriers when working with refugees, especially when one lacks both experience and expertise. In this case, it is clear that the teacher, the school counselor, the school nurse, and even the social worker did not have sufficient understanding or experience in working with Southeast Asian refugees. For example, the social worker's failure to understand Vietnamese phrases and Mrs. Nguyen's limited English proficiency placed serious limitations on their ability to communicate accurately (Schwartz, Rodriguez, Santiago-Rivera, et al., 2010). The social worker might have avoided much of the misunderstanding if an interpreter had been present. In addition, the school personnel may have misinterpreted many culturally sanctioned forms of behavior on the part of the Vietnamese. Phuoc's reluctance to disrobe in front of strangers (the nurse) may have been prompted by cultural taboos rather than by attempts to hide the injuries. Traditional Asian culture dictates strongly that family matters are handled within the family. Many Asians believe that family affairs should not be discussed publicly, and especially not with strangers. Disrobing publicly and telling others about the scars or the trauma of the Thai pirates would not be done readily. Yet such knowledge is required by educators and social service agencies that must make enlightened decisions.

Third, both school and social service personnel are obviously unenlightened about indigenous healing beliefs and practices. In the case of Vang Xiong, we saw how knowledge and understanding of cultural beliefs led to appropriate and helpful treatment. In the case of the Nguyen family, lack of understanding led to charges of child abuse. But is this really a case of child abuse? When Mrs. Nguyen said "Thùôc Nam," what was she referring to? What did the fresh bruises along Phuoc's spinal column, forehead, and bridge of the nose mean? And didn't Mrs. Nguyen admit that her husband used the bamboo sticks and bag of coins to beat Phuoc?

In Southeast Asia, traditional medicine derives from three sources: Western medicine (Thùôc Tay), Chinese or Northern medicine (Thùôc Bac), and Southern medicine (Thùôc Nam). Many forms of these treatments continue to exist among Asian Americans and are even more prevalent among the Vietnamese refugees who brought the treatments to the United States (Hong & Domokos-Cheng Ham, 2001). Thùôc Nam, or traditional medicine, involves using natural fruits, herbs, plants, animals, and massage to heal the body. Massage treatment is the most common cause of misdiagnosis of child abuse because it leaves bruises on the body. Three common forms of massage treatment are Băt Gió ("catching the wind"), Cao Gió ("scratching the wind," or "coin treatment"), and Giác Hoi ("pressure massage," or "dry cup massage"). The latter involves steaming bamboo tubes so that the insides are low in pressure, applying them to a portion of the skin that has been cut, and sucking out "bad air" or "hot wind." Cao Gió involves rubbing the patient with a mentholated ointment and then using coins or spoons to strike or scrape lightly along the ribs and both sides of the neck and shoulders. Băt Gió involves using both thumbs to rub the temples and massaging toward the bridge of the nose at least 20 times. Fingers are used to pinch the bridge of the nose. All three treatments leave bruises on the parts of the body treated.

If the social worker could have understood Mrs. Nguyen, he would have known that Phuoc's 4-day absence from school was due to illness and that he was treated by his parents via traditional folk medicine. Massage treatments are a widespread custom practiced not only by Vietnamese but also by Cambodians, Laotians, and Chinese. These treatments are aimed at curing a host of physical ailments, such as colds, headaches, backaches, and fevers. In the mind of the practitioner, such treatments have nothing to do with child abuse. Yet the question still remains: Is it considered child abuse when traditional healing practices result in bruises? This is a very difficult question to answer because it raises a larger question: Can culture justify a practice, especially when it is harmful? Although unable to answer this second question directly (we encourage you to engage in dialogue about it), we point out that many medical practitioners in California do not consider it child abuse because (a) medical literature reveals no physical complications as a result of Thùôc Nam; (b) the intent is not to hurt the child but to help him or her; and (c) it is frequently used in conjunction with Western medicine. However, we would add that health professionals and educators have a responsibility to educate parents concerning the potential pitfalls of many folk remedies and indigenous forms of treatment.

THE PRINCIPLES OF INDIGENOUS HEALING

Ever since the beginning of human existence, all societies and cultural groups have developed not only their own explanations of abnormal behaviors but also their culture-specific ways of dealing with human problems and distress (Gone, 2010; Harner, 1990; Solomon & Wane, 2005). Within the United States, counseling and psychotherapy are the predominant psychological healing methods. In other cultures, however, indigenous healing approaches continue to be widely used. Although there are similarities between Euro-American helping systems and the indigenous practices of many cultural groups, there are major dissimilarities as well. Western forms of counseling, for example, rely on sensory information defined by the physical plane of reality (Western science), whereas most indigenous methods rely on the spiritual plane of existence in

> Ever since the beginning of human existence, all societies and cultural groups have developed not only their own explanations of abnormal behaviors but also their culture-specific ways of dealing with human problems and distress.

seeking a cure. In keeping with the cultural encapsulation of our profession, Western healing has been slow to acknowledge and learn from these age-old forms of wisdom (Constantine, Myers, Kindaichi, & Moore, 2004; Gone, 2010; C. C. Lee, 1996). In its attempt to become culturally responsive, however, the mental health field must begin to put aside the biases of Western science, to acknowledge the existence of intrinsic help-giving networks, and to incorporate the legacy of ancient wisdom that may be contained in indigenous models of healing.

The work and writings of Lee (C. C. Lee, 1996; C. C. Lee & Armstrong, 1995; C. C. Lee, Oh, & Mountcastle, 1992) are especially helpful in this regard. C. C. Lee has studied what is called the *universal shamanic tradition*, which encompasses the centuries-old recognition of healers within a community. The anthropological term *shaman* refers to people often called witches, witch doctors, wizards, medicine men or women, sorcerers, and magic men or women. These individuals are believed to possess the power to enter an altered state of consciousness and journey to other planes of existence beyond the physical world during their healing rituals (Garrett et al., 2011; Moodley, 2005). Such was the case of Mrs. Thor, a shaman who journeyed to the spirit world in order to find a cure for Vang.

A study of indigenous healing in 16 non-Western countries found that three approaches were often used (C. C. Lee et al., 1992). First, there is heavy reliance on the use of communal, group, and family networks to shelter the disturbed individual (Saudi Arabia), to problem solve in a group context (Nigeria), and to reconnect them with family or significant others (Korea). Second, spiritual and religious beliefs and traditions of the community are used in the healing process. Examples include reading verses from the Koran and using religious houses or churches. Third, use of shamans (called *piris* and *fakirs* in Pakistan and Sudan), who are perceived to be the keepers of timeless wisdom, constitutes the norm. In many cases, the person conducting a healing ceremony may be a respected elder of the community or a family member. Two representative indigenous healing approaches are exemplified in the Hawaiian ho'oponopono and the Native American sweat lodge ceremony.

Ho'oponopono

An excellent example that incorporates these approaches is the Native Hawaiian *ho'oponopono* healing ritual (Nishihara, 1978; Rezentes, 2006). Translated literally, the word means "a setting to right, to make right, to correct." In cultural context, *ho'oponopono* attempts to restore and maintain good relations among family members and between the family and the supernatural powers. It is a kind of family conference (family therapy) aimed at restoring good and healthy harmony in the family. Many Native Hawaiians consider it to be one of the soundest methods of restoring and maintaining good relations that any society has ever developed. Such a ceremonial activity usually occurs among members of the immediate family but may involve the extended family and even nonrelatives if they were involved in the *pilikia* (trouble). The process of healing includes the following:

1. The ho'oponopono begins with *pule weke* (opening prayer) and ends with *pule ho'opau* (closing prayer). The pule creates the atmosphere for the healing and

involves asking the family gods for guidance. These gods are not asked to intervene, but to grant wisdom, understanding, and honesty.

2. The ritual elicits *'oia'i'o* or (truth telling), sanctioned by the gods, and makes compliance among participants a serious matter. The leader states the problem, prays for spiritual fusion among members, reaches out to resistant family members, and attempts to unify the group.
3. Once this occurs, the actual work begins through *mahiki*, a process of getting to the problems. Transgressions, obligations, righting the wrongs, and forgiveness are all aspects of ho'oponopono. The forgiving/releasing/severing of wrongs, the hurts, and the conflicts produces a deep sense of resolution.
4. Following the closing prayer, the family participates in *pani*, the termination ritual in which food is offered to the gods and to the participants.

In general, we can see several principles of indigenous Hawaiian healing: (a) Problems reside in relationships with people and spirits; (b) harmony and balance in the family and in nature are desirable; (c) healing must involve the entire group and not just an individual; (d) spirituality, prayer, and ritual are important aspects of healing; (e) the healing process comes from a respected elder of the family; and (f) the method of healing is indigenous to the culture (Rezentes, 2006).

Native American Sweat Lodge Ceremony

Another example of indigenous healing increasingly being employed by Western cultures in medicine, mental health, substance abuse, and correctional facilities is the Native American sweat lodge ceremony (sweat therapy) (Garrett & Portman, 2011; Garrett et al., 2011). Among Native Americans, the sweat lodge and the ensuing rituals are filled with cultural and spiritual symbolism and meaning. The sweat lodge itself is circular or oval and symbolizes the universe and/or womb from which life originates; the stone pit represents the power of the creator, and the stones (healing power of the earth) are heated by the sacred fire; the water used in the ceremony is essential for all life; the steam that rises when water is thrown on the stones represents both the prayers of the participants and ancient knowledge; and the sweat of the participants is part of the purification process. Consistent with most indigenous mandates, the sweat lodge ceremony is conducted under the following conditions as described by Garrett et al. (2011):

1. The lodge is constructed from materials garnered from Mother Earth. Permission is sought from the wood, bark, rocks, and other materials to participate in the sacred ritual. The reciprocity involved in requesting permission and giving thanks is part of the belief in the interrelationship of all things and the maintenance of balance and harmony.
2. A Fire Keeper has the responsibility of tending the sacred fire from which the stones will be heated.
3. Participants strip themselves of all clothing and jewelry and enter on their hands and knees to show respect for Mother Earth. They then sit in a sacred circle (hoop of life).

4. The ceremony begins in silence (true voice of the Creator); then invocation and thanks are given to the Great Spirit, Mother Earth, the four directions, spirits, and all relations in nature.
5. Water or an herbal mixture is then poured on the heated rocks, producing a purifying steam.
6. The ritualized cleansing of the body is meant to ensure harmony, balance, and wellness in the person. The participants purify themselves by joining with the powers of Mother Earth and the Universal Circle that connects living and nonliving beings.
7. Unlike most Western forms of healing, the sweat lodge ceremony takes place in the presence of a person's support network: the family, clan, and community. Not only does the ceremony cleanse the body, mind, and spirit, but it also brings together everyone to honor the energy of life.

As mentioned previously, sweat therapy has been increasingly adopted in Western society as a form of treatment. Its use, however, is based on other Western therapeutic rationales rather than that ascribed to Native Americans.

Indigenous healing can be defined as helping beliefs and practices that originate within the culture or society. It is not transported from other regions, and it is designed for treating the inhabitants of the given group. Those who study indigenous psychologies do not make an a priori assumption that one particular perspective is superior to another (Mikulas, 2006). The Western ontology of healing (counseling/therapy), however, does consider its methods to be more advanced and scientifically grounded than those found in many cultures. Western healing has traditionally operated from several assumptions: (a) reality consists of distinct and separate units or objects (therapist and client, observer and observed); (b) reality consists of what can be observed and measured via the five senses; (c) space and time are fixed and absolute constructs of reality; and (d) science operates from universal principles and is culture free (Highlen, 1996). Although these guiding assumptions of Western science have contributed much to human knowledge and to the improvement of the human condition, most non-Western indigenous psychologies appear to operate from a different perspective. For example, many non-Western cultures do not separate the observer from the observed and believe that all life forms are inter-related with one another, including mother nature and the cosmos; that the nature of reality transcends the senses; that space and time are not fixed; and that much of reality is culture bound (Walsh & Shapiro, 2006). Let us briefly explore several of these parallel assumptions and see how they are manifested in indigenous healing practices.

> *Indigenous healing* can be defined as helping beliefs and practices that originate within the culture or society. It is not transported from other regions, and it is designed for treating the inhabitants of the given group. Those who study indigenous psychologies do not make an a priori assumption that one particular perspective is superior to another.

Holistic Outlook, Interconnectedness, and Harmony

The concepts of separation, isolation, and individualism are hallmarks of the Euro-American worldview. On an individual basis, modern psychology takes a reductionist approach to describing the human condition (i.e., id, ego, and superego; belief, knowledge, and skills; cognitions, emotions, and behaviors). In Western science, the experimental design is considered the epitome of methods used to ask and answer questions about the human condition or the universe. The search for cause and effect is linear and allows us to identify the independent variables, the dependent variables, and the effects of extraneous variables that we attempt to control. It is analytical and reductionist in character. The attempt to maintain objectivity, autonomy, and independence in understanding human behavior is also stressed. Such tenets have resulted in separation of the person from the group (valuing of individualism and uniqueness), science from spirituality, and man/woman from the universe.

Most non-Western indigenous forms of healing take a holistic outlook on well-being, in that they make minimal distinctions between physical and mental functioning and believe strongly in the unity of spirit, mind, and matter. The interrelatedness of life forms, the environment, and the cosmos is a given. As a result, the indigenous peoples of the world tend to conceptualize reality differently. The psychosocial unit of operation for many culturally diverse groups, for example, is not the individual but the group (collectivism). In many cultures, acting in an autonomous and independent manner is seen as the problem because it creates disharmony within the group.

Illness, distress, or problematic behaviors are seen as an imbalance in people relationships, a disharmony between the individual and his or her group, or as a lack of synchrony with internal or external forces. Harmony and balance are the healer's goal. Among American Indians, for example, harmony with nature is symbolized by the circle, or hoop of life (Garrett & Portman, 2011; McCormick, 2005; Sutton & Broken Nose, 2005). Mind, body, spirit, and nature are seen as a single unified entity, with little separation between the realities of life, medicine, and religion. All forms of nature, not just the living, are to be revered because they reflect the creator or deity. Illness is seen as a break in the hoop of life, an imbalance, or a separation between the elements. Many indigenous beliefs come from a metaphysical tradition. They accept the interconnectedness of cosmic forces in the form of energy or subtle matter (less dense than the physical) that surrounds and penetrates the physical body and the world.

> Illness, distress, or problematic behaviors are seen as an imbalance in people relationships, a disharmony between the individual and his or her group, or as a lack of synchrony with internal or external forces. Harmony and balance are the healer's goal.

Both the ancient Chinese practice of acupuncture and chakras in Indian yoga philosophy involve the use of subtle matter to rebalance and heal the body and mind (Highlen, 1996). Chinese medical theory is concerned with the balance of yin (cold) and yang (hot) in the body, and it is believed that strong emotional states, as well as an imbalance in the type of foods eaten, may create illness (Pedersen &

Pope, 2010; So, 2005). As we saw in the case of Phuoc Nguyen, treatment might involve eating specific types or combinations of foods or using massage treatment to suck out "bad" or "hot" air. Such concepts of illness and health can also be found in the Greek theory of balancing body fluids (blood, phlegm, black bile, and yellow bile) (Bankart, 1997).

Likewise, the Afrocentric perspective also teaches that human beings are part of a holistic fabric—that they are interconnected and should be oriented toward collective rather than individual survival (Boyd-Franklin, 2003, 2010; Graham, 2005). The indigenous Japanese assumptions and practices of Naikan and Morita therapy attempt to move clients toward being more in tune with others and society, to move away from individualism, and to move toward interdependence, connectedness, and harmony with others (Bankart, 1997; C. P. Chen, 2005). Naikan therapy, which derives from Buddhist practice, requires clients to reflect on three aspects of human relationships: (a) what other people have done for them, (b) what they have done for others, and (c) how they cause difficulties to others (Walsh & Shapiro, 2006). The overall goal is to expand awareness of how much we receive from others, how much gratitude is due them, and how little we demonstrate such gratitude. This ultimately leads to a realization of the interdependence of the parts to the whole. Working for the good of the group ultimately benefits the individual.

Belief in Metaphysical Levels of Existence

Some time back two highly popular books—*Embraced by the Light* (Eadie, 1992) and *Saved by the Light* (Brinkley, 1994)—and several television specials described fascinating cases of near-death experiences. All had certain commonalities: The individuals who were near death felt like they were leaving their physical bodies, observed what was happening around them, saw a bright beckoning light, and journeyed to higher levels of existence. Although the popularity of such books and programs might indicate that the American public is inclined to believe in such phenomena, science has been unable to validate these personal accounts and remains skeptical of their existence. Yet many societies and non-Western cultures accept, as given, the existence of different levels or planes of consciousness, experience, or existence. They believe the means of understanding and ameliorating the causes of illness or problems of life are often found in a plane of reality separate from the physical world of existence.

Asian psychologies posit detailed descriptions of states of consciousness and outline developmental levels of enlightenment that extend beyond that of Western psychology. Asian perspectives concentrate less on psychopathology and more on enlightenment and ideal mental health (Pankhania, 2005; Walsh & Vaughan, 1993). The normal state of consciousness in many ways is not considered optimal and may be seen as a "psychopathology of the average" (Maslow, 1968). Moving to higher states of consciousness has the effect of enhancing perceptual sensitivity and clarity, concentration, and sense of identity, as well as emotional, cognitive, and perceptual processes. Such movement, according to Asian philosophy, frees one from the negative pathogenic forces of life. Attaining enlightenment and liberation can be achieved through the classic practices of meditation and yoga.

Research findings indicate that yoga and meditation are the most widely used of all therapies (Walsh & Shapiro, 2006). They have been shown to reduce anxiety, specific phobias, and substance abuse (Kwee, 1990; Shapiro, 1982; West, 1987); to benefit those with medical problems by reducing blood pressure and aiding in the management of chronic pain (Kabat-Zinn, 1990); to enhance self-confidence, sense of control, marital satisfaction, and so on (Alexander, Rainforth, & Gelderloos, 1991); and to extend longevity (Alexander, Langer, Newman, Chandler, & Davies, 1989). Today, meditation and yoga in the United States have become accepted practices among millions, especially for relaxation and stress management. For practitioners of meditation and yoga, altered states of consciousness are unquestioned aspects of reality.

According to some cultures, nonordinary reality states allow some healers to access an invisible world surrounding the physical one. Puerto Ricans, for example, believe in *espiritismo* (spiritism), a world where spirits can have major impacts on the people residing in the physical world (Chavez, 2005). *Espiritistas*, or mediums, are culturally sanctioned indigenous healers who possess special faculties allowing them to intervene positively or negatively on behalf of their clients. Many cultures strongly believe that human destiny is often decided in the domain of the spirit world. Mental illness may be attributed to the activities of hostile spirits, often in reaction to transgressions of the victim or the victim's family (C. C. Lee, 1996; Mullavey-O'Byrne, 1994). As in the case of Mrs. Thor, shamans, mediums, or indigenous healers often enter these realities on behalf of their clients in order to seek answers, to enlist the help of the spirit world, or to aid in realigning the spiritual energy field that surrounds the body and extends throughout the universe.

Ancient Chinese methods of healing and Hindu chakras also acknowledge another reality that parallels the physical world. Accessing this world allows the healer to use these special energy centers to balance and heal the body and mind. Occasionally, the shaman may aid the helpee or novice to access that plane of reality so that he or she may find the solutions. The *vision quest*, in conjunction with the sweat lodge experience, is used by some American Indians as religious renewal or as a rite of passage (Garrett et al., 2011; Heinrich, Corbin, & Thomas, 1990; D. P. Smith, 2005). Behind these uses, however, is the human journey to another world of reality. The ceremony of the vision quest is intended to prepare the young man for the proper frame of mind; it includes rituals and sacred symbols, prayers to the Great Spirit, isolation, fasting, and personal reflection. Whether in a dream state or in full consciousness, another world of reality is said to reveal itself. Mantras, chants, meditation, and the taking of certain drugs (peyote) all have as their purpose a journey into another world of existence (Duran, 2006).

Spirituality in Life and the Cosmos

Native American Indians look on all things as having life, spiritual energy, and importance. A fundamental belief is that all things are connected. The universe consists of a balance among all of these things and a continuous flow of cycling of this energy. Native American Indians believe that we have a sacred relationship with the universe that is to be honored. All things are connected, all things have life, and all things are worthy of re-spect and reverence. Spirituality focuses on the harmony that comes from our connection with all parts of the universe—in which everything has the purpose and value exemplary of personhood, including plants (e.g., "tree people"), the land ("Mother Earth"), the winds ("the Four Powers"), "Father Sky," "Grandfather Sun," "Grandmother Moon," "The Red Thunder Boys." Spiritual being essentially requires only that we seek our place in the universe; everything else will follow in good time. Because everyone and everything was created with a specific purpose to fulfill, no one should have the power to interfere or to impose on others the best path to follow. (J. T. Garrett & Garrett, 1994, p. 187)

The sacred Native American beliefs concerning spirituality are a truly alien concept to modern Euro-American thinking. The United States has had a long tradition in believing that one's religious beliefs should not enter into scientific or rational decisions (Duran, 2006). Incorporating religion in the ra-tional decision-making process or in the conduct of therapy has generally been seen as unscientific and unprofessional. The schism between religion and sci-ence occurred centuries ago and has resulted in a split between science/psy-chology and religion (Fukuyama & Sevig, 1999). This is reflected in the oft quoted phrase, "separation of Church and State." The separation has become a serious barrier to mainstream psychology's incorporation of indigenous forms of healing into mental health practice, especially when religion is confused with spirituality. Although people may not have a formal religion, indigenous helpers believe that spirituality is an intimate aspect of the human condition. Western psychology acknowledges the behavioral, cognitive, and affective realms, but it makes only passing reference to the spiritual realm of existence. Yet indigenous helpers believe that spirituality transcends time and space, mind and body, and our behaviors, thoughts, and feelings (Lee & Armstrong, 1995; D. P. Smith 2005).

These contrasting worldviews are perhaps most clearly seen in definitions of "the good life" and how our values are manifested in evaluating the worth of others. In the United States, for example, the pursuit of happiness is most likely manifested in material wealth and physical well-being, whereas other cultures value spiritual or intellectual goals. The worth of a person is anchored in the num-ber of separate properties he or she owns and in his or her net worth and ability to acquire increasing wealth. Indeed, it is often assumed that such an accumulation of wealth is a sign of divine approval (Condon & Yousef, 1975). In cultures where spiritual goals are strong, people's worth is unrelated to material possessions but rather resides within individuals, emanates from their spirituality, and is a function of whether they live the "right life." People from capitalistic cultures often do not understand self-immolations and other acts of suicide in countries such as India. They are likely to make statements such as, "Life is not valued there" or, better yet, "Life is cheap." These statements indicate a lack of understanding about actions that arise from cultural forces rather than personal frustrations; they may be symbolic of a spiritual-valuing rather than a material-valuing orientation.

One does not have to look beyond the United States, however, to see such spiritual orientations; many racial/ethnic minority groups in this country are strongly spiritual. African Americans, Asian Americans, Latino/Hispanic Americans, and Native Americans all place strong emphasis on the interplay and interdependence of spiritual life and healthy functioning (Boyd-Franklin, 2010; Garrett & Portman, 2011). Puerto Ricans, for example, may sacrifice material satisfaction in favor of values pertaining to the spirit and the soul. The Lakota Sioux often say *Mitakuye Oyasin* at the end of a prayer or as a salutation. Translated, it means "to all my relations," which acknowledges the spiritual bond between the speaker and all people present and extends to forebears, the tribe, the family of man, and mother nature. It speaks to the philosophy that all life forces, Mother Earth, and the cosmos are sacred beings and that the spiritual is the thread that binds all together.

Likewise, a strong spiritual orientation has always been a major aspect of life in Africa, and this was also true during the slavery era in the United States.

> Highly emotional religious services conducted during slavery were of great importance in dealing with oppression. Often signals as to the time and place of an escape were given then. Spirituals contained hidden messages and a language of resistance (e.g., "Wade in the Water" and "Steal Away"). Spirituals (e.g., "Nobody Knows the Trouble I've Seen") and the ecstatic celebrations of Christ's gift of salvation provided Black slaves with outlets for expressing feelings of pain, humiliation, and anger. (Hines & Boyd-Franklin, 1996, p. 74)

The African American church has a strong influence over the lives of Black people and is often the hub of religious, social, economic, and political life (Boyd-Franklin, 2010). Religion is not separated from the daily functions of the church, as it acts as a complete support system for the African American family, with the minister, deacons, deaconesses, and church members operating as one big family. A strong sense of peoplehood is fostered via social activities, choirs, Sunday school, health-promotion classes, day care centers, tutoring programs, and counseling. To many African Americans the road to mental health and the prevention of mental illness lie in the health potentialities of their spiritual life.

Mental health professionals are becoming increasingly open to the potential benefits of spirituality as a means for coping with hopelessness, identity issues, and feelings of powerlessness (Fukuyama & Sevig, 1999). As an example of this movement, the Association for Counselor Education and Supervision (ACES) adopted a set of competencies related to spirituality. They define *spirituality* as:

> the animating force in life, represented by such images as breath, wind, vigor, and courage. Spirituality is the infusion and drawing out of spirit in one's life. It is experienced as an active and passive process. Spirituality is also described as a capacity and tendency that is innate and unique to all persons. This spiritual tendency moves the individual towards knowledge,

love, meaning, hope, transcendence, connectedness, and compassion. Spirituality includes one's capacity for creativity, growth, and the development of a values system. Spirituality encompasses the religious, spiritual, and transpersonal. (American Counseling Association, 1995, p. 30)

Interestingly enough, it appears that many in the United States are experiencing a "spiritual hunger," or a strong need to reintegrate spiritual or religious themes into their lives (Gallup, 1995; Hage, 2004; Thoresen, 1998). For example, it appears that there is a marked discrepancy between what patients want from their doctors and what doctors supply. Often, patients want to talk about the spiritual aspects of their illness and treatment, but doctors are either unprepared or disinclined to do so (Hage, 2004). Likewise, most mental health professionals feel equally uncomfortable, disinclined, or unprepared to speak with their clients about religious or spiritual matters.

Thoresen (1998) reported in a meta-analysis of over 200 published studies that the relationship between spirituality and health is highly positive. Those with higher levels of spirituality have lower disease risk, fewer physical health problems, and higher levels of psychosocial functioning. It appears that people require faith as well as reason to be healthy and that psychology may profit from allowing the spirit to rejoin matters of the mind and body (Strawbridge, Cohen, Shema, & Kaplan, 1997).

In general, indigenous healing methods have much to offer to Euro-American forms of mental health practice. The contributions are valuable not only because multiple belief systems now exist in our society but also because counseling and psychotherapy have historically neglected the spiritual dimension of human existence. Our heavy reliance on science and on the reductionist approach to treating clients has made us view human beings and human behavior as composed of separate noninteracting parts (cognitive, behavioral, and affective). There has been a failure to recognize our spiritual being and to take a holistic outlook on life. Indigenous models of healing remind us of these shortcomings and challenge us to look for answers in realms of existence beyond the physical world.

REFLECTION AND DISCUSSION QUESTIONS

1. What thoughts do you have about the role of spirituality and religion in psychology and mental health?
2. Should therapists avoid discussing these matters with clients and leave it to the clergy?
3. What are the possible positive and negative outcomes of doing so?
4. Would you feel comfortable talking about religion with your clients?
5. If you were in therapy, how important would it be to discuss your religious or spiritual beliefs?
6. Are you a religious person?

The Dangers of Uncritical Acceptance of Religious Belief Systems: The Middle Ages

Although we have discussed the important role that indigenous healing plays in many societies and cultures, there are downsides reflected in our historical past where an uncritical acceptance of religious belief systems may actually harm rather than heal or enlighten. Such was the case during a period known as the Middle Ages, when supernatural explanations of human behavior led to a total eclipse of science and resulted in the deaths of many innocent people, primarily those accused of being witches (women, the mentally ill, those with disfigurements, gypsies, and scientists who voiced beliefs that differed from the Church). It is not our intent to give a detailed account of the harmful role Christianity played during the Middle Ages, but that infamous period in our history contains many lessons. Suffice it to say that there exists good reason for why modern science and the mental health professions have viewed the role of religion in explaining natural events with skepticism.

Early Christianity did little to promote science and in many ways actively discouraged it. The church demanded uncompromising adherence to its tenets. Christian fervor brought with it the concepts of heresy and punishment; certain truths were deemed sacred, and those who challenged them were denounced as heretics. Scientific thought that was in conflict with church doctrine, especially during the Middle Ages, was not tolerated. Because of this atmosphere, rationalism and scholarly scientific works went underground for many years, preserved mainly by Arab scholars and European monks. Natural and supernatural explanations of illness were fused. Rational and scientific thought gave way to an emphasis on the supernatural. Religious dogma included the beliefs that nature was a reflection of divine will and beyond human reason and that earthly life was a prelude to the "true" life (after death). Scientific inquiry—attempts to understand, classify, explain, and control nature—was less important than accepting nature as a manifestation of God's will.

During the Middle Ages, people came to believe that many illnesses were the result of supernatural forces, although they had natural causes. In many cases, the mentally ill were treated gently and with compassion in monasteries and at shrines, where they were prayed over and allowed to rest. In other cases, treatment could be quite brutal, especially if illnesses were believed to be due to God's wrath. Because illness was then perceived to be punishment for sin, the sick person was assumed to be guilty of wrongdoing, and relief could come only through atonement or repentance. During this period, treatment of the mentally ill sometimes consisted of torturous exorcistic procedures seen as appropriate to combat Satan and eject him from the possessed person's body. Prayers, curses, obscene epithets, and the sprinkling of holy water—as well as such drastic and painful "therapy" as flogging, starving, and immersion in hot water—were used to drive out the devil. Although the practice of exorcism is ancient, it is still recognized in Catholicism, Eastern Orthodox, and some Protestant sects. The Church of England has an official exorcist in each diocese. In general, possessed persons are not considered evil in themselves, so exorcism is seen as treatment rather than punishment.

Belief in the power of the supernatural became so prevalent and intense that it frequently affected whole populations. Beginning in Italy early in the 13th century, large numbers of people were affected by various forms of *mass madness*, or group hysteria, in which a great many people exhibit similar symptoms that have no apparent physical cause. One of the better known manifestations of this disorder was *tarantism*, a dance mania characterized by wild raving, jumping, dancing, and convulsions. The hysteria was most prevalent during the height of the summer and was attributed to the sting of a tarantula. A victim would leap up and run out into the street or marketplace, jumping and raving, to be joined by others who believed that they had also been bitten. The mania soon spread throughout the rest of Europe, where it became known as Saint Vitus' Dance. Another form of mass madness was *lycanthropy*, a mental disorder in which victims imagine themselves to be wolves and imitate wolves' actions. (Motion pictures about werewolves—people who assume the physical characteristics of wolves during the full moon—are modern reflections of this delusion.) While the Church explained these events by using supernatural explanations, scientists explain them as a form of mass hysteria. They believe that the stress and fear of the times created conditions ripe to accept a supernatural explanation. During the 13th century, for example, there was enormous social unrest. Devastating events without apparent explanations were visited upon a population that felt no control over their lives. The bubonic plague had destroyed one third of the population of Europe. War, famine, and pestilence were rampant, and the social order of the times was crumbling.

During the 15th and 16th centuries, the authority of the church was increasingly challenged by social and religious reformers. Reformers such as Martin Luther attacked the corruption and abuses of the clergy, precipitating the Protestant Reformation of the 16th century. Church officials viewed such protests as insurrections that threatened their power. According to the church, Satan himself fostered these attacks. By doing battle with Satan and with people supposedly influenced or possessed by Satan, the church actively endorsed an already popular belief in demonic possession and witches. To counter the threat, Pope Innocent VIII issued a papal bull (decree) in 1484 calling on the clergy to identify and exterminate witches. This resulted in the 1486 publication of the extremely influential *Malleus Maleficarum* (The Witch's Hammer). The mere existence of this document acted to confirm the existence of witches, and it also outlined means of detecting them. For example, red spots on the skin (birthmarks) were supposedly made by the claw of the devil in sealing a blood pact and thus were damning evidence of a contract with Satan. Such birth defects as clubfoot and cleft palate also aroused suspicion.

Witch hunts occurred in both colonial America and in Europe. It has been estimated that some twenty thousand people (mainly women) were killed as witches in Scotland alone and that more than one hundred thousand throughout Europe were executed as witches from the middle of the 15th to the end of the 17th century. The witchcraft trials of 1692 in Salem, Massachusetts, are infamous. Several hundred people were accused, many were imprisoned and tortured, and 20 were killed. It would seem reasonable to assume that the mentally ill would be especially prone to being perceived as witches. Indeed, psychiatric historians argue that mental disorders were at the roots of witchcraft persecutions (Alexander & Selesnick, 1966; Deutsch, 1949; Zilboorg & Henry, 1941).

CONCLUSIONS

The role of demons, witches, and possessions in explaining abnormal behavior has been part and parcel of many cultures and societies. There is good reason why Western science has viewed religion with skepticism. Until recently, the mental health profession has also been largely silent about the influence or importance of spirituality and religion in mental health. Thus, during therapy or work with clients, therapists have generally avoided discussing such topics. It has been found, for example, that many therapists (a) do not feel comfortable nor competent in discussing spiritual or religious issues with their clients, (b) are concerned they will appear proselytizing or judgmental if they touch on such topics, (c) believe they may usurp the role of the clergy, and (d) may feel inauthentic addressing client concerns, especially if they are atheists or agnostics (Gonsiorek, Richards, Pargament, & McMinn, 2009; Knox, Catlin, Casper, & Schlosser, 2005).

Yet it has been found that greater than 80% of Americans say that religion is important in their lives, that in both medical and mental health care patients express a strong desire for providers to discuss spiritual and faith issues with them, and that racial/ethnic minorities believe that spiritual issues are intimately linked to their cultural identities (Gallup Organization, 2009). More compelling are findings that reveal a positive association between spirituality/religion and optimal health outcomes, longevity, and lower levels of anxiety, depression, suicide, and substance abuse (Cornah, 2006). Studies on the relationship of spirituality and health found that higher levels of spirituality were associated with lower disease risk, fewer physical health problems, and higher psychosocial functioning (Thoresen, 1998). On a therapeutic level, these findings provide a strong rationale for psychology to incorporate spirituality into their research and practice.

Surveys support the inescapable conclusion that many in the United States are experiencing a spiritual hunger, or a strong need to reintegrate spiritual or religious themes into their lives (Hage, 2004). Many mental health professionals are becoming increasingly open to the potential benefits of spirituality in the treatment of clients. As part of that process, psychologists are making distinctions between spirituality and religion. *Spirituality* is an animating life force that is inclusive of religion and speaks to the thoughts, feelings, and behaviors related to a transcendent state. *Religion* is narrower, involving a specific doctrine and particular system of beliefs. Spirituality can be pursued outside a specific religion because it is transpersonal and includes one's capacity for creativity, growth, and love (Cornish, & Wade, 2010). Mental health professionals are increasingly recognizing that people are thinking, feeling, behaving, social, cultural, and spiritual beings and that the human condition is broad, complex, and holistic.

REFLECTION AND DISCUSSION QUESTIONS

1. How does one balance the basic tenets of science with our religious beliefs and the roles they play in people's lives?
2. Are science, religion, and spirituality necessarily antagonistic to one another?

Implications for Clinical Practice

We have repeatedly stressed that the worldviews of culturally diverse clients may often be worlds apart from the dominant society. When culturally diverse clients attribute disorders to causes quite alien from Euro-American diagnosis, when their definitions of a healer are different from that of conventional therapists, and when the role behaviors (process of therapy) are not perceived as therapeutic, major difficulties are likely to occur in the provision of therapeutic services.

As a Western-trained therapist, for example, how would you treat clients who believed (a) that their mental problems were due to spirit possession, (b) that only a shaman with inherited powers could deal with the problem, and (c) that a cure could be effected only via a formal ritual (e.g., chanting, incense burning, symbolic sacrifice) and a journey into the spirit world? Most of us have had very little experience with indigenous methods of treatment and would find great difficulty in working effectively with such clients. There are, however, some useful guidelines that might help bridge the gap between contemporary forms of therapy and traditional non-Western indigenous healing.

1. Do not invalidate the indigenous belief systems of your culturally diverse client. On the surface, the assumptions of indigenous healing methods might appear radically different from our own. When we encounter them, we are often shocked, find such beliefs to be unscientific, and are likely to negate, invalidate, or dismiss them. Such an attitude will invalidate our clients as well. Entertaining alternative realities does not mean that the therapist must subscribe to that belief system. It does mean, however, that the helping professional must avoid being judgmental. This will encourage and allow the client to share his or her story more readily, to feel validated, and to encourage the building of mutual respect and trust. Remember that cultural storytelling and personal narratives have always been an intimate process of helping in all cultures.
2. Become knowledgeable about indigenous beliefs and healing practices. Therapists have a professional responsibility to become knowledgeable and conversant about the assumptions and practices of indigenous healing so that a process of desensitization and normalization can occur. By becoming knowledgeable and understanding of indigenous helping approaches, the therapist will avoid equating differences with deviance. Despite different explanations, many similarities exist between Western and non-Western healing practices.
3. Realize that learning about indigenous healing and beliefs entails experiential or lived realities. Although reading books about non-Western forms of healing and attending seminars and lectures on the topic is valuable and helpful, understanding culturally different

perspectives must be supplemented by lived experience. We suggest that you consider attending cultural events, meetings, and activities of the different cultural groups in your community. Such actions allow you to observe culturally different individuals interacting in their community and to see how their values are expressed in relationships.

4. Avoid overpathologizing and underpathologizing a culturally diverse client's problems. Therapists or counselors who are culturally unaware and who believe primarily in a universal psychology may often be culturally insensitive and inclined to see differences as deviance. They may be guilty of overpathologizing a culturally different client's problems by seeing it as more severe and pathological than it truly may be. There is also a danger, however, of underpathologizing a culturally diverse client's symptoms. While being understanding of a client's cultural context, having knowledge of culture-bound syndromes and being aware of cultural relativism are desirable, being oversensitive to these factors may predispose the therapist to minimize problems.

5. Be willing to consult with traditional healers or to make use of their services. Mental health professionals must be willing and able to form partnerships with indigenous healers or to develop community liaisons. Such an outreach has several advantages: (a) Traditional healers may provide knowledge and insight into client populations that would prove of value to the delivery of mental health services; (b) such an alliance will ultimately enhance the cultural credibility of therapists; and (c) it allows for referral to traditional healers (e.g., shamans, religious leaders) when treatment is rooted in cultural traditions.

6. Recognize that spirituality is an intimate aspect of the human condition and a legitimate aspect of mental health work. Spirituality is a belief in a higher power, which allows us to make meaning of life and the universe. It may or may not be linked to a formal religion, but there is little doubt that it is a powerful force in the human condition. A counselor or therapist who does not feel comfortable dealing with the spiritual needs of clients or who believes in an artificial separation of the spirit (soul) from the everyday life of the culturally different client may not be providing the needed help. Just as therapists might inquire about the physical health of their clients, they should feel free and comfortable to inquire about their client's values and beliefs as they relate to spirituality. We do not, however, advocate indoctrination of the client nor prescribing any particular pathway to embracing, validating, or expressing spirituality and spiritual needs.

7. Be willing to expand your definition of the helping role to community work and involvement. More than anything else, indigenous healing is community oriented and community focused. Culturally competent mental health professionals must begin to expand their definition of the helping role to encompass a greater community involvement. The in-the-office setting is often nonfunctional in minority communities. Culturally sensitive helping requires making home visits, going to community centers, and visiting places of worship and other areas within the community. The type of help most likely to prevent mental health problems allows clients to build and maintain healthy connections with their family, their god(s), and their universe.

PART IV

Racial/Cultural Identity Development in Multicultural Counseling and Therapy

Racial/Cultural Identity Development in People of Color: Therapeutic Implications

CHAPTER FOCUS QUESTIONS

1. What factors are influential in the development of racial/cultural identity in people of color?
2. What does it mean to be African American, Asian American, Latino/a American, or Native American?
3. How do sociopolitical forces come into play in the identity development of people of color?
4. How does the level or stage of racial consciousness affect the attitudes, beliefs, and behaviors toward oneself, toward members of one's minority group, and toward majority group members?
5. How does the racial consciousness of a person of color impact the counseling/therapy situation?
6. What are the characteristic therapeutic challenges most likely to occur when working with a client of color in the conformity stage, dissonance stage, resistance and immersion stage, introspection stage, and integrative awareness stage?

Case Study: Sansei (Third-Generation) Japanese American Female

For nearly all my life I have never seriously attempted to dissect my feelings and attitudes about being a Japanese American woman. Aborted attempts were made, but they were never brought to fruition, because it was unbearably painful. Having been born and raised in Arizona, I had no Asian

(continued)

(continued)

friends. I suspect that given an opportunity to make some, I would have avoided them anyway. That is because I didn't want to have anything to do with being Japanese American. Most of the Japanese images I saw were negative. Japanese women were ugly; they had "cucumber legs," flat yellow faces, small slanty eyes, flat chests, and were stunted in growth. The men were short and stocky, sneaky and slimy, clumsy, inept, "wimpy looking," and sexually emasculated. I wanted to be tall, slender, large eyes, full lips, and elegant looking; I wasn't going to be typical Oriental! . . .

At Cal [University of California, Berkeley], I've been forced to deal with my Yellow-White identity. There are so many "yellows" here that I can't believe it. I've come to realize that many White prejudices are deeply ingrained in me; so much so that they are unconscious. . . . To accept myself as a total person, I also have to accept my Asian identity as well. But what is it? I just don't know. Are they the images given me through the filter of White America, or are they the values and desires of my parents?

Yesterday, I had rude awakening. For the first time in my life I went on a data with a Filipino boy. I guess I shouldn't call him a "boy," as my ethnic studies teacher says it is derogatory toward Asians and Blacks. I only agreed to go because he seemed different from the other "Orientals" on campus. (I guess I shouldn't use that word either.) He's president of his Asian fraternity, very athletic and outgoing . . . When he asked me, I figured, "Why not?" It'll be a good experience to see what it's like to date an Asian boy. Will he be like White guys who will try to seduce me, or will he be too afraid to make any move when it comes to sex? . . . We went to San Francisco's Fisherman's Wharf for lunch. We were seated and our orders were taken before two other White women. They were, however, served first. This was painfully apparent to us, but I wanted to pretend that it was just a mix-up. My friend, however, was less forgiving and made a public fuss with the waiter. Still, it took an inordinate amount of time for us to get our lunches, and the filets were overcooked (purposely?). My date made a very public scene by placing a tip on the table, and then returning to retrieve it. I was both embarrassed but proud of his actions.

This incident and others made me realize several things. For all my life I have attempted to fit into White society. I have tried to convince myself that I was different, that I was like all my other White classmates, and that prejudice and discrimination didn't exist for me. I wonder how I could have been so oblivious to prejudice and racism. I now realize that I cannot escape from my ethnic heritage and from the way people see me. Yet I don't know how to go about resolving many of my feelings and conflicts. While I like my newly found Filipino "male" friend (he is sexy), I continue to have difficulty seeing myself married to anyone other than a White man. (Excerpts from a Sansei student journal, 1989)

This Sansei (third-generation) Japanese American female is experiencing a racial awakening that has strong implications for her racial/cultural identity development. Her previous belief systems concerning Euro-Americans and Asian Americans are being challenged by social reality and the experiences of being a visible racial/ethnic minority. First, a major theme involving societal portrayals of Asian Americans is clearly expressed in the student's beliefs about racial/cultural characteristics: She describes the Asian American male and female in highly unflattering terms. She seems to have internalized these beliefs and to be using White standards to judge Asian Americans as being either desirable or undesirable. For the student, the process of incorporating these standards has not only attitudinal but behavioral consequences as well. In Arizona, she would not have considered making Asian American friends even if the opportunity presented itself. In her mind, she was not a "typical Oriental"; she disowned or felt ashamed of her ethnic heritage, and she even concludes that she would not consider marrying anyone but a White male.

Second, her denial that she is an Asian American is beginning to crumble. Being immersed on a campus in which many other fellow Asian Americans are in attendance forces her to explore ethnic identity issues—a process she has been able to avoid while living in a predominantly White area. In the past, when she encountered prejudice or discrimination, she had been able to deny it or to rationalize it away. The differential treatment she received at a restaurant and her male friend's labeling it as "discrimination" make such a conclusion inescapable. The shattering of illusions is manifest in a realization that (a) despite her efforts to "fit in," it is not enough to gain social acceptance among many White Americans; (b) she cannot escape her racial/cultural heritage; and (c) she has been brainwashed into believing that one group is superior over another.

Third, the student's internal struggle to cast off the cultural conditioning of her past and the attempts to define her ethnic identity are both painful and conflicting. When she refers to her "Yellow-White" identity; writes about the negative images of Asian American males but winds up dating one; uses the terms "Oriental" and "boy" (in reference to her Asian male friend) but acknowledges their derogatory racist nature; describes Asian men as "sexually emasculated" but sees her Filipino date as "athletic," "outgoing," and "sexy"; expresses embarrassment at confronting the waiter about discrimination but feels proud of her Asian male friend for doing so; and states that she finds him attractive but could never consider marrying anyone but a White man, we have clear evidence of the internal turmoil she is undergoing. Understanding the process by which racial/cultural identity develops in persons of color is crucial for effective multicultural counseling/therapy.

Fourth, it is clear that the Japanese American female is a victim of ethnocentric monoculturalism. As we mentioned previously, the problem being experienced by the student does not reside in her but in our society. It resides in a society that portrays racial/ethnic minority characteristics as inferior, primitive, deviant, pathological, or undesirable. The resulting damage strikes at the self-esteem and self-group identity of many culturally different individuals in our society; many, like the student, may come to believe that their racial/cultural heritage or characteristics are burdens to be changed or overcome. Understanding racial/cultural identity development and its relationship to therapeutic practice are the goals of this chapter.

RACIAL/CULTURAL IDENTITY DEVELOPMENT MODELS

The historic work on racial/cultural identity development among minority groups has led to major breakthroughs in the field of multicultural counseling/therapy (Atkinson, Morten, & Sue, 1998; W. E. Cross, 1971, 1995; W. E. Cross, Smith, & Payne, 2001; Helms, 1984, 1995; J. Kim, 1981; A. S. Ruiz, 1990). Most would agree that Asian Americans, African Americans, Latino/Hispanic Americans, and American

Indians have distinct cultural heritages that make each different from the other. Yet such cultural distinctions can lead to a monolithic view of minority group attitudes and behaviors (Atkinson, Morten, & Sue, 1998). The erroneous belief that all Asians are the same, all Blacks are the same, all Hispanics are the same, or all American Indians are the same has led to numerous therapeutic problems.

First, therapists may often respond to the culturally diverse client in a very stereotypic manner and fail to recognize within-group or individual differences. For example, research indicates that Asian American clients seem to prefer and benefit most from a highly structured and directive approach, rather than an insight/feeling-oriented one (Hong & Domokos-Cheng Ham, 2001; B. S. K. Kim, 2011; Root, 1998; Sandhu, Leung, & Tang, 2003). Although such approaches may generally be effective, they are often blindly applied without regard for possible differences in client attitudes, beliefs, and behaviors. Likewise, conflicting findings in the literature regarding whether people of color prefer therapists of their own race seem to be a function of our failure to make such distinctions. Preference for a racially or ethnically similar therapist may really be a function of the cultural/racial identity of the minority person (within-group differences) rather than of race or ethnicity per se.

Second, the strength of racial/cultural identity models lies in their potential diagnostic value (Helms, 1984; Vandiver, 2001). Premature termination rates among minority clients may be attributed to the inappropriateness of transactions that occur between the helping professional and the culturally diverse client. Research now suggests that reactions to counseling, the counseling process, and counselors are influenced by cultural/racial identity and are not simply linked to minority group membership. The high failure-to-return rate of many clients seems to be intimately connected to the mental health professional's inability to assess the cultural identity of clients accurately (Ivey, D'Andrea, & Ivey, 2011).

A third important contribution derived from racial identity models is their acknowledgment of sociopolitical influences in shaping minority identity (à la the Sansei student). Most therapeutic approaches often neglect their potential sociopolitical nature. The early models of racial identity development all incorporated the effects of racism and prejudice (oppression) upon the identity transformation of their victims. Vontress (1971), for instance, theorized that African Americans moved through decreasing levels of dependence on White society to emerging identification with Black culture and society (Colored, Negro, and Black). Other similar models for Blacks have been proposed (W. E. Cross, 1971; W. S. Hall, Cross, & Freedle, 1972; B. Jackson, 1975; C. W. Thomas, 1970, 1971). The fact that other minority groups, such as Asian Americans (Maykovich, 1973; S. Sue & Sue, 1971), Hispanics (A. S. Ruiz, 1990; Szapocznik, Santisteban, Kurtines, Hervis, & Spencer, 1982), women (Downing & Roush, 1985; McNamara & Rickard, 1989), lesbians/gays (Cass, 1979), and disabled individuals (Olkin, 1999), have similar processes may indicate experiential validity for such models as they relate to various oppressed groups.

Black Identity Development Models

Early attempts to define a process of minority identity transformation came primarily through the works of Black social scientists and educators (W. E.

Cross, 1971; B. Jackson, 1975; C. W. Thomas, 1971). Although there are several Black identity development models, the Cross model of psychological nigrescence (the process of becoming Black) is perhaps the most influential and well documented (W. E. Cross, 1971, 1991, 1995; W. S. Hall et al., 1972). The original Cross model was developed during the civil rights movement and delineates a five-stage process in which Blacks in the United States move from a White frame of reference to a positive Black frame of reference: *preencounter, encounter, immersion-emersion, internalization, and internalization-commitment.*

- The *preencounter* stage is characterized by individuals (African Americans) who consciously or unconsciously devalue their own Blackness and concurrently value White values and ways. There is a strong desire to assimilate and acculturate into White society. Blacks at this stage evidence self-hate, low self-esteem, and poor mental health (Vandiver, 2001).

- In the *encounter* stage, a two-step process begins to occur. First, the individual encounters a profound crisis or event that challenges his or her previous mode of thinking and behaving; second, the Black person begins to reinterpret the world, resulting in a shift in worldviews. Cross points out how the slaying of Martin Luther King, Jr., was such a significant experience for many African Americans. The person experiences both guilt and anger over being brainwashed by White society.

- In the third stage, *immersion-emersion*, the person withdraws from the dominant culture and becomes immersed in African American culture. Black pride begins to develop, but internalization of positive attitudes toward one's own Blackness is minimal. In the emersion phase, feelings of guilt and anger begin to dissipate with an increasing sense of pride.

- The next stage, *internalization*, is characterized by inner security as conflicts between the old and new identities are resolved. Global anti-White feelings subside as the person becomes more flexible, more tolerant, and more bicultural/multicultural.

- The last stage, *internalization-commitment*, speaks to the commitment that such individuals have toward social change, social justice, and civil rights. It is expressed not only in words but also in actions that reflect the essence of their lives.

It is important to note, however, that Cross's original model makes a major assumption: The evolution from the preencounter stage to the internalization stage reflects a movement from psychological dysfunction to psychological health (Vandiver, 2001).

Confronted with evidence that these stages may mask multiple racial identities, questioning his original assumption that all Blacks at the preencounter stage possess self-hatred and low self-esteem, and aware of the complex issues related to race salience, W. E. Cross (1991) revised his theory of nigrescence in his book *Shades of Black*. His changes, which are based on a critical review of the literature on Black racial identity, have increased the model's explanatory powers and promise high predictive validity (Vandiver, Fhagen-Smith, Cokley, Cross, & Worrell, 2001; Worrell, Cross, & Vandiver, 2001). In essence, the revised model contains nearly all the features from the earlier formulation, but it differs in several significant ways.

First, Cross introduces the concept of *race salience*, the degree to which race is an important and integral part of a person's approach to life. The Black person may function with "race" consciousness playing either a large role in his or her identity or a minimal one. In addition, salience for Blackness can possess positive (pro-Black) or negative (anti-Black) valence. Instead of using the term "pro-White" in the earlier preencounter stage, Cross now uses the term *race salience*. Originally, Cross believed that the rejection of Blackness and the acceptance of an American perspective were indicative of only one identity, characterized by self-hate and low self-esteem. His current model now describes two identities: (a) preencounter assimilation and (b) preencounter anti-Black. The former has low salience for race and a neutral valence toward Blackness, whereas the latter describes individuals who hate Blacks and hate being Black (high negative salience). In other words, it is possible for a Black person at the preencounter stage who experiences the salience of race as very minor and whose identity is oriented toward an "American" perspective not to be filled with self-hate or low self-esteem.

The sense of low self-esteem, however, is linked to the preencounter anti-Black orientation. According to Cross, such a psychological perspective is the result of miseducation and self-hatred. The miseducation is the result of the negative images about Blacks portrayed in the mass media; among neighbors, friends, and relatives; and in the educational literature (Blacks are unintelligent, criminal, lazy, and prone to violence). The result is an incorporation of such negative images into the personal identity of the Black person. Interestingly, the female Sansei student described earlier in this chapter, though Japanese American, would seem to possess many of the features of Cross's preencounter anti-Black identity.

Second, the immersion-emersion stage once described one fused identity (anti-White/pro-Black) but is now divided into two additional ones: anti-White alone and anti-Black alone. While Cross speaks about two separate identities, it appears that there are three possible combinations: anti-White, pro-Black, and an anti-White/pro-Black combination.

Third, Cross has collapsed the fourth and fifth stages (internalization and internalization-commitment) into one: internalization. He observed that minimal differences existed between the two stages except one of "sustained interest and commitment." This last stage is characterized by Black self-acceptance and can be manifested in three types of identities: (a) Black nationalist (high Black positive race salience), (b) biculturalist (Blackness and fused sense of Americanness), and (c) multiculturalist (multiple identity formation, including race, gender, sexual orientation, etc.).

Although Cross's model has been revised significantly and the newer version is more sophisticated, his original 1971 nigrescence theory continues to dominate the racial identity landscape. Unfortunately, this has created much confusion among researchers and practitioners. We encourage readers to familiarize themselves with his most recent formulation (W. E. Cross, 1991, 1995).

Asian American Identity Development Models

Asian American identity development models have not advanced as far as those relating to Black identity. One of the earliest heuristic, "type" models was developed by S. Sue and D. W. Sue (1971a) to explain what they saw as clinical differences among Chinese American students treated at the University of California, Berkeley, Counseling Center: (a) *traditionalist*—a person who internalizes conventional Chinese customs and values, resists acculturation forces, and believes in the "old ways"; (b) *marginal person*—a person who attempts to assimilate and acculturate into White society, rejects traditional Chinese ways, internalizes society's negativism toward minority groups, and may develop racial self-hatred (à la the Sansei student); and (c) *Asian American*—a person who is in the process of forming a positive identity, who is ethnically and politically aware, and who becomes increasingly bicultural.

Kitano (1982) also proposed a type model to account for Japanese American role behaviors with respect to Japanese and American cultures: (a) positive-positive, in which the person identifies with both Japanese and White cultures without role conflicts; (b) negative-positive, in which there is a rejection of White culture and acceptance of Japanese American culture, with accompanying role conflicts; (c) positive-negative, in which the person accepts White culture and rejects Japanese culture, with concomitant role conflict; and (d) negative-negative, in which one rejects both.

These early type models suffered from several shortcomings (F. Y. Lee, 1991). First, they failed to provide a clear rationale for why an individual develops one ethnic identity type over another. Although they were useful in describing characteristics of the type, they represented static entities rather than a dynamic process of identity development. Second, the early proposals seem too simplistic to account for the complexity of racial identity development. Third, these models were too population specific in that they described only one Asian American ethnic group (Chinese American or Japanese American); and one wonders whether they are equally applicable to Korean Americans, Filipino Americans, Vietnamese Americans, and so on. Last, with the exception of a few empirical studies (F. Y. Lee, 1991; D. W. Sue & Frank, 1973), testing of these typologies is seriously lacking.

In response to these criticisms, theorists have begun to move toward the development of stage/process models of Asian American identity development (J. Kim, 1981; F. Y. Lee, 1991; Sodowsky, Kwan, & Pannu, 1995). Such models view identity formation as occurring in stages, from less healthy to more healthy evolutions. With each stage there exists a constellation of traits and characteristics associated with racial/ethnic identity. They also attempt to explain the conditions or situations that might retard, enhance, or impel the individual forward.

After a thorough review of the literature, J. Kim (1981) used a qualitative narrative approach with third-generation Japanese American women to posit a progressive and sequential stage model of Asian American identity development: ethnic awareness, White identification, awakening to social political consciousness, redirection to Asian American consciousness, and incorporation. Her model integrates the influence of acculturation, exposure to cultural differences, environmental negativism to racial differences, personal methods of handling race-related conflicts, and the effects of group or social movements on the Asian American individual.

1. The *ethnic awareness* stage begins around the ages of 3 to 4, when the child's family members serve as the significant ethnic group model. Positive or neutral attitudes toward one's own ethnic origin are formed, depending on the amount of ethnic exposure conveyed by the caretakers.
2. The *White identification* stage begins when children enter school, where peers and the surroundings become powerful forces in conveying racial prejudice that negatively impacts their self-esteem and identity. The realization of "differentness" from such interactions leads to self-blame and a desire to escape racial heritage by identifying with White society.
3. The *awakening to social political consciousness* stage means the adoption of a new perspective, often correlated with increased political awareness. J. Kim (1981) believed that the civil rights and women's movements and other significant political events often precipitate this new awakening. The primary result is an abandoning of identification with White society and a consequent understanding of oppression and oppressed groups.
4. The *redirection* stage means a reconnection or renewed connection with one's Asian American heritage and culture. This is often followed by the realization that White oppression is the culprit for the negative experiences of youth. Anger against White racism may become a defining theme, with concomitant increases of Asian American self-pride and group pride.
5. The *incorporation* stage represents the highest form of identity evolution. It encompasses the development of a positive and comfortable identity as Asian American and consequent respect for other cultural/racial heritages. Identification for or against White culture is no longer an important issue.

Latino/Hispanic American Identity Development Models

Although a number of ethnic identity development models have been formulated to account for Latino/a identity (Bernal & Knight, 1993; Casas & Pytluk, 1995; Szapocznik et al., 1982), the one most similar to those of African Americans and Asian Americans was proposed by A. S. Ruiz (1990). His model was formulated from a clinical perspective via case studies of Chicano/Latino subjects. Ruiz made several underlying assumptions. First, he believed in a culture-specific explanation of identity for Chicano, Mexican American, and Latino/a clients. Although models about other ethnic group development or the more general ones were helpful, they lacked the specificity of Latino/a cultures. Second, the marginal status of Latinos is highly correlated with maladjustment. Third, negative experiences of forced assimilation are considered destructive to an individual. Fourth, having pride in one's cultural heritage and ethnic identity is positively correlated with mental health. Last, pride in one's ethnicity affords the Hispanic greater freedom to choose freely. These beliefs underlie the five-stage model.

1. *Causal stage:* During this period messages or injunctions from the environment or significant others either affirm, ignore, negate, or denigrate the ethnic heritage of the person. Affirmation about one's ethnic identity is lacking, and the person may experience traumatic or humiliating experiences related to ethnicity. There is a failure to identify with Latino/a culture.

2. *Cognitive stage:* As a result of negative/distorted messages, three erroneous belief systems about Chicano/Latino heritage become incorporated into mental sets: (a) Ethnic group membership is associated with poverty and prejudice; (b) assimilation to White society is the only means of escape; and (c) assimilation is the only possible road to success.

3. *Consequence stage:* Fragmentation of ethnic identity becomes very noticeable and evident. The person feels ashamed and is embarrassed by ethnic markers, such as name, accent, skin color, cultural customs, and so on. The unwanted self-image leads to estrangement and rejection of one's Chicano/Latino heritage.

4. *Working-through stage:* Two major dynamics distinguish this stage. First, the person becomes increasingly unable to cope with the psychological distress of ethnic identity conflict. Second, the person can no longer be a "pretender" by identifying with an alien ethnic identity. The person is propelled to reclaim and reintegrate disowned ethnic identity fragments. Ethnic consciousness increases.

5. *Successful resolution stage:* This last stage is exemplified by greater acceptance of one's culture and ethnicity. There is an improvement in self-esteem and a sense that ethnic identity represents a positive and success-promoting resource.

The Ruiz model has a subjective reality that is missing in many of the empirically based models. This is expected, since it was formulated through a clinical population. It has the added advantage of suggesting intervention focus and direction for each of the stages. For example, the focus of counseling in the causal stage is disaffirming and restructuring of the injunctions; for the cognitive stage, it is the use of cognitive strategies attacking faulty beliefs; for the consequence stage, it is reintegration of ethnic identity fragments in a positive manner; for the working-through stage, ethnocultural identification issues are important; and for the successful resolution stage, the promotion of a positive identity becomes important.

A RACIAL/CULTURAL IDENTITY DEVELOPMENT MODEL

Earlier writers (Berry, 1965; Stonequist, 1937) have observed that minority groups share similar patterns of adjustment to cultural oppression. In the past several decades, Asian Americans, Hispanics, and American Indians have experienced sociopolitical identity transformations so that a *Third World consciousness* has emerged, with cultural oppression as the common unifying force. As a result of studying these models and integrating them with their own clinical observations, Atkinson, Morten, and Sue (1979, 1989, 1998) proposed a five-stage Minority Identity

> The R/CID model defines five stages of development that oppressed people experience as they struggle to understand themselves in terms of their own culture, the dominant culture, and the oppressive relationship between the two cultures: *conformity, dissonance, resistance and immersion, introspection,* and *integrative awareness.*

Development model (MID) in an attempt to pull out common features that cut across the population-specific proposals. D. W. Sue and D. Sue (1990, 1999) later elaborated on the MID, renaming it the Racial/Cultural Identity Development model (R/CID) to encompass a broader population. As discussed shortly, this model may be applied to White identity development as well.

The R/CID model proposed here is not a comprehensive theory of personality, but rather a conceptual framework to aid therapists in understanding their culturally different clients' attitudes and behaviors. The model defines five stages of development that oppressed people experience as they struggle to understand themselves in terms of their own culture, the dominant culture, and the oppressive relationship between the two cultures: *conformity, dissonance, resistance and immersion, introspection,* and *integrative awareness.* At each level of identity, four corresponding beliefs and attitudes that may help therapists better understand their minority clients are discussed. These attitudes/beliefs are an integral part of the minority person's identity and are manifest in how he or she views (a) the self, (b) others of the same minority, (c) others of another minority, and (d) majority individuals. Table 11.1 outlines the R/CID model and the interaction of stages with the attitudes and beliefs.

Conformity Stage

Similar to individuals in the preencounter stage (W. E. Cross, 1991), minority individuals are distinguished by their unequivocal preference for dominant cultural values over their own. White Americans in the United States represent their reference group, and the identification set is quite strong. Lifestyles, value systems, and cultural/physical characteristics that most resemble White society are highly valued, whereas those most like their own minority group may be viewed with disdain or may hold low salience for the person. We agree with Cross that minority people at this stage can be oriented toward a pro-American identity without subsequent disdain or negativism toward their own group. Thus, it is possible for a Chinese American to feel positive about U.S. culture, values, and traditions without evidencing disdain for Chinese culture or feeling negatively about oneself (absence of self-hate). Nevertheless, we believe that such individuals represent a small proportion of persons of color at this stage. Research on their numbers, on how they have handled the social-psychological dynamics of majority-minority relations, on how they have dealt with their minority status, and on how they fit into the stage models (progression issues) needs to be conducted.

We believe that the conformity stage continues to be most characterized by individuals who have bought into societal definitions about their minority status in society. Because the conformity stage represents, perhaps, the most damning

Table 11.1   The Racial/Cultural Identity Development Model

Stages of Minority Development Model	Attitude Toward Self	Attitude Toward Others of the Same Minority	Attitude Toward Others of a Different Minority	Attitude Toward Dominant Group
Stage 1— Conformity	Self-depreciating or neutral due to low race salience	Group-depreciating or neutral due to low race salience	Discriminatory or neutral	Group-appreciating
Stage 2— Dissonance	Conflict between self-depreciating and group appreciating	Conflict between group-depreciating views of minority hierarchy and feelings of shared experience	Conflict between dominant-held and group depreciating	Conflict between group-appreciating
Stage 3— Resistance and immersion	Self-appreciating	Group-appreciating experiences and feelings of culturocentrism	Conflict between feelings of empathy for other minority	Group-depreciating
Stage 4— Introspection	Concern with basis of self-appreciation	Concern with nature of unequivocal appreciation	Concern with ethnocentric basis for judging others	Concern with the basis of group depreciation
Stage 5— Integrative awareness	Self-appreciating	Group-appreciating	Group-appreciating	Selective appreciation

Source: From D. R. Atkinson, G. Morten, and D. W. Sue, *Counseling American minorities: A cross cultural perspective,* 5th ed. Copyright © 1998 Wm. C. Brown Publishers, Dubuque, IA. All rights reserved. Reprinted by permission.

indictment of White racism and because it has such a profound negative impact on persons of color, understanding its sociopolitical dynamics is of utmost importance for the helping professional. Those in the conformity stage are really victims of larger social-psychological forces operating in our society. The key issue here is the dominant-subordinate relationship between two different cultures (Atkinson, Morten, et al., 1998; Freire, 1970; D. W. Sue, 2003). It is reasonable to believe that members of one cultural group tend to adjust themselves to the group possessing the greater prestige and power in order to avoid feelings of inferiority. Yet it is exactly this act that creates ambivalence in the minority individual. The pressures for assimilation and acculturation (melting-pot theory) are strong, creating possible culture conflicts. These individuals are victims of *ethnocentric monoculturalism* (D. W. Sue, 2004): (a) belief in the superiority of one group's cultural heritage—its language, traditions, arts-crafts, and ways of behaving (White) over all others; (b) belief in the inferiority of all other lifestyles (non-White); and (c) the power to impose such standards onto the less powerful group.

The psychological costs of racism on persons of color are immense. Constantly bombarded on all sides by reminders that Whites and their way of life are superior and that all other lifestyles are inferior, many minorities begin to wonder whether they themselves are not somehow inadequate, whether members of their own group are not to blame, and whether subordination and segregation are not justified. K. B. Clark and M. K. Clark (1947) first brought this to the attention of social scientists by stating that racism may contribute to a sense of confused self-identity among Black children. In a study of racial awareness and preference among Black and White children, they found that (a) Black children preferred playing with a White doll over a Black one, (b) the Black doll was perceived as being "bad," and (c) approximately one third, when asked to pick the doll that looked like them, picked the White one.

It is unfortunate that the inferior status of minorities is constantly reinforced and perpetuated by the mass media through television, movies, newspapers, radio, books, and magazines. This contributes to widespread stereotypes that tend to trap minority individuals: Blacks are superstitious, childlike, ignorant, fun loving, dangerous, and criminal; Hispanics are dirty, sneaky, and criminal; Asian Americans are sneaky, sly, cunning, and passive; Indians are primitive savages. Such portrayals cause widespread harm to the self-esteem of minorities who may incorporate them (D. W. Sue, 2003). The incorporation of the larger society's standards may lead minority group members to react negatively toward their own racial and cultural heritage. They may become ashamed of who they are, reject their own group identification, and attempt to identify with the desirable "good" White minority. In the *Autobiography of Malcolm X* (A. Haley, 1966), Malcolm X relates how he tried desperately to appear as White as possible. He went to painful lengths to straighten and dye his hair so that he would appear more like White males. It is evident that many minorities do come to accept White standards as a means of measuring physical attractiveness, attractiveness of personality, and social relationships. Such an orientation may lead to the phenomenon of racial self-hatred, in which people dislike themselves for being Asian, Black, Hispanic, or Native American. People at the conformity stage seem to possess the following characteristics.

1. Attitudes and beliefs toward the self (self-depreciating attitudes and beliefs): Physical and cultural characteristics identified with one's own racial/cultural group are perceived negatively, as something to be avoided, denied, or changed. Physical characteristics (black skin color, "slant-shaped eyes" of Asians), traditional modes of dress and appearance, and behavioral characteristics associated with the minority group are a source of shame. There may be attempts to mimic what is perceived as White mannerisms, speech patterns, dress, and goals. Low internal self-esteem is characteristic of the person.

2. Attitudes and beliefs toward members of the same minority (group-depreciating attitudes and beliefs): Majority cultural beliefs and attitudes about the minority group are also held by the person in this stage. These individuals may have internalized the majority of White stereotypes about their group. In the case of Hispanics, for example, the person may believe that members of his or her own group have high rates of unemployment because "they are lazy, uneducated, and unintelligent." Little thought or validity is given to other viewpoints, such as unemployment's being a function of job discrimination,

prejudice, racism, unequal opportunities, and inferior education. Because persons in the conformity stage find it psychologically painful to identify with these negative traits, they divorce themselves from their own group. The denial mechanism most commonly used is, "I'm not like them; I've made it on my own; I'm the exception."

3. Attitudes and beliefs toward members of different minorities (discriminatory): Because the conformity-stage person most likely strives for identification with White society, the individual shares similar dominant attitudes and beliefs not only toward his or her own minority group but toward other minorities as well. Minority groups most similar to White cultural groups are viewed more favorably, whereas those most different are viewed less favorably. For example, Asian Americans may be viewed more favorably than African Americans or Latino/Hispanic Americans in some situations. Although a stratification probably exists, we caution readers that such a ranking is fraught with hazards and potential political consequences. Such distinctions often manifest themselves in debates over which group is more oppressed and which group has done better than the others. Such debates are counterproductive when used to (a) negate another group's experience of oppression, (b) foster an erroneous belief that hard work alone will result in success in a democratic society, (c) shortchange a minority group (i.e., Asian Americans) from receiving the necessary resources in our society, and (d) pit one minority against another (divide and conquer) by holding one group up as an example to others.

4. Attitudes and beliefs toward members of the dominant group (group-appreciating attitude and beliefs): This stage is characterized by a belief that White cultural, social, and institutional standards are superior. Members of the dominant group are admired, respected, and emulated. White people are believed to possess superior intelligence. Some individuals may go to great lengths to appear White. Consider again the example from the *Autobiography of Malcolm X*, in which the main character would straighten his hair and primarily date White women. Reports that Asian women have undergone surgery to reshape their eyes to conform to White female standards of beauty may (but not in all cases) typify this dynamic.

Dissonance Stage

No matter how much one attempts to deny his or her own racial/cultural heritage, an individual will encounter information or experiences that are inconsistent with culturally held beliefs, attitudes, and values. An Asian American who believes that Asians are inhibited, passive, inarticulate, and poor in people relationships may encounter an Asian leader who seems to break all these stereotypes (e.g., the Sansei student). A Latino/a who feels ashamed of his or her cultural upbringing may encounter another Latino/a who seems proud of his or her cultural heritage. An African American who believes that race problems are due to laziness, untrustworthiness, or personal inadequacies of his or her own group may suddenly encounter racism on a personal level. Denial begins to break down, which leads to a questioning and challenging of the attitudes/beliefs of the conformity stage. This was clearly what happened when the Sansei student encountered discrimination at the restaurant.

In all probability, movement into the dissonance stage is a gradual process. Its very definition indicates that the individual is in conflict between disparate pieces of information or experiences that challenge his or her current self-concept. People generally move into this stage slowly, but a traumatic event may propel some individuals to move into dissonance at a much more rapid pace. W. E. Cross (1971) stated that a monumental event such as the assassination of a major leader like Martin Luther King, Jr., can often push people quickly into the ensuing stage.

1. Attitudes and beliefs toward the self (conflict between self-depreciating and self-appreciating attitudes and beliefs): There is now a growing sense of personal awareness that racism does exist, that not all aspects of the minority or majority culture are good or bad, and that one cannot escape one's cultural heritage. For the first time the person begins to entertain the possibility of positive attributes in the minority culture and, with it, a sense of pride in self. Feelings of shame and pride are mixed in the individual, and a sense of conflict develops. This conflict is most likely to be brought to the forefront quickly when other members of the minority group may express positive feelings toward the person: "We like you because you are Asian [or Black, American Indian, or Latino]." At this stage, an important personal question is being asked: "Why should I feel ashamed of who and what I am?"

2. Attitudes and beliefs toward members of the same minority (conflict between group-depreciating and group-appreciating attitudes and beliefs): Dominant-held views of minority strengths and weaknesses begin to be questioned as new, contradictory information is received. Certain aspects of the minority culture begin to have appeal. For example, a Latino/Hispanic male who values individualism may marry, have children, and then suddenly realize how Latino cultural values that hold the family as the psychosocial unit possess positive features. Or the minority person may find certain members of his group to be very attractive as friends, colleagues, lovers, and so forth.

3. Attitudes and beliefs toward members of a different minority (conflict between dominant-held views of minority hierarchy and feelings of shared experience): Stereotypes associated with other minority groups are questioned, and a growing sense of comradeship with other oppressed groups is felt. It is important to keep in mind, however, that little psychic energy is associated with resolving conflicts with other minority groups. Almost all energies are expended toward resolving conflicts toward the self, the same minority, and the dominant group.

4. Attitudes and beliefs toward members of the dominant group (conflict between group-appreciating and group-depreciating attitudes): The person experiences a growing awareness that not all cultural values of the dominant group are beneficial. This is especially true when the minority person experiences personal discrimination. Growing suspicion and some distrust of certain members of the dominant group develop.

Resistance and Immersion Stage

The minority person tends to endorse minority-held views completely and to reject the dominant values of society and culture. The person seems dedicated to reacting against White society and rejects White social, cultural, and institutional standards as having no personal validity. Desire to eliminate oppression of the individual's minority group becomes an important motivation of the individual's behavior. During the resistance and immersion stage, the three most active types of affective feelings are *guilt*, *shame*, and *anger*. There are considerable feelings of guilt and shame that in the past the minority individual has sold out his or her own racial and cultural group. The feelings of guilt and shame extend to the perception that during this past "sell-out," the minority person has been a contributor and participant in the oppression of his or her own group and other minority groups. This is coupled with a strong sense of anger at the oppression and feelings of having been brainwashed by forces in White society. Anger is directed outwardly in a very strong way toward oppression and racism. Movement into this stage seems to occur for two reasons. First, a resolution of the conflicts and confusions of the previous stage allows greater understanding of social forces (racism, oppression, and discrimination) and his or her role as a victim. Second, a personal questioning of why people should feel ashamed of themselves develops. The answer to this question evokes feelings of guilt, shame, and anger.

> During the resistance and immersion stage, the three most active types of affective feelings are *guilt*, *shame*, and *anger*.

1. Attitudes and beliefs toward the self (self-appreciating attitudes and beliefs): The minority individual at this stage is oriented toward self-discovery of one's own history and culture. There is an active seeking out of information and artifacts that enhance that person's sense of identity and worth. Cultural and racial characteristics that once elicited feelings of shame and disgust become symbols of pride and honor. The individual moves into this stage primarily because he or she asks the question, "Why should I be ashamed of who and what I am?" The original low self-esteem engendered by widespread prejudice and racism that was most characteristic of the conformity stage is now actively challenged in order to raise self-esteem. Phrases such as "Black is beautiful" represent a symbolic relabeling of identity for many Blacks. Racial self-hatred begins to be actively rejected in favor of the other extreme: unbridled racial pride.

2. Attitudes and beliefs toward members of the same minority (group-appreciating attitudes and beliefs): The individual experiences a strong sense of identification with and commitment to his or her minority group as enhancing information about the group is acquired. There is a feeling of connectedness with other members of the racial and cultural group, and a strengthening of new identity begins to occur. Members of one's group are admired, respected, and often viewed now as the new reference group or ideal. Cultural values of the minority group are accepted without question. As indicated, the pendulum

swings drastically from original identification with White ways to identification in an unquestioning manner with the minority group's ways. Persons in this stage are likely to restrict their interactions as much as possible to members of their own group.

3. Attitudes and beliefs toward members of a different minority (conflict between feelings of empathy for other minority group experiences and feelings of culturocentrism): Although members at this stage experience a growing sense of comradeship with persons from other minority groups, a strong culturocentrism develops as well. Alliances with other groups tend to be transitory and based on short-term goals or some global shared view of oppression. There is less of an attempt to reach out and understand other racial-cultural minority groups and their values and ways, and more of a superficial surface feeling of political need. Alliances generally are based on convenience factors or are formed for political reasons, such as combining together as a large group to confront an enemy perceived to be larger.

4. Attitudes and beliefs toward members of the dominant group (group depreciating attitudes and beliefs): The minority individual is likely to perceive the dominant society and culture as an oppressor and as the group most responsible for the current plight of minorities in the United States. Characterized by both withdrawal from the dominant culture and immersion in one's cultural heritage, there is also considerable anger and hostility directed toward White society. There is a feeling of distrust and dislike for all members of the dominant group in an almost global anti-White demonstration and feeling. White people, for example, are not to be trusted because they are the oppressors or enemies. In extreme form, members may advocate complete destruction of the institutions and structures that have been characteristic of White society.

Introspection Stage

Several factors seem to work in unison to move the individual from the resistance and immersion stage into the introspection stage. First, the individual begins to discover that this level of intensity of feelings (anger directed toward White society) is psychologically draining and does not permit one to really devote more crucial energies to understanding oneself or one's own racial-cultural group. The resistance and immersion stage tends to be a reaction against the dominant culture and is not proactive in allowing the individual to use all energies to discover who or what he or she is. Self-definition in the previous stage tends to be reactive (against White racism), and a need for positive self-definition in a proactive sense emerges.

Second, the minority individual experiences feelings of discontent and discomfort with group views that may be quite rigid in the resistance and immersion stage. Often, in order to please the group, the individual is asked to submerge individual autonomy and individual thought in favor of the group good. Many group views may now be seen as conflicting with individual ones. A Latino/a individual who may form a deep relationship with a White person may experience considerable pressure from his or her culturally similar peers to break off the relationship because that White person is the "enemy." However, the personal experiences of the individual may, in fact, not support this group view.

It is important to note that some clinicians often confuse certain characteristics of the introspective stage with parts of the conformity stage. A minority person from the former stage who speaks against the decisions of his or her group may often appear similar to the conformity person. The dynamics are quite different, however. Although the conformity person is motivated by global racial self-hatred, the introspective person has no such global negativism directed at his or her own group.

1. Attitudes and beliefs toward the self (concern with basis of self-appreciating attitudes and beliefs): Although the person originally in the conformity stage held predominantly to majority group views and notions to the detriment of his or her own minority group, the person now feels that he or she has too rigidly held onto minority group views and notions in order to submerge personal autonomy. The conflict now becomes quite great in terms of responsibility and allegiance to one's own minority group versus notions of personal independence and autonomy. The person begins to spend more and more time and energy trying to sort out these aspects of self-identity and begins increasingly to demand individual autonomy.

2. Attitudes and beliefs toward members of the same minority (concern with the unequivocal nature of group appreciation): Although attitudes of identification are continued from the preceding resistance and immersion stage, concern begins to build up regarding the issue of group-usurped individuality. Increasingly, the individual may see his or her own group taking positions that might be considered quite extreme. In addition, there is now increasing resentment over how one's group may attempt to pressure or influence the individual into making decisions that may be inconsistent with the person's values, beliefs, and outlooks. Indeed, it is not unusual for a minority group to make it clear to individual members that if they do not agree with the group, they are against it. A common ploy used to hold members in line is exemplified in questions such as "How Asian are you?" and "How Black are you?"

3. Attitudes and beliefs toward members of a different minority (concern with the ethnocentric basis for judging others): There is now greater uneasiness with culturocentrism, and an attempt is made to reach out to other groups in finding out what types of oppression they experience and how this has been handled. Although similarities are important, there is now a movement toward understanding potential differences in oppression that other groups might have experienced.

4. Attitudes and beliefs toward members of the dominant group (concern with the basis of group depreciation): The individual experiences conflict between attitudes of complete trust for the dominant society and culture and attitudes of selective trust and distrust according to the dominant individual's demonstrated behaviors and attitudes. Conflict is most likely to occur here because the person begins to recognize that there are many elements in U.S. American culture that are highly functional and desirable, yet there is confusion as to

how to incorporate these elements into the minority culture. Would the person's acceptance of certain White cultural values make the person a sellout to his or her own race? There is a lowering of intense feelings of anger and distrust toward the dominant group but a continued attempt to discern elements that are acceptable.

Integrative Awareness Stage

Minority persons in this stage have developed an inner sense of security and now can own and appreciate unique aspects of their culture as well as those in U.S. culture. Minority culture is not necessarily in conflict with White dominant cultural ways. Conflicts and discomforts experienced in the previous stage become resolved, allowing greater individual control and flexibility. There is now the belief that there are acceptable and unacceptable aspects in all cultures and that it is very important for the person to be able to examine and to accept or reject those aspects of a culture that are not seen as desirable. At the integrative awareness stage, the minority person has a strong commitment and desire to eliminate all forms of oppression.

1. Attitudes and beliefs toward the self (self-appreciating attitudes and beliefs): The culturally diverse individual develops a positive self-image and experiences a strong sense of self-worth and confidence. Not only is there an integrated self-concept that involves racial pride in identity and culture, but the person develops a high sense of autonomy. Indeed, the client becomes bicultural or multicultural without a sense of having "sold out one's integrity." In other words, the person begins to perceive his or her self as an autonomous individual who is unique (individual level of identity), a member of one's own racial-cultural group (group level of identity), a member of a larger society, and a member of the human race (universal level of identity).

2. Attitudes and beliefs toward members of same minority (group-appreciating attitudes and beliefs): The individual experiences a strong sense of pride in the group without having to accept group values unequivocally. There is no longer the conflict over disagreeing with group goals and values. Strong feelings of empathy with the group experience are coupled with awareness that each member of the group is also an individual. In addition, tolerant and empathic attitudes are likely to be expressed toward members of one's own group who may be functioning at a less adaptive manner to racism and oppression.

3. Attitudes and beliefs toward members of a different minority (group-appreciating attitudes): There is now literally a reaching out toward different minority groups in order to understand their cultural values and ways of life. There is a strong belief that the more one understands other cultural values and beliefs, the greater is the likelihood of understanding among the various ethnic groups. Support for all oppressed people, regardless of similarity to the individual's minority group, tends to be emphasized.

4. Attitudes and beliefs toward members of the dominant group (attitudes and beliefs of selective appreciation): The individual experiences selective trust

and liking from members of the dominant group who seek to eliminate oppressive activities of the group. The individual also experiences openness to the constructive elements of the dominant culture. The emphasis here tends to be on the fact that White racism is a sickness in society and that White people are also victims who are in need of help.

THERAPEUTIC IMPLICATIONS OF THE R/CID MODEL

Let us first point out some broad general clinical implications of the R/CID model before discussing specific meanings within each of the stages. First, an understanding of cultural identity development should sensitize therapists and counselors to the role that oppression plays in a minority individual's development. In many respects, it should make us aware that our role as helping professionals should extend beyond the office and should deal with the many manifestations of racism. Although individual therapy is needed, combating the forces of racism means a proactive approach for both the therapist and the client. For the therapist, social justice advocacy and systems intervention are often the answers. For culturally diverse clients, it means the need to understand, control, and direct those forces in society that negate the process of positive identity. Thus, a wider sociocultural approach to therapy is mandatory.

Second, the model will aid therapists in recognizing differences between members of the same minority group with respect to their cultural identity. It serves as a useful assessment and diagnostic tool for therapists to gain a greater understanding of their culturally different client. In many cases, an accurate delineation of the dynamics and characteristics of the stages may result in better prescriptive treatment. Therapists who are familiar with the sequence of stages are better able to plan intervention strategies that are most effective for culturally different clients. For example, a client experiencing feelings of isolation and alienation in the conformity stage may require an approach different from the one he or she would require in the introspection stage.

Third, the model allows helping professionals to realize the potentially changing and developmental nature of cultural identity among clients. If the goal of multicultural counseling/therapy is intended to move a client toward the integrative awareness stage, then the therapist is able to anticipate the sequence of feelings, beliefs, attitudes, and behaviors likely to arise. Acting as a guide and providing an understandable end point will allow the client to understand more quickly and work through issues related to his or her own identity. We now turn our attention to the R/CID model and its implications for the therapeutic process.

Conformity Stage: Therapeutic Implications

For the vast majority of those in the conformity stage (belief in the superiority of White ways and the inferiority of minority ways), several therapeutic implications can be derived. First, persons of color are most likely to prefer a White therapist over a minority therapist. This flows logically from the belief that Whites are more competent and capable than are members of their own race. Such a racial preference can be manifested in the client's reaction to a minority therapist via negativism, resistance, or open hostility. In some instances, the client may even request a change in therapist (preferably someone White). On the other hand, the conformity individual who is seen by a White therapist may be quite pleased about it. In many cases, the minority client, in identifying with White culture, may be overly dependent on the White therapist. Attempts to please, appease, and seek approval from the helping professional may be quite prevalent.

Second, most conformity individuals will find that attempts to explore issues of race, racism, or cultural identity or to focus upon feelings are very threatening. Clients in this stage generally prefer a task-oriented, problem-solving approach because an exploration of identity may eventually touch upon feelings of low self-esteem, dissatisfaction with personal appearance, vague anxieties, and racial self-hatred and may challenge the client's self-deception that he or she is not like the other members of his or her own race.

Whether you are a White or a minority counselor working with a conformity individual, the general goal may be the same. There is an obligation to help the client sort out conflicts related to racial/cultural identity through some process of re-education. Somewhere in the course of counseling or therapy, issues of cultural racism, majority-minority group relations, racial self-hatred, and racial cultural identity need to be dealt with in an integrated fashion. We are not suggesting a lecture or a solely cognitive approach, to which clients at this stage may be quite intellectually receptive, but exercising good clinical skills that take into account the client's socioemotional state and readiness to deal with feelings. Only in this manner will the client be able to distinguish the difference between positive attempts to adopt certain values of the dominant society and a negative rejection of one's own cultural value (a characteristic of the integrative awareness stage).

Although the goals for the White and the minority therapist are the same, the way a therapist works toward them may be different. For example, a minority therapist will likely have to deal with hostility from the racially and culturally similar client. As we saw in Chapter 3, a minority therapist working with a client of his or her own race or any person of color may symbolize all that the client is trying to reject. Because therapy stresses the building of a coalition, establishment of rapport, and to some degree a mutual identification, the process may be especially threatening. The opposite may be true of work with a White therapist. The client of color may be overeager to identify with the White professional in order to seek approval. However, rather than being detrimental to multicultural counseling/therapy, these two processes can be used quite effectively and productively. If the minority therapist can aid the client in working through his or her feelings of antagonism and if the majority therapist can aid the client in working through his or her need to overidentify, then the client will be moved closer to awareness than to self-deception. In the former case, the therapist can take a nonjudgmental stance toward the client and provide a positive minority role model. In the latter, the White therapist needs to model positive attitudes toward cultural diversity. Both need to guard against unknowingly reinforcing the client's self-denial and rejection.

Dissonance Stage: Therapeutic Implications

As individuals become more aware of inconsistencies between dominant-held views and those of their own group, a sense of dissonance develops. Preoccupation and questions concerning self, identity, and self-esteem are most likely brought in for therapy. More culturally aware than their conformity counterparts, dissonance clients may prefer a counselor or therapist who possesses good knowledge of the client's cultural group, although there may still be a preference for a White helper. However, the fact that minority helping professionals are generally more knowledgeable of the client's cultural group may serve to heighten the conflicting beliefs and feelings of this stage. Since the client is so receptive toward self-exploration, the therapist can capitalize on this orientation in helping the client come to grips with his or her identity conflicts.

Resistance and Immersion Stage: Therapeutic Implications

Minority clients at this stage are likely to view their psychological problems as products of oppression and racism. They may believe that only issues of racism are legitimate areas to explore in therapy. Furthermore, openness or self-disclosure to therapists not of one's own group is dangerous because White therapists are "enemies" and members of the oppressing group.

Clients in the resistance and immersion stage believe that society is to blame for their present dilemma and actively challenge the establishment. They are openly suspicious of institutions such as mental health services because they view them as agents of the establishment. Very few of the more ethnically conscious and militant minorities will use mental health services because of its identification with the status quo. When they do, they are usually suspicious and hostile toward the helping professional. A therapist working with a client at this stage of development needs to realize several important things.

First, he or she will be viewed by the culturally different client as a symbol of the oppressive society. If you become defensive and personalize the attacks, you will lose your effectiveness in working with the client. It is important not to be intimidated or afraid of the anger that is likely to be expressed; often, it is not personal and is quite legitimate. White guilt and defensiveness can serve only to hinder effective multicultural counseling/therapy. It is not unusual for clients at this stage to make sweeping negative generalizations about White Americans. The White therapist who takes a nondefensive posture will be better able to help the client explore the basis of his or her racial tirades.

In general, clients at this stage prefer a therapist of their own race. However, the fact that you share the same race or culture as your client will not insulate you from the attacks. Again, as outlined in Chapter 3, minority therapists working with a same-race client at the stage of resistance can encounter unique challenges. For example, an African American client may perceive the Black counselor as a sellout of his or her own race, or as an Uncle Tom. Indeed, the anger and hostility directed at the minority therapist may be even more intense than that directed at a White one.

Second, realize that clients in this stage will constantly test you. In earlier chapters we described how minority clients will pose challenges to therapists in order to test their trustworthiness (sincerity, openness, and nondefensiveness) and expertise (competencies). Because of the active nature of client challenges, therapy sessions may become quite dynamic. Many therapists find that this stage is frequently the most difficult to deal with because counselor self-disclosure is often necessary for establishing credibility.

Third, individuals at this stage are especially receptive to approaches that are more action-oriented and aimed at external change (challenging racism). Also, group approaches with persons experiencing similar racial/cultural issues are well received. It is important that the therapist be willing to help the culturally different client explore new ways of relating to both minority and White persons.

Introspection Stage: Therapeutic Implications

Clients at the introspection stage may continue to prefer a therapist of their own race, but they are also receptive to help from therapists of other cultures as long as the therapists understand their clients' worldview. Ironically, clients at this stage may, on the surface, appear similar to conformity persons. Introspection clients are in conflict between their need to identify with their minority group and their need to exercise greater personal freedom. Exercising personal autonomy may occasionally mean going against the wishes or desires of the minority group. This is often perceived by minority persons and their group as a rejection of their own cultural heritage. This is not unlike conformity persons, who also reject their racial/cultural heritage. The dynamics between the two groups, however, are quite dissimilar. It is very important for therapists to distinguish the differences. The conformity person moves away from his or her own group because of perceived negative qualities associated with it. The introspection person wants to move away on certain issues but perceives the group positively. Again, self-exploration approaches aimed at helping the client integrate and incorporate a new sense of identity are important. Believing in the functional values of White American society does not necessarily mean that a person is selling out or going against his or her own group.

Integrative Awareness Stage: Therapeutic Implications

Clients at this stage have acquired an inner sense of security as to self-identity. They have pride in their racial/cultural heritage but can exercise a desired level of personal freedom and autonomy. Other cultures and races are appreciated, and there is a development toward becoming more multicultural in perspective. Although discrimination and oppression remain a powerful part of their existence, integrative awareness persons possess greater psychological resources to deal with these problems. Being action- or systems-oriented, clients respond positively to the designing and implementation of strategies aimed at community and societal change. Preferences for therapists are based not on race, but on those who can share, understand, and accept their worldviews. In other words, attitudinal similarity between therapist and client is a more important dimension than membership-group similarity.

CONCLUSIONS

The R/CID framework is a useful heuristic tool for counselors who work with culturally diverse populations. The model reminds therapists of several important clinical imperatives: (a) Within-group differences are very important to acknowledge in clients of color because not all members of a racial/cultural group are the same. Depending on their levels of racial consciousness, the attitudes, beliefs, and orientations of clients of color may be quite different from one another. (b) A culturally competent counselor needs to be cognizant of and to understand how sociopolitical factors influence and shape identity. Identity development is not solely due to cultural differences but to how the differences are perceived in our society. (c) The model alerts clinicians working with clients of color to certain likely challenges associated with each stage or level of racial/cultural consciousness. Not only may it serve as a useful diagnostic tool, but it provides suggestions of what may be the most appropriate treatment intervention. (d) Other socially marginalized or devalued groups undergo similar identity processes. For example, formulations for women, LGBT groups, those with disabilities, and so forth, can now be found in the psychological literature. Mental health professionals hoping to work with these specific populations would be well served to become familiar with these models as well.

One important aspect relatively untouched in the clinical and research literature is the racial identity development of helping professionals. We have spent considerable time describing the identity development of people of color from the perspective of clients. We have, however, in Chapter 3 indicated that the level of racial consciousness of the minority therapist may impact that of the client of color. In the next chapter we address the issue of White identity development and discuss how it may impact clients of color. But it is equally important for counselors of color to consider their own racial consciousness and how it may interact with a client from their own group. We present several questions for you to consider in the reflection and discussion questions to follow.

REFLECTION AND DISCUSSION QUESTIONS

1. What types of conflicts and/or challenges confront a therapist of color at the conformity stage when working with a client of color at the resistance and immersion stage? How would they perceive one another? How may they respond to one another? What therapeutic issues are likely to arise? What needs to be done in order for the therapist to be helpful?

2. Can you discuss other stage combinations and their implications for therapists and clients of color working with one another?

3. Does a counselor of color have to be at the integrative awareness stage to be helpful to clients of color?

Research on racial/cultural identity development has slowed considerably since the 1990s (Ponterotto & Mallinckrodt, 2007; Yoon, 2011), and little change in the models presented in this chapter has occurred. In some respects, this reflects the widespread acceptance of the importance of identity development and how much it has become a part of the social-psychological and mental health landscape. On the other hand, it also reflects the considerable confusion about the theory and measurement of racial/cultural identity. Indeed, a special issue of the *Journal of Counseling Psychology* in 2007 (Cokley, 2007; Helms, 2007) discussed in detail the conceptual and methodological challenges confronting the field. Although many measures have been developed in an attempt to assess and/or test the conceptual models, most have proven limited because of the sometimes nuanced aspects of measurement. It is clear that we have encountered an impasse that can be broken only through the development of more sophisticated and better measures of racial and ethnic identity.

Implications for Clinical Practice

We have already given considerable space to outlining specific therapeutic suggestions, so a repeat of these would be redundant. Rather, in proposing the R/CID model, we have been very aware of some major cautions and possible limitations that readers should take into account in working with minority clients.

1. Be aware that the R/CID model should not be viewed as a global personality theory with specific identifiable stages that serve as fixed categories. The process of cultural identity development is dynamic, not static. One of the major dangers is to use these stages as fixed entities. In actuality, the model should serve as a conceptual framework to help us understand development.

2. Do not fall victim to stereotyping in using these models. Most minority clients may evidence a dominant characteristic, but there are mixtures from other stages as well. Furthermore, situations and the types of presenting problems may make some characteristics more manifest than others. It is possible that minority clients may evidence, for example, conformity characteristics in some situations but resistance and immersion characteristics in others.

3. Know that minority development models are conceptual aids and that human development is much more complex. A question often raised in the formulation of cultural identity development models is whether identity is a linear process. Do individuals always start at the beginning of these stages? Is it possible to skip stages? Can people regress? In general, our clinical experience has been that minority and majority individuals in this society do tend to move at some gross level through each of the identifiable stages. Some tend to move faster than others, some tend to stay predominately at only one stage, and some may regress.

4. Know that identity development models begin at a point that involves interaction with an oppressive society. Most of these are weak in formulating a stage prior to conformity characteristics. Recent Asian immigrants to the United States are a prime example of the inadequacy of cultural identity development models. Many of the Asian immigrants tend to hold very

positive and favorable views of their own culture and possess an intact racial/cultural identity already. What happens when they encounter a society that views cultural differences as being deviant? Will they or their offspring move through the conformity stage as presented in this model?

5. Be careful of the implied value judgments given in almost all development models. They assume that some cultural resolutions are healthier than others. For example, the R/CID model obviously does hold the integrative awareness stage as a higher form of healthy functioning.

6. Be aware that racial/cultural identity development models seriously lack an adequate integration of gender, class, sexual orientation, and other sociodemographic group identities. William Cross has made some beginning attempts to do so.

7. Know that racial/cultural identity is not a simple, global concept. A great deal of evidence is mounting that suggests that although identity may sequentially move through identifiable stages, affective, attitudinal, cognitive, and behavioral components of identity may not move in a uniform manner. For example, it is entirely possible that the emotions and affective elements associated with certain stages do not have a corresponding one-to-one behavioral impact.

8. Begin to look more closely at the possible therapist and client stage combinations. As mentioned earlier, therapeutic processes and outcomes are often the function of the identity stage of both therapist and client. White identity development of the therapist can either enhance or retard effective therapy.

White Racial Identity Development: Therapeutic Implications

CHAPTER FOCUS QUESTIONS

1. What does it mean to be White? As a White person, how would you answer this question? As a person of color, how would you answer it?
2. As a White person, how aware are you of your own Whiteness and the way it affects your life? As a person of color, why do you think it is so difficult for Whites to understand themselves as racial/cultural beings?
3. What emotional reactions do you experience when the question is asked, "What does it mean to be White?" Why do you think you are reacting that way?
4. What is White privilege? In what ways do you benefit from it? In what ways are you disadvantaged by it? How aware are you of White privilege?
5. How does one's White racial identity development stage affect the therapeutic process? How would it possibly affect the definitions of normality-abnormality, assessment, diagnosis, and treatment of culturally diverse clients?
6. As a White person, how would you develop a nonracist White identity?
7. As a White helping professional, what would you need to do in order to prevent your Whiteness from interfering with your work with clients of color?

WHAT DOES IT MEAN TO BE WHITE?

42-Year-Old White Businessman

Q: What does it mean to be White?

A: Frankly, I don't know what you're talking about!

Q: Aren't you White?

A: Yes, but I come from Italian heritage. I'm Italian, not White.

Q: Well then, what does it mean to be Italian?

A: Pasta, good food, love of wine [obviously agitated]. This is getting ridiculous!

OBSERVATIONS: Denial and/or conflicted about being White. Claims Italian heritage, but unable to indicate more than superficial understanding of ethnic meaning. Expresses annoyance at the question.

26-Year-Old White Female College Student

Q: What does it mean to be White?

A: Is this a trick question? [pause] I've never thought about it. Well, I know that lots of Black people see us as being prejudiced and all that stuff. I wish people would just forget about race differences and see one another as human beings. People are people, and we should all be proud to be Americans.

OBSERVATIONS: Seldom thinks about being White. Defensive about prejudicial associations with Whiteness. Desires to eliminate or dilute race differences.

65-Year-Old White Male Retired Construction Worker

Q: What does it mean to be White?

A: That's a stupid question [sounds irritated]!

Q: Why?

A: Look, what are you . . . Oriental? You people are always blaming us for stereotyping, and here you are doing the same to us.

Q: When you say "us," to whom are you referring?

A: I'm referring to Americans who aren't colored. We are all different from one another. I'm Irish, but there are Germans, Italians, and those Jews. I get angry at the colored people for always blaming us. When my grandparents came over to this country, they worked 24 hours a day to provide a good living for their kids. My wife and I raised five kids, and I worked every day of my life to provide for them. No one gave me nothing! I get angry at the Black people for always whining. They just have to get off their butts and work rather than going on welfare. At least you people [reference to Asian Americans] work hard. The Black ones could learn from your people.

OBSERVATIONS: Believes that the question stereotypes Whites, and expresses resentment with being categorized. Views White people as ethnic groups. Expresses belief that anyone can be successful if they work hard enough. Believes African Americans are lazy and that Asian Americans are successful. Strong anger directed toward minority groups.

34-Year-Old White Female Stockbroker

Q: What does it mean to be White?

A: I don't know [laughing]. I've never thought about it.

Q: Are you White?

A: Yes, I suppose so [seems very amused].

Q: Why haven't you thought about it?

A: Because it's not important to me.

Q: Why not?

A: It doesn't enter into my mind because it doesn't affect my life. Besides, we are all unique. Color isn't important.

OBSERVATIONS: Never thought about being White because it's unimportant. People are individuals, and color isn't important.

These are not atypical responses given by White Euro-Americans when asked this question. When people of color are asked the same question, their answers tend to be more specific:

29-Year-Old Latina Administrative Assistant

Q: What does it mean to be White?

A: I'm not White; I'm Latina!

Q: Are you upset with me?

A: No. . . . It's just that I'm light, so people always think I'm White. It's only when I speak that they realize I'm Hispanic.

Q: Well, what does it mean to be White?

A: Do you really want to know? . . . Okay, it means you're always right. It means you never have to explain yourself or apologize. . . . You know that movie [*Love Story*, which features the line, "Love means never having to say you're sorry"]? Well, being White is never having to say you're sorry. It means they think they're better than us.

OBSERVATIONS: Strong reaction to being mistaken for being White. Claims that being White makes people feel superior and is reflected in their disinclination to admit being wrong.

39-Year-Old Black Male Salesman

Q: What does it mean to be White?

A: Is this a school exercise or something? Never expected someone to ask me that question in the middle of the city. Do you want the politically correct answer or what I really think?

Q: Can you tell me what you really think?

A: You won't quit, will you [laughing]? If you're White, you're right. If you're Black, step back.

Q: What does that mean?

A: White folks are always thinking they know all the answers. A Black man's word is worth less than a White man's. When White customers come into our dealership and see me standing next to the cars, I become invisible to them. Actually, they may see me as a well-dressed janitor [laughs] or actively avoid me. They will search out a White salesman. Or when I explain something to a customer, they always check out the information with my White colleagues. They don't trust me. When I mention this to our manager, who is White, he tells me I'm oversensitive and being paranoid. That's what being White means. It means having the authority or power to tell me what's really happening even though I know it's not. Being White means you can fool yourself into thinking that you're not prejudiced, when you are. That's what it means to be White.

OBSERVATIONS: Being White means you view minorities as less competent and capable. You have the power to define reality. You can deceive yourself into believing you're not prejudiced.

21-Year-Old Chinese American Male College Student (Majoring in Ethnic Studies)

Q: What does it mean to be White?

A: My cultural heritage class was just discussing that question this week.

Q: What was your conclusion?

A: Well, it has to do with White privilege. I read an article by a professor at Wellesley. It made a lot of sense to me. Being White in this society automatically guarantees you better treatment and unearned benefits and privileges than minorities. Having white skin means you have the freedom to choose the neighborhood you live in. You won't be discriminated against. When you enter a store, security guards won't assume you will steal something. You can flag down a cab without the thought they won't pick you up because you're a minority. You can study in school and be assured your group will be portrayed positively. You don't have to deal with race or think about it.

Q: Are White folks aware of their White privilege?

A: Hell, no! They're oblivious to it.

OBSERVATIONS: Being White means having unearned privileges in our society. It means you are oblivious to the advantages of being White. (D. W. Sue, 2003, pp. 115–120)

REFLECTION AND DISCUSSION QUESTIONS

1. In small groups, analyze the seven responses given by the people to the question "What does it mean to be White?" Are there any themes that seem to emanate from the responses?
2. In what ways are the White responses different from those of people of color? Why do you think this is so?
3. How would you answer this question? What reactions do you experience personally when asked? What reactions do you have to the answers given by people? Why?

THE INVISIBLE WHITENESS OF BEING

The responses given by White Euro-Americans and persons of color are radically different from one another. Yet the answers given by both groups are quite common and representative of the range of responses students give in our diversity and multicultural classes. White respondents would rather not think about their Whiteness, are uncomfortable or react negatively to being labeled White, deny its importance in affecting their lives, and seem to believe that they are unjustifiably accused of being bigoted simply because they are White.

Strangely enough, Whiteness is most visible to people of color when it is denied, evokes puzzlement or negative reactions, and is equated with normalcy. Few people of color react negatively when asked what it means to be Black, Asian American, Latino/a, or a member of their race. Most could readily inform the questioner about what it means to be a person of color. There seldom is a day, for example, in which we (the authors) are not reminded of being racially and culturally different from those around us. Yet Whites often find the question about Whiteness quite disconcerting and perplexing.

It appears that the denial and mystification of Whiteness for White Euro-Americans are related to two underlying factors. First, most people seldom think about the air that surrounds them and about how it provides an essential life-giving ingredient, oxygen. We take it for granted because it appears plentiful; only when we are deprived of it does it suddenly become frighteningly apparent. Whiteness is transparent precisely because of its everyday occurrence—its institutionalized normative features in our culture—and because Whites are taught to think of their lives as morally neutral, average, and ideal (D. W. Sue, 2004). To people of color, however, Whiteness is not invisible because it may not fit their normative qualities (e.g., values, lifestyles, experiential reality). Persons of color find White culture quite visible because even though it is nurturing to White Euro-Americans, it may invalidate the lifestyles of multicultural populations.

Second, Euro-Americans often deny that they are White, seem angered by being labeled as such, and often become very defensive (e.g., saying, "I'm not White; I'm Irish," "You're stereotyping, because we're all different," or "There isn't anything like a White race"). In many respects, these statements have validity. Nonetheless, many White Americans would be hard pressed to describe their Irish, Italian, German, or Norwegian heritage in any but the most superficial manner. One of the reasons is related to the processes of assimilation and acculturation. Although there are many ethnic groups, being White allows for assimilation. While persons of color are told to assimilate and acculturate, the assumption is that there exists a receptive society. Racial minorities are told in no uncertain terms that they are allowed only limited access to the fruits of our society. Thus, the accuracy of whether Whiteness defines a race is largely irrelevant. What is more relevant is that Whiteness is associated with unearned privilege—advantages conferred on White Americans but not on persons of color. It is our contention that much of the denial associated with being White is related to the denial of White privilege, an issue we explore in a moment.

UNDERSTANDING THE DYNAMICS OF WHITENESS

Our analysis of the responses from both Whites and persons of color leads us to the inevitable conclusion that part of the problem of race relations (and by inference multicultural counseling and therapy) lies in the different worldviews of both groups. It goes without saying that the racial reality of Whites is radically different from that of people of color (D. W. Sue, 2010a). Which group, however, has the more accurate assessment related to this topic? The answer seems to be contained in the following series of questions: If you want to understand oppression, should you ask the oppressor or the oppressed? If you want to learn about sexism, do you ask men or women? If you want to understand homophobia, do you ask straights or gays? If you want to learn about racism, do you ask Whites or persons of color? It appears that the most accurate assessment of bias comes not from those who enjoy the privilege of power, but from those who are most disempowered (Hanna, Talley, & Guindon, 2000; Neville, Worthington, & Spanierman, 2001). Taking this position, the following assumptions are made about the dynamics of Whiteness.

First, it is clear that most Whites perceive themselves as unbiased individuals who do not harbor racist thoughts and feelings; they see themselves as working toward social justice and possessing a conscious desire to better the life circumstances of those less fortunate than they. Although admirable qualities, this self-image serves as a major barrier to recognizing and taking responsibility for admitting and dealing with one's own prejudices and biases. To admit to being racist, sexist, or homophobic requires people to recognize that the self-images they hold so dear are based on false notions of the self.

Second, being a White person in this society means chronic exposure to ethnocentric monoculturalism as manifested in White supremacy (Zetzer, 2011). It is difficult, if not impossible, for anyone to avoid inheriting the racial biases, prejudices, misinformation, deficit portrayals, and

> To admit to being racist, sexist, or homophobic requires people to recognize that the self-images they hold so dear are based on false notions of the self.

stereotypes of their forebears (Cokley, 2006). To believe that one is somehow immune from inheriting such aspects of White supremacy is to be naive or to engage in self-deception. Such a statement is not intended to assail the integrity of Whites but to suggest that they also have been victimized. It is clear to us that no one was born wanting to be racist, sexist, or homophobic. Misinformation is not acquired by free choice but is imposed upon White people through a painful process of cultural conditioning. In general, lacking awareness of their biases and preconceived notions, counselors may function in a therapeutically ineffective manner.

Third, if White helping professionals are ever able to become effective multi-cultural counselors or therapists, they must free themselves from the cultural conditioning of their past and move toward the development of a nonracist White identity. Unfortunately, many White Euro-Americans seldom consider what it means to be White in our society. Such a question is vexing to them because they seldom think of race as belonging to them—nor of the privileges that come their way by virtue of their white skin (Foster, 2011; Furman, 2011). Katz (1985) points out a major barrier blocking the process of White Euro-Americans investigating their own cultural identity and worldview:

> Because White culture is the dominant cultural norm in the United States, it acts as an invisible veil that limits many people from seeing it as a cultural system. . . . Often, it is easier for many Whites to identify and acknowledge the different cultures of minorities than accept their own racial identity. . . . The difficulty of accepting such a view is that White culture is omnipresent. It is so interwoven in the fabric of everyday living that Whites cannot step outside and see their beliefs, values, and behaviors as creating a distinct cultural group. (pp. 616–617)

As we witnessed in Chapter 6, the invisible veil allows for racial, gender, and sexual orientation microaggressions to be delivered outside the level of awareness of perpetrators (D. W. Sue, 2010a). Ridley (1995) asserts that this invisible veil can be unintentionally manifested in therapy with harmful consequences to minority clients:

> Unintentional behavior is perhaps the most insidious form of racism. Unintentional racists are unaware of the harmful consequences of their behavior. They may be well-intentioned, and on the surface, their behavior may appear to be responsible. Because individuals, groups, or institutions that engage in unintentional racism do not wish to do harm, it is difficult to get them to see themselves as racists. They are more likely to deny their racism. (p. 38)

The conclusion drawn from this understanding is that White counselors and therapists may be unintentional racists: (a) They are unaware of their biases, prejudices, and discriminatory behaviors; (b) they often perceive themselves as moral, good, and decent human beings and find it difficult to see themselves as racist;

(c) they do not have a sense of what their Whiteness means to them; and (d) their therapeutic approaches to multicultural populations are likely to be more harmful (unintentionally) than helpful. These conclusions are often difficult for White helping professionals to accept because of the defensiveness and feelings of blame they are likely to engender. Nonetheless, we ask that White therapists and students not be turned off by the message and lessons of this chapter. We ask you to continue your multicultural journey in this chapter as we explore the question, "What does it mean to be White?"

MODELS OF WHITE RACIAL IDENTITY DEVELOPMENT

A number of multicultural experts in the field have begun to emphasize the need for White therapists to deal with their concepts of Whiteness and to examine their own racism (Ponterotto, Utsey, & Pedersen, 2006; D. W. Sue, 2010; Todd & Abrams, 2011). These specialists point out that while racial/cultural identity development for minority groups proves beneficial in our work as therapists, more attention should be devoted toward the White therapist's racial identity. Since the majority of therapists and trainees are White middle-class individuals, it would appear that White identity development and its implication for multicultural counseling/therapy would be important aspects to consider, both in the actual practice of clinical work and in professional training.

For example, research has found that the level of White racial identity awareness is predictive of racism and internal interpersonal characteristics (Burkard et al., 2003; Miville, Darlington, Whitlock, & Mulligan, 2005; Pope-Davis & Ottavi, 1994; Spanierman, Poteat, Beer, & Armstrong, 2006; Vinson & Neimeyer, 2000, 2003; Y. Wang, Davidson, Yakushko, Savoy, Tan, & Bleier, 2003): (a) the less aware subjects were of their White identity, the more likely they were to exhibit increased levels of racism; (b) the higher the level of White identity development, the greater the reported multicultural counseling competence, more positive opinions toward minority groups, and better therapeutic alliances; (c) higher levels of mature interpersonal relationships and a better sense of personal well-being were associated with higher levels of White identity consciousness; and (d) as a group, women were more likely than men to exhibit higher levels of White consciousness and were less likely to be racist.

It was suggested that this last finding was correlated with women's greater experiences with discrimination and prejudice. Evidence also exists that multicultural counseling/therapy competence is correlated with White racial identity attitudes (Neville et al., 2001). Other research suggests that a relationship exists between a White Euro-American therapist's racial identity and his or her readiness for training in multicultural awareness, knowledge, and skills (Carney & Kahn, 1984; Helms, 1990; Sabnani, Ponterotto, & Borodovsky, 1991; Utsey, Gernat, & Hammar, 2005). Since developing multicultural sensitivity is a long-term developmental task, the work of many researchers has gradually converged toward a conceptualization of the stages/levels/statuses of consciousness of racial/ethnic identity development for White Euro-Americans. A number of these models describe the salience of identity for establishing relationships between the White therapist and the culturally different client, and some have now linked stages of identity with stages for appropriate training (Bennett, 1986; Carney & Kahn, 1984; Sabnani et al., 1991).

The Hardiman White Racial Identity Development Model

One of the earliest integrative attempts at formulating a White racial identity development model is that of Rita Hardiman (1982). Intrigued with why certain White Americans exhibit a much more nonracist identity than do other White Americans, Hardiman studied the autobiographies of individuals who had attained a high level of racial consciousness. This led her to identify five White developmental stages: (a) naiveté—lack of social consciousness, (b) acceptance, (c) resistance, (d) redefinition, and (e) internalization.

1. The naiveté stage (lack of social consciousness) is characteristic of early childhood, when we are born into this world innocent, open, and unaware of racism and the importance of race. Curiosity and spontaneity in relating to race and racial differences tend to be the norm. A young White child who has almost no personal contact with African Americans, for example, may see a Black man in a supermarket and loudly comment on the darkness of his skin. Other than the embarrassment and apprehensions of adults around the child, there is little discomfort associated with this behavior for the youngster. In general, awareness and the meaning of race, racial differences, bias, and prejudice are either absent or minimal. Such an orientation becomes less characteristic of the child as the socialization process progresses. The negative reactions of parents, relatives, friends, and peers toward issues of race, however, begin to convey mixed signals to the child. This is reinforced by the educational system and mass media, which instill racial biases in the child and propel him or her into the acceptance stage.

2. The acceptance stage is marked by a conscious belief in the democratic ideal—that everyone has an equal opportunity to succeed in a free society and that those who fail must bear the responsibility for their failure. White Euro-Americans become the social reference group, and the socialization process consistently instills messages of White superiority and minority inferiority into the child. The underemployment, unemployment, and undereducation of marginalized groups in our society are seen as support that non-White groups are lesser than Whites. Because everyone has an equal opportunity to succeed, the lack of success of minority groups is seen as evidence of some negative personal or group characteristic (low intelligence, inadequate motivation, or biological/cultural deficits). Victim blaming is strong, as the existence of oppression, discrimination, and racism is denied. Hardiman believes that although the naiveté stage is brief in duration, the acceptance stage can last a lifetime.

3. Over time, the individual begins to challenge assumptions of White superiority and the denial of racism and discrimination. Moving from the acceptance

stage to the resistance stage can prove to be a painful, conflicting, and uncomfortable transition. The White person's denial system begins to crumble because of a monumental event or a series of events that not only challenge but also shatter the individual's denial system. A White person may, for example, make friends with a minority coworker and discover that the images he or she has of "these people" are untrue. They may have witnessed clear incidents of unfair discrimination toward persons of color and may now begin to question assumptions regarding racial inferiority. In any case, the racial realities of life in the United States can no longer be denied. The change from one stage to another might take considerable time, but once completed, the person becomes conscious of being White, is aware that he or she harbors racist attitudes, and begins to see the pervasiveness of oppression in our society. Feelings of anger, pain, hurt, rage, and frustration are present. In many cases, the White person may develop a negative reaction toward his or her own group or culture. Although they may romanticize people of color, they cannot interact confidently with them because they fear that they will make racist mistakes. This discomfort is best exemplified in a passage by Sara Winter (1977):

> We avoid Black people because their presence brings painful questions to mind. Is it OK to talk about watermelons or mention "black coffee"? Should we use Black slang and tell racial jokes? How about talking about our experiences in Harlem, or mentioning our Black lovers? Should we conceal the fact that our mother still employs a Black cleaning lady? . . . We're embarrassedly aware of trying to do our best but to "act natural" at the same time. No wonder we're more comfortable in all-White situations where these dilemmas don't arise. (p. 1)

According to Hardiman (1982), the discomfort in realizing that one is White and that one's group has engaged in oppression of racial/ethnic minorities may propel the person into the next stage.

4. Asking the painful question of who one is in relation to one's racial heritage, honestly confronting one's biases and prejudices, and accepting responsibility for one's Whiteness are the culminating marks of the *redefinition stage*. New ways of defining one's social group and one's membership in that group become important. The intense soul-searching is most evident in Winter's (1977) personal journey as she writes,

> In this sense we Whites are the victims of racism. Our victimization is different from that of Blacks, but it is real. We have been programmed into the oppressor roles we play, without our informed consent in the process. Our unawareness is part of the programming: None of us could tolerate the oppressor position, if we lived with a day-to-day emotional awareness of the pain inflicted on other humans through the instrument of our behavior. . . . We Whites benefit in concrete ways, year in and year out, from the present racial

arrangements. All my life in White neighborhoods, White schools, White jobs, and dealing with White police (to name only a few), I have experienced advantages that are systematically not available to Black people. It does not make sense for me to blame myself for the advantages that have come my way by virtue of my Whiteness. But absolving myself from guilt does not imply forgetting about racial injustice or taking it lightly (as my guilt pushes me to do). (p. 2)

There is realization that Whiteness has been defined in opposition to people of color—namely, by standards of White supremacy. By being able to step out of this racist paradigm and redefine what her Whiteness meant to her, Winter is able to add meaning to developing a nonracist identity. The extremes of good/bad or positive/negative attachments to "White" and "people of color" begin to become more realistic. The person no longer denies being White, honestly confronts one's racism, understands the concept of White privilege, and feels increased comfort in relating to persons of color.

5. The internalization stage is the result of forming a new social and personal identity. With the greater comfort in understanding oneself and the development of a nonracist White identity comes a commitment to social action as well. The individual accepts responsibility for effecting personal and social change without always relying on persons of color to lead the way. As Winter (1977) explains,

> To end racism, Whites have to pay attention to it and continue to pay attention. Since avoidance is such a basic dynamic of racism, paying attention will not happen naturally. We Whites must learn how to hold racism realities in our attention. We must learn to take responsibility for this process ourselves, without waiting for Blacks' actions to remind us that the problem exists, and without depending on Black people to reassure us and forgive us for our racist sins. In my experience, the process is painful but it is a relief to shed the fears, stereotypes, immobilizing guilt we didn't want in the first place. (p. 2)

The racist-free identity, however, must be nurtured, validated, and supported in order to be sustained in a hostile environment. Such an individual is constantly bombarded by attempts to be resocialized into the oppressive society.

There are several potential limitations to the Hardiman (1982) model: (a) the select and limited sample that she uses to derive the stages and to enumerate the characteristics makes potential generalization suspect; (b) the autobiographies of White Americans are not truly representative, and their experiences with racism may be bound by the era of the times; (c) the stages are tied to existing social identity development theories, and the model proposes a naive stage that for all practical purposes exists only in children ages 3 to 4 years (it appears tangential in her model and might better be conceptualized as part of the acceptance stage of socialization); and (d) there have been no direct empirical or other postmodern methods of exploration concerning the model to date. Despite these cautions and potential limitations, Hardiman has contributed greatly to our understanding of White identity development by focusing attention on racism as a central force in the socialization of White Americans.

The Helms White Racial Identity Development Model

Working independently of Hardiman, Janet Helms (1984, 1990, 1994, 1995) created perhaps the most elaborate and sophisticated White racial identity model yet proposed. Helms is arguably the most influential White identity development theorist. Not only has her model led to the development of an assessment instrument to measure White racial identity, but it also has been scrutinized empirically (Carter, 1990; Helms & Carter, 1990) and has generated much research and debate in the psychological literature. Like Hardiman (1982), Helms assumes that racism is an intimate and central part of being a White American. To her, developing a healthy White identity requires movement through two phases: (a) abandonment of racism and (b) defining a nonracist White identity. Six specific racial identity statuses are distributed equally in the two phases: contact, disintegration, reintegration, pseudoindependence, immersion/emersion, and autonomy. Originally, Helms used the term *stages* to refer to the six; but because of certain conceptual ambiguities and the controversy that ensued, she has abandoned its usage.

1. *Contact status:* People in this status are oblivious to and unaware of racism, believe that everyone has an equal chance for success, lack an understanding of prejudice and discrimination, have minimal experiences with persons of color, and may profess to be color-blind. Such statements as "People are people," "I don't notice a person's race at all," and "You don't act Black" are examples. Although there is an attempt to minimize the importance or influence of race, there is a definite dichotomy of Blacks and Whites on both a conscious and an unconscious level regarding stereotypes and the superior/inferior dimensions of the races. Because of obliviousness and compartmentalization, it is possible for two diametrically opposed belief systems to coexist: (a) Uncritical acceptance of White supremacist notions relegates minorities into the inferior category with all the racial stereotypes, and (b) there is a belief that racial and cultural differences are considered unimportant. This allows Whites to avoid perceiving themselves as dominant group members or as having biases and prejudices. Such an orientation is aptly stated by Peggy McIntosh (1989) in her own White racial awakening:

> My schooling gave me no training in seeing myself as an oppressor, as an unfairly advantaged person, or as a participant in a damaged culture. I was taught to see myself as an individual whose moral state depended on her individual moral will. . . . Whites are taught to think of their lives as morally neutral, normative, and average, and also ideal, so that when we work to benefit others, this is seen as work which will allow "them" to be more like "us." (p. 8)

2. *Disintegration status:* Although in the previous status the individual does not recognize the polarities of democratic principles of equality and the unequal treatment of minority groups, such obliviousness may eventually break down. The White person becomes conflicted over irresolvable racial moral dilemmas that are frequently perceived as polar opposites: believing one is nonracist, yet not wanting one's son or daughter to marry a minority group member; believing that all men are created equal, even though society treats Blacks as second-class citizens; and not acknowledging that oppression exists and then witnessing it (e.g., the beating of Rodney King). Conflicts between loyalty to one's group and humanistic ideals may manifest themselves in various ways. The person becomes increasingly conscious of his or her Whiteness and may experience dissonance and conflict, resulting in feelings of guilt, depression, helplessness, or anxiety. Statements such as "My grandfather is really prejudiced, but I try not to be" and "I'm personally not against interracial marriages, but I worry about the children" are representative of personal struggles occurring in the White person.

   Although a healthy resolution might be to confront the myth of meritocracy realistically, the breakdown of the denial system is painful and anxiety provoking. Attempts at resolution, according to Helms, may involve (a) avoiding contact with persons of color, (b) not thinking about race, and (c) seeking reassurance from others that racism is not the fault of Whites.

3. *Reintegration status:* This status can best be characterized as a regression in which the pendulum swings back to the most basic beliefs of White superiority and minority inferiority. In their attempts to resolve the dissonance created from the previous process, there is a retreat to the dominant ideology associated with race and one's own socioracial group identity. This ego status results in idealizing the White Euro-American group and the positives of White culture and society; there is a consequent negation and intolerance of other minority groups. In general, a firmer and more conscious belief in White racial superiority is present. Racial/ethnic minorities are blamed for their own problems.

> I'm an Italian grandmother. No one gave us welfare or a helping hand when we came over [immigrated]. My father worked day and night to provide us with a decent living and to put all of us through school. These Negroes are always complaining about prejudice and hardships. Big deal! Why don't they stop whining and find a job? They're not the only ones who were discriminated against, you know. You don't think our family wasn't? We never let that stop us. In America everyone can make it if they are willing to work hard. I see these Black welfare mothers waiting in line for food stamps and free handouts. You can't convince me they're starving. Look at how overweight most of them are. . . . Laziness—that's what I see. (Quoted from a workshop participant)

4. *Pseudoindependence status:* This status represents the second phase of Helms's model, which involves defining a nonracist White identity. As in the Hardiman model, a person is likely to be propelled into this phase

because of a painful or insightful encounter or event that jars the person from the reintegration status. The awareness of other visible racial/ethnic minorities, the unfairness of their treatment, and a discomfort with their racist White identity may lead individuals to identify with the plight of persons of color. There is an attempt to understand racial, cultural, and sexual orientation differences and a purposeful and conscious decision to interact with minority group members. However, the well-intentioned White person at this status may suffer from several problematic dynamics: (a) Although intending to be socially conscious and helpful to minority groups, the White individual may unknowingly perpetuate racism by helping minorities adjust to the prevailing White standards; and (b) choice of minority individuals is based on how similar they are to him or her, and the primary mechanism used to understand racial issues is intellectual and conceptual. As a result, understanding has not reached the experiential and affective domains. In other words, understanding Euro-American White privilege; sociopolitical aspects of race; and issues of bias, prejudice, and discrimination tend to be more an intellectual exercise.

5. *Immersion/emersion status:* If the person is reinforced to continue a personal exploration of himself or herself as a racial being, questions become focused on what it means to be White. Helms states that the person searches for an understanding of the personal meaning of racism and the ways in which one benefits from White privilege. There is an increasing willingness to confront one's own biases, to redefine Whiteness, and to become more activistic in directly combating racism and oppression. This status is different from the previous one in two major ways: It is marked by (a) a shift in focus from trying to change Blacks to changing the self and other Whites and (b) increasing experiential and affective understanding that was lacking in the previous status. This latter process is extremely important. Indeed, Helms believes that a successful resolution of this status requires an emotional catharsis or release that forces the person to relive or reexperience previous emotions that were denied or distorted. The ability to achieve this affective/experiential upheaval leads to a euphoria, or even a feeling of rebirth, and is a necessary condition to developing a new, nonracist White identity. As Winter (1977) states,

> Let me explain this healing process in more detail. We must unearth all the words and memories we generally try not to think about, but which are inside us all the time: "nigger," "Uncle Tom," "jungle bunny," "Oreo," lynching, cattle prods, castrations, rapists, "black pussy," and black men with their huge penises, and hundreds more. (I shudder as I write.) We need to review three different kinds of material: (1) All our personal memories connected with blackness and black people, including everything we can recall hearing or reading; (2) all the racist images and stereotypes we've ever heard, particularly the grossest and most hurtful ones; (3) any race-related things we ourselves said, did, or omitted doing which we feel bad about today. . . . Most whites begin with a good deal of

amnesia. Eventually the memories crowd in, especially when several people pool recollections. Emotional release is a vital part of the process. Experiencing feelings seems to allow further recollections to come. I need persistent encouragement from my companions to continue. (p. 3)

6. *Autonomy status: :* Increasing awareness of one's own Whiteness, reduced feelings of guilt, acceptance of one's role in perpetuating racism, and renewed determination to abandon White entitlement lead to an autonomy status. The person is knowledgeable about racial, ethnic, and cultural differences; values the diversity; and is no longer fearful, intimidated, or uncomfortable with the experiential reality of race. Development of a nonracist White identity becomes increasingly strong. Indeed, the person feels comfortable with his or her nonracist White identity, does not personalize attacks on White supremacy, and can explore the issues of racism and personal responsibility without defensiveness. A person in this status "walks the talk" and actively values and seeks out interracial experiences. Characteristics of the autonomy status can be found in the personal journey of Kiselica (1998):

> I was deeply troubled as I witnessed on a daily basis the detrimental effects of institutional racism and oppression on ethnic-minority groups in this country. The latter encounters forced me to recognize my privileged position in our society because of my status as a so-called Anglo. It was upsetting to know that I, a member of White society, benefited from the hardships of others that were caused by a racist system. I was also disturbed by the painful realization that I was, in some ways, a racist. I had to come to grips with the fact that I had told and laughed at racist jokes and, through such behavior, had supported White racist attitudes. If I really wanted to become an effective, multicultural psychologist, extended and profound self-reckoning was in order. At times, I wanted to flee from this unpleasant process by merely participating superficially with the remaining tasks . . . while avoiding any substantive self-examination. (pp. 10–11)

Helm's model is by far the most widely cited, researched, and applied of all the White racial identity formulations. Part of its attractiveness and value is the derivation of "defenses," "protective strategies," or what Helms (1995) formally labels *information-processing strategies* (IPSs), which White people use to avoid or assuage anxiety and discomfort around the issue of race. Each status has a dominant IPS associated with it: *contact* = obliviousness or denial; *disintegration* = suppression and ambivalence; *reintegration* = selective perception and negative out-group distortion; *pseudoindependence* = reshaping reality and selective perception; *immersion/emersion* = hypervigilance and reshaping; and *autonomy* = flexibility and complexity. Table 12.1 lists examples of IPS

Table 12.1 White Racial Identity Ego Statuses and Information-Processing Strategies

1. *Contact status:* Satisfaction with racial status quo, obliviousness to racism and one's participation in it. If racial factors influence life decisions, they do so in a simplistic fashion. Information-processing strategy (IPS): Obliviousness.

    Example: "I'm a White woman. When my grandfather came to this country, he was discriminated against, too. But he didn't blame Black people for his misfortunes. He educated himself and got a job. That's what Blacks ought to do. If White callers [to a radio station] spent as much time complaining about racial discrimination as your Black callers do, we'd never have accomplished what we have. You all should just ignore it" (quoted from a workshop participant).

2. *Disintegration status:* Disorientation and anxiety provoked by irresolvable racial moral dilemmas that force one to choose between own-group loyalty and humanism. May be stymied by life situations that arouse racial dilemmas. IPS: Suppression and ambivalence.

    Example: "I myself tried to set a nonracist example [for other Whites] by speaking up when someone said something blatantly prejudiced—how to do this without alienating people so that they would no longer take me seriously was always tricky—and by my friendships with Mexicans and Blacks who were actually the people with whom I felt most comfortable" (Blauner, 1993, p. 8).

3. *Reintegration status:* Idealization of one's socioracial group, denigration, and intolerance for other groups. Racial factors may strongly influence life decisions. IPS: Selective perception and negative out-group distortion.

    Example: "So what if my great-grandfather owned slaves. He didn't mistreat them; and besides, I wasn't even here then. I never owned slaves. So I don't know why Blacks expect me to feel guilty for something that happened before I was born. Nowadays, reverse racism hurts Whites more than slavery hurts Blacks. At least they got three square [meals] a day. But my brother can't even get a job with the police department because they have to hire less-qualified Blacks. That [expletive] happens to Whites all the time" (quoted from a workshop participant).

4. *Pseudoindependence status:* Intellectualized commitment to one's own socioracial group and deceptive tolerance of other groups. May make life decisions to "help other racial groups." IPS: Reshaping reality and selective perception.

    Example: "Was I the only person left in America who believed that the sexual mingling of the races was a good thing, that it would erase cultural barriers and leave us all a lovely shade of tan? . . . Racial blending is inevitable. At the very least, it may be the only solution to our dilemmas of race" (Allen, 1994, p. C4).

5. *Immersion/emersion status:* Search for an understanding of the personal meaning of racism and the ways by which one benefits and a redefinition of Whiteness. Life choices may incorporate racial activism. IPS: Hypervigilance and reshaping.

    Example: "It's true that I personally did not participate in the horror of slavery, and I don't even know whether my ancestors owned slaves. But I know that because I am White, I continue to benefit from a racist system that stems from the slavery era. I believe that if White people are ever going to understand our role in perpetuating racism, then we must begin to ask ourselves some hard questions and be willing to consider our role in maintaining a hurtful system. Then, we must try to do something to change it" (quoted from a workshop participant).

6. *Autonomy status:* Informed positive socioracial group commitment, use of internal standards for self-definition, capacity to relinquish the privileges of racism. May avoid life options that require participation in racial oppression. IPS: Flexibility and complexity.

    Example: "I live in an integrated [Black-White] neighborhood, and I read Black literature and popular magazines. So I understand that the media presents a very stereotypic view of Black culture. I believe that if more of us White people made more than a superficial effort to obtain accurate information about racial groups other than our own, then we could help make this country a better place for all peoples" (quoted from a workshop participant).

Source: Helms, 1995, p. 185.

statements likely to be made by White people in each of the six ego statuses. Understanding these strategic reactions is important for White American identity development, for understanding the barriers that must be overcome in order to move to another status, and for potentially developing effective training or clinical strategies.

The Helms model, however, is not without its detractors. In an article critical of the Helms model and of most "stage" models of White racial identity development, Rowe, Bennett, and Atkinson (1994) raised some serious objections. First, they claim that Helms's model is erroneously based on racial/ethnic minority identity development models (discussed in the previous chapter). Because minority identity development occurs in the face of stereotyping and oppression, it may not apply to White identity, which does not occur under the same conditions. Second, they believe that too much emphasis is placed on the development of White attitudes toward minorities and that not enough is placed on the development of White attitudes toward themselves and their own identity. Third, they claim that there is a conceptual inaccuracy in putting forth the model as developmental via stages (linear) and that the progression from less to more healthy seems to be based on the author's ethics. Last, Rowe (2006) attacks the Helms model of White racial identity development because it is based upon the White Racial Identity Attitude Scale (Helms & Carter, 1990), which he labels as "pseudoscience" because he asserts that the psychometric properties are not supported by the empirical literature. It is important to note that the critique of the Helms (1984) model has not been left unanswered. In subsequent writings, Helms (1994, 1995) has disclaimed the Rowe et al. (1994) characterization of her model and has attempted to clarify her position.

The continuing debate has proven beneficial for two reasons. First, the Helms model has evolved and changed (whether because of these criticisms or not) so that it has become even more intricate and clear. For example, Helms denies ever being a stage theorist, but to prevent continuing future confusion, she now prefers the term *status* and describes her thinking on this issue in detail (Helms, 1995). Second, in responding to the Helms model, Rowe et al. (1994) offered an alternative means of conceptualizing White identity that has contributed to the increasing understanding of White identity development.

Briefly, Rowe et al. (1994) prefer to conceptualize White racial identity as one of *types* or *statuses* rather than *stages*. They take care in explaining that these types are not fixed entities but are subject to experiential modification. They propose two major groupings covering seven types of racial consciousness: unachieved (avoidant, dependent, and dissonant) and achieved (dominative, conflictive, reactive, and integrative). Movement from type to type is dependent on the creation of dissonance, personal attributes, and the subsequent environmental conditions encountered by the person. As a result, the primary gateway for change involves the dissonant type. Persons can move among all types except two unachieved ones, avoidant and dependent. These latter two are characterized by a lack of internalized attitudes. Space does not permit an extended discussion of the model; we have chosen to summarize these types and their characteristics in Table 12.2.

Table 12.2 Rowe, Bennett, and Atkinson's Model of White Racial Consciousness Types and Their Characteristics

I. Unachieved
  A. Avoidant types ignore, avoid, deny, or minimize racial issues. They do not consider their own racial identity, nor are they seemingly aware of minority issues.
  B. Dependent types have minimal racial attitudes developed through personal experience or consideration. They most often follow the lead of significant others in their lives, such as a child would with his or her parent.
  C. Dissonant types often feel conflict between their belief systems and contradictory experiences. This type may break away from these attitudes depending on the degree of support or the intensity of the conflict. As such, it is a transitory status for the person.
II. Achieved
  A. Dominative types are very ethnocentric and believe in White superiority and minority inferiority. They may act out their biases passively or actively.
  B. Conflictive types oppose direct and obvious discrimination but would be unwilling to change the status quo. Most feel that discrimination has been eliminated and that further efforts constitute reverse racism.
  C. Reactive types have good awareness that racism exists but seem unaware of their personal responsibility in perpetuating it. They may overidentify with or be paternalistic toward minorities.
  D. Integrative types "have integrated their sense of Whiteness with a regard for racial/ethnic minorities . . . [and] integrate rational analysis, on the one hand, and moral principles, on the other, as they relate to a variety of racial/ethnic issues" (Rowe et al., 1994, p. 141).

THE PROCESS OF WHITE RACIAL IDENTITY DEVELOPMENT: A DESCRIPTIVE MODEL

Analysis of the models just discussed reveals some important differences. First, the identity development models seem to focus on a more definite and sequential movement through stages or statuses. They differ, however, in where they place the particular stages or statuses in the developmental process. Given that almost all models now entertain the possibility that development can vary (looping and recycling), the consciousness development model allows greater latitude conceptually for movement to various types. Rowe et al. (1994) seem to offer a more fluid process of racial experience by White people. Consequently, the model is also less bound by the context or era of the times (identity formed during the civil rights movement versus current times). The addition of nonachieved statuses is missing in the development theories and may capture more closely the "passive" feel that some Whites experience in their racial identity development (Todd & Abrams, 2011).

However, the essential concept of developing a positive White identity is conspicuously absent from the consciousness model. It lacks richness in allowing White people to view their developmental history better and to gain a sense of their past, present, and future. Struggling with racial identity and issues of race requires a historical perspective, which development theories offer. It is with this in mind that we have attempted to take aspects of White racial identity/consciousness development into consideration when formulating a descriptive model with practical implications.

In our work with White trainees and clinicians, we have observed some very important changes through which they seem to move as they work toward multicultural competence (Sue, 2011). We have been impressed with how Whites seem to go through parallel racial/cultural identity transformations. This is especially true if we accept the fact that Whites are as much victims of societal forces (i.e., they are socialized into racist attitudes and beliefs) as are their minority counterparts (D. W. Sue, 2003). No child is born wanting to be a racist! Yet White people do benefit from the dominant-subordinate relationship in our society. It is this factor that Whites need to confront in an open and honest manner.

Using the formulation of D. W. Sue and D. Sue (1990) and D. W. Sue et al. (1998), we propose a seven-step process that integrates many characteristics from the other formulations. Furthermore, we make some basic assumptions with respect to those models:

1. Racism is an integral part of U.S. life, and it permeates all aspects of our culture and institutions (ethnocentric monoculturalism).
2. Whites are socialized into the society and therefore inherit all the biases; stereotypes; and racist attitudes, beliefs, and behaviors of the larger society.
3. How Whites perceive themselves as racial beings follows an identifiable sequence that can occur in a linear or nonlinear fashion.
4. The status of White racial identity development in any multicultural encounter affects the process and outcome of interracial relationships.
5. The most desirable outcome is one in which the White person not only accepts his or her Whiteness but also defines it in a nondefensive and nonracist manner.

Seven-Step Process

1. *Naiveté phase:* This phase is relatively neutral with respect to racial/cultural differences. Its length is brief and is marked by a naive curiosity about race. As mentioned previously, racial awareness and burgeoning social meanings are absent or minimal, and the young child is generally innocent, open, and spontaneous regarding racial differences. Between the ages of 3 to 5, however, the young White child begins to associate positive ethnocentric meanings to his or her own group and negative ones to others. Bombarded by misinformation through the educational channels, mass media, and significant others in his or her life, a sense of superiority is instilled in the concept of Whiteness and the inferiority of all other groups and their heritage. The following passage describes one of the insidious processes of socialization that leads to propelling the child into the conformity phase.

> It was a late summer afternoon. A group of White neighborhood mothers, obviously friends, had brought their 4- and 5-year-olds to the local McDonald's for a snack and to play on the swings and slides

provided by the restaurant. They were all seated at a table watching their sons and daughters run about the play area. In one corner of the yard sat a small Black child pushing a red truck along the grass. One of the White girls from the group approached the Black boy and they started a conversation. During that instant, the mother of the girl exchanged quick glances with the other mothers, who nodded knowingly. She quickly rose from the table, walked over to the two, spoke to her daughter, and gently pulled her away to join her previous playmates. Within minutes, however, the girl again approached the Black boy and both began to play with the truck. At that point, all the mothers rose from the table and loudly exclaimed to their children, "It's time to go now!" (Taken from D. W. Sue, 2003, pp. 89–90)

2. *Conformity phase:* The White person's attitudes and beliefs in this phase are very ethnocentric. There is minimal awareness of the self as a racial being and a strong belief in the universality of values and norms governing behavior. The White person possesses limited accurate knowledge of other ethnic groups, but he or she is likely to rely on social stereotypes as the main source of information. As we saw, Hardiman (1982) described this phase as an acceptance of White superiority and minority inferiority. Consciously or unconsciously, the White person believes that White culture is the most highly developed and that all others are primitive or inferior. The conformity phase is marked by contradictory and often compartmentalized attitudes, beliefs, and behaviors. A person may believe simultaneously that he or she is not racist but that minority inferiority justifies discriminatory and inferior treatment, and that minority persons are different and deviant but that "people are people" and differences are unimportant (Helms, 1984). As with their minority counterparts at this phase, the primary mechanism operating here is one of denial and compartmentalization. For example, many Whites deny that they belong to a race that allows them to avoid personal responsibility for perpetuating a racist system. Like a fish in water, Whites either have difficulty seeing or are unable to see the invisible veil of cultural assumptions, biases, and prejudices that guide their perceptions and actions. They tend to believe that White Euro-American culture is superior and that other cultures are primitive, inferior, less developed, or lower on the scale of evolution.

It is important to note that many Whites in this phase of development are unaware of these beliefs and operate as if they are universally shared by others. They believe that differences are unimportant and that "people are people," "we are all the same under the skin," "we should treat everyone the same," "problems wouldn't exist if minorities would only assimilate," and discrimination and prejudice are something that others do. The helping professional with this perspective professes color-blindness, views counseling/therapy theories as universally applicable, and does not question their relevance to other culturally different groups. The primary mechanism used in encapsulation is denial—denial that people are different, denial that discrimination exists, and denial of one's own prejudices. Instead, the locus of the problem is seen to reside in the minority individual or group. Minorities would not encounter problems if they would only assimilate and acculturate (melting pot), value education, or work harder.

3. *Dissonance phase:* Movement into the dissonance phase occurs when the White person is forced to deal with the inconsistencies that have been compartmentalized or encounters information/experiences at odds with denial. In most cases, individuals are forced to acknowledge Whiteness at some level, to examine their own cultural values, and to see the conflict between upholding humanistic nonracist values and their contradictory behavior. For example, a person who may consciously believe that all people are created equal and that he or she treats everyone the same suddenly experiences reservations about having African Americans move next door or having one's son or daughter involved in an interracial relationship. These more personal experiences bring the individual face-to-face with his or her own prejudices and biases. In this situation, thoughts that "I am not prejudiced," "I treat everyone the same regardless or race, creed, or color," and "I do not discriminate" collide with the denial system. Additionally, some major event (e.g., the assassination of Martin Luther King, Jr., the Rodney King beating) may force the person to realize that racism is alive and well in the United States.

The increasing realization that one is biased and that Euro-American society does play a part in oppressing minority groups is an unpleasant one. Dissonance may result in feelings of guilt, shame, anger, and depression. Rationalizations may be used to exonerate one's own inactivity in combating perceived injustice or personal feelings of prejudice; for example, "I'm only one person—what can I do?" or "Everyone is prejudiced, even minorities." As these conflicts ensue, the White person may retreat into the protective confines of White culture (encapsulation of the conformity phase) or move progressively toward insight and revelation (resistance and immersion phase).

Whether a person regresses is related to the strength of positive forces pushing an individual forward (support for challenging racism) and negative forces pushing the person backward (fear of some loss) (D. W. Sue, 2011; Todd & Abrams, 2011). For example, challenging the prevailing beliefs of the times may mean risking ostracism from other White relatives, friends, neighbors, and colleagues. Regardless of the choice, there are many uncomfortable feelings of guilt, shame, anger, and depression related to the realization of inconsistencies in one's belief systems. Guilt and shame are most likely related to the recognition of the White person's role in perpetuating racism in the past. Guilt may also result from the person's being afraid to speak out on the issues or to take responsibility for his or her part in a current situation. For example, the person may witness an act of racism, hear a racist comment, or be given preferential treatment over a minority person but decide not to say anything for fear of violating racist White norms. Many White people rationalize their behaviors by believing that they are powerless to make changes. Additionally, there is a tendency to retreat into White culture. If, however, others (which may include some family and friends) are more accepting, forward movement is more likely.

4. *Resistance and immersion phase:* The White person who progresses to this phase will begin to question and challenge his or her own racism. For the first time, the person begins to realize what racism is all about, and his or her eyes are suddenly open. Racism is seen everywhere (e.g., advertising, television, educational materials, interpersonal interactions). This phase of development is marked by a major questioning of one's own racism and that of others in society. In addition, increasing awareness of how racism operates and its pervasiveness in U.S. culture and institutions is the major hallmark of this level. It is as if the person awakens to the realities of oppression; sees how educational materials, the mass media, advertising, and other elements portray and perpetuate stereotypes; and recognizes how being White grants certain advantages denied to various minority groups.

There is likely to be considerable anger at family and friends, institutions, and larger societal values, which are seen as having sold him or her a false bill of goods (democratic ideals) that were never practiced. Guilt is also felt for having been a part of the oppressive system. Strangely enough, the person is likely to undergo a form of racial self-hatred at this phase. Negative feelings about being White are present, and the accompanying feelings of guilt, shame, and anger toward oneself and other Whites may develop. The White liberal syndrome may develop and be manifested in two complementary styles: the paternalistic protector role or the overidentification with another minority group (Helms, 1984; Ponterotto, 1988). In the former, the White person may devote his or her energies in an almost paternalistic attempt to protect minorities from abuse. In the latter, the person may actually want to identify with a particular minority group (e.g., Asian, Black) in order to escape his or her own Whiteness. The White person will soon discover, however, that these roles are not appreciated by minority groups and will experience rejection. Again, the person may resolve this dilemma by moving back into the protective confines of White culture (conformity phase), again experience conflict (dissonance), or move directly to the introspective phase.

5. *Introspective phase:* This phase is most likely a compromise of having swung from an extreme of unconditional acceptance of White identity to a rejection of Whiteness. It is a state of relative quiescence, introspection, and reformulation of what it means to be White. The person realizes and no longer denies that he or she has participated in oppression and benefited from White privilege or that racism is an integral part of U.S. society. However, individuals at this phase become less motivated by guilt and defensiveness, accept their Whiteness, and seek to redefine their own identity and that of their social group. This acceptance, however, does not mean a less active role in combating oppression. The process may involve addressing the questions, "What does it mean to be White?" "Who am I in relation to my Whiteness?" and "Who am I as a racial/cultural being?"

The feelings or affective elements may be existential in nature and involve feelings of disconnectedness, isolation, confusion, and loss. In other words, the person knows that he or she will never fully understand the minority experience but feels disconnected from the Euro-American group as well. In some ways, the introspective phase is similar in dynamics to the dissonance phase, in that both represent a transition from one perspective to another. The process used to answer the previous questions and to deal with the ensuing feelings may involve a searching, observing, and questioning attitude. Answers to these questions involve dialoging and observing one's own social group and actively creating and experiencing interactions with various minority group members as well.

6. *Integrative awareness phase:* Reaching this level of development is most characterized as (a) understanding the self as a racial/cultural being, (b) being aware of sociopolitical influences regarding racism, (c) appreciating racial/cultural diversity, and (d) becoming more committed toward eradicating oppression. The formation of a nonracist White Euro-American identity emerges and becomes internalized. The person values multiculturalism, is comfortable around members of culturally different groups, and feels a strong connectedness with members of many groups. Most important, perhaps, is the inner sense of security and strength that needs to develop and that is needed to function in a society that is only marginally accepting of integrative, aware White persons.

7. *Commitment to antiracist action phase:* Someone once stated that the ultimate White privilege is the ability to acknowledge it but do nothing about it. This phase is most characterized by social action. There is likely to be a consequent change in behavior and an increased commitment toward eradicating oppression. Seeing "wrong" and actively working to "right" it requires moral fortitude and direct action. Objecting to racist jokes; trying to educate family, friends, neighbors, and coworkers about racial issues; and taking direct action to eradicate racism in the schools and workplace and in social policy (often in direct conflict with other Whites) are examples of actions taken by individuals who achieve this status. Movement into this phase can be a lonely journey for Whites because they are oftentimes isolated by family, friends, and colleagues who do not understand their changed worldview. Strong pressures in society to not rock the boat, threats by family members that they will be disowned, avoidance by colleagues, threats of being labeled a troublemaker or not being promoted at work are all possible pressures for the White person to move back to an earlier phase of development. To maintain a nonracist identity requires Whites to become increasingly immunized to social pressures for conformance and to begin forming alliances with persons of color or other liberated Whites who become a second family to them. As can be seen, the struggle against individual, institutional, and societal racism is a monumental task in this society.

OVERCOMING PERSONAL RACISM AND DEVELOPING A NONRACIST WHITE IDENTITY: PERSONAL STRATEGIES AND ACTIONS

Although White racial identity development models tell us much about the characteristics most likely to be exhibited by individuals as they progress through these phases, they are very weak in giving guidance about how to develop a nonracist White identity. Possible answers seem to lie in the social-psychological literature

The seven basic principles of prejudice reduction are:

- having intimate and close contact with others
- cooperation rather than competition on common tasks
- sharing mutual goals
- exchanging accurate information rather than stereotypes
- sharing an equal status relationship
- support for prejudice reduction by authorities and leaders
- feeling a sense of connection and belonging with one another

about the basic principles or conditions needed to reduce prejudice through intergroup contact first formulated by Gordon Allport (1954) in his classic book *The Nature of Prejudice*. His work has been refined and expanded by other researchers and scholars (Aboud, 1988; Amir, 1969; Cook, 1962; Gaertner, Rust, Dovidio, Bachman, & Anastasio, 1994; J. M. Jones, 1997). D. W. Sue (2003) has summarized these findings into the basic principles of prejudice reduction: (a) having intimate and close contact with others, (b) cooperation rather than competition on common tasks, (c) sharing mutual goals, (d) exchanging accurate information rather than stereotypes, (e) sharing an equal status relationship, (f) support for prejudice reduction by authorities and leaders, and (g) feeling a sense of connection and belonging with one another. To this we might add the contributions of White racial identity development theorists who have indicated the importance of understanding oneself as a racial/cultural being. It has been found, for example, that the level of White racial awareness is predictive of racism (Pope-Davis & Ottavi, 1994; Wang et al., 2003); the less aware that participants were of their White racial identity, the more likely they exhibited increased levels of racism.

These seven basic principles arose primarily through studies of how to reduce intergroup conflict and hostility, but several seem consistent with reducing personal prejudice through experiential learning and the acquisition of accurate information about other groups. Translating these principles into roles and activities for personal development has come from recommendations put forth by the American Psychological Association (n.d.), the President's Initiative on Race (1998, 1999), educators and trainers (Ponterotto et al., 2006; Young & Davis-Russell, 2002), and from studies on difficult racial dialogues (D. W. Sue, Lin, Torino, et al., 2009; D. W. Sue, Rivera, Capodilupo, et al., 2010). D. W. Sue (2003) outlines basic learning situations/activities most likely to enhance change in developing a nonracist White identity.

Principle 1: Learn About People of Color From Sources Within the Group

- First, you must experience and learn from as many sources as possible (not just the media or what your neighbor may say) in order to check out the validity of your assumptions and understanding.
- If you want to understand racism, White people may not be the most insightful or accurate sources. Acquiring information from persons of color allows you to understand the thoughts, hopes, fears, and aspirations from the perspective of people of color. It also acts as a counterbalance to the worldview expressed by White society about minority groups.

Principle 2: Learn From Healthy and Strong People of the Culture

- A balanced picture of racial/ethnic minority groups requires that you spend time with healthy and strong people of that culture. The mass media and our educational texts (written from the perspectives of Euro-Americans) frequently portray minority groups as uncivilized or pathological or as criminals or delinquents.
- You must make an effort to fight such negative conditioning and ask yourselves what are the desirable aspects of the culture, the history, and the people. This can come about only if you have contact with healthy representatives of that group.
- Since you seldom spend much intimate time with persons of color, you are likely to believe the societal projection of minorities as being law breakers and unintelligent, prone to violence, unmotivated, and uninterested in relating to the larger society.
- Frequent minority-owned businesses, and get to know the proprietors.
- Attend services at a variety of churches, synagogues, temples, and other places of worship to learn about different faiths and to meet religious leaders.
- Invite colleagues, coworkers, neighbors, or students of color to your home for dinner or a holiday.
- Live in an integrated or culturally diverse neighborhood, and attend neighborhood organizational meetings and attend/throw block parties.
- Form a community organization on valuing diversity, and invite local artists, authors, entertainers, politicians, and leaders of color to address your group.
- Attend street fairs, educational forums, and events put on by the community.

Principle 3: Learn From Experiential Reality

- Although listening to readings, attending theater, and going to museums are helpful to increase understanding, you must supplement your factual understanding with the experiential reality of the groups you hope to understand. These experiences, however, must be something carefully planned to be successful.
- It may be helpful to identify a cultural guide: someone from the culture who is willing to help you understand his or her group; someone willing to introduce you to new experiences; someone willing to help you process your thoughts, feelings, and behaviors. This allows you to more easily obtain valid information on race and racism issues.

Principle 4: Learn From Constant Vigilance of Your Biases and Fears

- Your life must become a "have to" in being constantly vigilant to manifestations of bias in both yourself and the people around you.
- Learn how to ask sensitive racial questions of your minority friends, associates, and acquaintances. Persons subjected to racism seldom get a chance to talk about it with a nondefensive and nonguilty person from the majority group.
- Most minority individuals are more than willing to respond, to enlighten, and to share *if they sense that your questions and concerns are sincere and motivated by a desire to learn and serve the group.*

Principle 5: Learn From Being Committed to Personal Action Against Racism

- Dealing with racism means a personal commitment to action. It means interrupting other White Americans when they make racist remarks, tell racist jokes, or engage in racist actions, even if this is embarrassing or frightening.
- It means noticing the possibility for direct action against bias and discrimination in your everyday life; in the family, at work, and in the community.
- It means taking initiative to make sure that minority candidates are fairly considered in your place of employment, advocate to teachers of your children to include multicultural material in the curriculum, volunteer in community organizations to have them consider multicultural issues, and contribute and work for campaigns of political candidates who will advocate for social justice.

The journey to developing a White nonracist identity is not an easy path to travel. Remember, racial identity and cultural competence are intimately linked to one another. Becoming a culturally competent helping professional requires more than "book learning" and both experiential learning and the need to take personal action. Are you ready for the challenge?

REFLECTION AND DISCUSSION QUESTIONS

1. Do these suggestions and strategies make sense to you? Are there others that come to mind?
2. What would make it difficult for you to personally implement? What barriers stand in the way? For example, what would make it difficult for you to interrupt a stranger or even a family member when a racist or sexist joke is made?
3. Have you ever been in a situation where you were the only White person in an activity or event full of Black, Asian, or Latino/a people? What feelings did you have? How did you feel? Were you uncomfortable or fearful?
4. What would you need in the way of support or personal moral courage to move toward developing a White nonracist identity?

Implications for Clinical Practice

It is important to stress again the need for White Euro-American counselors to understand the assumptions of White racial identity development models. We ask readers to seriously consider the validity of these assumptions and to engage one another in a dialogue about them. Ultimately, the effectiveness of White therapists is related to their ability to overcome sociocultural conditioning and to make their Whiteness visible. The following guidelines and suggestions will help you do so.

1. Accept the fact that racism is a basic and integral part of U.S. life and permeates all aspects of our culture and institutions. Know that as a White person you are socialized into U.S. society and, therefore, inherit the biases, stereotypes, and racist attitudes, beliefs, and behaviors of the society

2. Understand that the level of White racial identity development in a cross-cultural encounter (e.g., working with minorities, responding to multicultural training) affects the process and outcome of an interracial relationship (including counseling/therapy).

3. Work on accepting your own Whiteness, but define it in a nondefensive and nonracist manner. How you perceive yourself as a racial being seems to be correlated strongly with how you perceive and respond to racial stimuli.

4. Spend time with healthy and strong people from another culture or racial group. As a counselor, the only contact we usually have comes from working with a narrow segment of the society. Thus, the knowledge we have about minority groups is usually developed from working with troubled individuals.

5. Know that becoming culturally aware and competent comes through lived experience and reality. Identify a cultural guide, someone from the culture who is willing to help you understand his or her group.

6. Attend cultural events, meetings, and activities led by minority communities. This allows you to hear from church leaders, to attend community celebrations, and to participate in open forums so that you may sense the strengths of the community, observe leadership in action, personalize your understanding, and develop new social relationships.

7. When around persons of color, pay attention to feelings, thoughts, and assumptions that you have when race-related situations present themselves. Where are your feelings of uneasiness, differentness, or outright fear coming from? Do not make excuses for these thoughts or feelings, dismiss them, or avoid attaching meaning to them. Only if you are willing to confront them directly can you unlearn the misinformation and nested emotional fears.

8. Dealing with racism means a personal commitment to action. It means interrupting other White Americans when they make racist remarks and jokes or engage in racist actions, even if it is embarrassing or frightening. It means noticing the possibility for direct action against bias and discrimination in your everyday life.

Multicultural Counseling and Specific Populations

While Section One addressed common principles, practices, and issues of multicultural counseling and therapy that are often applicable across groups, this section is divided into four parts that recognize the unique challenges and group differences between socially marginalized groups in our society. Section Two was created for several reasons.

- First, we recognize that while issues of culture-conflict, prejudice, and discrimination occur to almost all socially devalued groups in our society, the histories and the unique challenges confronting people of color, for example, may differ substantially from that of women, those who live in poverty, and for religious minorities.
- Second is the recognition that the terms *multiculturalism, diversity*, and *multicultural counseling competence* are broad terms that include race, gender, social class, religious orientation, sexual orientation, and many other sociodemographic groups in our society. To not acknowledge this fact is to render certain groups invisible, thereby invalidating their existence as unique.
- Third, numerous instructors continue to find the coverage of specific populations helpful to their students. The extensive coverage in Section Two allows instructors freedom to use all of the chapters in this section or to selectively choose those that fit their course requirements.
- Last, but importantly, was our attempt to provide a guideline of how to approach the use of population-specific chapters through an open and

flexible assessment process that avoids stereotypical and rigid therapeutic applications (see Part V).

Section Two contains the following four parts:

- Part V: Understanding Specific Populations
- Part VI: Counseling and Therapy With Racial/Ethnic Minority Group Populations
- Part VII: Counseling and Special Circumstances Involving Racial/Ethnic Populations
- Part VIII: Counseling and Therapy With Other Multicultural Populations

Understanding Specific Populations

Culturally Competent Assessment

David Sue and Diane M. Sue

"Bias is a very real issue," said Francis Lu, a psychiatrist at the University of California at San Francisco. "We don't talk about it—it's upsetting. We see ourselves as unbiased and rational and scientific." . . . Psychiatrist Heather Hall, a colleague of Lu's, said she had to correct the diagnoses of about 40 minorities over a two-year period. . . . Advocates for cultural competence say both clinicians and patients are unwilling to acknowledge that race might matter: "In a cross-cultural situation, race or ethnicity is the white elephant in the room," said Lillian Comas-Diaz. (Vedantam, 2005, p. 1)

Accurate assessment, diagnosis, and case conceptualization, key prerequisites to the provision of appropriate treatment, are dependent upon the characteristics, values, and worldviews of both the therapist and the client (American Psychological Association, Presidential Task Force on Evidence-Based Practice, 2006). Most clinicians recognize that client variables, such as gender, racial or cultural background, and socioeconomic status, can significantly affect assessment, diagnosis, and conceptualization. However, we often forget that as clinicians we are not "objective" observers of our clients. Instead, we each have our own set of beliefs, values, and theoretical assumptions. To reduce error, a clinician must be aware of potential biases that can affect clinical judgment, including the influence of *stereotypes* (i.e., generalizations based on limited or inaccurate information). Unfortunately, our current methods of assessment and diagnosis often do not adequately consider these factors, especially with respect to therapist variables. Additionally, many of our instruments and processes for assessment and diagnosis do not address client variables in a meaningful manner.

If we are to follow best-practice guidelines and the ethical standards of our profession, broad background factors, including the worldview of the client, must be considered. How can this be accomplished? First and foremost, it is critical that

---

Significant portions of this chapter are adapted from D. Sue & D. M. Sue (2008), *Evidence-based practices in a diverse society.*

we operate from the perspective that a thorough understanding of clients' beliefs, expectations, and experiences is an essential aspect of the assessment and case conceptualization process. We believe that culturally competent assessment occurs through a combination of evidence-based guidelines for assessment and a cultural competency framework.

In this chapter, we will cover (a) the impact of therapist variables on assessment and diagnosis, emphasizing the dangers of stereotyping; (b) ways in which culturally competent practices can reduce diagnostic errors; (c) contextual and collaborative assessment; and (d) ideas for infusing cultural competence into standard intake and assessment procedures. Careful consideration of these factors when using evidence-based guidelines to conduct assessment will ensure that clinicians form an accurate and complete picture of the problems and issues facing each client. This chapter serves as an important foundation to understanding and using the information contained in the 13 specific population chapters to follow.

We will demonstrate how culturally competent assessment should be conducted—in a manner that considers the unique background, values, and beliefs of each client. We hope that as you proceed though the final chapters of this book—chapters describing general characteristics and special challenges faced by various oppressed populations—you will remember that we are providing this information so you will have some knowledge of specific research or sociopolitical and cultural factors that *might* be pertinent to a client or family from this population. However, it is critical that when counseling diverse clientele you actively work to avoid succumbing to stereotypes (i.e., basing your opinions of the client on limited information or prior assumptions). Instead, your task is to develop an in-depth understanding of each individual client, taking into consideration the individual's unique personal background and worldview. By doing this, you will be in a position to develop an individually tailored treatment plan that effectively addresses presenting problems in a culturally sensitive manner.

> Assessment is a two-way street, influenced by both client and therapist variables.

THERAPIST VARIABLES AFFECTING DIAGNOSIS

Assessment is best thought of as a two-way street, influenced by both client and therapist variables. Because humans filter observations through their own set of values and beliefs, we begin our discussion by focusing on therapist self-assessment.

A treatment team observing a clinical interview erupted in laughter when the foreign-born psychiatric resident attempted to find out what caused or precipitated the client's problem. In poor and halting English, the resident asked, "How brought you to the hospital?" The patient responded, "I came by car." (Chambliss, 2000, pp. 186)

Later, during the case conference, the psychiatric resident attributed the patient's response to concrete thinking, a characteristic sometimes displayed by people with schizophrenia. The rest of the treatment team, however, believed the response was due to a poorly worded question. This example illustrates what can occur when therapists focus solely on the client without considering the impact of therapist variables. Personal characteristics, attitudes, and beliefs can (and do) influence how and what is assessed, as well as interpretations of clinical data. Counselors and other mental health professionals are often unaware of how strongly personal beliefs can affect clinical judgment (Garb, 1997).

In one study, 108 psychotherapists read an intake report involving a male client whose sexuality was revealed through references to his previous and present partners; all clinical data was identical with the exception of references to sexual orientation. Details suggesting heterosexual or same-sex orientation had little impact on clinical ratings; however, therapists given data suggesting the client was bisexual were more likely to "detect" emotional disturbance. The researchers concluded that these differential diagnostic perceptions were the result of stereotypes of bisexual men being "confused and conflicted" (Mohr, Weiner, Chopp, & Wong, 2009).

In conducting culturally competent assessment, we must not only be aware of the influence of stereotypes but also be alert for common diagnostic errors such as:

• *Confirmatory strategy*—the search for evidence or information supporting one's hypothesis and ignoring data that is inconsistent with this perspective. Mental health professionals have been found to use a confirmatory strategy when working with clients, including searching for information that confirms beliefs based on their worldviews or theoretical orientation (Osmo & Rosen, 2002). In a similar manner, our views or stereotypes regarding the characteristics and values of ethnic minority and other diverse groups can act as blinders when working with clients from these groups. To combat this type of error when working with a client to conceptualize (i.e., understand and interpret) the presenting problem, clinicians can make sure that any hypotheses formulated are tested with the client. When determining if these *possible* interpretations resonate with the client, it is critical that the therapist be open to both confirmatory and disconfirmatory information (i.e., data that confirms or disconfirms their belief or hypothesis).

• *Attribution errors* occur when the therapist holds a different perspective of the problem than that of the client. For example, a therapist might see a problem as stemming from a personal characteristic or trait of the client rather than considering environmental or sociocultural explanations (e.g., poverty, discrimination, oppression). Attribution error can be reduced by performing a thorough assessment that includes sociocultural and environmental factors and testing hypotheses regarding extrapsychic (i.e., residing outside the person) as well as intrapsychic (i.e., residing within the person) influences.

• *Judgmental heuristics* are commonly used quick-decision rules. They can be problematic because they short-circuit our ability to engage in self-correction. For example, if we quickly identify our client as "defensive" or "overreactive," these characterizations will reduce our attempt to gather additional or contradictory information. In one study (Stewart, 2004), 300 clinicians received identical vignettes regarding hypothetical clients, with the only difference being the clients' stated birth order. Birth order influenced the judgment of the clinicians, including the expected prognosis for the client, even though there is little research support for personality differences associated with birth order. These kinds of beliefs or associations occur automatically and need to be identified and addressed. This tendency can be reduced by acknowledging the existence of judgmental heuristics, questioning the basis for quick decisions, assessing additional factors, and evaluating the accuracy of opinions regarding clients.

• *Diagnostic overshadowing* can occur when the presence of a problem is minimized because attention is diverted to a more salient characteristic. For example, individuals who are gay or lesbian can have a number of psychological issues that have nothing to do with their sexual orientation. In diagnostic overshadowing, a therapist may perceive the presenting problem as having to do with conflicts over sexual orientation and not address other critical issues. Other salient characteristics are race, religious affiliation, and visible disabilities. We must be aware of our beliefs and values as we work with clients and their specific presenting problems. We are all susceptible to making errors in clinical judgment during assessment; therefore, it is important to adopt a tentative stance and test out our observations. Those who remember that errors in judgment are possible can reduce their effect by using a self-corrective model. In the next section, for example, we discuss why it is important to consider whether the current focus on cultural competence may, in fact, be creating new sources of errors—errors resulting from applying cultural information in a stereotypic, "one-size-fits-all" manner.

CULTURAL COMPETENCE AND PREVENTING DIAGNOSTIC ERRORS

Regina, a mixed-race (Asian/White) student felt that her therapist had "this kind of book-learned . . . image of some kind of immigrant family, instead of . . . an emotional understanding of what it's like to be, like, Asian in [specific small city, in the intermountain West]." (D. F. Chang & Berk, 2009, p.527)

"You shouldn't expect a lot of African American clients to be in touch with their feelings and do some real intrapsychic work. Sometimes you have to be more directive and problem-focused in dealing with Black people." (Constantine & Sue, 2007, p. 146)

Given the growing multicultural nature of the United States population, all mental health organizations now promote cultural competence and the ability to work effectively with multicultural clients. However, is it possible that this focus on cultural differences is creating unintended consequences? Is the emphasis on understanding cultural factors leading to problems such as stereotyping or the blind application of cultural information? The two examples above illustrate the problems that can occur when general cultural information is applied to clients without assessing for individual differences. Surprisingly, in the second case, it was a supervisor giving stereotype-based advice to her supervisee.

Multicultural awareness can, in fact, lead to diagnostic overshadowing if clinician attention to race or other diversity issues results in neglect of other important aspects of the client (Vontress & Jackson, 2004). As clinicians working with diverse populations, we need to consider all aspects of each client's life and not automatically assume that presenting problems are based on racial or diversity issues. In fact, it would be irresponsible for a clinician to focus on a client's diversity or environmental stressors when there are other significant concerns (Weinrach & Thomas, 2004).

Some mental health professionals have argued that the emphasis on culture and the development of culture-specific approaches have led to led to fragmentation, confusion, and controversy in the field of counseling and psychotherapy. Diversity training has been accused of producing "professionally sanctioned stereotyping," in which cultural attributes are given primary consideration, rather than a focus on the understanding the uniqueness and life circumstances of the individual client (Freitag, Ottens, & Gross, 1999; D. W. Sue & D. Sue, 2003). Although it is important to understand group-specific differences, it is equally critical that we avoid a "cookbook" approach, in which the characteristics of different groups are memorized and applied to all clients who belong to a specific group (C. C. Lee, 2006; Speight, Myers, Cox, & Highlen, 1991).

Do guidelines for increasing cultural competence (e.g., increasing knowledge and information regarding different cultural group and developing multicultural clinical skills) contribute to assessment errors, such as confirmatory bias, diagnostic overshadowing or stereotyping? These errors certainly can happen and are most likely to occur when clinicians fail to use self-correcting strategies or fail to consider the individuality of each client. It is our belief that effective culturally competent assessment can, in fact, minimize the dangers of stereotyping or placing inordinate weight on race or other diversity issues.

Cultural competence is defined in different ways. We will use the definition focusing on the following three components: (a) self-awareness (i.e., self-reflection and awareness of one's values and biases); (b) knowledge of culturally diverse groups (e.g., marginalized status, characteristics, strengths, norms, and values); and (c) specific clinical skills, including the ability to generate a wide variety of verbal and nonverbal helping responses, form a therapeutic alliance, and intervene at the individual, group, institutional and societal levels. We believe that *appropriate* use of these aspects of cultural competence can *prevent* diagnostic and treatment errors due to inaccurate assumptions and stereotypes.

Cultural Competence: Self-Awareness

Self-awareness is considered important with respect to both cultural competency and evidence-based practice. For example, therapists may be unaware that stereotypes are affecting their views and/or responses to clients or that differences between themselves and their clients are affecting the therapeutic process. For example, studies have found that mental health professionals pathologize clients who display nontraditional gender role behavior (Seem & Johnson, 1998) and rate female clients as less competent than males (Danzinger & Welfel, 2000).

Such judgments (or inferential errors) constitute deviations from culture competence and the evidence-based practice model of self-reflection and self-awareness regarding the impact of one's values and beliefs. The identification of one's biases or taking the time to self-reflect can help reduce such errors. Self-awareness questions such as "Which identities allow me to experience privilege?" "Which identities expose me to oppression?" and "How do I feel about these experiences?" provide clinicians the opportunity to reflect on how their own backgrounds and experiences have shaped their worldviews (Singh & Chun, 2010, p. 36).

Further, we need to develop self-awareness regarding our assessment processes and identify our values, theoretical orientation, and beliefs about different groups whose social, cultural, or ethnic backgrounds differ from our own. Do I hold assumptions about gender roles, sexual orientation, older individuals, ageism, political philosophy, or "healthy" family structure that may influence my clinical judgment? Do I hold certain stereotypes or impressions of the client or cultural groups to which the client belongs? Such self-assessment is a necessary step in working with clients who differ from us and is an important component of counselor competence (Ridley, Mollen, & Kelly, 2011).

Cultural Competence: Knowledge

The knowledge component of cultural competence requires counselors to be aware of different worldviews (e.g., that the majority of cultures in the world have a collectivistic and interdependent orientation; that the structure of some families is hierarchical in nature). Such knowledge is crucial in working with ethnic minority populations. In our special-population chapters, you will encounter descriptions such as the following:

- African American families often show adaptability in family roles, strong kinship bonds, and a strong religious orientation.
- American Indian/Alaska Native families are often structured with the extended family as the family basic unit; children are frequently raised by aunts, uncles, and grandparents who live in separate households.
- Asian American families are hierarchical and patriarchal in structure, with males typically having higher status than females.
- Latino/a American families strongly value family unity (*familismo*). The extended family can include not only relatives but also godparents and close friends.

This type of cultural knowledge is useful in helping counselors understand family patterns commonly seen among different ethnic minority populations; such information can be particularly helpful when patterns contrast with the family and relationship structure typical of White American families. However, these descriptions are "modal" cultural characteristics—that is, they may or may not be applicable to a particular client. Knowledge also involves awareness that significant within-group differences can exist—individuals can vary in terms of acculturation, identification with cultural values, and unique personal experiences, to name a few.

Cultural information should not be applied rigidly; it is necessary to determine the degree of fit between general cultural information and the individual client in front of us. Gone (2009), for example, points out that it is not enough to know that a client is American Indian; you need to ask, "What kind of Indian are you?" In other words, you need to learn what tribe the client is affiliated with (if any), the nature of connections with the tribe, and, if the client is closely connected, the particular values and practices of the tribal culture. Among ethnic minorities, within- and between-group differences are quite large—some individuals and families are quite acculturated, whereas others retain a more traditional cultural orientation (B. S. K. Kim, 2007). Cultural differences, such as the degree of assimilation, socioeconomic background, family experiences, and educational level, affect each individual in a unique manner.

Knowledge of cultural values associated with specific groups can help us generate hypotheses about the manner in which a client (or family members) might view a disorder, for example. However, the accuracy of such cultural hypotheses must be assessed with each client. Thus, it is critical that we communicate with the client in order to confirm (or disconfirm) any hypotheses generated from our cultural "knowledge." In our opinion, the cultural competence component of "knowledge" requires not only that we be *open* to the worldview of others but that we take care to remember that every client has a unique life story.

Cultural Competence: Multicultural Skills

The multicultural skills component of cultural competence requires that counselors effectively apply a variety of helping skills when forming a therapeutic alliance. As discussed in our chapter on evidence-based practice, it is important to individualize the choice of helping skills and avoid a blind application of techniques to all situations and all populations. The manner of developing an effective therapeutic bond will differ from individual to individual and may differ from ethnic group to ethnic group. It is important to individualize relationship skills and to consistently evaluate the effectiveness of our verbal and nonverbal responses to the client.

Research-based information regarding ethnic minorities (e.g., African Americans prefer an egalitarian therapeutic relationship; Asian Americans prefer a more formal relationship and concrete suggestions from the counselor; Latino/a Americans do better with a more personal relationship with the counselor; American Indians/Alaska Natives prefer a relaxed, client-centered listening style) can alert counselors to possible variations in therapeutic style that may enhance therapeutic progress. However, the applicability of the information needs to be evaluated for each client. The therapist's task is to help clients identify strategies for dealing with problems within cultural constraints and to develop the skills to negotiate cultural differences with the larger society. To achieve this, the counselor must sometimes be willing to adopt a variety of helping modes, such as advisor, consultant, and advocate.

In summary, errors in assessment can occur because of biases, mistakes in thinking, and stereotypes that exist within the clinician. In the past, assessment practices focused only on the client; potential counselor biases or inaccurate assumptions were not taken into consideration. It is now clear that effective assessment requires that therapist characteristics also be considered. Do cultural competency guidelines contribute to stereotypes? Some mental health practitioners believe that this is the case. However, we would argue precisely the opposite. If used appropriately, cultural competency and evidence-based practice guidelines that focus on awareness of one's values and biases, appropriate use of cultural knowledge, and the value of understanding the unique background and experience of each client help *prevent* stereotyping.

CONTEXTUAL AND COLLABORATIVE ASSESSMENT

Self-awareness is an important first step in reducing errors in multicultural assessment. However, this is only one part of the equation. Only through close collaboration with the client can we accurately identify the specific issues involved in the presenting problem and eliminate the blind application of cultural knowledge. This can best be accomplished with a collaborative approach in which clients are given opportunities to share their beliefs, perspectives, and expectations, as well as their explanations of problems. If a client's belief about the presenting problem differs from that of the therapist, treatment based only on the therapist's views is often ineffective. We will begin by sharing some ideas regarding how a therapist might introduce the assessment and case conceptualization process in a manner that helps facilitate dialogue and a collaborative relationship.

What we are going to do today is gather information about you and the problem that brings you in for counseling. In doing so, I will need your help. In therapy we will work together to decide what concerns to address and what solutions you feel comfortable with. Some of the questions I ask may seem very personal, but they are necessary to get a clear picture of what may be going on in your life. As I mentioned before, everything that we discuss is confidential, with the exceptions that we already went over. I will also ask about your family and other relationships and about your values and beliefs, since they might be related to your concerns or might help us decide the best strategies to use in therapy. Sometimes our difficulties are not just due to personal issues but are also due to expectations from our parents, friends, or society. The questions I will be asking will help us put together a more complete picture of what might be happening with you and what might be causing the symptoms you came here to address. When we get to that point, we can talk together to see if my ideas about what might be going on seem to be on the right track. If there are any important issues I don't bring up, please be sure to let me know. Do you have any questions before we begin?

Assessment and diagnosis are critical elements in the process of devising a treatment plan. An introduction such as the one just presented helps set the stage for a collaborative and contextual intake interview. Clients are informed that family, environmental, and social-cultural influences will be explored. Many clinical assessments and interviews do not consider these factors and, therefore, must be modified. To remedy this shortcoming, we stress the importance of both the *collaborative approach*, in which the client and the therapist work together to construct an accurate definition of the problem, and the *contextual viewpoint*, which acknowledges that both the client and the therapist are embedded in systems such as family, work, and culture. These perspectives are gaining support within various mental health professions. For example, ethical principles regarding informed consent regarding therapy emphasize the need to give clients information necessary to make sound decisions and, thus, be collaborators in the therapy process (Behnke, 2004).

The importance of collaboration is also stressed in the report of the President's New Freedom Commission on Mental Health (2003), in which clients are described as "consumers" and "partners" in the planning, selection, and evaluation of services. As we have already discussed extensively, contextualism is also important in recognizing that both therapist and client operate from their own experiences and worldviews. Just as clients may have socialization experiences or experiences with prejudice or discrimination that play a role in the presenting concerns (American Psychological Association, 2003), therapists may hold worldviews or have had experiences that influence their perceptions of the client or the client's issues.

Karen Seeley is a mental health practitioner who describes herself as a "white, middle-class North American therapist." She recognized that she differed from ethnic minority clients in terms of culture, nationality, race, and personal history and that these differences could inhibit communication in therapy and produce inaccurate assessment. She was also aware that the therapeutic techniques developed for "mainstream Westerners" may be inappropriate in multicultural situations. She strives to use cultural knowledge not as "an end in itself, but as a starting point from which to investigate each client's particular cultural formation and identity." Seeley (2004) demonstrates many of the qualities of cultural competence starting with self-awareness, as illustrated in her work with clients:

Case Study: Diane

Diane sought treatment when she began to feel emotionally destabilized by the psychological problems of an acquaintance. Diane worked off campus an the assistant manager of a bookstore. One of her employees had developed a severe eating disorder, and Diane had become increasingly distressed as she witnessed the employee's deterioration. In addition, Diane began to experience a loss of appetite and became convinced that she, too, was developing an eating disorder. In the intake interview, Diane did not present significant anorexic symptoms. At first glance, she seemed to need help differentiating herself from others. (p.126)

During the second session, Diane expressed even greater emotional distress because her employee had announced that she would be leaving her job to receive treatment for anorexia. Diane shared that she felt responsible for her employee's condition and explained how she had tried very hard to get her to eat. She felt a great sense of failure when she was unable to do so. In conceptualizing the case, Seeley needed to determine why her client was so distressed and so involved in the employee's struggles with anorexia. Were Diane's symptoms the result of obsessive tendencies or possibly related to unhealthy identity and boundary aspects of her relationship with her employee? In other words, was the presenting problem an internal (i.e., intrapsychic) phenomenon? Because Diane was an immigrant raised in Samoa, Seeley wanted to entertain the possibility of cultural involvement in Diane's behavior and emotional distress.

Seeley conducted an ethnographic inquiry by asking Diane about work relationships in Samoa, especially between supervisors and employees. Diane explained how the work relationship was "like a family" and how supervisors assume responsibility for the well-being of their employees. When asked how she viewed the relationship with her current employee in Samoan terms, she compared it to a "mother-daughter" relationship. In addition, Diane explained how eating and food are a very important part of social relationships in Samoa, describing how a good host is responsible for making sure that everyone eats and has enough to eat.

With this additional information, Seeley hypothesized that Diane's feelings of "excessive responsibility" were probably the result of cultural influences rather than obsessive tendencies or boundary issues. When Seeley presented this hypothesis to Diane, she agreed that this could be the cause of her distress regarding the employee's welfare. After discovering the roots of her symptoms, Diane began an exploration of the differences in expectations in employer-employee relationships in the United States compared to Samoa. This process helped Diane reduce her feelings of responsibility and distress, with a resultant reduction in depressive symptoms. Seeley's use of a cultural inquiry allowed her to conceptualize the problem accurately. We believe this case demonstrates a highly effective use of cultural competency guidelines.

Collaborative Conceptualization Model

Case Study: Erica

Erica is a biracial (North American father and Korean mother) college student who was raised in Korea. She sought counseling to relieve feeling of loneliness and anxiety at the university. Erica speaks unaccented fluent English and considers herself bicultural. When asked to describe her background and her current problem, she was reluctant to give much information. The counselor entertained the possibility that cultural constraints might be involved in Erica's difficulty to talk about mental health issues and inquired about how she would describe her problems in a Korean setting. Erica responded that in Korea people did not convey their problems to others; it would be considered selfish and self-centered. With Erica's help, the problem was conceptualized as a conflict between Korean norms and values and those of the United States. Erica's roommates believed she was too "passive and meek" and encouraged her to be more assertive. Erica explained that in Korea people were "tuned into" her needs, so she did not need to directly verbalize them. Erika began to realize that her social anxiety and loneliness were related to differing cultural expectations and concluded that she would need to learn new ways of communicating. (Seeley, 2004)

The preceding example illustrates the importance of collaborative assessment and the value of obtaining clients' input regarding social and cultural elements that may be associated with presenting problems. Gambrill (2005) identifies ways in which therapists can enhance the accuracy and effectiveness of assessment, conceptualization, and treatment planning. First, as we have emphasized previously, therapists need to be aware of the impact of their own values, worldviews, and beliefs on their practice. Similarly, clients' unique characteristics, values, and circumstances should always be considered. Additionally, clients should be encouraged to actively participate in the assessment and conceptualization process. In other words, case conceptualization, as well as assessment, is best done in a collaborative manner in which therapist self-awareness, client involvement, and the scientific method are all utilized. With this approach, the therapist and the client can choose intervention strategies that involve the integration of the best research studies, clinical expertise, and client input.

> Case conceptualization, as well as assessment, is best done in a collaborative manner in which therapist self-awareness, client involvement, and the scientific method are all utilized.

Collaborative conceptualization (modified from Spengler, Strohmer, Dixon, & Shivy, 1995, to include client involvement) includes the following steps:

1. *Use both clinician skill and client perspective to understand the problem.* Clinical expertise is essential in assessment, developing hypotheses, eliciting client participation, and guiding conceptualization. Therapists bring experience, knowledge, and clinical skill to this process; clients bring an understanding of their own background and their perspective of the problem. Therapists should be aware of their values, biases, preferences, and theoretical assumptions and how these factors might influence their work with clients.

2. *Collaborate and jointly define the problem.* Within this framework, the clinician and the client, either jointly or independently, formulate conceptualizations of the problem. A joint process generally leads to more accurate conceptualization. In cases where definitions of the problem differ, these differences are discussed, and the agreed-upon aspects of the problem can receive primary focus. In some cases, the therapist can reframe the client's conceptualization in a manner that results in mutual agreement.

3. *Jointly formulate a hypothesis regarding the cause of the problem.* The therapist can tentatively address possibilities regarding what is causing or maintaining the

problem with questions such as "Could the problems you are having with your children be due to the values that they are being exposed to?" "Are you trying too hard to be accepted by society and denying your own identity?" "You mentioned before that you get really down on yourself when you feel you aren't living up to your parent's expectations. Do you think that might have anything to do with how you've been feeling lately?" or "I remember you saying that it's been hard to be so far away from others who share your religious background. Do you think that has anything to do with your depression?" When perceptions or explanations of the problem differ, these differences can be acknowledged and an attempt made to identify and focus on similarities.

4. *Jointly develop ways to confirm or disconfirm the hypothesis regarding the problem, continuing to consider alternative hypotheses.* The therapist might say, "If your depression is due, in part, to a lack of activity, how would we determine if this is the case?" or "How can we figure out if your parents' wanting you to get all As in college is part of what is going on?" or "What else might be involved in your feeling depressed?"

5. *Test out the hypothesis using both the client and the therapist as evaluators.* The therapist might ask, "You explored the positive aspects of your identity. Did that reduce your depressive feelings?" or "You mentioned you felt more depressed this week when you were thinking how you were not as good as other people. Do you think that these critical thoughts might be contributing to your depression?" or "It sounds like you were really feeling down after you talked to your parents this week and shared that you had gotten a B on your calculus exam. What do you think that might mean in terms of what is going on with your depression?"

6. *If the conceptualization appears to be valid, develop a treatment plan.* The therapist might say, "You mentioned you felt better when you spent some time with friends this week. It sounds to me like you confirmed your hypothesis that being alone increases your depression. You also noticed that you tend to spend less time thinking negative thoughts about yourself when you're around others. Let's talk about how that important information can be used when we decide how to best treat your depression."

7. *If the hypothesis is not borne out, therapist and client collect additional data and formulate new, testable hypotheses.* The therapist might say, "It's good we checked out that idea that there is a connection between your negative thoughts and being home alone. You mentioned that when you went out walking, you started thinking about the times you've been rejected and your depression seemed to get even worse. Can I ask you to share some of the thoughts that were going through your head when you were walking?"

We believe it is of critical importance to go through a collaborative process such as this; therapist and client can adopt a scientific framework as they work to conceptualize the problem and then have an equal voice in evaluating the problem definition. Unless there is substantial agreement on the definition of a problem, therapeutic progress is likely to be less than optimal.

Collaborating on Intervention Strategies

There is a movement away from relying on "practitioners' ideology" or preferences for treatment options to interventions that have received research support

(Edmond, Megivern, Williams, Rochman, & Howard, 2006). As mentioned in Chapter 9 on evidence-based practice, we believe that intervention strategies should be based on research on the facilitating qualities possessed by therapists (empathy, warmth, and genuineness), client characteristics (motivation, personality, and support systems), and techniques. Interventions should not be rigidly applied but instead should be modified according to client characteristics and feedback. Consensus between therapist and client regarding the course of therapy allows the therapeutic relationship to strengthen. In addition, using a collaborative approach allows clients to develop confidence that the therapist understands their issues and is using methods that are likely to achieve desired goals. Thus, collaboration improves treatment outcome by enhancing clients' hope and optimism.

INFUSING CULTURAL COMPETENCE INTO STANDARD CLINICAL ASSESSMENTS

Many interview forms and diagnostic systems place little emphasis on collaboration or contextualism. Instead, the traditional medical model is usually followed and diagnosis is primarily made through the identification of symptoms, without attempts to validate impressions or determine the meaning of the symptoms for the client. In this approach, problems are seen to reside in the individual, with little attention being given to family, community, or environmental influences. If a therapist recognizes and values the importance of a collaborative and contextual approach, modification in standard assessment intake forms can be made. We will suggest ways in which cultural and environmental factors can be added to standard intake interviews.

Culturally Sensitive Intake Interviews

Nearly everyone in the mental health field conducts intake interviews, diagnostic interviews are usually conducted during the first session or sessions. Typically, the client is informed that the assessment session is not a therapy session but rather a time to gather information in order get to know the client and more fully understand the client's concerns. The specific relationship-building skills previously addressed in the chapter on evidence-based practice are extremely important in the context of assessment as well as therapy. For example, it is important that the clinician ask questions and respond to answers in a supportive and empathetic manner.

Intake forms generally include questions concerning client demographic information, the presenting problem, history of the problem, previous therapy, psychosocial history, educational and occupational experiences, family and social supports, medical and medication history, risk assessment, diagnosis, and goals for treatment. Many of the questions are focused primarily on the individual, with little consideration of situational, family, sociocultural, or environmental issues. We realize that it is difficult to modify standard intake forms used by clinics and other mental health agencies, but consideration can be given to these contextual factors when gathering data or making a diagnosis. Common areas of inquiry found in standard diagnostic evaluations and the rationale for each area are presented below (Rivas-Vazquez, Blais, Rey, & Rivas-Vazquez, 2001), together with suggestions for specific contextual queries that can be used to supplement the standard interview for ethnic minorities and other diverse populations.

• *Identifying information:* Asking about the reason for seeking counseling allows the therapist to gain an immediate sense of the client and reason for seeking therapy. Other information gathered includes age, gender, ethnicity, marital status, and referral source. It is important to inquire about cultural groups to which the client feels connected. For ethnic minorities or immigrants, the degree of acculturation or adherence to traditional values is important. For other areas of diversity, such as religion, sexual orientation, age, gender, or disability, it is important to consider whether any of these factors are important in understanding the client or any of the difficulties the client is facing. When relevant, ask about the primary language used in the home or the degree of language proficiency of the client or family members. Determine whether an interpreter is needed. (It is important not to rely on family members to translate when assessing clinical matters.)

• *Presenting problem:* To understand the source of distress in the client's own words, obtain his or her perception of the problem and assess the degree of insight the client has regarding the problem and the chronicity of the problem. Some questions clinicians can consider include: What is the client's explanation for his or her disorder? Does it involve somatic, spiritual, or culture-specific causes? Among all groups potentially affected by disadvantage, prejudice, or oppression, does the client's own explanation involve internalized causes (e.g., internalized heterosexism among gay males or lesbians or self-blame in a victim of a sexual assault) rather than external, social, or cultural explanations? What does the client perceive are possible solutions to the problem?

• *History of the presenting problem:* To assist with diagnostic formulation, it is helpful to have a chronological account of and perceived reasons for the problem. It is also important to determine levels of functioning prior to the problem and since it developed and to explore social and environmental influences. When did the present problem first occur, and what was going on when this happened? Has the client had similar problems before? How was the client functioning before the problem occurred? What changes have happened since the advent of the problem? Are there any family issues, value conflicts, or societal issues involving such factors as gender, ability, class, ethnicity, or sexual orientation that may be related to the problem?

• *Psychosocial history:* Clinicians can benefit from understanding the client's perceptions of past and current functioning in different areas of living, as well as early socialization and life experiences, including expectations, values, and beliefs from the family that may play a role in the presenting problem. How does the client describe his or her level of social, academic, or family functioning during childhood and adolescence? Were there any traumas during this period? Were there any past experiences or problems in socialization with the family or community that may be related to the current problem? McAuliffe and Ericksen (1999) describe some questions that can be used, when appropriate, to assess social background, values, and beliefs: "How has your gender role or social class influenced your expectations and life plans?" "Do religious or spiritual beliefs play a role in your life?" "How would you describe your ethnic heritage; how has it affected your life?" "What was considered to be appropriate behavior in childhood, adolescence, and as an adult?" "How does your family respond to differences in beliefs about gender, acculturation, and other diversity issues?" "What changes would you make in the way your family functions?"

• *Abuse history:* Despite the potential importance of determining if the client is facing any harmful or dangerous situations, many mental health professionals do not routinely inquire about abuse histories, even in populations known to be at increased risk of abuse. In one study, even when the intake form included a section on abuse, less than one third of those conducting intake interviews inquired about this topic (Young, Read, Barker-Collo, & Harrison, 2001). It is extremely important to address this issue since background information such as a history of sexual or physical abuse can have important implications for diagnosis, treatment, and safety planning. The following questions involve domestic violence for women (Stevens, 2003, p. 6) but can and should be expanded for use with other groups, including men and older adults:

Have you ever been touched in a way that made you feel uncomfortable?
Have you ever been forced or pressured to have sex?
Do you feel you have control over your social and sexual relationships?
Have you ever been threatened by a (caretaker, relative, partner)?
Have you ever been hit, punched, or beaten by a (caretaker, relative, or partner)?
Do you feel safe where you live?
Have you ever been scared to go home? Are you scared now?

If during the intake process a client discloses a history of having been abused and there are no current safety issues, the therapist can briefly and empathetically respond to the disclosure and return to the issue at a later time in the conceptualization or therapy process. Of course, developing a safety plan and obtaining social and law enforcement support may be necessary when a client discloses current abuse issues.

• *Strengths:* It is important to identify culturally relevant strengths, such as pride in one's identity or culture, religious or spiritual beliefs, cultural knowledge and living skills (e.g., hunting, fishing, folk medicine), family and community supports, and resiliency in dealing with discrimination and prejudice (P. A. Hays, 2009). The focus on strengths often helps put a problem in context and defines support systems or positive individual or cultural characteristics that can be activated in the treatment process. This is especially important for ethnic group members and individuals of diverse populations subjected to negative stereotypes. What are some attributes that they are proud of? How have they successfully handled problems in the past? What are some strengths of the client's family or community? What are sources of pride, such as school or work performance, parenting, or connection with the community? How can these strengths be used as part of the treatment plan?

• *Medical history:* It is important to determine whether there are medical or physical conditions or limitations that may be related to the psychological problem and important to consider when planning treatment. Is the client currently taking any medications, using herbal substances, or using any form of folk medicine? Has the client had any major illnesses or physical problems that might have affected his or her psychological state? How does the client perceive these conditions? Is the client engaging in appropriate self-care? If there is some type of physical limitation or disability, how has this influenced daily living? How have family members, friends, or society responded to this condition?

• *Substance abuse history:* Although substance use can affect diagnosis and treatment, this potential concern is often underemphasized in clinical assessment. Because substance-use issues are common, it is important to ask about drug and alcohol use. What is the client's current and past use of alcohol, prescription medications, and illegal substances, including age of use, duration, and intensity? If the client drinks alcohol, how much is consumed? Does the client (or family members) have concerns about the client's substance use? Has drinking or other substance use ever affected the social or occupational functioning of the client? What are the alcohol- and substance-use patterns of family members and close friends?

• *Risk of harm to self or others:* Even if clients do not share information about suicidal or violent thoughts, it is important to consider the potential for self-harm or harm to others. What is the client's current emotional state? Are there strong feelings of anger, hopelessness, or depression? Is the client expressing intent to harm himself or herself? Does there appear to be the potential to harm others? Have there been previous situations involving dangerous thoughts or behaviors? Asking a client a simple question such as "How likely is it that you will hurt yourself?" may yield accurate self-predictions of future self-harm (Peterson, Skeem, & Manchak, 2011).

Diversity considerations can easily be infused into the intake process. Such questions can help the therapist understand the client's perspective on various issues. Questions that might provide a more comprehensive account of the client's perspective include (Dowdy, 2000):

• *"How can I help you?"* This addresses the reason for the visit and client expectations regarding therapy. Clients can have different ideas of what they want to achieve. Unclear or divergent expectations between client and therapist can hamper therapy.

• *"What do you think is causing your problem?"* This helps the therapist to understand the client's perception of the factors involved. In some cases, the client will not have an answer or may present an explanation that may not be plausible. The task of the therapist is to help the client examine different areas that might relate to the problem, including interpersonal, social, and cultural influences. However, one must be careful not to impose an "explanation" on the client.

• *"Why is this happening to you?"* This question taps into the issue of causality and possible spiritual or cultural explanations for the problem. Some may believe the problem is due to fate or is a punishment for "bad behavior." If this question does not elicit a direct answer or if you want to obtain a broader perspective, the therapist can inquire, "What does your mother (husband, family members, friends) believe is happening to you?"

- *"What have you done to treat this condition?" "Where else have you sought treatment?"* These questions can lead to a discussion of previous interventions, the possible use of home remedies, and the client's evaluation of the usefulness of these treatments. Responses can also provide information regarding previous providers of treatment and client perceptions of prior treatment.

- *"How has this condition affected your life?"* This question helps identify individual, interpersonal, health, and social issues related to the concern. Again, if the response is limited, the clinician can inquire about the impact on each of these specific areas.

Implications for Clinical Practice

Although there is increased focus on cultural competence in assessment, difficulties in effective implementation of culturally competent practices are prevalent. N. D. Hansen et al. (2006) conducted a random sample survey of 149 clinicians regarding the importance of multicultural competencies and, more importantly, whether they practiced these recommendations. Although the participants rated competencies such as "using DSM cultural formulations," "prepare a cultural formulation," "use racially/ethnically sensitive data-gathering techniques," and "evaluating one's own multicultural competence" as very important, they were much less likely to actually use these competencies in their practice.

What accounts for this discrepancy between the ratings of importance of multicultural competencies and the actual use of recommended practices? We believe that a contributing factor is the continued reliance on counseling and psychotherapy practices that were developed without consideration of diversity issues or the impact of therapist qualities on assessment and conceptualization. Many intake interviews and clinical assessments continue to reflect the view that a disorder resides in the individual. Until assessments ask specific questions such as those discussed in this chapter, cultural competency will receive only lip service.

Knowledge of cultural variables and sociopolitical influences affecting members of different groups can sensitize therapists regarding *possible* cultural, social, or environmental influences on individual clients. As you read the following chapters dealing with a variety of specific populations, we hope you do not see the information as an end in itself, but rather as a means to assist you to create hypotheses when working collaboratively with clients in the assessment and conceptualization process. As we advise repeatedly throughout the chapters, it is important not to stereotype clients or overgeneralize based on the information presented. Clients must be seen in their totality, as unique individuals, as people who share similarities with their reference groups, and as Homo sapiens who share the human condition with everyone.

PART VI

Counseling and Therapy with Racial/Ethnic Minority Group Populations

Counseling African Americans

Through the media and even in school, I could see that in many people's eyes, Blacks and Whites were not equal. I sometimes felt that I was under attack, but this did nothing but build my strength, character, and resilience. (Murphy, 2005, p. 315)

The fact that several school personnel made derogatory remarks about [Black] parents in front of researchers made us wonder what they would say in our absence. At the end of a parent-teacher conference, which lasted only 5 minutes, the teacher commented that the brevity of the conference did not matter because the parent "wouldn't have understood it anyway." (Harry, Klingner, & Hart, 2005)

Two national Republicans used terms such as "tar baby" and "boy" to refer to President Obama. Both later apologized. (Jonsson, 2011)

Several White elementary school teachers decided to "honor" Black History Month by having students carry portraits of O. J. Simpson, Dennis Rodman, and RuPaul in [a] school parade celebrating influential African Americans. Children from other classes displayed photos of more appropriate black role models, such as Nelson Mandela, Harriet Tubman, and President Barack Obama. (Nittle, 2010, p. 1)

The African-American population was 38.9 million in 2010, representing 13% of the total population. The poverty rate for African Americans remains nearly two times higher than that of all households (23.5% versus 13%) (U.S. Census Bureau, 2010c), and the unemployment rate is nearly twice as high (13.6% versus 7.4%) (U.S. Department of Labor, 2012). Their disadvantaged status, as well as racism and poverty, contributes to the following statistics. In the 25-to-29 age group, nearly 12% of African American men were in prison or jail, as compared with 1.7% of White males (Associated Press, 2006, May 21). Approximately 23% of African American adults do not have a high school diploma (Fry, 2010). Infant mortality for Black mothers is twice that of Whites, and the lifespan of African Americans is 5 to 6 years shorter than that of White Americans (Centers for Disease Control, 2006). The median wealth of white households is 20 times that of African American households (Pew Research Center, 2011b).

Although these statistics are grim, much of the literature is based on the economically disadvantaged rather than on other segments of the African American population (Holmes & Morin, 2006). This focus on those living in poverty masks the great diversity that exists among African Americans and the significant variance in socioeconomic status, educational level, cultural identity, family structure, and reactions to racism. Although Black males (38%) are experiencing greater downward mobility out of the middle class compared with the 21% of White males reporting recently decreased earnings (Acs, 2011), over 38% of African American households are middle class versus 44% of all households (U.S. Census, 2010). Many middle- and upper-class African Americans embrace the values of the dominant society, believe that advances can be made through hard work, feel that race has a relative rather than a pervasive influence on their lives, and take pride in their heritage. As Hugh Price, former president of the National Urban League, observed, "This country is filled with highly successful Black men who are leading balanced, stable, productive lives working all over the labor market" (Holmes & Morin, 2006, p. 1). However, even among this group of successful African American men earning $75,000 a year or more, 6 in 10 reported being victims of racism and having someone close to them murdered or incarcerated.

CHARACTERISTICS AND STRENGTHS

In the following sections we consider the characteristics, values, and strengths of African Americans and their implications in treatment. The African American population is becoming increasingly heterogeneous in terms of ethnic and racial identity, social class, educational level, and political orientation, so it is important to remember that the following are generalizations; their applicability needs to be assessed for each client.

Ethnic and Racial Identity

Many believe that minorities go through a sequential process of racial identity or consciousness. For many African Americans, the process involves a transformation from a non-Afrocentric identity to one that is Afrocentric (although some African Americans consistently embrace a Black identity through early socialization). The Cross (1991, 1995) model, which was described in detail in Chapter 12, identifies the stages of preencounter, encounter, immersion-emersion, and internalization. These stages are associated with differences in perspective regarding the self and relationships with others, beginning with the acceptance of White standards and deprecation of Black culture and culminating in an appreciation of both Black culture and aspects of the White culture.

Implications

African Americans who are at the preencounter level are less likely to report racial discrimination, whereas those in the immersion stage tend to be younger and least satisfied with societal conditions (Hyers, 2001). African Americans with the greatest internalization of Black racial identity report the highest self-esteem (Pierre & Mahalik, 2005). African American preferences for counselor ethnicity are often related to their current stage of racial identity (Atkinson & Lowe, 1995). Parham and Helms (1981) found that African Americans at the preencounter stage preferred a White counselor, whereas those in later stages preferred an African American counselor. In a study involving 128 Black college students, over 75% indicated that they would have no preference regarding the race of the counselor for issues such as depression, anxiety, drug or alcohol problems, meeting new people, overcoming loneliness, and dealing with anger. However, half indicated preference for a Black counselor for racial issues and problems with personal relationships. Elevated cultural mistrust and strong internalized Afrocentric attitudes were associated with stronger preference for a Black counselor (Townes, Chavez-Korell, & Cunningham, 2009).

> Often, the most important counselor characteristic for African Americans is the cultural sensitivity of the counselor.

Often, the most important counselor characteristic for African Americans is the cultural sensitivity of the counselor. Culturally sensitive counselors (those who acknowledge the possibility that race or culture might play a role in the client's problem) are seen as more competent than culture-blind counselors (who focus on factors other than race when dealing with the presenting problem) (Pomales, Claiborn, & LaFromboise, 1986; Want, Parham, Baker, & Sherman, 2004). Among a group of working-class African American clients, the degree of therapeutic alliance with White counselors was affected not only by the client's stage of racial identity but also by similarities in gender, age, attitudes, and beliefs. Additionally, clients facing issues related to parenting, drug use, or anxiety looked for therapists with understanding of these specific issues (Ward, 2005).

Family Structure

Increasingly, African American families are headed by single parents. About one third of African American households are headed by married couples, compared with half of all households (U.S. Census Bureau, 2005c). The African American family is often described as matriarchal; among lower-class African American families, 63% are headed by women versus 33% of all U.S. households (Z. E. Taylor, Larsen-Rife, Conger, Widaman, & Cutrona, 2010). Black children are significantly less likely than other children to be living with two married parents (35% versus 84% for Asian children, 64% for Hispanic children, and 75% for White children) (Child Trends, 2010). In 2008, 72% of all births to Black women were outside of marriage, compared with 29% for non-Hispanic White women (Black Demographics.com, 2011).

Implications

A counselor's reaction to a client's family structure may be affected by a Eurocentric, nuclear-family orientation. Similarly, many assessment forms and evaluation processes are based on a middle-class Euro-American perspective of what constitutes a family. For family therapy to be successful, counselors must first identify their own set of beliefs and values regarding appropriate roles and communication patterns within a family and take care not to impose these beliefs on other families. We have to be able to put on "different lenses" and move from a deficit model to an asset or strengths perspective when evaluating families (Rockymore, 2008). A supportive parenting style that includes warmth, communication, and consistent discipline appears to be protective against drug use by African American youth (Gibbons et al., 2010). However, physical discipline or critical comments, unless unduly harsh, should not necessarily be viewed negatively (each situation should be assessed individually). For example, although African American parents, especially those of the working class, are more likely than White parents to use physical punishment to discipline their children (Pinderhughes, Dodge, Bates, Pettit, & Zelli, 2000), such punishment or seemingly "critical" behavior by African American family members may, in fact, be perceived by children as signs of caring and concern (Rosenfarb, Bellack, & Aziz, 2006). Differences in family functioning should not be automatically seen as deficits (Gorman & Balter, 1997). Traditional parent education approaches are often inappropriate for African American families. In fact, they may perpetuate the view that minorities have deficient child-rearing skills. Culturally sensitive parent education programs designed for African Americans focus on single parenting, drug abuse, different types of discipline, and strategies for dealing with culture conflicts and responding to racism. In working with economically disadvantaged African American families, the counselor may need to assume various roles, including advocate, case manager, problem solver, and facilitating mentor (Ahai, 1997), and to help the family navigate community systems, including the educational or judicial system.

Kinship Bonds With Extended Family and Friends

Case Study: Johnny

A mother. Mrs. J., brought her 13-year-old son, Johnny, in for counseling due to recent behavioral problems at home and in school. After asking "Who is living in the home?" the therapist learned that Johnny lived with his mom, a stepfather, and five brothers and sisters. Also, the mother's sister, Mary, and three children had been staying with the family while their apartment was repaired. The mother also had a daughter living with an aunt in another state. The aunt was helping the daughter raise her child. When asked, "Who helps you out?" Mrs. J. responded that her mother sometimes helps watch the children, but that, more frequently, a neighbor (who has children of a similar age) watches the younger children when Mrs. J. works during school hours.

Further questioning revealed that Johnny's problem developed soon after his aunt and cousins moved in. Before this, Johnny had been his mother's primary helper and took charge of the children until the stepfather returned home from work. The changes in the family structure that occurred when the sister and her children moved in was stressful for Johnny. Family treatment included Mrs. J. and her children, the stepfather, Mary and her children, and Mrs. J.'s mother. Pressures on Johnny were discussed, and alternatives were considered. Mrs. J.'s mother agreed to temporarily take in Mary and her children. To deal with these additional disruptions in the family, follow-up meetings were conducted to help clarify roles in the family system. Johnny once again assumed the role of helping his mother and stepfather watch the younger children. Within a period of months, his behavioral problems at home and school disappeared.

Implications

Because of the possibility of extended or nontraditional family arrangements, questions should be directed toward clarifying who is living in the home and who helps out. Therapists should work to strengthen and increase functionality of the original family structure rather than attempt to change it. One of the strengths of the African American family is that men, women, and children are allowed to adopt multiple roles within the family. For example, as in the case of Johnny, older children might adopt a caretaking role, and friends or grandparents might help raise children. In such cases, therapy might focus on enhancing the working alliance among caregivers (Montague, 1996; Muroff, 2007; Robbins & Szapocznik, 2000).

Spiritual and Religious Values

Case Study: D.

D. is a 42-year-old African American woman recently divorced after 20 years of marriage and raising two children with little support from her ex-husband. She presented with depressive-like symptoms—feelings of loneliness, lack of energy, lack of appetite, and crying spells . . . . Although part of the treatment focused on traditional psychological interventions, such as cognitive restructuring, expression of feelings, and changing behaviors, D's treatment also included participation in two church-related programs, including the women's ministry, a program that provided social support and decreased emotional and social isolation. Treatment also involved participation in "The Mother to Son Program," a program targeting single mothers parenting African American boys. This program provides support for mothers, as well as rites of passage programs and mentoring relationships for their sons. (Queener & Martin, 2001, p. 120)

Spirituality and religion play an important role in many African American families; church participation provides comfort, economic support, and opportunities for self-expression, leadership, and community involvement. Among a sample of low-income African American children, those whose parents regularly attended church had fewer problems (Christian & Barbarin, 2001). Support systems connected with the church (including friends and club involvement) were found to promote resilience in African American undergraduates exposed to racial microaggressions (Watkins, Labarrie, & Appio, 2010). The African American church often functions as a religious, social, and political hub for African Americans. It is an important support system that includes social events and other community events that serve to foster a sense of "peoplehood" (Boyd-Franklin, 2010).

Implications

Spiritual beliefs are important to many African Americans and serve as a protective factor in response to stressors. If a client is heavily involved in church activities or has strong religious beliefs, the counselor might consider enlisting church leaders to help the client (or family) deal with social and economic stressors or conflicts involving the family, school, or community. Church personnel often have enhanced understanding of the family dynamics and living conditions of parishioners. In addition, churches often sponsor parenting programs or activities that enrich family life.

Educational Characteristics

Case Study: Jackie

Jackie, a 10-year-old African American female, came in with her mother presenting with anger problems, low mood, suicidal thoughts, and family discord. She had always been a stellar student, but her grades had begun to fall from straight As to Bs and Cs. Jackie notes that "she is not smart enough to keep up with the other kids." (Muroff, 2007, p. 131)

African American parents encourage their children to develop career and educational goals at an early age in spite of the obstacles produced by racism and economic conditions. The gap in educational attainment between African American and White children is gradually narrowing. In 2009, over 90% of African Americans (ages 16 to 24) had completed high school or were still enrolled in school (Child Trends, 2011). The high school graduation rate for African Americans has increased to 84.14% versus 87.1% for White Americans, although only 19% receive a bachelor's degree compared with 30% for White Americans (U.S. Census Bureau, 2011e). However, some academic concerns persist. Especially at risk are

African American boys, who often lose interest in academics during middle and high school. However, in a study of 1,225 school-aged African American males (6th to 10th graders), 62% aspired to go to college, similar to rates for White male students. Black males with plans to attend college frequently reported positive feelings about their school and teachers (Toldson, Braithwaite, & Rentie, 2009). In contrast, community violence, parent absenteeism, and school discord affect the school performance of inner-city youth (Bemak, Chi-Ying, & Siroskey-Sabdo, 2005).

The educational environment is often negative for African American youth. They are two to five times more likely to be suspended from school and often receive harsher consequences than their White peers (Monroe, 2005). School personnel often hold stereotypes of African American parents as being neglectful or incompetent and blame children's problems on a lack of parental support for schooling. As one teacher stated, "The parents are the problem! They [the African American children] have absolutely no social skills, such as not knowing how to walk, sit in a chair, . . . it's cultural" (Harry, Klinger, & Hart, 2005, p. 105); but when these researchers visited the homes of parents who were criticized, they often observed parental love, effective parenting skills, and family support for education.

Implications

Factors associated with school failure, especially in African American males, must be identified and system-level intervention strategies applied. Traditional educational practices often do not meet the needs of diverse populations. For example, many African American youths display an animated, persuasive, and confrontational communication style, while schools often have norms of quiet conformity; teacher-focused instruction; and individualized, competitive activities. White teachers may perceive the typical communication patterns, physical movement, and walking style of African American youth as aggressive or noncompliant (Duhaney, 2000; Monroe, 2005). It is important for educators to recognize culturally based behaviors that are not intended to be disruptive. If teachers are not sensitive to these cultural differences, they may respond inappropriately to minority group members (Bordeau, 2004). Students often learn best when curricula and classroom styles are modified, taking cultural factors into consideration.

African American Youth

Case Study: LeaJay Harper

LeaJay Harper says she was a typically rebellious teenager raised by a single mother. She left home at 17 and lived on the streets, surviving on stale donated bread and sleeping on church porches. When she was 18, she was arrested for stealing a $ 10 bag of McDonald's food. "I was hungry." she said. She went to jail. (Mulady, 2011, p.1)

For many urban African American adolescents, life is complicated by problems of poverty, illiteracy, and racism. African American youth are more likely to be victims of violence, such as stabbings or shootings, but are reluctant to report these incidents because of fear of the police or of being accused of "snitching" (S. Schwartz et al., 2010). Most African American youth feel strongly that race is still a factor in how people are judged (Pew Research Center, 2010a). Young African American children are well aware of occupational status. In one study, they identified service jobs as those performed by "only Black people" and high-status jobs as those performed by White Americans (Bigler & Averhard, 2003).

Issues presented in counseling may differ to some extent between males and females. Although African American adolescent females display higher self-confidence, lower levels of substance use, and more positive body images than other groups of adolescent girls (Belgrave, Chase-Vaughn, Gray, Addison, & Cherry, 2000), they often encounter sexism as well as racism. While striving to succeed in relationships and careers, African American adolescent females not only are burdened by living in a male-dominated society but undergo the stressors associated with being African American or living in poverty (Talleyrand, 2010). Acute awareness of issues of racism and sexism is reflected in the following comment:

> Well, in this time I think it's really hard to be an African American woman . . . we are what you call a double negative; we are Black and we are a woman and it's really hard . . . society sees African American females as always getting pregnant and all that kind of thing and being on welfare. (Shorter-Gooden & Washington, 1996, p. 469)

In interviews with young African American females, Shorter-Gooden and Washington (1996) found that the struggle over racial identity was a more salient factor than gender identity in establishing self-definition. These adolescents believed that they had to be strong and were determined to overcome obstacles resulting from societal misperceptions involving Blackness. About half were raised by single mothers, and most indicated the importance of the mother-daughter relationship. Careers were important to two thirds of the group, and most reported that their parents had instilled strong motivation to succeed academically.

Unfortunately, there is a growing trend toward incarceration of African American girls and young women. They are the fastest growing incarcerated group of young people in the United States. In California, the arrest rate is 49 per 1,000 for Black girls, compared with 9 per 1,000 for White girls and 15 per 1,000 for Latinas (Pfeffer, 2011). In general, the crimes committed are not violent and are frequently associated with poverty, homelessness, and maltreatment within the home. Further, zero tolerance policies in schools disproportionately affect African American girls, who may be disciplined for talking back, interpersonal conflict, or truancy. LeaJay Harper, quoted at the beginning of this section, was arrested a second time for stealing pajamas and underwear for her young daughter. Instead of jail time, she was sent to a six-month treatment program and now runs the Young Mothers United Program at the Center for Young Women's Development in San Francisco, helping other African American girls and young women who are at risk of losing their children due to arrests for similar nonviolent offences (Mulady, 2011).

Implications

African American youth often do not come to counseling willingly. They may have been referred by social agencies or brought in by their parents. Because of this, lack of cooperation may be an issue:

Case Study: Michael

Michael is a 19-year-old African American male brought to counseling by his aunt, Gloria, with whom he has lived for the past 2 years. Gloria is concerned about Michael's future . . . . Although Michael graduated from high school and is employed part-time at a fast-food restaurant, he is frustrated with this work and confused about his future. He believes that Black men 'don't get a fair shake" in life and is discouraged about his prospects about getting ahead. . . Michael's aunt . . . . is concerned that Michael's peers are involved in gangs and illegal activities. She thinks the rap music he listens to is beginning to fill his head with hate and anger. . . . Michael's major issues center around a need to develop a positive identity as an African American man and discover his place in the world. (Frame & Williams, 1996, p. 22)

Frame and Williams (1996) suggested several strategies for working with African American youth such as Michael. The first is based on the African tradition of storytelling and involves the use of metaphors. In response to statements like "Black men don't get a fair shake," counselors can encourage clients to identify family phrases or Biblical stories that instill hope. Additional metaphors can be generated from the writings of prominent African Americans. To assist Michael with his struggle to overcome societal barriers, he could be encouraged to envision himself as a crusader for human rights and other socially appropriate ways of directing his anger. The counselor could also engage Michael in discussions about rap music; issues addressed in the lyrics could be explored, as well as healthy outlets for feelings of anger or despair. Family and community support for Michael could be generated by including extended family, the pastor, teachers, and other important individuals in Michael's life and encouraging them to discuss their own struggles and search for identity. Use of techniques such as these, derived from African American experiences, can lead to personal empowerment.

In counseling young African American women, issues involving racial identity and conflict should be explored. Counselors can help African American females counteract negative images associated with being Black and being female; enhancing internal strength by developing pride and dignity in Black womanhood can serve as a buffer to racism and sexism and can prevent the incorporation of negative images into their own belief systems (Jordan, 1997).

Cultural Strengths

Protective factors and strengths among African Americans include positive ethnic identity; familial, extended kin, and community support systems; flexible family roles; achievement orientation; and spiritual beliefs and practices (Kaslow et al., 2010; LaTaillade, 2006). Family and religious protective factors have been hypothesized to account for finding that African Americans have lower levels of heavy and binge drinking than any ethnic group, with the exception of Asian Americans (Substance Abuse and Mental Health Services Administration (2011). Additionally, African American adolescents have the lowest rates of substance use compared to Whites and other ethnic groups (Johnston, O'Malley, Bachman, & Schulenberg, 2010).

The African American family structure has many strengths. Among families headed by females, the rearing of children is often undertaken by a large number of relatives, older children, and close friends. For many, the extended family network provides emotional and economic support. African American families are characterized by flexibility in family roles, strong kinship bonds, a strong work and achievement ethic, and strong religious orientation (Hildebrand, Phenice, Gray, & Hines, 1996; Rockymore, 2008; McCollum, 1997). Kinship support diminishes risks of internalizing or externalizing problem behaviors in children and can ameliorate conditions such as poor parenting (Taylor, 2010). Among low-income single mothers, many displayed substantial parenting involvement with their children and emphasized achievement, self-respect, and racial pride with their children (Rockymore, 2008).

Despite the challenges of racism and prejudice, many African American families have been able to instill positive self-esteem in their children by means of role flexibility. African American men and women value such behaviors as assertiveness; within a family, males are more accepting of women's work roles and are more willing to share in the responsibilities traditionally assigned to women. Many women demonstrate a "Strong Black Woman" image that includes pride in racial identity, self-reliance, and capability in handing challenges—all while nurturing the family. Although self-efficacy can be a strength, excessive investment in meeting the expectations of such a role can lead to emotional suppression and difficulty expressing vulnerability or distress (Harrington, Crowther, & Shipherd, 2010).

SPECIFIC CHALLENGES

In the following sections we consider challenges often faced by African Americans and consider their implications in treatment. Remember that these are generalizations and that their applicability needs to be assessed for each individual.

Racism and Discrimination

Many African Americans perceive ongoing racism in the United States. Sixty-one percent of African Americans believe that the federal response to the disaster caused by Hurricane Katrina would have been faster if White populations had been involved (Washington, 2005). Forty-three percent of African Americans report there is "a lot" of anti-Black discrimination in the United States, as opposed to only 13% of Whites. Such lack of trust and feelings of discrimination also affect views of social and health systems (Miller, Seib, & Dennie, 2001). Whereas about half of Whites believe Blacks have equal societal opportunities, 81% of Blacks believe more change is necessary (Pew Research Center, 2010a). Many African Americans believe that racial profiling occurs frequently (Carlson, 2004). In situations involving suspected racial profiling, Black men often report thinking, "Maybe I am being treated this way because I am Black," and needing to decide, "Do I protest it or just take it?" (Fausset & Huffstutter, 2009, p. 1). Exposure to these kinds of microaggressions are not uncommon among African Americans (D. W. Sue, Capodilupo, & Holder, 2008). Often cultural mistrust, or "healthy cultural paranoia," can serve as a coping strategy with respect to racism (Phelps, Taylor, & Gerard, 2001). African Americans also face *colorism*, differential treatment based on skin color that often occurs unconsciously. For example, individuals with lighter skin color are seen as more intelligent or attractive (Kelly & Greene, 2010). Colorism can also affect the housing and employment opportunities of darker African Americans.

Viglione, Hannon, and DeFina (2011) found that Black women with lighter skin received shorter sentences than women with darker skin who committed similar crimes. Many contend that the high rates of arrest and conviction among African Americans are associated with racism; youth affected by these issues (their fathers are incarcerated) have increased risk of poverty, school failure, emotional distress, and criminal activity, including frequent use of marijuana, cocaine, and crystal meth. This effect can further exacerbate the cycle of racial inequality, substance abuse, and imprisonment (Roettger, Swisher, Kuhl, & Chavez, 2011). The experience of perceived racial discrimination is associated with decreased levels of self-esteem and life satisfaction and increased depressive symptoms in African American and Caribbean Black youth (Seaton, Caldwell, Sellers, & Jackson, 2011). Some African American adolescents report drug use as a way of coping with feelings of anger in reaction to racial discrimination (Gibbons et al., 2010).

Racial socialization can help buffer the negative effects of racist discrimination (Fischer & Shaw, 1999). African American parents differ in the ways in which they address racism with their children. Some address racism and prejudice directly and help their children identify with their own race, whereas others consider race to be of minor importance and ignore the topic of race and focus on human values or discuss the issue only if brought up by their children. Neal-Barnett & DeAngelis, 1997 found ignoring racial issues in socialization left children vulnerable to anxiety when African American peers accused them of "acting White." They also had fewer opportunities to develop coping strategies when faced with discrimination. Similarly, protective factors for African American youth include parental focus on increasing positive feelings about self and enhancing a sense pride in one's culture (Belgrave et al., 2000).

Implications

Since the mental health environment is a microcosm of the larger society, the mental health professional should be willing to address and anticipate possible mistrust from African American clients (Obasi & Leong, 2009; Whaley, 2001). Therapists should carefully assess both the problems confronting a client and the client's response to the problem situation, including the way he or she usually deals with racism. It may be necessary to encourage consideration of more productive options, such as taking a conscious, problem-solving approach. A. C. Jones (1985) described four interactive factors that should be considered in working with African American clients (see Figure 14.1). The first factor involves reactions to racial oppression. Most African Americans have faced racism, and the possibility that this factor plays a role in the present problem should be examined. Vontress and Epp (1997) described this factor as "historical hostility," a reaction in response to current and past suffering endured by the group. Problems are often perceived through this filter. Other interactive factors described by Jones include the possible influence of African American culture and traditions on the client's behavior; the degree to which the client has adopted majority culture values, and the personal experiences of the individual. Individual experiences with racial oppression can vary significantly among African Americans. For some, such experiences are even more significant than racial identity. The task of the

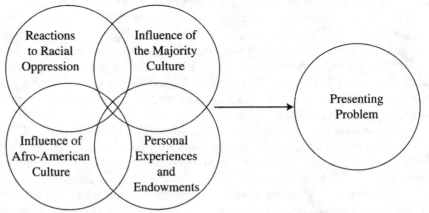

Figure 14.1 The Interaction of Four Sets of Factors in the Jones Model

Source: From "Psychological Functioning in Black Presenting Americans: A Conceptual Problem Guide for Use in Psychotherapy," by A. C. Jones, 1985, *Psychotherapy, 22,* p. 367. Copyright 1982 by *Psychotherapy.* Reprinted by permission of the Editor, *Psychotherapy.*

therapist is to help the client understand the effects of such issues and allow such understanding to guide conscious, growth-producing choices. Therapists may also decide to discuss the positive benefits of racial socialization with the parents of African American children.

Implications for Clinical Practice

The first therapy sessions are crucial in determining whether a client will return. African Americans have a high rate of therapy termination (Fortuna, Alegria, & Gao, 2010; Lester, Resick, Young-Xu, & Artz, 2010). Termination often reflects a counselor's inability to establish an effective therapeutic alliance. African American clients tend to prefer an egalitarian therapeutic relationship, so it is critically important to answer questions, explain the counseling and assessment process, and enlist the assistance of the client. Prior experiences may render issues of trust very important. The counselor can deal with these issues by discussing them directly and by being open, authentic, and empathetic. Clients often make a decision regarding continuation of therapy based on their personal evaluation of the counselor. As one African American client stated, *"I am assessing to see if that person [counselor] is willing to go that extra mile and speak my language and talk about my Blackness"* (Ward, 2005, p. 475). Counselors may need to have a broader role and more flexible style when working with African American clients, including being more directive, serving in an educative function, and helping the client deal with agencies or with issues involving health and employment. Although the order of these elements can be modified and some can be omitted, these steps may be helpful to the counselor and the client:

1. During the first session, it may be beneficial to bring up the reaction of the client to working with a counselor of a different ethnic background. (Although African Americans show a same-race preference, being culturally competent has been shown to be even more important.) A statement such as, "Sometimes clients feel uncomfortable working with a counselor of a different race. Would this be a problem for you?"
2. Determine clients' values and preferences by identifying their expectations and worldview and what they believe counseling entails, as well as exploring their feelings about counseling. Determine how they view the problem and possible solutions.
3. If clients are there involuntarily, discuss how counseling can be made useful for them. Explain your relationship with the referring agency and the limits of confidentiality.
4. Assess the positive assets of the client, such as family (including relatives and nonrelated friends), community resources, and church.
5. Help the client define goals and appropriate means of attaining them. Assess ways in which the client, family members, and friends have handled similar problems successfully.
6. Establish an egalitarian relationship. Many African Americans are comfortable establishing a close personal connection with the counselor. This may be accomplished by self-disclosure. If the client appears hostile or aloof, discussing some noncounseling topics may be useful.

(continued)

(continued)

7. After the therapeutic alliance has been formed, collaboratively determine interventions (a number of culturally adapted evidence-based therapies have been found to be effective with African Americans). Problem-solving and time-limited approaches may be most acceptable.
8. Analysis of the client's racial identity and family structure can be helpful in deciding if alternative treatment modes and approaches might be beneficial.
9. Determine any external factors that might be related to the presenting problem. Determine whether and how the client has responded to discrimination and racism, both in unhealthy and healthy ways. Do not dismiss issues of racism as "just an excuse"; instead, help the client identify alternative means of dealing with the problems.
10. Examine issues around racial identity (many clients at the preencounter stage will not believe that race is an important factor). For some, increased Afrocentric identification will be an important factor in establishing a positive self-identity. In these cases, elements of African/African American culture can be incorporated in counseling through readings, movies, music, and discussions of prominent African Americans.

Counseling American Indians and Alaska Natives

Some American Indians want to abolish Columbus Day and instead have a holiday that honors indigenous people. . . . It bothers these young Indians that people still believe Christopher Columbus discovered America when there already were indigenous people living here. (Hanson, 2006, p. 1)

In 1887, the U.S. government determined that Indians were incapable of managing their own land, so they placed the property in a trust, promising the Indians that they would receive income from their land. They never did. In 1999, a Federal judge ruled that the government had breached its sacred trust duties. (Maas, 2001)

Of the 175 Indian languages once spoken in the United States, only about 20 are still passed on to younger generations. James Jackson, Jr., remembers his experience in a boarding school when a teacher grabbed him when he was speaking his native language and threatened to wash out his mouth with soap: "That's where we lost it [our language]." (Brooke, 1998)

In 2010, the University of North Dakota agreed to retire the fighting Sioux name and logo to comply with a ban from the NCAA (National Collegiate Athletic Association). Do the Native-themed mascots or logos impact the psychological well-being of American Indians? The American Psychological Association (2005) believes such symbols and imagery undermine respectful and accurate images of the American Indians' culture.

American Indians/Alaska Natives form a highly heterogeneous group composed of 565 distinct tribes, some consisting of only four or five members (Bureau of Indian Affairs, 2011). The American Indian and Alaska Native population was 2.9 million in 2010, representing 0.9% of the total population (U.S. Census Bureau, 2010h). An additional 1.81 million Americans report having Indian roots. About 34% of American Indians live on reservations, whereas 57% reside in metropolitan areas (Bureau of Indian Affairs, 2011). Fewer American Indians are high school graduates than the general U.S. population (71% versus 80%). The poverty rate is double the U.S. average, with income only 62% of the mean income of all households (U.S. Census Bureau, 2006). American Indians differ in their degree of acculturation. Although most do not live on reservations or with their tribes, many are returning because of casino jobs or a more nurturing environment. One man who returned described his need for a more "friendly place, friendly face, and friendly greetings" (Shukovsky, 2001, p. A1).

Because American Indian/Alaska Natives comprise such a small percentage of the U.S. population, they are relatively "invisible," which makes information about them susceptible to stereotypes (Bureau of Indian Affairs, 2011). This is one of the reasons many are opposed to the use of Indian-themed mascots and logos. American Indians want the ability to define themselves. American Indian high school and college students who viewed such images reported higher levels of depression, lower self-esteem, and decreased feelings of community worth (Fryberg, Markus, Oyserman, & Stone, 2008). In examining online responses to this controversy, Steinfeldt et al. (2010) found hostile attitudes from non-Indian respondents: "If the nickname is taken away, we should take away Indian educational programming and funding" and "We are being victimized by reverse racism and PC society."

Health statistics reveal significant concerns. The alcoholism mortality rate is over twice as high for Indians as that for the U.S. population as a whole (Centers for Disease Control and Prevention, 2008). Rates of obesity and diabetes are also much higher (U.S. Department of Health and Human Services, 2007). Injury-related deaths (motor vehicle crashes, suicides, homicides, drownings) occur more frequently compared to the overall U.S. rate. Injuries and violence account for 75% of all deaths for American Indian/Alaska Native Americans between the ages of 1 and 19 (Centers for Disease Control and Prevention, 2007). These populations also suffer disproportionately from depression and substance abuse (Office of Minority Health and Health Disparities, 2007). Among Native American women at a private care facility in New Mexico, mood disorders were reported by 21%, 47% had an anxiety disorder, and 14% had alcohol dependence or abuse. These rates are 2 to 2.5 times higher than found in the general population (Duran et al., 2004).

What constitutes an Indian is often an area of controversy. The U.S. Census depends on self-report of racial identity. Congress has formulated a legal definition: An individual must have an Indian blood quantum of at least 25% to be considered an Indian. This definition has caused problems both within and outside the Indian community. Some tribes have developed their own criteria and specify either tribal enrollment or blood quantum levels. Ken Hansen, chairman of the Samish tribe, stated, "It is a fundamental right of any nation, including tribal nations, to define their own membership. If a person meets the criteria for membership in a tribe, they are Indian" (Shukovsky, 2001, p. A13). Tribal definitions typically allow inclusion of the 60% of American Indians who have mixed heritage, including Black, White, and Latino/a backgrounds (Trimble, Fleming, Beauvais, & Jumper-Thurman, 1996).

CHARACTERISTICS AND STRENGTHS

In the following sections we consider the characteristics, values, and strengths of American Indian/Native Alaska populations and consider their implications in treatment. Remember that these are generalizations and that their applicability needs to be assessed for particular clients and their families.

Tribal Social Structure

For the many Indians, including those living both on and off reservations, the tribe is of fundamental importance. The tribe and the reservation, an interdependent system, provides Indians with a sense of belonging and security. Tribal connections are significant because individuals see themselves as an extension of their tribe. Status and rewards are obtained by adherence to tribal structure. Indians judge themselves in terms of whether their behaviors are of benefit to the tribe. Personal accomplishments are honored and supported if they serve to benefit the tribe.

Implications

Interventions with American Indian/Alaska Native families and individuals should include an assessment of the importance of tribal relationships in any decision-making process. In a study of 401 American Indian youth (half tribal-based and half urban-based), urban-based youth were more likely to identify personal, familial, and environmental strengths than were tribal-based youth, whereas the latter identified more tribal strengths (Stiffman et al., 2007). The tribe is very important for many Indians, even among those who do not reside on the reservation. Many use the word *here* to describe the reservation and the word *there* to describe everything that is outside. The reservation is a place to conduct ceremonies and social events and to maintain cultural identity. Indians who leave the reservation to seek greater opportunities sometimes report losing their sense of personal identity (Lone-Knapp, 2000).

> Interventions with American Indian/Alaska Native families and individuals should include an assessment of the importance of tribal relationships in any decision-making process.

Family Structure

It is difficult to describe "the Indian family." It varies from the matriarchal structures seen in the Navajo, where women govern the family, to patriarchal structures, in which men are the primary authority figures. Some generalizations can be made, however. A high fertility rate, out-of-wedlock births, and strong roles for women are commonly seen. For most tribes, the extended family is the basic unit. Children are often partially raised by relatives, such as aunts, uncles, and grandparents, who live in separate households (M. T. Garrett, 2006).

Implications

The concept of the extended family is often misunderstood by those in the majority culture who operate under the concept of the nuclear family.

Misinterpretations are possible if a counselor believes that parents should raise and be responsible for their own children. The extended family often includes distant relatives and even friends. It is not unusual for children to stay in multiple households. In work with children, counselors should determine the roles of various family members so that interventions can include appropriate individuals. The emphasis on collectivism is strong. If the goals or techniques of therapy lead to discord with the family or tribe, they will not be effective. Interventions may need to include the input of family, relatives, friends, elders, or tribal leaders.

Cultural and Spiritual Values

Because of the great diversity and variation among American Indians, it is difficult to describe a set of values that encompasses all groups. However, certain generalizations can be made regarding Indian values (M. T. Garrett, 2006; M. T. Garrett & Portman, 2011; Garwick & Auger, 2000).

1. *Sharing:* Among Indians, honor and respect are gained by sharing and giving, in contrast with the dominant culture where status is gained by the accumulation of material goods.

   Implications: Once enough money is earned, Indians may stop working and spend time and energy in ceremonial activities. The accumulation of wealth is not a high priority but is a means to enjoy the present. Interventions targeting alcohol or drug use should take into consideration this emphasis on sharing.

2. *Cooperation:* Indians work hard to prevent discord and disharmony and believe that the tribe and the family take precedence over the individual. Indian children are often sensitive to the opinions and attitudes of their peers and may actively avoid disagreements or contradictions. Most do not like to be singled out and made to perform in school unless the whole group benefits.

   Implications: Instead of going to work or school, Indians may prioritize assisting a family member needing help. Indian children may be seen as unmotivated in school because of their reluctance to compete with peers.

3. *Noninterference:* Indians are taught to not interfere with others and to observe rather than react impulsively. Rights of others are respected. This belief in noninterference extends to parenting style.

   Implications: Culture significantly shapes parent-child relationships. Indians are more indulgent and less punitive than parents from other ethnic groups (MacPhee, Fritz, & Miller-Heyl, 1996). Euro-American parenting styles may conflict with American Indian values. One culturally sensitive parent education program developed for American Indians included (a) use of the oral tradition of storytelling to teach lessons to children; (b) understanding the spiritual nature of child rearing and the spiritual value of children; and (c) use of the extended family in child rearing. The eight-session program included social time for parents and children before each session, including storytelling and a potluck meal. The program applies traditional teaching methods, such as nurturing, use of nature to teach lessons, and use of harmony as a guiding principle for family life (Gorman & Balter, 1997).

4. *Time orientation:* Indians show greater focus on the present than on the future. Ideas of punctuality or planning for the future may be unimportant. Life is to be lived in the here and now.

   Implications: Tasks may be approached from a logical perspective rather than according to deadlines. In contrast, the majority culture values delay of gratification and planning for future goals. In working with these issues, the counselor should acknowledge such value differences and help the individual or family develop strategies to negotiate value conflicts.

5. *Spirituality:* The spirit, mind, and body are all interconnected. Illness involves disharmony between these elements. Positive emotions can be curative; healing can take place through events such as talking to an old friend on the phone or watching children play (Garrett & Wilbur, 1999).

   Implications: Traditional curative approaches attempt to restore spirit-mind-body harmony. The sweat lodge and vision quest are often used to re-establish connections between the mind, body, and spirit. To treat a problem successfully, all of these elements may need to be considered and addressed. Counselors can help clients identify factors involved in disharmony; determine curative events, behaviors, and feelings; and use client-generated solutions to create balance.

6. *Nonverbal communication:* Learning occurs by listening rather than talking. Indian families tend to ask few direct questions. Direct eye contact with an elder may be seen as a sign of disrespect.

   Implications: Differences in nonverbal communication can lead to misunderstandings. For example, lack of eye contact or direct communication may be viewed as a sign of disrespect. It is important to determine whether specific behaviors are due to cultural values or are actual problems.

Cultural Strengths

American Indian/Alaska Native populations had to endure extermination and assimilation efforts and were able to do so because of cultural values and strengths such as spirituality; respect for traditional values; extended family networks; allegiance to the family, community, and tribe; respect for elders; respect for the environment and the land; and the promotion of such themes as belonging, mastery, independence, and generosity (Gilgun, 2002). The values of listening and observing rather than reacting can enhance communication and decrease conflict. Spiritual and traditional practices also act as a protective factor (Garroutte et al., 2003). The respect shown for the environment and the interconnection between humans and the environment is something that can be emulated by all cultures. Additionally, the focus on the present is increasingly recognized as an asset, particularly among those who incorporate mindfulness activities into clinical practice (Chiesa & Serretti, 2011).

SPECIFIC CHALLENGES

In the following sections we consider challenges often faced by American Indian populations and that consider their implications in treatment. Remember that these are generalizations and that their applicability needs to be assessed for each client.

Historical and Sociopolitical Background

In North America, wars and diseases that resulted from contact with Europeans decimated the American Indian population; by the end of the 18th century, only about 10% of the original population remained. Additionally, Indians suffered massive loss of their land. The experience of American Indians in America is not comparable to that of any other ethnic group. In contrast to immigrants, who arrived with few resources and struggled to gain equality, American Indians originally had resources. However, their land and status were severely eroded by imperial, colonial, and then federal and state policies (K. W. Johnson et al., 1995). For years, extermination and seizure of lands seemed to be the primary governmental policy toward Indians. The words of one Delaware tribal member reflect these experiences: "I admit that there are good White men, but they bear no proportion to the bad; the bad must be the strongest, for they rule."

In the 1830s, more than 125,000 Indians from different tribes were forced from their homes in many different states to a reservation in Oklahoma. The move was traumatic for Indian families and, in many cases, disrupted their cultural traditions. Assaults against the Indian culture also occurred via attempts to "civilize" Indians. Many Indian children were removed from their families and placed in English-speaking boarding schools. They were not allowed to speak their own language and were forced to spend 8 continuous years away from their families and tribes. Children were also removed from their homes and placed with non-Indian families until the Indian Child Welfare Act of 1978 prohibited these practices (Blanchard, 1983; Choney, Berryhill-Paapke, & Robbins, 1995; K. W. Johnson et al., 1995).

> One of the most serious failings of the present system is that Indian children are often removed from the custody of their natural parents by non-tribal government authorities who have no basis for intelligently evaluating the cultural and social premises underlying Indian home life and child rearing. Many of the individuals who decide the fate of our children are at best ignorant of our cultural values, and at worst contemptuous of the Indian way and convinced that removal, usually to a non-Indian household or institution, can only benefit an Indian child. (*Congressional Record*, 1997)

Chief Calvin Isaac of the Mississippi Band of Choctaw Indians spoke these words during the 1998 congressional hearings regarding possible amendments to the Indian Child Welfare Act. Statistics were cited indicating that over 90% of American Indian children were still being placed by state courts and child welfare workers into non-Indian homes (*Congressional Record*, 1997). Amendments to the original act dramatically reduced this type of placement, although further changes to either strengthen or weaken the act are periodically proposed.

These events have had a tremendous negative impact on family and tribal cohesion and prevented the transmission of cultural values from parents to children. Gone (2009) believes that the experiences of colonization, coercive assimilation experiences in boarding schools, and the widespread loss of indigenous languages and customs have resulted in unresolved grief—"soul wounds"—that lead to behavioral dysfunction and substance abuse. "I find that pain . . . is buried inside you. . . . If you disclose it, it's your healing . . . But if you bury it, and don't want to say anything about it, then it's going to affect your life" (Gone, 2009, p. 756). The following case study illustrates some of the disruptions caused by a boarding school experience.

Case Study: Mary

Mary was born on the reservation. She was sent away to school when she was 12 and did not return to the reservation until she was 20. By the time she returned, her mother had died from pneumonia. She didn't remember her father, the medicine man of the tribe, very well. Shortly after she returned, she became pregnant by a non-Indian man she met at a bar. Mary's father . . . looked forward to teaching and leaving to his grandson, John, the ways of the medicine mam . . . John felt his grandfather was out of step with the 20th century . . . Mary . . . could not validate the grandfather's way of life . . . [because] she remembered having difficulty fitting in when she returned to the reservation . . . In response to the growing distance between her father and her son, she became more and more depressed and began to drink heavily. (Sage, 1977, p. 48)

In the past, the tribe, through the extended family, was responsible for the education and training of children. The sense of tribal identity developed through this tradition was significantly eroded by governmental policies. In addition, even recent history is full of broken treaties, the seizure or misuse of Indian land, and battles led by local or federal officials to remove or severely limit fishing and hunting rights. Thus, American Indians are often suspicious of the motives of the majority culture; many still do not expect to be treated fairly by non-Indians (Cruz & Spense, 2005; K. W. Johnson et al., 1995).

Implications

When working with American Indian children and families, it is important to consider the historical sociopolitical relationship between American Indians and the local, state, and federal government. The counselor should understand not only the national history of oppression but also local issues and specific tribal history (Dana, 2000).

The historic disruption of Indian families resulting in the Indian Child Welfare Act has important implications for how Indians might view child protective services or respond to runaway youth. Currently, decisions regarding the placement of American Indian children are held in tribal courts. Testimony from expert witnesses familiar with the specific Indian cultural group must be obtained before children can be removed from their homes. Additionally, if children are removed from their parents, residence with extended family members, other tribal members, or other Indian families is given primary consideration.

Educational Concerns

There is a high rate of school failure among American Indian/Alaska Native populations (Whitesell, Mitchell, Spicer, and the Voices of Indian Teen Project Team, 2009). American Indian children appear to do well during the first few years of school. However, by the fourth grade, a pattern of academic decline and truancy develops; a significant drop in achievement motivation often occurs in middle school. Although some have argued that traditional cultural values and beliefs are incompatible with those of the educational system, there is increasing support for the view that perceived barriers to mobility are the culprit for reduced academic performance. In other words, academic success is not perceived as leading to rewards or success. Some contend that once Indian children realize their "Indianness," achievement motivation drops (Wood & Clay, 1996). In addition, many youth see that jobs are available in casinos or on the reservation, so they do not see the value in pursuing a "White man's education." Many American Indians/Alaska Natives never finish high school. Only 11% have a bachelor's degree, versus 24% of the U.S. population (U.S. Census Bureau, 2006). Such educational gaps are believed to perpetuate the cycle of poverty and reduced opportunities and may contribute to the high suicide rate among American Indian adolescents (Keane, Dick, Bechtold, & Manson, 1996).

Implications

The blame for school failure has generally been placed on the individual rather than on the school environment. However, many Indians who leave school report feeling "pushed out" and express mistrust of teachers who represent the same White community that historically exerted control over the economic, social, and religious lives of Indians (Deyhle & Swisher, 1999). At a systems level, positive changes could occur if public schools and institutions of higher education (a) recognized the sociocultural history of Indians and related perceptions of schools as a potentially hostile environment and (b) increased efforts to accommodate some of the social and cultural differences of American Indian students, including adapting curricula to reflect students' cultural background (Reyhner, 2002). The perceived lack of reward for academic achievement must also be addressed. Schools must help students bridge the two worlds of Native American and White cultures. Some tribes have given up on the public school system and have developed their own learning centers and community colleges.

Acculturation Conflicts

When I attended the university, that's the first time I saw a powwow. . . . It's only now [that] I start learning my culture.

I don't know the meaning of the symbols of our culture. Instead, I know the symbols of the Catholic faith. (Gone, 2009, p. 757)

Not only do Indian children and adolescents face the same developmental issues faced by other youth, but they also may experience conflict over exposure to two very different cultures, factors that may result in failure to develop a positive self-image or strong ethnic identity (Garrett & Portman, 2011). Many youth are caught between expectations of their parents to maintain traditional values and the necessity to adapt to the majority culture (Rieckmann, Wadsworth, & Deyhle, 2004). In one study of American Indian adolescents, the most serious problems identified involved family relationships, grades, and concerns about the future. In addition, boys frequently cited their Indianness or being Indian as a problem. One third of the girls surveyed reported feeling that they did not want to live (Bee-Gates, Howard-Pitney, LaFramboise, & Rowe, 1996).

Many Indians are acculturated and hold the values of the larger society. The degree to which a client identifies with the native culture should always be considered. Five levels of cultural orientation were formulated by M. T. Garrett and Pichette (2000):

1. *Traditional:* The individual may speak little English and practice traditional tribal customs and methods of worship.
2. *Marginal:* The individual may be bilingual but has lost touch with his or her cultural heritage yet is not fully accepted in mainstream society.
3. *Bicultural:* The person is conversant with both sets of values and can communicate in a variety of contexts.
4. *Assimilated:* The individual embraces only the mainstream culture's values, behaviors, and expectations.
5. *Pantraditional:* The individual has been exposed to and adopted mainstream values but is making a conscious effort to return to the "old ways."

Implications

Counselors can discuss the client's tribal affiliation (if any), languages spoken, self-identity, and residential background and whether there is a current relationship to a tribe or tribal culture (M. T. Garrett & Pichette, 2000). The types of problems and the therapeutic process and goals appropriate for someone living on a rural reservation may be very different from those appropriate for an urbanized Indian who retains few traditional beliefs. Individuals with a traditional orientation may be unfamiliar with expectations of the dominant culture and may want to develop the skills and resources to deal with mainstream society. In contrast, assimilated or marginal American Indians may want to examine value and self-identity conflicts and may face issues such as (a) lack of pride in or denial of Indian heritage, (b) pressure to adopt majority cultural values, (c) guilt over not knowing or participating in the Indian culture, (d) negative views regarding American Indians, and (e) a lack of an extended support or belief system.

Level of acculturation is also likely to guide selection of therapeutic interventions. For example, acculturated American Indians have found success with all components of cognitive behavior therapy (CBT), whereas those who are traditionally oriented are responsive to the short-term focus, activity schedule, and homework assignments in CBT but have difficulty with the underlying theoretical assumptions regarding the association between thoughts and emotional symptoms (Jackson, Schmutzer, Wenzel, & Tyler, 2006). In these cases, cultural adaptations that involve modified explanations for CBT may be useful.

Alcohol and Substance Abuse

Substance abuse is one of the greatest problems faced by American Indian/Alaska Native populations. Although rates of alcohol use vary across tribes and regions, American Indians have the highest weekly alcohol consumption of any ethnic group (Chartier & Caetano, 2010). Thus, alcoholism is a significant concern for many tribes (Hasin, Stinson, Ogburn, & Grant, 2007; Spillance & Smith, 2009). It is common to begin drinking at an early age. Thus, it is not surprising that rates of alcohol and drug use (including experimentation with inhalants) are also high among American Indian youth (Ding, Chang, & Southerland, 2009). In Alaska, 32% of American Indians/Alaska Natives of childbearing age reported heavy drinking, which is responsible for the disproportionately high percentage of cases of fetal alcohol syndrome reported in this population (Centers for Disease Control and Prevention, 1994). However, it must be remembered that there is variability in alcohol-use patterns between specific subgroups; for example, Southwest Indians, especially females, have low rates of alcohol consumption (Chartier & Caetano, 2010).

A variety of explanations has been put forth regarding possible reasons for the high levels of alcohol abuse (see Figure 12.1). Although drinking alcoholic beverages may initially have been incorporated into cultural practices as an activity of sharing, giving, and togetherness (Swinomish Tribal Mental Health Project, 1991), heavy alcohol use is associated with other factors, such as low self-efficacy and feelings of powerlessness (M. J. Taylor, 2000). Substance abuse is also related to low self-esteem, cultural identity conflicts, lack of positive role models, childhood maltreatment, social pressure to use substances, hopelessness about life, and a breakdown in the family (Swinomish Tribal Mental Health Project, 1991; Yee et al., 1995).

Implications

Successful drug treatment programs have incorporated appropriate cultural elements. Community-oriented programs engage the entire community rather than specific individuals and have the advantage of directly involving community leaders (Hawkins, Cummins, & Marlatt, 2004). One tribal community reduced their alcoholism rate from 95% to 5% in 10 years by creating a community culture in which alcoholism was not tolerated, while revitalizing traditional culture (Thomason, 2000). Many tribes have developed similar programs to deal with alcohol- and substance-abuse issues.

Domestic Violence

The rate of domestic violence, along with physical and sexual assault, is quite high in many native communities. Statistics indicating that American Indian women suffer a higher rate of violence (3.5 times higher) than the national average (Bhungalia, 2001) may underestimate exposure to violence because many women do not report assaults. American Indian/Alaska Native women are often sexually and physically abused beginning early in life; abuse is especially high among lesbian and bisexual women (D'Oro, 2010). The high incidence of domestic violence may result from changes in traditional status and roles for men and women, as well as stressors associated with social and economic marginalization.

Implications

During counseling, it may be difficult to determine whether domestic violence is occurring within a family or couple. American Indian women who are abused may remain silent because of cultural barriers, a high level of distrust of White-dominated agencies, fear of familial alienation, and the historical failure of state and tribal agencies to prosecute domestic crimes (Bhungalia, 2001). Jurisdictional struggles between state and tribal authorities can also result in a lack of help for women. Many tribes acknowledge the problem of family violence and have developed community-based domestic violence interventions using strategies from the Indian cultural perspective rather than resources from the majority culture (Hamby, 2000). When working with a domestic-violence issue with an American Indian woman, tribal issues, tribal programs, and family support options should be identified.

Suicide

Robert Jensen was the first. The lanky 17-year-old Sioux Indian, who'd been drinking heavily and having run-ins with the police all summer, slipped into his family's dank basement last Aug. 30. Over toward the corner, past the rusted-out furnace and broken sewer line, he threaded a braided leather belt over a board nailed between floor beams, buckled it around his neck and hanged himself.

On Nov. 16, in the same basement with the same type of belt, Robert's 16-year-old cousin and best friend, Charles Gerry, hanged himself. Three other Indian youths have since taken their lives. . . . In the 5 months since Robert's death, 43 reservation boys and girls have attempted suicide. ("Rash of Indian Suicides," 1998)

Sixteen-year-old Franci Jackson considered hanging herself with a rope when she felt she couldn't take any more bullying at school, the teen from Frazer told a U.S. Senate field panel taking testimony on the epidemic. . . . But then she changed her mind.

"I thought of my mom and dad and how much they love me. And if I leave, what would they do without me? But most kids don't think," she said in tears. Six students had killed themselves in the previous year with another 20 attempting suicide. (Associated Press, 2011)

The high incidence of suicide among American Indians is thought to be the result of alcohol abuse, poverty, boredom, and family breakdown. American Indian/Alaska Native youth have twice the rate of attempted and completed suicide as other youth (D'Oro, 2011). Adolescence to adulthood is the time of greatest risk for suicide, especially among young males (EchoHawk, 1997; Middlebrook, LeMaster, Beals, Novins, & Manson, 2001). Among a sample of 122 American Indian middle-school children living on a North Plains reservation, 20 percent had made a nonfatal suicide attempt and of this group, nearly half had attempted suicide two or more times (LaFromboise, Medoff, Lee, & Harris, 2007).

Implications

There are many societal and economic issues facing American Indians. For those who live on a reservation or identify with a tribe, community activities sometimes exist focused on reducing suicidal ideation and promoting resilience in youth. Effective programs need to be culturally consistent. For example, many Indians believe that mental health issues are due to unbalanced spiritual relationships (Limb & Hodge, 2010). In traditional Indian belief systems, there is not only a seen world but an unseen world. Events that disrupt the unseen world disturb the harmony in the seen world. Therefore, if intervention focuses only on the seen world, change will not occur (Cruz, 2005). A promising culturally tailored suicide intervention program was implemented by LaFromboise and Howard-Pitney (1995) at the request of the Zuni Tribal High School. Scores on a suicide probability measure indicated that 81% of the students were in the moderate to severe risk ranges. Of the participants, 18% reported having attempted suicide, and 40% reported knowing of a relative or friend who had committed suicide. The program involved the development of suicide intervention and prevention skills through role-playing. Other components included building self-esteem, identifying emotions and stressors, recognizing and eliminating negative thoughts or emotions, receiving information on suicide and intervention strategies, and setting personal and community goals. The program was effective in reducing feelings of hopelessness and suicidal probability ratings. Intervention programs may need to be developed based on the needs of individual tribes. For example, although suicidal ideation among the Pueblo was associated with the suicidal behavior of friends, low self-esteem and depression were the most significant factors for adolescents from Northern Plain tribes (LaFromboise, 2006).

Implications for Clinical Practice

1. Explore the client's ethnic identity, tribal affiliation, and adherence to cultural values, as well as family members' association with a tribe or reservation. In addition, determine the appropriateness of a mind-body-spirit emphasis. Keep in mind that many American Indians adhere completely to mainstream values, whereas others, especially those living on or near reservations, are more likely to hold to traditional values.
2. Understand the extensive history of oppression experienced by American Indians and learn about local issues associated with the client's tribe or reservation.
3. Evaluate using a client-centered listening style initially, and determine when to use more structure and questions. Try not to hurry the individual. Allow sufficient time for clients to finish statements and thoughts.
4. Assess the problem from the perspective of the individual, family, extended family, and, if appropriate, the tribal community; attempt to determine the role of cultural and experiential factors.
5. If necessary, address basic needs first, such as problems involving food, shelter, child care, and employment. Identify possible resources, such as Indian Health Services or tribal programs.
6. Be alert for problems such as domestic violence, substance abuse, depression, and suicidality during assessment.
7. Identify possible environmental contributors to problems such as racism, discrimination, poverty, and acculturation conflicts.
8. Help children and adolescents determine whether cultural values or an unreceptive environment contribute to their problem. Strategize different ways of dealing with these conflicts.
9. Help determine concrete goals that incorporate cultural, family, extended family, and community perspectives.
10. Determine whether child-rearing practices are consistent with traditional Indian methods and how they may conflict with mainstream methods.
11. In family interventions, identify extended family members, determine their roles, and request their assistance when appropriate.
12. Generate possible solutions with the client; consider the possible consequences of change from individual, family, and community perspectives. When appropriate, include strategies that may involve cultural elements and that focus on holistic factors (mind, body, spirit).

Counseling Asian Americans and Pacific Islanders

Among traditionally oriented Chinese Americans, depression is described with terms such as discomfort, pain, dizziness, or other physical symptoms, rather than as feelings of sadness. Many feel that a diagnosis of depression is "morally unacceptable" or "experientially meaningless." (Kleinman, 2004)

Calling Asian Indians the new "model minority" isn't a compliment. It's an attempt to fit them into a box for political purposes. . . . The phase "model minority" inherently pits one minority group against others. . . . After all, if one community is the "model," then the others are problematic and less desirable. (Srivastavana, 2009, p. 1)

I did not dare to talk to my parents if I have some problems because I am afraid they will feel worried about me. I see my parents work so hard, and I don't want to bother them with those problems. (Yeh, Kim, Pituc, & Atkins, 2008, p. 42)

The Asian American population is growing rapidly and, as of 2010, is currently almost 15 million, representing 5% of the total population. An additional 2,600,000 census respondents checked Asian and one other ethnic group. Native Hawaiian and other Pacific Islanders number 1.2 million and comprise 0.4% of the total population. More than half of Pacific Islanders reported multiple races (U.S. Census Bureau, 2010f). More than 60% of Asian Americans are immigrants; more than two thirds speak a language other than English at home and about 40% do not speak English "very well." In fact, with the exception of Japanese Americans, Asian American populations are now principally composed of internationally born individuals. There are about 3.8 million Asians of Chinese descent in the United States, 2.8 million Asian Indians, 1.7 million Vietnamese, 1.6 million Koreans, and 1.3 million Japanese (U.S. Census Bureau, 2010f). Between-group differences within the Asian American population are quite large, since the population is composed of at least 40 distinct subgroups that differ in language, religion, and values (Sandhu, 1997). They include the larger Asian groups in the United States (Chinese, Filipinos, Koreans, Asian Indians, and Japanese), refugees and immigrants from Southeast Asia (Vietnamese, Laotians, Cambodians, and Hmongs), and Pacific Islanders (Hawaiians, Guamanians, and Samoans). Compounding the difficulty in making any generalization about the Asian American population are within-group differences. Individuals diverge on variables such as migration and relocation experiences, degree of assimilation or acculturation, identification with the home country, facility in their native language and in English, family composition, educational background, religion, and degree of adherence to religious beliefs.

CHARACTERISTICS AND STRENGTHS

In the following section, we present some of the cultural values, behavioral characteristics, and expectations that Asian Americans might have about therapy and consider the implications of these factors in treatment. The accuracy of these group generalizations must be determined for each individual client or family.

Asian Americans: A Success Story?

The contemporary image of Asian Americans is that of a highly successful minority that has "made it" in society (Yin, 2000). Indeed, a close analysis of census data (U.S. Census Bureau, 2011) seems to support this contention. Of those over the age of 25, over half of Asian/Pacific Islanders have a bachelor's degree, versus 30% of their White counterparts; 20% have an advanced degree, compared with 10% of Whites (U.S. Census Bureau, 2011c). Additionally, Asian Americans have the lowest high school dropout rate (2%) among all racial and ethnic groups (Child Trends, 2011). Words such as *intelligent*, *hardworking*, *enterprising*, and *disciplined* are frequently applied to this population (Morrissey, 1997). The median income of Asian American families was $64,308, versus $49,445 for the U.S. population as a whole (U.S. Census Bureau, 2011d).

However, a closer analysis of the status of Asian Americans reveals disturbing contrasts with popular views of their success story. First, in terms of economics, references to the higher median income of Asian Americans do not take into account (a) the higher percentage of Asian American families having more than one wage earner, (b) between-group differences in education and income, and (c) a higher prevalence of poverty despite the higher median income (12.5% for Asian Americans and 15.1% for Pacific Islanders, versus 9.4% for non-Hispanic Whites) (U.S. Census, 2010f). Rates of poverty are particularly high among Hmong, Guamanian, Indonesian, and Cambodian immigrants (Iwasaki, 2006). Second, in the area of education, Asian Americans show a disparate picture of extraordinarily high educational attainment and a large, undereducated mass. Among the Hmong, only 40% have completed high school, and fewer than 14% of Tongan, Cambodian, Laotian, and Hmong adults have a bachelor's degree (U.S. Census Bureau, 2005a). When averaged out, this bimodal distribution indicates how misleading statistics can be.

Third, there is now widespread recognition that Chinatowns, Manilatowns, and Japantowns in San Francisco and New York represent ghetto areas with prevalent unemployment, poverty, health problems, and juvenile delinquency. People outside these communities seldom see the deplorable social conditions that exist behind the bright neon lights, restaurants, and quaint shops. Fourth, although Asian Americans underutilize mental health services, it is not clear if this is due to low rates of socioemotional difficulties, discriminatory mental health practices, or cultural values inhibiting self-referral (Asai & Kameoka, 2005; Ting & Hwang, 2009). It is possible that much of the mental illness, adjustment problems, and juvenile delinquency among Asians is hidden. The discrepancy between official and real rates of adjustment difficulties may be due to cultural factors, such as the shame and disgrace associated with admitting to emotional problems, the handling of problems within the family rather than relying on outside resources, and the manner of symptom formation, such as a low prevalence of acting-out disorders.

Fifth, Asian Americans have been exposed to discrimination and racism throughout history and continue to face anti-Asian sentiments. Even fourth- and fifth-generation Asian Americans are sometimes identified as "foreign" (D. W. Sue, Bucceri, Lin, Nadal, & Torino, 2009). In a survey of a representative sample of 1,216 adults to determine their attitudes toward Asian Americans, several disturbing findings were reported (Committee of 100, 2001). Nearly one third of respondents indicated that Chinese Americans would be more loyal to China than to the United States, and nearly half of all the people surveyed believed that Chinese Americans would pass secret information to China. About a quarter of the sample would disapprove if someone in their family married an Asian American, and 17% would be upset if a "substantial" number of Asian Americans moved into their neighborhood. Perceived racial discrimination is associated with higher psychological distress, state and trait anxiety, depression, and suicidal ideation (Hwang & Goto, 2009).

It is important for those who work with Asian Americans to look behind the success myth and to understand the historical and current experiences of Asians in America. The matter is even more pressing for counselors when we realize that Asian Americans underutilize counseling and other mental health facilities. The approach of this chapter is twofold. First, we attempt to indicate how the interplay of social and cultural forces has served to shape and define the lifestyle of recent immigrants/refugees and American-born Asians. Second, we explore how an understanding of Asian American values and social experiences suggests a need for modifications in counseling and psychotherapeutic practices when working with some members of this population.

> It is important for those who work with Asian Americans to look behind the success myth and to understand the historical and current experiences of Asians in America. The matter is even more pressing for counselors when we realize that Asian Americans underutilize counseling and other mental health facilities.

Collectivistic Orientation

> I was born and raised in Korea and came to the United States in 1968. . . . I must move back to Seoul to take care of my aging mother. I am a man of Asian values (filial piety), and my children are young college graduates of American values (career advancement and development). (Choi, 1999, p. 7)

Instead of promoting individual needs and personal identity, Asian families tend to have a family and group orientation. Children are expected to strive for family goals and not engage in behaviors that might bring dishonor to the family. Asian American parents tend to show little interest in children's viewpoints regarding family matters. Instead, the emphasis is on adherence to "correct" values, family harmony, and adapting to the needs of family members, especially elders (P. H. Chen, 2009; Rothbaum, Morelli, Pott, & Liu-Constant, 2000). Asian American adolescents appear to retain the expectation to assist, support, and respect their family even when exposed to a society that emphasizes adolescent autonomy and independence (Fuligni et al., 1999). Whereas Euro-American parents rated being "self-directed" as the most important attribute in children's social competence, Japanese American parents chose "behaves well" (O'Reilly, Tokuno, & Ebata, 1986). Chinese American parents also believed that politeness and calmness are important childhood characteristics (Jose, Huntsinger, & Liaw, 2000). Asian American families do differ, however, in the degree to which they place individual needs over family needs. For example, in the case just given, the client accepted the fact that his adult children would not return home to stay with his wife (their mother) while he was in Korea taking care of his mother. Although he decries American society, in which individualism prevails over collectivism, he acknowledges that his children have honored the family by being successful and that they define family obligations in a different manner.

Implications

Because of a possible collectivistic orientation, it is important to consider the family and community context during assessment and problem definition. It is important to be open to different family orientations and to not automatically consider interdependence as a sign of enmeshment. After doing a client-centered analysis of the problem, counselors can ask, "How does your family see the problem?" It is important to determine whether the client is aware of the effects of conflicting expectations. For traditionally oriented Asian Americans, a focus on individual client needs and wishes may run counter to the values of collectivism. Goals and treatment approaches may need to include a family focus (e.g., "How important is it for you to consult your family before deciding how to deal with the problem?" and "How would achieving your goals affect you, your family, friends, and social community?"). Questions such as these allow the therapist to assess the degree of collectivism in the family. Acculturated Asian Americans with an individualistic orientation can often benefit from traditional counseling approaches, but family issues should also be considered, since acculturation conflicts are common.

Hierarchical Relationships

Traditional Asian American families tend to be hierarchical and patriarchal in structure, with males and older individuals occupying a higher status (Kim, 2011). Communication flows downward from parents to children; children are expected to defer to their elders as a matter of obligation and duty (A. Lau, Fung, & Yung, 2010). Sons are expected to carry on the family name and tradition. Even when they marry, their primary allegiance is to the parents. Even third-generation Asian Americans feel the pressure of parental obligations (Ina, 1997). Between-group differences do exist. Japanese Americans are the most acculturated. The majority are third- or fourth-generation Americans. Filipino American families tend to be more egalitarian, whereas Korean, Southeast Asian, and Chinese American families tend to be more patriarchal and traditional in orientation (Blair & Qian, 1998).

Implications

In family therapy, it is important to determine the family structure and communication pattern. Does it appear to be egalitarian or hierarchical? Modern Chinese societies are moving toward more egalitarian relationships between husband and wife and between parents and children (Chen, 2009). If the structure is not clear, addressing the father first and then the mother may be most productive. If English is a problem, use an interpreter with the parents. Having children interpret for the parents can be counterproductive because it upsets the hierarchical structure. For very traditionally oriented families, having communication between family members directed to the therapist may be more congruent with cultural values than having family members address one another. It is also important to assess possible status changes within the family. It is not uncommon among Asian immigrants for women to retain their occupational status while men are either underemployed or unemployed. Such loss of male status may result in family conflict, particularly if males attempt to maintain their status by becoming even more authoritarian. In such cases, it may be helpful to cast societal factors as the problem that needs to be addressed.

Parenting Styles

Amy Chua, author of the book *Battle Hymn of the Tiger Mom*, raised a storm of criticism when she described her child-rearing strategies, including banning sleepovers, play dates, watching TV, or playing computer games and considering any grade less than an A as unacceptable. Her children are required to complete all of their school work and must practice their musical instruments three hours each day (One daughter, Sophia, played at Carnegie Hall at age 14 and the other daughter, Lulu, is a gifted violinist. (Corrigan, 2011)

Asian American parenting styles tend to be more authoritarian and directive than those in Euro-American families (B.Kim, 2011), although a relaxed style is often used with children younger than the age of 6 or 7 (Jose et al., 2000; Meston et al., 1999). Shame, the induction of guilt, and love withdrawal are often used to control and train the children (Lau, Fung, Wang, & Kang, 2009). Problem behavior in children is thought to be due to a lack of discipline. While praise is considered to be a valuable means of reinforcing children's behaviors, many Asian families consider instruction to be the main parenting strategy (Paiva, 2008). As one parent stated, "I don't understand why I should reward things they should already be doing. Studying hard is a normal responsibility. Listening to parents is a must. Why should they feel proud when they are merely meeting a basic obligation?" (A. Lau, 2010, p. 887). Criticism rather than praise is believed to be effective in changing behaviors. However, differences in parenting style between Asian American groups have been found. Japanese and Filipino American families tend to have the most egalitarian relationships, whereas Korean, Chinese, and Southeast Asian Americans are more authoritarian (Blair & Qian, 1998).

Implications

Egalitarian or Western-style parent-effectiveness training strategies may run counter to traditional child-rearing patterns. Traditional Asian American families exposed to Western techniques or styles may feel that their parenting skills are being criticized. Instead of attempting to establish egalitarian relationships, there can be a focus on identifying different aspects of parenting, such as teaching and modeling. The therapist can help refocus parenting to utilize the more positive aspects of Asian child-rearing strategies, framing the change as helping the children with problems rather than altering poor parenting. It is also important to commiserate with parents regarding the difficulties they encounter raising children in a society with different cultural standards.

Emotionality

> As a child, I was taught not to call attention to myself, because an upright nail gets pounded down. I was taught to be helpful and to accommodate the needs of others. I believed that the mature person was loving, kind, and kept their opinions private. (Yabusaki, 2010, p. 3)

Strong emotional displays, especially in public, are considered signs of immaturity or lack of self-control; control of emotions is considered a sign of strength (B. S. K. Kim, 2011). In many Asian families, there is generally less open display of emotions (Rothbaum et al., 2000). Instead, care and concern are shown by attending to the physical needs of family members. Fathers frequently maintain an authoritative and distant role and are not generally emotionally demonstrative or involved with children. Their role is to provide for the economic and physical needs of the family. Mothers are more responsive to the children but use less nurturance and more verbal and physical punishment than do Euro-American mothers (Kelly & Tseng, 1992). However, mothers are expected to meet the emotional needs of the children and often serve as the intermediary between the father and the children. When the children are exposed to more open displays of emotions from Western society, they may begin to question the comparative lack of emotion displayed by their parents.

Implications

Counseling techniques that focus directly on emotions may be uncomfortable and produce shame for traditional Asian Americans. Emotional behavior can be recognized in a more indirect manner. For example, if a client shows discomfort, the therapist could respond by saying either "You look uncomfortable" or "This situation would make someone uncomfortable." In both cases the discomfort would be recognized. We have found that many Asian Americans are more responsive to the second, more indirect acknowledgment of emotions. It is also helpful to focus on behaviors more than emotions and to identify how family members are meeting each other's needs. Among traditional Asian American couples, care and concern may be demonstrated by taking care of the physical needs of the partner rather than by verbally expressing concern. Western therapies that emphasize verbal and emotional expressiveness may not be appropriate in work with Asian couples or families.

Holistic View on Mind and Body

A female Asian American client described her symptoms, including dizziness, loss of appetite, an inability to complete household chores, and insomnia. She asked the therapist if her problem could be due to "nerves." The therapist suspected depression, since her symptoms included many of the physical manifestations of the disorder. She asked the client if she felt depressed and sad. At this point, the client paused and looked confused. She finally stated that she feels very ill and that these physical problems are making her sad. Her perspective was that it is natural to feel sad when sick. When the therapist followed up by asking if there was a family history of depression, the client displayed even more discomfort and defensiveness. Although the client never directly contradicted the therapist, she never returned. (Tsui & Schultz, 1985)

Because the mind and body are considered inseparable, Asian Americans may express emotional difficulties through somatic complaints (Conrad & Pacquiao, 2005; Ryder, Yang, & Heini, 2002). Physical complaints are a common and culturally accepted means of expressing psychological and emotional stress. It is believed that physical problems cause emotional disturbances and that symptoms will disappear once the physical illness is treated. Instead of mentioning anxiety or depression, Asian clients often mention headaches, fatigue, restlessness, and disturbances in sleep and appetite (Wong, Tran, Kim, Kerne, & Calfa, 2010; Yeung, Chang, Gresham, Nierenberg, & Fava, 2004). Even psychotic patients typically focus on somatic complaints and seek treatment for these physical ailments (Nguyen, 1985).

Implications

Treat somatic complaints as real problems. Inquire about medications or other treatments that may have been used to treat the symptoms. To address possible psychological factors, counselors can ask questions such as, "Dealing with headaches and dizziness can be quite troublesome; how are these affecting your mood or relationships with others?" This approach both legitimizes the physical complaints and allows an indirect way to assess psychosocial factors. It is beneficial to develop an approach that deals with both somatic complaints and the consequences of being "ill."

Academic and Occupational Goal Orientation

> I want to write. I have to write. . . . This is not the choice my parents would make, and surely not the choice they would wish me to make. . . . I must not let it deter my progress or shut down my dreams, my purpose. (Ying, Coombs, & Lee, 1999, p. 357)

There is great pressure for children to succeed academically and to have a successful career, since both are indicative of a successful upbringing. As a group, Asian Americans perform better academically than do their Euro-American counterparts. Although Asian American students have high levels of academic achievement, they also have more fear of academic failure and spend twice as much time each week studying compared with their non-Asian peers (Eaton & Dembo, 1997). Their achievement often comes with a price. Asian American adolescents report feeling isolated, depressed, and anxious and report little praise for their accomplishments from their parents (Lorenzo, Pakiz, Reinherz, & Frost, 1995). Asian American parents often have specific career goals in mind for their children (generally in technical fields or the hard sciences). Because choice of vocation may reflect parental expectations rather than personal talent, Asian college students are sometimes uncertain about realistic career options (Lucas & Berkel, 2005). Deviations from either academic excellence or "appropriate" career choices can produce conflict between family members.

Implications

Counselors can inquire about and discuss conflicts between parental academic or career goals and the client's strengths, interests, and desires. When working with parents, counselors can encourage the recognition of all positive behaviors and contributions made by their children, rather than just academic performance.

For career or occupational conflicts, counselors can acknowledge the importance parents place on their children achieving success, while indicating that there are many career options that can be considered. Differences of opinion can be presented as a culture conflict. The counselor can help the client brainstorm ways to present other possibilities to the parents. Because Asian American students often lack clarity regarding vocational interests, they may need additional career counseling assistance (Lucas & Berkel, 2005).

Cultural Strengths

Asian Americans have cultural values that have provided resiliency and strength. The family orientation provides means to achieve honor by demonstrating respect for parents and elders and supporting siblings in their endeavors. These prescriptions produce a collective support system that can shield the individual and family from sources of stress. Because the achievements and success of an individual are considered a source of pride for the family rather than the individual, group harmony is primary. The ability to reconnect with cultural traditions is provided by the presence of communities such as Chinatowns, Manilatowns, Koreatowns, and Japantowns. Enculturation or identification with racial and ethnic background can result in pride and serve as a buffer against prejudice and discrimination and family conflicts (Hwang, Woods, & Fujimoto, 2010; B. S. K. Kim, 2011). Pacific Islanders have faced a history of colonization and oppression. Despite these challenges and obstacles, cultural strengths, such as collectivity, harmony in family relationships, and respect for elders, have been important in their resilience. Pacific Islanders can rely on the community and family during times of stress (Vakalahi, 2009). Korean American college students were found to have strong cognitive flexibility. In dealing with conflicts with parents, these individuals used creative means to prevent or resolve problems in a way that accommodated traditional cultural expectations and their own personal needs (Ahn, Kim, & Park, 2009).

SPECIFIC CHALLENGES

In the following sections we consider challenges often faced by Asian Americans and consider their implications in treatment. Remember that these are generalizations and that their applicability needs to be assessed for each client.

Racial Identity Issues

> White privilege was a concept I was unaware of, even though it was intricately woven into the fabric of my life. If someone had asked me then, I would probably have said that I have not experienced racism, and I did not feel oppressed in any way. This is not to say I had not experienced racism. I just never thought of those encounters as racism because, most of the times, they were subtle. I reacted to racial microaggressions with

confusion, fear, and frustration, although I never understood my emotions. (Lo, 2010, p. 26)

As Asian Americans are progressively exposed to the standards, norms, and values of the wider U.S. society, increasing assimilation and acculturation are frequently the result. Bombarded on all sides by peers, schools, and the mass media, which uphold Western standards, Asian Americans are frequently placed in situations of extreme culture conflict and experience pain and agony regarding behavioral and physical differences (B. S. K. Kim, 2011). Asian American college women report lower self-esteem and less satisfaction with their racially defined features than do their Caucasian counterparts (Mintz & Kashubeck, 1999). C.-R. Lee (1995) described his experiences as "straddling two worlds and at home in neither" and how he felt alienated from both American and Korean cultures. As with other adolescents, those of Asian American descent also struggle with the question of "Who am I?" In the case above, Lo talks about the struggles encountered during his racial identity development. Individuals undergoing acculturation conflicts may respond in the following manner (Huang, 1994):

1. *Assimilation:* Seeking to become part of the dominant society to the exclusion one's own cultural group
2. *Separation or enculturation:* Identifying exclusively with the Asian culture
3. *Integration/biculturalism:* Retaining many Asian values while simultaneously learning the necessary skills and values for adaptation to the dominant culture
4. *Marginalization:* Perceiving one's own culture as negative but feeling inept at adapting to the majority culture

Implications

Although identity issues can be a problem for some Asian Americans, others believe that ethnic identity is not salient or important. Assessing the ethnic self-identity of clients is important because it can affect conceptualization of presenting problems and the choice of techniques used in therapy. Those who adhere to Asian values have a more negative view toward seeking counseling (Kim, 2007). Acculturated Asian American college students hold beliefs similar to those of counselors, whereas less acculturated students do not (Mallinckrodt, Shigeoka, & Suzuki, 2005). Assimilated Asian clients are generally receptive to Western styles of counseling and may not want reminders of their ethnicity. Traditionally identified Asians are more likely to be recent immigrants who retain strong cultural values and are more responsive to a culturally adapted counseling approach. Bicultural Asian Americans adhere to some traditional values, while also incorporating many Western values.

> Although identity issues can be a problem for some Asian Americans, others believe that ethnic identity is not salient or important. Assessing the ethnic self-identity of clients is important because it can affect conceptualization of presenting problems and the choice of techniques used in therapy.

Acculturation Conflicts

Children of Asian descent who are exposed to different cultural standards often attribute their psychological distress to their parents' backgrounds and different values. The issue of not quite fitting in with their peers yet being considered "too Americanized" by their parents is common. Parent-child conflicts are among the most common presenting problems for Asian American college students seeking counseling (R. M. Lee, Su, & Yoshida, 2005) and are often related to dating and marriage issues (Ahn, Kim, & Park, 2009). Chinese immigrant mothers report a larger acculturation gap with sons compared with daughters (Buki, Ma, Strom, & Strom, 2003). The larger the acculturation gap between parents and children, the greater the number of family problems. Parents may complain, "My children have lost their cultural heritage" (Hwang, Woods, & Fugimoto, 2010). The inability to resolve differences in acculturation results in misunderstandings, miscommunication, and conflict (R. M. Lee, Choe, Kim, & Ngo, 2000). Parents may feel at a loss in terms of how to deal with their children. Some respond by becoming more rigid. One Asian Indian daughter described her parents as displaying a "museumization of practices." On a trip to India, she discovered that there was a wide difference between her parents' version of "Indian" and what Indians in India actually did; her parents' version was much more restrictive (Das Gupta, 1997).

Implications

To prevent negative interpersonal exchanges between parents and their children, problems can be reframed or conceptualized as due to acculturation conflicts. In this way, both the parents and their children can discuss cultural standards and the expectations from larger society. Although family therapy would seem to be the ideal medium in which to deal with problems for Asian Americans, certain difficulties exist. Most therapy models are based on Euro-American perspectives of egalitarian relationships and require verbal and emotional expressiveness. Some models assume that a problem in a family member is reflective of dysfunction between family members. In addition, the use of direct communication between child and parents, confrontational strategies, and nonverbal techniques such as "sculpting" may be an affront to the parents.

Assess the structure of the Asian American family. Is it hierarchical or more egalitarian? What is their perception of healthy family functioning? How are decisions made in the family? How are family members showing respect for each other and contributing to the family? Focus on the positive aspects of the family and reframe conflicts to reduce confrontation. Expand systems theory to include societal factors such as prejudice, discrimination, poverty, and conflicting cultural values. Issues revolving around the pressures of being an Asian American family in this society need to be investigated. Describe the session as a solution-oriented one and explain that family problems are not uncommon. As much as possible, allow sensitive communications between family members to come through the therapist. The therapist can function as a culture broker in helping the family negotiate conflicts with the larger society.

Expectations Regarding Counseling

Because psychotherapy may be a foreign concept for some Asian Americans, it is important to carefully explain the nature of the assessment and treatment process and the necessity of obtaining personal information and information regarding family dynamics. Asian American clients may expect concrete goals and strategies focused on solutions. Even acculturated Asian American college students have a preference for the counselor to serve a helper role offering advice, consultation, and the facilitation of family and community support systems (Atkinson, Kim, & Caldwell, 1998). Mental health professionals must be careful not to impose techniques or strategies. Counselors often believe that they should adopt an authoritarian or highly directive stance with Asian American clients. What is actually expected by Asian clients is an active role by the counselor in structuring the session and guidelines on the types of responses that they will be expected to make. It can be helpful for the therapist to accept the role of being the expert regarding therapy, while the client is given the role of expert regarding his or her life. In this way clients can assist the therapist by facilitating understanding of the problem and possible means of approaching the problem (S.W.-H. Chen & Davenport, 2005).

Implications

Carefully describe the client's role in the therapy process, indicating that problems can be individual, relational, environmental, or a combination of these and that you will perform an assessment of each of these areas. Introduce the concept of *co-construction*—that in counseling, problems are identified and solutions are developed with the help of both the client and the counselor. The therapist might explain, "In counseling we try to understand the problem as it affects you, your family, friends, and community, so I will ask you questions about these different areas. With your help we will also consider possible solutions that you can try out." Co-construction reduces the chance that the therapist will impose his or her theoretical framework on the client.

The counselor should direct therapy sessions but should ensure full participation from clients in developing goals and intervention strategies. Suggestions can be given and different options presented for consideration by the client. Clients can also be encouraged to suggest their own solutions and then select the option that they believe will be the most useful in dealing with the problem. The opportunity for Asian American clients to try interventions on their own promotes the cultural value of self-sufficiency. The consequences for any actions taken should be considered, not only for the individual client, but also for the family. Focusing on specific problems brought in by clients and helping clients develop their own goals allows clients to present their concerns and reduces the chance that the therapist's worldview will be imposed on clients. The client's perspective is also important in determining what needs to be done if cultural or family issues are involved.

Therapy should be time limited, should focus on concrete resolution of problems, and should deal with the present or immediate future. Cognitive-behavioral and other solution-focused strategies are useful in working with Asian Americans (Chen & Davenport, 2005). However, as with other Euro-centric approaches, these approaches may need to be altered because the focus is on the individual, whereas the unit of treatment for Asian Americans may actually be the family, community, or society. Cognitive-behavioral approaches can be modified to incorporate a collectivistic rather than an individualistic perspective. For example, assertiveness training can be altered for Asian clients by first considering possible cultural and social factors that may affect assertiveness (e.g., values placed on modesty or minority status). Then situations where assertiveness might be functional, such as in class or when seeking employment, can be identified, as well as situations where a traditional cultural style might be more appropriate (e.g., with parents or other elders). Additionally, possible cultural or societal influences that affect social anxiety or assertiveness can be discussed. Finally, the client can practice role-playing to increase assertiveness in specific situations. This concrete alteration of a cognitive-behavioral approach considers cultural factors and allows clients to establish self-efficacy.

Racism and Discrimination

Asian Americans continue to face issues of racism and discrimination (Hwang & Goto, 2009). Very negative stereotypes of this group are still held by a large number of American adults. In a sample of 444 Chinese American adolescents, it was found that discrimination in early adolescence was related to depression, alienation, and lower academic performance in middle adolescence (Brenner & Kim, 2009). Asian Americans report significantly more workplace discrimination than do their White counterparts (M. P. Bell, Harrison, & McLaughlin, 1997). Southeast Asian refugees who experienced racial discrimination reported high rates of depression (Noh, Beiser, Kaspar, Hou, & Rummens, 1999).

Implications

A therapist must assess the effects of possible environmental factors, such as racism, on mental health issues in Asian Americans and help insure that clients not internalize issues based on discriminatory practices. Instead, the focus should be on how to deal with racism and on possible efforts to change the environment. If a problem occurs in school, the therapist can help assess the school's academic and social receptivity to Asian students. The same can be done with discriminatory practices at the client's place of employment. Intervention may have to occur at a systems level, with the therapist serving in the role of advocate for the client.

Implications for Clinical Practice

[A] one-size-fits-all approach to clinical work with Asian Americans is potentially problematic. Instead, it is important for clinicians to identify within-group differences among their Asian American clients based on their mental illness, lay beliefs, and level of enculturation. (Wong et al., 2010, p. 328)

There is a range of acceptable practices in working with Asian American clients. Qualities such as attitudinal similarity between the counselor and the Asian American client and agreement on the cause and treatment of a disorder are more important than racial match in promoting counselor credibility and the working alliance (O. Meyer, Zane, & Cho, 2011). Counselors who demonstrate multicultural competence by addressing the cultural beliefs of clients are viewed as more competent by Asian Americans (S. Wang & Kim, 2010). Helping Asian American clients formulate culturally acceptable strategies can improve their problem-solving abilities and facilitate the development of skills for successful interactions within the larger society, including balancing conflicting values. Many of the counseling skills learned in current mental health programs, such as cognitive behavioral therapies (Lau, Chan, Li, & Au, 2010), can be effective, especially if modifications are made for less acculturated clients. Considerations in working with Asian American clients include:

1. Be aware of cultural differences between the therapist and the client regarding counseling, appropriate goals, and process. Use strategies appropriate to the collectivistic, hierarchical, and patriarchal orientation of Asian Americans, when needed.
2. Build rapport by discussing confidentiality and explaining the client role, including the process of co-constructing the problem definition and solutions.
3. Identify and incorporate the client's beliefs about the etiology and appropriate treatment regarding the disorder.
4. Assess not just from an individual perspective but include family, community, and societal influences on the problem. Obtain the worldview, degree of acculturation, and ethnic identity of the Asian American client.
5. Conduct a positive assets search. What strengths, skills, problem-solving abilities, and social supports are available to the individual or family? How have problems been successfully solved in the past?
6. Consider or reframe the problem, when possible, as one involving issues of culture conflict or acculturation.
7. Determine whether somatic complaints are involved, and assess their influence on mood and relationships. Discuss somatic as well as psychological issues.
8. Take an active role, but allow Asian Americans to choose and evaluate suggested interventions. Asian Americans may prefer an immediate resolution to a problem rather than in-depth exploration.
9. Use problem-focused, time-limited approaches that have been modified to incorporate possible cultural factors.
10. Self-disclosure regarding strategies the counselor has used in the past to solve problems similar to those faced by the client can be helpful.

11. With family therapy, the therapist should be aware that Western-based theories and techniques may not be appropriate for Asian families. Determine the structure and communication patterns among the members. It may be helpful to address the father first and to initially have statements by family members directed to the therapist. Focus on positive aspects of parenting, such as modeling and teaching.

12. In couples counseling, assess for societal or acculturation conflicts, and determine their perspective on what an improved relationship would look like. Problems often occur when there are differences in acculturation among the partners. Determine the ways that caring, support, or affection is shown, including providing for economic needs.

13. With Asian children and adolescents, common problems involve acculturation conflicts with parents, feeling guilty or stressed over poor academic performance, negative self-image or identity issues, and struggles between interdependence and independence.

14. Consider the need to act as an advocate or to engage in systems-level intervention in cases of institutional racism or discrimination.

Counseling Latinos

Diane M. Sue and David Sue

I can remember having to hide when I was a kid. . . . I would come home and my parents would be maybe 20 or 30 minutes late, and I would cry until they got home because I was afraid they had been deported. (Modie, 2001, p. A6)

It was sometimes hard to adjust. When I went outside, I was in America but inside my house, it was Mexico. My father was the leader of the house. It wasn't that way for some of my American friends. (Middleton, Arrendondo, & D'Andrea, 2000, p. 24)

Jennifer Cortes received the panicked call just after 11 A.M. Immigration officers were at Bellingham's Northwest Health Care Linen where her husband, Ezequiel Rosas-Cortes, worked sorting laundry. . . . Agents turned Jennifer away as they arrested her husband, an illegal immigrant. (Gambrell, 2006, p. A1)

A thick scar below his right elbow reminds him of his first days in the fields, when he slipped and fell on some sharp farming tools. . . . Like many farmworker children, Gonzales went to work to help his family pay the bills. He was a good student until he dropped out at age 15. He hasn't given up hope . . . but his family comes first. (Kramer, 1998, p. A6)

In this chapter, we use the term *Latino/a* in reference to individuals living in the United States with ancestry from Mexico, Puerto Rico, Cuba, the Dominican Republic, and Central or South American Spanish-speaking counties. However, Latino/a is only one of many terms used for self-identification by members of this population. For example, more than half of the Latino/a youth (ages 16 to 25) in one sample self-identified first by their family's country of origin (i.e., Mexican, Cuban), while approximately 20% self-identified as "Hispanic" or "Latino/a," and 24% self-identified as "American." Among youth who are third-generation or higher, about half chose "American" as their first term of self-description (Pew Research Center, 2009). The U.S. Census uses the term *Hispanic* as an ethnic descriptor rather than the term *Latino/a*.

Throughout Latin America, the immigration of European, African, and Asian populations and subsequent mixture with indigenous groups has resulted in a wide range of phenotypes. Thus, the physical traits of Latinos vary greatly and include characteristics of indigenous groups, Blacks, Asians, and fair-skinned Europeans. Latinos are currently the largest minority group in the United States, comprising 16.3% of the total U.S. population. Because of immigration patterns and high birthrates (one in four infants born in the United States is Latino/a), more than half of the growth in the total U.S. population between 2000 and 2010 resulted from increases in the Latino/a population. According to the U.S. Census, there are 50.5 million Hispanic Americans, of whom 63% are of Mexican origin, 9.2% from Puerto Rico or of Puerto Rican descent, 3.5% have Cuban ancestry, and 16% originate from Central and South America (2011d).

Approximately 37% of Latinos are immigrants; about 11% of foreign-born Latinos have become U.S. citizens. Approximately one fourth of Latino/a adults are undocumented immigrants; about two thirds of all undocumented immigrants are from Mexico (Marrero, 2011). It is not surprising that half of all Latino/a American adults express concern that they, a family member, or a close friend will be deported (Pew Hispanic Center, 2007). Those who are undocumented occupy the lowest rung of the labor pool and are often taken advantage of because they have no legal status.

Although Latino/a groups share many characteristics, there are many between-group and within-group differences. Many are strongly oriented toward their ethnic group, whereas others are quite acculturated to mainstream values. About three-fourths of U.S.-born Latinos are third-generation or higher, with many descended from the large wave of Latin Americans who began immigrating in the 1960s. In certain states and cities Latinos make up a substantial percentage of the population. Mexican Americans are the dominant Latino/a group in metropolitan areas throughout the United States. Most Puerto Ricans reside in the Northeast, and most Cubans live in Florida (Lopez & Dockterman, 2011).

Approximately 41% of the adult Latino/a population have no official high school diploma (Fry, 2010). About 14% of Latinos have a bachelor's degree or higher; however, 21% have less than a ninth-grade education (U.S. Census Bureau, 2011d). Median wealth of non-Latino White households is 18 times that of Latino households (Pew Hispanic Center, 2011). Latinos are overrepresented among the poor, have high unemployment, and often live in substandard housing. Many hold semiskilled or unskilled occupations (U.S. Census Bureau, 2010a). Latino/a household wealth fell 66% from 2005 to 2009 (from a median of $18,359 to $6,234), primarily because many Latinos live in states severely affected by the housing crisis (Pew Hispanic Center, 2011).

CHARACTERISTICS AND STRENGTHS

In the following sections we consider the characteristics, values, and strengths of Latino/a individuals and consider their implications in treatment. These are generalizations and their applicability needs to be assessed for each client or family.

Cultural Values and Characteristics

The development and maintenance of interpersonal relationships are central to the Latino/a culture (Dingfelder, 2005; Hernandez, Garcia, & Flynn, 2010; Kuhlberg, Pena, & Zayas, 2010). There is typically deep respect and affection among a large network of family and friends. Family unity, respect, and tradition (*familismo*) are an important aspect of life for Latinos. Cooperation among family members is stressed. For many Latinos, the extended family includes not only relatives but also close friends and godparents. Each member of the family has a role: grandparents (wisdom), mother (self-denial), father (responsibility), children (obedience), and godparents (resourcefulness) (Lopez-Baez, 2006; P. Ruiz, 1995).

Implications

Familismo refers not only to family cohesiveness and interdependence but also to loyalty and placing the needs of close friends and family members before personal needs (Baumann, Kuhlberg, & Zayas, 2010). Counselors can inquire about clients' connectedness with extended and nuclear family members and the value placed on *familismo*. Because of these strong familial and social relationships, Latinos often wait until resources from extended family and close friends are exhausted before seeking help. Even in cases of severe mental illness, many Latinos wait months before obtaining assistance (Urdaneta, Saldana, & Winkler, 1995).

Although there are many positive features of the extended family, emotional involvement and obligations with numerous family and friends can function as a source of stress, particularly when decisions are made that impact the individual negatively (Aguilera, Garza, & Munoz, 2010). Problem definition may need to incorporate the perspectives of both nuclear and extended family members, and solutions may need to bridge cultural expectations and societal demands. Additionally, family responsibilities sometimes take precedence over outside concerns, such as school attendance or work obligations (Avila & Avila, 1995; C. G. Franklin & Soto, 2002). For example, older children may be kept home to care for ill siblings, attend family functions, or work (Headden, 1997; Hildebrand, Phenice, Gray, & Hines, 1996). Under these circumstances, problematic behaviors (i.e., absenteeism) can be addressed by framing them as a conflict between cultural and societal expectations.

Family Structure

Latinos often live in households having five or more members (U.S. Census Bureau, 2010e). Traditional Latino/a families are hierarchical in form, with special authority given to parents, older family members, and males. Within the family, sex roles are clearly delineated. The father is typically the primary authority figure (Lopez-Baez, 2006). Children are expected to be obedient and are typically not involved in family decisions; parents may expect adolescents to work to help meet family financial obligations (Lefkowitz, Romo, Corona, Au, & Sigman, 2000). Parents reciprocate by providing for children through young adulthood and even after marriage. This type of reciprocal relationship is a lifelong expectation. Older children are expected to care for and protect their younger siblings; older sisters often function as surrogate mothers. The sexual behaviors of adolescent females are severely restricted, whereas male children are afforded greater freedom. Marriage and parenthood often occur early in life and are viewed as stabilizing influences. Also, in traditionally oriented Latino/a marriages, emphasis is placed on social activities involving extended family and friends rather than on activities as a couple (Negy & Woods, 1992).

Implications

Assessment of family structure should consider the family hierarchy and how decisions are made within the family unit. Conflicts among family members often involve differences in acculturation and conflicting views of roles and expectations for family members, as well as clashes between cultural values and mainstream societal expectations (Baumann, Kuhlberg, & Zawas, 2010). In less acculturated families, counselors may find success by helping family members reframe these issues as responses to acculturation stress; they can then negotiate conflicting cultural norms and values (Szapocznik & Kurtines, 1993). Counselors can help clients consider ways in which they can demonstrate their allegiance to the family without significantly compromising their own acculturation. One such approach is demonstrated in the following case:

> During family therapy, a Puerto Rican mother indicated to her son, "You don't care for me anymore. You used to come by every Sunday and bring the children. You used to respect me and teach your children respect. Now you go out and work, you say, always doing this or that. I don't know what spirit [que diablo] has taken over you." (Inclan, 1985, p. 332)

In response, the son explained that he was sacrificing and working hard because he wanted to be a successful provider and someone of whom his children could be proud. The son has adopted future-oriented, mainstream U.S. values, stressing hard work and individual achievement. The mother was disappointed because she believed her son should spend time with her, encourage the family to gather together, and prioritize the family over individual desires. This clash in values was at the root of the problem. In working with this family, the therapist provided alternative ways of viewing the conflict. He explained how our views are shaped by the values that we hold. He asked the mother about her socialization and early childhood values. The son expressed how difficult it was to lose his parents' respect but also his belief that he needed to work hard and focus on the future in order to succeed in the United States. The therapist pointed out that different adaptive styles may be necessary for different situations and that what "works best" may be dependent on the social context. Both mother and son acknowledged that they demonstrate love and affection in different ways. As a result of the sessions, mother and son better understood the nature of their conflicts and were able to improve their relationship.

Gender Role Expectations

Latinos often experience conflicts over gender roles. In traditional Latino/a culture, men are expected to be strong, dominant, and the provider for the family (*machismo*), whereas women are expected to be nurturant, submissive to the male, and self-sacrificing (*marianismo*). As head of the family, the father expects family members to be obedient. Individuals with greater ethnic identity are more likely to subscribe to traditional male and female roles (Abreu, Goodyear, Campos, & Newcomb, 2000). Areas of possible gender role conflict for males (especially among immigrants) include (Avila & Avila, 1995; Constantine, Gloria, & Baron, 2006):

1. *Lack of confidence in areas of authority:* Latino men may lack confidence interacting with agencies and individuals outside of the family; this can result in feelings of inadequacy and concern about diminished authority, especially if the wife or children are more fluent in English.
2. *Feelings of isolation and depression because of the need to be strong:* Talking about concerns or stressors may be seen as a sign of weakness. This difficulty discussing feelings can produce isolation and anger or depression.
3. *Conflicts over the need to be consistent in his role:* As ambiguity and stress increase, there may be more rigid adherence to traditional roles.

For women, conflicts may involve (a) expectations associated with traditional roles, (b) anxiety or depression over not being able to live up to these standards, and (c) inability to express feelings of anger (Lopez-Baez, 2006; Zanipatin, Welch, Yi, & Bardina, 2005). Latina immigrants are often socialized to feel inferior and to expect suffering or martyrdom. With greater exposure to the dominant culture, such views may be questioned. Certain roles may change more than others. Some women may be very modern in their views regarding education and employment but remain traditional in the area of sexual behavior and personal relationships. Others remain very traditional in all areas.

Many Latinas assert their influence indirectly and "behind the scenes," thus preserving the appearance of male control (L. L. Hayes, 1997). Acculturation can increase role conflict. For example, in families where both husband and wife are acculturated, there may be less avoidance of conflict and more open expression of feelings during arguments (Flores, Tschann, Marin, & Pantoja, 2004). Some caution that Latino/a gender roles may be misunderstood and are not as negative, inflexible, or rigid as they are sometimes described. For example, the concept of *machismo* includes being a good provider; additionally egalitarian decision making appears to be increasing among more acculturated Latinos (G. M. Gonzalez, 1997).

Implications

Therapists should explore the client's degree of adherence to traditional gender norms, as well as the gender role views among family members (Andrés-Hyman,

> Counselors must be able to help the family, especially males, deal with the anxiety associated with role change. When dealing with gender role conflicts, counselors who believe in equal relationships must be careful not to impose their views on clients.

Ortiz, Añez, Paris, & Davidson, 2006). It is important to consider the potential impact of acculturation on marital relationships, particularly when women function independently in the work setting or when dealing with schools and other agencies. For both males and females, role conflict is likely to occur if the male is unemployed, if the female is employed, or both. Counselors must be able to help the family, especially males, deal with the anxiety associated with role change. When dealing with gender role conflicts, counselors who believe in equal relationships must be careful not to impose their views on clients. Instead, if a Latina client desires greater independence, the counselor can help her consider the consequences of change, including potential problems within her family and community, and work toward this goal within a cultural framework. It is helpful to frame conflicts in gender roles as an external issue involving differing expectations between cultural and mainstream values and to encourage problem solving to deal with the different sets of expectations.

Spiritual and Religious Values

> Mrs. Lopez, age 70, and her 30-year-old daughter sought counseling because they had a very conflictual relationship. . . . The mother was not accustomed to a counseling format. . . . At a pivotal point in one session, she found talking about emotional themes overwhelming and embarrassing. . . . In order to reengage her, the counselor asked what resources she used when she and her daughter quarreled. She . . . prayed to Our Lady of Guadalupe. (Zuniga, 1997, p. 149)

The therapist subsequently employed a culturally adapted strategy of having Mrs. Lopez use prayer and spiritual guidance to understand her daughter and to find solutions to their conflicts. The use of a cultural perspective allowed the sessions to continue. Religion (often, but not always, Catholicism) is important to many Latinos. Prayers requesting guidance from patron saints can be a source of comfort in times of stress. Latinos often believe that life's misfortunes are inevitable and feel resigned to their fate (*fatalismo*). Consequently, Latinos may take a seemingly passive approach to problems and lack experience assertively addressing challenges. Also, some Latino/a groups believe that evil spirits cause mental health problems and rely on indigenous healing practices.

Implications

During assessment, it is important to consider religious or spiritual beliefs, including exploration of the spiritual meanings of presenting problems

(Andrés-Hyman et al., 2006). If there is a strong belief in fatalism, instead of attempting to change this view, the therapist can acknowledge this attitude and help the individual or family determine the most adaptive response to the situation. A therapist might say, "Given that the situation is unchangeable, how can you and your family deal with this?" in an attempt to have the client develop problem-solving skills within certain parameters. The strong reliance on religion can be a resource (e.g., evoking God's support through prayer to facilitate problem solving). Fatalism can be countered by stressing *"Ayudate, que Dios te ayudara,"* which is the equivalent of "God helps those who help themselves" (Organista, 2000). Indigenous healing practices can also be incorporated into the therapeutic process.

Educational Characteristics

Peer pressure to drop out can be nearly overwhelming in the Latino/a community, as DeAnza Montoya, a pretty Santa Fe teen, can attest. In her neighborhood, it was considered "anglo" and "nerdy" to do well in school. . . . "In school they make you feel like a dumb Mexican," she says, adding that such slights only bring Latinos closer together. (Headden, 1997, p. 64)

Many Latino/a students do not fare well in the public school system. Latino/a students have increased likelihood of dropping out of school; this is particularly true among first-generation (immigrant) youth and those who are third-generation or higher (Pew Research Center, 2009). In 2009, 18% of Latinos (ages 16 to 24) were not enrolled in school and had not completed high school (Child Trends, 2011). Approximately 41% of Latino/a adults do not have a regular high school diploma, including 52% of those who are foreign-born. Additionally, the vast majority (90%) of Latinos who drop out of high school never attain a General Educational Development (GED) credential and thus are not eligible to attend college or vocational programs or to enter the military (Fry, 2010).

A number of problems contribute to the high dropout rate of Latino/a students. Educational difficulties are sometimes related to limited English proficiency. Spanish is the primary language spoken in over half of Latino/a households; others speak Spanish on a more limited basis. Although most second-generation Latinos are bilingual (exposed to Spanish in the home and to English in school), their command of both English and Spanish may be marginal. The high pregnancy rate for Latina girls also contributes to school dropout rates. Although teen pregnancy among 15- to 19-year-old Latinas is decreasing, the birth rate (70 live births per 1,000 in this age group) is significantly higher than other groups (Hamilton, Martin, & Ventura, 2009). However, there is some optimism regarding education. Between 1993 and 2003, the college enrollment of Latino/a students rose nearly 70% (D. Hayes,

2006). Additionally, many Latino/a youth value education and are optimistic about the future (Pew Research Center, 2009).

Implications

Although teachers often attempt to accommodate Latino/a cultural learning styles and adapt lessons for students with limited English skills, the move against bilingual education and the rapid immersion of Spanish-speaking students in English can exacerbate academic difficulties. Also, Latino/a students are sometimes placed in special education classes merely because of poor English skills and the use of tests not standardized for Spanish-speaking populations (Middleton et al., 2000). Many immigrant parents do not realize they have the right to question school decisions. Difficulty communicating with Spanish-speaking parents compounds the problem. Some are unable to attend conferences because of work requirements, and this may be interpreted as a lack of caring about the child's education. To engage parents, conferences can be scheduled at flexible hours and interpreters made available. Face-to-face communication or other personal contact is more successful than written material (even if written in Spanish) since many parents have limited Spanish literacy skills. Trust develops slowly, and it is important to identify and support the family's strengths rather than focusing on its shortcomings (Espinosa, 1997). Altering instructional strategies to fit cultural values (i.e., cooperation) is also important.

Cultural Strengths

> Asked how she persevered against the odds, Cinthya speaks with emotion about her family. "It's my parents," she said. "They have sacrificed so much to give us the opportunity to go to school, to grow." (New Journalism on Latino Children, 2010, p. 1)

Cinthya grew up in poverty. She is now attending Columbia University working on her public health degree. She credits her success to her family. Most Latino/a children grow up in two-parent families, often supported by a strong kinship system. *Familismo* and the related sense of connectedness and loyalty among immediate and extended family can be a source of significant social and emotional support for individuals and families (Hernadez, Garcia, & Flynn, 2010; Kuhlberg, Pena, & Zayas, 2010). Traditional Latino/a values place a great deal of emphasis on creating a harmonious atmosphere and accord within the family system. *Personalismo* refers to a personalized communication style that is characterized by interactions that are respectful, interdependent, and cooperative. *Simpatico* refers to the relational style displayed by many Latinos—a style emphasizing social harmony and a gracious, hospitable, and personable atmosphere (Holloway, Waldrip, & Ickes, 2009). Many Latino/a individuals have a strong system of spiritual and religious beliefs; their faith can be nurtured as a source of strength when dealing with personal or family issues (Andrés-Hyman et al., 2006).

SPECIFIC CHALLENGES

In the following sections we consider challenges often faced by Latino/a individuals and consider their implications in treatment. Remember that these are generalizations and that their applicability needs to be assessed for each client.

Stigma Associated With Mental Illness

Depressive symptoms are common among Latinas, with 53% reporting moderate to severe symptoms versus 37% of White women (Diaz-Martinez, Interian, & Waters, 2010). Mexican-American males and Puerto Ricans of both genders have high rates of weekly alcohol consumption and binge-drinking; additionally, alcoholism among Latinos is more likely to be chronic (Chartier & Caetano, 2010). Statistics such as these confirm the need for mental health support among Latinos. However, the cultural stigma associated with mental illness, including fear that psychiatric medications can cause addiction, results in reluctance to seek treatment. Latino/a immigrants are also more likely to fear embarrassment or social discrimination from family, friends, and employers if they acknowledge psychological distress and are more likely to express psychological distress via somatic symptoms.

"When Latinos think of mental illness, they just think one thing: *loco*," says Clara Morato, whose son, Rafaelo, was diagnosed with bipolar disorder at age 18 (Dichoso, 2010, p. 1). *Machismo* may also be a barrier to seeking treatment due to concerns about lost time from work (Vega, Rodriguez, & Ang, 2010). Additionally, Latinos underutilize resources for their children. Although most young children are citizens, one or both parents may be undocumented and, therefore, reluctant to seek assistance (Capps et al., 2005).

Implications

Clinicians can anticipate and help counteract the stigma associated with mental illness by taking the time to build rapport and provide psychoeducation about therapeutic approaches (Vega, Rodriguez, & Ang, 2010). Comas-Diaz (2010), a Puerto Rican multicultural therapist, advocates exploring the client's heritage, history of cultural translocation, and views about counseling early in therapy and encourages a flexible therapeutic style that might include roles familiar to the client, such as

> Developing a culturally relevant therapeutic alliance, providing psychoeducation about how treatment is conducted and how goals are developed in a collaborative manner, and using a flexible, culture-centered approach can help clients overcome stigma associated with seeking help and reluctance to participate openly in treatment.

healer, advisor, coach, teacher, guide, advocate, consultant, and mentor. Developing a culturally relevant therapeutic alliance, providing psychoeducation about how treatment is conducted and how goals are developed in a collaborative manner, and using a flexible, culture-centered approach can help clients overcome stigma associated with seeking help and reluctance to participate openly in treatment.

Acculturation Conflicts

As with many ethnic minority groups, Latinos are frequently faced with societal values that may be distinctly different from their own. Additionally, the severing of ties to family and friends, the loss of supportive resources, language inadequacy, unemployment, and culture conflict all function as stressors for recent immigrants (Hovey, 2000). Some maintain their traditional orientation, whereas others assimilate and exchange their native cultural practices and values for those of the host culture. Differences in acculturation between family members can produce stress within the family unit as seen in the following case:

> Juan, a 46-year-old Latino, was born in Mexico and has lived in the United States for 10 years. He works as a cook, has been married for over 20 years, and has five children. Juan has frequent conflicts with his wife and children, believing that they want freedom from him and that they have become too "Americanized." He strongly believes in the cultural values of *familismo* (family connectedness), *machismo* (being head of the family, with responsibility for providing for the family), and *respeto* (respect) from his children. As husband and father, he believes that he should set the rules in the family and that his wife and children should respect his rules. Juan often feels stressed, angry, hopeless, and depressed and has had suicidal thoughts and thoughts of hurting his wife. When angry, he resorts to threats and physical violence. (Santiago-Rivera et al., 2008)

Juan's therapist recognized that traditional cognitive-behavior therapy (an evidence-based treatment for depression) might not adequately address the environmental stressors, acculturation conflicts, and feeling of isolation and powerlessness Juan was experiencing. Instead, the therapist modified another evidence-based treatment (behavioral activation therapy). He encouraged Juan to participate in free or low-cost activities (e.g., socializing with and attending church services with his wife and children), thus enhancing family relationships and building social networks within the community. Differences between Juan's upbringing in Mexico and the American culture faced by his children were also discussed in therapy, increasing Juan's understanding of issues faced by his wife and children. At the end of therapy, Juan was no longer depressed and reported improved relationships with his wife and children (Santiago-Rivera et al., 2008).

Those who either completely reject or accept the values of the host culture appear to experience greater stress (Miville, Koonce, Darlington, & Whitlock,

2000). Miranda and Umhoefer (1998a, 1998b) found that both highly and minimally acculturated Mexican Americans score high on social dysfunction, alcohol consumption, and acculturative stress. They concluded that a bicultural orientation (i.e., maintaining some components of the native culture while incorporating practices and beliefs of the host culture) may be the "healthiest" resolution for acculturation; those with bicultural values are able to accept and negotiate aspects of both cultures. Some of the issues involved in acculturation conflict are evident in the following case:

> A Latino teenager, Mike, was having difficulty knowing "who he was" or what group he belonged with. His parents had given him an Anglo name to ensure his success in American society. They only spoke to him in English because they were fearful that he might have an accent. During his childhood, he felt estranged from his relatives because his grandparents, aunts, and uncles could speak only Spanish. At school, he did not fit in with his non-Latino peers, but also felt different from the Mexican American students who would ask him why he was unable to speak Spanish. Mike's confusion over his ethnic identity resulted in significant distress. (Avila & Avila, 1995)

During their early teen years, Latino/a children begin to have questions about their identity and whether they should adhere to mainstream or traditional values. Few role models exist for Latino/a children. The representation of Latinos on English-language channels often involves characters who behave criminally or are violent. The mixed heritage of many Latino/a Americans raises additional identity questions. Should those of Mexican heritage call themselves "Mexican," "American," "Mexican American," "Chicano," "Latino," or "Hispanic"? What about those with indigenous, Asian, or African ancestry? An ethnic identity provides a sense of belonging and group membership. Many Latino/a youngsters undergo the process of searching for an identity. This struggle in combination with acculturative stresses may be responsible for findings such as:

1. Among Latino/a adolescents, length of time living in the United States is associated with lower self-esteem. Parent-adolescent conflict is a strong risk factor for internalizing symptoms and lowered self-esteem, particularly among more acculturated adolescents whose families demonstrate minimal focus on *familismo*, the importance of family ties (Smokowski, Rose, & Bacallao, 2010).

2. Latino/a adolescents have a higher risk of behaviors such as alcohol, tobacco, and other substance use; aggressive behavior; and suicide (Smokowski, Rose, & Bacallao, 2010). Latino/a children born in the United States have higher rates of delinquency and substance use and are more likely than immigrant youth to carry a weapon, be gang associated, or imprisoned (Pew Research Center, 2009).

3. Latina adolescents have the highest rate of attempted suicide of any other adolescent group, with 15% reporting attempted suicide (Baumann, Kuhlberg, & Zayas, 2010).

4. Experimentation with inhalants is increasing among low-income Latino youth (Ding, Chang, & Southerland, 2009). Latino adolescents have the highest rate of drug use of any subgroup (Johnston, O'Malley, Bachman, & Schulenberg, 2010). Latino students report minimal concern about potential negative consequences of substance use and less confidence using refusal skills (R. A. Shih, Miles, Tucker, Zhou, & D'Amico, 2010). Stress related to acculturation appears to be a significant factor in alcohol-use patterns for Latinos (Chartier & Caetano, 2010).

Implications

The client's degree of acculturation has important implications for treatment, especially during initial therapy sessions, and can influence both perceptions of and responses to counseling. For example, Latinos with minimal acculturation may have difficulty being open and self-disclosing or discussing their issues in depth and may believe that counseling will take only one session (Dittman, 2005). The therapeutic alliance can be enhanced by beginning the counseling relationship in a more formal manner and working to build trust before comprehensive exploration of the presenting problem or extensive interviewing regarding sensitive topics. Discussion of preferences for a female or a male provider can also be discussed during the initial session (Andrés-Hyman et al., 2006).

Acculturation can be assessed by inquiring about the client's background, generational status, residential history, reasons for immigration, primary language, religious orientation and strength of religious beliefs, the extent of extended family support, and other information related to acculturation. The therapist needs to determine the degree of adherence both to traditional values and to those of the majority culture (Dingfelder, 2005). Second-generation Latino/a Americans are often marginal in both native and majority cultures. They are often bilingual (exposed to Spanish at home and English at school) but frequently have less-than-optimal use of either language.

Ethnic identity issues should be recognized and incorporated during assessment and treatment for Latino/a youth and adults. Conflicts between mainstream values and ethnic group values can be discussed, and clients can help brainstorm methods for bridging these differences. It should be stressed that ethnic identity is part of the normal development process. In many cases, a bicultural perspective may be the most functional, since such a perspective does not involve the wholesale rejection of either culture.

Counselors should also inquire about potential acculturations conflicts, including their impact on client symptoms or family conflicts. Identification with core cultural values appears to serve as a protective factor and source of strength for Latino/a children and adolescents (Dettlaff & Johnson, 2011). However, although values such as *familismo* can be a source of strength for youth, distress may feel unbearable when there is parent-child discord (Hernandez, Garcia, & Flynn, 2010).

Research attempting to identify the risk factors accounting for the high incidence of suicide attempts among Latinas, particularly among girls whose mothers place high value on *familismo*, suggests that although *familismo* can be a protective factor with respect to emotional and behavioral health, conflicts that result from adolescent strivings for autonomy and resultant parent-child conflict can be a risk factor, particularly for those accustomed to close parent-child relationships and harmony in the family unit (Kuhlberg, Pena, & Zayas, 2010). Adolescents may question family obligations and parental rules and viewpoints and desire input into decisions. Such behavior may be viewed as disrespectful by parents and extended family.

Females may feel overprotected by parents and question rules or expectations, such as staying at home to care for others and being monitored on dates or forbidden to date; such acculturation conflict may be particularly distressing to girls, since gender socialization for females emphasizes their role in maintaining harmonious relationships. Both biculturalism and *familismo* are related to higher self-esteem and greater flexibility in negotiating both cultures among Latino/a adolescents (Smokowski, Rose, & Bacallao, 2010). Effective interventions for parent-child conflict include enhancing bicultural understanding and promoting adaptive interpersonal behaviors (e.g., improved communication, increased parental affection, and emotional connection) (Kuhlberg, Pena, & Zayas, 2010).

Racism and Discrimination

Arizona state law allows the state superintendent of Public Education to disallow any ethnic studies class that "promotes resentment towards a race or class of people . . . (or) advocates ethnic solidarity instead of treatment of pupils as individuals. (Martinez & Guitierrez, 2010, p. 1)

Because of the anti-immigration rhetoric, Latinos are now seen as the ethnic group suffering from the most discrimination. Almost 80 percent of Latinos believe that there is "a lot" or "some" discrimination against their group. (Pew Research Center, 2010b)

Stressors such as racism and discrimination can lead to emotional difficulties, particularly when combined with acculturation conflicts (Gee, Ryan, Laflamme, & Holt, 2006). Sociopolitical factors such as anti-immigration sentiment affect not only Latino/a immigrants but also Latinos whose families have resided in the United States for many generations. Legislators in Arizona and Alabama recently enacted some of the broadest measures against undocumented immigrants in U.S. history. Such recent legislation includes making it a crime for noncitizens to be without documents (i.e., a visa or immigration forms) authorizing their presence in the United States and requiring law enforcement officers and other officials (including school personnel) to verify immigration status. These laws (supported by the majority of U.S. citizens) have been heavily criticized for promoting racial profiling.

Additionally, Arizona has implemented a state law banning any ethnic studies classes that "advocate ethnic solidarity instead of treatment of pupils as individuals" and instructors with "heavy accents" teaching English classes (Martinez & Gutierrez, 2010; Navarette, 2011). Latino/a adolescents are particularly vulnerable to the effects of acculturation conflict and societal racism. In a national poll, 16% of Latino/a Americans indicated that prejudice was the most important issue facing them (Krupin, 2001). Perceived discrimination among Mexican American adolescents increased psychological distress and such behaviors as drug use, fights, and sexual promiscuity (Flores, Tschann, Dimas, Pasch, & de Groat, 2010). Many youth attempt to deal with family distress, discrimination, and feelings of hopelessness by involvement in gang activities (Baca & Koss-Chioino, 1997).

Implications

Clinicians must assess not only intrapsychic issues but also the degree to which external conditions are involved in mental health issues. Thus, it is important to be sensitive to sociopolitical issues (e.g., anti-immigrant sentiments) and client experiences with disenfranchisement and discrimination (Andrés-Hyman et al., 2006). For example, highly educated Latinos report demoralizing situations in which their academic success is questioned or they are assumed to be less qualified than they actually are (Rivera, Forquer, & Rangel, 2010). Additionally, many clients may be dealing with issues related to unemployment and poverty, including stressful interactions with bureaucracies (Vasquez, 1997).

Careful assessment of the source of emotional distress is necessary before appropriate action can be taken. This should be done early in the treatment process, as illustrated by the case of a migrant worker in his mid-50s who was fearful of leaving his home because he heard threatening voices. In working with him, A. Ruiz (1981) initiated an analysis of possible external causes, suggesting that the client undergo a complete physical examination, with special attention to exposure to pesticides and other agricultural chemicals that might result in mental symptoms. Additionally, interviews revealed that the client was quite anxious due to fears of deportation, suspiciousness of outside authorities, and recent encounters with creditors.

Linguistic Issues

Considerable evidence suggests that assessment results can be influenced by linguistic differences or misunderstandings. Assessments should always be conducted in the primary language of the client and interpreted within a sociocultural context.

Implications

It is essential that clinicians consider the validity of tests for Latino/a clients and the influence of cultural or social factors as well as language barriers, discrimination, immigration stress, and poverty (H. M. González et al., 1997). Because of the lack of bilingual counselors, problems in diagnosis can occur with clients who are not proficient in English. For example, Marcos (1973) reported that Mexican American clients were considered to have greater psychopathology when interviewed in English than when interviewed in Spanish. However, interpreters themselves may present difficulties in the counseling process, such as distortions in communication.

Implications for Clinical Practice

Several writers (Andres-Hyman et al., 2006; Bean, Perry, & Bedell, 2001; Paniagua, 1994; P. Ruiz, 1995; Velasquez et al., 1997) have made suggestions about initial counseling sessions with Latino/a clients.

1. Assess the acculturation level of the client and family members and modify your interactions and assessment accordingly.
2. It is important to engage in a respectful, warm, and mutual introduction with the client. Less acculturated clients may expect a more formal relationship and see the counselor as an authority figure. Paniagua (1994) recommends interviewing the father for a few minutes during the beginning of the first session, showing recognition of the father's authority and sensitivity to cultural factors in counseling.
3. Determine whether a translator is needed. Be careful not to interpret slow speech or long silences as indicators of depression or cognitive dysfunction. The client may be struggling with English communication skills.
4. Give a brief description of what counseling is and the role of each participant. Such information is particularly important for less acculturated clients, who may expect to meet for only one or two sessions or expect that medication will be prescribed.
5. Explain the notion of confidentiality. Even immigrants with legal status have inquired about whether the information shared during counseling would "end up in the hands of the Border Patrol or other immigration authorities" (Velasquez et al., 1997, p. 112). Immigrant families may also be uncertain about the limits of confidentiality, especially as it applies to child abuse or neglect issues. Physical discipline is used in some Latino/a families. Parents may be fearful about how their child-rearing practices will be perceived.
6. Have clients state in their own words the problem or problems as they see them. Determine the possible influence of religious or spiritual beliefs. Use paraphrasing to summarize the problem as you understand it and make sure that the client knows you understand it.
7. Consider whether there are cultural or societal aspects to the problem. What are the impacts of racism, poverty, and acculturative stress on the problem?
8. Determine the positive assets and resources available to the client and his or her family. Have they, other family members, or friends dealt with similar problems?
9. Help the clients prioritize the problems and determine what they perceive as important goals. What are their expectations? How will they know when the goals have been achieved?
10. Discuss possible negative consequences of achieving the indicated goals for the individual, family, and community.

(continued)

(continued)

11. Discuss the possible participation of family members in therapy. Within the family, determine the hierarchical structure, as well as the degree of acculturation of the different members.

12. Assess possible problems from external sources, such as the need for food, shelter, or employment or stressful interactions with agencies. Provide necessary assistance in developing and maintaining environmental supports.

13. Explain the treatment to be used, why it was selected, and how it will help achieve the goals (culturally adapted evidence-based therapies for Latinos should be considered). Consistently evaluate the client's or family's response to the therapeutic approach you have chosen.

14. With the client's input, determine a mutually agreeable length of treatment. It is better to offer time-limited, solution-based therapies.

15. Remember that *personalismo* is a basic cultural value for many Latinos. Although initial meetings may be quite formal, once trust has developed, clients often develop a close personal bond with the counselor, may treat the counselor as a close friend or family member, and may give gifts or extend invitations to family functions. These behaviors are culturally based and not evidence of dependency or a lack of boundaries.

Counseling Individuals of Multiracial Descent

Hector is a 16-year-old boy whose mother is European American and whose father immigrated to the United States from Mexico. Hector was referred for counseling because he was acting out in school and making frequent racist remarks. He appeared to be White and openly claimed only his White identity. . . . He frequently joked about "Mexicans." Hector admitted that although he knew he made racist remarks, he did not like strangers to make derogatory comments about Mexicans or Mexican Americans. (McDowell et al., 2005, p. 408)

"I feel like she's black. I'm black and I'm her mother, and I believe in the one-drop theory. . . . " Halle Berry, whose mother is Caucasian, is speaking about her own daughter. Halle Berry self-identified as Black on the U.S. Census, as did President Barack Obama, whose mother was also of White European ancestry. (S. L. Brown, 2011)

An adult male of Latino/Middle Eastern descent tried to organize a university celebration of El Dia de los Muertos (Day of the Dead), a holiday during which Mexican families remember the dead and the continuity of life. In doing so, he received responses such as "Why are you doing that?" I'm like, because it comes from my culture. And they just look at me and they're like, "What exactly are you?" (Miville, Constantine, Baysden, & So-Lloyd, 2005, p. 511)

Multiracial individuals are often faced with the "What are you?" question. For years, multiracial individuals have fought for the right to identify themselves as belonging to more than one racial group. Our society, however, is one that tends to force people to choose one racial identity over another or imposes a singular racial identity upon them. In the case of Hector, described previously, counseling helped him better understand the source of his ambivalent feelings about his Mexican heritage. He admitted making jokes before someone else could do so at his expense. People of mixed-race heritage are often ignored, neglected, and considered nonexistent in educational materials, media portrayals, and psychological literature (Root, 1992a, 1996; M. M. Torres, 1998). One multiracial psychology intern (Japanese mother and Irish father) working in a Black community was asked by his supervisor how his clients felt about working with a "White" psychologist.

> Our society is one that tends to force people to choose one racial identity over another or imposes a singular racial identity upon them.

When the supervisor noticed the confusion on the intern's face he stated, "I know you are Asian but you look White" (Murphy-Shigematsu, 2010).

Such dynamics can lead to major psychological and social stressors in terms of identity formation. There are often related feelings of existing between the margins of two or more cultures, as well as a sense of discrepancy between the multiracial individual's self-identity and the one imposed by others. The intern considered the supervisor's reaction to him to be a microaggression and felt it interfered with their working relationship. Unfortunately, mental health professionals often receive little training in working with multiracial clients who are distressed or confused by having monoracial categories imposed upon them (Gillem, Lincoln, & English, 2007). In fact, counselors may have conscious and unconscious attitudes, biases, and stereotypes similar to the layperson regarding race mixing (miscegenation) and "racial contamination." Attitudes against interracial marriage continue to exist. In a recent poll, 46% of Mississippi Republicans thought that interracial marriage should be illegal (Webster, 2011).

In more ways than one, the 2000 U.S. Census set in motion a complex psychological and political debate because for the first time it allowed people to check more than one box for their racial identities and to be counted as multiracial (Nittle, 2011). Proponents of the change have argued that it is unfair to force multiracial people to choose only one identity because such practices (a) create alienation and identity confusion, (b) deny racial realities, (c) undermine pride in being multiracial, and (d) ignore important personal information (e.g., medical advantages of knowing one's racial heritage).

Custom, history, and prejudices, however, continue to affect perceptions regarding those who are multiracial. Additionally, many civil rights organizations, including the National Association for the Advancement of Colored People (NAACP), believe that multiracial categorization will dilute the strength of their constituencies, and because census numbers on race and ethnicity figure into sociopolitical calculations involving antidiscrimination laws, dispersal of funds for minority programs may be adversely affected. Caught in the struggle—often with significant social and emotional consequences—are persons of mixed racial heritage.

MULTIRACIALISM IN THE UNITED STATES

Mental health professionals can increase their understanding of multiracialism and related issues by increasing awareness of facts such as (J. J. Johnson, 1992; Root, 1992b; U.S. Census Bureau, 2010h; Wehrly, Kenney, & Kenney, 1999):

- The biracial baby boom in the United States started in 1967, when the last laws against race mixing (antimiscegenation) were repealed. As a result, there was a rapid increase in interracial marriage and a subsequent rise in the number of biracial children in the United States. One of seven marriages now involves partners from different racial or ethnic backgrounds.

- Nine million people reported more than one race in the census, whereas the vast majority (97%) of the U.S. population reported only one race. Ninety-two percent of those who reported multiple races indicated a mixture of two races; White and Black (1.8 million) was the largest multiple-race combination, followed by White and "some other race" (1.7 million), White and Asian (1.6 million), and White and American Indian or Alaska Native (1.4 million) (U.S. Census Bureau, 2010h).

- Census figures may underestimate the multiracial population since many multiracial individuals choose to self-identify with only one race. For example, 16% of Americans consider themselves to be mixed race, but only 1% self-identify with more than one racial group (D'Vera, 2011). Accurate counting of multiracial heritage is further complicated by the fact that 30% to 70% of African Americans are multiracial by multigenerational history; the vast majority of Latinos and Filipinos are multiracial, as are the majority of American Indians and Native Hawaiians.

- When gender is taken into consideration, Latinas, Asian American women, and American Indian women are more likely than their male counterparts to marry interracially. Black and White men have a higher interracial marriage rate than males of other races. The highest rate of interracial marriage is between White men and Asian women, and the lowest is between White men and Black women.

Implications

These statistics raise major questions regarding the monoracial versus multiracial climate of our society. For example, why are the offspring of a Black-White union considered Black by our society? Why not White? Why is it easy for us to accept the notion that children of certain mixed couples (e.g., Asian/White, Native American-White) are multiracial but that other combinations that involve African Americans are not? Why do some people of mixed-race heritage choose to identify themselves with only one race? Are certain interracial relationships more acceptable than others? Why? What accounts for the fact that Asian American women and Latinas are more likely than their male counterparts to marry outside of their ethnic group?

Mental health professionals who work with multiracial clients need to understand the implications of these questions if they are to be effective in work with racially mixed clients. They need to examine their own attitude regarding interracial couples and multiracial children (Gillem et al., 2007; Kenney, 2002). In our journey to understand the implications of the issues confronting multiracial individuals, we concentrate on several themes that have been identified as important in working with this population.

The "One Drop of Blood" Rule

Alvin Poussaint, an African American Harvard psychiatrist, stood before a packed audience and posed a pointed question to them: "Do you know how powerful

> *Hypodescent*, or the "One Drop Rule," is a class-based social system that maintains the myth of monoracialism by assigning the person of mixed racial heritage to the least desirable racial status (Root, 1996).

Black blood is?" After an awkward silence, he answered, "It is so powerful that one tiny drop will contaminate the entire bloodstream of a White person!" What Poussaint was referring to is called *hypodescent*, or the "One Drop Rule," a class-based social system that maintains the myth of monoracialism by assigning the person of mixed racial heritage to the least desirable racial status (Root, 1996). This system was further institutionalized by an 1894 Supreme Court decision (*Plessy v. Ferguson*) that a person who was seven-eighths White and one-eighth Black and "maintained that he did not look Negro" was nonetheless to be classified as Negro (Davis, 1994).

In essence, the hypodescent concept stemmed from a variety of self-serving motives. Initially, it was an attempt by White European immigrants to maintain racial purity and superiority by passing laws against interracial marriages (antimiscegenation laws), primarily directed at Blacks and Native Americans. As early as the 1660s, laws were passed making it a crime for "Negro slaves" to marry "freeborn English women" (Wehrly et al., 1999). Interestingly, such laws were also clear evidence of gender bias. Men of color could not have access to valued property (White women), whereas White men were allowed sexual access to Black women (Pascoe, 1991). Hypodescent thinking and laws not only maintained racial purity but also generated additional property for slave owners. Africans were purchased as slave laborers; the more slaves an owner possessed, the greater his wealth and access to free labor. Thus, economically, it was beneficial to classify offspring of a Black-White union as "Negro" because it increased owners' wealth. Also, the prevalent beliefs of the time were that "Negroes and Indians" were subhuman creatures, uncivilized, lower in intellect, and impulsively childlike. One drop of Black blood in a person would make him or her contaminated and Black.

The rule of hypodescent applies to other racial/ethnic minority groups as well, but it appears to predominate with African Americans. Although groups of color are often averse to discussing social desirability differences between them, conventional wisdom and some data suggest that African Americans are often considered less desirable than their Asian American counterparts (L. A. Jackson et al., 1996), although Asian Americans are still considered significantly less desirable than Whites. It also appears that whether one is a man or a woman of a minority group affects how he or she is perceived by society. For example, images of Asian American women are much more favorable (e.g., petite, exotic, and sexually pleasing) than are their male counterparts (e.g., passive, emasculated, inhibited, and unattractive; D. Sue, 2005).

These findings offer an explanation for why interracial marriages between Asian Americans and European Americans occur more frequently than marriages between Blacks and Whites; why mixed-race children of the former union are more likely to be considered multiracial, whereas those of the latter are more likely to be considered Black; and why Asian American women are more likely than their male counterparts to marry outside their racial group (Jackman,

Wagner, & Johnson, 2001; Lewandowski & Jackson, 2001). These double standards not only lead to hard feelings and resentments between African Americans and Asian Americans but also create friction among men and women within the Asian American population as well as other racial minority groups. It is important to understand that such antagonism between racial/ethnic minority groups and between the sexes of a group originate from these biased sociopolitical processes. The true cause is society's ongoing and differential acceptance and stereotyping of minority groups.

Implications

Many multiracial individuals face forces that impose a racial identity upon them. Such identities are likely to be determined not only by their racial heritage but also by the societal status associated with their particular background (Moss & Davis, 2008). In fact, any mixed-racial heritage is generally considered "lower status" than that of European Americans. Multiracial children, when asked their heritage, have been found to answer one way internally and another way to the questioner (Cross, 1991). The external answer may be an attempt to fit in, to not violate the expectations of the interrogator, or to take the path of least resistance. For example, answering that one is biracial is often not satisfactory to the questioner and is likely to result in further probing. Unable to identify their conflicts and feelings about being multiracial and about the frequent questions about their identity, children often settle for the answer most likely to end the questions, responding by giving the "most acceptable" monoracial identity. However, such answers often result in internal disharmony, a false sense of self, social marginality, and guilt (McDowell et al., 2005; Winn & Priest, 1993).

SPECIFIC CHALLENGES

In the following sections we consider challenges often faced by multiracial populations and consider their implications in treatment. Remember that these are generalizations and that their applicability needs to be assessed for each client.

Racial/Ethnic Ambiguity: "What Are You?"

I don't even like to identify myself as a race anymore. My family has been pulling me in two directions about what I am. I just want to be a person. (Saulny, 2011a, p. 2)

Racial/ethnic ambiguity occurs when people are not easily able to distinguish the monoracial category of the multiracial individual from phenotypic characteristics. Phenotypic traits play a major role in how people perceive others. If African American traits are dominant, the One Drop Rule will automatically classify the person as Black, regardless of the answer of the multiracial individual; the questioner might think, *"She says she's mixed, but she is really Black."* For multiracial individuals with ambiguous features, the "What are you?" question becomes a constant dilemma, a question that the multiracial person may not possess the language or sophistication to answer properly.

Historically, there have been many negative societal associations with the process and dynamics that produce a multiracial child (interracial marriages and relationships). Therefore, the language associated to describe such offspring is often unfamiliar or associated with negative connotations. Such terms as *Mulatta/o* (African/European), *Afroasian* (African/Asian), *Mestiza/o* (Indian/Spanish) are confusing to most people, including the multiracial child (Root, 1992a, 1996). More contemporarily, multiracial individuals are sometimes referred to as "mutts" or "half-breeds."

The "What are you?" question requires the individual to justify his or her existence in a world rigidly built on the concepts of racial purity and monoracialism. This is reinforced by a multiracial person's attempt to answer such a question by discerning the motives of the interrogator: "Why is the person asking?" "Does it really matter?" "Are they really interested in the answer, or am I going to violate their expectations?" "Do they see me as an oddity?" If the person answers "American," this will only lead to further inquiry (Ramirez, 1996). If the answer is "mixed," the interrogator will query further: "What ethnicity are you?" If the answer is "part White and Black," other questions follow: "Who are your parents?" "Which is Black?" "Why did they marry?" The multiracial person begins to feel picked apart and fragmented by such questioning about his or her racial background (Root, 1990). The problem with giving an answer is that it is often "not good enough."

The communication from our society is quite clear: "There is something different about you." We cannot stress enough how often multiracial persons face a barrage of questions about their racial identities, from childhood to adulthood (Houston, 1997; Wehrly et al., 1999). The inquisition can result in invalidation, conflicting feelings of loyalties to the racial/ethnic identities of parents, internal trauma, and confused identity development.

Implications

Multiracial children often feel quite isolated and may find little support, even from their parents. This is especially true for monoracial parents, who themselves are not multiracial. How, for example, does a White mother married to a Black husband raise her child? White? Black? Mixed? Other? Parents of interracial marriages may fail to understand the challenges encountered by their children, gloss over differences, or raise the child as if he or she were monoracial. The child may, therefore, lack role models and feel even greater loneliness. Even being a multiracial parent may not result in greater empathy or understanding of the unique challenges faced by multiracial children, especially if the parents (themselves victims of a monoracial system) have not adequately resolved their own identity conflicts. Therapists can help interracial couples prepare their children for questions regarding racial heritage (Kenney, 2002).

The problem is compounded by the gender of the parents and the multiracial child. One clinical study of 10 families found that when the mother is White and the father Black, daughters are more likely to identify with the mother's racial background; and when the mother is Black and the father White, boys and girls will likely identify with being Black. In almost all of these cases, the children expressed shame at not including their father's heritage as part of their identity and experienced anxiety, depression, and difficulty coping. Interestingly, it was found that the one child raised as biracial seemed to be the most emotionally healthy of the entire group (Bowles, 1993).

Existing Between the Margins

Kayci Baldwin remembers how her Black father and White mother were concerned about her acceptance by other children. After some initial struggles regarding her racial identity, Kayci now actively embraces her multicultural identity and is involved with a nationwide multicultural teen group. (Associated Press, 2009)

Root (1990) asserted that mixed-race people begin life as "marginal individuals" because society refuses to view the races as equal and because their ethnic identities are ambiguous. They are often viewed as fractionated people—composed of fractions of a race, culture, or ethnicity. A person who is Asian, White European, and African may not be completely accepted by any of these groups. Multiracial people may encounter prejudice and discrimination not only from the dominant group but also from secondary ethnic groups (Sanchez, Shih, & Garcia, 2009). Physical appearance may strongly influence their sense of group belonging and racial self-identification (AhnAllen, Suyemoto, & Carter, 2006). Also, racial identity is often influenced by environmental factors, such as where one grows up (i.e., in an integrated neighborhood and school versus in an ethnic community). Although being multiracial does not itself lead to emotional problems, societal reaction to race mixture can introduce stressors. Issues of racial identity and racial discrimination among multiracial adolescents have been associated with substance abuse and other problem behaviors (Choi, Harachi, Gillmore, & Catalano, 2006). However, many young mixed-race adults are rejecting the traditional color definition and adopting a more fluid sense of identity (Saulny, 2011a).

In Chapter 11 we spent considerable time discussing racial/cultural identity development among minority group members. Criticisms leveled at these theories include the following: (a) They were developed from a monoracial perspective rather than a multiracial one; (b) they falsely assume that multiracial individuals will be accepted by their parent culture or cultures; and (c) their linear nature is inadequate to describe the complexity of the many possible multiracial resolutions (Kerwin & Ponterotto, 1995; Poston, 1990; Root, 1990, 1992a, 1996).

In an early model of biracial identity development, Poston (1990) described five stages. At the *personal identity* stage, biracial children's sense of self is largely independent of ethnic heritage; at the *choice of group categorization* stage, the youngster feels pressure (from parents, peers or societal forces) to identify with one racial orientation. At the *enmeshment/denial* stage, negative feelings may emerge, either consciously or unconsciously, regarding the denial of one's racial heritage (i.e., the racial heritage not "selected"). At the *appreciation* stage, the person begins to value the racial roots of both parents; and at the *integration* stage, wholeness and integration of both identities occur. Multiracial individuals confront the process of resolving marginality and developing a healthy identity throughout their lives (Gillem et al., 2007). Perhaps the most sophisticated of the multiracial identity development models is the one proposed by Root (1990, 1998). We focus here on Root's descriptions of the four possible healthy resolutions of marginality.

1. The multiracial individual *accepts the identity assigned by society*. For example, the child of a Black-Japanese union is likely to be considered Black by friends, peers, and family. Root believes that this can be a positive choice if the person is satisfied with the identity, receives family support, and is active rather than passive in evidencing the identity. The individual in this situation, however, may have a very fluid identity that changes radically in different situations. If the person, for example, travels or moves to another community or region of the country, the assigned racial identity may become Japanese or even mixed.

2. The person may choose to resolve marginality through *identification with both groups*. "I think a lot of us are chameleons. We can sit in a group of White people and feel different, but still fit in. . . . But we can turn around and sit in a group of Black people, even though we are not Black in the same way" (Miville et al., 2005, p. 512). In this case, the person is able to shift from one identity (White American) when with one group to another identity (African American) when with a different group. This method of adaptation is healthy as long as individuals do not lose their sense of self-integrity, view the ability to move in two worlds as positive, and can relate well to positive aspects of both identities and cultures.

3. The person may decide to *choose a single racial identity* in an active manner. Although it may appear similar to the first option, it differs in two ways: (a) It is the individual, not society, who makes the choice of racial group identity, and (b) the identity is less prone to shifting when the situational context changes. However, as indicated in the case of the Latino/Middle Eastern individual at the beginning of the chapter, self-identity may not be accepted by other groups. Actively choosing a single racial identity can be a positive option when the individual does not deny his or her other racial heritage and when the group with whom the individual chooses to identify does not marginalize the person.

4. Identification with a *mixed-race heritage* or *multiracial identity* is another option. "I think it [being multiracial] has made me expertly cued to cultural cues. Kind of as an observer, I'm always trying to learn, 'ok, what's going on here, how does one act here, and what are the cultural norms'" (Suyemoto, 2004, p. 216). In fact, bicultural/biracial or multicultural/multiracial identification rather than identifying with only one race is increasing in frequency

(Brunsma, 2005; Suzuki-Crumly & Hyers, 2004). A multicultural identity allows equal valuing of all aspects of one's racial/cultural heritage, the ability to relate to both groups, and feelings of being well integrated.

Implications

There are several important distinctions between multiracial and monoracial identity development models. First, for those who are multiracial, resolutions occur not only between dominant-subordinate group relations (culture-conflicts) but often within individual racial identities as well (e.g., White/Asian, Native American/ Black). Second, resolutions often involve more than conflicts between two racial groups. Third, the complexity of multiple resolutions may differ depending on gender, the type of multiracial combination, and other group identity factors, such as socioeconomic status, age, and sexual orientation. Fourth, identities may shift— with the degree of fluidity displayed depending on the situational context. Last, multiracial identity development models entertain the notion that there is more than one resolution that can lead to healthy adjustment.

In therapy with multiracial individuals, identity issues sometimes come to the surface (although it should not be assumed that this is the source of a client's problem). If feelings of marginality are producing distress, positive resolution can occur with any of the choices discussed. Therapists should be aware that a growing number of multiracial individuals are choosing "multiracial" as their ethnic identity. This choice should not be considered pathological and interpreted as confusion or an inability to commit to an integrated identity (Suyemoto, 2004).

Stereotypes and Myths

There is considerable evidence that the myths and stereotypes associated with multiracial individuals and interracial couples involved attempts to prevent the mixing of races through stigmatizing such mixture (Wehrly et al., 1999). Unfortunately, sociopsychological research on this topic has often perpetuated and reinforced inaccurate beliefs about race mixing and mixed-race people. Even now, the perception that multiracial children are somehow inferior or more prone to major social and psychological problems is not uncommon (Jackman et al., 2001). However, studies indicate that multiracial individuals are as well adjusted as their monoracial peers (Sanchez et al., 2009; Shih & Sanchez, 2005).

Interracial unions were often portrayed as unhappy and unstable, Early research and writings on the characteristics and dynamics of interracial relationships and marriages focused primarily on negative attributes. It was believed that individuals who chose to marry outside their racial group were somehow deficient, lacked in self-esteem, or harbored feelings of inferiority (Beigel, 1966); rebelling against parental authority (Saxton, 1968); or experiencing mental problems (Brayboy, 1966). Stereotypes have fluctuated depending on the race and the gender of each partner. A White person who violated social norms against interracial marriages might be described as experimenting with the "exotic," attempting to express a liberal view, possessing low self-esteem, or being a social/occupational failure unable to attract a member of his or her own race (Rosenblatt, Karis, & Powell, 1995). Members of a minority group were often seen as trying to elevate themselves socially, economically, and psychologically.

Sexual stereotypes also played a major role in the perception of men and women who are involved in interracial relationships/marriages. As previously mentioned, there seems to be more positive views of Asian American women than their male counterparts (S. Sue & Sue, 1971). These are still quite pervasive beliefs, whether conscious or unconscious. African Americans, especially males, are often stereotyped as possessing "primitive sexuality" and as being "passionate, potent, and sexually virile" (Frankenberg, 1993). While Asian American men are not viewed as a competitive threat, African American men with their "aggressive and promiscuous sexual behaviors" have been viewed with greater suspicion. History is replete with incidents reflecting society's hostility and antagonism toward Black men.

Stereotypes of multiracial individuals were also largely negative. Due to historical legal and social prohibitions against interracial relationships, it is not difficult to see why negative stereotypes developed. For decades, multiracial individuals were viewed as products of an "unholy and immoral union" and thus doomed to an immoral, troubled, and marginal existence, likely to suffer identity problems and low self-esteem, as well as social isolation. On the other hand, multiracial individuals are sometimes described as inordinately beautiful or handsome, but even these stereotypes are associated with myths of eroticism and promiscuity.

Implications

In general, early myths about mixed marriages implied that these unions were the result of unhealthy motives by the partners and that multiracial offspring were doomed to suffer deficiencies and pathologies. The early studies of mixed-race individuals and the assumptions were problematic. First, if partners in mixed marriages and their multiracial offspring experienced identity issues, conflicts, and psychological problems, it is likely that these difficulties were the result of an intolerant and hostile society. In other words, they would have resulted from bias, discrimination, and racism rather than from anything inherent in the marriage or the "unhealthy" qualities of those involved. Second, we already know that to a large extent research is influenced by and reflects societal views. It seems likely, therefore, that early researchers most likely asked questions and designed studies with a problem-oriented orientation and a focus on identifying pathology, rather than the healthy and functional traits of the group. Third, in the case of interracial relationships/marriages, current research now suggests that these marriages are based on the same ingredients as other marriages: love, companionship, and compatible interests and values (Lewandowski & Jackson, 2001; Porterfield, 1982; Rosenblatt et al., 1995). Additionally, research reveals the beneficial sociopsychological traits associated with a multiracial heritage, including an increased sense of uniqueness, greater variety in one's life, greater tolerance and understanding of people, increased ability to deal with racism and to interact and build alliances with diverse people and groups (Sanchez et al., 2009; Saulny, 2011a; Wehrly et al., 1999).

A MULTIRACIAL BILL OF RIGHTS

Countless numbers of times I have fragmented and fractionalized myself in order to make the other more comfortable in deciphering my behavior, my words, my loyalties, my choice of friends, my appearance, my parents, and so on. And given my multiethnic history, it was hard to keep track of all the fractions, to make them add up to one whole. It took me over 30 years to realize that fragmenting myself seldom served a purpose other than to preserve the delusions this country has created around race. Reciting the fractions to the other was the ultimate act of buying into the mechanics of racism in this country. Once I realized this, I could ask myself other questions. How exactly does a person be one-fourth, one-eighth, or one-half something? To fragment myself and others, "She is one-half Chinese and one-half White" or "He is one-quarter Native, one-quarter African American, and one-half Spanish," was to unquestioningly be deployed to operate the machinery that disenfranchised myself, my family, my friends, and others I was yet to meet. (Root, 1996, pp. 4–5)

These words were written by Maria Root, a leading psychologist in the field of multiracial identity and development, who expressed concerns about the way in which society has historically relegated multiracial persons to deviant status, minimized their contributions to society, and ignored their existence because they do not fit into a monoracial classification. In her personal and professional journey, Root (1996) developed a *Bill of Rights for Racially Mixed People* that is composed of three major affirmations: resistance, revolution, and change.

1. *Resistance* refers to the multiracial individual's right to resist the belief systems imposed by society, the data on which they are based, and the rationalizations used to justify the status quo regarding race relations. It means refusing to fragment, marginalize, or disconnect from others and the self. The following four assertions embody resistance.

   I have the right not to:
   • Justify my existence in this world.
   • Keep the races separate within me.
   • Be responsible for people's discomfort with my physical ambiguity.
   • Justify my ethnic legitimacy.

2. *Revolution* refers to multiracial people or to anyone who enters into an interracial relationship and chooses to "cross the boundaries" of race relations. According to Root, these individuals are often seen as "race traitors" who can create an emotional/psychic earthquake that challenges the reality of our oppressive racial system. The following four assertions embody revolution.

   I have the right to:
   • Identify myself differently than strangers expect me to.
   • Identify myself differently from how my parents identify me.

- Identify myself differently than my brothers and sisters.
- Identify myself differently in different situations.

3. *Change* refers to the active attempt to build connections, wholeness, and a sense of belonging to one another. Although the two other sets of assertions are attempts to free one from the racialized existence of a monoracial system, *connections* acknowledge that our social fates are intertwined and dependent on one another. According to Root, this sense of belonging serves as a force against perpetrating atrocities against fellow human beings. The following four assertions embody change:

I have the right to:
- Create a vocabulary to communicate about being multiracial.
- Change my identity over my lifetime—and more than once.
- Have loyalties and identify with more than one group of people.
- Choose freely whom I befriend and love.

Implications

Root's Bill of Rights is much more complex and meaningful than is described here. It has major implications for mental health providers because it challenges our notions of a monoracial classification system, reorients our thoughts about the many myths of multiracial persons, makes us aware of the systemic construction and rationalizations of race, warns us about the dangers of fractionating identities, and advocates freedom of choice for the multiracial individual. For the mental health provider, much insight can be derived from the twelve assertions contained in the Bill of Rights.

MULTIRACIAL STRENGTHS

Although a multicultural identity can result in challenges, many cite advantages, such as having access to and support from several cultural communities (Sanchez et al., 2009). In the present day there is much greater acceptance of interracial marriage, especially among young adults (Pew Research Center, 2010a). Multiracial individuals are quite visible on television, in movies, and in advertising. Support groups have arisen. For example, Michelle Lopez-Mullin, president of the Multiracial and Biracial Student association, has one parent who is Chinese and Peruvian and one who is White and American Indian and finds pride in her identity (Saulny, 2011a). Instead of feeling marginalized, many multiracial individuals possess enhanced cultural competence and feel comfortable in more than one cultural setting. They may be able to "borrow from their various racial backgrounds, culling out strengths specific to these cultures, and using them to support their well-being" (Pedrotti, Edwards, & Lopez, 2008, p. 199). And as in the case of Michelle Lopez-Mullin, pride may develop for multiple cultural groups.

Implications for Clinical Practice

Although monoracial minority group members experience many of the issues faced by multiracial individuals, the latter, in addition to dealing with racism, are likely to experience unique stressors related to their multiple racial/ethnic identities. For example, most monoracial minorities find their own groups receptive and supportive of them. Multiracial individuals may be placed in the awkward situation of not being fully accepted by any group. Likewise, monoracial minority group children can expect psychological and emotional support from their parents—the parents share common experiences with their children, can act as mentors, and relate to the experiences their children encounter with respect to minority status. However, multiracial children may be the products of monoracial parents. Some helpful guidelines working with multiracial clients include the following:

1. Become aware of your own stereotypes and preconceptions regarding interracial relationships and marriages. When you see a racially mixed couple, do you pay extra attention to them? What thoughts and images do you have? Only when you are able to become aware of your biases will you be able to avoid imposing them upon your clients.

2. When working with multiracial clients, avoid stereotyping. As with interracial relationships, cultural conditioning creates beliefs about racially mixed people. In general, these images are based on mistaken convictions that may deny the mixed-race heritage of the person and his or her uniqueness.

3. It is important to see multiracial people in a holistic fashion rather than as fractions of a person. This means being careful when dealing with the "What are you?" question. It is important to emphasize the positive qualities of the total person rather than seeing the person as parts.

4. Remember that being a multiracial person often means coping with marginality, isolation, and loneliness. These feelings are not the result of internal problems but are generally brought about by external factors related to prejudice. Nevertheless, mixed-race persons often experience strong feelings of loneliness, rejection, forced-choice situations, guilt/shame from not fully integrating all aspects of their racial heritage, and anger. These feelings have often been submerged and hidden because there is no one to share them with who understands. As mentioned earlier, mixed-race children often come from homes with monoracial parents.

5. Identify the strengths regarding multicultural identity as well as the challenges faced by the individuals and the resources available to them.

6. With mixed-race clients, emphasize the freedom to choose one's identity. Root's Bill of Rights is helpful here. There is no one identity suitable for everyone. The racial identity models discussed in this chapter all have limitations, and it is important to note that identities are often changing and fluid rather than fixed. Remember that many multicultural individuals have resolved their identity in a healthy manner and that it is not a factor in their presenting problem.

7. Take an active psychoeducational approach. Multiracial individuals are often subjected to a rigid monoracial system that stereotypes and fits them into rigid categories. Oftentimes, children may learn to internalize the stereotypes and accept an identity imposed upon them.

(continued)

(*continued*)

Somewhere in the counseling process, clients can be helped to understand the forces of oppression, and the counselor can empower them to take an active part in formulating their identities.

8. Since mixed-race people have historically been portrayed as possessing deficiencies, stress their positive attributes and the advantages of being multiracial and multicultural.

9. Recognize that family counseling may be especially valuable in working with mixed-race clients, especially if they are children. Frequently, parents (especially if monoracial) are unaware of the unique conflicts related to their child's multiracial journey. Parents can be taught to empower their children, convey positive aspects of being multiracial, and help them integrate a healthy identity.

10. When working with multiracial clients, ensure that you possess basic knowledge of the history and issues related to hypodescent thinking (the One Drop Rule), ambiguity (the "What are you?" question), marginality, and racial/cultural identity. The knowledge cannot be superficial but must entail a historical, political, social, and psychological understanding of the treatment of race, racism, and monoracialism in this society. In essence, these four dynamics form the context within which the multiracial individual operates on a continuing basis.

PART VII

Counseling and Special Circumstances Involving Racial/Ethnic Populations

Counseling Arab and Muslim Americans

A large group of teenagers were asked to identify what role in a movie or on television a person from different ethnic backgrounds would be most likely to play. For Arab Americans, the roles were that of a terrorist or a convenience store clerk. This result was obtained even though the study predated the September 11, 2001, terrorist attacks. (Zogby, 2001a)

A New York City cab driver was slashed on the throat, lip, and forearm after answering affirmatively after being asked by a drunken passenger if he was a Muslim. (Hays, 2010)

Elkugia, who was born in Libya, was voted homecoming queen for her high school. While playing basketball for her high school team, she wears a headscarf, a long jersey, and athletic pants instead of shorts. Her clothing reflects her Muslim faith and is a "form of modesty." (Iwasaki, 2006)

Arabs are individuals who originate from countries located in the Middle East and North Africa and whose primary language is Arabic. Arabs began immigrating to the United States in the late 1800s. About one quarter of Arab Americans are Muslims, followers of the Islamic religion. Although the populations of Arabic-speaking countries include large numbers of Muslims, most Arab Americans are Christian (M. L. Jackson & Nassar-McMillan, 2006). Although Arab Americans and Muslims have always encountered prejudice and discrimination, negative behavior directed toward these groups accelerated following the September 11, 2001, attacks.

Muslims and "Arab-appearing" individuals have since been subjected to increased discrimination and attacks. In a letter to his constituents, U.S. Congressman Virgil Goode wrote, "I fear that in the next century we will have many more Muslims in the United States if we do not adopt the strict immigration policies that I believe are necessary to preserve the values and beliefs traditional to the United States of America" (Frommer, 2006, p. 1). Goode wrote this letter in response to a request made by a newly elected Muslim congressman to use the Quran (the Islamic holy book) during his swearing-in ceremony.

Arab Americans, descending from about 20 different countries, are heterogeneous in terms of race, religion, and political ideology. Approximately 56% of Arab Americans trace their ancestry to Lebanon, while 14% are from Syria, 11%

from Egypt, 9% from Palestine, 4% from Jordan, 2% from Iraq, and 4% from other countries (El-Badry, 2006). Because of categorization systems used in the U.S. Census, it is difficult to determine the precise size of the Arab American population. It is estimated that there are over 3,500,000 Arab Americans, with 94% living in metropolitan areas, such as Los Angeles, Detroit, New York, Chicago, and Washington, D.C. (Arab American Institute, 2011). The majority of Arab Americans are native-born U.S. citizens. Arab Americans can have African, Asian, or European ancestry.

The majority of Arab Americans arrived in two major waves (Nassar-McMillan & Hakim-Larson, 2003; Suleiman, 1999). The first lasted from 1875 to World War II and primarily involved Arab Christians from Lebanon and Syria who immigrated for economic reasons. The second wave began after World War II and has included Palestinians, Iraqis, and Syrians who left in order to escape the Arab-Israeli conflicts and civil war. This latter group included larger numbers of Muslims. The aftermath of the September 11 attacks initially reduced Arab immigration. However, it has once again increased, and more than 40,000 immigrants from Muslim countries, such as Egypt, Pakistan, and Morocco, were admitted to the United States in 2005 (Elliott, 2006).

In comparison with the U.S. population as a whole, Arab Americans are more likely to be married (61% versus 54%), male (57% versus 49%), young, and highly educated (46% have bachelor's degree versus 28% of the total adult population) (Arab American Institute, 2011). Sixty-nine percent indicate they speak a language other than English at home, but 65% speak English "very well." The majority work as executives, professionals, and office and sales staff. Forty-two percent work in management positions. Arab American income is higher than the national median income ($59,012 versus $52,029) (Arab American Institute, 2011). However, the poverty rate is also higher (17% versus 12%; U.S. Census Bureau, 2005f). Arab Americans participate in a variety of religions. More than 33% are Roman Catholic, 25% are Muslim, 18% are Eastern Orthodox, and 10% are Protestant (Arab American Institute, 2003).

CHARACTERISTICS AND STRENGTHS

In the following sections we consider the characteristics, values, and strengths of Arab and Muslim Americans and consider their implications in treatment. Remember that these are generalizations and their applicability needs to be assessed for each client.

Cultural and Religious Values

Muslims are followers of Islam. The name of their religion means "submission to God." The *Quran*, the Islamic holy book, is considered to be the literal word of God. Islam is one of the fastest growing religions in the United States with approximately one fourth of U.S. Muslims being converts to the faith (U.S. Department of State, 2002). Within Islam, there are two major sects—Sunni and Shiite. The Sunnis are the largest group, accounting for about 90% of Muslims worldwide. The remaining 10% are Shiites. Most Muslims in America are Sunni, whereas those in Iraq, Bahrain, Lebanon, and Iran are mainly Shiite. It is estimated that about 4 to 6 million Muslims are living in the United States; not all Muslims descend from Arabic-speaking countries. There are about 1 billion Muslims worldwide of whom only about 200 million are Arab (Amri, 2010). Of the 2.6 million Muslims in the United States (Pew Research Center, 2011), 28% are White, 35% are African Americans, 18% are Asians, and 18% are Arab or "other race" (Younis, 2009). Hate crimes again Muslims are second only to those perpetrated against Jewish Americans (FBI, 2010). The lives of Muslims are governed by laws derived from the Quran, which deals with social issues, family life, economics and business, sexuality, and other aspects of life. Adherence to Islam is demonstrated by individual accountability and a declaration of faith ("There is no god but God and Muhammad is his messenger"). Muslims engage in the ritual of prayer five times a day and annually fast during daylight hours during the holy month of Ramadan—a time for inner reflection, devotion to God, and spiritual renewal. Almsgiving and a pilgrimage to Mecca are additional signs of devotion (Nobles & Sciarra, 2000). Some Muslim women, particularly those of Arab descent, wear traditional clothing because of the Islamic teachings of modesty.

Family Structure and Values

Family structure and values of Arab Americans and Muslim Americans differ widely, depending on the specific country of origin and acculturation level. An Arab American engineer living in San Francisco made the following observation: "American values are, by and large, very consistent with Islamic values, with a focus on family, faith, hard work, and an obligation to better self and society" (U.S. Department of State, 2002, p. 1). Some generalizations can be made about the values of Arab Americans. Family obligations and interdependence among members are very important. This group orientation can result in pressure for conformity and high expectations for children. Parents expect to remain part of their child's life for as long as possible.

In traditionally oriented families, the oldest son is trained to become the head of the extended family. Family roles are complementary, with men serving as providers and head of the family and women maintaining the home and rearing children. Mothers are likely to behave affectionately toward their children, whereas fathers may be aloof, generating both fear and respect (Dwairy, 2008). In traditional Arab American families, there is a strong sense of a community and an identity that revolves around culture and God. Hospitality is considered to be very important (Hodge, 2002; Nobles & Sciarra, 2000). Treatment for personal problems may be considered shameful and disclosed only to close family or friends; outside help may be sought only as a last resort. In general, boys are advised by older males, and girls are advised by older females. Opposite-sex discussions with other than a family member may be problematic (M. L. Jackson & Nassar-McMillan, 2006).

> Counselors should be aware that traditional Arab families are hierarchical, with men considered to be the head of the family.

Implications

Counselors should be aware that traditional Arab families are hierarchical, with men considered to be the head of the family. Although Western media often portray women as powerless victims of emotional and physical abuse, in most Arab and Muslim families, women are treated with honor and respect (Ibrahim & Dykeman, 2011). Problems can occur with acculturation conflicts involving the struggle to adhere to traditional familial patterns (culturally collective support) or to seek individual fulfillment.

Cultural Strengths

Arab and Muslim Americans tend to be collectivistic rather than individualistic in orientation. Family and community supports can be protective factors in dealing with prejudice and discrimination from the larger society. Family resources can be brought to bear on personal issues and problems. Newer immigrants receive support and acceptance within Arab communities. Similarly, being part of a religious community can also provide guidance in dealing with problems and issues. Being a Muslim provides not only religious beliefs but also a code of behavior that encompasses cultural, racial, gender, and familial considerations.

SPECIFIC CHALLENGES

In the following sections we consider challenges often faced by Arab and Muslim Americans and consider their implications in treatment. Remember that these are generalizations and their applicability needs to be assessed for each client.

Stereotypes, Racism, and Discrimination

Arab Americans of all ages are caught in the cross-fire of the sociopolitical tensions between the United States and the Arab world. (Winerman, 2006)

Rita Zaweidah, the co-founder of the Arab American Community Coalition of Washington State explains, "When somebody is picked up or arrested or they've done something, they don't just mention that it is a male that was picked up. It's a Muslim male. You never see them saying a Christian male or an Irish male or an English male or female or whatever else. But for some reason when it's anything regarding the Middle East, the religion is the first word somewhere in that sentence." (Zaki, 2011)

Arabs, Arab Americans, and Muslims are often stereotyped in movies as sheiks, barbarians, or terrorists (Nassar-McMillan, Lambert, & Hakim-Larson, 2011). As was mentioned in the poll of teenagers at the beginning of the chapter, Arabs are expected in the roles of terrorist or convenience store clerk. Islam has been portrayed as a violent religion. In fact, in 2006, Pope Benedict XVI created a storm of protests from the Muslim world when he read a quote from a 14th-century emperor: "Show me just what Muhammad brought that was new, and there you will find only evil and inhuman, such as his command to spread by the sword the faith he preached." The pope later professed "total and profound respect for all Muslims" and said he was trying to make the point that religion and violence do not go together. Nonetheless, followers of Islam were deeply hurt by his statement.

The terrorist attacks on September 11, 2001, also had a profound impact on how Arab and Muslim Americans were viewed in the United States. After September 11, hate crimes increased, with thousands of Arab and Muslim American males subjected to deportation hearings, airline passenger profiling, vandalism, physical violence, and increased discrimination (Moradi & Hasan, 2004). Many have felt cautious regarding qualities that might draw attention to themselves, such as their dress or their names. Some women who previously wore headscarves discontinued the practice or stayed inside their homes. The vast majority of Arab and Muslim Americans were angered, upset, and dismayed by the terrorist attacks, as were all Americans, and even supported retaliation against countries supporting the terrorist attacks (Zogby, 2001b). At the same time, they were aware of the increased negative response by the public to Muslims or those of Arab descent. Unfortunately, many of the fears regarding discrimination have been realized. In a report covering incidents involving Arab Americans occurring between September 11, 2001, and October 11, 2002 (American-Arab Anti-Discrimination Committee, 2003), the following were reported:

- More than 700 violent incidents were directed at Arab Americans or those perceived to be Arab Americans or Muslims during the first 9 weeks after the September 11 attacks.
- More than 800 cases of employment discrimination against Arab Americans occurred.
- More than 80 cases of illegal or discriminatory removal from aircrafts after boarding occurred (removal based on perceived ethnicity).
- Thousands of Arab men were required to submit to a "voluntary interview" by government officials.
- Numerous instances of denial of services and housing occurred.

Behavioral changes occurred because of the scrutiny given to Arab Americans and Muslims. A Muslim woman stopped giving to Muslim charities, assuming that her donation would be monitored by authorities. An Imam (leader of prayer at a mosque) in Sacramento shaved part of his beard. Among Muslims who worship at a mosque, nearly 100% reported being called a profane name in public, being profiled at airports, or having been visited by authorities. Because of the harassment and resulting fear, some stopped attending prayer services (Sahagun, 2006).

Muslim women face added stressors since their traditional garments are clearly identifiable (Winerman, 2006). Although more than 10 years have passed since the September 11 attacks, Arab and Muslim Americans remain wary. Their concerns may be warranted. Results from a recent poll indicated that 36% of Americans believe that Muslims are too extreme in their religious beliefs and 28% believe they are sympathetic to the Al Qaeda terrorist group (Newport, 2011).

Implications

Because many Americans have negative views of Muslims and Arab Americans, mental health professionals should examine their own attitudes toward these groups.

- Have you been influenced by the negative stereotypes regarding individuals of these groups? Would you feel less safe if your plane had Arab-looking passengers or if you noticed a fellow passenger carrying a Quran? What would your reaction be if a client came in wearing traditional clothing?
- It is important to realize that Arab Americans, especially those who appear to be from an Arab country or who are Muslims, are bombarded by negative stereotypes, prejudice, and discrimination.
- Therapists should be informed regarding antidiscrimination policies, provide clients with information about recourses for discriminatory policies, and support client efforts to challenge discrimination. If clients are encountering job or housing discrimination, the therapist can discuss their legal rights and assist them in taking appropriate actions, such as reporting hate crimes to the police.
- The website for the American-Arab Anti-Discrimination Committee (ADC) offers legal resources and information on addressing discrimination in these and other areas. Mental health professionals should ask about discriminatory actions directed toward clients and be willing to explore these experiences and help seek solutions.

Acculturation Conflicts

A 14-year-old Middle Eastern Muslim boy was suspended from school for the use of alcohol and skipping school. He had been receiving good grades and had no previous behavioral problems. His problems stemmed from acculturation conflicts and the stigma associated with the 9/11 terrorist attacks. (Measham, Guzder, Rousseau, & Nadeau, 2010)

As with many groups that face discrimination and prejudice, some Arab and Muslim Americans do not acknowledge their religion or ethnic background and have changed their names to be more "American sounding." Although some Arab Americans are bicultural and accept both their Arab and American identities (Nobles & Sciarra, 2000), others try to hide their religious and ethnic identities by wearing American-style clothing. Many have completely assimilated, especially those from the first wave of Arab American immigration, who were primarily

Christian. More recent immigrants are more likely to maintain their traditional identity and live in ethnic communities and are more likely to be Muslim and practice their religion in an open fashion (Amri, 2010). Some women in this group may wear the *hijab*, or head scarf, as a sign of modesty. Traditionally oriented Arab and Muslim Americans may avoid certain aspects of American society, preferring to maintain contact with individuals from their own religious group or country of origin. The September 11 attacks appeared to strengthen the ethnic identity of many Arab Americans, with 88% of those polled after the attacks responding that they were proud of their heritage and 84% indicating that their ethnic heritage is important in defining their identity. More than 80% said that securing Palestinian rights is personally important to them (Zogby, 2001b).

> Because culture, values, and religion can differ significantly within the Arab and Muslim American communities, therapists need to determine the background and beliefs of each client or family, rather than responding in a stereotypical manner.

Implications

Because culture, values, and religion can differ significantly within the Arab and Muslim American communities, therapists need to determine the background and beliefs of each client or family, rather than responding in a stereotypical manner. Some individuals may be highly acculturated or assimilated, whereas others may adhere strongly to traditional cultural and religious standards (especially Arab American Muslims). Generational acculturation conflicts are common, with children acculturating more quickly than parents. This may be especially problematic for traditionally oriented Arab Americans who adhere to a hierarchical family structure in which the children are expected to "behave appropriately."

Implications for Clinical Practice

Arab Americans are a very diverse group in terms of religion, culture, country of origin, and degree of acculturation. There is similar diversity within the Muslim community. Recent Muslim immigrants are likely to adhere more strictly to Islamic principles, whereas those who have lived in the United States for much of their lives are more likely to have a moderate perspective (Ibrahim & Dykeman, 2011). In general, non-Arab Americans and non-Muslims possess little knowledge about these groups and have likely been exposed to misinformation. Because of this, many individuals view the action of extremist Islamic groups as representing the view of Muslims and Arab Americans. As mental health workers, we need to understand Arab culture and Muslim beliefs. The following are recommendations for working with Arab American and Muslim clients (Amri, 2010; Ibrahim & Dykeman, 2011):

(continued)

(*continued*)

1. Identify your attitudes about Arab Americans and Muslims.
2. Recognize that many face discrimination and violence because of their Arab background or their religious beliefs.
3. Be ready to help those who have been discriminated against in seeking legal recourse.
4. Cross-gender counselor pairing may be problematic with Arab or Muslim clients. Counselor should inquire if gender of the therapist is a factor to be considered.
5. Recognize that Arab and Muslim Americans are diverse groups. Recent immigrants are more likely to hold stronger traditional values and beliefs. Collaborate with each client or family to gain an understanding of their lifestyle and beliefs, including their religion and the importance of religion in their lives. Religion may not be a factor in the presenting problem,
6. Determine the structure of the family through questions and observation. With traditional families, try addressing the husband or male first. Traditional families may appear highly interdependent, a common cultural characteristic. Determine if acculturation conflicts are producing stress within the family.
7. Be careful of self-disclosures that may be interpreted as weakness. Positive self-disclosures may enhance the therapeutic alliance.
8. In traditionally oriented Arab Americans families, there may be reluctance to share family issues or to express negative feelings with a therapist.
9. There may be greater acceptance to holistic approaches that incorporate family members and the religious or social community, especially with clients who hold more traditional values.
10. Be open to exploring spiritual beliefs and the use of prayer or fasting to reduce distress.
11. Cognitive-behavioral strategies may be productive for Muslims if distressing thoughts are modified in accordance with Islamic beliefs (Khodayarifard & McClenon, 2011).

Counseling Jewish Americans

Thirty percent believe that American Jews are more loyal to Israel than to America, and 29 percent believe that Jews are responsible for the death of Christ. More than a quarter of African-Americans (28%) hold anti-Semitic beliefs, and more than a third of foreign-born Hispanics (35%) have such attitudes. (Anti-Defamation League, 2009)

On July 28, 2006, Naveed Haq, a Muslim, went to the Jewish Federation Office in Seattle, shot one woman to death and wounded five others. His motive for the shooting was a belief that Jews are responsible for conflicts in the Middle East.

David Duke spoke to a group of Holocaust deniers at a conference on the Holocaust convened by Iran's president in 2006. During his speech, the former Imperial Wizard of the Ku Klux Klan and Louisiana State Representative claimed that the Holocaust was a hoax perpetrated by European Jews to justify the occupation of Palestine and the creation of Israel. (Fathi, 2006)

Jewish Americans have long been targets of discrimination and prejudice. That such prejudice continues to this day is revealed in the astonishing statistics that of the 1,376 hate crimes motivated by religious bias, the vast majority (more than 70%) have been anti-Semitic. The second highest, 9.3%, were anti-Islamic (FBI, 2010). Prejudicial reactions against Jews not only involve overt actions such as vandalism, assaults, or direct displays of anti-Semitism but also surface during the celebration of religious holidays or when worldwide events involve Israel or conflicts in the Middle East.

Such prejudice is also revealed in personal statements, such as in 2006 when actor and director Mel Gibson said, "Jews are responsible for all the wars in the world" (Gibson has since apologized for his statement), or when, during a contentious discussion involving the termination of Judith Regan, an editor employed by HarperCollins Publishers, Ms. Regan purportedly made a statement complaining that a "Jewish cabal" was against her, referring to members of the publishing firm and their decisions not to publish a controversial book by O. J. Simpson that Ms. Regan had produced (S. Hall, 2006). Although Jewish Americans have experienced centuries of discrimination both within the

United States and throughout the world, they have received little attention in the multicultural literature.

Jewish Americans include (a) people who practice Judaism and have a Jewish ethnic background, (b) people who have converted to Judaism but who do not have Jewish parents, and (c) individuals with a Jewish ethnic background who do not practice Judaism but still maintain cultural identification and connection to their Jewish descent (Schlosser, 2006). Although most Jewish Americans do not follow all religious traditions (only 40% indicate that religion plays a major role in their lives), many retain strong Jewish connections by celebrating the major holy days of Yom Kippur, Hanukkah, and Passover. Also, some regularly attend synagogue services and follow the tradition of keeping kosher homes (Younis, 2009).

The Jewish population in the United States is estimated to be 5.2 million. It is the largest Jewish community in the world outside of Israel (where there is a Jewish population of 7.8 million); there are also large Jewish populations in Canada and Argentina. Since 1990, the Jewish population in the United States decreased from 5.5 million to 5.2 million. Many are concerned about this decline in the Jewish population in the United States. According to the 2000–2001 National Jewish Survey, this population decline is due to aging (many are older than age 65), falling birth rate, intermarriage, and assimilation. Approximately 52% of Jewish women between the ages of 30 to 34 have not had any children, compared with 27% of all American women; the fertility rate of Jewish women is below that needed to maintain the population. Interfaith marriage rates are about 50%; only one third of these couples raise their children in the Jewish faith, compared with the 96% who marry within their faith (Berkofsky, 2006).

Approximately 85% of Jewish Americans were born in the United States, and almost all are native English speakers. Some speak Hebrew, Yiddish, or the language of their country of origin. Most of those born outside the United States are from the former Soviet Union. Jews are a highly educated group, with 62% of those 18 and older possessing at least a bachelor's degree, versus 22.4% of non-Jews. Their income level and household wealth is also higher than that of the total population (Burstein, 2007). Most Jewish individuals consider themselves to be a minority group and indicate that their heritage is "very" or "somewhat" important to them. About half report "strong emotional ties" to Israel. Jewish Americans were in the forefront of the civil rights movement in the 1960s. In fact, half of the White Freedom Riders and civil rights attorneys involved in the movement were Jewish Americans. In general, Jews describe themselves politically as "liberal" or "very liberal." Jewish Americans are well represented in all aspects of American society in terms of business, education, politics, entertainment, and the arts.

The earliest Jews to arrive in the United States immigrated from Spain and Portugal. The second group of Jewish immigrants emigrated from Germany and Eastern Europe because of persecution and/or economic reasons. By World War I, 250,000 German-speaking Jews had arrived in America. Eastern European Jews came to America as a result of overpopulation, poverty, and persecution. Between 1880 and 1942, more than 2 million Jews from Russia, Austria, Hungary, and

Romania entered the United States and constituted the largest group of Jews in the United States. Because of their historical and political background, Jewish immigrants have tended to be strong supporters of liberal policies in America (Singer, 2002; Zollman, 2006).

CHARACTERISTICS AND STRENGTHS

In the following sections we consider the characteristics, values, and strengths of individuals who are Jewish and consider their implications in treatment. Remember that these are generalizations and their applicability needs to be assessed for particular clients and their families.

Spiritual and Religious Values

Judaism, with its belief in one omnipotent God who created humankind, was one of the earliest monotheistic religions. According to Judaism, God established a covenant with the Jewish people and revealed his commandments to them in the *Torah*, the holy book. The most important commandments are the Ten Commandments. One of the most important Jewish holidays is Yom Kippur, the Day of Atonement. It is a time set aside to atone for sins during the past year. Rosh Hashanah, the start of the Jewish New Year, is another High Holiday in Judaism, This holiday, celebrated 10 days before Yom Kippur, represents the creation of the world or Universe. Even those who are not religious often attend synagogue services and spend time with family during these celebrations.

Within Judaism, the degree of adherence to religious tradition varies. Those who are traditional (Orthodox Judaism) follow all Jewish traditions. Many others are adherents of the progressive movement (Reform Judaism), which advocates the freedom of individuals to make choices about which traditions to follow (Altman, Inman, Fine, Ritter, & Howard, 2010; Rich, 2004). Individuals who wish to convert to Judaism go through the process of (a) studying Judaism and the observance of the commandments, (b) immersion in a ritual bath, and for males, (c) circumcision (symbolic circumcision may be allowed by some sects).

As previously noted, individuals consider themselves to be Jewish not only when they practice Judaism but also if they are nonreligious but of Jewish parentage or upbringing. About half who identify as Jewish adhere to Judaism. However, many others celebrate some Jewish holidays, considering such celebration a cultural rather than a religious activity. These individuals still consider themselves Jewish because of the commonality of history, culture, and experiences. Friedman, Friedlander, and Blustein (2005) conducted interviews with 10 Jewish adults to understand their perspective regarding identity. All participants indicated a fluidity of identity over the years. One stated, "When I was a kid, it made me feel a little bit different in certain situations, but now I would be very proud to be associated with Jewish people and to be Jewish. I would say it has gotten stronger." Another commented on their Jewish identity by responding, "[I]t's the dips and valleys in my life . . . it is pretty much a constant, but it does go up and down" (p. 79).

Among the participants, identity was influenced by childhood experiences, such as participating in Jewish holiday traditions with family members, eating in a kosher dining room, or engaging in discussions with parents about Judaism. As adults, some expressed feelings of guilt for not consistently practicing religious customs. Some had a deep Jewish identity but did not engage in Jewish rituals. However, most expressed pride about being Jewish. From this phenomenological study, Jewish identity appears to be defined differently by those who practice Judaism versus individuals who are secular and do not engage in Jewish religious practices. For many, Jewish identity revolves around common experiences and history, rather than religion.

Cultural Strengths

Judaism is a guidebook on how to live your life and be a good person. . . .
 I keep Kosher because that's what I grew up with and it's something that is a comfort to me. . . . My grandma and all my relatives went through and died for their religion. . . . (Altman et al., 2010, p. 167)

Judaism is more than just a religion. It is a culture with a set of traditions and historical experiences that provide Jewish individuals with a sense of connection and commonality and feelings of acceptance (Schlosser, 2006). Some believe the sociocultural connection is even stronger than the religious aspects of Judaism, although the latter provide ideals that Jews can aspire to. Religious behavior and traditions, such as lighting Shabbat candles, can be calming since they remind individuals of their history and their community (Altmann et al., 2010). These aspects of Judaism serve as protective factors against the discrimination and prejudice that Jews face. Among orthodox Jews, higher levels of religious beliefs are associated with positive mental health. This may be due to emotional and spiritual support from having a personal relationship with God (Rosmarin, Pirutinsky, Pargament, & Krumrei, 2009).

SPECIFIC CHALLENGES

In the following sections we consider challenges often faced by those who are Jewish and consider their implications in treatment. Remember that these are generalizations and their applicability needs to be assessed for each client.

Historical and Sociopolitical Background

Dating back to the Middle Ages, the Jewish people have experienced persecution, oppression, and second-class status, as well as being targeted for massacre or expulsion from their homes (e.g., during the Christian Crusades, the Spanish Inquisition, the Holocaust, and so on). For centuries, they have been stereotyped as hungry for wealth, power, and control and scapegoated during periods of financial distress. An older Jewish woman asked her therapist, "Have you heard of the Holocaust?" (Hinrichsen, 2006, p. 30). The Holocaust represents an incredibly traumatic period in Jewish history. During this period, Nazi Germans murdered approximately 6 million Jewish men, women, and children. There were many more who survived inhumane treatment after being imprisoned in forced labor and concentration camps and whose lives have been affected forever.

> What constitutes Jewish identity is complex and highly personal. An important aspect is a sense of shared cultural and historical experiences.

What constitutes Jewish identity is complex and highly personal. An important aspect is a sense of shared cultural and historical experiences. *Holocaust deniers*, individuals who do not acknowledge or who question the existence of the genocide that occurred during the Holocaust, not only invalidate the loss and suffering of Holocaust victims and their families but also strike at an important part of Jewish identity. It is distressing when this tragic history is ignored or invalidated. It is also hurtful when our society recognizes Christian holidays and religious expectations but ignores those of the Jewish faith.

A well-known mental health practitioner and educator, Stephen Weinrach (2002), was proud of his Jewish identity and became an outspoken critic of the mental health organization to which he belonged for being blind to the plight of Jewish Americans. He wrote:

Issues that have concerned Jews have failed to resonate with the counseling profession, including, for the most part, many of the most outspoken advocates for multicultural counseling. . . . The near universal failure of those committed to multicultural counseling to rail against anti-Semitism and embrace the notion of Jews as a culturally distinct group represents the most painful wound of all. (p. 310)

In his article, Weinrach made the following observations regarding the mental health profession:

- Counseling associations ignore requests from Jewish members to reschedule meetings when the meetings conflict with Jewish holidays (e.g., the National Board for Certified Counselors scheduled the National Counseling Exam on Yom Kippur, a day when work is not permitted).
- Texts on multicultural counseling often do not address Jewish Americans as a diverse group. Only 8% of multicultural courses in APA doctoral programs in counseling covered Jews as a distinct cultural group (Priester et al., 2008).
- Few articles in counseling journals have involved Jewish Americans, and, in some texts, Jewish Americans have been portrayed in a stereotypic manner.

In our opinion, Weinrach has made some valid points. In writing this chapter, we found very few articles on clinical issues involving Jewish Americans or their history of oppression, although numerous articles were easily located for the other diverse groups covered in this text. We must recognize the degree of prejudice and discrimination faced by Jewish Americans and reexamine policies that may be insensitive to their concerns.

Prejudice and Discrimination

Although Jewish individuals have achieved great success, it is evident that they remain targets of prejudice, discrimination, and even violence. About 60% have reported being discriminated against, a rate similar to that reported by African Americans (Berkofsky, 2006; J. J. Goldberg, 2000).

- Anti-Semitic views toward American Jews often arise in conjunction with negative reaction to Israeli actions in the Middle East (Cohen, Jussim, Harber, & Bhasin, 2009).
- In a national poll of American voters (Council for the National Interest, 2006), 39% of Americans believe that the "Israeli lobby" was a key factor responsible for the United States going to war in Iraq and confronting Iran. Among Jewish Americans, 77% disagreed with this view.
- In a survey of Americans (Anti-Defamation League, 2005), it was found that that 14% of the adults surveyed hold "hard-core" anti-Semitic beliefs. Many believe that Jewish Americans wield too much power. One third believe that those who are Jewish are more loyal to Israel than to America.
- Examples of microaggressions against Jewish Americans include automatically assigning intelligence to a Jew; giving preference to Christians; lack of recognition of Jews during multicultural discussions; and assuming that Jews are wealthy and have control over U.S. policy and decisions in Hollywood (Schlosser, 2009a).

Implications

It is evident that Jewish Americans continue to face a great deal of prejudice, even with the successes they have had in American society. It is critical to be aware of the prejudice and discrimination to which Jewish American clients have been exposed. A 78-year-old woman seeking treatment for depression asked the counseling intern, "Are you Jewish?" (Hinrichsen, 2006, p. 30). When the intern inquired about the question, the client stated that she had experienced discrimination from non-Jews and was uncertain whether the intern would understand her difficulties.

> Jewish Americans continue to face a great deal of prejudice, even with the successes they have had in American society. It is critical to be aware of the prejudice and discrimination to which Jewish American clients have been exposed.

Anti-Semitic attitudes within ethnic minority populations may be especially troubling to those who are Jewish; that is, it can be especially hurtful when such attitudes are held by others who have experienced oppression, prejudice, and discrimination. Several reasons may exist regarding the anti-Semitic attitudes of foreign-born Hispanic immigrants and African Americans toward Jewish Americans. First, many do not perceive Jews as a disadvantaged minority. Also, some may resent the fact that the Jewish community has historically supported affirmative action policies and are more likely to favor advancement based on merit (E. Shapiro, 2006).

Ethnic Identity Issues

For many Jewish individuals, their identity is tied to historical events, such as the Holocaust and the oppression historically faced by the Jewish people. It can also involve cultural traditions and ancestry—not just religious beliefs. There is no single Jewish identity; instead there is a range, from individuals who are proud of their Jewish heritage to those who have internalized anti-Semitism and, therefore, hide their Jewish background from others to those who feel confused and alienated from mainstream culture. While some do not publically self-identify as Jewish, others are bicultural and take pride in both American and Jewish identities. Schlosser (2009b) believes that Jews go through the following stages of ethnic identity development:

- Lack of awareness of one's Jewish identity
- Gradual awareness of Jewish identity
- Comparison of Jewish identity with other religions, such as Christianity
- Development of a sense of Jewishness
- Integration of Jewish identity with other identities

Implications

Counselors should recognize that American Jews may have identity concerns that deal with anti-Semitism, living under Christian privilege, the Shoah (Holocaust), and the invisibility of Judaism. Jews are highly diverse in regard to cultural and ethnic identity and adherence to religious orthodoxy. The counselor should not assume that all Jewish clients see Jewish identity or practice Judaism in the same manner (Schlosser, 2006).

Implications for Clinical Practice

In *Jewish Issues in Multiculturalism: A Handbook for Educators and Clinicians*, Langman (1999) indicates it is difficult to use culturally appropriate interventions because of the diversity of the Jewish culture. However, he does offer some guiding principles of importance for mental health providers. First, it is very important to be respectful of and knowledgeable about Jewish culture. Because most clinicians are from a Christian background, the traditions, values, and religious rituals that are important to Jewish Americans are often overlooked or are dismissed. As we discussed in Chapter 6, therapists might inadvertently commit microaggressions due to their lack of understanding. For example, Langman provides the example of a Jewish client who requested that an appointment not be scheduled during Yom Kippur, to which the therapist responded: "What? Do you need to pray or something?" The client felt humiliated, devalued, ashamed, and unsupported.

(continued)

(*continued*)

Second, therapists should strive to understand the full spectrum of Jewish identities within the Jewish population, including those of religious as well as nonreligious Jews. As our prior section indicates, knowledge of the history of anti-Semitism, its effects on identity, and possible repercussions of internalized anti-Semitism should be recognized. Langman discusses the latter as an insidious social conditioning process that makes some Jewish Americans ashamed of their ethnic and religious heritage. In this respect, he views the sociopolitical process that equates Jewish differences as deviance to be the culprit and encourages counselors not to "blame the victim."

Third, Langman makes it clear that therapists need to be aware of their own values, assumptions, and biases that may be detrimental to their Jewish clients. He cites research that indicates that Jews are viewed as being "cold," "hostile," and "obstructive," whereas White non-Jews are seen as being more "warm," "friendly," and "helpful." He encourages counselors to explore any feelings of negativism toward Jewish Americans, Jewish culture, Judaism, and/or Israel.

Finally, although about half of Jewish Americans are not associated with a synagogue or have only slight connections to a Jewish congregation, it may be desirable to consult with a rabbi when working with clients who are strongly religious, particularly those who maintain Orthodox beliefs. In some cases, religious doubts or issues regarding religiously prohibited behaviors or behaviors associated with guilt or shame may be best addressed with guidance from religious leaders as part of the therapeutic process. Such consultation is easier when the counselor has spent time cultivating relationships with the Jewish community. Counselors should also consider the following (Altman et al., 2010):

1. As members of mental health professions, we must be aware of policies or expectations that do not take Jewish American concerns into consideration, such as scheduling meetings or appointments on Jewish holidays.
2. We need to examine our attitudes and beliefs regarding Jewish Americans. Are their problems invisible to us? Is our failure to acknowledge the discrimination experienced by those of the Jewish faith due to a Christian-centered worldview, a lack of knowledge, or a reflection of anti-Semitism?
3. It is important to remember that Jewish Americans are the most targeted religious group for hate crimes and discrimination. Because many Jewish Americans are well educated and economically secure, we often do not understand that they may suffer from discrimination or hate.
4. Jewish American mental health professionals should also feel free to bring up their concerns when they are subjected to insensitivity or discrimination.
5. Jewish counselors should take care not to make assumptions about a client's Jewish identity and issues based on the counselor's own sense of identity or beliefs regarding Judaism (Friedman et al., 2005).

Counseling Immigrants and Refugees

The Latino community in a small central Washington college town nervously hid behind closed doors Friday following an immigration raid. . . . Relatives were left scrambling to find child care for the children left behind. . . . As Brientos's husband prepared to leave for work . . . immigration agents arrived at the trailer park with guns drawn. . . . They were shouting orders and knocking down doors. (Dininny, 2011, p. 1)

Latino students have started vanishing from Alabama public schools in the wake of a court ruling that upheld the state's tough new law cracking down on illegal immigration. . . . Several districts with large immigrant enrollments . . . reported a sudden exodus of children from Latino families, some of whom told officials they would leave the state to avoid trouble with the law, which requires schools to check students' immigration status. (Reeves, 2011, p. 1)

There are about 33.5 million immigrants living in the United States, which is about 12% of the population. About half have arrived since 1990. The reasons for migration include escape from poverty, seeking a higher quality of life, and political unrest (Negy, Schwartz, & Reig-Ferrer, 2009). Approximately half of those who immigrated to the United States since 1965 are from Latin America and one fourth from Asia; many others come from Europe, Canada, the Middle East, and Africa (Pew Research Center, 2009). Many immigrants, particularly those from undeveloped countries, earn lower wages and have a high incidence of poverty.

Although the percentage of immigrants with a bachelor's or other advanced degree is slightly higher compared with adults born in the United States, 33% of U.S. adult immigrants have not completed high school (compared with 12.5% of the total adult population). Immigrant students had a high school dropout rate of 21% in 2009, rates significantly higher than the national average. Although immigrants account for 10% of high school students, they account for 27% of high school dropouts (Child Trends, 2011). Children of immigrant families have high rates of poverty (35%), and almost half are uninsured (Wight, Thampi, & Chau, 2011).

It is estimated that 36% of immigrants are legally admitted as permanent residents or have temporary visas (e.g., work or student visas). Individuals with permission to reside and work in the United States hold a *green card* and are required to carry a copy of the card with them. Although U.S. citizenship is not required to legally remain in the United States, 32% of immigrants have gone through the process of becoming *naturalized citizens*—they have met requirements to become U.S. citizens (Camarota, 2010).

In 2010, there were an estimated 11.2 million undocumented immigrants in the United States (Pew Research Center, 2011). This primarily includes individuals who entered the United States without permission and those who stayed after obtaining temporary legal admission. Of the unauthorized immigrants in the United States, 76% are Latino/a (primarily from Mexico), 11% are from Asia, 4% from the Caribbean, 2% from the Middle East, and the remainder from other countries. They make up about 5.4% of the labor force in low-skilled, low-paying jobs (Passel & Cohn, 2009). About 60% of the farmworkers who help pick billions of dollars worth of agricultural products are undocumented immigrants. Nearly 25% of workers who butcher meat, poultry, and fish are undocumented, including many women. Most undocumented immigrants subsist on poverty-level wages and are exposed to exploitation and abuse in the workplace. A high percentage of women working in these food industries are subject to sexual abuse (Southern Poverty Law Center, 2010).

In our society, immigrants have received a mixed reception from both the government and the public. Not only are immigrants faced with the stress of adjusting to a new country, but they are often exposed to a hostile environment once reaching the United States. For example, Mexican immigrants were blamed for the 2009 outbreak of swine flu (Alexander, 2009). In a poll, 70% of White Americans supported the provisions of the Arizona anti-immigration law that requires state and local law enforcement officials to question people about their immigration status if they believe the person might be in the country illegally (Murray, 2010).

Although the public is divided regarding perceptions of how immigrants affect the economy and their place in the nation, approximately half agree that "immigrants today are a burden on our country because they take our jobs, housing, and health care." Only one third agree that "immigrants today strengthen our country because of their hard work and talents." In contrast, Latinos (78%) are less likely to resent the presence of immigrants and more likely to say that immigration strengthens the country (Pew Research Center, 2010b). The strong backlash against the Bush administration's (2004) proposal to pass a guest worker program for undocumented immigrants resulted in plans to build a physical border between Mexico and the United States and the formation of citizen's vigilante groups (e.g., Minute Men).

Immigrants have made positive social, political, and cultural contributions to U.S. society for generations. Immigrants often demonstrate significant loyalty to their chosen "homeland" and have brought with them both ingenuity and a strong work ethic. Many immigrants are from countries with a collectivistic orientation; they often serve as role models of interdependence and cooperation with multiple extended family and community supports. Immigrants are often supportive of each other and promote group identification and acceptance of differences. These kinds of supports can help ameliorate stressors involved in living in a new culture, especially one that stresses the individual. The attributes from the various ethnic and cultural groups to which immigrants belong strengthen the diversity of our nation.

CHALLENGES FACING IMMIGRANTS

In the following sections we consider challenges often faced by immigrants and consider their implications in treatment. Remember that these are generalizations and their applicability needs to be assessed for each client.

Historical and Sociopolitical Factors

Historically, many U.S. immigration policies and laws have been unfair and exclusionary (Chung & Bemak, 2007). Until 1952, only White persons were allowed to become naturalized citizens. With the Immigration Act of 1965, people from any nation were finally allowed to become naturalized citizens. In part, this change was facilitated by the U.S. civil rights movement. However, attempts to decrease immigrant rights continue. For example, in 2006, the Ohio legislature passed a law (subsequently overturned for being unconstitutional) that allowed election officials at polling places to make inquiries of registered voters who appeared to be immigrants (e.g., Are you a native or a naturalized citizen? Where were you born? What official documentation do you possess to prove your citizenship?). They were then required to provide documentation and to declare, under oath, that they were the person named in the documentation.

Many citizens are opposed to the number of immigrants entering the United States and the idea of providing a path to citizenship for illegal immigrants. In the latter case, the argument is often made that illegal immigrants violated the law by not following immigration policy and procedures and that they are a drain on the social system. Those on the other side of the debate counter that businesses have benefited from and continue to rely on the work provided by undocumented workers, many of whom have lived in the United States for decades, paying taxes and contributing to their communities.

As previously mentioned, the 2010 census estimated 11.2 million undocumented immigrants living in the United States. Anti-immigration laws and the recent economic downturn have not, in fact, led to a significant reduction in this population because many of these immigrants are now remaining in the United States rather than following the historic pattern of periodic (or permanent) return to their homeland (Marrero, 2011). According to the Department of Homeland Security, only about 39% of undocumented immigrants arrived after the year 2000; most are well integrated into society and have children born in the United States—children whose dominant language is English and who have never visited their parent's homeland. Having established their lives in the United States and having children who only know life in the United States is a powerful reason for these immigrants to want to remain in the country. The work of these undocumented immigrants is indispensable in agriculture, construction, child care, and in the restaurant and hotel industry (Marrero, 2011).

Although the vast majority of undocumented workers pay taxes and only minimally use health care, welfare, or other social services (Massey, Durand, & Malone, 2002), many states and communities have passed or are in the process of passing laws against the provision of social and other services to this population. For example, in 2005, a bill (House Bill 4437) passed in the House of Representatives combined border protection, illegal immigration control, and antiterrorism efforts. If this bill had also passed the Senate and been signed into law, faith-based groups or "good Samaritans" could have been prosecuted for assisting undocumented immigrants. Additionally, undocumented immigrants would have been classified as "aggravated felons," thus allowing local law enforcement officials to expel them from the country.

More recently, legislation was enacted in Arizona that made it a crime for noncitizens to be in Arizona without official documents authorizing their presence in the United States; further, law enforcement officers must verify immigration status when lawfully stopping, detaining, or arresting someone they believe might be in the United States illegally. This law, supported by the majority of U.S. citizens and Arizona residents, has been criticized as a form of "racial profiling." Additionally, new laws in Arizona banned instructors with "heavy accents" from teaching English classes (Martinez & Gutierrez, 2010; Navarrette, 2011). Even before these recent laws, polls indicated that a large number of Latino/a adults in the United States were concerned that they, a family member, or a close friend would be deported (Pew Hispanic Center, 2007). These laws and actions are likely to continue to provoke fear and unease within the immigrant population, as well as decrease the likelihood of immigrants reporting crimes or abuse.

Prejudice and Discrimination

The sign outside of one of Philadelphia's famous cheesesteak restaurants reads "This is AMERICA: WHEN ORDERING 'PLEASE SPEAK ENGLISH.'" The owner put up the sign due to frustration about customers (primarily immigrants from Latin America and Asia) who were unable to order in English. This sign has been challenged by members of the City's Commission on Human Relations, who argue that the sign discourages customers of "certain backgrounds" from eating there. (Associated Press, 2006a)

The September 11, 2001, terrorist attacks had a dramatic impact on attitudes toward immigrants. The resulting emphasis on preventing the entry of terrorists into the United States resulted in not only Arab or Muslim Americans being viewed with suspicion but also anyone "appearing foreign." Immigrants became regarded as possible terrorists. Since the trauma of September 11, the movement toward legalization of undocumented immigrants has slowed, and there has been a dramatic decline in admission of refugees (Patrick, 2004). The nativism movement, promoting the position that only U.S. "natives" (understood to be people of European descent) belong in the United States, is receiving greater support

(American Friends Service Committee, 2006a, 2006c). Similarly, the English-only movement, viewed by many immigrants and others as being exclusionary, is strengthening.

Although immigrants already use less than half of available health care resources as compared with the average U.S. citizen (National Immigration Law Center, 2006), the climate of fear has led to even further decreases in the utilization of medical or government services by immigrants. Many immigrants, even those who are permanent legal residents, fear deportation or not being granted citizenship. Many are afraid that seeking assistance might suggest an inability to live here independently. There is also concern among immigrants that agencies might contact authorities if services are sought. Children of immigrants born in the United States are citizens, but many harbor great fear and anxiety regarding the immigration status of their parents, siblings, or other close family members.

It is clear that societal and governmental reactions to immigrants are influenced by social conditions. They become more negative when economic conditions result in a loss of jobs or limited housing. In areas experiencing economic stress, negative feelings toward immigrants increase. Conflicts are sometimes seen between immigrants and U.S.-born ethnic minorities. In some U.S. cities, the confrontations have been violent. Most have involved issues regarding jobs, schools, and housing, particularly when there is a perception that immigrants are taking jobs and other resources away from U.S.-born citizens. As Ada Edwards, a radio director, noted, "In some communities there is a . . . shortage in low-income housing. So, when you have low-income groups and they're all [competing] for the same house, they start working against each other instead of looking at the problem of availability of low-income housing" (as cited in American Friends Service Committee, 2006b, p. 2). The debate over a path to citizenship for undocumented immigrants has also gained prominence in recent years and has led to a number of large pro-immigration demonstrations. Unfortunately, it has also fueled anti-immigrant feeling in some quarters. Over half of Latinos polled in a national survey reported they have seen an increase in discrimination because of the debate over immigration policy (Suro & Escobar, 2006).

Implications

Mental health professionals should be aware that immigrant clients or their families may see the therapist as an arm of government. The therapist should also be aware of the rights or exclusions associated with immigrant status (N. Bernstein, 2006):

- Hospitals are required to provide emergency care to anyone, including undocumented immigrants. Other treatments depend on local laws. Information regarding other immigrant issues can be obtained from the National Immigration Law Center.
- Free community clinics exist that will treat individuals regardless of immigration status.
- Immigrants can ask for interpreter services from health care providers.

Most documented immigrants are not eligible to receive Medicaid, food stamps, or social security benefits during their first five years in the United States or longer, regardless of how much they have paid in taxes.

Cultural and Acculturation Conflicts

Some of the most difficult challenges faced by immigrants are their adjustment and adaptation to new cultural customs within a completely different society and the mixed reception they receive from U.S. citizens. Placed in unfamiliar settings, adjusting to climactic differences, and lacking community and social support, many experience severe culture shock (Chung & Bemak, 2007). Feelings of isolation, loneliness, disorientation, helplessness, anxiety, and depression often characterize the immigration experience. The only sources of comfort and support may be a small circle of relatives or friends, who also may be adjusting to a different way of life. Immigrants need to negotiate the educational system, acquire language proficiency, and seek employment. All three of these major challenges require immigrants to attain knowledge and understanding of the workings of U.S. society, sometimes an overwhelming task. Immigrants often come from countries in which there are gender inequities and spousal abuse; help-seeking barriers may be present because of self-blame, concern for the children, or lack of knowledge regarding abuse (Ting & Panchanadeswaran, 2009).

Implications

In additional to traditional mental health services, psychoeducational approaches are often required to assist immigrants to acquire (a) education and training for themselves and their children; (b) knowledge of employment opportunities, job search skills, and the ability to manage financial demands; (c) language proficiency to ensure success in this society; and (d) strategies to manage family relationship conflicts. Counselors often need to take on multiple roles, including educator (providing information on services and educating immigrants about their rights and responsibilities) and advocate (helping negotiate the institutional structures of the health care, education, and employment systems). To effectively assist immigrants, it is important to understand the life circumstances of immigrant groups, to have liaisons within the immigrant community, and to be familiar with community resources aimed at helping immigrants adjust to a new world.

Gender Issues and Domestic Violence

Male immigrants often face the loss of status and develop a sense of powerlessness. They may have lost their assigned roles within the family and society as a whole and may be unemployed or underemployed. Because women often find it easier to gain employment, the resulting changes in the balance of power increase the risk of domestic violence as men attempt to reestablish their authority and power. Among many immigrant groups, women are socialized to sacrifice their own personal needs for the good of their husbands and children. Such training leads to ignoring or denying their own pains or symptoms so that their family needs are taken care of (Ro, 2002). Fear of reporting partner abuse is made more difficult because of economic dependence or fear of retaliation (Quiroga & Flores-Ortiz, 2000).

Implications

As with other cases involving family violence, the following steps are recommended (J. L. Lum, 1999).

- Assess the lethality of the situation. If there is a high degree of danger, develop a safety plan. The woman should know where she and her children can stay if she needs to leave home. The therapist should help identify shelters or other resources available for the particular immigrant group to which the woman belongs.
- If the degree of violence is nonlethal and the woman does not want to leave the home, provide psychoeducational information on abusive relationships, the cycle of violence, and legal recourse. Give crisis numbers or other contact information to use if the violence escalates.
- Convey an understanding of both the cultural and situational obstacles the client faces. Forming a strong therapeutic relationship is especially important if no support is available from other family members or friends. In congruence with cultural perspectives, the woman's role may be defined as the one who protects and cares for everyone's welfare.
- Attempt to expand support systems for the client, especially within the client's community. Support groups and services are now available for a number of different immigrant groups.

Barriers to Seeking Treatment

Multiple barriers exist for immigrants in their utilization of social and mental health services. As mentioned earlier, immigrants utilize health care services much less than U.S. citizens. Mental health providers need to understand how cultural, linguistic, and informational barriers can affect immigrants.

In a survey of health care providers, several barriers to accessing services were identified:

- *Communication difficulties due to language differences:* More than half of the providers identified language barriers as the major source of difficulty regarding service delivery. This affects critical areas, such as obtaining accurate information during assessment and testing. The providers also mentioned that it is difficult to obtain interpreter services, especially given the diversity of dialects within some ethnic groups. This barrier most commonly involves Latino/a and Asian immigrants, who are the least likely to have learned English (Weisman et al., 2005).
- *Lack of knowledge of mainstream service delivery:* Many immigrants lack knowledge about how the health care system operates in the United States. Extra

time is required when providers try to explain clinic practices and paperwork. Often, apparent noncompliance in following through with recommendations is due to poor understanding of services.

- *Cultural factors:* Many immigrant groups are hesitant to speak about "family issues" or issues of personal concern because of the cultural importance of privacy (Chung & Bemak, 2007). Women who were abused by their husbands or have been sexually assaulted may not talk about these issues because of cultural norms and shame, as well as fear of deportation. A stigma exists for many immigrants in seeking help for mental health problems. Emotional dysfunctions may be labeled "craziness," or there may be fear that difficulties will be blamed on the family.
- *Lack of resources:* Many immigrant families are poor and lack transportation to go to the service location. In addition, there may be a lack of time to attend sessions, due to the economic necessity to work as many hours as possible or to limited flexibility in work schedules.

Linguistic and Communication Issues

If immigrants are not fluent in English, the use of interpreters may be necessary. Many therapists and interpreters are not aware of the dynamics involved or the impact on the traditional dyadic therapeutic relationship when adding another individual. Mental health professionals need to know some of these issues when using interpreters. Most interpreters receive little or no training in working with distressed or traumatized individuals, and they may experience uncontrollable feelings of emotional distress when hearing traumatic stories, especially when their backgrounds are similar to those of the clients (K. E. Miller, Zoe, Pazdirek, Caruth, & Lopez, 2005).

Sometimes revelations produce a "reexperiencing of their own trauma," resulting in a tendency to disengage emotionally. For example, one interpreter discovered that in order to protect herself from distressing feelings as she was interpreting for traumatized clients, she became dismissive and casual when describing the violent events brought up by the clients. In another case, a therapist observed, "I had one interpreter start shaking. It was too much for her. The client had been raped, and it was a woman interpreter and a woman client. . . . She just became incredibly upset and angry" (K. E. Miller et al., 2005, p. 34).

> Therapists also report developing reactions to interpreters. Some initially think of the interpreters as "translation machines," whose interpersonal qualities are unimportant. Eventually, however, therapists often realize that interpreters form part of a three-person alliance.

Therapists also report developing reactions to interpreters. Some initially think of the interpreters as "translation machines," whose interpersonal qualities are unimportant. Eventually, however, therapists often realize that interpreters form part of a three-person alliance. Clients sometimes initially develop a stronger attachment to the interpreter than to the therapist. Because of this, therapists need to deal with feelings of "being left out" and to accept that their relationships with clients might develop in a slower fashion. Therapists can choose to use interpreters as important cultural resources by obtaining the interpreter's thoughts regarding issues discussed in sessions. In general, many therapists are appreciative of interpreters and do not perceive any long-term negative effects on therapeutic progress. Some even mention that the presence of an interpreter can mitigate the intensity of the emotional impact from hearing traumatic stories. Sometimes, however, interpreters interject their own opinions, intervene directly with clients, or question interventions because they do not understand the therapeutic approach (K. E. Miller et al., 2005).

Implications

These results indicate the necessity of specific training in the best practices for both therapists and interpreters (H. R. Searight & Searight, 2009; Yakushko, 2010).

- Interpreters should receive brief training regarding specific mental disorders and the interventions employed in therapy, particularly treatment of trauma, grief, and loss.
- Because interpreters can be affected emotionally by traumatic experiences discussed in therapy, therapists should discuss self-care strategies for the interpreters, as well as ways of dealing with exposure to traumatic reports.
- Clients clearly do not regard interpreters as translation machines. Therefore, interpreters should be trained in the relationship skills that are needed in therapy. In the triadic relationship, interpersonal skills such as empathy and congruence are necessary.
- Therapists should also receive training on how to work effectively with interpreters and become conversant with different models of interpreting. Some prefer simultaneous translation, whereas others prefer delayed translation.

Therapists should also be aware that, in many cases, the therapeutic alliance may form first with the interpreter. Many therapists who have worked with interpreters understand that for non-English-speaking clients, interpreters are the bridge between the therapist and the client and are critical in assessment and the provision of therapy.

COUNSELING REFUGEES

Deng fled the civil war in Sudan and has been in the United States for the past 2 years. He is 28 years old and spent 4 years in a refugee camp before coming to the United States. He describes fleeing burning villages outside of Darfur and seeing many people from his own family and community slaughtered, raped, and beaten. He remembers running and hiding, being near starvation, drinking muddy water, avoiding crocodiles and once a lion, and being alarmed when bombs dropped nearby. . . . He wonders what happened to his family and friends and feels guilty for having escaped. He arrived in the United States without parents or family and with no possessions. (Chung & Bemak, 2007, p. 133)

Deng's escape from Sudan and the trauma he experienced are not uncommon for refugees. In contrast to other immigrants who voluntary left their country of origin, *refugees* are individuals who flee their country of origin in order to escape persecution due to race, religion, nationality, political opinion, or membership in a particular social group (Chung & Bemak, 2007). *Asylees*, individuals who meet the criteria for refugee status, are physically present in the United States or at a point of entry when granted permission to reside in the United States. Similar to refugees, asylum seekers have been uprooted from their countries of origin, often after suffering years of persecution or torture directed toward themselves, their family and friends, or even their entire community.

Predetermined allotments for specific geographical locations limit the number of refugees and asylees accepted by the U.S. government; these limits change from year to year (Rytina, 2005). During 2005, for example, more than 53,813 refugees from Somalia, Laos, Cuba, Russia, Liberia, Ukraine, Sudan, Vietnam, Iran, and Ethiopia were admitted to the United States. In addition, more than 25,000 individuals (including their immediate family members) were granted *asylum;* the countries contributing the greatest number to this group were China, Colombia, Haiti, and Venezuela (Batalova, 2006).

In 2010, the 73,293 refugees admitted to the United States were primarily from three countries: Iraq, Burma, and Bhutan; in addition, 21,113 individuals (primarily from China, Ethiopia, and Haiti) were granted asylum (Martin, 2011). Some 1.5 million refugees from Southeast Asia arrived in the United States between 1975 and 1995, most from Vietnam, Cambodia, and Laos (Chung, Bemak, & Okazaki, 1997). The vast majority of Vietnamese, who left just before the fall of Saigon in 1975, had only a few days to decide whether to leave their country. Refugees frequently spend years in resettlement camps, waiting to be resettled in any country willing to accept them.

What characterizes the life experience of many refugees is their premigration trauma, often life-threatening in nature. The impact of trauma is likely to be exacerbated by the challenges of adjustment to a new world. Being displaced from their country of origin, refugees often express concern about adapting to a new culture and country. Losing their cultural identity is also a worry. Lacking a support or community group, many refugees feel estranged and isolated. Many report feelings of homesickness and concerns over the breakup of family and community ties. There are often worries about the future, difficulties communicating in English, and unemployment. Refugees want their children to learn their native language and to maintain family and cultural traditions. The Americanization of children is of special concern to many refugee parents, given the U.S. societal emphasis on openness and individuality. Parents may worry about the academic and social adjustment of their children and what they perceive to be a lack of discipline in American society. Because of the need to work, many have inflexible, low-wage jobs that prevent them from monitoring their children (Weine et al., 2006).

Effects of Past Persecution, Torture, or Trauma

Trauma, loss, and feelings of displacement are very common among refugees. Posttraumatic stress disorder (PTSD) and elevated rates of mood and anxiety disorders are frequent in this population (Nickerson, Bryant, Silove, & Steel, 2010), including nightmares and symptoms involving dissociation, intrusive thoughts, and hypervigilance (Chung & Bemak, 2007). It is important to note, however, that the vast majority of refugees are able to make a healthy transition to life in the United States. Although many of the challenges faced by refugees are similar to those encountered by other immigrants, differences do exist. In general, refugees are under more stress than other immigrants (Chung, Bemak, Ortiz, & Sandoval-Perez, 2008). Most immigrants had time to prepare for their move to the United States, whereas for most refugees the escape was sudden and traumatic (Bemak, Chung, & Bornemann, 1996). Family members are often left behind. With the exception of undocumented immigrants, who often have experienced robbery, beatings, and sexual assault, refugees have typically been exposed to more trauma than other immigrants.

The premigration experiences of many refugees are filled with the atrocities of war, torture and killing, sexual assault, incarceration, and a continuing threat of death. For example, Central American refugees from El Salvador, Guatemala, Nicaragua, and Honduras related violent experiences, such as witnessing beatings and killings, fearing for their own lives or that of family members, being injured, or being victims of sexual assault. These Central American refugees reported feelings of isolation and exhibited high levels of mistrust with service providers (Asner-Self & Marotta, 2005). Refugees often experience emotional reactions related to the destruction of their family and social networks, sometimes as a result of genocide. Many report that memories of war intrude into their daily lives.

Implications

To see loved ones raped, beaten, and killed can have lasting, long-term consequences. It may be difficult to share such traumatic experiences with a therapist. Women may be even more affected if they have been sexually abused or assaulted. In some countries, sexually assaulted women are shunned and considered unfit for marriage. In order to have a strong therapeutic relationship with traumatized refugees, it is especially important to establish trust and to recognize that the disclosure of traumatic experiences takes time. There may be a hesitation to relay experiences of torture due to feelings of fear, shame, or humiliation. Clients should be allowed to go at their own pace in bringing up these experiences. Questions related to exposure to weapons, violence, or other stressful incidents

> In order to have a strong therapeutic relationship with traumatized refugees, it is especially important to establish trust and to recognize that the disclosure of traumatic experiences takes time. There may be a hesitation to relay experiences of torture due to feelings of fear, shame, or humiliation. Clients should be allowed to go at their own pace in bringing up these experiences.

might allow for greater comfort in revealing traumatic experiences (Asner-Self & Marotta, 2005).

It is important to consider the cultural perspective of refugees regarding mental and physical disorders to determine how their views might be different from the dominant culture. Many immigrants take a somatic view of psychological disorders—that mental disorders are the result of physical problems. If somatic symptoms are brought up, the therapist can work first with the somatic complaints. Also, because there may be a lack of understanding of PTSD symptoms, therapists can help clients understand why they occur. Symptoms can be framed as normal reactions to trauma that anyone in their situation might develop. Therapists can reassure clients that the symptoms can be treated and are not signs that they are "going crazy."

Safety Issues and Coping With Loss

Refugees often come from politically unstable situations. In such cases, issues of safety are salient and must be addressed. Some clients may have faced the adversarial experience of having to prove that they were persecuted before being allowed into the United States. Because of this, they may be reluctant to relate experiences for fear of being disbelieved. The loss of friends, family, and status is very troubling to immigrants and refugees. Refugees often feel guilty about leaving other family members behind and may go through a bereavement process. Many will not be able to resume their previous level of occupational and social functioning. It is important to identify their perceptions about what is lost.

Implications

Based on negative experiences with governmental powers in their homeland, refugees may also be concerned about providing information or may be very wary of how information will be used. Confidentiality and the reason for assessment should be carefully discussed. Additionally, since problem behaviors or mental difficulties may be seen as a source of shame for the individual or the family, knowing that the information obtained will be confidential may offer some relief. It is helpful to acknowledge the difficulty involved in sharing private information, with reassurance that it is necessary in order to develop the best solutions. To determine the possibility that cultural constraints exist, the counselor might also state something like the following: "Sometimes people in counseling believe that family issues should stay in the family. How do you feel about this belief?"

To understand the loss experienced by refugees, it may be beneficial to obtain a migration narrative as part of the assessment. This provides an understanding of the individual's social and occupational life prior to leaving his or her country of origin. Information regarding family life, friends, and activities can be gathered by asking questions such as, "How would you describe your daily life in your country of origin? What did you like and dislike about your country? What was family life like? What kind of job or family roles did you have? What was your community like? How did you decide to leave your country?" Therapists can also inquire about experiences with transit from their homeland and any traumas associated with this process. "What happened before, during, and after you left your country? What differences do you see between living in your country and living in America? What do you see as advantages and disadvantages of living in either country?" It is important to understand experiences with resettlement camps and whether family members were separated. In addition, one should inquire about clients' experiences with prejudice and discrimination in their homeland and since arriving in the United States. This process gives a clearer picture of the perceived losses and experiences of refugees (Weisman et al., 2005).

Implications for Clinical Practice

Many immigrants hold cultural belief systems that are collectivistic and thus consider interpersonal relationships and social networks to be of paramount importance. The Western worldview, however, is individualistic and stresses the importance of autonomy, mastery, and control of the environment. Mental health systems that value independence over interdependence, separate mental functioning from physical functioning, attribute causation as internally located, and that seek to explain events from a Western empiricist approach can be at odds with the cultural belief systems of immigrants. Counselors may inadvertently impose their belief systems on immigrant populations and communicate a disrespect or invalidation of their worldview. A counselor should also perform a self-assessment with respect to immigrants by asking themselves questions such as, "How do I feel about immigrants and refugees coming to our country?" "What are my feelings about illegal immigrants?" (Villalba, 2009). It is important for therapists to consider the following (Burnett & Thompson, 2005):

1. Remember that immigrants face multiple stressors, including the stress of moving to and living in another country; learning another language; and negotiating new social, economic, political, educational, and social systems. It is often a confusing and frightening experience. Mental health providers who understand the complexities of this situation can do much to reassure clients by demystifying the process.
2. Be aware that the client may have day-to-day stressors, such as limited resources, a need for permanent shelter, lack of employment, or frustrating interactions with agencies. Allow time to understand and to provide support related to these immediate needs, or help the client locate resources related to specific needs (Grey & Young, 2008).
3. Do not assume that the client has an understanding of mental health services or counseling. Give a description of what counseling is and the role of therapist and client.
4. Inquire about client beliefs regarding the cause of their difficulties, listening for socio-political, cultural, religious, or spiritual interpretations. Understanding and validating clients' conceptualizations of presenting problems within their cultural matrix is an important aspect of providing culturally relevant services.
5. Allow time for clients to share their backgrounds, their premigration stories, and changes in their lives since immigrating.

(continued)

(*continued*)

6. Use psychoeducation to explain the symptoms of disorders, the psychotherapeutic approach, and how chosen strategies will help the client make desired changes. Modify evidence-based therapies to include cultural beliefs (Nickerson et al., 2010).

7. Keep current regarding what is happening at the local, state, and federal level relative to immigration issues, particularly the tone of the debate. As our review indicates, sociopolitical conditions and public policy can have either positive or detrimental impact on the life experiences of immigrants.

8. Families may be impacted by poverty, fear of immigration raids, parents working multiple jobs, and a lack of an extended family network. In addition, acculturation conflicts can occur. In some families, children have learned to threaten parents with dialing 911 when physically disciplined (Leidy, Guerra, & Toro, 2010).

9. Mental health providers should consider offering services within the immigrant community rather than outside of it. These services should be made culturally relevant and partially staffed by members of the immigrant community.

10. In the course of assessment and diagnosis of mental disorders, take into account environmental factors, language barriers, and potential exposure to discrimination and hostility. When necessary, use skilled and knowledgeable interpreters.

11. Be knowledgeable about refugee experiences and psychological strategies commonly used to cope with stress. Understand symptom manifestations likely to indicate posttraumatic stress and other mental disorders that may arise from experiences of war, imprisonment, persecution, rape, and torture. These symptoms could be nightmares, avoidance, hopelessness, and negative beliefs about the self and others. Develop your own system of self-care to decrease the effects of intense work with clients with traumatic histories.

PART VIII

Counseling and Therapy With Other Multicultural Populations

Counseling LGBT Individuals

CHAPTER

22

Jacob Williams, a preschool student, was playing when a little girl who had been observing him asked where his dad was. Jacob responded by saying he didn't have a father but had two moms. The little girl was confused but later walked up to one of the two mothers and said she had "figured it out." She had two granddads, so Jacob could have two moms. (Wingert & Kantrowitz, 2000)

Because of the repeal of the "don't ask, don't tell" policy, transgender people believe they should not be denied the ability to serve in the armed forces. Military officials argue that they are not discriminating against transgender individuals—it is just that because they suffer from a gender identity disorder, they are not fit for military service. (Perkins, 2011)

"Transgender people are second-class citizens, and bisexuals are below even them. We're the white trash of the gay world, a group whom it is socially acceptable not to accept. Feeling awkward among straights is what it feels like to be bi. Being distrusted among gays is what it feels like, too." (Pajor, 2005, p. 575)

In this chapter we will discuss lesbian, gay, bisexual, or transgender (LGBT) Americans—individuals who have an affectional and/or sexual attraction to a person of the same sex (gay men and lesbians); individuals who have an affectional and/or sexual attraction to members of both sexes (bisexuals); and individuals whose gender identification is inconsistent with their biological sex (transgender) (LGBT may also be referred to as LGBTQ. The *Q* represents individuals who identify as queer or who are questioning their sexuality.) It is estimated that there are approximately 9 million LGBT Americans; in addition, about 19 million Americans have engaged in same-sex behaviors. In fact, around one fourth of the adult population acknowledges some same-sex attraction. An estimated 3.5% of American adults identify as lesbian, gay, or bisexual, with 0.3% identifying as transgender. The bisexual population (the majority of whom are women) is slightly larger than the lesbian or the gay male population (Gates, 2011).

The mood of the country reveals contradictory attitudes and actions toward sexual minorities. Overall, there appears to be increased acceptance of LGBT individuals and their lifestyles. In a national survey, a large majority supported job protection, antidiscrimination in housing, and health benefits for gay men and lesbians (American Enterprise Institute, 2004). A growing number of states have passed laws allowing same-sex marriages (CNN, 2011). The Obama administration supported the "Respect for Marriage Act," a legislative effort to repeal the "Defense of Marriage Act," the 1996 federal law banning gay marriage (Murashko, 2011). In 2011, 53% of Americans supported recognizing same-sex marriage in the same manner as traditional marriages, as compared to 2% supporting this position in 1996. Younger Americans appear to be the most accepting, with 70% of those between the ages of 18 and 34 supporting same-sex marriage (Newport, 2011).

New York City is making it easier for transgender individuals to change the sex listed on their birth certificates, even without undergoing sex-change operations (Caruso, 2006). President Obama signed a memorandum that hospitals participating in Medicare or Medicaid programs "may not deny visitation privileges on the basis of race, color, national origin, religion, sex, sexual orientation, gender identity, or disability" and California Governor Jerry Brown signed a bill requiring schools to modify the social studies curricula to include the contributions of LGBT individuals (Lin, 2011).

Even with progress occurring on these fronts, however, discrimination and violence against sexual minorities remain high. In this chapter, we focus on identity development and strengths of LGBT individuals, as well as some of the major issues and challenges facing sexual minorities, including the coming-out process, societal misconceptions, and the reality of ongoing prejudice and discrimination.

UNDERSTANDING SEXUAL MINORITIES

Cross-gender behaviors and appearance are highly stigmatized in school and in our society. LGBT individuals live in a heterosexual and *cisgender* society (i.e., expecting normative gender behavior) where they face the challenge of developing a healthy self-identity in the midst of societal norms that view their sexual orientation or gender identification as "abnormal." This contrast can significantly affect the transition from childhood to adolescence to adulthood, as well as family relationships and personal identity development.

Sexual Identity Issues

Once LGBT individuals recognize heterosexual and transgendered societal realities, the discovery of being "different" can be agonizing. As one individual observed: "Imagine learning about love and sexuality in a heterosexual world when your preference is for people of the same gender" (Parker & Thompson, 1990). Awareness of sexual orientation for gay males and lesbians tends to occur in the early teens, with sexual experiences and self-identification typically occurring during the mid-teens and same-sex relationships during the late teens (Blake, Ledsky, Lehman, & Goodenow, 2001). Female youth were more consistent with their identity than males. Bisexual youth display more cognitive dissonance related to sexual orientation than do consistently gay or lesbian youth and report greater identity confusion and lower levels of self-disclosure and community connection (Balsam & Mohr, 2007). In a longitudinal study of 156 gay, lesbian, and bisexual youth, 57% consistently self-identified as gay/lesbian and 15% consistently identified as bisexual, while 18% of bisexuals transitioned to gay/lesbian (Rosario, Schrimshaw, Hunter, & Braun, 2006).

Gender dysphoria (i.e., discontent with the biological sex one is born with) and sexual orientation are not the same thing; the sexual orientation of a transgender person can be heterosexual, same-sex, or bisexual (Wester, McDonough, White, Vogel, & Taylor, 2010; Zucker & Cohen-Ketteris, 2008). Like sexual orientation, however, gender identity is an important aspect of one's total being. Transgender people feel a marked incongruence between the gender with which they self-identify and the gender assigned to them based on physical characteristics at birth (Meyer-Bahlburg, 2009). They often report feeling "different" at an early age. One activist described gender dysphoria as "one of the greatest agonies . . . when your anatomy doesn't match who you are inside" (Wright, 2001).

Because transgender individuals have a long-standing conviction that nature somehow placed them in the wrong body, they often wish to replace their physical sexual characteristics with those of the opposite sex; thus, sex reassignment surgery is considered. Such surgeries have produced variable results; many females who undergo sexual reassignment express satisfaction with the outcome of surgery, whereas males who change to female are less likely to feel satisfied; this may be because adjusting to life as a man is easier than adjusting to life as a woman or perhaps because man-to-woman changes engender more negative reactions (Lawrence, 2008). Although gender dysphoria is still considered a mental disorder (American Psychiatric Association, 2012), transgender individuals are hoping that they can follow the successful path taken by the gay and lesbian movement and eventually eliminate such classification.

The struggle for identity involves one's internal perceptions, which likely contrast with external perceptions and the assumptions others make about one's sexual orientation. LGBT individuals struggle with accepting their own internal identity, which they may perceive to contrast with society's definition of what is healthy. In addition, they must identify and combat internalized heterosexism, internalized homophobia, and internalized transphobia (Chaney, Filmore, & Goodrich, 2011). A resolution often occurs when the individual ceases struggling to be "straight" and begins to establish a new identity, self-concept, and understanding of what constitutes a good life. During this period, individuals (and members of their families) often deal with issues of grief over letting go of the old, sometimes idealized, identity (Browning, Reynolds, & Dworkin, 1998).

> Heterosexual activity does not mean one is a heterosexual, nor does same-sex activity indicate homosexuality.

Implications

Adolescence is a time of exploration and experimentation. Heterosexual activity does not mean one is a heterosexual, nor does same-sex activity indicate homosexuality.

Many LGBT youth describe feeling "different" from early childhood. When their sexual identity is acknowledged, they must deal with the stigma associated with being gay, lesbian, bisexual, or transgender. Many feel alone and isolated, having no one to talk to. Additionally, they may feel emotionally disconnected from others, fearing that discovery of their secret will lead to rejection and disapproval.

Many pretend to be straight or avoid discussing sexuality. Because of fear of the consequences of disclosure during their struggle with identity issues, LGBT youth (and adults) face this process alone, without the potential support and nurturance of peers, parents, and other family members or of others who have gone through the same struggle. Mental health professionals can help LGBT youth develop coping and survival skills and expand environmental supports, but first the individual needs to be comfortable disclosing his or her struggles and seeking such support.

LGBT Youth

Youth who are LGBT or who are questioning their sexual orientation face a variety of stressors. Discrimination and harassment in the school environment is common. In a large survey of middle and high school students, nearly 9 out of 10 LGBT students reported experiencing harassment at school in the past year, and two thirds reported feeling unsafe because of their sexual orientation. Forty percent of LGBT students reported being physically harassed, and nearly 19% had been physically assaulted in school because of their sexual orientation; 53% were exposed to cyberbullying through text messages, e-mails, and Internet postings on social networking sites such as Facebook. Safety concerns led one third of the LGBT students surveyed to skip school (GLSEN, 2009). Additionally, gay, lesbian, and bisexual students receive harsher punishments than their heterosexual peers for similar school or public offenses (Himmelstein & Bruckner, 2011).

LGBT youth are five times more likely than their heterosexual peers to attempt suicide, especially in unsupportive environments (Hatzenbeuhler, 2011). Higher rates of suicide attempts have been found among Black and Latino/a LGBT youth (Meyer, Dietrich, & Schwartz, 2008). LGBT youth also have increased risk for substance use and abuse (McCabe, Hughes, Bostwick, West, & Boyd, 2009), especially when there is also a history of childhood abuse or victimization (McCabe, Wilsnack, West, & Boyd, 2010).

Implications

Mental health professionals need to address the problems of LGBT youth at both the systems and individual levels. To improve the school environment, professionals can advocate for inclusion of gay and transgender issues in the curriculum, addressing self-management and social skills relevant to LGBT youth, provision of adequate social services, and a nondiscriminatory school environment. Although most schools have policies that prohibit antigay discrimination or harassment, only 30% offer any education regarding sexual and gender diversity and less than 30% of school districts provide training for teachers and staff regarding challenges facing LGBT students (Rienzo, Button, Sheu, & Li, 2006). It is important to encourage schools to consistently enforce policies that protect LGBT youth from harassment and violence.

Support groups for LGBT students to discuss concerns in a safe and confidential environment are also important. Programs such as gay-straight alliances, along with antibullying policies that specifically apply to LGBT youth, not only reduce harassment but also reduce the risk of suicide (Hatzenbeuhler, 2011). LGBT youth need safe places to meet others and to socialize. Community-based supports involving hotlines; youth clubs; or groups such as Parents, Families, and Friends of Gays and Lesbians (PFLAG) can be helpful. Such organizations defuse possible harassment and violence in school and allow gay students to gain support and create openly gay lives (Peyser & Lorch, 2000).

LGBT Couples and Families

As opposition to gay marriage has eased over the past decade, the number of openly gay and lesbian couples has nearly doubled to about 650,000. Approximately one out of five same-sex couples are raising children (Yen, 2011). The intimate relationships of gay and lesbian couples appear to be similar to those of heterosexual individuals, although lesbian couples share a more egalitarian relationship than many heterosexual couples (Riggle, Whitman, Olson, Rostosky, & Strong, 2008). A common reality for the vast majority of same-sex couples is that in most states, same-sex couples are prohibited from marrying. Denise Penn, a bisexual, acutely feels this contradiction. Although her neighbors seemed quite accepting of her partners or friends of either sex, she was shaken when a ban on gay marriage came up for a state vote and her "accepting" neighbors displayed signs reading "PROTECT MARRIAGE" (Leland, 2000).

Many LGBT couples and individuals have a keen interest in becoming parents. However, the right of gays and lesbians to adopt children has been challenged in many states (Stone, 2006). In fact, in Massachusetts, some agencies discontinued adoption services to protest a state law allowing gay men and lesbian women to adopt children (LeBlanc, 2006). Research findings indicate that children raised by LGBT couples are as mentally healthy as children with heterosexual parents and that there is no reason to believe that a heterosexual family structure is necessary for healthy child development. Despite myths to the contrary, there is no evidence of sexual identity confusion or increased likelihood of displaying a same-sex sexual orientation (Dingfelder, 2005). In fact, children raised by lesbian mothers are well adjusted, perform better academically, and have fewer behavioral problems than their peers (Gartrell & Bos, 2010).

Implications

In addition to the typical relationship difficulties faced by heterosexual couples and families, LGBT individuals also face prejudice and discrimination from society. Conflicts sometimes occur when individuals in LGBT relationships differ in terms of internalized homophobia or the extent to which they are "out" to others in their social, work, or family networks. They may be uncomfortable showing public displays of affection or may feel the need to hide their sexual orientation or their relationship (Blando, 2001).

In work with LGBT parents or determining their suitability as adoptive parents, mental health professionals should determine their own attitudes and beliefs regarding LGBT individuals. The empirical data indicates that LGBT parenting styles and child-rearing practices do not differ from those of their heterosexual counterparts. In addition to normal developmental issues, children of LGBT parents may benefit from support when explaining their nontraditional family to peers. Many hope that changes in school curricula encouraging respect for diversity and diverse lifestyles will help with this challenge.

Strengths of LGBT Individuals

> Queer people of color not only survive experiences of oppression, they develop resilience and coping skills in the process. (Singh & Chun, 2010, p. 38)

Although LGBT people face discrimination, prejudice, and disadvantaged status in society, many show considerable resilience in the face of adversity and develop such strategies as maintaining hope and seeking social support (Singh, Hays, & Watson, 2011). Many cite positive aspects of being a lesbian or a gay man, such as belonging to a supportive community, being able to create families of choice, serving as positive role models, living authentically, being involved in social justice and activism, and freedom from gender-specific roles (Riggle et al., 2008). Even going through the process of identity development can be a strength—many LGBT individuals move though the process of internalized heterosexism, identity confusion, and identity comparison toward identity tolerance, and finally identity acceptance, identity pride, and identity synthesis (Akerlund & Cheung, 2000). The egalitarian relationship frequently seen in lesbian couples not only promotes resilience in their children but also provides a positive model for respectful interpersonal relationships (Bos & Gartrell, 2010).

SPECIFIC CHALLENGES

In the following sections we consider challenges faced by LGBT individuals and consider their implications in treatment. Societal pressures and related struggles are reflected in the increased incidence of substance abuse as well as anxiety and depressive disorders. Gay youth are especially vulnerable because of pressures within the school and peer environment as well as struggles with "coming out." Adults face issues related to letting others know "who they really are" as well as settling down with a partner, getting married, and having children—things that heterosexual individuals take for granted.

Coming Out

The decision to *come out* is extremely difficult and is often influenced by the overwhelming sense of isolation the individual feels. The process of maintaining secrets about sexual orientation or gender identity issues can seriously affect relationships with friends and family. Coming out to parents and friends can lead to rejection, anger, and grief. This is especially difficult for adolescents who are emotionally and financially dependent on their family. About two thirds of youth come out to their mothers, about one third to their fathers, and 42% come out to both parents (Savin-Williams, 2001). Coming out is an ongoing process for LGBT individuals—each time they need to determine with whom and when to disclose. During initial stages of this process, self-esteem, life satisfaction, and happiness may decrease as they face negative reactions from others (Chaney et al., 2011).

Coming out is often more difficult for ethnic minorities who face the stigma of being "multiple minorities." Black and Latino gay and lesbian youth are more reluctant to disclose their sexual orientation than are their White counterparts (Rosario et al., 2004). Gay Mexican American men have a greater degree of internalized homophobia, partly because of the cultural value of *machismo*. In Latino communities there is strong negative reaction to gay men and frequent use of epithets such as *maricon* (sissy) and *joto* (fag) (Estrada, Rigali-Oiler, Arciniega, & Tracey, 2011). Latino men report racism, discomfort, and rejection from the gay community; Latino men with darker skin or more Indian features were more likely to face rejection (Ibanez, Van Oss Marin, Flores, Millett, & Diaz, 2009).

E. S. Lindsey (2005), who is an African American, was asked to write a chapter on sexual diversity for the 2005 edition of *Our Bodies, Ourselves*. She notes, "In the mainsteam media, both gay and straight, coming out is portrayed in an extremely idealized and simplistic way. The gay person, always white and middle class, decides he or she is gay, tells families and friends, who might experience a little homophobia . . . and ends up marching proudly down the main thoroughfare of a progressive major metropolitan area" (p. 186). The experience for people of color is often different when coming out—they frequently face both rejection from their communities and racism from the majority culture. Among the working poor, it also means the possibility of losing their jobs. Transgendered individuals face additional challenges when coming out, since their process involves preparing for coming out to friends, family, and coworkers, having them adjust to a changing physical appearance, and developing coping responses to possible negative reactions (Budge, Tebbe, & Howard, 2010).

Implications

The decision of when to come out should be carefully considered. To whom does the individual want to reveal the information? What are the possible effects and consequences (both long and short term) of self-disclosure for the individual and the recipient of the information? What new sources of support are available if negative reactions are encountered? If the individual is already in a relationship, how will the disclosure affect his or her partner? In some cases, the client may conclude that it is not yet a good time to disclose. If a client has considered the implications of coming out and desires to take this step, the counselor can offer specific help and preparation in determining how this should be accomplished. Role-plays and the discussion of possible reactions can be practiced.

Clients needing support during the disclosure process may choose to disclose or pursue follow-up discussion during a counseling session. Disclosure to parents may provoke feelings of both grief (e.g., loss of their visions of their child's future, including weddings and grandchildren) and guilt (i.e., believing their parenting was responsible). Parents may need support in dealing with the societal stigma of having a LGBT family member and may benefit from receiving information and education regarding myths and stereotypes. If parents or other family members are rejecting, the individual must strengthen other sources of social support. This may be particularly important for ethnic minorities, who may be additionally affected by cultural and class variables. Prior to and during the coming-out process the counselor can help the client deal with both external and internalized heterosexism—such societal beliefs are at the core of homophobia (Scott, 2011). Thus, rather than allowing clients to internalize self-blame, counselors can help clients understand that it is societal prejudice that is the problem.

Prejudice and Discrimination

About one-quarter of LGBT staff, faculty, and students reported experiencing harassment . . . with transgender individuals receiving even higher levels of harassment. . . . About one third have considered leaving their institutions. . . . 43 percent of transgender students, faculty, and staff . . . feared for their physical safety. (Rankin, Weber, Blumenfeld, & Frazer, 2010, p. 4)

We have alluded to the overwhelming prejudice and discrimination facing LGBT youth and adults. More than 94% of LGBT adults report hate crime victimization (Herek, Cogan, & Gillis, 2002). Such victimization was highlighted following the tragic suicide of a Rutgers University student who was victimized by antigay harassment and cyberbullying initiated by his college roommate, who secretly recorded and publicized a sexual interaction between the student and another man (Lederman, 2011). In addition to openly antigay harassment (Burn, Kadlec, & Rexler, 2005), LGBT individuals are commonly subjected to subtle heterosexism, such as the common practice of equating the word *gay* with *stupid* or automatically making the assumption that most people are heterosexual; practices such as these create feelings of denigration and invalidation (Burn et al., 2005).

Perceived discrimination based on sexual orientation, especially among those who keep silent about their experiences, increases risk of depression (McLaughlin, Hatzenbuehler, & Keyes, 2010). Sexual assaults in adulthood were reported by 12% of gay men and 13% of bisexual men, compared to 2% of heterosexual men. Among women, the rates of sexual assault were 16% for lesbians, 17% for bisexual women, and 8% for heterosexual women (Balsam, Rothblum, & Beauchaine, 2005). Bisexual individuals sometime experience hostility from heterosexuals as well as from the gay community (Brewster & Moradi, 2010); mental distress is particularly pronounced among bisexual women (Fredriksen-Boldsen, Kim, Barkan, Balsam, & Mincer, 2010).

Transgender individuals face being viewed as mentally ill, delusional, or self-destructive not only by the public, but also by mental health workers (Mizock & Fleming, 2011). LGBT individuals also face microaggressions that invalidate their sexual orientation, including the common use of language and terms that demonstrate heteronormality and heterosexual privilege (Smith, Shin, & Officer, 2011).

Misconceptions about LGBT Individuals

LGBT individuals have been historically labeled as suffering from psychopathology, with resultant attempts to therapeutically intervene to change sexual orientation. In 2009, the American Psychological Association (2009b) reviewed research on sexual orientation and concluded, "Same-sexual attractions, behaviors, and orientation per se are normal and positive variants of human sexuality. . . . They are not indicators of mental or developmental disorders. . . . Gay men, lesbians, and bisexual individuals can live satisfying lives as well as form stable, committed relations and families that are equivalent to heterosexual relationships in essential respects" (p. 54). A resolution was adopted stating that clients should no longer be told that it is possible to change sexual orientation and that, instead, therapists should provide psychoeducation regarding sexual orientation and assistance to increase family and social support (APA, 2009a). Numerous studies (Berube, 1990; Gonsiorek, 1982; Hooker, 1957; Reiss, 1980) have demonstrated few adjustment differences between individuals with a same-sex versus heterosexual orientation. As one researcher concluded, "Homosexuality in and of itself is unrelated to psychological disturbance or maladjustment" (Gonsiorek, 1982, p. 74).

It is likely that societal stressors such as prejudice and discrimination account for the findings that LGBT youth report elevated rates of major depression, generalized anxiety disorder, and substance abuse (Rienzo et al., 2006) and that LGBT adults are at higher risk for substance- and alcohol-related problems (Cochran, Keenan, Schober, & Mays, 2000; Kennedy, 2005; McCabe et al., 2009). Although gay men report high rates of major depression, lesbians appear to fare better and report mental health equal to that of their heterosexual counterparts (DeAngelis, 2002).

A number of research studies reveal that bias continues to exist among mental health professionals. In one study, 97 counselors read a fictitious intake report about a bisexual woman seeking counseling, with no indication that the problem involved her sexual orientation. The problems involved career choice, issues with parents over independence, ending a two-year relationship with another woman, and problems with her boyfriend. Thus, issues involved were boundaries with parents, career choice, and romantic relationships. Counselors with the most negative attitude regarding bisexuality believed her problems stemmed from her sexual orientation and rated her lower in psychosocial functioning (Mohr, Israel, & Sedlacek, 2001).

Other studies (Garnets, Hancock, Cochran, Goodchilds, & Peplau, 1998; Shelton & Delgado-Romero, 2011) have similarly shown that it is not uncommon for therapists to engage in biased and inappropriate practices or to hold beliefs that affect the therapeutic alliance with LGBT clients, including:

1. Assuming that a client is heterosexual, thereby making it harder to bring up issues regarding sexual orientation.
2. Believing that same-sex orientation is sinful or a form of mental illness.
3. Failing to understand that a client's problem, such as depression or low self-esteem, can be a result of experiences with discrimination or internalization of society's view of homosexuality.
4. Focusing on sexual orientation when it is not relevant. Problems may be completely unrelated to sexual orientation, but some therapists continue to focus on this topic.
5. Attempting to have clients renounce or change their sexual orientation. For example, a lesbian was asked by the therapist to date men.
6. Trivializing or demeaning homosexuality. A therapist responded to a lesbian who brought up that she was "into women" that he didn't care, since he had a client who was "into dogs."
7. Lacking an understanding of identity development in lesbian women and gay men, or viewing homosexuality solely as sexual activity.
8. Not understanding the impact of possible internalized negative societal pressures or homophobia on identity development.
9. Underestimating the consequences of "coming out" for the client, and making the suggestion to come out without careful discussion of the pros and cons of this disclosure.
10. Misunderstanding or underestimating the importance of intimate relationships for gay men and lesbians. One therapist reportedly advised a lesbian couple who were having problems in their relationship to not consider it a permanent relationship and consider going to a gay bar to meet others.
11. Using the heterosexual framework inappropriately when working with lesbian and gay male relationships. One couple was given a book to read dealing with heterosexual relationships.
12. Presuming that clients with a different sexual orientation cannot be good parents, and automatically assuming that their children's problems are a result of the orientation.
13. Overidentifying with LGBT clients through excessive displays of acceptance or "understanding."

Implications

Although mental health organizations have acknowledged that homosexuality is not a mental disorder, it is recognized that a "need for better education and training of mental health practitioners" exists (American Psychological Association, Division 44/Committee on Lesbian, Gay, and Bisexual Concerns Joint Task Force, 2000; Shelton & Delgado-Romero, 2011). Heterosexist bias in therapy needs to be acknowledged and changed. Fortunately, curricular changes in mental health training programs have resulted in increasing emphasis on the concerns and challenges of LGBT individuals as well as on the positive characteristics and supportive relationships found in these groups.

Some of these changes may be having an effect. In a survey of psychologists, 92% reported viewing the LGBT lifestyle and identity as "acceptable," and 58% reported a gay-affirmative approach to therapy (Kilgore, Sideman, Amin, Baca, & Bohanske, 2005); however, it is uncertain whether these responses reflect actual changes in attitudes and practices or if, instead, they are simply reflective of "politically correct" responding.

It is important for therapists to continue to examine possible stereotypes or negative attitudes regarding LGBT clients and to monitor behavior and interactions for possible microaggressions. LGBT clients report perceiving counselors more positively and feeling a greater willingness to disclose personal information, including sexual orientation, when the counselor refrained from heterosexist language (e.g., using the term *partner* instead of *boyfriend* or *girlfriend* or *husband* or *wife*) (Dorland & Fischer, 2001). Workshops and training in the use of nondiscriminatory intake forms and identifying psychological and health issues faced by many LGBT clients are helpful means of increasing the effectiveness of health care providers (Blake, Ledsky, Lehman, & Goodenow, 2001).

Aging

> Kelly Glossip was accepted in a senior citizens home but turned it down, "I'm used to being out, so the idea of going into senior housing in a straight environment is horrifying. . . . I know that I would have to go completely back in the closet." (Watkins, 2010, p. 1)

> The two older women often sit next to each other in identical recliners. . . . Evenings they hold hands under a blanket on the sofa watching TV. . . . They've been partners for 18 years. More than anything, they want to stay together in old age. (King, 2001, p. B1)

The two women—Selma Kannel, 75, and Nancy King, 67—are worried about their remaining years. If one experiences declining health, will her partner be allowed to make health care decisions, if needed, and will people respond to their relationship negatively? Older LGBT are fearful of having to go to retirement or assisted-living communities where prejudice may exist. These problems will only increase because up to 3 million LGBT individuals in the United States are older than age 65, and this number is expected to double in 15 years (Pearlman, 2006). Older LGBT individuals are less likely to have revealed their sexual orientation to others when compared to younger generations (Donahue & McDonald, 2005).

If still in the closet, many individuals attempt to hide long-term relationships when dealing with health or government agencies. One man accompanied his partner, who was dying of cancer, to see the surgeon. Initially the physician was surprised to see the male patient accompanied by a man and became hostile but eventually understood the relationship and talked to him as if he were the next of kin (King, 2001). In addition, as with other segments of U.S. society, ageism exists in gay and lesbian communities. All of these issues can produce a great deal of concern among

With older LGBT individuals, issues of coming out (or coming out again) may need to be addressed as needs for health care or social services increase. Counselors can assist in the development of coping skills, expanded social support systems, and advocacy in locating services for older LGBT adults.

older LGBT adults as they confront declining health and a diminishing social support system.

Implications

With older LGBT individuals, issues of coming out (or coming out again) may need to be addressed as needs for health care or social services increase. Counselors can assist in the development of coping skills, expanded social support systems, and advocacy in locating services for older LGBT adults. Such advocacy groups are increasing in number. One organization, Senior Action in a Gay Environment (SAGE), provides counseling, educational and recreational activities, and discussion groups for older LGBT individuals. The Gay and Lesbian Association of Retiring Persons (GLARP) operates retirement communities for LGBT individuals and provides them with support and education on aging (Donahue & McDonald, 2005).

In addition, LGBT-friendly teleconferences exist for homebound seniors. Project Visibility, a culturally competent training program for staff and administrators of nursing homes and assisted-living facilities, counters stereotypes and fosters compassionate care for older LGBT adults living in these facilities (Mellskog, 2011). Many organizations have added the transgender community to their mission statements. The mental health professional needs to be aware of these resources and advocate changes in laws regarding LGBT partnership rights.

Implications for Clinical Practice

1. Examine your own views regarding heterosexuality, and determine their impact on work with LGBT clients. Understand heterosexual and cisgender privilege. A way to personalize this perspective is to assume that some of your family, friends, or coworkers may be LGBT.
2. Read the "Appropriate Therapeutic Responses to Sexual Orientation" (American Psychological Association, 2009b), "Report of the APA Task Force on Gender Identity and Gender Variance" (American Psychological Association, 2009c), and ALGBTIC's "Competencies for Counseling Transgender Clients" (Burnes et al., 2009).
3. Develop partnerships, consultation, or collaborative efforts with local and national LGBT organizations.
4. Ensure that your intake forms, interview procedures, and language are free of heterosexist bias and include a question on sexual behavior, attraction, or orientation. Be aware that LGBT clients may have specific concerns regarding confidentiality.
5. Do not assume that presenting problems are necessarily the result of sexual orientation. Typical presenting problems include relationship difficulties, self-esteem issues, depression, and anxiety (Lyons, Bieschke, Dendy, Worthington, & Georgemiller, 2010). Societal issues may or may not play a role in these problems.

6. Remember that mental health issues may result from stress due to prejudice and discrimination; internalized homophobia; the coming-out process; a lack of family, peer, school, or community support; being a victim of sexual or other physical assault; suicidal ideation or attempts; and substance abuse. Ethnic minority LGBT individuals may be dealing with rejection from their ethnic communities as well as marginalization within the gay community.

7. Realize that LGBT couples may have problems similar to those of their heterosexual counterparts but may also display unique concerns, such as differences in the degree of comfort with public demonstrations of their relationship or reactions from their family of origin.

8. Assess spiritual and religious needs. Many LGBT individuals have a strong religious faith but encounter exclusion. Religious support is available. For example, for individuals of the Christian faith, the Fellowship United Methodist Church accepts all types of diversity and is open to gay congregation members. LGBT individuals who have strong religious beliefs but who belong to a nonaffirming church can explore different options, such as joining an affirming religious group or more liberal sects of their own religion or developing their own definitions of what it means to be gay or religious (Sherry, Adelman, Whilde, & Quick, 2010). It is much easier to adapt to a different religious group than to change one's sexual orientation (Haldeman, 2010).

9. Because many LGBT clients have internalized the societal belief that they cannot have long-lasting relationships, have materials available that portray healthy and satisfying LGBT relationships.

10. Recognize that a large number of LGBT clients have been subject to hate crimes as well as ongoing microaggression. Depression, anger, posttraumatic stress, and self-blame may result. These conditions need to be assessed and treated.

11. For clients still dealing with internalized homosexuality, it may help to focus on helping them establish a new affirming identity. Many LGBT individuals avoid discrimination by assuming a heterosexual identity and avoiding the issue of sexuality with others, whereas others are able to reveal their true identity. The consequences of each of these reactions need to be considered both from individual and societal perspectives.

12. A number of therapeutic strategies can be useful with internalized homophobia, prejudice, and discrimination. They can include identifying and correcting cognitive distortions, coping skills training, assertiveness training and utilizing social supports. It can be helpful to ask questions such as, "Have you had incidences where you thought you were treated differently because you are a sexual minority person?" (Kashubeck-West, Szymanski, & Meyer, 2008, p. 617). Help LGBT clients identify and replace heterosexist and cisgender messages with positive affirming messages about their identity.

13. To increase awareness of internalized heterosexism, ask LGBT clients to talk about their coming-out experiences; thoughts and feelings about their sexuality; feelings of homophobia; experiences with heterosexism in school, family, work, and religion; degree of interactions with other LGBT individuals; and the availability of support (Kashubeck-West et al., 2008).

14. Systems-level intervention is often needed in schools, employment situations, or religious organizations. Diversity workshops can help organizations acquire accurate information regarding sexual diversity. Counselors may need to be advocates for change.

15. Transgender individuals may need assistance on topics such as making name changes, referrals to medical professionals for hormone or surgical options, and the name and location of support groups (Bess & Stabb, 2009).

Counseling Older Adult Clients

I saw a pic of Steven Tyler in *Stuff* Mag the other day, his face looks all flabby; Ozzy looks like he's about 65. . . . He mumbles and slurs like an 85-year-old; Harrison Ford used to be so hot! Now, he's all old, gray, and yucky, like me (Pop Culture Information Society, 2002)

Stereotypes of older adults as being asexual are incorrect. Romantic relationships are common in later life. In Internet personal ads, older men seek physical attractiveness and younger women while older women were more selective, seeking status and security. (Alterovitz & Mendelsohn, 2009)

Individuals aged 65 and older currently constitute 16.2% of the U.S. population. However, this group is growing and is expected to constitute 20% of the population by 2030. During the past decade, the age-85-and-older group, the fastest growing segment of the adult population, has increased by 38%. Because females live longer than males, at age 85, there are only 39 men for every 100 women (U.S. Census Bureau, 2011a). Because of the "graying" of adults, definitions of old are changing. Most baby boomers define old as being age 70 or older, although 25% believe that a person is not old until they reach the age of 80 (Carroll, 2011).

We are an aging society, yet we are poorly prepared to handle our current aged population and are certainly not equipped for the coming baby boomer generation (Palmore, 2005). The older adult population is underserved and little understood. Information is lacking on therapies and medications for older individuals. As a group, older adults are less likely to receive new treatments for heart attacks or other illnesses, and older women are less likely to receive radiation and chemotherapy after breast cancer surgery. This is surprising, since a healthy male 65 years of age has a 28% chance of living to 90 and 11% chance of living to 95. Among women who reach the age of 65, 40% will live to age 90 and 19% to the age of 95 (Life Expectancy Tables, 2010).

CHARACTERISTICS AND STRENGTHS

In the following sections we consider the characteristics and strengths of older adults and treatment implications. Remember that the applicability of this information needs to be assessed for individual clients and their families.

Physical and Economic Health

> She calls it "being sidelined." Greta Hale, an 82-year-old grand-mother of five, looks forward to visiting her large family but often feels like an outsider when she does. On holidays, she often sits alone while younger generations buzz about, preparing meals, telling jokes, and engaging in lively debates. "My hearing is not so good anymore," she explains. Otherwise spry and healthy, Ms. Hale wants to partici-pate but avoids doing so because, she admits, "I don't always under-stand what people are saying. I think maybe it's just easier for them to pretend I'm not there." She considers this one of the more difficult aspects of aging. (Wallhagen, Pettengill, & Whiteside, 2006, p. 40)

Older adults often have physical impairments, such as hearing or vision loss or cardiovascular disease (McDonnall, 2011). Ethnic minority older Americans tend to have more chronic, debilitating diseases, such as diabetes and heart disease (Costantino, Malgady, & Primavera, 2009). About 30% of adults between the ages of 65 and 74 have some hearing impairment, and this increases to about half of those older than 75 (Wallhagen et al., 2006). Up to 25% of older adults have insomnia or difficulty falling asleep (Silvertsen et al., 2006).

Approximately 9% of those between the ages of 65 and 69 require assist-ance with self-care; at the age of 85 and older, about 50% require assistance. In all age categories, women are more likely to need assistance than are men (U.S. Census Bureau, 2005b). The majority of older individuals, however, are quite healthy and able to live independent lives requiring only minimal assist-ance. In fact, the percentage of adults aged 75 and older requiring nursing home care has decreased from 10.2% in 1990 to 7.4% in 2006; only 16% re-quire such care at age 85 (Cohen, 2011; El Nasser, 2009).

When providing mental health services for older adults, counselors/therapists should consider the possibility that physical limitations exist. To ensure that the counseling environment is appropriate for older clients, rooms should have adequate light and be free from extraneous noise, as well as any limiting environmental barriers. If the client uses eyeglasses or hearing aids, make sure they are present in the session.

Implications

When providing mental health services for older adults, counselors/therapists should consider the possibility that physical limitations exist. To ensure that the counseling environment is appropriate for older clients, rooms should have adequate light and be free from extraneous noise, as well as any limiting environmental barriers. If the client uses eyeglasses or hearing aids, make sure they are present in the session. Due to the frequency of physical conditions (e.g., cardiovascular disease, hypertension), it is critical to work with medical providers to rule out the possibility that physical conditions, medications, or medication interactions are causing or contributing to emotional symptoms. Also, poverty, unemployment, poor living conditions, discrimination, or lack of receptivity among health care providers can significantly contribute to mental health concerns and may need to be addressed.

Sexuality in Later Years

The topic of sexuality and the aging process is often given little consideration. Underlying this neglect is the belief that sexuality should not be considered in the aged. As one physician noted,

> I recently worked in an infectious disease clinic where I met a patient in her late 60s who was infected with the human immunodeficiency virus (HIV). My surprise at seeing an older woman with an infection associated with unprotected sex or injecting drug use made me realize I had preconceptions about aging and the elderly. . . . My attitudes could be construed as sexist [ageist] in nature. (McCray, 1998, pp. 1035–1036)

More than 10% of all new cases of AIDS occur in individuals older than 50 (UCSF Center for AIDS Prevention Studies, 2006). In our youth-oriented society, older adults are not expected to be interested in sex. One psychology intern remarked, "You never think the same about your older clients [or your grandparents] after you have an 80-year-old woman telling you how much she enjoys oral sex" (Zeiss, 2001, p. 1). Some consider sexual activity among older persons to be rare or even inappropriate. However, sexual interest and activity continue well into the 80s and 90s for many individuals (Kun & Schwartz, 1998; Lindau et al., 2007). In a study of 3,005 older people, 53% between the ages of 65 and 74 were sexually active, as were 26% between the ages of 75 and 85. Women reported significantly less sexual activity than men; in part, this was due to reduced likelihood of having a spousal or intimate relationship, as well as sexual problems such as low desire, difficulty with vaginal lubrication, and inability to reach orgasm. The most prevalent sexual problem in older men was erectile dysfunction (Lindau et al., 2007).

Changes do occur in sexual functioning in both older men and women. In men, erections occur more slowly and require more continuous stimulation, although they can be maintained for longer periods without the need for ejaculation. The refractory period increases, so that it may take a day or two for the man to become sexually responsive again. Antihypertensive drugs, vascular diseases, and diabetes are common causes of impotence in men. For women, aging is associated with a decline in estrogen resulting in decreases in vaginal lubrication. However, sexual responsiveness of the clitoris is similar to that of younger women. Sexual activities remain important for older men and women. Medical and psychological methods have been successful in treating sexual dysfunctions in older adults.

Age does not appear to be related to sexual satisfaction. In one survey involving 600 older women, most respondents voiced positive reactions to their sexual experiences such as, "Physical satisfaction is not the only aim of sex. . . . It is the nearness of someone throughout the lonely nights" and "I believe sex is a wonderful outlet for love and physical health and worth trying to keep alive in advancing age. . . . It makes one feel youthful and close to one's mate and pleased to 'still work'" (B. Johnson, 1995, p. A23).

Implications

As with younger adults, sexual concerns should be addressed. Emotional stressors (retirement, caregiving, and lifestyle changes) as well as physical changes can produce problems in sexual functioning and should also be considered. The mental health professional should determine the reason for any difficulties (encouraging the client to consult with medical professionals, when appropriate). Many treatments and medications are now available to improve sexual functioning in older adults. Knowledge of these advances is important when counseling this population.

Strengths

Most older adults have good emotional stability and high levels of affective well-being. Although they may have less control over their environment, many show flexibility in their ability to adjust to different situations. They also show greater facility in understanding and managing emotions than younger individuals (Scheibe & Carstensen, 2010). The majority of older adults are mentally alert and engaged and possess years of life and work experience. Interestingly, more than half of the individuals selected to serve as chief executive officers (CEOs) in Fortune 500 companies are older than age 55 (Begley, 2010).

Many, especially ethnic and minority group members, place a high value on religious beliefs, a factor contributing to a sense of hope and optimism, meaning and purpose in life, and better mental health (American Psychological Association, 2009). In a 16-year longitudinal study involving adults aged 70 to 100, most were satisfied with aging, felt younger than their chronological age, and downgraded the importance of age-related changes. Only when they approached death did they become less satisfied with aging (Kotter-Gruhn, Kleinspehn-Ammerlahn, Gerstorf, & Smith, 2009).

SPECIFIC CHALLENGES OF OLDER ADULTS

In the following sections we consider challenges often faced by older populations and consider their implications in treatment.

Prejudice and Discrimination

Older individuals are subject to negative stereotypes and discrimination (Alterovitz & Mendelsohn, 2009). *Ageism*, very common in our society, is defined as negative attitudes toward the process of aging or toward older individuals. Women who are older are even more likely to be viewed negatively by society as a whole, and many internalize ageist norms (Hatch, 2005). In a review of attitudes toward older individuals, Palmore (2005) found that older adults were thought to be rigid and inadaptable in their thought processes; lacking in health, intelligence, and alertness; and either as having no sexual interest or, if they were sexually active, as engaging in activity inappropriate for their age. Older adults are also viewed as "all alike" (i.e., stereotyped), possessing such characteristics as being rigid, sickly, dependent, and depressed (American Psychological Association, 2009a). Jokes about old age abound and are primarily negative in nature.

The entertainment industry, news broadcasts, and advertising media are dominated by younger individuals. Information about older people is often presented by youthful reporters who may not understand the experiences of older generations. One exception is Donald M. Murray, who at the age of 81 wrote about issues of age, emphasizing some of the positive aspects of aging. In one column he extolled the virtues of old age:

> I am not elderly, I am old and proud of it. I am aged, like a good cheese. I am a walking history book, an elder of the tribe, tested, tempered, wise. . . . I can leave parties early. . . . I enjoy melancholy, even revel in it. (as cited in Frankel, 1998, p. 16)

Implications

Ageism influences how both the general public and mental health professionals perceive older persons. Negative stereotypes often result in older adults feeling invisible or less valued. Many older individuals come to accept ageist views and suffer a loss of self-esteem. In fact, many internalize negative societal beliefs. Unfortunately, mental health professionals also display age bias (Weiss, 2005), expressing reluctance to work with older adults and perceiving this population to be less interesting, having a poorer prognosis, more set in their ways, and less likely to benefit from mental health services. Additionally, mental health problems in older adults are sometimes inaccurately attributed to aging; such beliefs can limit referrals for needed services.

Multiple Discrimination

Minority status in combination with older age can produce a double burden. Unfortunately, even minority members who have experienced discrimination themselves can display ageism. For example, older lesbian women may still encounter discrimination on the basis of their sexual orientation. Some remain distressed over their lack of acceptance from the heterosexual community and even family members. They observe that neighbors interact with them but do not invite them over. In addition, they may feel isolated from the lesbian community:

> I was shocked and hurt when one of them [a young lesbian] who considers herself quite liberated didn't want to dance with me at a local lesbian bar, but she did dance with others. (Jacobson & Samdahl, 1998, p. 242)

The woman attributed this rejection to her being older than the other women. She points out that in lesbian newsletters or activities, there is seldom anything about older women. Because of institutionalized heterosexism, lesbian, gay, bisexual, or transgender (LGBT) older adults are often forced to hide their sexual orientation from health providers (American Psychological Association, 2009a).

Implications

The therapist should assess for potential problems of multiple discrimination when working with older adults who have disabilities or who are from different cultural groups or social classes, or are sexual minorities. Counselors can help clients come to terms with factors associated with ageism and find different sources of social support. They can also actively work to change negative societal attitudes.

Mental Deterioration

> After 49 years of teaching in Whatcom County schools, including the last 26 as a substitute, Mitch Evich has come across all kinds of students. "Recently I've worked in classes that were lovely, you can't beat them," Evich said. "Of course, other classes, I wish I could," he said with a laugh. Evich, now 81, has no immediate plans on ending his substitute teaching career. (Lane, 1998, p. A1)

A common view of older persons is that they are mentally incompetent. Although there is some cognitive slowing associated with normal aging (e.g., periodic memory difficulties, such as forgetting names or phone numbers or misplacing objects), the majority of older adults do not demonstrate significant mental decline.

A common view of older persons is that they are mentally incompetent. Although there is some cognitive slowing associated with normal aging (e.g., periodic memory difficulties, such as forgetting names or phone numbers or misplacing objects), the majority of older adults do not demonstrate significant mental decline. In fact, most are still mentally sharp and benefit from the store of knowledge that they have acquired over a lifetime. Even when cognitive slowing occurs, older adults often use various strategies to compensate for deficits (Krendl, Heatherton, & Kensinger, 2009). Memory for perceptual information, highly practiced responses, and general knowledge hold up well while working memory falls off more rapidly (Craik, 2008). Multitasking involving activities that compete for attention (e.g., talking on a cell phone while crossing the street) becomes more difficult for many older adults, although passive tasks are not affected (Nagamatsu et al., 2011; Neider et al., 2011).

Approximately one in seven adults aged 71 or older have dementia (i.e., memory impairment and declining cognitive functioning), including the 2.4 million in this age group diagnosed with Alzheimer's disease (National Institute on Aging, 2007). Alzheimer's disease is now the fifth leading cause of death among American adults aged 65 and older; the risk of Alzheimer's disease and other dementias increases with age (Centers for Disease Control and Prevention, 2011). Women usually live longer than men, so they are more likely to develop dementia; among 65-year-olds, the lifetime risk of developing dementia is approximately 11% for men and 19% for women (Gatz, 2007).

Implications

For older adults demonstrating significant cognitive decline and for those suspected of having a neurodegenerative condition such as Alzheimer's disease, the traditional mental status exam can give some indication of problem areas. However, a more frequently used assessment is the Mini-Mental State Examination (MMSE). This test takes about 5 to 10 minutes to administer and has normative and validity data. It is comprised of eleven items and assesses orientation, registration, attention and calculation, recall, language, and visual motor integrity. Early detection of cognitive declines allows for treatment and advance planning (e.g., legal matters or dealing with potential problems, such as driving).

Other steps in evaluating dementia and other cognitive changes include:

- Obtain a self-report from the client regarding possible changes in memory or other cognitive function.
- Obtain reports from family members and friends regarding the client's cognitive performance. Be especially alert to discrepancies.
- Take a careful history of the onset and progression of the cognitive changes.
- Coordinate with medical professionals who can assess for possible side effects of medication or other physical conditions that may be related to cognitive declines.
- Assess for depression, since it can also result in dementia-like performance or the overreporting of cognitive problems. Remember that depression and dementia can also occur together.

Although dementia has a gradual progression, the effects of this disorder can quickly impact both the affected individual and family members. In the early stages, memory problems are often the primary symptoms. Delusions and hallucinations may also occur in later stage dementia. Family members may not understand that individuals with dementia may not retain what they are told. They may become frustrated when the individual with the disorder is forgetful or needs extra assistance following through with tasks. Some may believe the behavior is willful or may try to assume responsibility over all aspects of the person's life, even when the older person can perform effectively in some areas.

Adult children may infantilize or dominate a parent with a cognitive decline, assuming that their actions are in the best interest of their parent but failing to take the parent's own preferences or values into consideration. Self-identity and autonomy are important to older adults, including those with dementia. Elderspeak, such as "Are we ready for our bath?" "You want to take your medicine now, don't you?" (Williams, Kemper, & Hummert, 2005, p. 15), is often used with exaggerated intonation and elevated pitch, along with terms such as *honey* and *good girl*. Many older adults consider elderspeak to be demeaning.

Caregiving may be stressful and may increase conflict among family members. When working with family members who care for a relative with dementia, a mental health professional should address the following issues:

1. The need for patience and understanding when working with individuals with dementia
2. The potential stresses on family members and the need to enhance coping strategies
3. Education of family members regarding specific neurological difficulties and the effects on cognition and behavior, available treatments, and strategies for dealing with agitation, wandering, and other safety issues
4. The family dynamics as they relate to the caregiving situation and how responsibilities should be allocated
5. Improvement of communication among family members, possibly including encouraging family members to avoid the use of elderspeak, oversimplification, or unnecessary repetition of requests
6. Financial and legal matters, such as power of attorney provisions

Elder Abuse and Neglect

Agnes, 85 years old, lost her husband last year. Because of her own problems with arthritis and congestive heart failure, Agnes moved in with her 55-year-old daughter, Emily. The situation is difficult for all of them. Sometimes Emily feels as if she's at the end of her rope, caring for her mother and worrying about her college-age son and her husband, who is about to be forced into early retirement. Emily has caught herself calling her mother names and accusing her mother of ruining her life. (American Psychological Association, 2001b, p. 1)

Maltreatment of older adults, including neglect and emotional, financial, physical, and sexual abuse, is a significant public health concern. Many cases of abuse or neglect go undetected, especially among those who are most vulnerable (e.g., individuals with dementia, depression, significant health concerns). Family circumstances most commonly associated with abuse and neglect include (a) previous traumatic experiences and a pattern of violence in the family, (b) stress (including marital stress) resulting from accommodating an older parent or relative in the family home, (c) financial burdens, (d) overcrowded quarters, and (e) low levels of social support (Acierno et al., 2010; U.S. Department of Health and Human Services, 1998). In addition, caregiver stress has been directly related to the time spent providing assistance (Bookwala & Schulz, 2000). It is also important to be alert for client self-neglect (e.g., unsafe driving, failure to eat or take medications), another common concern that can have serious consequences (Mosqueda & Dong, 2011).

Implications

It is essential that counselors be familiar with the complex ethical and legal issues pertaining to defining and reporting elder abuse and neglect, including self-neglect (Zeranski & Halgin, 2011), and with best practice guidelines (Molinari, 2011). To reduce the prevalence of elder abuse and neglect, several steps can be taken with the general public and those caring for older adults (American Psychological Association, 2001b). First, continued public education can bring the problem out in the open and increase awareness of the risk factors involved in abuse. Second, respite care (e.g., family members, friends, or hired workers help with care) can help reduce caregiver burnout. Third, increasing social contact and support is also likely to help keep stress manageable. Assistance may also be possible from religious or community organizations as well as organizations focused on particular medical conditions.

Substance Abuse

"I wouldn't get up in the morning," she said. "I realized I was using alcohol to raise my spirits. It raises your spirits for a little while, and then you become depressed. . . . With people dying around you, you feel more lonely and isolated." (Wren, 1998, p. 12)

Alcohol abuse can begin after a loss. Genevieve May, a psychiatrist, started abusing alcohol after the death of her husband. Finding that this was not the solution, Dr. May entered the Betty Ford Center and was successfully treated at age 83. It is estimated that 17% of adults aged 60 and older abuse alcohol or prescription drugs; some of the misuse of prescription drugs may involve confusion over or misunderstanding of the directions. Because older adults take an average of five different prescription drugs a day, the chance of negative drug interactions or reactions with alcohol increases dramatically (Guerra, 1998). Often these reactions resemble psychological or organic conditions. Older problem drinkers are more likely to be unmarried, report more stress, have more financial problems, report persistent interpersonal conflicts with others, and have fewer social resources (Brennan & Moos, 1996). It is estimated that the number of older adults who need treatment for substance abuse will increase from 1.7 million in 2001 to 4.4 million in 2020 (Gfroerer, Penne, Pemberton, & Folsom, 2003).

In a national survey, a sharp increase was reported in older Americans being treated for substance abuse. Although about three fourths had initiated the abuse before the age of 25, there was an increase in those who reported initiating substance use within five years of admission. Among older Americans, the abuse of heroin had doubled from 7.2% to 16%, cocaine from 2.9% to 11.4%, prescription medications from 0.7% to 3.5%, and marijuana from 0.6% to 2.9% (Substance Abuse and Mental Health Services Administration, 2010).

Implications

Older adults rarely seek treatment for substance abuse problems because of shame and perhaps because they feel uncomfortable in programs that deal with "street" drugs, such as heroin or crack cocaine. As compared to younger substance abusers, older patients respond better to more structured program policies, more flexible rules regarding discharge, more comprehensive assessment, and more outpatient mental health aftercare (Moos, Mertens, & Brennan, 1995). Late-onset alcohol and drug abuse problems seem to be related to such stressors as the death of a spouse, family member, or friend; retirement issues; family conflicts; physical health problems; or financial concerns. Many of these stressors are typical issues faced in later life. Early intervention to identify and provide support for these issues can reduce substance abuse risk.

Depression and Suicide

Depression is one of the most common psychiatric complaints among older adults. Although physical changes associated with aging (e.g., hearing or vision loss or cardiovascular disease) can sometimes lead to depression (McDonnall, 2011), depression is not a normal consequence of aging. Stressful life changes, such as the death of friends and relatives, increasing social isolation, or financial distress, can increase the risk of depression. Depression is more strongly associated with feelings of "being old" than with actual age or health status (Rosenfeld, 2004). The rate of depression increases with age for males, whereas the rate of depression in women decreases after the age of 60.

In men, depression is associated with vascular disease, erectile dysfunction, and decreased testosterone. Among older men, the highest rates of depression are for those who never married (20.6%) or who are separated or divorced (19.2%). The prevalence of depression among older women is highest among those who are separated or divorced (23.1%) or widowed (15.4%). For both males and females, depression is most common among those in stressful relationships (St. John & Montgomery, 2009). Depression needs to be identified and treated, since it is also seen as an independent risk factor for cardiovascular and cerebrovascular disease. Not only does late-life depression significantly affect older adults' physical health, it can also affect social connections and overall functioning as well as increase risk of suicide (Beyer, 2007).

Among older women, suicide is most prevalent among Asian females. Suicide rates are exceptionally high among older men, with risk increasing with increasing age; White males aged 85 or older have the highest suicide rate of any group (Centers for Disease Control and Prevention, 2010). It is unclear whether this group has less resilience and fewer coping strategies or whether it is because life changes associated with advanced age (e.g., loss of employment, physical changes, loss of control) are a greater stressor for men. Factors associated with suicide included being separated, divorced, or alone; suffering depression; having an anxiety disorder; having physical or medical problems; and dealing with family conflict or loss of a relationship.

Implications

It is important to avoid assuming that depression is a normal consequence of aging (American Psychological Association, 2009a). Although 139 people over 100 years of age scored higher for depression than individuals in their 80s or 60s, they reported that they were in good spirits (Scheetz, Martin, & Poon, 2012). However, in many cases, major depression tends to be unrecognized in older adults and is a significant predictor of suicide. It is, therefore, essential to assess for depression and suicidality when working with older adults. The best instrument for screening for depression is the Geriatric Depression Scale, which was specifically developed for older adults. It has age-related norms and omits somatic symptoms that may be associated with physical problems rather than depression.

Because depression often co-occurs with physical illnesses, such as cardiovascular disease, stroke, diabetes, and cancer, health providers often believe that the mood disturbance is a normal consequence of problems, so they are less likely to refer for mental health treatment. Many older individuals who committed suicide had visited a primary care physician very close to the time of suicide (45% within 1 week, and 73% within 1 month) (Juurlink et al., 2004). There is an urgent need to detect and adequately treat depression in order to reduce suicide among older individuals.

A number of biological and psychological treatments are effective in treating depression in older adults. Antidepressants such as the selective serotonin reuptake inhibitors (SSRIs) have fewer side effects and are more likely to be continued, an important consideration since rates of noncompliance with medication are high among older adults (Cooper et al., 2005). Evidence-based therapies, such as cognitive-behavioral therapy, dialectical behavior therapy, and interpersonal therapy, are also useful in reducing depression with this population (Gorenstein et al., 2005). Interpersonal therapy has been demonstrated to reduce suicidal and death ideation (Heisel, Duberstein, Talbot, King, & Tu, 2009). Approximately 80% of older adults with depression overcome it if they are given appropriate treatment.

Implications for Clinical Practice

Many older adults develop meaningful support systems in the community and have positive contact with family members. Social contacts are important, and engaging in either paid or volunteer work can enhance the self-esteem and life satisfaction of older individuals (Acquino, Russell, Cutrona, & Altmaier, 1996). Issues that older adults face may include retirement and other changing roles; loss and illness of loved ones; more limited financial resources; caretaking responsibilities; social isolation; health and physical problems, including sensory impairment; and the cultural devaluation of their group (Corna, Wade, Streiner, & Cairney, 2009; I. A. James, 2008; Myers & Harper, 2004). The American Counseling Association contains end-of-life care provisions (quality of care, counselor competence, and confidentiality) in its ethics code and should be consulted when working with terminally ill clients and their loved ones (Werth & Crow, 2009).

The following are suggestions in offering mental health services to older adults (American Psychological Association, 2004; Knight & McCallum, 1998; Pennington, 2004).

1. Obtain specific knowledge and skills in counseling older adults, and critically evaluate your own attitudes about aging.
2. Be knowledgeable about legal and ethical issues that arise when working with older adults (e.g., competency issues).
3. Determine the reason for evaluation and the social factors affecting the problem, such as recent losses, financial stressors, and family issues.
4. Show older adults respect, and give them as much autonomy as possible, regardless of mental status or the issues involved. When communicating with older adults
   - Give full attention to the individual.
   - Talk to rather than about the person.
   - Use respectful language (not elderspeak), but don't be overly sweet.
   - Treat the person as an adult.
   - Take the individual's concerns seriously.
5. Determine the older adult's views of the problem, his or her belief system, stage-of-life issues, educational background, and social and ethnic influences.
6. Assist in interpreting the impact on their lives of cultural issues, such as ethnic group membership, gender, and sexual orientation.
7. Presume competence in older adult clients unless the contrary is obvious.
8. If necessary, slow the pace of therapy to accommodate cognitive slowing.
9. Involve older adults in decisions as much as possible. If there are cognitive limitations, it may be necessary to use legally recognized individuals to assist with decision making.
10. Use multiple assessments, and include relevant sources (client, family members, significant others, and health care providers).
11. Determine the role of family caregivers, educate them about emotional or neurocognitive disorders, and help them develop strategies to reduce burnout.
12. When working with an older couple, help negotiate issues regarding time spent alone and together (especially after retirement). Arguments over recreation are common. There is often too much "couple time" and no "legitimate" reason for separateness.

13. Recognize that it is important to help individuals who are alone establish support systems in the community.

14. Help the older adult develop a sense of fulfillment in life by discussing the positive aspects of their experiences. Success can be defined as having done one's best or having met and survived challenges. A life review is often helpful.

15. Infections and medication side effects can be particularly troublesome for older adults. A physical evaluation may be needed to determine whether mental symptoms have physical causes.

16. For adults very close to the end of their lives, help them deal with a sense of attachment to familiar objects by having them decide how heirlooms, keepsakes, and photo albums will be distributed and cared for. Counseling can significantly improve the quality of life for older adults or help them resolve late-life issues.

Counseling Women

Diane M. Sue and David Sue

You never see someone that looks like me as a scientist. No matter how long I stay here. When I walk through the campus, no one's ever gonna look at me and just think that I'm a physicist. . . . I guess the things that made other people find it hard to see me as a scientist are making it hard for me to see myself as a scientist, too. (Soffa Caldo, Chicana college senior, quoted in Ong, 2005, p. 593)

Alasdair Thompson, leader of a local business group, suggested that women earned less than men because "once a month they have sick problems." This suggestion that women are less productive because of menstruation resulted in his firing. (Checker, 2011)

Approximately 66 percent of family caregivers are women. Among this group, 45 percent indicate they did not have a choice about assuming the role of caregiver. More than one-third of female caregivers also have children or grandchildren under 18 years old living with them. (National Alliance for Caregiving, 2009)

There were 156,964,211 females in the United States in 2010, compared to 151,781,326 males. The ratio of women to men increases with age; among those aged 85 or older, there are about twice as many women as men (U.S. Census Bureau, 2011a). Although women constitute more than half of the population, we include them in the special populations section because within the patriarchal structure of U.S. society, women have been historically subjected to prejudice and discrimination as well as a disadvantaged status. For centuries, governmental leadership and legal decision makers (e.g., the Supreme Court) as well as religious leaders have been primarily male—such power imbalances are deeply ingrained in the social context of our society. Contemporarily, females continue to face oppressive conditions and experience high levels of economic and psychological stress.

In this chapter we focus on many feminist issues. *Feminism*, a frequently misunderstood term, refers to efforts directed toward gender equality—equal economic, social, and political rights and opportunities for women. Early feminists focused on voting and property rights, whereas contemporary feminists advocate for reproductive rights; parental leave and quality child care; psychosocial safety for women (e.g., targeting domestic violence and sexual assault); and ending wage disparity, sexist power structures, and other forms of discrimination. Many feminists focus on the social forces that contribute to gender oppression as well as related socialization practices.

Feminist therapists believe that the patriarchal nature of U.S. society contributes to many of the problems faced by women and that psychological symptoms are often the result of women's subordinate status in society; feminist case conceptualizations incorporate the intersection of multicultural influences and recognize racism and other forms of oppression. Interventions based on a feminist perspective focus on goals, such as empowerment, identifying personal strengths, and discovering areas for self-growth outside of traditional roles (Diaz-Martinez, Interian, & Waters, 2010).

SPECIFIC CHALLENGES

In the following sections we consider societal challenges faced by women and consider their implications in treatment. We conclude with a discussion of women's strengths. Remember that these are generalizations and their applicability needs to be assessed for each client.

Societal Pressures

Historically, women have taken on caregiving roles while simultaneously fulfilling stereotyped feminine social roles in which they are evaluated according to physical beauty, modesty, and their potential as marriage partners. Contemporarily, large numbers of women are employed outside the home, balancing expectations of traditional female roles within the home with varying work expectations outside the home. Although the "marriageability" focus has lessened in recent years (i.e., more women view marriage as an option rather than an economic or social necessity), females are still socialized based on these historic cultural values.

Ongoing socialization experiences affect women's self-perceptions. For example, the more women are treated as sexual objects (e.g., subjected to sexualized evaluation such as sexualized gazes or overt visual inspection and related sexual comments), the more they feel devalued and trivialized (Hill & Fischer, 2008). Such objectivization is pervasive. Melissa Farley, a clinical psychologist who conducted a study on the buying of sex (broadly defined as purchases such as prostitution, pornography, phone sex, lap dances, etc.) found that it was exceedingly difficult to locate men who do not participate in at least some of these activities. She voices concern about the burgeoning demand for (and proliferation of) such products and services and the resultant dehumanization and commoditization of women (Bennetts, 2011).

There are ongoing concerns about the film industry's overrepresentation of males and the sexualization and marginalization of females, even in family-oriented films (Smith & Choueiti, 2011). The stereotyped standards of beauty expressed through advertisements and the mass media also have a strong impact on the health and self-esteem of girls and women. The sexualization of young girls, sometimes as early as the preschool years, is particularly troublesome (Machia & Lamb, 2009). When females are exposed to stereotyped societal messages via toys (e.g., dolls), television, music videos, song lyrics, magazines, and advertising, they begin to (a) believe that their primary value comes from being attractive, (b) define themselves according to media-influenced body standards, and (c) see themselves as sexualized objects (American Psychological Association, Task Force on the Sexualization of Girls, 2007; Moffitt & Szymanski, 2011).

Additionally, societal pressure for females to be thin leads to the internalization of an unrealistic "thin ideal" with resultant body dissatisfaction, disordered eating patterns, and frequent dieting (Hill & Fischer, 2009; Sinclair, 2006). In one sample of 4,745 middle and high school students, many more females were unhappy with their bodies (42% of females versus 25% of males) and reported self-esteem issues due to body shape or weight (36% of females versus 24% of males) (Ackard, Fulkerson, & Neumark-Sztainer, 2007). The need to meet societal standards for thinness or beauty becomes more intense when girls experience the physical changes associated with puberty. Underweight models and digitally "enhanced" photos further convey unrealistic messages about ideal body size. Exposure to such photos is strongly associated with increased depression, body dissatisfaction, and disordered eating in young women (Grabe, Ward, & Hyde, 2008; Moffitt & Szymanski, 2011). Not surprisingly, the lifetime prevalence of eating disorders, such as anorexia nervosa, bulimia nervosa, and binge-eating disorder, are much higher among women (Hudson, Hiripi, Pope, & Kessler, 2007).

In addition to the focus on physical attributes, females are socialized to focus on meeting the needs of others, taking on the role of nurturer and caregiver. They are influenced by beliefs that "good mothers" should stay home with their children or be available if needed by their children during work hours. Women often experience "role overload" and exhaustion due to disproportionate responsibility for child care, household chores, and care of elders. For example, women are 2.5 times more likely than men to do housework and among couples with children, women are twice as likely as men to be responsible for child care (Bureau of Labor Statistics, 2011). Such family responsibilities can affect women's employment status as well as career commitment (Bertrand, Goldin, & Katz, 2010). Women are also more likely to take on primary caretaking responsibilities for older or disabled family members (National Alliance for Caregiving, 2009). Young women appear to be well aware of these social realities. In one study, college women believed that, regardless of their educational attainment or career status, they would have more domestic responsibilities than their husbands and have lower salaries than their male counterparts (Fetterolf & Eagly, 2011).

Implications

Interventions directed at changing the unrealistically thin female image promoted by advertisers, magazines, and other mass media can help reduce body dissatisfaction in females. Programs aimed at preventing or altering disturbed eating patterns generally involve (a) learning to develop a more positive attitude toward one's body; (b) becoming aware of unhealthy societal messages of "what it means to be female" (e.g., girls must be thin, pretty, and sexy); (c) determining the consequences of internalized gender-related societal messages (e.g., distorted expectations and negative self-statements); (d) developing healthier eating and exercise habits; (e) increasing comfort in expressing feelings to peers, family members, and significant others; (f) choosing appropriate self-care messages (e.g., "Being healthy is important, so I will eat and exercise appropriately"); (g) developing plans to implement health-based changes; and (h) identifying healthy strategies to deal with stress and pressure (Richardson & Paxton, 2010).

Similarly, women can be encouraged to develop as much balance as possible in their lives by emphasizing the importance of personal well-being in meeting the various role demands. Counselors can also help women who are overwhelmed with caretaking responsibilities to negotiate more equal sharing of responsibilities, including seeking support from other family members or outside sources.

Discrimination, Harassment, and Victimization

Women continue to experience both sexism and gender-based discrimination in social and professional settings, with the vast majority of women reporting experiences with sexual harassment, being disrespected due to their gender, or being subjected to sexist behavior by strangers (Lord, 2010). As mentioned in our discussion of microaggressions in Chapter 6, sexism can be overt (i.e., blatantly unequal and unfair treatment), covert (i.e., unequal, harmful treatment conducted in a hidden manner, such as gender-biased hiring practices), or subtle (i.e., unequal treatment that is so normative that it is unquestionably accepted).

Sexual harassment (broadly defined as verbal or physical conduct of a sexual nature, sometimes with explicit or implicit expectations that a woman submit to sexual requests) continues to be quite prevalent in school and work environments. Intimidating, hostile, or sexually offensive work environments (e.g., displaying sexually suggestive pictures, telling sexual jokes) are also examples of sexual harassment. A recent national survey indicates that sexual harassment in the schools remains a significant concern—one that has effects not only on girls' psychological well-being but also on their learning (American Association of University Women, 2011). In the past decade, official complaints of sexual harassment in the workplace have declined, with many large companies claiming zero incidents of harassment (Equal Employment Opportunity Commission, 2010). This may, in part, be due to increased educational efforts and explicit policies prohibiting harassment. However, there is concern that the decline may, in fact, result from reduced reporting due to fear of retaliation or other social consequences (e.g., enhanced scrutiny, social disapproval, job loss, interrupted career advancement). Although harassment can be extremely distressing and affect academic and work performance, many women are hesitant to report such behavior.

In addition, sexual victimization and intimate partner violence disproportionately affect women and account for 27% of the violence experienced by females (U.S. Department of Commerce, 2011). Many women affected by intimate partner violence report significant ongoing psychological distress (Zahnd, Aydin, Grant, & Holtby, 2011). Up to half of one sample of college women reported experiencing some form of sexual aggression (Yeater, Treat, Viken, & McFall, 2010). Among women veterans who served in Iraq and Afghanistan, 31% reported experiencing unwanted sexual attention, and more than half reported exposure to offensive sexual behavior, such as sexual stories and jokes; additionally, half reported gender harassment that was not sexually based (Street, Vogt, & Dutra, 2009). Such abuse or harassment can have long-term effects, including chronic headaches, pelvic pain, gastrointestinal distress, and other physical symptoms, as well as emotional symptoms, such as anxiety, depression, disordered eating, and posttraumatic stress disorder (Chen et al., 2010; Lee et al., 2009; Paras et al., 2009; Steiger et al., 2010).

Implications

Students and employees can benefit from knowing how to identify harassment and exactly what steps to take if harassment occurs (e.g., request that the behavior stop; seek help from parents, counselors, or administrative staff; record details of the event). Similarly, strategies for assertively reacting to overt or covert sexism can empower females who are confronted with offensive or discriminatory behaviors.

Violence and sexual harassment against females can lead to a number of mental health problems. It is important for counselors to ask about experiences with discrimination, harassment, or gender-based violence and to consider the effect of such events in case conceptualization. Even among adolescents, screening should be performed for intimate partner abuse, especially in cases where suicidal thoughts, use of drugs, or disordered eating patterns exist. Prevention strategies targeting dating violence are sometimes implemented in high school and college settings (Yeater et al., 2010). The American Psychological Association (2007) recommends support for policy initiatives, including legal and legislative reform addressing the issue of violence against women; improved training for mental health workers to recognize and treat those affected by such violence; dissemination of information regarding violence against women to churches, community groups, educational institutions, and the general public; and the exploration of psychoeducational and sociocultural interventions to change male objectification of women.

> Violence and sexual harassment against females can lead to a number of mental health problems. It is important for counselors to ask about experiences with discrimination, harassment, or gender-based violence and to consider the effect of such events in case conceptualization.

Educational Barriers

> Over a third of students surveyed in grades 3–12 agreed with the statement that "people think that the most important thing for girls is to get married and have children." (National Coalition for Women and Girls in Education, 2008, pp. 1–2)

Although women make up 51% of the U.S. population, they are underrepresented in positions of power and are affected by implicit bias, gender stereotyping, and discrimination. For example, in *Beyond Bias and Barriers: Fulfilling the Potential of Women in Academic Science and Engineering,* the National Academies (2006) report that women face barriers in the fields of science and engineering. In many cases, the culture of masculinity (including images of dominance and forcefulness) are deeply entrenched in "masculine" fields of study within institutions of higher education (de Pillis & de Pillis, 2008). Some progress has been made in promoting gender equality, but inequities continue.

The National Coalition for Women and Girls in Education (2008) reports that (a) girls and women continue to be underrepresented in such areas as math and science; (b) female students continue to receive less attention, encouragement, and praise than male students do; and (c) sexual harassment of females continues to be pervasive (about 40% of high school students report that teachers and other school employees have sexually harassed them; 62% of female college students also report being harassed). Teachers are often unaware that they may be promoting sexism by providing differential responses to male and female students (Frawley, 2005). In one study of third-grade teachers who believed they had a gender-free style, it was found that boys were allowed to speak out of turn, whereas girls were not; boys were less likely to be confronted when involved in disagreements; and when girls spoke out of turn, they were reminded to raise their hands (Garrahy, 2001).

Implications

In the educational arena, mental health professionals can advocate for changes at the system levels. Coursework for teachers can include demonstrations and discussion of responses that may inadvertently convey gender-restrictive messages. Attitudes and negative gender stereotypes do affect performance (Johns, Schmader, & Martens, 2005). In a series of studies, Brown and Josephs (1999) found that gender-specific performance concerns can influence academic functioning. Women who were told a math test would indicate they were weak in math performed worse than women who believed the test was designed to confirm strong math skills. Thus, the stereotype that women are bad at math affected their performance. Many studies have similarly documented how performance can be significantly affected by *stereotype threat* (i.e., anxiety that one's performance will confirm negative, stereotype-based expectations); such anxiety can lead to avoidance of areas of perceived weakness, thus perpetuating racial and gender gaps in performance.

Another study investigating the influence of stereotype threat found that female engineering students who interacted with men behaving in a sexist manner
prior to taking an engineering test performed more poorly than women exposed
to a nonsexist male prior to the test; this effect was found for engineering tests but
not for English tests (i.e., an area not expected to be affected by stereotype threat)
(Logel et al., 2009). Attitudes and expectations regarding stereotyped personality
characteristics and appropriate career choices need to be addressed in educational
programs and with individual clients. Small changes in the culture of mathematics,
science, or engineering departments (e.g., hiring female faculty, mentoring systems for female staff and students, combating negative stereotypes) can help attract women to these fields as well as maintain their interest, enthusiasm, and
sense of belonging (Hill, Corbett, & St. Rose, 2010).

Economic and Employment Barriers

Although women make up 55% of college students and account for a greater percentage of associate, bachelor's, and master's degrees, females make less than their
male counterparts across all racial groups. This disparity (found across educational, experiential, and job categories) is most pronounced between White men
and White women, with women earning 77 cents for each dollar earned by men
(U.S. Census Bureau, 2011). This gap affects not only women but the families
they are supporting. The poverty rate for single mothers with children is 37%—
the highest of any demographic group in the United States. Women with a low
income are especially at risk for depression or domestic violence, or are likely to
become exclusive caregivers of children or older family members (Levy & O'Hara,
2010). Women continue to predominate in low-wage, traditionally female occupations; additionally, pay disparities and differential career advancement occur even
in female-dominant fields. For example, women account for 79% of elementary
and secondary school teachers but only 44% of principals (National Coalition for
Women and Girls in Education, 2008).

Many organizations continue to operate under a value system that emphasizes
power and control rather than relationship skills. Nontraditional career fields are
often not hospitable to women; thus, many women remain in "feminine" careers.
Women are underrepresented not only in fields such as science and engineering but
also in managerial and executive level jobs—occupations associated with "masculine"
qualities, such as being assertive, independent, and influencing others, rather than
"feminine" qualities, such as being concerned with relationships, sensitivity, nurturance, and kindness (de Pillis & de Pillis, 2009; Madera, Hebl, & Martin, 2009).

Potential career barriers are often apparent to women even before they reach
the workplace. For example, college women report that gender role stereotypes
and underrepresentation of women in certain fields influence career choices.
College women not only believe that they will have more difficulty getting hired
than men but also expect to experience discrimination, harassment, and differential treatment. Minority college women perceive even more pronounced career
barriers due to gender and ethnic stereotyping and discrimination (Luzzo &
McWhirter, 2001; Ong, 2005).

College women are also aware that when a woman behaves in a manner that is not considered to be feminine, negative consequences may result. These expectations closely approximate reality. For example, if a woman displays a task-oriented style of leadership that violates the gender norm of modesty, she may be rated as competent but only at the expense of lower social attraction and likability ratings; men displaying the same leadership style are rated high in both competence and likeability (Rudman, 1998). Interestingly, college students given descriptions of fictional top executives said to be responsible for bringing success to their organizations evaluated the fictional female leaders more favorably, describing them as more sensitive and more competent; students assumed that these successful women had a more employee-focused leadership style and had the strength to overcome gender-based challenges along their career path (Rosette & Tost, 2010). In other words, the college students recognized that female executives are required to work much harder to rise to the top.

> Women leaders often confront divergent expectations—they are expected to be assertive and in control but are simultaneously criticized for these same traits.

Women leaders often confront divergent expectations—they are expected to be assertive and in control but are simultaneously criticized for these same traits. Even successful businesswomen report barriers to advancement on the corporate ladder, including the following (Lyness & Thompson, 2000):

1. Women were made to feel that they somehow needed to change, that they were hired or promoted due to "token-hiring practices," and that they were not a "good fit" for senior management. They perceived discomfort from male colleagues, did not have female role models, and felt they had to perform at a higher level than their male counterparts.

2. Male coworkers heightened cultural boundaries by emphasizing male camaraderie and differences from women, often relying on a "good old boys network," and excluding women from information necessary for job performance. Such informal networking provided multiple advantages to male managers.

3. Women executives received less frequent and less effective mentoring than their male counterparts, including limited access to potential mentors, mentors unwilling to work with them, and the misinterpretation of a mentorship request as a sexual invitation.

Implications

Counselors can encourage continued education and job training for women working in minimum-wage jobs and, when needed, provide information regarding quality child care as well as assistance locating food, clothing, and affordable housing. Counselors should consider the worldview of women living in poverty and the "web of stress with which low-income women contend." Therapists can use multicultural therapy models such as *feminist relational advocacy*, a therapeutic approach focused on listening to women's narratives, recognizing the role of oppression in creating emotional distress, recognizing strengths, and providing advocacy as well as emotional and practical support (Goodman, Glenn, Bohlig, Banyard, & Borges, 2009). When possible, mental health services should be provided in convenient locations serviced by public transportation. Child care and other on-site programs for family members can increase participation in the mental health system.

Mental health professionals should also help expand the career choices available to women. In doing so, a comprehensive, skills-based approach is most effective. One program for college women (K. R. Sullivan & Mahalik, 2000) focused on increasing career self-efficacy by enhancing understanding of the impact of gender socialization on career choice and development; learning about the career paths of successful women (e.g., reading about and discussing women's unique career development and observing and interviewing successful women regarding their career decision-making processes and insights); promoting skills to manage anxiety through relaxation and adaptive self-talk; and counteracting internalized stereotypes by identifying and challenging self-defeating thoughts.

Ageism

The number of women aged 65 and older is expected to double and reach 40 million by 2030 (U.S. Census Bureau, 2011a). Given the emphasis on youth and beauty that exists in our society, women face additional barriers as they age, including age discrimination at work; preferential treatment of younger females in stores, restaurants, and other public establishments; reduced dating opportunities (e.g., men often prefer to date younger women); and a sense of being "invisible" (Committee on Women in Psychology, 1999). In addition, older women often confront changing roles (e.g., an "empty nest," loss of career, increased caretaking of aging family members, accommodating a partner's retirement). Responses to midlife changes such as menopause can be influenced by both ageism and sexism, as well as cultural meanings ascribed to menopause (e.g., beliefs that sexual attractiveness and youth are lost at menopause).

Many women report that midlife transitions were not as stressful as they anticipated. Among women between the ages of 40 and 59, nearly three fourths reported feeling "very happy" or "happy." Most were enjoying midlife because of increased independence, freedom from worrying about what others think, freedom from parenting, and the ability to define their own identity based on their own interests (McQuaide, 1998). Instead of being concerned about a midlife crisis, aging, the empty nest syndrome, or menopause, many middle-aged women report going through a midlife review process, as well as having confidence, a strong sense of identity, and a sense of power over their lives (Gibbs, 2005; Hunter, Sundel, & Sundel, 2002). These findings indicate that transitions through midlife may be easier than previously assumed. Differences in transition experiences may be found with women experiencing the stress of poverty or caretaking responsibilities.

Implications

It is important not to assume that all women experience a "midlife crisis" and to be aware that women may differ significantly in how they experience life transitions. The life path of women is quite variable. For example, some women are grandmothers in their late 30s or early 40s, whereas others are new mothers in their 40s. Thus, women may experience various midlife transitions (e.g., a simultaneous sense of loss and sense of freedom when children leave home) at significantly different ages. The personal meaning and reaction to these events should be understood for each individual. Counselors can help women negotiate the loss of prior roles by affirming new commitments in life and by assisting women to develop the personal meaning of life experiences through self-exploration. It is helpful to normalize feelings of anxiety or doubt associated with life transitions and to reframe such experiences as opportunities for greater personal and spiritual development.

Depression

Depression is one of the most prevalent psychiatric disorders and a leading cause of worldwide disability (Andrade et al., 2010); women have a 70% increased lifetime risk of experiencing a major depressive episode compared with men (Kessler, Chiu, Demler, & Walters, 2005). In part, gender differences in depression are believed to be influenced by varying hormone levels and hormone secretion patterns beginning in puberty and continuing throughout the transition to menopause (Graziottin & Serafini, 2009). Additionally, gender socialization and early social learning are believed to contribute to gender differences in stress hormone regulation and the metabolic effects of stress (Dedovic, D'Aguiar, & Pruessner, 2009). Women are particularly vulnerable to severe depression during and following menopause (Graziottin & Serafini, 2009), particularly if they need to continue working full time, have compromised health, or have negative views regarding aging (Woods, Mitchell, Percival, & Smith-DiJulio, 2009).

Various stressors such as sexual abuse and unequal gender roles (Chen et al., 2010; Vigod & Stewart, 2009), as well as perceived discrimination based on gender, especially among those who do not talk to others about their experiences (McLaughlin, Hatzenbuehler, & Keyes, 2010), also contribute to the high prevalence of depression in women. Other factors encountered by females that are linked with the development of depression include:

- The presence of stress, especially acute stress and stress involving interpersonal problems and dependency (i.e., the need to depend on others) (Hammen, 2006; Muscatell, Slavich, Monroe, & Gotlib, 2009; Stader & Hokanson, 1998).
- Work environments that involve chronic stress and few decision-making opportunities (i.e., conditions experienced by many women in the workplace) (Bonde, 2008; Verboom et al., 2011)
- Exposure to targeted rejection (i.e., active, intentional social exclusion or rejection) (Slavich, Way, Eisenberger, & Taylor, 2010).

Gender-specific socialization practices can influence feelings of self-worth. Although men are socialized to value autonomy, self-interest, and achievement-oriented goals, females are taught to value social goals and interdependent functioning (e.g., caring about others, not wanting to hurt others). Because women's self-perceptions are strongly influenced by the opinions of others, they are more vulnerable to interpersonal stress, particularly stressors involving close friends or family. Women often try to maintain relationships at the cost of their own needs and wishes. Failures in relationships are often seen as personal failures, compounding stress and affecting mood. Additionally, gender role expectations can decrease women's sense of control over life situations and diminish their sense of personal worth. Ruminating (i.e., repeatedly thinking about concerns or events) further increases depressive symptoms among females (Hankin, 2009). Additionally, adolescent girls experiencing depression are more likely to generate interpersonal stress, which in turn can result in ongoing depressive symptoms (Rudolph, Flynn, Abaied, Groot, & Thompson, 2009).

Women who are also affected by stressors such as racism, ageism, or exposure to poverty have increased vulnerability to depression. For example, among African American women, everyday encounters with discrimination were linked with increases in depressive symptoms (Schulz et al., 2006; Wagner & Abbott, 2007). Community-based focus-group discussions involving African American women with histories of violent victimization underscored the role of interpersonal violence in the development of depression among these women (Nicolaidis et al., 2010).

Because minority-group females frequently encounter discrimination and prejudice, they may perceive daunting obstacles to achieving their life goals. African American teenagers who were interviewed concerning their multiple minority status were quite aware of the discrimination that they face.

> I'm a black female and black females are the lowest. The black female has a hard time, for one, because she's black, two, because she's a female, and I think it would take more for me to strive to get what I want. (Olsen, 1996, p. 113)

African American teenagers in this study were aware of the negative messages regarding their ethnicity and also the disparagement of the female gender.

Implications

In therapy it is important to address the stressors faced by clients, identifying societal and cultural factors as well as individual influences. It is important to assess for environmental factors, such as poverty, racism, economic conditions, and abusive relationships, as well as specific experiences with overt, covert, or subtle sexism. Women often benefit from psychoeducation regarding the power differential in society, unrealistic gender expectations, and the impact of these expectations on mood. Identifying internalized stereotypes and related self-defeating thoughts and substituting more positive self-statements can reduce depression. Establishing strong social support networks and locating assistance with specific needs (e.g., financial, health, child care) can help women who are experiencing stressful life circumstances (Knowlton & Latkin, 2007).

Evidence-based therapies involving exposure to positive activities; facilitating social interactions; improving social, communication, and assertiveness skills; and identifying role conflicts can help women decrease depressive symptoms and find relationships more satisfying (Lejuez, Hopko, Acierno, Daughters, & Pagoto, 2011; Levenson et al., 2010;). Similarly, practice altering negative, self-critical thoughts and negative self-biases (DeRubeis, Siegle, & Hollon, 2008) and using mindfulness strategies (i.e., calm awareness of present experience, thoughts, and feelings; having an attitude of acceptance rather than being judgmental, evaluative, or ruminative) to disrupt the cycle of negative thinking can reduce depressive symptoms (Gilbert & Christopher, 2010). Therapy focused on improving interpersonal relationships and enhancing social support has been helpful in decreasing depression in women affected by intimate partner violence (Zlotnick, Capezza, & Parker, 2011).

Depression in women is associated with an increased risk of cardiovascular disease, the leading cause of death in women. Consequently, counselors may choose to educate clients about the risk and likelihood of developing coronary heart disease (CHD) and risk factors, such as smoking, a high-fat diet, sedentary lifestyle, and obesity. For women who become depressed after menopause, it is important to provide information on the physiological processes involved with menopause and to discuss the impact of sociocultural attitudes toward women and aging.

Gender Bias in Therapy

It is important for counselors to recognize the sexist nature of our society and to be aware of possible biases when working with female clients (Diaz-Martinez et al., 2010). For example, does the counselor believe there are certain attributes associated with a healthy feminine identity? In past research, qualities such as being more submissive, emotional, and relationship-oriented were identified as positive qualities in women (Atkinson & Hackett, 1998). If counselors adhere to stereotypic, societal standards, consciously or unconsciously, these attitudes may be conveyed to clients during counseling. One study of family therapy sessions revealed that counselors interrupted women more often than they interrupted men (Werner-Wilson, Price, Zimmerman, & Murphy, 1997). Even though the therapists were not aware of this behavior, they were engaged in subtle sexism. Gender-based microaggressions such as this not only can be destructive to the therapeutic alliance (Owen, Tao, & Rodolfo, 2010) but can also significantly affect a female client's sense of empowerment.

Biases can also occur during diagnosis, especially for ethnic minority women (American Psychological Association, 2007a). Many contend that some personality disorders are based on exaggerated gender characteristics. Self-dramatization and exaggerated emotional expressions; intense fluctuations in mood, self-image, and interpersonal relationships; and reliance on others and the inability to assume responsibilities are characteristics of histrionic, borderline, and dependent personality disorders, respectively. Not surprisingly, women are much more likely to be diagnosed with these disorders.

Another problematic diagnosis is premenstrual dysphoric disorder, a new diagnostic category involving serious symptoms of depression, irritability, and tension that appear the week before menstruation and remit soon after the onset of menses. Those critical of this diagnostic category contend that premenstrual dysphoric disorder is a socially constructed condition affected by cultural beliefs and conditioned social and gender role expectations; critics strongly oppose designating symptoms of a normal biological function as a psychiatric disorder (Chekoudjian, 2009; Offman & Kleinplatz, 2004).

Many psychological theories are gender biased. For example, the concepts of "codependency" and "enmeshment," descriptors more frequently applied to women, involve behaviors influenced by cultural expectations and gender-based socialization practices—devotion to home and relationships, connectedness, nurturance, and placing the needs of the family over personal needs. Gender bias is also inherent in family systems therapeutic models; these approaches generally fail to recognize the effects of gender-based power imbalance, including unequal distribution of power within families. Also, disturbances are often interpreted as problems in the system rather than due to stressors experienced by individual family members. Under this theoretical conceptualization, women who are abused are seen as contributors to the system dysfunction.

EMBRACING GENDER STRENGTHS

Women display affiliative qualities, such as being concerned with relationships, sensitivity, nurturance, and kindness (de Pillis & de Pillis, 2009), characteristics often undervalued in our society. Such relationship strengths result in effective teamwork and better rapport within family systems and within society at large. Women have a strong capacity for developing and maintaining strong social support networks. Many women also demonstrate skill at understanding how others are feeling and responding accordingly; thus, they are skilled at anticipating emotional consequences of decisions. Women often show talent in terms of creativity, problem solving, and mental flexibility and are frequently guided by strong values.

Gender-based characteristics such as emotional self-regulation and an orientation to relationships are assets in work settings (Raffaelli, Crocket, & Shen, 2005). Women are more likely than men to display a transformational leadership style—an energetic, passionate approach to projects and the ability to energize others to work toward clearly articulated goals (Vinkenburg, van Engen, Eagly, & Johannesen-Schmidt, 2011). Women employees and leaders are more likely to display an open, consensus-building, and collegial approach to work; to encourage participation, teamwork, and cooperative efforts amongst colleagues; and to share power (Caliper, 2005). These qualities are increasingly recognized as important attributes in a work environment (Rosette & Tost, 2010). Fortunately, as Kanyoro observed, "There is a new growing appreciation of those traits that women use to keep families together and to organize volunteers to unite and make change in the shared life of communities. These newly admired leadership qualities of shared leadership, nurturance, and doing good for others are today not only sought after but also indeed needed to make a difference in the world" (quoted in Lowen, 2011, p. 1).

Implications for Clinical Practice

Both male and female counselors should self-assess for possible sexist beliefs, assumptions, or behaviors and take care not to limit client growth by fostering traditional gender roles. Each female client should be provided the opportunity to choose the life path that is best for her, despite societal gender expectations or political correctness. Problems identified by female clients should be viewed within a societal context in which devaluation of women is a common occurrence; gender-based considerations should be considered integral aspects of problem conceptualization and treatment planning. Guidelines for counselors working with female clients include (American Psychological Association, 2007; Fitzgerald & Nutt, 1998; Szymanski, Carr, & Moffitt, 2011):

1. Remain aware of potential biases in the diagnosis and treatment of women and the tendency for women to internalize problems beginning at an early age.
2. Recognize that many counseling theories and practices are male-centered and may require modifications when working with women. For example, cognitive-behavioral therapeutic approaches can be modified to include a focus on internalized societal messages or unrealistic standards of beauty.
3. Possess up-to-date information regarding the biological, psychological, and sociological issues that affect women, including a strong understanding of the physiological and social implications of reproductive processes, such as menstruation, pregnancy (including unplanned pregnancy), birth, infertility and miscarriage, and menopause.
4. Assess sociocultural factors to determine their role in the presenting problem; consider the influence of gender role socialization; overt, covert, and subtle sexism; discrimination and harassment; and economic, educational, and employment barriers.
5. Help clients realize the impact of power imbalances, gender expectations, and societal definitions of attractiveness on mental health.
6. Emphasize the unique strengths and talents that women bring to work and interpersonal relationships, including the effectiveness of democratic, people-oriented leadership styles.
7. Help clients correct cultural misperceptions that males are superior in math, science, and technology, and discuss women's achievements in leadership positions and in nontraditional fields (e.g., science, math, technology, engineering) as well as strategies women have used to overcome barriers in these fields. Exposure to successful female role models is important for both girls and women.
8. Encourage females to take challenging coursework in math and science and to recognize that academic achievement is an ongoing, cumulative process.
9. Assess for the possible impact of abuse or trauma-related experiences.

10. Clients may need assistance developing financial independence and other supports necessary to leave unhappy marriages or abusive relationships.

11. Do not allow traditional definitions of "good leadership" to mask the talents and strengths women bring to the workplace. Systems-level intervention may be needed to create work environments that optimize the contributions of female leaders and employees.

12. Counselors can educate women about how negative gender-based stereotypes and stereotype threat undermine women's confidence and lead to reduced performance—such knowledge can reduce the influence of negative stereotypes (Johns, Schmader, & Martens, 2005).

13. Be alert for signs of depression. Keep in mind that maternal depression can have a significant effect on children's behavior and well-being (Tully, Iacono, & McGue, 2008).

14. Encourage women to identify and address their own needs and to practice assertively setting boundaries when confronted with unrealistic demands.

15. Be ready to take an advocacy role in initiating systems-level changes as they relate to sexism and sexual harassment.

Counseling and Poverty

Laura Smith

We're people with lives and things in our lives that are affecting our health. . . . Talking about our mental health is not the same as someone who feels down sometimes. If you don't have a roof over your head, if you don't have your electric bill paid, then how are you going to take care of your mental health? There is not a traditional mental health strategy that gets at that. (Participant in the ROAD [Reaching Out About Depression] project, Goodman et al., 2007, p. 286)

[W]hen the therapist and client come from different class backgrounds, they do not always view situations, family relationships, nor solutions from the same viewpoint. . . . I did not find that these therapists were particularly unsympathetic or knowingly unkind. What I did find was that the therapists . . . were unaware of their own class values. (Chalifoux, 1996, p. 32)

Poverty does not constitute a cultural designation in the true sense of the word, yet the challenges and landmarks of life in poverty diverge enough from mainstream life to warrant consideration by counseling professionals. Part of this consideration requires that counselors who come from middle-class (and more affluent) backgrounds learn about life in poverty, about which most of them know very little. Equally as important, however, is learning about the class-related biases, attitudes, assumptions, and procedures that are often embedded in the worldviews of people who hold social class privilege and the ways that these assumptions are manifested within psychological theory, research, and practice. Without an awareness of the social, cultural, and interpersonal discrimination that accompanies poverty, counselors will be unable to work most effectively with poor clients—and may even unintentionally contribute to their oppression.

> Without an awareness of the social, cultural, and interpersonal discrimination that accompanies poverty, counselors will be unable to work most effectively with poor clients—and may even unintentionally contribute to their oppression.

As these considerations are profiled in the following sections, they will be presented within the context of *social class stratification theory* (Beeghley, 2008). This context is significant in that Americans tend not to be well-acquainted with social class theory—many of us are more familiar with numerical calculations such as socioeconomic status (SES) and often think of poverty only in terms of inadequate financial resources. Financial resources are indeed critical to understanding life in poverty; a social class framework, however, positions poverty as more than a lack of purchasing power. Rather, poverty is understood to be the bottom-most rung in a hierarchical system of sociocultural power relations that goes beyond differences in income. Within this hierarchy, social class oppression is called *classism* (Lott & Bullock, 2007), and it operates to limit (or to enhance) access to many kinds of socially valued assets. As will be described in a subsequent section, these assets include the availability of essential services and resources (e.g., education and health care), entrée to mainstream opportunities and experiences, cultural inclusion/exclusion, and representation within our nation's system of participatory democracy (Smith, 2010).

CHARACTERISTICS AND STRENGTHS

As of 2010, the U.S. Census Bureau's survey results estimated that American poverty had increased during the previous year from 13.2% of the population to 14.3%, resulting in the largest number of poor Americans (43.6 million) since poverty estimates have been published (U.S. Census Bureau, 2010c). The trends and data summarized here provide a demographic snapshot of American poverty today:

* The poverty rate increased for Whites from 8.6% to 9.4%; for Blacks, from 24.7% to 25.8%; and for Latinos, from 23.2% to 25.3%. For Asians, the 2009 poverty rate of 12.5% did not change significantly from the previous year (U.S. Census Bureau, 2010c).
* Women are 40% more likely to live in poverty than men and 60% more likely to live in extreme poverty (or to have resources that amount to less than half the poverty rate) (Legal Momentum, 2003). Within White, Black, Mexican, Puerto Rican, Cuban, Native American, Asian, and Pacific Islander ethnicities, women of every group are more likely to be poor than the men of the same background (Elmelech & Lu, 2004).
* Twenty-four percent of lesbians live in poverty, as opposed to 19% of straight women; the poverty rates of gay men are approximately equal to those of straight men (Albelda, Badgett, Schneebaum, & Gates, 2009).
* Twenty-one percent of America's children live in poverty (15.3 million children), and 9% live in extreme poverty (Wight, Chau, & Aratani, 2011).
* Twelve percent of White children live in poor families, along with 36% of Black children, 15% of Asian children, 34% of Native American children, and 33% of Latino/a children (Wight, Chau, & Aratani, 2011).

The preceding statements use the word *poverty* with reference to specific numerical criteria, such as the federal poverty threshold. Different branches of the U.S. government compute such designations slightly differently, yet such calculations (and hence, figures such as the ones just given) always underestimate the number of families who are struggling economically. For example, the Department of Health and Human Services (HHS) 2011 guidelines specify that a family of four must earn less than $22,350 per year to fall beneath the poverty line; therefore, a family of four attempting to live on $22,351 per year would *not* be counted among the poor. These data effectively illustrate, however, a significant characteristic of American social class structure: positions of lower socioeconomic power and access—that is, life in poverty—intersect meaningfully with marginalization along other dimensions of identity, such as race, gender, and sexual orientation.

Strengths of People Living in Poverty

Presenting the strengths of people living in poverty is a somewhat self-contradictory undertaking. On one hand, the question may seem to suggest that poor people are somehow inherently different from the rest of us—and research evidence supports the opposite contention. Certainly, an individual *can* suffer a financial downturn for a variety of personal reasons. Nevertheless, the fact that particular cultural groups are consistently overrepresented among the poor supports the notion that poverty generally derives from people's historical and sociopolitical contexts rather than from individual constitutional peculiarities (e.g., Belle, 1990; Carmon, 1985; Costello, Compton, Keeler, & Angold, 2003). Similarly, the elevated levels of stress, deprivation, and physical wear and tear that are characteristically detected among poor people would theoretically be expected to affect almost anyone who was constrained to survive life in poverty.

On the other hand, when people *do* survive poverty, they demonstrate many strengths that are often not part of the stereotypical image that people in other classes have of the poor. For example, Banyard (2008) wrote of the patience, persistence, and determination of homeless women as they struggled to make decent lives for their children—women who have often been stereotyped with the classist, racist label *welfare queen*. The words of these homeless mothers illustrated Banyard's characterization of them as not only surviving but tenaciously creating survival strategies, solving problems, and maintaining hope as they prioritized their children and their roles as mothers:

> [Y]ou have an allotted time to get out of the [shelter]. That's stressful, knowing that the clock's ticking. . . . You've worked all your life, and then you're stuck on welfare, and then your children ask for things. (p. 1)

> We just, we think of it again, and think of another route. You know, like taking another street. You know, it's not like you'll hit a highway . . . but it won't be a dead end street. (p. 2)

You know, it's like I run this race, I fall down. I'm not just going to lay there. Even if I lose, I'm going to get up and still try to make it to the finish line. (p. 2)

Obviously, most of us would wish for a world in which mothers, fathers, and children did not have to demonstrate their ability to survive homelessness. However, it is important to take stock of the strengths that people in poverty demonstrate as they are forced to do so, as Banyard (2008) explained:

If we assume that women in poverty are lazy and unmotivated (common stereotypes), we are likely to design policies that focus exclusively on giving them, as individuals, penalties for not finding a job. If we, on the other hand, assume that many women possess the desire to make a better life for themselves and their families, and listen to their stories of how hard it is to feed and house a family on minimum wage or to find affordable childcare, then we design policies which encourage work by supporting a living wage and educational opportunities for low-income workers and increasing accessible, affordable childcare for their children. (p. 2)

SPECIFIC CHALLENGES

Most of us can readily appreciate that a scarcity of the essential resources and services that support life—healthy food, safe communities, good schools, adequate health care, a roof over one's head—would lead in obvious ways to discomfort, distress, and crisis for poor families. What may not be as obvious is the additional bias and injury that accrue to people in poverty as the result of institutional and cultural classism. As is the case with other forms of oppression, classist attitudes often exist at an unconscious level within the worldviews of well-intentioned individuals and can consequently be perpetuated by counselors who are unaware of the implications of their actions. Understanding classism, therefore, is an essential component of multiculturally competent practice. The sections that follow profile some examples of classist discrimination.

The Cultural Invisibility and Social Exclusion of the Poor

The American author and poet Dorothy Allison (1994), who was raised in poverty, observed, "My family's life was not on television, not in books, not even in comic books" (p. 17), a perception that has subsequently been borne out by the social psychological literature. Bullock, Wyche, and Williams (2001) found that poor people rarely appear within televised media representations—and when they do, it is most often through reality shows that depict them as lazy, promiscuous, dysfunctional, and/or drug-addicted. Similarly, the experiences of working-class people are largely without representation in popular culture, and there are few poor or working-class voices in the national discourse on public policy issues. When they are included, usually with regard to specific topics, such as organized labor, they are often presented in a negative light.

Increasingly, the poor are being physically as well as metaphorically excluded from mainstream cultural life. A report entitled "Homes Not Handcuffs" documented the rise in civic ordinances that restrict the sharing of food, make it illegal to sit or sleep in public spaces, and drive homeless people away from public areas, often resulting in the loss of people's personal documents, medications, and other property (National Law Center on Homelessness and Poverty and the National Coalition for the Homeless, 2009). Ehrenreich (2009) called this trend "the criminalization of poverty" (para. 2).

Educational Inequities

Although education is often promoted as a pathway out of poverty, American educational disparities are such that the families with the greatest need are often relegated to the least adequate educational resources. Jonathan Kozol has chronicled the interface of class, race, and schooling in America in books including *The Shame of the Nation* (2005), finding that children who attend public schools in poor communities are more likely to be taught by poorly paid, uncertified teachers and to have fewer computers, fewer library books, fewer classes, fewer extra-curricular opportunities, and fewer teachers than those students in wealthier communities. According to "Losing Ground," a report by the National Center for Public Policy and Higher Education, the relatively small number of poor students who make it to college campuses will find that the costs of a college education have escalated at a rate higher than both inflation and family income. As a result, the graduation rates of low-income students are reduced, whereas students from middle-class and wealthy families continue to attend college in record numbers.

Environmental Injustice

Waste dumps, "dirty industries," and other pollution-producing operations are frequently located in the urban and rural areas, where poor people and people of color live. U.S. Environmental Protection Agency (EPA) administrator Lisa Jackson called these neighborhoods "hot spots of emissions, hot spots of contamination" as she discussed efforts to address the resulting elevated risk of asthma and other pollution-related conditions (Eilperin, 2010, para. 17).

Disparities in the Judicial System

Mentioned regularly in media descriptions of legal proceedings, bail represents one of the more overt forms of classist discrimination: The poor remain in

> Mentioned regularly in media descriptions of legal proceedings, bail represents one of the more overt forms of classist discrimination: The poor remain in prison cells while wealthier people accused of the same crimes go home.

prison cells, while wealthier people accused of the same crimes go home. Moreover, funding for legal aid services is sufficient only to provide counsel to a small proportion of the Americans who need it, with the result that millions of poor people are priced out of the U.S. civil legal process for the vast majority of their legal concerns (Rhode, 2004). Reiman (2007) has argued that the criminal justice system itself is deeply classist, in that it portrays crime per se as the misdeeds of the poor. In other words, street crimes such as burglary, theft, and selling drugs are the contents of the typical police blotter and are tallied in national crime rate statistics. This practice serves to deflect attention from the crimes that actually cause the most death, destruction, and suffering in our country, crimes that derive from the actions of people with social class privilege: corporate fraud, the creation of toxic pollutants, profiteering from unhealthy or unsafe products, and risky high-level financial ventures where the American public ends up bearing the consequences of the risk.

Classism and the Minimum Wage

Without people working in minimum-wage jobs to carry them along, the lives of middle-class and wealthy Americans would come to a standstill. Our society relies upon the people who ring up our purchases, work in child care, change hospital beds, clean offices, and serve food—yet the citizens who perform these necessary jobs cannot earn enough money to lift their families above the poverty line. The federal minimum wage of $7.25 per hour does not allow a full-time worker to lift his or her family of four out of poverty, a conclusion that emerges from examining the cost of living around the country via Penn State's Living Wage Calculator. This tool calculates the minimum cost of essential food, medical, housing, and transportation requirements in almost every U.S. city and county and is available online at www.livingwage.geog.psu.edu. This observation goes hand in hand with a finding by the National Coalition for the Homeless (2005): As many as 25% of people in U.S. homeless shelters have jobs. The unlivable level of the minimum wage gives rise to inherent ethical contradictions, suggesting that classist attitudes toward poor may influence public debate (or lack thereof) regarding this issue.

Health Care Inequities

The health disparities research is resoundingly clear: Poor people face elevated rates of nearly every sort of threat to survival, including heart disease, diabetes, exposure to toxins, cognitive and physical functional decline, and homicide, among many others (e.g., Belle, Doucet, Harris, Miller, & Tan, 2000; Scott, 2005). The Kaiser Commission (2010) reported that by 2009 the number of Americans without health insurance had grown to 50 million. The majority of these individuals come from low-income families, yet 61% come from families where one or more members work full time. Not surprisingly, people without access to medical care often have no choice but to allow preventable conditions to escalate into serious ones and to leave serious problems untreated. Correspondingly, a 2009 Harvard study found that nearly 45,000 U.S. deaths annually are associated with a lack of health insurance (Wilper, Woolhandler, Lasser, McCormick, Bor, & Himmelstein, 2009).

Negative Attitudes and Beliefs

Wealthy people can become national celebrities on the basis of the wealth they own, with the media chronicling their everyday activities. Moreover, intellectualism and critical thinking are largely presented as the exclusive province of more affluent Americans within popular culture. By contrast, social psychological research indicates that traits such as *crude, irresponsible, lazy, stupid, dirty*, and *immoral* are attributed more often to poor people than to middle-class people (Cozzarelli, Wilkinson, & Tagler, 2001; Landrine, 1985; Lott & Saxon, 2002).

Training Implications

Collectively, the manifestations of classism discussed previously operate to create a physically challenging, socially excluded life experience for men, women, and children living in poverty. Like other forms of oppression, therefore, classism can be understood to undermine the physical and emotional well-being of people withstanding its impact. The social exclusion of the poor was captured by psychologist Bernice Lott (2002) in describing the primary characteristic of classism as *cognitive and behavioral distancing* from the poor. In particular, Lott linked this phenomenon to psychologists' lack of attention to poverty, which is often apparent even in the context of their consideration of other cultural issues. As a consequence, psychological theory, research, and practice tend to be largely inaccessible by poor people and not particularly relevant to their experiences (Smith, 2010). In addition, counselors who offer services in poor communities may find that their work is compromised by previously unexamined classist assumptions. Aponte (1994), a family therapist who devoted his career to working with poor clients, suggested that "therapy with the poor must have all the sophistication of the best psychological therapies. It must also have the insight of the social scientist and the drive of the community activist" (p. 9). The following suggestions can help guide counselors in improving their skills in the context of poverty (Smith, 2005, 2009).

1. *Supplement your knowledge of social class, poverty, and related issues.* Although most counselors do not receive focused training experiences regarding poverty, helpful resources exist by which counselors, supervisors, and trainees can deepen their understanding of social class, the circumstances faced by poor Americans, and the implications of both for clinical work. Some useful starting points include:
   * *Psychology and Economic Injustice* (Lott & Bullock, 2007)

- *The Color of Wealth* (Lui, Leondar-Wright, Brewer, & Adamson, 2006)
- *Class Matters: Where We Stand* (hooks, 2000)
- The APA Task Force on Resources for the Inclusion of Social Class in Psychology Curricula (American Psychological Association, 2008).

2. *Increase your understanding and awareness of social class privilege.* Many counselors-in-training receive multicultural training experiences that facilitate their awareness of race-related identity—and enhancing class awareness is an analogous process, although it is seldom addressed as such. To aid counselors in this effort, Liu, Pickett, and Ivey (2007) developed a list of self-statements corresponding to White middle-class privilege. These statements included "I can be assured that I have adequate housing for myself and my family" and "My family can survive an illness of one or more members" (p. 205). The authors also presented a case example to which counselors can refer in applying class-related considerations within counseling practice.

3. *Learn about the everyday realities of life in poverty.* Students in some professions (such as social work) receive training that educates them regarding welfare procedures, housing offices, food stamps, and other aspects of government bureaucracy; this training helps prepare them to encounter clients with nowhere to turn for health services, shelter, or child care. Mental health counselors, who often lack this preparation, can find themselves disoriented by the unfamiliar deprivations of life in a poor community. Because such information is often locally specific and subject to change, city and state government websites and Internet searches are a good way to gather it.

4. *Learn to see the everyday signs of social class stratification and bias.* Although social class is not often discussed openly in the United States, the signs of its existence are all around us if we begin to open our eyes to it. Sometimes these signs can be seen readily, as in the aforementioned public fascination with the lives of wealthy people or in people's interest in wearing clothing that features corporate or designer logos. Others are more subtle, such as those that are manifested through *classist microaggressions* (Smith & Redington, 2010). These expressions of class-based derogation are directly analogous to microaggressions based on other marginalized identities (Sue et al., 2007). Classist microaggressions include the use of class-referenced words to indicate favorable or unfavorable evaluations, such as describing an object or a person as *classy* or *high-class* in a complimentary fashion or describing it as *low-class* or *low-rent* to discredit it. Other classist microaggressions illustrate specific intersections with other identities. Hartigan (2005) discussed the meanings inherent in the name-calling directed toward poor White Americans, such as *White trash*, *trailer trash*, *rednecks*, or *hillbillies*, whereas Rose (2008) analyzed a microaggression that derives from oppression according to race, class, and gender: *welfare queen*.

Implications for Clinical Practice

In addition to increasing their awareness of poverty and social class privilege, counselors can improve the effectiveness and relevance of their work in the context of poverty according to the following guidelines:

1. Integrate a social justice framework within counseling practice. Many counselors who go to work in poor communities will encounter bleak urban landscapes, crowded schools, and crumbling housing developments for the first time. How are counselors to incorporate the impact of such environmental and contextual dimensions within psychotherapeutic practice, which often seems concerned primarily with an individual's emotional interior? The application of a social justice model to counseling practice makes room within case conceptualization and treatment design for counselors' analyses of the systemic aspects and origins of client distress. Feminist and multicultural examinations of social justice practice can be found within other chapters of this book, as well as in works by Aldarondo (2007), Goodman, Liang, Helms, Latta, Sparks, and Weintraub (2004), Miller and Stiver (1997), and Nelson and Prilleltensky (2005).

2. Adopt a flexible approach to treatment. As multicultural psychologists have long contended, the conventional roles and behaviors of psychological practice are at best culture-bound and at worst oppressive to clients from marginalized groups (D. W. Sue et al., 1998). As mentioned, life in poverty can be vastly different from the middle-class existence portrayed in many counseling skills textbooks; counselors must, therefore, be willing to use these resources flexibly. Dumont (1992) wrote about his experience with clients living in poverty, having come to practice in a community mental health center as a psychoanalytically trained psychiatrist. Contending with the pathological social and environmental forces—racism, pollution, involuntary unemployment, and malnutrition—that predominated in his clients' lives, he concluded that "the 50-minute hour of passive attention, of pushing toward the past, of highlighting the shards of unconscious material in free association, just does not work" (p. 6).

   Along these lines, when counselors are willing to learn from community members about the interventions that might be most useful to them, different kinds of supplementary (or alternative) modalities can emerge. These interventions might involve the development of new practices and modalities in accordance with local needs, such as group discussions offered as part of community gatherings, psychoeducational groups in local classrooms, and collaborative events with homeless shelters (Smith, 2005; Smith, Chambers, & Bratini, 2009). Other modalities might involve the formation of community partnerships that combine counseling practice with peer counseling and local social justice advocacy (Goodman et al., 2007). The initiation of participatory-action research projects has also been explored as a means by which the well-being of poor communities can be enhanced in concert with social justice activism (Smith & Romero, 2010).

3. Be willing to incorporate problem solving and resource identification within sessions—but don't assume that this will be the focus of the work. People living in poverty are often only a paycheck or an accident away from a health or housing crisis. Even in the absence of crisis, they may be constrained to devote time and energy to such exigencies as securing child care

(continued)

(continued)

and making food stamps last until the end of the month. Counselors have indicated that they often feel that discussion of such issues is not sufficiently "deep" and does not therefore qualify as the "real" work that they are there to do (Schnitzer, 1996). Such a response bears traces of class bias in that it discounts as superficial some of the most pressing realities of poor clients' lives. This bias can also work in the other direction, however, in that middle-class counselors can be so unsettled by their clients' lack of resources that they assume that clients' psychological realities are oriented entirely around securing them. The latter assumption undermines the therapeutic encounter as well, in that it can hinder counselors from engaging poor clients in exploring the same kinds of feelings, fears, hopes, or other emotional issues that clients in any setting are likely to find important (Smith, 2005)—and it should go without saying that many poor clients come to speak with counselors about precisely these issues. The suggestion that emerges from this balancing act has much in common with good multicultural counseling in general: Be accountable for understanding the unique aspects of clients' sociocultural context, and be open to addressing them; however, do not assume that this knowledge constitutes a "recipe" for working with them.

4. Incorporate an advocacy role into your work. Atkinson, Thompson, and Grant (1993) identified *advocate* as one of the systems intervention roles in which counselors should be competent, and at no time is that role more relevant than when working in the context of oppression. Moreover, given that research has conclusively demonstrated the damage that poverty exacts upon people's physical and emotional well-being, advocating for the eradication of poverty and the greater cultural inclusion of the poor *is* advocating for psychological well-being. Such advocacy can be expected to benefit a large portion of society, given that over half of Americans are likely to spend at least a year below the poverty line at some point during their lives (Hacker, 2006). Opportunities for advocacy include support for broadened access to mental and physical health care for poor families and participation in the living wage movement, which would raise the minimum wage to a level that allows workers to lift their families out of poverty.

Counseling Persons With Disabilities

The mother of a child with Down syndrome explains how hurtful words can be. Use of expressions such as "spaz," "lame," "brain dead," "gimp," or "cripple" is demoralizing and communicates the message that it is okay to engage in this type of demeaning description. (Hertzog, 2010)

A 77-year-old woman has been on kidney dialysis for 10 years; she also has seizures, arthritis, and significant hearing loss. Communication with the social worker is not going well due to the woman's impaired hearing. The daughter explains that her mother has hearing aids but does not wear them because they hurt her ears. The social worker directs all her questions to the daughter, leaving the mother wondering what is being discussed. (Desselle & Proctor, 2000)

In 1988, I became obviously disabled. I walk with crutches and a stiff leg. Since that time, I no longer fulfill our cultural standard of physical attractiveness. But worse, there are times when people who know me don't acknowledge me. When I call their name and say, "Hello," they often reply, "Oh, I didn't see you." I have also been mistaken for people who do not resemble me. For example, I was recently asked, "Are you a leader in the disability movement?" While I hope to be that someday, I asked her, "Who do you believe I am?" She had mistaken me for a taller person with a different hair color, who limps but does not use a walking aid. The only common element was our disability. My disability had become my persona. This person saw it and failed to see me. (Buckman, 1998, p. 19)

Danielle Buckman, the woman in the last vignette, is a psychotherapist who teaches university courses on counseling people with disabilities. Due to her own struggle with multiple sclerosis, she has firsthand experiences with discriminatory reactions from the general public. Since Ms. Buckman is in midlife, she also expresses concern about the triple whammy of gender, disability, and aging issues. Attitudes toward individuals with disabilities range from ignorance and lack of understanding to being overprotective or overly sympathetic to disdainful and dismissive. People often do not know how to respond to people with disabilities. In the second vignette, the social worker was talking to the daughter as if the mother were not present. The daughter felt frustrated and responded,

You are not even trying to communicate with my mother. . . . She can understand you if you look at her and speak slowly and clearly. . . . Imagine how you would feel if you and your spouse went to the doctor to consult about a major surgery you were scheduled for and the doctor directed the conversation only to your spouse as if you were not intelligent enough to know what was being discussed. (Desselle & Proctor, 2000, p. 277)

There are about 54 million individuals with some level of disability (physical or mental), of whom 35 million have a disability that severely affects daily functioning. Because of the traumatic brain injuries from the wars in Iraq and Afghanistan, the incidence of individuals with physical disabilities is increasing (Terrio, Nelson, Betthauser, Harwood, & Brenner, 2011). Of the 72.3 million families in the United States, about 21 million have at least one member with a disability (U.S. Census Bureau, 2005). Rates of disability are higher among African Americans (26.4%) and American Indian/Alaska Native groups (27%) compared with non-Hispanic Whites (16.2%) (Cornish, Gorgens, Olkin, Palomibi, & Abels, 2008).

Individuals with severe disability have high unemployment and poverty rates (U.S. Census Bureau, 2010a). Up to 90% of individuals with psychiatric disabilities are unemployed—the highest unemployment of all disability groups (Larson et al., 2011). In children, disability is more common in boys and children from low-income families (Sullivan, 2009). Children with disabilities are more likely to suffer from maltreatment, such as physical and sexual abuse and neglect (Algood, Hong, Gourdine, & Willams, 2011; Lightfoot, Hill, & LaLiberte, 2011). Women with disabilities are also at risk for abuse and may not report these incidents because of internalized oppression and marginalization (Robinson-Whelen et al., 2010).

In the following sections we consider background information and challenges often faced by individuals with disabilities and consider their implications in treatment. Remember disabilities vary greatly in terms of severity as well as specific condition. Therefore, applicability of the information presented needs to be considered for each client.

UNDERSTANDING DISABILITIES

There are many myths associated with people with disabilities (American Friends Service Committee, 1998; CSD Council for Students with Disabilities, 2006; LSU Office of Disability Services, 2011):

1. *Most are in wheelchairs.* Among the millions of people with disabilities, only about 10% use wheelchairs, crutches, or walkers. Most have more invisible disabilities, such as cardiovascular problems, arthritis and rheumatism, back and spine problems, hearing impairment, asthma, epilepsy, neurodevelopmental disorders (e.g., academic or intellectual impairment), and mental illness.

2. *People with disabilities are a drain on the economy.* It is true that many individuals of working age with disabilities are not working. However, the

majority of those who are unemployed want to work. Discrimination often hampers their efforts to join the workforce.

3. *Employees with disabilities have a higher absentee rate than employees without disabilities.* Studies have found that employees with disabilities may actually have fewer attendance problems than nondisabled employees.

4. *The greatest barriers to people with disabilities are physical ones.* In actuality, negative attitudes and stereotypes are the greatest impediments and the most difficult to change.

5. *Persons who have disabilities are brave and courageous.* Individuals with disabilities react to situations like anyone else does. They demonstrate a variety of emotional reactions in adapting to their condition. Some adapt well, whereas others have more difficulty coping.

6. *Government health insurance covers people with disabilities.* Many disabled individuals have private insurance, whereas a smaller number have no health insurance. Medicaid provides coverage for only a small percentage, usually those with extreme disability.

As mentioned previously, not all disabilities are apparent. Individuals with "invisible" disabilities (e.g., some mental disorders or physical conditions such as traumatic brain injury) are often responded to with frustration and resentment from friends, family members, and employers. When an individual looks healthy, others may not believe the person has a disability and may blame the individual for difficulties that are displayed. With a visible disability, prejudice and discrimination can occur, but accommodations are more likely to be made. However, with a less visible disabling condition, such as a traumatic brain injury, misattributions are common (e.g., blaming difficulties in recovery on the individual's personality or unwillingness to cooperate). There may also be unrealistic hopes for full recovery. Invisible disabilities can be assessed by consulting with family and friends about the client's pre-injury behaviors, abilities, personality, and attitudes to determine whether the changes in these characteristics are due to the injury. If this is the case, the counselor can educate family members about the nature of the condition and how unrealistic expectations sometimes develop with unobservable injuries (McClure, 2011).

Models of Disability

There are three models of disability, each affecting the way disabling conditions are perceived (Artman & Daniels, 2010; Olkin, 1999). First, the *moral model* focuses on the "defect" as representing some form of sin or moral lapse. The disability may be perceived as a punishment or test of faith. The individual or family members may respond with feelings of shame and responsibility. In some cultures, disabilities are believed to result from such factors as evil spirits, curses, or retribution form unhappy ancestors. Second, the *medical model* regards disability as a defect or loss of function that resides in the individual. Action is taken to cure or rehabilitate the condition. In some cultural groups, intervention targets rebalancing mind-body disharmony. The medical model has been responsible for many technological advances and treatments targeting a variety of conditions. Additionally, this approach dismisses the notion that moral issues have caused the disability. Third, the *minority model* views disability as an external problem involving an environment that is filled with negative societal attitudes and that fails to accommodate the needs of individuals with special needs. This perspective emphasizes the oppression, prejudice, and discrimination encountered by individuals who are disabled— experiences very similar to those of other minority groups.

Implications

Much of the research indicates that empowering individuals and caregivers increases life satisfaction. Unfortunately, the stress and prejudice associated with disabilities increases the risk for psychiatric or substance abuse problems (Turner, Lloyd, & Taylor, 2006). If mental health issues appear to be related to the disability, it is important to identify the way the disability is viewed by the client and by family members; such information may influence problem definition and intervention strategies. If the disability is seen as a moral issue (e.g., a test of faith), religious support may offer meaningful relief. Goals may include reducing guilt, giving meaning to the experience, generating support from the religious community, and developing problem-solving approaches.

From the medical model perspective, the client (or family) may want to focus on improving the client's condition, using technology or other interventions to help "normalize" functioning. Mental health professionals not only can help clients and family members obtain technological resources but can also enhance independent living skills and advocate for appropriate accommodations in school or work environments. Incorporating perspectives from the minority model can be useful; counselors can emphasize how societal attitudes play a large role in the problems faced by individuals with disabilities and focus on environmental supports directed at maximizing the potential of the client. An emphasis on self-empowerment and self-advocacy can help inoculate clients against societal prejudices and discrimination and help protect their self-esteem.

Life Satisfaction

I should have picked up the pieces and made the adjustment, and not dwell on it. . . . The problem is the rest of the world is dwelling on it. Every time you go out there, you're reacting to this ridiculous attitude problem, the architectural barriers, the financial discrimination, and this place won't hire you and this company won't insure you and that potential lover won't look at you. . . . So that reopens the wound maybe twenty times a day and yet you're supposed to have made the adjustment. (Noonan et al., 2004, p. 72)

Because of an auto accident, Gary Talbot went from being an "able-bodied man to able-bodied wheelchair user." He evaluates his life this way: "I don't like the fact that I can't walk down the street or go jogging or climb a hill or ride a bike. [But] there's so much I can do and that I've been able to do that I just wouldn't change anything about my life. (Rosenbaum, 2010a)

Ratings of life satisfaction among individuals with disabilities tend to be lower than among those without disabilities. However, these ratings depend on the type of disability and the timing of the ratings. Some individuals adjust well, whereas others remain chronically distressed. In one study of the life satisfaction of people with traumatic spinal cord injuries, 37% indicated they were "very satisfied" and 31% "somewhat satisfied" with their lives. This compares to 50% "very satisfied" and 40% "somewhat satisfied" among the general population. An interesting aspect of the study was that those who perceived themselves as "in control" reported the greatest satisfaction (Chase, Cornille, & English, 2000).

Having close social relationships and paid employment are also associated with increased life satisfaction (Crompton, 2010). Individuals with disabilities often rate activities such as communication, thinking, and relating socially as more important than being able to walk or to dress oneself. Unfortunately, many health professionals display a negative attitude toward disability. Only 18% of physicians and nurses imagined that they would be glad to be alive if they had a high-level spinal cord injury; in sharp contrast, 92% of those with this condition reported satisfaction with their lives (Gerhart, Koziol-McLain, Lowenstein, & Whiteneck, 1994).

> Mental health and health care providers often underestimate the potential quality of life for individuals with disabilities. Signs of depression or suicidal thoughts may be accepted as normal because of low expectations regarding life opportunities.

Implications

Mental health and health care providers often underestimate the potential quality of life for individuals with disabilities. Signs of depression or suicidal thoughts may be accepted as normal because of low expectations regarding life opportunities. Interventions may be considered useless. The research seems to show that many individuals with disabilities feel quite satisfied with their lives and that increasing their sense of control is important. Self-efficacy can be enhanced by encouraging as much personal control and decision making as possible. If depressive or suicidal thoughts or wishes surface, they should be addressed. Some support the right of individuals with disabilities to engage in assisted suicide. However, other organizations argue that individuals with disabilities are an oppressed group and express concern that they may be coerced to end their lives (Batavia, 2000).

Sexuality and Reproduction

Men and women with disabilities often express concerns over sexual functioning and reproduction. They worry about their sexual attractiveness and how to relate to or find a partner. Some may not know whether it is possible to have children or may have questions about the genetic implications of procreating. Mental health professionals who are uncomfortable with these topics may minimize or overlook these areas of concern.

Implications

Clearly, both clients and therapists need to be educated on these subjects as they relate to the specific disabilities. Many individuals who have a disability receive the societal message that they should not be sexual or that they are sexually unattractive. This concern should be addressed and assessed both individually and for couples, if applicable. Therapists can emphasize that sexual relationships are based on communication and emotional responsiveness to one another and can help individuals or couples develop new ways of achieving sexual satisfaction. Old messages regarding sexuality may have to be replaced with new ones. Sexual pleasure is possible even with a loss of sensation in the genitals (e.g., with spinal cord injuries). Many women with spinal cord injuries are still capable of orgasms and sexual pleasure from stimulation of the genitals or other parts of the body (Lindsey, Rivera, & Sipski-Alexander, 2007). Such injury also does not preclude the ability to become pregnant or deliver a child. Among men with spinal cord injuries, many are able to attain an erection and ejaculate, although they may have to learn new forms of stimulation (Klebine & Lindsey, 2007).

Spirituality and Religiosity

Spirituality and religious beliefs can be a source of inner strength and support. One woman with a disability wrote, "It sort of helps me to identify myself, thinking I am a woman created by God and I am so precious and I am so loved and I have so much beauty inside of me" (Nosek & Hughes, 2001, p. 23). Religion and spirituality (connection to a higher power) are associated with increased life satisfaction and functional ability for individuals with traumatic brain injuries (Waldron-Perrine et al., 2011).

Implications

The mental health professional should determine the role, if any, that religious beliefs or spirituality play in the life of a client with a disability. The spirituality of the woman in the previous example enhanced her sense of self. Such beliefs can be a source of support for clients and their caregivers. Therapists can ask clients about their religious or spiritual beliefs and how their beliefs help them confront challenges and incorporate their beliefs into treatment (Waldron-Perrine et al., 2011). In some cases, individuals may believe that their disability is a punishment from God or may blame God for not preventing the injury. These issues should also be addressed and resolved. Therapists can consult with or refer to religious leaders when working with clients who are attempting to come to terms with a disability.

Strengths

Many individuals with disabilities who have lived through natural disasters show resiliency and adaptation. Instead of responding, "Where were they when we needed them?" they were more likely to think, "What are my possibilities? What options do I have?" (Fox, White, Rooney, & Cahill, 2010)

Because of the broad variety of disabilities and because individuals with disabilities can come from any population, we will focus on personal characteristics that enhance daily living and satisfaction with life. Among those with spinal cord injuries, coping strategies, hope, and optimism are associated with a higher quality of life (Kortte, Gilbert, Gorman, & Wegener, 2010). Individuals with traumatic brain injuries who feel a connection to a higher power show greater life satisfaction and functional ability.

Qualities such as creativity, resilience, self-control, and the ability to make positive connections with others and find meaning in life are strengths that can be tapped in the therapy process (Dunn & Brody, 2008). Many individuals already possess these strengths; however, these attributes can also be developed or enhanced in counseling by focusing on changing perceptions regarding the disability, improving self-confidence, and focusing on ways to empower the client (Shallcross, 2011) and encourage active decision making (Artman & Daniels, 2010).

THE AMERICANS WITH DISABILITIES ACT

The Americans With Disabilities Act (ADA) was signed into law in 1990, extending the federal mandate of nondiscrimination to individuals with disabilities and to state and local governments and the private sector. The ADA defines *disability* as "a physical or mental impairment that substantially limits one or more of the major life activities of such individual." It protects individuals with intellectual impairment, hearing or vision impairment, orthopedic conditions, learning disabilities, speech impairment, AID/HIV, and other health or physical conditions. Psychiatric disorders covered include major depression, bipolar disorder, panic and obsessive-compulsive disorders, some personality disorders, schizophrenia, and rehabilitation from drug addiction.

The ADA was intended to address the following issues:

1. Historically, society has tended to isolate and segregate individuals with disabilities; despite some improvements, such forms of discrimination continue to be a serious and pervasive social problem.
2. Individuals with disabilities are also subjected to and affected by intentional exclusion; the discriminatory effects of architectural, transportation, and communication barriers and failure to make modifications to existing facilities and practice; overprotective rules and policies; exclusionary

qualification standards and criteria; segregation; and relegation to lesser services, programs, activities, benefits, jobs, or other opportunities.

3. Unlike individuals experiencing discrimination on the basis of race, color, sex, national origin, religion, or age, individuals subjected to discrimination on the basis of disability had no legal recourse.

4. Census data, national polls, and other studies have documented that people with disabilities, as a group, occupy an inferior status in our society and are severely disadvantaged socially, vocationally, economically, and educationally.

5. The nation's goals regarding individuals with disabilities are to ensure equality of opportunity, full participation, independent living, and economic self-sufficiency. The act prohibits discrimination in employment, telecommunications, transportation, and public services and accommodations (Atkinson & Hackett, 1998).

Under the ADA, employers are allowed to inquire about candidates' ability to perform the job but not about their disability. They also are not allowed to discriminate against an individual with a disability during employment or promotion if the individual is otherwise qualified; employers cannot use tests that will cause individuals to be screened out due to their disability. Additionally, employers are required to make "reasonable" accommodations for people with disabilities (Vacc & Clifford, 1995). The following is an example of adjustments and accommodations made for an employee:

> Mike Johnson wasn't asking for special treatment at work, but his bosses thought they'd better provide it anyway. Two months after being hospitalized for bipolar disorder, Johnson, an accomplished, 35-year-old sales executive, told his boss that he was feeling "stressed out." The boss also noticed that Johnson overbooked his schedule during his manic phases and would wake up late and miss appointments during depressive periods. (Sleek, 1998, p. 15)

Mike Johnson's employer was able to retain a valuable executive with bipolar disorder by developing a flexible work schedule that allowed him to accommodate variations in productivity and to have time off for therapy. Although the ADA has improved opportunities for individuals with disabilities, the law has been whittled away by court decisions that have supported businesses rather than people with disabilities. For these reasons, the National Council on Disability has promoted a bill to "restore the original intent" of the ADA (American Association of People with Disabilities, 2006).

Implications

Mental health professionals should know applicable federal and state laws, including the rights of individuals with disabilities in school and work settings. Mental health professionals also need to ensure that the services they provide address both legal and ethical standards. It is important not to provide unequal service or to deny treatment to clients with disabilities; if the individual requires treatment outside your area of specialization, you can help facilitate a referral to a more qualified provider. Also, be alert for criteria that may screen out clients with disabilities, such as requiring a driver's license for payment by check. Policies, practices, and procedures in your office can be modified to take into consideration those with disabilities, such as ensuring service animals are permitted in your building.

You may need to provide auxiliary aids and services, such as readers, sign-language interpreters, Braille materials, large-print materials, and videotapes or audiotapes to facilitate communication with some clients. Evaluate your office for structural and architectural barriers that prevent individuals from getting the services they need. In one study, a large majority of individuals with disabilities reported difficulties obtaining care because of office layout or other environmental barriers (Centers for Disease Control and Prevention, 2006). Evaluate the accessibility of your office, including availability of ramps, parking spaces, reachable elevator control buttons, and wide doorways. When remodeling or building new offices, hire an architect or contractor familiar with ADA requirements.

SPECIFIC CHALLENGES

In the following sections we consider challenges often faced by individuals with disabilities and consider their implications in treatment. Remember that these are generalizations and that their applicability needs to be assessed for each client.

Prejudice and Discrimination

Ableism is an all-too-common discriminatory practice in which individuals without disabilities are favored or given preferential treatment, thereby implying that those with a disability are somehow inferior (Keller & Galgay, 2010). Additionally, individuals who have disabilities may be evaluated based on an insidious deficit perspective (i.e., a belief that something is wrong with them). For example, employers believe that individuals with physical disabilities are less competent than individuals without a disability (Wang, Barron, & Hebl, 2010). Rohmer and Louvet (2009) make the point that "visible disability appears to be a superordinate social category"; that is, disability appears to be a highly salient characteristic. For example, individuals with observable physical disabilities are often referred to using language such as "confined to a wheel chair" or "wheelchair bound" (Artman & Daniels, 2010).

Prejudicial terms such as *retarded* or *lame* are often used without conscious awareness of the impact of these words on individuals with disabilities. Other reactions may be a result of not understanding the nature of specific disabilities. For example, most people without hearing loss do not understand that hearing aids can amplify all sounds, resulting in jumbled hearing, which is why individuals with hearing impairment may choose not to wear them. The public often has low expectations for individuals with disabilities and assumes that disability in one area also affects other skills. Additionally, able-bodied individuals often do not consider the structural and psychological barriers that individuals with disabilities have to face.

Implications

It is important for counselors to understand that individuals with disabilities are people first; like members of any group, they may demonstrate a wide range of functional difficulties as well as varying accomplishments. Mental health professionals need to be in the forefront of assisting individuals with disabilities to maximize their educational and employment opportunities. Approximately 9% of students enrolled in postsecondary educational institutions have some form of disability (Haller, 2006). Mental health professionals can prepare these students for success at the college level by teaching them to be self-advocates, including identifying their disability status and requesting accommodations when attending college.

The greatest prejudice may be displayed with hidden disabilities, such as psychiatric conditions. As a person with schizophrenia stated, "I don't want to tell anybody, because people who aren't ill, they do have a tendency sometimes to treat you different. . . . We've got to disguise ourselves a lot." (Goldberg, Killeen, & O'Day, 2005). Educating employers and workplace colleagues about specific conditions can work to allay fears (Law, 2011). Independence for individuals with intellectual disabilities or severe mental health issues can be encouraged by teaching them skills such as interviewing for jobs, managing money, doing laundry, or performing other daily living skills (Ericksen-Radtke & Beale, 2001).

Mental health professionals need to recognize that they are also subject to disability prejudice and address their discomfort with disabilities. Several suggestions are helpful (American Psychological Association, 2001a; Landsberger & Diaz, 2010):

1. Instead of thinking about a "disabled person," change the focus and use the phrase "person with a disability." This emphasizes the individual rather than the limitation.
2. Do not sensationalize disability by referring to the achievements of well-known individuals with disabilities as "superhuman" or "extraordinary." Such references create unfair expectations. Most individuals with disabilities have the same range of skills as do individuals without disabilities. Avoid the use of phrases that evoke pity and conjure up a nonfunctional status, such as "afflicted with," "suffering from," or "a victim of."
3. Respond to individuals with a disability according to their skills, personality, and other personal attributes rather than their disability. Increase your understanding of the individual's specific condition and related resources, but take care not to assume that the disability is a primary concern. (See Table 26.1 for additional suggestions when working with clients with various disabilities.)

Table 26.1   Things to Remember When Interacting With Individuals With Disabilities

1. People with physical disabilities:

   - Do not use or move items such as wheelchairs, crutches, and canes without permission. They are considered part of the individual's "personal space."
   - Ask if assistance is required before providing it; if your offer is accepted, ask for instructions on how to help and then follow them.
   - Address the individual directly; it is important to attend to the client rather than someone who might have accompanied him or her.
   - Sit at eye level to facilitate comfort in communication.
   - Make certain there is easy access to your office.

2. People with vision loss:

   - Identify yourself and anyone else who is present when greeting them. If the individual does not extend a hand, offer a verbal welcome.
   - Offer the use of your arm to guide—rather than steer or push—the individual.
   - Give verbal instructions to facilitate navigation.
   - If a service dog is present, do not pet or play with the dog.
   - Ask about preference regarding presentation of information (e.g., large print, Braille, audiotapes) at the beginning.
   - Let the individual know if you are moving about or if the conversation is to end.
   - Give verbal cues when offering a seat. Place the individual's hand on the back of the chair, and he or she will not need further help.

3. People who are deaf or hard of hearing:

   - Ask about the individual's preferred communication (some use American Sign Language and identify culturally with the deaf community, whereas others may prefer to communicate orally, read lips, or rely on residual hearing).
   - Address the individual directly, rather than a person accompanying the client.
   - Realize that talking very loud does not enhance communication.
   - To get attention, call the person by name. If there is no response, lightly touch the individual on the arm or shoulder.
   - Do not pretend to understand if you do not.
   - Use certified interpreters to facilitate communication; their role is to relay information.
   - Try to avoid using family members as interpreters.
   - Make direct eye contact, and keep your face and mouth visible.
   - Use open-ended questions rather than depending on nodding by the client.

4. People with speech impediments:

   - Allow the individual to finish speaking before you speak.
   - Realize that communication may take longer, and plan accordingly. Do not rush.
   - Face the individual, and give full eye contact.
   - Address the individual directly.
   - Do not pretend to understand if you do not.
   - When appropriate, use yes-or-no questions.
   - Check with the client, if needed, to ensure understanding.
   - Remember that a speech impediment does not mean the client has limited intelligence.

Source: Adapted from United Cerebral Palsy (2001).

SUPPORTS FOR INDIVIDUALS WITH DISABILITIES

In the past, programs for persons with neurodevelopmental disabilities (e.g., autism, intellectual impairment, learning disabilities) were limited to efforts at "rehabilitation" rather than assistance in maximizing potential and developing independent living skills. There has been gradual recognition that deficiencies in experiences and opportunities can significantly limit the individual's development and that services are most effective when they enable independence, self-determination, and productive participation in society. To accomplish this task, it is important for students with disabilities to complete school and learn job skills. Many schools offer vocational educational programs and school-to-work transition programs. Such programs assess the student's skills and interests and provide a curriculum tailored to needed job skills as well as general vocational skills (Levinson & Palmer, 2005). (See Table 26.2 for components in the program.)

Many school-to-work transition programs have shown promising results. The Bridges from School to Work program and Project Search provide students with disabilities the opportunity to learn work-related skills through local employment opportunities (District of Columbia Public Schools, 2011).

Table 26.2 Key Vocational Skills

Academic Skills
- Reading and writing (e.g., sight-word vocabulary, spelling, handwriting, typing)
- Math (e.g., basic computation, time, money, measurement)
- Problem solving
- Listening comprehension
- Speaking
- Computer skills

Communication Skills
- Accurately following directions
- Communicating information
- Understanding and processing information
- Requesting or offering assistance

Social and Interpersonal Skills
- Making necessary phone calls to employers and other professionals
- Displaying appropriate workplace behavior and etiquette
- Knowing appropriate topics for discussion in the workplace
- Knowing when and when not to socialize on the job

Occupational and Vocational Skills
- Using a time card and punch clock
- Arriving to work on time
- Calling when sick
- Using appropriate voice tone and voice volume
- Social interaction with coworkers (i.e., getting along; problem solving; making friends; and recognizing personal, professional, and sexual boundaries)

Some programs for individuals with moderate to severe intellectual or physical disabilities provide prevocational orientations for both the family and the student. Information on job preparation, job expectations, and skills training is followed by internships in local businesses and feedback on performance from employers. Such programs have been successful both in helping youth with disabilities make the transition to employment or further education and by opening doors in the business community (Fabian, Lent, & Willis, 1998).

Implications

There has been a shift in the orientation of programs for people with disabilities from remediation or "making them as normal as possible" to identifying and strengthening interests and skills. Mental health professionals working with individuals with disabilities should be aware of programs offering employment and educational assistance. It is also important for mental health professionals to be aware of the ways current technology is enhancing the quality of life and employment opportunities for many individuals with disabilities. Vocational and support group information is easily accessible via the Internet.

COUNSELING ISSUES WITH INDIVIDUALS WITH DISABILITIES

Helping professionals often display the same attitude as the general public toward individuals with disabilities and may feel uncomfortable or experience guilt or pity when working with this population. As when working with other oppressed groups, counselors must examine their views of clients with disabilities and identify and question prejudicial assumptions. A client's disability should not be the sole focus of counseling. However, environmental contributions to problems the client is experiencing (e.g., frustrations with architectural barriers or with negative stereotypes or prejudices) should be identified and addressed in counseling. It is also important to be aware of validity issues when using standardized assessment tools with individuals who have disabilities and to consider the effects of any physical impairments, including hearing or vision difficulties, on test performance.

Implications

As with all clients, comprehensive, nonbiased assessment is essential for clients who have disabilities. Kemp and Mallinckrodt (1996) point out some of the errors that can occur in assessment and counseling relationships with individuals with disabilities. First, errors of omission may be made. The counselor may fail to ask questions about critical aspects of the client's life because the assumption is made that the issue is unimportant due to the presence of the disability. For example, sexuality and relationship issues may be ignored because of the belief that the individual lacks the ability or interest to pursue these intimacies. Affective issues may also be avoided, since the counselor may be uncomfortable addressing the impact of the disability on the client. The counselor may also display lowered expectations of the client's capabilities.

> It is important not to succumb to the "spread" phenomenon that often exists with disabilities. This refers to believing that the disability encompasses unrelated aspects of the individual.

Second, errors of commission may be made. In such cases, an unjustified assumption is made that certain issues *should* be important because of the disability, when, in fact, they are not important issues for the client. Personal problems faced by the client may be assumed to result from the disability. Career and academic counseling may become a focus even when it is not what the client wants to discuss. Therapists also make errors by not addressing the disability at all, encouraging dependency and the "sick" role, or failing to confront countertransference issues (e.g., wanting to "rescue" the client).

It is generally appropriate to ask a client about the disability, including any related concerns. In doing so, it is important not to succumb to the "spread" phenomenon that often exists with disabilities. This refers to believing that the disability encompasses unrelated aspects of the individual. Therapists can also ask if there are ways that the disability is part of the presenting problem. Such an approach allows the therapist to address the disability directly. If the disability is of recent origin, factors such as coping strategies, recent challenges, whether the client blames himself or herself or others for the injury, and the amount of social support available can be assessed (Rabasca, 1999).

Family Counseling

Family caregivers now operate as integral parts of the health care system and provide services that were once performed by professional health care providers. It is, therefore, sometimes important to help reduce the impact of stressors on caregivers and other family members. Additionally, emotional issues, such as distress, guilt, self-punishment, or anger, may need to be dealt with. Family members may feel angry about their caretaking responsibilities or somehow feel responsible for the disabling condition (Resch et al., 2010).

Implications

Clients with a disability and their family members can work together to create positive changes that enhance both client well-being and family functioning. M. R. Hulnick and Hulnick (1989) suggest focusing on choices that can be made. For example, the counselor can ask questions such as "What are you doing that perpetuates the situation?" and "Are you aware of other choices that would have a different result?" These questions are empowering, since clients realize that they have the ability to make choices. Instead of viewing the disability or caretaking as a problem, reframing can be used to identify opportunities through questions such as "In what ways could you use this situation to your advancement?" or "What can you learn from this experience?"

Among family caregivers, several attributes led to greater satisfaction for themselves and the individual with the disability (Elliot, Shewchuk, & Richards, 1999). One approach employed by satisfied caregivers was using problem-solving strategies when encountering difficulties; these caretakers were skillful at defining the problem, generating and evaluating alternatives, implementing solutions, and assessing outcomes. This approach helped increase self-efficacy among family members and improved their ability to cope with stress. A second characteristic of satisfied caregivers was the ability to develop a more positive orientation toward the demands of the situation. These approaches can improve the emotional health of both the caregivers and family members with disabilities.

Reframing can also be useful. One psychologist who is blind believes that he may be less threatening to clients who are self-conscious or that clients might connect with him due to the fact that he has faced and overcome difficult issues (Clay, 1999). Albert Ellis, the founder of rational-emotive therapy, faced the challenges of diabetes, tired eyes, deficient hearing, and other physical handicaps but successfully used cognitive approaches, such as reframing, to deal with his disabilities. For example, because he could not keep his eyes open for any length of time, he focused on the positive aspects of conducting therapy sessions with his eyes closed, telling himself that with his eyes shut he could (a) focus "unusually well" on his clients' verbalizations (e.g., tone of voice, hesitations), (b) more easily identify their irrational thoughts, (c) help clients feel more relaxed, and (d) serve as a healthy model of an individual with a disability (Ellis, 1997). Ellis was thus able to redefine his disability as a useful feature in conducting therapy.

Implications for Clinical Practice

1. Identify your beliefs, assumptions, and attitudes about individuals with disabilities.
2. Understand the prejudice, discrimination, inconveniences, and barriers faced by individuals with disabilities and the problems faced by individuals with "invisible" disabilities.
3. Assess the impact of multiple discrimination on ethnic minorities and other diverse populations.
4. Redirect internalized self-blame for the disability to societal attitudes.
5. Employ the appropriate communication format, and address the client directly rather than through conversation with an accompanying individual.
6. Determine whether the disability is related to the presenting problem or whether it will impact assessment or treatment strategies. If it is not an issue, continue with your usual methods of assessment and case conceptualization.

(continued)

(*continued*)

7. If the disability is related to the problem, identify whether the client adheres to the moral model (disability results from a moral lapse), medical model (disability is a physical limitation), or minority model (disability results from societal failure to accommodate individual differences).

8. If formal tests are employed, provide appropriate accommodations. Interpret the results with care since standardization does not take into account various physical disabilities.

9. Recognize that family members and other social supports are important. Include them in your assessment, case conceptualization, goal formation, and selection of techniques.

10. Identify environmental changes or accommodations that may be needed, and then assist the client or family with necessary planning to implement changes.

11. Help family members reframe the problem so that positives can be identified. Focus on and strengthen the positive attributes of the client and family members.

12. Develop self-advocacy skills for both the client and family members.

13. Realize that mental health professionals may need to serve as advocates or consultants to initiate changes in academic and work settings.

References

Aboud, F. E. (1988). *Children and prejudice*. Cambridge, MA: Basil Blackwell.

Abreu, J. M., Goodyear, R. K., Campos, A., & Newcomb, M. D. (2000). Ethnic belonging and traditional masculinity ideology among African Americans, European Americans and Latinos. *Psychology of Men and Masculinity, 1,* 75–86.

Acierno, R., Hernandez, M. A., Amstadter, A. B., Resnick, H. R., Steve, K., Muzzy, W., & Kilpatrick, D. G. (2010). Prevalence and correlates of emotional, physical, sexual, and financial abuse and potential neglect in the United States: The National Elder Mistreatment study. *American Journal of Public Health, 100,* 292–297.

Ackard, D. M., Fulkerson, J. A., & Neumark-Sztainer, D. (2007). Prevalence and utility of DSM-IV eating disorder diagnostic criteria among youth. *International Journal of Eating Disorders, 40,* 409–417.

Ackerman, S. J., Benjamin, L. S., Beutler, L. E., Gelso, C. J., Goldfried, M. R., Hill, C., Lambert, M. J., Norcross, J. C., Orlinsky, D. E. & Rainer, J. (2001). Empirically supported therapy relationships: Conclusions and recommendation of the Division 29 Task Force. *Psychotherapy, 38,* 495–497.

Acquino, J. A., Russell, D. W., Cutrona, C. E., & Altmaier, E. M. (1996). Employment status, social support, and life satisfaction among the elderly. *Journal of Counseling Psychology, 43,* 480–489.

Acs, G. (2011). Waking up from the American dream. Retrieved from http://www.pewtrusts.org/uploadedFiles/wwwpewtrustsorg/Reports/Economic_Mobility/Pew_PollProject_Final_SP.pdf

Aguilera, A., Garza, M. J., & Munoz, R. F. (2010). Group cognitive-behavioral therapy for depression in Spanish: Culture-sensitive manualized treatment in practice. *Journal of Clinical Psychology: In Session, 66,* 857–867.

Ahai, C. E. (1997). A cultural framework for counseling African Americans. In C. C. Lee (Ed.), *Multicultural issues in counseling* (2nd ed., pp. 73–80). Alexandria, VA:

Ahn, A. J., Kim, B. S. K., & Park, Y. S. (2009). Asian cultural values gap, cognitive flexibility, coping strategies, and parent-child conflicts among Korean Americans. *Asian American Journal of Psychology, S(1), 1,* 29–44.

Ahn, H., & Wampold, B. E. (2001). Where oh where are the specific ingredients? A meta-analysis of component studies in counseling and psychotherapy. *Journal of Counseling Psychology, 48,* 251–257.

AhnAllen, J. M., Suyemoto, K. L., & Carter, A. S. (2006). Relationship between physical appearance, sense of belonging and exclusion, and racial/ethnic self-identification among multiracial Japanese European Americans. *Cultural Diversity and Ethnic Minority Psychology, 12,* 673–686.

Ahuvia, A. (2001). Well-being in cultures of choice: A cross-cultural perspective. *American Psychologist, 56*(1), 77.

Akerlund, M., & Cheung, M. (2000). Teaching beyond the deficit model: Gay and lesbian issues among African American, Latinos, and Asian Americans. *Journal of Social Work Education, 36,* 279–291.

Albelda, R. Badgett, M.V.L., Schneebaum, A., & Gates, G. J. (2009). *Poverty in the lesbian, gay, and bisexual community.* Retrieved from http://www.law.ucla.edu/williamsinstitute/pdf/LGBPovertyReport.pdf

Aldarondo, E. (2007). *Advancing social justice through clinical practice.* Mahwah, NJ: Erlbaum.

Alexander, B. (2009). Amid swine flu outbreak, racism goes viral. Retrieved from http://www.msnbc.msn.com/id/30467300/

Alexander, C., Langer, E., Newman, R., Chandler, H., & Davies, J. (1989). Transcendental meditation, mindfulness and longevity: An experimental study with the elderly. *Journal of Personality and Social Psychology, 57,* 950–964.

Alexander, C., Rainforth, M., & Gelderloos, P. (1991). Transcendental meditation, self actualization and psychological health: A conceptual overview and statistical meta-analysis. *Journal of Social Behavior and Personality, 6,* 189–247.

Alexander, F. G., & Selesnick, S. T. (1966). *The history of psychiatry.* New York, NY: Harper & Row.

Alexander, R., & Moore, S. E. (2008). The benefits, challenges, and strategies of African American faculty teaching at predominantly White institutions. *Journal of African American Studies, 12,* 4–18.

Algood, C. L., Hong, J. S., Goudine, R. M., & Williams, A. B. (2011). Maltreatment of children with developmental disabilities: An ecological systems analysis. *Child and Youth Services Review.* doi: 10.1016/j.childyouth.2011.02.003

Allen, A. (1994, May 29). Black unlike me: Confessions of a white man confused by racial etiquette. *Washington Post,* p. C1.

Allison, D. (1994). *Skin.* Ithaca, NY: Firebrand.

Allison, K. W., Crawford, I., Echemendia, R., Robinson, L., & Knepp, D. (1994). Human diversity and professional competence: Training in clinical and counseling psychology revisited. *American Psychologist, 49,* 792–796.

Allport, G. W. (1954). *The nature of prejudice.* Reading, MA: Addison-Wesley.

Allport, G. W. (1961). *Pattern and growth in personality.* New York, NY: Holt, Rinehart & Winston.

Alterovitz, S. S.-R., & Mendelsohn, G. A. (2009). Partner preferences across the life span: Online dating by older adults. *Psychology and Aging, 24,* 513–517.

Altman, A. N., Inman, A. G., Fine, S. G., Ritter, H. A., & Howard, E. R. (2010). Exploration of Jewish ethnic identity. *Journal of Counseling and Development, 88,* 163–173.

American Association of People with Disabilities. (2006). Bipartisan legislation introduced to restore ADA protections. *AAPD News,* pp. 1, 3.

American Association of University Women. (2011). *Crossing the line: Sexual harassment at school.* Retrieved from http://www.aauw.org/learn/research/crossingtheline.cfm

American-Arab Anti-Discrimination Committee. (2003). Report on hate crimes and discrimination against Arab Americans. Retrieved from http://www.adc.org/hate_crimes.htm

American Counseling Association. (1995). Summit results in formation of spiritual competencies. *Counseling Today,* p. 30.

American Counseling Association. (2005). *Code of ethics.* Alexandria, VA: Author

American Enterprise Institute. (2004). AEI study on homosexuality and gay marriage. Retrieved from http://www.aei.org/include/pub_print.asp?pubID=20867

American Friends Service Committee. (1998). *People with disabilities.* Philadelphia, PA: Affirmative Action Office.

American Friends Service Committee. (2006a). Immigrants and racial/ethnic tensions. Retrieved from http://www.afsc.org/immigrants-rights/learn/racial-ethnic.htm

American Friends Service Committee. (2006b). Immigration law and policy. Retrieved from http://www.afsc.org/immigrants-rights/learn/law-policy.htm

American Friends Service Committee. (2006c). Understanding anti-immigrant movements. Retrieved from http://www.afsc.org/immigrants-rights/learn/anti-immigrant.htm

American Psychiatric Association. (2000). *Diagnostic and Statistical Manual of Mental Disorders–Fourth Edition, Text Revision (DSM-IV-TR)*. Washington, DC: Author.

American Psychiatric Association (2012). DSM-5 development. Retrieved from http://www.dsm5.org/proposedrevision/Pages/GenderDysphoria.aspx

American Psychological Association. (n.d.). *Racism and psychology*. Washington, DC: Author.

American Psychological Association. (1993). Guidelines for providers of psychological services to ethnic, linguistic, and culturally diverse populations. *American Psychologist, 48*, 45–48.

American Psychological Association. (2001a). *Aging and human sexuality resource guide*. Washington, DC: Author.

American Psychological Association. (2001b). *Elder abuse and neglect: In search of solutions*. Washington, DC: Author.

American Psychological Association. (2003). Guidelines on multicultural education, training, research, practice, and organizational change for psychologists. *American Psychologist, 58*, 377–402.

American Psychological Association. (2005). *APA resolution recommending the immediate retirement of American Indian mascots, symbols, images, and personalities by schools, colleges, universities, athletic teams, and organizations*. Retrieved from http://www.apa.org/about/governance/council/policy/mascots.pdf

American Psychological Association. (2007). Guidelines for the psychological practice with girls and women. *American Psychologist, 62*, 949–979.

American Psychological Association. (2008, March 16). Report of the Task Force on Resources for the Inclusion of Social Class in Psychology Curricula. Retrieved from http://www.apa.org/pi/ses/resources/publications/social-class-curricula.pdf

American Psychological Association. (2009a). *Insufficient evidence that sexual orientation change efforts work*. Retrieved from http://www.apa.org/news/press/releases/2009/08/therapeutic.aspx

American Psychological Association. (2009b). *Multicultural competency in geropsychology*. Washington, DC: American Psychological Association.

American Psychological Association. (2001). Resolution on male violence against women. Retrieved from http://www.apa.org/about/governance/council/policy/male-violence.aspx

American Psychological Association, Division 44/Committee on Lesbian, Gay, and Bisexual Concerns Joint Task Force on Guidelines for Psychotherapy with Lesbian, Gay, and Bisexual Clients. (2012). Guidelines for psychotherapy with lesbian, gay, and bisexual clients. *American Psychologist, 67*, 10–42.

American Psychological Association. (2009c). *Report of the Task Force on Gender Identity and Gender Variance*. Washington, DC: American Psychological Association.

American Psychological Association Presidential Task Force on Evidence-Based Practice. (2006). Evidence-based practice in psychology. *American Psychologist, 61*, 271–285.

American Psychological Association, Task Force on the Sexualization of Girls. (2007). *Report of the Task Force on the Sexualization of Girls*. Retrieved from www.apa.org/pi/wpo/sexualization.html

American Psychological Association, (2007a). Task Force on Socioeconomic Status. (2007). *Report of the APA Task Force on Socioeconomic Status*. Washington, DC: American Psychological Association. Cited in chapter 5

Amri, S. (2010). Counseling Arab and Middle Eastern population: Perspectives from an Arab-American counselor. Retrieved from http://www.counseling.org/handouts/2010/596.pdf

Amir, Y. (1969). Contact hypothesis in ethnic relations. *Psychological Bulletin, 71*, 319–342.

Anderson, S. H., & Middleton, V. A. (2011). *Explorations in diversity*. Belmont, CA: Cengage.

Andrade, P., Noblesse, L. H., Temel, Y., Ackermans, L., Lim, L. W., Steinbusch, H. W., & Visser-Vandewalle, V. (2010). Neurostimulatory and ablative treatment options in major depressive disorder: A systematic review. *Acta Neurochirugia, 152*, 565–577.

Andrés-Hyman, R. C., Ortiz, J., Añez, L. M., Paris, M., & Davidson, L. (2006). Culture and clinical practice: Recommendations for working with Puerto Ricans and other Latinas (os) in the United States. *Professional Psychology: Research and Practice, 37*, 694–701.

Anti-Defamation League. (2005). ADL survey: Anti-Semitism declines slightly in America: 14 Percent of Americans hold 'strong' anti-Semitic beliefs. Retrieved from http://www.adl.org/PresRele/ASUS_12/4680_12.htm

Anti-Defamation League. (2009). *American attitudes towards Jews in America*. Washington, DC: Martila Communications.

Antony, M. M., & Roemer, L. (2011). *Behavior therapy*. Washington, DC: American Psychological Association.

Apfelbaum, E. P., Sommers, S. R., & Norton, M. I. (2008). Seeing race and seeming racist: Evaluating strategic colorblindness in social interaction. *Journal of Personality and Social Psychology, 95*, 918–932.

Aponte, H. J. (1994). *Bread and spirit: Therapy with the new poor*. New York, NY: Norton.

Arab American Institute. (2003). Religious Affiliations of Arab Americans. Retrieved from http://www.aaiusa.org

Arab American Institute. (2011). Arab American demographics. Retrieved from http://www.aaiusa.org/pages/demographics/

Arnett, J. J. (2009). The neglected 95%: Why American psychology needs to become less American. *American Psychologist, 63*, 602–614.

Artman, L. K., & Daniels, J. A. (2010). Disability and psychotherapy practice: Cultural competence and practical tips. *Professional Psychology: Research and Practice, 41*, 442–448.

Asai, M. O., & Kameoka, V. A. (2005). The influence of Sekentei on family caregiving and underutilization of social services among Japanese caregivers. *Social Work, 50*, 111–118.

Asner-Self, K. K., & Marotta, S. A. (2005). Developmental indices among Central American immigrants exposed to war-related trauma: Clinical implications for counselors. *Journal of Counseling and Development, 83*, 163–172.

Associated Press. (2006, May 21). U.S. report: 2.2 million now in prison, jails. Retrieved from http://www.msnbc.msn.com/id/12901873/

Associated Press. (2006, June 12). Philly eatery's English-only sign under fire. Retrieved from http://www.msnbc.msn.com/id/13272368/

Associated Press. (2009, May 28). Multiracial America is fastest growing group. Retrieved from http://www.msnbc.msn.com/id/30986649/ns/us_news-life/t/multiracial-america-fastest-growing-group/#.Tyv1tsUS2Ag

Associated Press. (2011). Senate hearing in Montana examines Indian suicides. Retrieved from http://ndnnews.com/2011/08/senate-hearing-in-mont-examines-indian-suicides/

Astor, C. (1997). Gallup poll: Progress in Black/White relations, but race is still an issue. *U.S. Society & Values*. Retrieved from http://usinfo.state.gov/journals/itsv/0897/ijse/gallup.htm

Atkinson, D. R., Bui, U., & Mori, S. (2001). Multiculturally sensitive empirically supported treatments—an oxymoron? In J. G. Ponterotto, J. M. Casas, L. A. Suzuki, & C. M. Alexander (Eds.), *Handbook of multicultural counseling* (pp. 542–574). Thousand Oaks, CA: Sage.

Atkinson, D. R., & Hackett, G. (1998). *Counseling diverse populations* (2nd ed.). Boston, MA: McGraw-Hill.

Atkinson, D. R., Kim, B. S. K., & Caldwell, R. (1998). Ratings of helper roles by multicultural psychologists and Asian American students: Initial support for the three-dimensional model of multicultural counseling. *Journal of Counseling Psychology, 45*, 414–423.

Atkinson, D. R., & Lowe, S. M. (1995). The role of ethnicity, cultural knowledge, and conventional techniques in counseling and psychotherapy. In J. G. Ponterotto, J. M. Casas, L. M. Suzuki, & C. M. Alexander (Eds.), *Handbook of multicultural counseling* (pp. 3–16). Thousand Oaks, CA: Sage.

Atkinson, D. R., Maruyama, M., & Matsui, S. (1978). The effects of counselor race and counseling approach on Asian Americans' perceptions of counselor credibility and utility. *Journal of Counseling Psychology, 25*, 76–83.

Atkinson, D. R., Morten, G., & Sue, D. W. (1979). *Counseling American minorities: A cross-cultural perspective*. Dubuque, IA: Brown.

Atkinson, D. R., Morten, G., & Sue, D. W. (1989). A minority identity development model. In D. R. Atkinson, G. Morten, & D. W. Sue (Eds.), *Counseling American minorities* (pp. 35–52). Dubuque, IA: W. C. Brown.

Atkinson, D. R., Morten, G., & Sue, D. W. (1998). *Counseling American minorities* (5th ed.). Boston, MA: McGraw-Hill.

Atkinson, D. R., Thompson, C. E., & Grant, S. K. (1993). A three-dimensional model for counseling racial/ethnic minorities. *Counseling Psychologist, 21*, 257–277.

Atkinson, D. R., & Wampold, B. E. (1993). Mexican Americans initial preferences for counselors: Simple choices can be misleading. *Journal of Counseling and Psychology, 49*, 245–248.

Avila, D. L., & Avila, A. L. (1995). Mexican Americans. In N. A. Vacc, S. B. DeVaney, & J. Wittmer (Eds.), *Experiencing and counseling multicultural and diverse populations* (3rd ed., pp. 119–146). Bristol, PA: Accelerated Development.

Axelton, J. A. (1993). *Counseling and Development in a Multicultural Society*. Pacific Grove, CA: Brooks/Cole.

Babbington, C. (2008). Poll shows gap between Blacks and Whites over racial discrimination. Retrieved from http://news.yahoo.com/page/election-2008-political-pulse-race-in-america

Baca, L. M., & Koss-Chioino, J. D. (1997). Development of a culturally responsive group counseling model for Mexican American adolescents. *Journal of Multicultural Counseling and Development, 25*, 130–141.

Bale, T. L., Baram, T. Z., Brown, A. S., Goldstein, J. M., Insel, T. R., McCarthy, M. M., . . . Nestler, E. J. (2010). Early life programming and neurodevelopmental disorders. *Biological Psychiatry, 68*, 314–319.

Balsam, K. F., & Mohr, J. J. (2007). Adaptation to sexual orientation stigma: A comparison of bisexual and lesbian/gay adults. *Journal of Counseling Psychology, 54*, 306–319.

Balsam, K. F., Rothblum, E. D., & Beauchaine, T. P. (2005). Victimization over the life span: A comparison of lesbian, gay, bisexual, and heterosexual siblings. *Journal of Consulting and Clinical Psychology, 73*, 477–487.

Banaji, M. R., & Greenwald, A. G. (1995). Implicit gender stereotyping in judgements of fame. *Journal of Personality and social Psychology, 68*, 181–198.

Bankart, C. P. (1997). *Talking cures: A history of Western and Eastern psycho therapies*. Pacific Grove, CA: Brooks/Cole.

Banks, J. A., & Banks, C. A. (1993). *Multicultural education*. Boston, MA: Allyn & Bacon.

Banyard, V. (2008). Welfare queens or courageous survivors? Strengths of women in poverty. Retrieved from http://www.unh.edu/discovery/sites/unh.edu.discovery/files/dialogue/2008/pdf/packet_banyard.pdf

Barongan, C., Bernal, G., Comas-Diaz, L., Iijima Hall, C. C., Nagayama Hall, G. C., LaDue, R. A., . . . Root, M. P. P. (1997). Misunderstandings of multiculturalism: Shouting fire in crowded theaters. *American Psychologist, 52*, 654–655.

Barrett, M. S., & Berman, J. S. (2001). Is psychotherapy more effective when therapists disclose information about themselves? *Journal of Consulting and Clinical Psychology, 69*, 597–603.

Batalova, J. (2006). Spotlight on refugees and asylees in the United States. Retrieved from http://www.migrationinformation.org/USFocus/print.ctf?ID=415

Batavia, A. I. (2000). The relevance of data on physician and disability on the right of assisted suicide. *Psychology, Public Policy, and Law, 6*, 546–558.

Baumann, A. A., Kuhlberg, J. A., & Zayas, L. H. (2010). Familism, mother-daughter mutuality, and suicide attempts of adolescent Latinas. *Journal of Family Psychology, 24*, 616–624.

Bautista, E. M. (2003). The impact of context, phenotype, and other identifiers on Latina/o adolescent ethnic identity and acculturation. *Dissertation Abstracts International: Section B: The Sciences and Engineering, 63*(7-B), 3464.

Bean, R. A., Perry, B. J., & Bedell, T. M. (2001). Developing culturally competent marriage and family therapists: Guidelines for working with Hispanic families. *Journal of Marital and Family Therapy, 27*, 43–54.

Bee-Gates, D., Howard-Pitney, B., LaFromboise, T., & Rowe, W. (1996). Help-seeking behavior of Native American Indian high school students. *Professional Psychology: Research and Practice, 27*, 495–499

Beeghley, L. (2008). *The structure of social stratification in the United States*. Boston, MA: Allyn & Bacon.

Begley, S. (2010). Science is reshaping what we know about getting older. Retrieved from http://www.newsweek.com/2010/06/18/this-is-your-brain-aging.html

Behnke, S. (2004). Informed consent and APA's new ethics code: Enhancing client autonomy, improving client care. *Monitor on Psychology, 35*, 80–81.

Behnken, B. D. (2011). *Fighting their own battles: Mexican Americans, African Americans, and the struggle for civil rights in Texas*. Charlotte, NC: University of North Carolina Press.

Beigel, H. G. (1966). Problems and motives in interracial relationships. *Journal of Sex Research, 2*, 185–205.

Belgrave, F. Z., Chase-Vaughn, G., Gray, F., Addison, J. D., & Cherry, V. R. (2000). The effectiveness of a culture- and gender-specific intervention for increasing resiliency among African American preadolescent females. *Journal of Black Psychology, 26*, 133–147.

Bell, L. A. (1997). Theoretical foundations for social justice education. In M. Adams, L. A. Bell, & P. Griffin (Eds.), *Teaching for diversity and social justice: A sourcebook* (pp. 3–15). New York, NY: Routledge.

Bell, M. P., Harrison, D. A., & McLaughlin, M. E. (1997). Asian American attitudes towards affirmative action in employment: Implications for the model minority myth. *Journal of Applied Behavioral Science, 33*, 356–377.

Belle, D. (1990). Poverty and women's mental health. *American Psychologist, 45*(3), 385–389.

Belle, D., Doucet, J., Harris, J., Miller, J., & Tan, E. (2000). Who is rich? Who is happy? *American Psychologist, 55*, 1160–1161.

Bemak, F., Chi-Ying, R., & Siroskey-Sabdo, L. A. (2005). Empowermentgroupsforaca-demic success: An innovative approach to prevent high school failure for at-risk, urban African. *Professional School Counseling, 8*, 377–389.

Bemak, F., Chung, R. C.-Y., & Bornemann, T. (1996). Counseling and psychotherapy with refugees. In P. Pedersen, J. Draguns, W. Lonner, & J. Trimble (Eds.), *Counseling across cultures* (4th ed., pp. 243–265). Thousand Oaks, CA: Sage.

Benish, S. G., Quintana, S., & Wampold, B. E. (2011). Culturally adapted psychotherapy and the legitimacy of myth: A direct-comparison meta-analysis. *Journal of Counseling Psychology, 58*, 279–289.

Bennett, M. J. (1986). A developmental approach to training for intercultural sensitivity. *International Journal of Intercultural Relations, 10*, 179–196.

Bennetts, L. (2011, July 25). The John next door. *Newsweek*, pp. 60–63.

Benokraitis, N. V. (1997). *Subtle sexism: Current practice and prospects for change*. Thousand Oaks, CA: Sage.

Berg, S. H. (2006). Everyday sexism and posttraumatic stress disorder in women. *Violence Against Women, 12*(10), 970–88.

Berke, D. M., Rozell, C. A., Hogan, T. P., Norcross, J. C., & Karpiak, C. P. (2011). What clinical psychologists know about evidence-based practice: Familiar-ity with online resources and research methods. *Journal of Clinical Psychology, 67*, 329–339.

Berkofsky, J. (2006). National Jewish Population Survey: 2000. A snapshot of American Jewry. Retrieved from http://www.myjewishlearning.com/history/Jewish_World_Today/Continuity/2000_NJPS.shtml

Berman, J. (1979). Counseling skills used by Black and White male and female counselors. *Journal of Counseling Psychology, 26*, 81–84.

Bernal, M. E., & Castro, F. G. (1994). Are clinical psychologists prepared for service and research with ethnic minorities? A report of a decade of progress. *American Psychologist, 49*, 797–805.

Bernal, M. E., & Knight, G. P. (1993). *Ethnic identity: Formation and transmission among Hispanics and other minorities*. Albany: State University of New York Press.

Bernal, G., & Sáez-Santiago, E. (2006). Culturally centered psychosocial interventions. *Journal of Community Psychology, 34*, 121–132.

Bernstein, B. (1964). Elaborated and restricted codes: Their social origins and some conse-quences. In J. J. Gumperz & D. Hymes (Eds.), The ethnography of communication. *American Anthropologist*66, 55–69.

Bernstein, N. (2006, March 3). Recourse grows slim for immigrants who fall ill. *New York Times*, p. A.14

Berry, B. (1965). *Ethnic and race relations*. Boston, MA: Houghton Mifflin.

Bérubé, A. (1990). *Coming out under fire: The history of gay men and women in World War II*. New York, NY: Free Press

Bertrand, M., Goldin, C., & Katz, L. F. (2010). Dynamics of the gender gap for young professionals in the financial and corporate sectors. *American Economic Journal: Applied Economics, 2*, 228–255.

Bess, J. A., & Stabb, S. D. (2009). The experiences of transgendered persons in psy-chotherapy: Voices and recommendations. *Journal of Mental Health Counseling, 31*, 264–282.

Beyer, J. L. (2007). Managing depression in geriatric populations. *Annals of Clinical Psychiatry, 19,* 221–238.

Bhungalia, L. (2001). Native American women and violence. *National NOW Times, 33,* 5, 13.

BigFoot, D. S., & Schmidt, S. R. (2010). Honoring children, mending the circle: cultural adaptation of trauma-focused cognitive-behavioral therapy for American Indian and Alaska Native children. *Journal of Clinical Psychology: In Session, 66,* 847–856.

Bigler, R. S., & Averhart, C. J. (2003). Race and the workforce: Occupational status, aspirations, and stereotyping among African American children. *Developmental Psychology, 39,* 572–580.

Black, L. (1996). Families of African origin: An overview. In M. McGoldrick, J. Giordano, & J. K. Pearce (Eds.), *Ethnicity and family therapy* (pp. 57–65). New York, NY: Guilford Press.

Black Demographics.com. (2011). African American Population. Retrieved from http://www.blackdemographics.com/population.html

Blair, S. L., & Qian, Z. (1998). Family and Asian students' educational performance. *Journal of Family Issues, 19,* 355–374.

Blake, S. M., Ledsky, R., Lehman, T., & Goodenow, C. (2001). Preventing sexual risk behaviors among gay, lesbian, and bisexual adolescents: The benefits of gay-sensitive HIV instruction in schools. *American Journal of Public Health, 91,* 940–946.

Blanchard, E. L. (1983). The growth and development of American Indians and Alaskan Native children. In G. J. Powell, J. Yamamoto, A. Romero, & A. Morales (Eds.), *The psychosocial development of minority group children* (pp. 96–103). New York, NY: Brunner/Mazel.

Blando, J. A. (2001). Twice hidden: Older gay and lesbian couples, friends, intimacy. *Generations, 25,* 87–89.

Blauner, B. (1993). But things are much worse for the negro people: Race and radicalism in my life and work. In J. H. Stanfield II (Ed.). *A history of race relations research: First generation recollections* (pp. 1–36). Newbury Park: Sage.

Bledsoe, S. E., Weissman, M. M., Mullen, E. J., Ponniah, K., Gameroff, M. J., Verdell, H., Mufson, L., Fitterling, H., & Wichramaratne, P. (2007). Empirically supported psychotherapy in social work training programs: Does the definition of evidence matter? *Research on Social Work Practice, 17,* 449–455.

Bloom, S. (1997). *Creating sanctuary.* New York, NY: Routledge.

Bonde, J. P. (2008). Psychosocial factors at work and risk of depression: A systematic review of the epidemiological evidence. *Occupational and Environmental Medicine, 65,* 438–445.

Bookwala, J., & Schulz, R. (2000). A comparison of primary stressors, secondary stressors, and depressive symptoms between elderly caregiving husbands and wives. *Psychology and Aging, 15,* 607–616.

Bordeau, W. C. (2004). Counseling at-risk Afro-American youth: an examination of contemporary issues and effective school-based strategies. New York, NY: Free Library. (2004). Retrieved from http://www.thefreelibrary.com/Counseling at-risk Afro-American youth: an examination of . . . -a0126313951

Bos, H., & Gartrell, N. (2010). Adolescents of the USA National Longitudinal Lesbian Family Study: Can family characteristics counteract the negative effects of stigmatization. *Family Process, 49,* 559–572.

Bowles, D. D. (1993). Bi-racial identity: Children born to African-American and White couples. *Clinical Social Work Journal, 21,* 417–427.

Boyd-Franklin, N. (2003). *Black families in therapy.* New York, NY: Guilford Press.

Boyd-Franklin, N. (2010). *Counseling Psychologist, 38,* 976–1000.

Boysen, G. A., & Vogel, D. L. (2008). The relationship between level of training, implicit bias, and multicultural competency among counselor trainees. *Training and Education in Professional Psychology, 2,* 103–110.

Brammer, R. (2012). *Diversity in counseling.* Belmont, CA: Cengage.

Brayboy, T. L. (1966). Interracial sexuality as an expression of neurotic conflict. *Journal of Sex Research, 2,* 179–184.

Brems, C. (2000). *Dealing with challenges in psychotherapy and counseling.* Belmont, CA: Brooks/Cole

Brennan, P. L., & Moos, R. H. (1996). Late-life drinking behavior. *Alcohol Health and Research World, 20,* 197–204.

Brenner, A. D., & Kim, S. Y. (2009). Experiences of discrimination among Chinese American adolescents and the consequences for socioemotional and academic development. *Developmental Psychology, 45,* 1682–1694.

Brewster, M. E., & Moradi, B. (2010). Perceived experiences of anti-bisexual prejudice: Instrument development and evaluation. *Journal of Counseling Psychology, 57,* 451–468.

Brinkley, D. (1994). *Saved by the light.* New York, NY: Villard Books.

Brondolo, E., Brady, N., Thompson, S., Tobin, J. N., Cassells, A., Sweeney, M., . . . Sweeney, M. (2008). Perceived racism and negative affect: Analysis of trait and state measures affect in a community sample. *Journal of Social and Clinical Psychology, 27,* 150–173.

Brooke, J. (1998, April 9). Indians strive to save their languages. *New York Times,* p. 1.

Brown, P. D. & O'Leary, K. D. (2000). Therapeutic alliance: Predicting continuance and success in group treatment for spouse abuse. *Journal of Consulting and Clinical Psychology, 68,* 340–345.

Brown, R. P., & Josephs, R. A. (1999). A burden of proof: Stereotype relevance and gender differences in math performance. *Journal of Personality and Social Psychology, 76,* 246–257.

Brown, S. L. (2011). All mixed up: 2010 Census reveals spike in multi-racial population. Retrieved from http://archive.theloop21.com/society/all-mixed-census-reveals-spike-multi-racial-population.

Browning, C., Reynolds, A. L., & Dworkin, S. H. (1998). Affirmative psychotherapy for lesbian women. In D. R. Atkinson & G. Hackett (Eds.), *Counseling diverse populations* (2nd ed., pp. 317–334). Boston, MA: McGraw-Hill.

Brunsma, D. L. (2005). Interracial families and racial identity of mixed-race children: Evidence from the early childhood longitudinal study. *Social Forces, 84,* 1131–1157.

Buckman, D. F. (1998). The see-through syndrome. *Inside MS, 16,* p. 19.

Budge, S. L., Tebbe, E. N., & Howard, K.A.S. (2010). The work experience of transgender individuals: Negotiating the transition and career decision-making process. *Journal of Counseling Psychology, 57,* 377–393.

Buki, L. P., Ma, T-C., Strom, R. D., & Strom, S. K. (2003). Chinese immigrant mothers of adolescents: Self-perceptions of acculturation effects on parenting. *Cultural Diversity and Ethnic Minority Psychology, 9,* 127–140.

Bullock, H. E., Wyche, K. F., and Williams, W. R. (2001). Media images of the poor. *Journal of Social Issues, 57,* 229–246.

Bureau of Indian Affairs. (2011). What we do. Retrieved from http://www.bia.gov/What-WeDo/index.htm

Bureau of Labor Statistics. (2011). American Time Use Survey Summary. Retrieved from http://www.bls.gov/news.release/atus.nr0.htm

Burkard, A. W., & Knox, S. (2004). Effect of therapist color-blindness on empathy and attributions in cross-cultural counseling. *Journal of Counseling Psychology, 51,* 1–29.

Burkard, A. W., Knox, S., Groen, N., Perez, M., & Hess, S. (2006). European American therapist self-disclosure in cross-cultural counseling. *Journal of Counseling Psychology, 53,* 15–25.

Burke, G. (2005, Oct. 24). Translating isn't kid stuff. *San Jose Mercury News,* p. 5B.

Burn, S. M. (2000). Heterosexuals' use of "fag" and "queer" to deride one another: A contributor to heterosexism and stigma. *Journal of Homosexuality, 40,* 1–11.

Burn, S. M., Kadlec, K., & Rexer, B. S. (2005). Effects of subtle heterosexism on gays, lesbians, and bisexuals. *Journal of Homosexuality, 49,* 23–38.

Burnes, T. R., Singh, A. A., Harper, A., Pickering, D. L., Moundas, S., . . . Hosea, J. (2009). ALGB TIC Competencies for counseling transgender clients. Retrieved from http://www.algbtic.org/ALGBTIC_Counseling_Transgender_Clients_Competencies.pdf

Burnett, A., & Thompson, K. (2005). Enhancing the psychosocial well-being of asylum seekers and refugees. In K. H. Barrett & W. H. George (Eds.), *Race, culture, psychology, and law* (pp. 205–224). Thousand Oaks, CA.: Sage.

Burstein, P. (2007). Jewish educational and economic success in the United States: A search for explanations. *Sociological Perspectives, 50,* 209–228.

Butler D., & Geis, F. L. (1990). Nonverbal affect responses to male and female leaders: Implications for leadership evaluations. *Journal of Personality and Social Psychology, 58,* 48–59.

Cain, D. J. (2010). *Person-centered psychotherapies.* Washington, DC: APA Press.

Caliper. (2005). The qualities that distinguish women leaders. Retrieved from http://www.calipercorp.com/cal_women.asp

Camarota, S. A. (2010). *Immigration and Economic Stagnation: An Examination of Trends 2000 to 2010.* Washington, DC: Center for Immigration Studies.

Capps, R., Fix, M., Ost, J., Reardon-Anderson, J., & Passel, J. S. (2005). The health and and wellbeing of young children of immigrants. *Immigrant families and workers: Facts and perspectives.* Washington, DC: Urban Institute.

Carlson, D. K. (2004). Racial profiling seen as pervasive, unjust. Retrieved from http://www.gallup.com/poll/12406/racial-profiling-seen-pervasive-unjust.aspx

Carmon, N. (1985). Poverty and culture: Empirical evidence and implications for public policy. *Sociological Perspectives, 28,* 403–417.

Carney, C. G., & Kahn, K. B. (1984). Building competencies for effective cross-cultural counseling: A developmental view. *Counseling Psychologist, 12,* 111–119.

Carroll, L. (2011). Elderly ignore heat warnings—because they are not old. Retrieved from http://www.msnbc.msn.com/id/43761917/ns/healthy-aging/

Carter, R. T. (1990). The relationship between racism and racial identity among White Americans: An exploratory investigation. *Journal of Counseling and Development, 69,* 46–50.

Carter, R. T. (1995). *The influence of race and racial identity in psychotherapy.* New York, NY: Wiley.

Carter, R. T. (Ed.). (2005). *Handbook of racial-cultural psychology and counseling.* Hoboken, NJ: Wiley.

Caruso, D. B. (2006, Nov. 8). New York City seeks to redefine the rules on gender identity. *Seattle Post-Intelligencer,* p. A14.

Casas, J. M., & Pytluk, S. D. (1995). Hispanic identity development. In J. G. Ponterotto, J. M. Casas, L. A. Suzuki, & C. M. Alexander (Eds.), *Handbook of multicultural counseling* (pp. 155–180). Thousand Oaks, CA: Sage.

Cashwell, C. S., Shcherbakova, J., & Cashwell, T. H. (2003). Effect of client and counselor ethnicity on preference for counselor disclosure. *Journal of Counseling and Development*, *81*, 196–201.

Cass, V. C. (1979). Homosexual identity formation: A theoretical model. *Journal of Homosexuality*, *4*, 219–235.

Castonguay, L. G., Goldfried, M. R., Wiser, S., Raue, P. J., & Hayes, A. M. (1996). Predicting the effect of cognitive therapy for depression: A study of unique and common factors. *Journal of Consulting and Clinical Psychology*, *64*, 497–504.

Centers for AIDS Prevention Studies, UCSF. (2006, May 11). What are the HIV prevention needs of adults over 50? Retrieved from http://www.caps.ucsf.edu/over50.html

Centers for Disease Control and Prevention. (1994). Prevalence and characteristic of alcohol consumption and fetal alcohol awareness—Alaska, 1991 and 1993. *Morbidity and Mortality Weekly Report*, *43*, 3–6.

Centers for Disease Control and Prevention. (2006). *National vital statistics reports: Health United States, 2006*. Washington, DC: U.S. Government Printing Office.

Centers for Disease Control and Prevention. (2007). Injuries among Native Americans: Fact sheet (2007). Retrieved from http://www.cdc.gov/ncipc/factsheets/nativemamericans.htm

Centers for Disease Control and Prevention. (2008). Alcohol-Attributable Deaths and Years of Potential Life Lost Among American Indians and Alaska Natives—United States, 2001–2005. Retrieved from http://www.cdc.gov/mmwr/preview/mmwrhtml/mm5734a3.htm

Centers for Disease Control and Prevention. (2010). Web-based Injury Statistics Query and Reporting System (WISQARS). National Center for Injury Prevention and Control, CDC (producer). Retrieved from www.cdc.gov/injury/wisqars/index.html

Centers for Disease Control and Prevention. (2011). The CDC Healthy Brain Initiative. Retrieved from http://www.cdc.gov/aging/pdf/HBISummary_508.pdf

Chalifoux, B. (1996). Speaking up: White working class women in therapy. In M. Hill & E. D. Rothblum (Eds.), *Classism and feminist therapy* (pp. 25–34). New York, NY: Harrington Park.

Chambliss, C. H. (2000). *Psychotherapy and managed care: Reconciling research and reality*. Boston: Allyn & Bacon.

Chambless, D. L., & Hollon, S. (1998). Defining empirically supported therapies. *Journal of Consulting and Clinical Psychology*, *66*, 7–18.

Chambless, D. L., & Ollendick, T. H. (2001). Empirically supported psychological interventions: Controversies and evidence. *Annual Review of Psychology*, *52*, 685–716.

Chaney, M. P., Filmore, J. M., & Goodrich, K. M. (2011). No more sitting on the sidelines. *Counseling Today*, 34–37.

Chang, D. F., & Berk, A. (2009). Making cross-racial therapy work: A phenomenological study of clients' experiences of cross-racial therapy. *Journal of Counseling Psychology*, *56*, 521–536.

Chang, E. T. (2001). Bitter fruit: The politics of Black-Korean conflict in New York City (Review). *Journal of Asian American Studies*, *4*(3), 295–298.

Chang, J., & Sue, S. (2005). Culturally sensitive research: Where have we gone wrong and what do we need to do now? In M. G. Constantine & D. W. Sue (Eds.), *Strategies for building multicultural competence in mental health and educational settings* (pp. 229–246). Hoboken, NJ: Wiley.

Chartier, K., & Caetano, R. (2010). Ethnicity and health disparities in alcohol research. Retrieved from http://findarticles.com/p/articles/mi_m0CXH/is_1–2_33/ai_n55302113/

Chase, B. W., Cornille, T. A., & English, R. W. (2000). Life satisfaction among persons with spinal cord injuries. *Journal of Rehabilitation*, *66*, 14–20.

Chavez, L. G. (2005). Latin American healers and healing: Healing as a redefinition process. In R. Moodley & W. West (Eds.), *Integrating traditional healing practices into counseling and psychotherapy* (pp. 85–99). Thousand Oaks, CA: Sage.

Chwalisz, K. (2001). A common factors revolution: Let's not "cut off our discipline's nose to spite its face." *Journal of Counseling Psychology*, *48*, 262–267.

Checker, L. (2011). CEO: Monthly "problems"—Why women earn less. Retrieved from http://msnbc.msn.com/ID/43655299/ns/business-personal-finance/#

Chekoudjian, C. B. (2009). The subjective experience of PMS: A sociological analysis of women's narratives (Unpublished master's thesis). University of South Florida, Tampa, FL. Retrieved from http://scholarcommons.usf.edu/etd/1895

Chen, C. P. (2005). Morita therapy: A philosophy of Yin/Yan coexistence. In R. Moodley & W. West (Eds.) *Integrating traditional healing practices into counseling and psychotherapy* (pp. 221–232). Thousand Oaks, CA: Sage.

Chen, E., Matthews, K. A., & Boyce, W. T. (2002). Socioeconomic differences in children's health: How and why do these relationships change with age? *Psychological Bulletin*, *128*, 295–329.

Chen, E. W.-C. (2009). *Encyclopedia of Asian American Issues Today*, *1*, 222–223

Chen, L. P., Murad, M. H., Paras, M. L., Colbenson, K. M., Sattler, A. L., . . . Zirakzadeh, A. (2010). Sexual abuse and lifetime diagnosis of psychiatric disorders: Systematic review and meta-analysis. *Mayo Clinic Proceedings*, *85*, 618–629.

Chen, P.-H. (2009). A counseling model for Self-relation coordination for Chinese clients with interpersonal conflicts. *Counseling Psychologist*, *37*, 987–1009.

Chen, S. W.-H., & Davenport, D. S. (2005). Cognitive-behavioral therapy with Chinese American clients: Cautions and modifications. *Psychotherapy: Theory, Research, Practice, Training*, *42*, 101–110.

Cheung, F. K., & Snowden, L. R. (1990). Community mental health and ethnic minority populations. *Community Mental Health Journal*, *26*, 277–291.

Chiesa, A., & Serretti, A. (2011). Mindfulness based cognitive therapy for psychiatric disorders: A systematic review and meta-analysis. *Psychiatry Research*, *87*, 441–453.

Child Trends. (2010). Family structure. Retrieved from www.childtrendsdatabank.org/?q=node/231

Chin, J. L. (2009). *Diversity in mind and in action*. Santa Barbara, CA: Praeger.

Choi, Y. H. (1999, September 7). Commentary: Asian values meet western realities. *The Los Angeles Times*, p. 7.

Choi, Y. H., Harachi, T. W., Gilmore, M. R., & Catalano, R. F. (2006). Are multiracial adolescents at greater risk? Comparisons of rates, patterns, and correlates of substance use and violence between monoracial and multiracial adolescents. *American Journal of Orthopsychiatry*, *76*, 86–97.

Choney, S. K., Berryhill-Paapke, E., & Robbins, R. R. (1995). The acculturation of American Indians: Developing frameworks for research and practice. In J. G. Ponterotto, J. M. Casas, L. A. Suzuki, & C. M. Alexander (Eds.), *Handbook of multicultural counseling* (pp. 73–92). Thousand Oaks, CA: Sage.

Choudhuri, D. D., Santiago-Rivera, A. L., & Garrett, M. T. (2012). *Counseling and diversity*. Belmont, CA: Cengage.

Christian, M. D., & Barbarin, O. A. (2001). Cultural resources and psychological adjustment of African American children: Effects of spirituality and racial attribution. *Journal of Black Psychology, 27*, 43–63.

Chung, R.C.Y., & Bemak, F. (2007). In M. G. Constantine (Ed.), *Clinical practice with people of color* (pp. 125–142). New York, NY: Teachers College Press.

Chung, R. C.-Y., Bemak, F., Ortiz, D. P., & Sandoval-Perez, P. A. (2008). Promoting the mental health of immigrants: A multicultural/social justice perspective. *Journal of Counseling and Development, 86*, 310–317.

Chung, R. C-Y. & Bernak, F. (2002). The relationship of culture and empathy in cross-cultural counseling. *Journal of Counseling and Development, 80*, 154–159.

Chung, R. C., Bemak, F. P., & Okazaki, S. (1997). Counseling Americans of Southeast Asian descent: The impact of the refugee experience. In C. Lee (Ed.), *Multicultural issues in counseling: New approaches to diversity* (2nd ed., pp. 207–231). Alexandria, VA: American Counseling Association.

Clark, K. B., & Clark, M. K. (1947). Racial identification and preference in Negro children. In T. M. Newcomb & E. L. Hartley (Eds.), *Readings in social psychology* (pp. 169–178). New York, NY: Holt, Reinhart & Winston.

Clark, L. L. (2010). *Seeing through our clients' eyes: An assessment of cultural competence in a community mental health agency.* (Doctoral dissertation). Retrieved from ProQuest Dissertations and Theses database (Accession Order No. AAT 3437082).

Clay, R. A. (1999). Four psychologists help others to see. *APA Monitor, 30*, 1–4.

CNN. (2011). Number of Americans in same-sex marriage states more than doubles. Retrieved from http://articles.cnn.com/2011–06–25/politics/new.york.gay.marriage_1_andrew-cuomo-couples-equal-rights-marriage licenses?_s=PM:POLITICS

Cochran, S. D., Keenan, C., Schober, C., & Mays, V. M. (2000). Estimates of alcohol use and clinical treatment needs among homosexually active men and women in the U.S. population. *Journal of Consulting and Clinical Psychology, 68*, 1062–1071.

Cohn, D. (2011). Multi-race and the 2010 Census. Retrieved from http://pewresearch.org/pubs/1953/multi-race-2010-census-obama

Cohen, F., Jussim L., Harber, K. D., & Bhasin, G. (2009). Modern anti-Semitism and Anti-Israeli attitudes. *Journal of Personality and Social Psychology, 97*, 290–306.

Cokley, K. (2006). The impact of racialized schools and racist (mis)education on African American Students' academic identity. In M. G. Constantine & D. W. Sue (Eds.), *Addressing Racism* (pp. 127–144). Hoboken, NJ: Wiley.

Cokley, K. (2007). Critical issues in the measurement of ethnic and racial identity: A referendum on the state of the field. *Journal of Counseling Psychology, 54*, 224–239.

Coleman, J. (2003, April 2). Bill would ban using children as interpreters. *San Jose Mercury News*, p. A 01.

Collins, B. E. (1970). *Social psychology*. Reading, MA: Addison-Wesley.

Comas-Diaz, L. (2010). On being a Latina healer: Voice, conscience and identity. *Psychotherapy Theory, Research, Practice, Training, 47*, 162–168.

Comas-Diaz, L., & Greene, B. (1994). Women of color with professional status. In L. Comas-Diaz & B. Greene (Eds.), *Women of color: Integrating ethnic and gender identities in psychotherapy* (pp. 347–388). New York, NY: Guilford Press.

Comaz-Diaz, L. & Jacobsen, F. M. (1995). Ethnocultural transference and counter-transference in the therapeutic dyad. *American Journal of Orthopsychiatry, 61*, 392–402.

Committee of 100. (2001). *American attitudes toward Chinese Americans and Asian Americans*. New York, NY: Author.

Committee on Women in Psychology. (1999). *Older psychologists survey*. Washington, DC: American Psychological Association.

Condon, J. C., & Yousef, F. (1975). *An introduction to intercultural communication*. New York, NY: Bobbs-Merrill.

Congressional Record. (1997). *Indian Child Welfare Act Amendments of 1997—Hon. George Miller*. Washington, DC: Author.

Conners, G. J., Carroll, K. M., DiClemente, C. C., Longabaugh, R., & Donovan, D. M. (1997). The therapeutic alliance and its relationship to alcoholism treatment participation and outcome. *Journal of Consulting and Clinical Psychology, 65*, 588–598.

Conrad, M. M., & Pacquiao, D. F. (2005). Manifestation, attribution, and coping with depression among Asian Indians from the perspectives of health care practitioners. *Journal of Transcultural Nursing, 16*, 32–40.

Constantine, M. G. (2002). Predictors of satisfaction with counseling: racial and ethnic minority clients' attitudes toward counseling and ratings of their counselors' general and multicultural counseling competence. *Journal of Multicultural Counseling and Development, 30*(4), 210–215.

Constantine, M. G. (2006). Institutional racism against African Americans. In M. G. Constantine & D. W. Sue (Eds.), *Addressing racism* (pp. 33–41). Hoboken, NJ: Wiley.

Constantine, M. G. (2007). Racial microaggressions against African American clients in a crossracial counseling relationship. *Journal of Counseling Psychology, 54*, 1–16.

Constantine, M. G., Gloria, A. M., & Baron, A. (2006). Counseling Mexican American college students. In C. C. Lee (Ed.), *Multicultural issues in counseling* (3rd ed., pp. 207–222). Alexandria, VA: American Counseling Association.

Constantine, M. G., Myers, L. J., Kindaichi, M., & Moore, J. L. (2004). Exploring indigenous mental health practices: The roles of healers and helpers in promoting well-being in people of color. *Counseling and Values, 48*, 110–125.

Constantine, M. G., & Sue, D. W. (2006). *Addressing racism*. Hoboken, NJ: Wiley.

Constantine, M. G., & Sue, D. W. (2007). Perceptions of Racial microaggressions among Black Supervisees in Cross-Racial Dyads. *Journal of Counseling Psychology, 54*, 142–153.

Cook, S. W. (1962). The systematic study of socially significant events: A strategy for social research. *Journal of Social Issues, 18*, 66–84.

Coombs, M. M., Coleman, D., & Jones, E. E. (2002). Working with feelings: The importance of emotion in both cognitive-behavioral and interpersonal therapy in the NIMH treatment of Depression Collaborative Research Program. *Psychotherapy: Theory/Research/Practice/Training, 39*, 233–244.

Cooper, C., Carpenter, I., Katona, C., Scholl, M., Wagner, C., Fialova, D., & Livingston, G. (2005). The Ad-HOC study of older adults' adherence to medication in 11 countries. *American Journal of Geriatric Psychiatry, 13*, 1067–1076.

Corey, G. (2012). *Theory and practice of counseling and psychotherapy* (9th ed.). Belmont, CA: Brooks/Cole.

Corna, L. M., Wade, T. J., Streiner, D. L., & Cairney, J. (2009). Transitions in hearing impairment and psychological distress in older adults. *Canadian Journal of Psychiatry, 54*, 518–525.

Cornah, D. (2006). *The impact of spirituality on mental health: A review of the literature*. London, UK: Mental Health Foundation.

Cornish, J. A. E., Gorgens, K. A., Olkin, R., Palomibi, B. J., & Abels, A. V. (2008). Perspectives on ethical practice with people who have disabilities. *Professional Psychology: Research and Practice, 39*, 488–497.

Corrigan, M. (2011). Tiger mothers: Raising children the Chinese way. Retrieved from http://www.npr.org/2011/01/11/132833376/tiger-mothers-raising-children

Cosgrove, L. (2006). The unwarranted pathologizing of homeless mothers: Implications for research and social policy. In R. L. Toporek, L. H. Gerstein, N. A. Fouad, G. Roysircar, & T. Israel (Eds.), *Handbook for social justice in counseling psychology* (pp. 200–214). Thousand Oaks, CA: Sage.

Costantino, G., Malgady, R. G., & Primavera, L. H. (2009). Congruence between culturally competent treatment and cultural needs of older Latinos. *Journal of Consulting and Clinical Psychology*, 77, 941–949.

Costello, E. J., Compton, S. N., Keeler, G., & Angold, A. (2003). Relationships between poverty and psychopathology: A natural experiment. *JAMA*, 290(15), 2023–2029.

Council for Students with Disabilities. (2006). Myths about people with disabilities. Retrieved from https://www.msu.edu/~csd/myths.html

Council for the National Interest. (2006). Poll: Forty percent of American voters believe the Israel Lobby has been a key factor in going to war in Iraq and now confronting Iran. Retrieved from http://www.cnionline.org/learn/polls/czandlobby/index2.htm

Cozzarelli, C., Wilkinson, A. V., and Tagler, M. J. (2001). Attitudes toward the poor and attributions for poverty. *Journal of Social Issues*, 57, 207–228.

Craik, F. I. M. (2008). Memory changes in normal and pathological aging. *Canadian Journal of Psychiatry*, 53, 343–345.

Craske, M. G. (2010). *Cognitive-behavioral therapy*. Washington, DC: American Psychological Association.

Crompton, S. (2010). Living with disability series: Life satisfaction of working-age women with disabilities. Retrieved from http://www.statcan.gc.ca/pub/11-008-x/2010001/article/11124-eng.htm

Cross, T. L., Bazron, B. J., Dennis, K. W., & Isaacs, M. R. (1989). *Towards a culturally competent system of care*. Washington, DC: Child and Adolescent Service System Program Technical Assistance Center.

Cross, W. E. (1971). The Negro-to-Black conversion experience: Towards a psychology of Black liberation. *Black World*, 30, 13–27.

Cross, W. E. (1991). *Shades of Black: Diversity in African American identity*. Philadelphia, PA: Temple University Press.

Cross, W. E. (1995). The psychology of Nigrescence: Revising the Cross model. In J. G. Ponterotto, J. M. Casas, L. A. Suzuki, & C. M. Alexander (Eds.), *Handbook of multicultural counseling* (pp. 93–122). Thousand Oaks, CA: Sage.

Cross, W. E., Smith, L., & Payne, Y. (2002). Black identity. In P. B. Pedersen, J. G. Draguns, W. J. Lonner, & J. E. Trimble (Eds.), *Counseling across cultures* (pp. 93–108). Thousand Oaks, CA: Sage.

Croteau, J. M., Lark, J. S., Lidderdale, M. A., & Chung, Y. B. (2005). *Deconstructing heterosexism in the counseling professions*. Thousand Oaks, CA: Sage.

Cruz, C. M., & Spence, J. (2005). Oregon tribal evidence based and cultural best practices. Retrieved from www.oregon.gov/OHA/mentalhealth/ebp/tribal-ebp-report.pdf

Cunningham, P. B., Foster, S. L., & Warner, S. E. (2010). Culturally relevant family-based treatment for adolescent delinquency and substance abuse: understanding within-session processes. *Journal of Clinical Psychology: In Session*, 66, 830–846.

Curtis, R., Field, C., Knann-Kostman, I., & Mannix, K. (2004). What 75 psychoanalysts found helpful and hurtful in their own analysis. *Psychoanalytic Psychology*, 21, 183–202.

Dana, R. H. (2000). The cultural self as a locus for assessment and intervention with American Indian/Alaska Natives. *Journal of Multicultural Counseling and Development, 28,* 66–82.

Danzinger, P. R., & Welfel, E. R. (2000). Age, gender and health bias in counselors: An empirical analysis. *Journal of Mental Health Counseling, 22,* 135–149.

Darwin, C. (1859). *On the origin of species by natural selection.* London, UK: Murray.

Das Gupta, M. (1997). "What is Indian about you?": A gendered, transnational approach to ethnicity. *Gender and Society, 11,* 572–596.

D'Augelli, A. R. (1989). Lesbians' and gay men's experiences of discrimination and harassment in a university community. *American Journal of Community Psychology, 17,* 317–321.

Davidson, M. M., Waldo, M., & Adams, E. M. (2006). Promoting social justice through preventive interventions in schools. In R. L. Toporek, L. H. Gerstein, N. A. Fouad, G. Roysircar, & T. Israel (Eds.), *Handbook for social justice in counseling psychology* (pp. 117–129). Thousand Oaks, CA: Sage.

Davis, J. F. (1991). *Who is Black?: One nation's definition.* University Park, PA: Pennsylvania State University Press

Davis, L. E., & Gelsomino, J. (1994). As assessment of practitioner cross-racial treatment experiences. *Social Work, 39,* 116–123.

Day, S. X. (2004). *Theory and design in counseling and psychotherapy.* Boston, MA: Houghton Mifflin.

Daya, R. (2005). Buddhist moments in psychotherapy. In R. Moodley & W. West (Eds.), *Integrating traditional healing practices into counseling and psychotherapy* (pp. 182–193). Thousand Oaks, CA: Sage.

DeAngelis, T. (2002). New data on lesbian, gay, and bisexual mental health. *APA Monitor, 33,* 46–47.

DeAngelis, T. (2005). Shaping evidence-based practice. *Monitor on Psychology, 36,* 26–31.

DeAngelis, Tori. (1997). Study shows black children more intimidated by peers. Retrieved from http://www.apa.org/monitor/dec97/peer.html

Dedovic, K., D'Aguiar, C., & Pruessner, J. C. (2009). What stress does to your brain: A review of neuroimaging studies. *Canadian Journal of Psychiatry, 54,* 5–15.

Deegear, J., & Lawson, D. M. (2003). The utility of empirically supported treatments. *Professional Psychology: Research and Practice, 34,* 271–277.

De Genova, N. (2006). *Racial transformations: Latinos and Asians remaking the United States.* Durham, NC: Duke University Press.

de Gobineau, A. (1915). *The inequality of human races.* New York, NY: Putnam.

de las Fuentes, C. (2006). Latina/o American populations. In M. G. Constantine (Ed.), *Clinical practice with people of color* (pp. 46–60). Hoboken, NJ: Wiley.

Demographic subgroup trends for various licit and illicit drugs, 1975–2009. Retrieved from http://www.monitoringthefuture.org/

DePaulo, B. M. (1992). Nonverbal behavior and self-presentation. *Psychological Bulletin, 111,* 203–243.

de Pillis, E., & de Pillis, L. (2008). Are engineering schools masculine and authoritarian? The mission statements say yes. Journal of Diversity in Higher Education, *1,* 33–44.

de Pillis, E. G. & de Pillis, L. G. (2008). *Journal of Diversity in Higher Education, 1,* 33–44.

DeRubeis, R. J., Siegle, G. J., & Hollon, S. D. (2008). Cognitive therapy vs. medications for depression: Treatment outcomes and neural mechanisms. *National Review of Neuroscience, 9,* 788–796.

Desselle, D. C., & Proctor, T. K. (2000). Advocating for the elderly hard-of-hearing population: The deaf people we ignore. *Social Work, 45,* 277–281.

Dettlaff, A. J., & Johnson, M. A. (2011). Child maltreatment dynamics among immigrant and U.S. born Latino children: Findings from the National Survey of Child and Adolescent well-being (NSCAW). *Children and Youth Services Review, 33*, 936–944.

Deutsch, A. (1949). *The mentally ill in America*. New York, NY: Columbia University Press.

Deyhle, D., & Swisher, K. (1999). Research in American Indian and Alaska Native education: From assimilation to self-determination. *Review of Research in Education, 22*, 113–194.

Diaz-Martinez, A. M., Interian, A., & Waters, D. M. (2010). The integration of CBT, multicultural and feminist psychotherapies with Latinas. *Journal of Psychotherapy Integration, 20*, 312–326.

Dichoso, S. (2010). Stigma haunts mentally ill Latinos. Retrieved from http://www.cnn.com/2010/HEALTH/11/15/latinos.health.stigma/index.html

Diller, J. V. (2011). *Cultural diversity*. Belmont, CA: Cengage.

Ding, K., Chang, G. A., & Southerland, R. (2009). Age of inhalant first time use and its association to the use of other drugs. *Journal of Drug Education. 39*, 261–272.

Dingfelder, S. F. (2005). Close the gap for Latino patients. *Monitor on Psychology, 36*, 58–61.

Dininny, S. (2011). Immigration raid shakes up Ellensburg. Associated Press. Retrieved from http://www.komonews.com/news/local/114400049.html

District of Columbia Public Schools. (2011). School-to-work programs nearly triple enrollment, increase capacity for DCPS Special Education students. Retrieved from http://www.dc.gov/DCPS/In+the+Classroom/Special+Education/Special+Education+News/School-towork+Programs+Nearly+Triple+Enrollment,+Increase+Capacity+for+DCPS+Special+Education+Students

Dittmann, M. (2005). Homing in on Mexican Americans' mental health access. *Monitor on Psychology, 36*, 70–72.

Doherty, W. J., & McDaniel, S. H. (2010). *Family therapy*. Washington, DC: American Psychological Association.

Dolliver, R. H., Williams, E. L., & Gold, D. C. (1980). The art of Gestalt therapy or: What are you doing with your feet now? *Psychotherapy: Theory, Research & Practice, 17*, 136–142.

Donahue, P., & McDonald, L. (2005). Gay and Lesbian aging: Current perspectives and future directions for social work practice and research. *Families in Society, 86*, 359–366.

Dorland, J. M., & Fischer, A. R. (2001). Gay, lesbian, and bisexual individuals' perceptions: An analogue study. *Counseling Psychologist, 29*, 532–547.

D'Oro, R. (2010). Stemming Native Americans' suicide rates. *Seattle Times*, p. A11.

D'Oro, R. (2011). Suicide rate remains high in Alaska, especially among Natives. Retrieved from http://www.adn.com/2011/01/12/1645956/report-says-suicide-remains-an.html

Dovidio, J. F., & Gaertner, S. L. (2000). Aversive racism and selective decisions: 1989–1999. *Psychological Science, 11*, 315–319.

Dovidio, J. F., Gaertner, S. L., Kawakami, K., & Hodson, G. (2002). Why can't we all just get along? Interpersonal biases and interracial distrust. *Cultural Diversity and Ethnic Minority Psychology, 8*, 88–102.

Dowdy, K. G. (2000). The culturally sensitive medical interview. *Journal of the American Academy of Physicians Assistants, 13*, 91–104.

Downing, N. E., & Roush, K. L. (1985). From passive acceptance to active commitment: A model of feminist identity development for women. *Counseling Psychologist, 13*, 695–709.

Draguns, J. G. (1976). Counseling across cultures. Common themes and distinct approaches. In P. B. Pedersen, W. J. Lonner, & J. G. Draguns (Eds.), *Counseling across cultures* (pp. 1–16). Honolulu, HI: University of Hawaii Press.

Draguns, J. G. (2002). Universal and cultural aspects of counseling and psychotherapy. In P. B. Pedersen, J. G. Draguns, W. J. Lonner, & J. E. Trimble (Eds.), *Counseling across cultures* (pp. 29–50). Thousand Oaks, CA: Sage.

Duarte-Velez, Y., Guillermo, B., & Bonilla, K. (2010). Culturally adapted cognitive-behavioral therapy: Integrating sexual, spiritual, and family identities in an evidence-based treatment of a depressed Latino adolescence. *Journal of Clinical Psychology: In Session, 66,* 895–906.

Duhaney, L. M. G. (2000). Culturally sensitive strategies for violence prevention. *Multicultural Education, 7,* 10–19.

Dumont, M. P. (1992). *Treating the poor: A personal sojourn through the rise and fall of community mental health.* Belmont, MA: Dymphna Press.

Dunn, D. S., & Brody, C. (2008). Defining the good life following acquired physical disability. *Rehabilitation Psychology, 53,* 413–425.

Duran, B., Sanders, M., Skipper, B., Waitzkin, H., Malcoe, L. H., Paine, S., & Yager, J. (2004). Prevalence and correlates of mental disorders among Native American women in primary care. *American Journal of Public Health, 94,* 71–77.

Duran, E. (2006). *Healing the soul wound.* New York, NY: Teachers College Press.

Dwairy, M. (2008). Counseling Arab and Muslim clients. In P. B. Pedersen, J. G. Draguns, W. J. Lonner, & J. E. Trimble (Eds.), *Counseling across cultures* (6th ed., pp. 147–160). Thousand Oaks, CA: Sage.

Dyche, L., & Zayas, L. H. (2001). Cross-cultural empathy and training the contemporary psychotherapist. *Clinical Social Work Journal, 29,* 245–258.

Eadie, B. J. (1992). *Embraced by the light.* Carson City, NV: Gold Leaf Press.

Eakins, B. W., & Eakins, R. G. (1985). Sex differences in nonverbal communication. In L. A. Samovar & R. E. Porter (Eds.), *Intercultural communication: A reader* (pp. 290–307). Belmont, CA: Wadsworth.

Eaton, M. J., & Dembo, M. H. (1997). Differences in the motivational beliefs of Asian Americans. *Journal of Educational Psychology, 89,* 433–440.

EchoHawk, M. (1997). Suicide: The scourge of Native American people. *Suicide and Life Threatening Behavior, 27,* 60–67.

Edmond, T., Megivern, D., Williams, C., Rochman, E., & Howard, M. (2006). Integrating evidence based practice and social work field education. *Journal of Social Work Education, 42,* 377–396.

Ehrenreich, B. (2009). Is it now a crime to be poor? Retrieved from http://www.nytimes.com/2009/08/09/opinion/09ehrenreich.html?

Eilperin, J. (2010). Environmental issues take center stage. Retrieved from http://www.washington post.com/wp-dyn/content/article/2010/11/21/April 2010112103782.html

El-Badry, S. (2006). Arab American demographics. Retrieved from http://www.allied-media-com/Arab-American/Arab%20american%

Eliade, M. (1972). *Shamanism: Archaic techniques of ecstasy.* New York, NY: Pantheon.

Elliott, A. (2006, September 10). Muslim immigration has bounced back. *Seattle Times,* p. A18.

Elliott, T. R., Shewchuk, R. M., & Richards, J. S. (1999). Caregiver social problem-solving abilities and family member adjustment to recentonset physical disability. *Rehabilitation Psychology, 44,* 104–123.

Ellis, A. (1997). Using rational emotive behavior therapy techniques to cope with disability. *Professional Psychology: Research and Practice, 28,* 17–22.

Ellis, A., & Ellis, D. J. (2011). *Rational emotive behavior therapy.* Washington, DC: American Psychological Association.

Elmelech, Y., & Lu, H. (2004). Race, ethnicity, and the gender-poverty gap. *Social Science Research, 33,* 158–182.

El Nasser, H. (2009, September 27). Fewer seniors live in nursing homes today. *USA Today*. Retrieved from http://www.usatoday.com/news/nation/census/2007–09–27-nursing-homes_N.htm

Equal Employment Opportunity Commission. (2010). Sexual Harassment Charges EEOC & FEPAs Combined: FY 1997–FY 2010. Retrieved from http://www.eeoc.gov/eeoc/statistics/enforcement/sexual_harassment.cfm

Ericksen-Radtke, M. M., & Beale, A. V. (2001). Preparing students with learning disabilities for college: Pointers for parents—part 2. *Exceptional Parent, 31*, 56–57.

Espinosa, P. (1997). School involvement and Hispanic parents. *Prevention Researcher, 5*, 5–6.

Estrada, F., Rigali-Oiler, M., Arciniega, M., & Tracy, T. J. G. (2011). Machismo and Mexican American men: An empirical understanding using a gay sample. *Journal of Counseling Psychology, 58*, 358–367.

Fabian, E. S., Lent, R. W., & Willis, S. P. (1998). Predicting work transition outcome for students with disabilities: Implications for counselors. *Journal of Counseling and Development, 76*, 311–316.

Fadiman, A. (1997). *The spirit catches you and you fall down*. New York, NY: Farrar, Straus & Giroux.

Faiver, C., Ingersoll, R. E., O'Brien, E., & McNally, C. (2001). *Explorations in counseling and spirituality*. Belmont, CA: Brooks/Cole.

Falicov, C. J. (2005). Mexican families. In M. Mc-Goldrick, J. Giordano, & N. Garcia-Preto (Eds.), *Ethnicity and family therapy* (pp. 229–241). New York, NY: Guilford Press.

Fang, C. Y., & Meyers, H. F. (2001). The effects of racial stressors and hostility on cardiovascular reactivity in African American and Caucasian men. *Health Psychology, 20*, 64–70.

Fathi, N. (2006, December 12). Iran opens conference on Holocaust. *New York Times*. Retrieved from http://www.nytimes.com/12/12/world/middleeast/12holocaust

Fausset, R., & Huffstutter, P. J. (2009). Black males' fear of racial profiling very real, regardless of class. Retrieved from http://www.latimes.com/news/nationworld/nation/la-na-racial-profiling25-2009jul25,0,7041188.story

Feagin, J. R., & Sikes, M. P. (1994). *Living with racism*. Boston, MA: Bacon.

Federal Bureau of Investigation. (2010). Hate crime statistics, 2009. Retrieved from http://www2.fbi.gov/ucr/hc2009/index.html

Fetterolf, J., & Eagly, A. H. (2011). Do young women expect gender equality in their future lives? An answer from a possible selves experiment. *Sex Roles, 65*, 83–93.

Fireside, H. (2004). *Separate and unequal: Homer Plessy and the Supreme Court decision that legalized racism*. Carroll & Graf: New York.

Fischer, A. R., & Shaw, C. M. (1999). African Americans' mental health and perceptions of racist discrimination: The moderating effects of racial socialization experiences and self-esteem. *Journal of Counseling Psychology, 46*, 395–407.

Flores, E., Tschann, J. M., Dimas, J. M., Pasch, L. A., & de Groat, C. L. (2010). Perceived racial/ethnic discrimination, posttraumatic stress symptoms, and health risk behaviors among Mexican American adolescents. *Journal of Counseling Psychology, 57*, 264–273.

Flores, E., Tschann, J. M., Marin, B. V., & Pantoja, P. (2004). Marital conflict and acculturation among Mexican American husbands and wives. *Cultural Diversity and Ethnic Minority Psychology, 10*, 39–52.

Fortuna, L. R., Alegria, M., & Gao, S. (2010). Retention in depression treatment among ethnic and racial minority groups in the United States. *Depression and Anxiety, 27*, 485–494.

Foster, D. M. (2011). Suppose to know better: On accepting privilege. In S. H. Anderson & V. A. Middleton (Eds.), *Explorations in diversity: Examining privilege and oppression in a multicultural society* (pp. 25–31). Belmont, CA: Cengage.

Foster, J. A., & MacQueen, G. (2008). Neurobiological factors linking personality traits and major depression. *La Revue Canadienne de Psychiatrie, 53,* 6–13.

Fouad, N. A., Gerstein, L. H., & Toporek, R. L. (2006). Social justice and counseling psychology in context. In R. L. Toporek, L. H. Gerstein, N. A. Fouad, G. Roysircar, & T. Israel (Eds.), *Handbook for social justice in counseling psychology* (pp. 1–16). Thousand Oaks, CA: Sage.

Fox, M. H., White, G. W., Rooney, C., & Cahill, A. (2010). The psychosocial impact of Hurricane Katrina on persons with disabilities and independent living staff living on the American Gulf Coast. *Rehabilitation Psychology, 55,* 231–240.

Fraga, E. D., Atkinson, D. R., & Wampold, B. E. (2002). Ethnic group preferences for multicultural counseling competencies. *Cultural Diversity and Ethnic Minority Psychology, 10,* 53–65.

Frame, M. W., & Williams, C. B. (1996). Counseling African Americans: Integrating spirituality in therapy. *Counseling and Values, 41,* 16–28.

Frank, J. W., Moore, R. S., & Ames, G. M. (2000). Historical and cultural roots of drinking problems among American Indians. *American Journal of Public Health, 90,* 344–351.

Frankel, M. (1998, May 24). The oldest bias. *New York Times Magazine,* pp. 16–17.

Frankenberg, R. (1993). *Euro-American women: Race matters.* Minneapolis, MN: University of Minnesota Press.

Franklin, A. J. (2004). *From brotherhood to manhood: How Black men rescue their relationships and dreams from the invisibility syndrome.* Hoboken, NJ: Wiley.

Franklin, C. G., & Soto, I. (2002). Editorial: Keeping Hispanic youth in school. *Children and Schools, 24,* 139–143.

Franklin, J. H. (1988). A historical note on black families. In H. P. McAdoo (Ed.), *Black families* (pp. 3–14). Newbury Park, CA: Sage.

Frawley, T. (2005). Gender bias in the classroom: Current controversies and implications for teachers. *Childhood Education, 81,* 221–227.

Fredriksen-Boldsen, K. I., Kim, H.-J., Barkan, S. F., Balsam, K. F., & Mincer, S. L. (2010). Disparities in health-related quality of life: A comparison of lesbian and bisexual women. *American Journal of Public Health, 100,* 2255–2261.

Freire, P. (1970). *Cultural action for freedom.* Cambridge, MA: Harvard Educational Review Press.

Freitag, R., Ottens, A., & Gross, C. (1999). Deriving multicultural themes from bibliotherapeutic literature: A neglected resource. *Counselor Education & Supervision, 39,* 120–133.

Freud, S. (1960). Psychopathology of everyday life. In J. Strachey (Ed. and Trans.), *The standard edition of the complete psychological works of Sigmund Freud* (6th ed.). London, UK: Hogarth Press.

Friedman, M. L., Friedlander, M. L., & Blustein, D. L. (2005). Toward an understanding of Jewish identity: A phenomenological study. *Journal of Counseling Psychology, 52,* 77–83.

Frommer, F. J. (2006, December. 20). Congressman criticized for Muslim letter. Retrieved from http://seattlepi.newsource.com/national/1133AP_Ellison_Quran.html

Fry, R. (2010). Hispanics, high school dropouts and the GED. Retrieved from http://pewhispanic.org/reports/report.php?ReportID=122

Fryberg, S. A., Markus, H. R., Oyserman, D., & Stone, J. M. (2008). Of warrior chiefs and Indian princesses: The psychological consequences of American Indian mascots. *Basic and Applied Social Psychology, 30,* 208–218.

Fuertes, J. N., & Brobst, K. (2002). Clients' ratings of counselor multicultural competency. *Cultural Diversity and Ethnic Minority Psychology, 8,* 214–223.

Fuertes, J. N., & Gelso, C. J. (2000). Hispanic counselors' race and accent and Euro Americans' universal-diverse orientation: A study of initial perceptions. *Cultural Diversity and Ethnic Minority Psychology, 6,* 211–219.

Fukuyama, M. A., & Sevig, T. D. (1999). *Integrating spirituality into multicultural counseling.* Thousand Oaks, CA: Sage.

Fuligni, A. J., Burton, L., Marshall, S., Perez-Febles, A., Yarrington, J., Kirsh, L. B., & Merriwether-DeVries, C. (1999). Attitudes toward family obligations among American adolescents with Asian, Latin American, and European backgrounds. *Child Development, 70,* 1030–1044.

Furman, R. (2011). White male privilege in the context of my life. In S. H. Anderson & V. A. Middleton (Eds.), *Explorations in diversity: Examining privilege and oppression in a multicultural society* (pp. 33–37). Belmont, CA: Cengage.

Gaertner, S. L. (1973). Helping behavior and racial discrimination among liberals and conservatives. *Journal of Personality and Social Psychology, 25,* 335–341.

Gaertner, S. L., & Dovidio, J. F. (2006). Understanding and addressing contemporary racism: From aversive racism to the common ingroup. *Journal of Social Issues, 61*(3), 615–639.

Gaertner, S. L., Rust, M. C., Dovidio, J. F., Bachman, B. A., & Anastasio, P. A. (1994). The contact hypothesis: The role of common ingroup identity on reducing intergroup bias. *Small Group Research, 25,* 224–249.

Gallo, L. C., & Matthews, K. A. (2003). Understanding the association between socioeconomic status and physical health: Do negative emotions play a role? *Psychological Bulletin, 129,* 10–51.

Gallup, G. (1995). *The Gallup poll: Public opinion 1995.* Wilmington, DE: Scholarly Resources.

Gallup Organization. (2009). *Religion.* Retrieved from http://www.gallup.com/poll/1690/Religion.aspx

Galton, F. (1869). *Hereditary genius: An inquiry into its laws and consequences.* London, UK: Macmillan.

Gambrell, J. (2006, October 13). Local wife says raided workers harmed no one. *Bellingham Herald,* pp. A1, A8.

Gambrill, E. (2005). *Critical thinking in clinical practice.* Hoboken, NJ: Wiley.

Garb, H. N. (1997) Race bias, social class bias, and gender bias in clinical judgment. *Clinical Psychology: Science and Practice, 4,* 99–120

Garber, B. D. (2004). Therapist alienation: Foreseeing and forestalling third-party dynamics: Undermining psychotherapy with children of conflicted caregivers. *Professional Psychology: Research and Practice, 35,* 357–363.

Garcia-Preto, N. (1996). Puerto Rican families. In M. McGoldrick, J. Giordano, & J. K. Pearce (Eds.), *Ethnicity and family therapy* (pp. 183–199). New York, NY: Guilford Press.

Garcia-Preto, N. (2005). Puerto Rican families. In M. McGoldrick, J. Giordano, & N. Garcia-Preto (Eds.), *Ethnicity and family therapy* (2nd ed., pp. 242–255). New York, NY: Guilford Press.

Garnets, L., Hancock, K. A., Cochran, S. D., Goodchilds, J., & Peplau, L. A. (1998). Issues in psychotherapy with lesbians and gay men: A survey of psychologists. In D. R. Atkinson & G. Hackett (Eds.), *Counseling diverse populations* (2nd ed., pp. 297–316). Boston, MA: McGraw-Hill.

Garrahy, D. A. (2001). Three third-grade teachers' gender-related beliefs and behavior. *Elementary School Journal, 102,* 81–94.

Garrett, J. T., & Garrett, M. W. (1994). The path of good medicine: Understanding and counseling Native American Indians. *Journal of Multicultural Counseling and Development*, *22*, 134–144.

Garrett, M. T. (2006). When Eagle speaks: Counseling Native Americans. In C. C. Lee (Ed.), *Multicultural issues in counseling: New approaches to diversity* (pp. 25–53). Alexandria, VA: American Counseling Association.

Garrett, M. T., & Pichette, E. F. (2000). Red as an apple: Native American acculturation and counseling with or without reservation. *Journal of Counseling and Development*, *78*, 3–13.

Garrett, M. T., & Portman, T. A. A. (2011). *Counseling Native Americans*. Belmont, CA: Cengage.

Garrett, M. T., Torres-Rivera, E., Brubaker, M., Portman, T. A. A., Brotherson, D., West-Olatunji, C., . . . Grayshield, L. (2011). Crying for a vision: The Native American Sweat Lodge ceremony as therapeutic intervention. *Journal of Counseling and Development*, *89*, 318–325. doi: 10.1002/j.1556-6678.2011.tb00096.x

Garrett, M. T., & Wilbur, M. P. (1999). Does the worm live in the ground? Reflections on Native American spirituality. *Journal of Multicultural Counseling & Development*, *27*, 193–207.

Garroutte, E. M., Goldberg, J., Beals, J., Herrell, R., Manson, S. M., & AI-SUPERPFP Team. (2003). Spirituality and attempted suicide among American Indians. *Social Science & Medicine*, *56*, 1571–1579.

Gartrell, N., & Bos, H. (2010). US National Longitudinal Lesbian Family Study: Psychological Adjustment of 17-Year-Old Adolescents. *Pediatrics*, *126*, 28–36.

Garwick, A. G., & Auger, S. (2000). What do providers need to know about American Indian culture? Recommendations from urban Indian family caregivers. *Families, Systems & Health*, *18*, 177–190.

Gates, G. J. (2011). How many people are lesbian, gay, bisexual, and transgender? Retrieved from http://wiwp.law.ucla.edu/research/census-lgbt-demographics-studies/how-many-people-are-lesbian-gay-bisexual-and-transgender/

Gatz, M. (2007). Genetics, dementia, and the elderly. *Current Directions in Psychological Science*, *16*, 123–127.

Gee, G. C., Ryan, A., Laflamme, D. J., & Holt, J. (2006). Self-reported discrimination among African descendants, Mexican Americans, and other Latinos in the New Hampshire REACH initiative: The added dimension of immigration. *American Journal of Public Health*, *96*, 1821–1828.

Gerhart, K. A., Koziol-McLain, J., Lowenstein, S. R., & Whiteneck, G. G. (1994). Quality of life following spinal cord injury: Knowledge and attitudes of emergency care providers. *Annals of Emergency Medicine*, *23*, 807–812.

Gibbons, F. X., Etcheverry, P. E., Stock, M. L., Gerrard, M., Weng, C.-Y., & O'Hara, R. E. (2010). Exploring the link between racial discrimination and substance use: What mediates? What buffers? *Journal of Personality and Social Psychology*, *99*, 785–801.

Gibbs, N. (2005). Midlife crisis? Bring it on! Retrieved from http://www.time.com/time/magazine/article/0,9171,1059032,00.html

Gibbs, L., & Gambrill, E. (2002). Evidence-based practice: Counterarguments to objections. *Research on Social Work Practice*, *12*, 452–476.

Gilbert, B. D., & Christopher, M. S. (2010). Mindfulness-based attention as a moderator of the relationship between depressive affect and negative cognitions. *Cognitive Therapy and Research*, *34*, 514–521.

Gilgun, J. F. (2002). Completing the circle: American Indian medicine wheels and the promotion of resilience of children and youth in care. *Journal of Human Behavior in the Social Environment*, *6*, 65–84.

Gillem, A. R., Lincoln, S. K., & English, K. (2007). Biracial populations. In M. G. Constantine (Ed.), *Clinical practice with people of color* (pp. 104–124). New York, NY: Teachers College Press.

Glassgold, J. M. (2009). The case of Felix: An example of gay-affirmative, cognitive-behavioral therapy. *Pragmatic Case Studies in Psychotherapy, 5*, 1–21.

Gloria, A. M., & Peregoy, J. J. (1996). Counseling Latino alcohol and other substance users/abusers. *Journal of Substance Abuse Treatment, 13*, 119–126.

Goldberg, J. J. (2000, May 5). A portrait of American Jews. *Jewish Journal*, pp. 1–2.

Goldberg, S. G., Killeen, M. B., & O'Day, B. (2005). The disclosure conundrum: How people with psychiatric disabilities navigate employment. *Psychology, Public Policy, and Law, 11*, 463–500.

Gone, J. P. (2009). A community-based treatment for Native American historical trauma: Prospects for evidence-based practice. *Journal of Consulting and Clinical Psychology, 17*, 751–762.

Gone, J. P. (2010). Psychotherapy and traditional healing for American Indians: Exploring the prospects for therapeutic integration. *Counseling Psychologist, 38*, 166–235.

Gonsiorek, J. C. (1982). Results of psychological testing on homosexual populations. *American Behavioral Scientist, 25*, 385–396.

Gonsiorek, J. C., Richards, P. S., Pargament, K. I., & McMinn, M. R. (2009). Ethical challenges and opportunities at the edge: Incorporating spirituality and religion into psychotherapy. *Professional Psychology: Research and Practice, 40*, 385–395.

Gonzalez, G. M. (1997). The emergence of Chicanos in the twenty-first century: Implications for counseling, research, and policy. *Journal of Multicultural Counseling and Development, 25*, 94–106.

Gonzalez, G. M., Castillo-Canez, I., Tarke, H., Soriano, F., Garcia, P., & Velasquez, R. J. (1997). Promoting the culturally sensitive diagnosis of Mexican Americans: Some personal insights. *Journal of Multicultural Counseling and Development, 25*, 156–161.

Goodman, J. (2009). Starfish, salmon, and whales: An introduction to the special section. *Journal of Counseling and Development, 87*, 259.

Goodman, L., Glenn, C., Bohlig, A., Banyard, V., & Borges, A. (2009). Feminist relational advocacy processes and outcomes from the perspective of low-income women with depression. *Counseling Psychologist, 37*, 848–876.

Goodman, L. A., Liang, B., Helms, J. E., Latta, R. E., Sparks, E., & Weintraub, S. (2004). Training counseling psychologists as social justice agents: Feminist and multicultural perspectives. *Counseling Psychologist, 32*, 793–837.

Goodman, L. A., Litwin, A., Bohlig, A., Weintraub, S. R., Green, A., Walker, J., . . . Ryan, N. (2007). Applying feminist theory to community practice: A multilevel empowerment intervention for low-income women with depression. In E. Aldarondo (Ed.), *Advancing social justice through clinical practice* (pp. 265–290). Mahwah, NJ: Erlbaum.

Gorman, J. C., & Balter, L. (1997). Culturally sensitive parent education: A critical review of quantitative research. *Review of Educational Research, 67*, 339–369.

Gossett, T. F. (1963). *Race: The history of an idea in America*. Dallas, TX: Southern Methodist University Press.

Gottesfeld, H. (1995). Community context and the underutilization of mental health services by minority patients. *Psychological Reports, 76*, 207–210.

Grabe, S., Ward, L. M., & Hyde, J. S. (2008). The role of the media in body image concerns among women: A meta-analysis of experimental and correlational studies. *Psychological Bulletin, 134*, 460–476.

Graham, M. (2005). Maat: An African-centered paradigm for psychological and spiritual healing. In R. Moodley & W. West (Eds.), *Integrating traditional healing practices into counseling and psychotherapy* (pp. 210–220). Thousand Oaks, CA: Sage.

Graziottin, A., & Serafini, A. (2009). Depression and the menopause: Why antidepressants are not enough. *Menopause International, 15,* 76–81.

Grey, N., & Young, K. (2008). Cognitive behavior therapy with refugees and asylum seekers experiencing traumatic stress symptoms. *Behavioural and Cognitive Psychotherapy, 36,* 3–19.

Grier, W., & Cobbs, P. (1968). *Black rage.* New York, NY: Basic Books.

Grier, W., & Cobbs, P. (1971). *The Jesus bag.* San Francisco, CA: McGraw-Hill.

Guerra, P. (1998, July). Older adults and substance abuse: Looking at the "invisible epidemic." *Counseling Today,* pp. 38, 43.

Gurin, P., Gurin, G., Lao, R., & Beattie, M. (1969). Internal-external control in the motivational dynamics of negro youth. *Journal of Social Issues, 25,* 29–54.

Gurung, R. A. R., & Mehta, V. (2001). Relating ethnic identity, acculturation, and attitudes toward treating minority clients. *Cultural Diversity and Ethnic Minority Psychology, 7,* 139–151.

Guthrie, R. V. (1997). *Even the rat was White: A historical view of psychology* (2nd ed.). New York, NY: Harper & Row.

Guzman, M. R., & Carrasco, N. (2011). *Counseling Latino/a Americans.* Belmont, CA: Cengage.

Hacker, J. S. (2006). *The great risk shift: The new insecurity and the decline of the American dream.* New York, NY: Oxford University Press.

Hage, S. M. (2004). A closer look at the role of spirituality in psychology training programs. *Professional Psychology: Research and Practice, 37,* 303–310.

Hage, S. M. (2005). Future considerations for fostering multicultural competence in mental health and educational settings: Social justice implications. In M. G. Constantine & D. W. Sue (Eds.), *Strategies for building multicultural competence in mental health and educational settings* (pp. 285–302). Hoboken, NJ: Wiley.

Haldeman, D. C. (2010). Reflections of a gay male psychotherapist. *Psychotherapy Theory: Research and Practice, 47,* 177–185.

Haley, A. (1966). *The autobiography of Malcolm X.* New York, NY: Grove Press.

Hall, E. T. (1959). *The silent language.* Greenwich, CT: Premier Books.

Hall, E. T. (1969). *The hidden dimension.* Garden City, New York, NY: Doubleday.

Hall, E. T. (1974). *Handbook for proxemic research.* Washington, DC: Society for the Ontology of Visual Communications.

Hall, E. T. (1976). *Beyond culture.* New York, NY: Anchor Press.

Hall, G. C. N. (2001). Psychotherapy research with ethnic minorities: Empirical, ethical, and conceptual issues. *Journal of Counseling and Clinical Psychology, 69,* 502–510.

Hall, P. A., Marshall, J., Mercado, A., & Tkachuk, G. (2011). Changes in coping style and treatment outcome following motor vehicle accident. *Rehabilitation Psychology, 56,* 43–51.

Hall, S. (2006). Judith Regan goes down fighting. Retrieved from http://www.eonline.com/print/index.jsp?uuid=1486440990ae-45e6

Hall, W. S., Cross, W. E., & Freedle, R. (1972). Stages in the development of Black awareness: An exploratory investigation. In R. L. Jones (Ed.), *Black psychology* (pp. 156–165). New York, NY: Harper & Row.

Halleck, S. L. (1971, April). Therapy is the handmaiden of the status quo. *Psychology Today, 4,* 30–34, 98–100.

Haller, B. A. (2006). Promoting disability-friendly campuses to prospective students: An analysis of university recruitment materials. *Disability Studies Quarterly, 26,* 1–10.

Halualani, R. T., Chitgopekar, A. S., Morrison, J. H. T. A., & Dodge, P. S. (2004). Diverse in name only? Intercultural interaction at a multicultural university. *Journal of Communication, 54*(2), 270–286.

Hamby, S. L. (2000). The importance of community in a feminist analysis of domestic violence among American Indians. *American Journal of Community Psychology, 28,* 649–669.

Hamilton, B. E., Martin, J. A., & Ventura, S. J. (2009). Births: Preliminary data for 2009. *National Vital Statistics Reports, 59*(3). Hyattsville, MD: National Center for Health Statistics.

Hammen, C. (2006). Stress generation in depression: Reflections on origins, research, and future directions. *Journal of Clinical Psychology, 62,* 1065–1082.

Haney-Lopez, I. F. (2003). *Racism on trial: The Chicano fight for justice.* Cambridge, MA: Harvard University Press.

Hankin, B. L. (2009). Development of sex differences in depressive and co-occurring anxious symptoms during adolescence: Descriptive trajectories and potential explanations in a multi-wave prospective study. *Journal of Clinical Child and Adolescent Psychology, 38,* 460–472.

Hanna, F. J., Talley, W. B., & Guindon, M. H. (2000). The power of perception: Toward a model of cultural oppression and liberation. *Journal of Counseling and Development, 78,* 430–446.

Hansen, J. C., Stevic, R. R., & Warner, R. W. (1982). *Counseling: Theory and process.* Toronto, Canada: Allyn & Bacon.

Hansen, N. D., Randazzo, K. V., Schwartz, A., Marshall, M., Kalis, D., Frazier, R., Burke, C., . . . & Novig, G. (2006). Do we practice what we preach? An exploratory survey of multicultural psychotherapy competencies. *Professional Psychology: Research and Practice, 37,* 66–74.

Hanson, L. (2006, October 9). Indian youths' march challenges Columbus "myth." Knight Ridder Tribune Business News, p. 1.

Hardiman, R. (1982). White identity development: A process oriented model for describing the racial consciousness of White Americans. *Dissertation Abstracts International, 43,* 104A. (University Microfilms No. 82-10330).

Harner, M. (1990). *The way of the shaman.* San Francisco, CA: Harper & Row.

Harrell, J. P. (2000). A multidimensional conceptualization of racism-related stresws: Implications for the well-being of people of color. *American Journal of Orthopsychiatry, 70,* 42–57.

Harrell, J. P., Hall, S., & Taliaferro, J. (2003). Physiological responses to racism and discrimination: An assessment of the evidence. *American Journal of Public Health, 93,* 243–248.

Harrington, E. F., Crowther, J. H., & Shipherd, J. C. (2010). Trauma, binge eating, and the "Strong Black Woman." *Journal of Consulting and Clinical Psychology, 78,* 469–479.

Harry, B., Klingner, J. K., & Hart, J. (2005). African American families under fire: Ethnographic views of family strengths. *Remedial and Special Education, 26,* 101–112.

Hartigan, J. (2005). *Odd tribes: Toward a cultural analysis of White people.* Durham, NC: Duke University Press.

Hasin, D. S., Stinson, F. S., Ogburn, E., & Grant, B. F. (2007). Prevalence, correlates, disability, and comorbidity of DSM-IV alcohol abuse and dependence in the United States: Results from the National Epidemiologic Survey on Alcohol and Related Conditions. *Archives of General Psychiatry, 64,* 830–842.

Hatch, L. R. (2005). Gender and ageism. *Generations, 29,* 19–25.

Hatzenbeuhler, M. L. (2011). The social environment and suicide attempts in lesbian, gay, and bisexual youth. *Pediatrics, 127,* 896–903.

Hawkins, E. H., Cummins, L. H., & Marlatt, G. A. (2004). Preventing substance abuse in American Indian and Alaska Native youth: Promising strategies for healthier communities. *Psychological Bulletin, 130*, 304–323.

Hayes, D. (2006). ACE report cites enrollment gains, retention problems. *Diverse Issues in Higher Education, 23*, 21.

Hayes, L. L. (1997, August). The unique counseling needs of Latino clients. *Counseling Today*, pp. 1, 10.

Hayes, P. A. (2009). Integrating evidence-based practice, cognitive-behavior therapy, and multicultural therapy: Ten steps for culturally competent practice. *Professional Psychology: Research and Practice, 40*, 354–360.

Hays, P. A. (2001). *Addressing cultural complexities in practice: A framework for clinicians and counselors*. Washington, DC: American Psychological Association.

Hays, T. (2010). Police: NY cabbie is asked if he's Muslim, stabbed. Retrieved from http://www.google.com/hostednews/ap/article/ALeqM5i5OdR6FH4zsmEVanHGR0y-jbOzngD9HQLPH02

Headden, S. (1997). The Hispanic dropout mystery. *US. News & World Report, 123*, 64–65.

Hecht, M. L., Jackson, R. L., & Ribeau, S. A. (2002). *African American communication: Exploring identity and culture* (2nd ed.). Mahwah, NJ: Erlbaum.

Heesacker, M., & Carroll, T. A. (1997). Identifying and solving impediments to the social and counseling psychology interface. *Counseling Psychologist, 25*, 171–179.

Heesacker, M., Conner, K., & Pritchard, S. (1995). Individual counseling and psychotherapy: Allocations from the social psychology of attitude change. *Counseling Psychologist, 23*, 611–632.

Heinrich, R. K., Corbin, J. L., & Thomas, K. R. (1990). Counseling Native Americans. *Journal of Counseling & Development, 69*, 128–133.

Heisel, M. J., Duberstein, P. R., Talbot, N. L., King, D. A., & Tu, X. M. (2009). Adapting interpersonal psychotherapy for older adults at risk for suicide: Preliminary findings. *Professional Psychology: Research and Practice, 40*, 156–164.

Helms, J. E. (1984). Toward a theoretical explanation of the effects of race on counseling: A Black and White model. *Counseling Psychologist, 12*, 153–165.

Helms, J. E. (1989). Expanding racial identity to cover the counseling process. *Journal of Counseling Psychology, 33*, 62–64.

Helms, J. E. (1990). *Black and White racial identity: Theory, research, and practice*. New York, NY: Greenwood Press.

Helms, J. E. (1994). How multiculturalism obscures racial factors in the therapy process: Comment on Ridley et al. (1994), Sodowsky et al. (1994), Ottavi et al. (1994), and Thompson et al. (1994). *Journal of Counseling Psychology, 41*, 162–165.

Helms, J. E. (1995). An update of Helms's White and people of color racial identity models. In J. G. Ponterotto, J. M. Casas, L. A. Suzuki, & C. M. Alexander (Eds.), *Handbook of multicultural counseling* (pp. 181–191). Thousand Oaks, CA: Sage.

Helms, J. E., & Carter, R. T. (1990). Development of the White racial identity attitude inventory. In J. E. Helms (Ed.), *Black and White racial identity: Theory, research and practice* (pp. 67–80). Westport, CT: Greenwood Press.

Helms, J. E., & Richardson, T. Q. (1997). How multiculturalism obscures race and culture as different aspects of counseling competency. In D. B. Pope-Davis & H. L. K. Coleman (Eds.), *Multicultural counseling competencies* (pp. 60–79). Thousand Oaks, CA: Sage.

Herek, G. M., Cogan, S. C., & Gillis, J. R. (2002). Victim experiences of hate crimes based on sexual orientation. *Journal of Social Issues, 58*, 319–399.

Hernandez, B., Garcia, J. I. R., & Flynn, M. (2010). The role of familism in the relation between parent-child discord and psychological distress among emerging adults of Mexican descent. *Journal of Family Psychology, 24*, 105–114.

Herring, R. D. (1997). *Counseling with Native American Indians and Alaskan Natives.* Thousand Oaks, CA: Sage.

Hertzog, J. (2010). "I just didn't know": The power of language. Retrieved from http://blog .govdelivery.com/usodep/2010/i-just-didnt-know-the-power-of-language.html

Highlen, P. S. (1994). Racial/ethnic diversity in doctoral programs of psychology: Challenges for the twenty-first century. *Applied and Preventive Psychology, 3*, 91–108.

Highlen, P. S. (1996). MCT theory and implications for organizations/systems. In D. W. Sue, A. E. Ivey, & P. B. Pedersen (Eds.), *A theory of multicultural counseling and therapy* (pp. 65–85). Pacific Grove, CA: Brooks/Cole.

Hildebrand, V., Phenice, L. A., Gray, M. M., & Hines, R. P. (1996). *Knowing and serving diverse families.* Englewood Cliffs, NJ: Prentice Hall.

Hill, C., Corbett, C., & St. Rose, A. (2010). *Why so few? Women in science, technology, engineering, and mathematic.* American Association of University Women. Retrieved from http://www.aauw.org/learn/research/upload/whysofew.pdf

Hill, D. B., & Willoughby, B. L. B. (2005). The development and validation of the genderism and transphobia scale. *Sex Roles, 53*(7/8), 531–544.

Hill, M. S., & Fischer, M. S. (2008). Examining objectification theory. *Counseling Psychologist, 36*, 745–776.

Hills, H. I., & Strozier, A. A. (1992). Multicultural training in APA approved counseling psychology programs: A survey. *Professional Psychology: Research and Practice, 23*, 43–51.

Hilsenroth, M. J., & Cromer, T. D. (2007). Clinician interventions related to alliance during the initial interview and psychological assessment. *Psychotherapy: Theory, Research, Practice, Training, 44*, 205–218.

Himmelstein, K. E. W., & Bruckner, H. (2011). Criminal-justice and school sanctions against nonheterosexual youth: A national longitudinal Study. *Pediatrics, 127* doi: 10.1542/peds.2009-2306

Hines, P. M., & Boyd-Franklin, N. (1996). African American families. In M. McGoldrick, J. Giodano, & J. K. Pearce (Eds.), *Ethnicity and family therapy* (pp. 66–84). New York, NY: Guilford Press.

Hines, P. M., & Boyd-Franklin, N. (2005). African American families. In M. McGoldrick, J. Giordano, & N. Garcia-Preto (Eds.), *Ethnicity and family therapy* (2nd ed., pp. 87–100). New York, NY: Guilford Press.

Hinrichsen, G. A. (2006). Why multicultural issues matter for practitioners working with older adults. *Professional Psychology: Research and Practice, 37*, 29–35.

Ho, M. K. (1987). *Family therapy with ethnic minorities.* Newbury Park, CA: Sage.

Ho, M. K. (1997). *Family therapy with ethnic minorities* (2nd ed.). Thousand Oaks, CA: Sage.

Hodge, D. R. (2002). Working with Muslim youth: Understanding the values and beliefs of Islamic discourse. *Children and Schools, 24*, 6–20.

Hojat, M., Louis, D. Z., Markham, F. W., Wender, R., Rabinowitz, C. & Gonnella, J. S. (2011). Physician's empathy and clinical outcomes for diabetic patients. *Academic Medicine, 86*, 359–364.

Hollingshead, A. R., & Redlich, E. C. (1968). *Social class and mental health.* New York, NY: Wiley.

Holloway, R. A., Waldrip, A. M., & Ickes, W. (2009). Evidence that a simpatico self-schema accounts for differences in the self-concepts and social behavior of Latinos versus Whites (and Blacks). *Journal of Personality and Social Psychology, 96*, 1012–1028.

Holmes, S. A., & Morin, R. (2006, June 3). Black men torn between promise and doubt. Retrieved from http://www.msnbc.nsn.com/id/print/1/displaymode/1098

Hong, G. K., & Domokos-Cheng Ham, M. (2001). *Psychotherapy and counseling with Asian American clients*. Thousand Oaks, CA: Sage.

Hooker, E. (1957). The adjustment of the male overt homosexual. *Journal of Projective Techniques, 21*, 18–31.

hooks, b. (2000). *Where we stand: Class matters*. New York, NY: Routledge.

Horrell, S. C. V. (2008). Effectiveness of cognitive-behavioral therapy with adult ethnic minority clients: A review. *Professional Psychology: Research and Practice, 39*, 160–168.

Houston, H. R. (1997). "Between two cultures": A testimony. *Amerasia Journal, 23*, 149–154.

Hovey, J. D. (2000). Acculturative stress, depression, and suicidal ideation in Mexican immigrants. *Cultural Diversity and Ethnic Minority Psychology, 6*, 134–151.

Howard, R. (1992). Folie à deux involving a dog. *American Journal of Psychiatry, 149*, 414.

Huang, L. N. (1994). An integrative approach to clinical assessment and intervention with Asian-American adolescents. *Journal of Clinical Child Psychology, 23*, 21–31.

Hudson, J. I., Hiripi, E., Pope, H. G., & Kessler, R. C. (2007). The prevalence and correlates of eating disorders in the National Comorbidity Survey Replication. *Biological Psychiatry, 61*, 348–358.

Huey, S. J., & Pan, D. (2006). Culture-responsive one-session treatment for phobic Asian Americans: A pilot study. *Psychotherapy: Theory, Research, Practice, Training, 43*, 549–554.

Hulnick, M. R., & Hulnick, H. R. (1989). "Life's challenges: Curse or opportunity?" Counseling families of persons with disabilities. *Journal of Counseling and Development, 68*, 166–170.

Hunter, S., Sundel, S. S., & Sundel, M. (2002). *Women at midlife: Life experiences and implications for the helping professions*. Washington, DC: NASW Press.

Hwang, W.-C., & Goto, S. (2009). The impact of perceived racial discrimination on the mental health of Asian American and Latino college students. *Asian American Journal of Psychology, S(1)*, 15–28.

Hwang, W.-C., Woods, J. J., & Fugimoto, K. (2010). Acculturative family distancing (AFD) and depression in Chinese American families. *Journal of Consulting and Clinical Psychology, 78*, 655–667.

Hyers, L. L. (2001). A secondary survey analysis study of African American ethnic identity orientation in two national samples. *Journal of Black Psychology, 27*, 139–171.

Ibanez, G. E., Van Oss Marin, B., Flores, S. A., Millett, G., & Diaz, R. M. (2009). General and gay-related racism experienced by Latino gay men. *Cultural Diversity and Ethnic Minority Psychology, 15*, 215–222.

Ibrahim, F. A., & Dykeman, C. (2011). Counseling Muslim Americans: Cultural and spiritual assessments. *Journal of Counseling and Development, 89*, 387–396.

Ina, S. (1997). Counseling Japanese Americans. In C. C. Lee (Ed.), *Multicultural issues in counseling* (2nd ed., pp. 189–206). Alexandria, VA: American Counseling Association.

Inclan, J. (1985). Variations in value orientations in mental health work with Puerto Ricans. *Psychotherapy, 22*, 324–334.

Irvine, J. J., & York, D. E. (1995). Learning styles and culturally diverse students: A literature review. In J. A. Banks & C. A. McGee Banks (Eds.), *Handbook of research on multicultural education* (pp. 484–497). New York, NY: Macmillan.

Ivey, A. E. (1981). Counseling and psychotherapy: Toward a new perspective. In A. J. Marsella & P. B. Pedersen (Eds.), *Cross-cultural counseling and psychotherapy*. New York, NY: Pergamon Press.

Ivey, A. E. (1986). *Developmental therapy*. San Francisco, CA: Jossey-Bass.

Ivey, A. E., D'Andrea, M. J., & Ivey, M. B. (2011). *Theories of counseling and psychotherapy: A multicultural perspective*. Boston, MA: Allyn &Bacon.

Ivey, A. E., D'Andrea, M., Ivey, M. B., & Simek-Morgan, L. (2007). *Theories of counseling and psychotherapy: A multicultural perspective* (2nd ed.). Boston, MA: Allyn & Bacon.

Ivey, A. E., & Ivey, M. B. (2003). *Intentional interviewing and counseling*. Pacific Grove, CA: Brooks/Cole.

Ivey, A. E., Ivey, M., Myers, J., & Sweeney, T. (2005). *Developmental counseling and therapy*. Boston, MA: Lahaska.

Iwamasa, G. Y. (1995). *Can multicultural sensitivity be taught to therapists in trainiong?* Symposium conducted at the Annual convention of the American Psychological Association. New York, NY.

Iwasaki, J. (2006a, Dec. 19). The best of both worlds. Retrieved from http://seattlepi. nwsource.com/printer2/index.asp ?ploc=t&ref

Jackman, C. F., Wagner, W. G., & Johnson, J. T. (2001). The attitudes toward multiracial children scale. *Journal of Black Studies, 27*, 86–99.

Jackson, B. (1975). Black identity development. *Journal of Educational Diversity, 2*, 19–25.

Jackson, L. A., Hodge, C. N., Gerard, D. A., Ingram, J. M., Ervin, K. S., & Sheppard, L. A. (1996). Cognition, affect and behavior in the prediction of group attitudes. *Personality and Social Psychology Bulletin, 22*, 306–316.

Jackson, L. C., Schmutzer, P. A., Wenzel, A., & Tyler, J. D. (2006). Applicability of cognitive-behavioral therapy with American Indian individuals. *Psychotherapy: Theory, Research, Practice, Training, 43*, 506–517.

Jackson, M. L., & Nassar-McMillan, S. (2006). Counseling Arab Americans. In C. C. Lee (Ed.), *Multicultural issues in counseling: New approaches to diversity* (3rd ed., pp. 235–247). Alexandria, VA: American Counseling Association.

Jacobson, S., & Samdahl, D. M. (1998). Leisure in the lives of old lesbians: Experiences with and responses to discrimination. *Journal of Leisure Research, 30*, 233–255.

Jaimes, A. (1992). *The state of Native America: Genocide, colonization, and resistance*. Boston, MA: South End Press.

James, E. (2008). Arab culture and Muslim stereotypes. *World and I, 23*(5), 4.

James, I. A. (2008). Stuff and nonsense in the treatment of older people: Essential reading for the over-45s. *Behavioural and Cognitive Psychotherapy, 36*, 735–747.

Jenkins, A. H. (1982). *The psychology of the Afro-American*. New York, NY: Pergamon Press.

Jensen, J. V. (1985). Perspective on nonverbal intercultural communication. In L. A. Samovar & R. E. Porter (Eds.), *Intercultural communication: A reader* (pp. 256–272). Belmont, CA: Wadsworth.

Johns, M., Schmader, T., & Martens, A. (2005). Knowing is half the battle: Teaching stereotype threat as a means of improving women's math performance, *Psychological Science, 16*, 175–179.

Johnson, B. (1995, January 19). Elderly women need not abandon sexuality. *Seattle Post-Intelligencer*.

Johnson, J. J. (1992). Developmental pathways: Toward an ecological theoretical formulation of race identity in Black-White biracial children. In M. P. P. Root (ed.), *Racially mixed people in America* (pp. 37–49). Newbury Park, CA: Sage.

Johnson, K. W., Anderson, N. B., Bastida, E., Kramer, B. J., Williams, D., & Wong, M. (1995). Macrosocial and environmental influences on minority health. *Health Psychology, 14*, 601–612.

Johnston, L. D., O'Malley, P. M., Bachman, J. G., & Schulenberg, J. E. (2010). *Demographic subgroup trends for various licit and illicit drugs, 1975–2009* (Monitoring the Future Occasional Paper No. 73). Ann Arbor, MI: Institute for Social Research. Retrieved from http://www.monitoringthefuture.org

Jones, A. C. (1985). Psychological functioning in Black Americans: A conceptual guide for use in psychotherapy. *Psychotherapy, 22*, 363–369.

Jones, C., & Shorter-Gooden, K. (2003). *Shifting: The double lives of Black women in America.* New York, NY: HarperCollins.

Jones, E. E., Kanouse, D., Kelley, H. H., Nisbett, R. E., Valins, S., & Weiner, B. (Eds.). (1972). *Attribution: Perceiving the causes of behavior.* Morristown, NJ: General Learning Press.

Jones, J. M. (1972). *Prejudice and racism.* Reading, MA: Addison Wesley.

Jones, J. M. (1997). *Prejudice and racism* (2nd ed.). Washington, DC: McGraw-Hill.

Jonsson, P. (2011). What were two republicans thinking, calling Obama "tar baby" and "boy"? Retrieved from http://www.csmonitor.com/USA/Politics/2011/0803/What-were-two-Republicans-thinking-calling-Obama-tar-baby-and-boy

Jordan, J. M. (1997). Counseling African American women from a cultural sensitivity perspective. In C. C. Lee (Ed.), *Multicultural issues in counseling* (2nd ed., pp. 109–122). Alexandria, VA: American Counseling Association.

Jordan, V. E. (2002, June). Speech given at Howard University's Rankin Memorial Chapel, Washington, DC.

Jose, P. E., Huntsinger, C. S., Huntsinger, P. R., & Liaw, L. (2004). Parental values and practices relevant to young children's social development in Taiwan and the United States. *Journal of Cross-Cultural Psychology, 31*, 677–702.

Jourard, S. M. (1964). *The transparent self.* Princeton, NJ: Van Nostrand.

Jung, C. G. (1960). The structure and dynamics of the psyche. In *Collected works (Vol. 8).* Princeton, NJ: Princeton University Press.

Juurlink, D. N., Herrmann, N., Szalai, J. P., Kopp, A., Redelmeier, D. A. (2004). Medical illness and the risk of suicide in the elderly. *Archives of Internal Medicine, 164*, 1179–1184.

Kabat-Zinn, J. (1990). *Full catastrophe living.* New York, NY: Delacorte.

Kail, R. V., & Cavanaugh, J. C. (2013). *Human development: A life-span view* (6th ed.). Belmont, CA: Brooks/Cole.

Kaiser Commission. (2010). The uninsured: A primer.

Kamarck, T., & Jennings, J. R. (1991). Biobehavioral factors in sudden cardiac death. *Psychological Bulletin, 109*, 42–75.

Kashubeck-West, S., Szymanski, D., & Meyer, J. (2008). Internalized heterosexism: Clinical implications and training considerations. *Counseling Psychologist, 36*, 615–630.

Kaslow, N. J., Leiner, A. S., Reviere, S., Jackson, E., Bethea, K., . . . Thompson, M. P. (2010). Suicidal, abused African American women's response to a culturally informed intervention. *Journal of Consulting and Clinical Psychology, 78*, 449–458.

Katz, J. (1985). The sociopolitical nature of counseling. *Counseling Psychologist, 13*, 615–624.

Keane, E. M., Dick, R. W., Bechtold, D. W., & Manson, S. M. (1996). Predictive and concurrent validity of the Suicide Ideation Questionnaire among American Indian Adolescents. *Journal of Abnormal Child Psychology, 24*, 735–747.

Kearney, L. K., Draper, M., & Baron, A. (2005). Counseling utilization of ethnic minority college students. *Cultural Diversity and Ethnic Minority Psychology, 11*, 272–285.

Keller, R. M., & Galgay, C. E. (2010). Microaggressive experience of people with disabilities. In D. W. Sue (Ed.), *Microaggressions and marginality* (pp. 241–267). Hoboken, NJ: Wiley.

Kelly, J. F., & Greene, B. (2010). Diversity within African American, female therapists: Variability in clients' expectations and assumptions about the therapist. *Psychotherapy: Theory, Research, Practice, Training, 47*, 186–197.

Kelly, M., & Tseng, H. (1992). Cultural differences in childrearing: A comparison of immigrant Chinese and Caucasian American mothers. *Journal of Cross-Cultural Psychology, 23*, 444–455.

Kemp, N. T., & Mallinckrodt, B. (1996). Impact of professional training on case conceptualization of clients with a disability. *Professional Psychology: Research and Practice, 27*, 378–385.

Kennedy, R. (2003). Highlights of the American Psychiatric Association 55th Institute on Psychiatric Services. Retrieved from http://www.medscape.com/viewarticle/471433

Kenney, K. R. (2002). Counseling interracial couples and multiracial individuals: Applying a multicultural counseling competency framework. *Counseling and Human Development, 35*, 1–11.

Kerwin, C., & Ponterotto, J. G. (1995). Biracial identity development: Theory and research. In J. Ponterotto, J. M. Casas, L. A. Suzuki, & C. M. Alexander (Eds.), *Handbook of multicultural counseling* (pp. 199–217). Newbury Park, CA: Sage.

Kessler, R. C., Chiu, W. T., Demler, O., & Walters, E. E. (2005). Prevalence, severity, and comorbidity of 12-month DSM-IV disorders in the National Comorbidity Survey Replication. *Archives of General Psychiatry, 62*, 617–627.

Khodayarifard, M., & McClenon, J. (2011). Family therapy in Iran: A case study of obsessive-compulsive disorder. *Journal of Multicultural Counseling and Development, 39*, 78–89.

Kilgore, H., Sideman, L., Amin, K., Baca, L., & Bohanske, B. (2005). Psychologists' attitudes and therapeutic approaches towards gay, lesbian, and bisexual issues continue to improve: An update. *Psychotherapy: Theory, Research, Practice, Training, 42*, 395–400.

Kim, B. S. K. (2007). Adherence to Asian and European American cultural values and attitudes toward seeking professional psychological help among Asian American college students. *Journal of Counseling Psychology, 54*, 474–480.

Kim, B. S. K. (2011). *Counseling Asian Americans*. Belmont, CA: Cengage.

Kim, B. S. K., & Atkinson, D. R. (2002). Asian American client adherence to Asian cultural values, counselor expression of cultural values, counselor ethnicity, and career counseling process. *Journal of Counseling Psychology, 49*, 3–13.

Kim, B. S. K., Hill, C. E., Gelso, C. J., Goates, M. K., Asay, P. A., & Harbin, J. M. (2003). Counselor self-disclosure, East Asian American client adherence to Asian cultural values, and counseling process. *Journal of Counseling Psychology, 50*, 324–332.

Kim, B. S. K., Li, L. C., & Liang, C. T. H. (2002). Effects of Asian American client adherence to Asian cultural values, session goal, and counselor emphasis of client expression on career counseling process. *Journal of Counseling Psychology, 49*, 342–354.

Kim, B. S. K., Liang, C. T. H., & Li, L. C. (2003). Counseling ethnicity, counselor nonverbal behavior, and seesion outcome with Asian American clients: Initial findings. *Journal of Counseling and Development, 81*, 202–209.

Kim, J. (1981). The process of Asian American identity development: A study of Japanese-American women's perceptions of their struggle to achieve personal identities as Americans of Asian ancestry. *Dissertation Abstracts International, 42*, 155 1A. (University Microfilms No. 81-18080).

Kim, J. G. S. (2002). Racial perceptions and psychological well being in Asian and Hispanic Americans. *Dissertation Abstracts International, 63(2-B)*, 1033B.

Kim, K. (1999). *Koreans in the hood: Conflict with African-Americans*. Baltimore, MD: Johns Hopkins University Press.

Kim, S. C. (1985). Family therapy for Asian Americans: A strategic structural framework. *Psychotherapy, 22*, 342–356.

King, M. (2001, October 7). Concerns of elder gays. *Seattle Times*, pp. B1, 9.

Kiselica, M. S. (1998). Preparing anglos for the challenges and joys of multiculturalism. *Counseling Psychologist, 26*, 5–21.

Kiselica, M. S. (1999a). Confronting my own ethnocentrism and racism: A process of pain and growth. *Journal of Counseling and Development, 77*, 14–17.

Kiselica, M. S. (Ed.). (1999b). *Confronting prejudice and racism during multicultural training*. Alexandria, VA: American Counseling Association.

Kiselica, M. S. (2003). My privileged and fulfilling life as a counselor educator. In R. L. Dingman & J. Weaver (Eds.), *Days in the lives of counselors* (pp. 151–159). Boston, MA: Allyn & Bacon.

Kitano, H. H. L. (1982). Mental health in the Japanese American community. In E. E. Jones & S. J. Korchin (Eds.), *Minority mental health* (pp. 149–164). New York, NY: Praeger.

Klebine, P., & Lindsey, L. (2007). Sexual function for men with spinal cord injury. Retrieved from http://www.spinalcord.uab.edu/show.asp?durki=22405

Kleinman, A. (2004). Culture and depression. *New England Journal of Medicine, 351*, 951–953.

Kluckhohn, F. R., & Strodtbeck, F. L. (1961). *Variations in value orientations*. Evanston, IL: Row, Patterson.

Knight, B. G., & McCallum, T. J. (1998). Adapting psychotherapeutic practice for older clients: Implications of the contextual, cohort-based, maturity, specific challenge model. *Professional Psychology: Research and Practice, 29*, 15–22.

Knowlton, A., & Latkin, C. (2007). Network financial support and conflict as predictors of depressive symptoms among a highly disadvantaged population. *Journal of Community Psychology, 35*, 13–28.

Knox, S., Burkard, A. W., Johnson, A. J., Suzuki, L. A., & Ponterotto, J. G. (2003). African American and European American therapists' experiences of addressing race in cross-racial psychotherapy dyads. *Journal of Counseling Psychology, 50*, 466–481.

Knox, S., Catlin, L., Casper, M., & Schlosser, L. Z. (2005). Addressing religion and spirituality in psychotherapy: Clients' perspectives. *Psychotherapy Research, 15*, 287–303.

Kochman, T. (1981). *Black and White styles in conflict*. Chicago, IL: University of Chicago Press.

Koltko-Rivera, M. E. (2004). The psychology of worldviews. *Review of General Psychology, 8*, 3–58.

Kort, B. (1997). Female therapist, male client: Challenging beliefs—a personal journey. *Women and Therapy, 20*, 97–100.

Kortte, K. B., Gilbert, M., Gorman, P., & Wegener, S. T. (2010). Positive psychological variables in the prediction of life satisfaction after spinal cord injury. *Rehabilitation Psychology, 55*, 40–47.

Kotter-Gruhn, D., Kleinspehn-Ammerlahn, A., Gerstorf, D., & Smith, J. (2009). Self-perceptions of aging predict mortality and change with approaching death: Results from the Berlin aging study. *Psychology and Aging, 24*, 654–667.

Kozol, J. (2006). *The shame of the nation*. New York, NY: Broadway Books.

Kramer, F. (1998, May 24). On nation's farms, some workers give up childhood—"I just want to go back to school," a youngster tells child-labor forum. *Seattle Times*, p. A6.

Kratochwill, T. R. (2002). Evidence-based interventions in school psychology: Thoughts on thoughtful commentary. *School Psychology Quarterly, 15*, 518–532.

Krendl, A. C., Heatherton, T. F., & Kensinger, E. A. (2009). Aging minds and twisting attitudes: An fMRI investigation of age differences in inhibiting prejudice. *Psychology and Aging, 24,* 530–541.

Krieger, N., & Sidney, S. (1996). Racial discrimination and blood pressure: The CARDIA study of young Black and White adults. *American Journal of Public Health, 86,* 1370–1378.

Krupin, S. (2001, July 25). Prejudice, schools key concerns of Hispanics. *Seattle Post Intelligencer,* p. A7.

Kuhlberg, J. A., Pena, J. B., & Zayas, L. H. (2010). Familism, parent-adolescent conflict, self-esteem, internalizing behaviors and suicide attempts among adolescent Latinas. *Child Psychiatry and Human Development, 41,* 425–440.

Kun, K. E., & Schwartz, R. W. (1998). Older Americans with HIV/AIDS. *SIECUS Report, 26,* 12–14.

Kwee, M. (1990). *Psychotherapy, meditation and health.* London, United Kingdom: East-West.

LaBarre, W. (1985). Paralinguistics, kinesics and cultural anthropology. In L. A. Samovar & R. E. Porter (Eds.), *Intercultural communication: A reader* (pp. 272–279). Belmont, CA: Wadsworth.

Labov, W. (1972) *Language in the inner city: Studies in the Black English vernacular.* Philadelphia, PA: University of Pennsylvania Press.

LaFromboise, T. D. (1998). American Indian mental health policy. In D. A. Atkinson, G. Morten, & D. W. Sue (Eds.), *Counseling American minorities: A cross-cultural perspective* (pp. 137–158). Boston, MA: McGraw-Hill.

LaFromboise, T. D. (2006). American Indian youth suicide prevention. *Prevention Researcher, 13,* 16–18.

LaFromboise, T. D., & Howard-Pitney, B. (1995). The Zuni Life Skills Development Curriculum. *Journal of Counseling Psychology, 42,* 479–486.

LaFromboise, T. D., Medoff, L., Harris, A., & Lee, C. C. (2007). Psychological and cultural correlates of suicidal ideation among American Indian early adolescents on a Northern Plains reservation. *Research in Human Behavior, 41,* 119–43.

Laing, R. D. (1967). *The divided self.* New York, NY: Pantheon.

Laing, R. D. (1969). *The politics of experience.* New York, NY: Pantheon.

Laird, J., & Green, R. (1996). *Lesbians and gays in couples and families.* San Francisco, CA: Jossey-Bass.

Lambert, M. J., & Barley, D. E. (2001). Research summary on the therapeutic relationship and psychotherapy outcome. *Psychotherapy, 38,* 357–361.

Landrine, H. (1985). Race x class stereotypes of women. *Sex Roles, 13,* 65–75.

Landsberger, S. A., & Diaz, D. R. (2010). Communicating with deaf patients: 10 tips to deliver appropriate care. *Current Psychiatry, 9,* 36–37.

Lane, M. (1988, June 22). At age 81, teacher's lessons are timeless. *Bellingham Herald,* p. A1.

Langman, P. F. (1999). *Jewish issues in multiculturalism: A handbook for educators and clinicians.* Northvale, NJ: Jason Aronson.

La Roche, M. J., Batista, C. & D'Angelo, E. (2011). A content analysis of guided imagery scripts: A strategy for the development of cultural adaptations. *Journal of Clinical Psychology, 67,* 45–57.

Larson, J. E., Ryan, C. B., Wassel, A. K., Kaszynski, K. L., Ibara, L., . . . Boyle, M. G. (2011). Analysis of employment incentives and barriers for individuals with psychiatric disabilities. *Rehabilitation Psychology, 56,* 145–149.

Lass, N. J., Mertz, P. J., & Kimmel, K. (1978). The effect of temporal speech alterations on speaker race and sex identification. *Language and Speech, 21,* 279–290.

LaTaillade, J. J. (2006). Considerations for treatment of African American couple relationships. *Journal of Cognitive Psychotherapy: An International Quarterly*, *20*, 341–354.

Lau, A. S., Fung, J. J., & Yung, V. (2010). Group parent training with immigrant Chinese families: Enhancing engagement and augmenting skills development. *Journal of Clinical Psychology: In Session*, *66*, 880–894.

Lau, J. S., Fung, J., Wang, S.-W., & Kang, S.-M. (2009). Explaining elevated social anxiety among Asian Americans: Emotional attunement and a cultural double bind. *Cultural Diversity and Ethnic Minority Psychology*, *15*, 77–85.

Lau, W.-Y., Chan, C. K.-Y., Li, J. C.-H., & Au, T. K.-F. (2010). Effectiveness of group cognitive-behavioral treatment for childhood anxiety in community clinics. *Behaviour Research and Therapy*, *48*, 1067–1077.

Law, N. (2011). Disability discrimination in the workplace on the rise. Retrieved from http://knowledgebase.findlaw.com/kb/2011/Jan/248758.html

Lawrence, A. A. (2008). Gender identity disorders in adults: Diagnosis and treatment. In D. Rowland & L. Incrocci (Eds.), *Handbook of sexual and gender identity disorders* (pp. 423–456). Hoboken, NJ: Wiley.

LeBlanc, S. (2006, March 11). Catholic group ends adoption role: Massachusetts law on gay parents is cited. *Chicago Tribune*, p. 4.

Lederman, J. (2011, February 2). Dharun Ravi wants Tyler Clementi case dismissed. Retrieved from http://www.huffingtonpost.com/2011/07/26/dharun-ravi-wants-tyler-c_n_909451.html

Lee, C. C. (1996). MCT theory and implications for indigenous healing. In D. W. Sue, A. E. Ivey, & P. B. Pedersen (Eds.), *A theory of multicultural counseling and therapy* (pp. 86–98). Pacific Grove, CA: Brooks/Cole.

Lee, C. C. (2006). Ethical issues in multicultural counseling. In B. Herlihy & G. Corey (Eds.), *ACA ethical standards casebook* (6th ed.). Alexandria, VA: American Counseling Association.

Lee, C. C. (2007). *Counseling for social justice*. Alexandria, VA: ACA.

Lee, C. C., & Armstrong, K. L. (1995). Indigenous models of mental health intervention: Lessons from traditional healers. In J. G. Ponterotto, J. M. Casas, L. A. Suzuki, & C. M. Alexander (Eds.), *Handbook of multicultural counseling* (pp. 441–456). Thousand Oaks, CA: Sage.

Lee, C. C., Oh, M. Y., & Mountcastle, A. R. (1992). Indigenous models of helping in non-western countries: Implications for multicultural counseling. *Journal of Multicultural Counseling and Development*, *20*, 1–10.

Lee, C.-R. (1995). *Native speaker*. New York, NY: Berkley.

Lee, E. (1996). Chinese families. In M. McGoldrick, J. Geordano, & J. K. Pearce (Eds.), *Ethnicity and family therapy* (pp. 249–267). New York, NY: Guilford Press.

Lee, F. Y. (1991). The relationship of ethnic identity to social support, self-esteem, psychological distress, and help-seeking behavior among Asian American college students. Unpublished doctoral dissertation, University of Illinois, Urbana-Champaign.

Lee, R. M., Choe, J., Kim, G., & Ngo, V. (2000). Construction of the Asian American Family Conflicts Scale. *Journal of Counseling Psychology*, *47*, 211–222.

Lee, R. M., Su, J., & Yoshida, E. (2005). Coping with intergenerational family conflict among Asian American college students. *Journal of Counseling Psychology*, *52*, 389–399.

Lefcourt, H. (1966). Internal versus control of reinforcement: A review. *Psychological Bulletin*, *65*, 206–220.

Lefkowitz, E. S., Romo, L. F. L., Corona, R., Au, T. K.-F., & Sigman, M. (2000). How Latino American and European American adolescents discuss conflicts, sexuality, and AIDS with their mothers. *Developmental Psychology, 36*, 315–325.

Legal Momentum. (2003). Reading between the lines: Women's poverty in the United State. Retrieved from http://www.legalmomentum.org/assets/pdfs/womeninpoverty.pdf

Leidy, M. S., Guerra, N. G., & Toro, R. I. (2010). Positive parenting, family cohesion, and child social competence among immigrant Latino families. *Journal of Family Psychology, 24*, 252–260.

Lejuez, C. W., Hopko, D. R., Acierno, R., Daughters, S. B., & Pagoto, S. L. (2011). Ten-year revision of the brief behavioral activation treatment for depression: Revised treatment manual. *Behavior Modification, 35*, 111–161.

Leland, J. (2000, March 20). Shades of gray. *Newsweek*, 46–49.

Leong, F. T. L. (1986). Counseling and psychotherapy with Asian-Americans: Review of literature. *Journal of Counseling Psychology, 33*, 196–206.

Leong, F. T. L., Wagner, N. S., & Kim, H. H. (1995). Group counseling expectations among Asian American students: The role of culture-specific factors. *Journal of Counseling Psychology, 42*, 217–222.

Leong, F. T. L., Wagner, N. S., & Tata, S. P. (1995). Racial and ethnic variations in help-seeking attitudes. In J. G. Ponterotto, J. M. Casas, L. A. Suzuki, & C. M. Alexander (Eds.), *Handbook of multicultural counseling* (pp. 415–438). Thousand Oaks, CA: Sage.

Lester, K., Resick, P. A., Young-Xu, Y., & Artz, C. (2010). Impact on race on early treatment termination and outcomes in posttraumatic stress disorder treatment. *Journal of Consulting and Clinical Psychology, 78*, 480–489.

Levenson, H. (2010). *Brief dynamic therapy*. Washington, DC: American Psychological Association.

Levenson, J. C., Frank, E., Cheng, Y., Rucci, P., Janney, C. A., . . . Fagiolini, A. (2010). Comparative outcomes among the problem areas of interpersonal psychotherapy. *Depression and Anxiety, 27*, 434–440.

Levinson, E. M., & Palmer, E. J. (2005). Preparing students with disabilities for school-to-work transition and postschool life. Retrieved from http://www.nasponline.org/resources/principals/Transition%20Planning%20WEB.pdf

Levy, L. B., & O'Hara, M. W. (2010). Psychotherapeutic interventions for depressed, low-income women: A review of the literature. *Clinical Psychology Review, 30*, 934–950.

Lewandowski, D. A., & Jackson, L. A. (2001). Perceptions of interracial couples: Prejudice at the dyadic level. *Journal of Black Psychology, 27*, 288–303.

Lewis, J. A., Lewis, M. D., Daniels, J. A., & D'Andrea, M. J. (1998). *Community counseling*. Pacific Grove, CA: Brooks/Cole.

Life Expectancy Tables. (2010). How long will you live? Retrieved from http://www.efmoody.com/estate/lifeexpectancy.html

Lightfoot, E., Hill, K., & LaLiberte, T. (2011). Prevalence of children with disabilities in the child welfare system and out of home placement: An examination of administrative records. *Children and Youth Services Review*. doi: 10.1016/j.childyouth.2011.02.019

Lilienfeld, S. O. (2007). Psychological treatments that cause harm. *Psychological Science, 2*, 53–70.

Limb, G. E., & Hodge, D. R. (2010). Helping child welfare workers improve cultural competence by utilizing spiritual genograms with Native American families and children. *Children and Youth Services Review, 32*, 239–245.

Lin, J. (2011). California Gov. Jerry Brown signs law requiring public schools to teach "gay history." Retrieved from http://www.cnsnews.com/news/article/california-gov-jerry-brown-signs-law-requiring-public-schools-teach-gay-history

Lin, Y. (2001). The effects of counseling styles and stages on perceived counselor effectiveness from Taiwanese female university clients. *Asian Journal of Counselling, 8*, 35–60.

Lindau, S. T., Schumm, L. P., Laumann, E. O., Levinson, W., O'Muircheartaigh, C. A., & Waite, L. J. (2007). A study of sexuality and health among older adults in the United States. *New England Journal of Medicine, 357*, 762–774.

Lindsey, E. S. (2005). Reexamining gender and sexual orientation: Revisioning the representation of queer and trans people in the 2005 edition of *Our Bodies, Ourselves. NWSA Journal, 17*, 184–189.

Lindsey, L., Rivera, P., & Sipski-Alexander, M. L. (2007). Sexuality for women with spinal cord injury. Retrieved from http://www.spinalcord.uab.edu/show.asp?durki=51275

Li-Repac, D. (1980). Cultural influences on clinical perception: A comparison between Caucasian and Chinese-American therapists. *Journal of Cross-Cultural Psychology, 11*, 327–342.

Liu, W. M., Ali, S. R., Soleck, G., Hopps, J., Dunston, K., & Pickett, T. (2004). Using social class in counseling psychology research. *Journal of Counseling Psychology, 51*, 3–18.

Liu, W. M., Hernandez, J., Mahmood, A., & Stinson, R. (2006). Linking poverty, classism, and racism in mental health: Overcoming barriers to multicultural competency. In M. G. Constantine & D. W. Sue (Eds.), *Addressing racism* (pp. 65–86). Hoboken, NJ: Wiley.

Liu, W. M., Pickett, T., & Ivey, A. E. (2007). White middle-class privilege: Social class bias and implications for training and practice. *Journal of Multicultural Counseling and Development, 35*, 194–206.

Lo, H.-W. (2010). My racial identity development and supervision: A self-reflection. *Training and Education in Professional Psychology, 4*, 26–28.

Locke, D. C. (1998). *Increasing multicultural understanding*. Thousand Oaks, CA: Sage.

Logel, C., Walton, G. M., Spencer, S. J., Iserman, E. C., von Hippel, W., & Bell, A. E. (2009). Interacting with sexist men triggers social identity threat among female engineers. *Journal of Personality and Social Psychology, 96*, 1089–1103.

London, P. (1988) *Modes and morals of psychotherapy*: New York, NY: Holt, Rinehart & Winston.

Lone-Knapp, F. (2000). Rez talk: How reservation residents describe themselves. *American Indian Quarterly, 24*, 635–640.

Lopez, M. H., & Dockterman, D. (2011). U.S. Hispanic country of origin counts for nation, top 30 metropolitan areas. Retrieved from http://pewhispanic.org/reports/report.php?ReportID=142

Lopez-Baez, S. I. (2006). Counseling Latinas: Culturally responsive interventions. In C. C. Lee (Ed.), *Multicultural issues in counseling* (3rd ed., pp. 187–194). Alexandria, VA: American Counseling Association.

Lopez-Baez, S. I., & Paylo, M. J. (2009). Social justice advocacy: Community collaboration and systems advocacy. *Journal of Counseling and Development, 87*, 276–283.

Lorant, V., Deliege, D., Eaton, W., Robert, A., Philippot, P., & Ansseau, M. (2003). Socioeconomic inequalities in depression: A meta-analysis. *American Journal of Epidemiology, 157*, 98–112.

Lord, T. Y. (2010). The relationship of gender-based public harassment to body image, self-esteem, and avoidance behavior. Dissertation Abstracts International: Section B: The Sciences and Engineering, Vol 70(8-B), 2010, 5171.

Lorenzo, M. K., Pakiz, B., Reinherz, H. Z., & Frost, A. (1995). Emotional and behavioral problems of Asian American adolescents: A comparative study. *Child and Adolescent Social Work Journal, 12*, 197–212.

Lorion, R. P. (1973). Socioeconomic status and treatment approaches reconsidered. *Psychological Bulletin, 79*, 263–280.

Lorion, R. P. (1974). Patient and therapist variables in the treatment of low-income patients. *Psychological Bulletin, 81*, 344–354.

Lott, B. (2002). Cognitive and behavioral distancing from the poor. *American Psychologist, 57*, 100–110.

Lott, B., & Bullock, H. E. (2007). *Psychology and economic injustice*. Washington, DC: American Psychological Association.

Lott, B., & Saxon, S. (2002). The influence of ethnicity, social class and context on judgments about U. S. women. *Journal of Social Psychology, 142*, 481–499.

Lowen, L. (2011). Qualities of women leaders: The unique leadership characteristics of women. Retrieved from http://womensissues.about.com/od/intheworkplace/a/Women-Leaders.htm

LSU Office of Disability Services. (2011). Dispelling myths about people with disabilities. Retrieved from http://appl003.lsu.edu/slas/ods.nsf/$Content/Myths?Open Document

Lucas, M. S., & Berkel, L. A. (2005). Counseling needs of students who seek help at a university counseling center: A closer look at gender and multicultural issues. *Journal of College Student Development, 46*, 251–266.

Lui, M., Leondar-Wright, B., Brewer, R., & Adamson, R. (2006). *The color of wealth*. Boston, MA: New Press.

Lui, W. M., & Pope-Davis, D. B. (2005). The working alliance, therapy ruptures and impasses, and counseling competence: Implications for counselor training and education. In R. T. Carter (Ed.), *Handbook of racial-cultural psychology and counseling* (pp. 148–167). Hoboken, NJ: Wiley.

Lum, D. (2011). *Culturally competent practice*. Belmont, CA: Cengage.

Lum, J. L. (1999). Family violence. In L. C. Lee & N. W. S. Zane (Eds.), *Handbook of Asian American psychology* (pp. 505–526). Thousand Oaks, CA: Sage.

Lum, R. G. (1982). Mental health attitudes and opinions of Chinese. In E. E. Jones & S. J. Korchin (Eds.), *Minority mental health*. New York, NY: Praeger.

Luzzo, D. A., & McWhirter, E. H. (2001). Sex and ethnic differences in the perception of educational and career-related barriers and levels of coping efficacy. *Journal of Counseling and Development, 79*, 61–67.

Lyness, K. S., & Thompson, D. E. (2000). Climbing the corporate ladder: Do female and male executives follow the same route? *Journal of Applied Psychology, 85*, 86–101.

Lyons, H. Z., Bieschke, K. J., Dendy, A. K., Worthington, R. L., & Georgemiller, R. (2010). Psychologists' competence to treat lesbian, gay and bisexual clients: State of the field and strategies for improvement. *Professional Psychology: Research and Practice, 41*, 424–434.

Maas, P. (2001, September 9). The broken promise. *Parade Magazine*, 4–6.

Machia, M., & Lamb, S. (2009). Sexualized innocence: Effects of magazine ads portraying adult women as sexy little girls. *Journal of Media Psychology, 21*, 15–24.

Mack, D. E., Tucker, T. W., Archuleta, R., DeGroot, G., Hernandez, A. A., & Oh Cha, S. (1997). Interethnic relations on campus: Can't we all get along? *Journal of Multicultural Counseling and Development, 25*(4), 256–268.

MacPhee, D., Fritz, J., & Miller-Heyl, J. (1996). Ethnic variations in personal social networks and parenting. *Child Development, 67*, 3278–3295.

Madera, J. M., Hebl, M. R., & Martin, R. C. (2009). Gender and letters of recommendation for academia: Agentic and communal differences. *Journal of Applied Psychology, 94*, 1591–1599.

Mallinckrodt, B., Shigeoka, S., & Suzuki, L. A. (2005). Asian and Pacific Island American students' acculturation and etiology beliefs about typical counseling presenting problems. *Cultural Diversity and Ethnic Minority Psychology, 11*, 227–238.

Marcos, L. R. (1973). The language barrier in evaluating Spanish-American patients. *Archives of General Psychiatry, 29*, 655–659.

Marrero, P. (2011, August 8). Migración mexicana permanece estable. *La Opinion.* Retrieved from http://www.impre.com/laraza/noticias/2011/8/3/migracion-mexicana-permanece-e-266040–2.html

Martin, D. C. (2011). Refugees and asylees: 2010. Retrieved from http://www.dhs.gov/xlibrary/assets/statistics/publications/ois_rfa_fr_2010.pdf

Martinez, M., & Gutierrez, T. (2010). Tucson teachers sue Arizona over new "anti-Hispanic" school law. Retrieved from http://www.cnn.com/2010/US/10/19/arizona.ethnic.studies.lawsuit/?hpt=T2

Maslow, A. H. (1968). *Toward a psychology of being.* Princeton, NJ: Van Nostrand.

Massey, D. S., Durand, J., & Malone, N. (2002). *Beyond smoke and mirrors: Mexican immigration in an era of economic integration.* New York, NY: Russell Sage Foundation.

Maykovich, M. H. (1973). Political activation of Japanese American youth. *Journal of Social Issues, 29*, 167–185.

McAuliffe, G. J., & Eriksen, K. P. (1999). Toward a constructivist and developmental identity for the counseling profession: The context-phase-stage style model. *Journal of Counseling and Development, 77*, 267–280.

McCabe, H. T., Wilsnack, S. E., West, B. T., & Boyd, C. J. (2010). Victimization and substance use disorders in a national sample of heterosexual and sexual minority women and men. *Addiction, 105*, 2130–2140.

McCabe, S. E., Hughes, T. L., Bostwick, W. B., West, B. T., & Boyd, C. J. (2009). Sexual orientation, substance use behaviors and substance dependence in the United States. *Addiction, 104*, 1333–1345.

McClain, P. D., Carter, N., DeFrancesco, V., Lyle, M., Nunnally, S. C., . . . Cotton, K. D. (2006). Racial distancing in a southern city: Latino immigrants' views of Black Americans. *Journal of Politics, 68*, 3–23. doi: 10.1111/j. 1468-2508. 2006.00446.x

McClure, J. (2011). The role of causal attributions in public misconceptions about brain injury. *Rehabilitation Psychology, 56*, 85–93.

McCollum, V. J. C. (1997). Evolution of the African American family personality: Considerations for family therapy. *Journal of Multicultural Counseling and Development, 25*, 219–229.

McCormick, R. (2005). The healing path: What can counselors learn from aboriginal people about how to heal? In R. Moodley & W. West (Eds.), *Integrating traditional healing practices into counseling and psychotherapy* (pp. 293–304). Thousand Oaks, CA: Sage.

McCray, C. C. (1998). Ageism in the preclinical years. *Journal of the American Medical Association, 279*, 1035.

McDonnall, M. C. (2011). Physical status as a moderator of depressive symptoms among older adults with dual sensory loss. *Rehabilitation Psychology, 56*, 67–76.

McDowell, T., Ingoglia, L., Serizawa, T., Holland, C., Dashiell, J. W. Jr, & Stevens, C. (2005). Raising multicultural awareness in family therapy through critical conversations. *Journal of Marital and Family Therapy, 31*, 399–412.

McGoldrick, M., Giordano, J., & Garcia-Preto, N. (2005). *Ethnicity and family therapy.* New York, NY: Guilford Press.

McIntosh, P. (1989, July/August). White privilege: Unpacking the invisible knapsack. *Peace and Freedom*, pp. 8–10.

McLaughlin, K. A., Hatzenbuehler, M. L., & Keyes, K. M. (2010). Responses to discrimination and psychiatric disorders among Black, Hispanic, female, and lesbian, gay, and bisexual individuals. *American Journal of Public Health, 100,* 1477–1484.

McNamara, K., & Rickard, K. M. (1989). Feminist identity development: Implications for feminist therapy with women. *Journal of Counseling and Development, 68,* 184–193.

McNeil, D. G. (2011, August 30). Panel hears grim details of venereal disease tests. *New York Times.* Retrieved from http://www.nytimes.com/2011/08/31/world/americas/31syphilis.html?scp=1&sq=McNeil%20syphilis&st=cse

McQuaide, S. (1998). Women at midlife. *Social Work, 43,* 21–31.

Measham, T., Guzder, J., Rousseau, C. M., & Naeau, L. (2010). Cultural considerations in child and adolescent psychiatry. *Cross-Cultural Psychiatry, 27,* 1–5.

Mehrabian, A. (1972). *Nonverbal communication.* Chicago, IL: Aldene-Atherton.

Mellskog, P. (2011, June 5). LGBT program for seniors gets $100,000 grant. *Longmont Weekly,* p. 7.

Meston, C. M., Heiman, J. R., Trapnell, P. D., & Carlin, A. S. (1999). Ethnicity, desirable responding, and self-reports of abuse: A comparison of European- and Asian-ancestry undergraduates. *Journal of Counseling and Clinical Psychology, 67,* 139–144.

Meyer, I. H., Dietrick, J., & Schwartz, S. (2008). Lifetime prevalence of mental disorders and suicide attempts in diverse lesbian, gay and bisexual populations. *American Journal of Public Health, 98,* 1004–1006.

Meyer, O., Zane, N., & Cho, Y. I. (2011). Understanding the psychological processes of the racial match effect in Asian Americans. *Journal of Counseling Psychology, 58,* 335–345. Retrieved from http://www.ncbi.nlm.nih.gov/pubmed/21574698

Middlebrook, D. L., LeMaster, P. L., Beals, J., Novins, D. K., & Manson, S. M. (2001). Suicide prevention in American Indian and Alaska Native communties: A critical review of programs. *Suicide and Life-Threatening Behavior, 31,* 132–149.

Middleton, R., Arrendondo, P., & D'Andrea, M. (2000, December). The impact of Spanish-speaking newcomers in Alabama towns. *Counseling Today,* 24.

Mikulas, W. L. (2006). Integrating the world's psychologies. In L. T. Hoshmand (Ed.), *Culture, psychotherapy and counseling* (pp. 91–111). Thousand Oaks, CA: Sage.

Miller, J. B., & Stiver, I. P. (1997). *The healing connection.* Boston, MA: Beacon Press.

Miller, K. E. (2005). Association between illness and suicide risk in older adults. *American Family Physician, 71,* 1404–1405.

Miller, K. E., Zoe, L. M., Pazdirek, L., Caruth, M., & Lopez, D. (2005). The role of interpreters in psychotherapy with refugees: An exploratory study. *American Journal of Orthopsychiatry, 75,* 27–39.

Miller, S. T., Seib, H. M., & Dennie, S. P. (2001). African American perspectives on health care: The voice of the community. *Journal of Ambulatory Care Management, 24,* 37–42.

Mindess, A. (1999). *Reading between the signs.* Yarmouth, ME: Intercultural Press.

Mintz, L. B., Bartels, K. M., & Rideout, C. A. (1995). Training in counseling ethnic minorities and race-based availability of graduate school resources. *Professional Psychology: Research and Practice, 26,* 316–321.

Mintz, L. B., & Kashubeck, S. (1999). Body image and disordered eating among Asian American and Caucasian college students: An examination of race and gender differences. *Psychology of Women Quarterly, 23,* 781–796.

Mio, J. S. (2005). Academic mental health training settings and the multicultural guidelines. In M. G. Constantine & D. W. Sue (Eds.), *Strategies for building multicultural competence in mental health and educational settings* (pp. 129–144). Hoboken, NJ: Wiley.

Mio, J. S., & Morris, D. R. (1990). Cross-cultural issues in psychology training programs: An invitation for discussion. *Professional Psychology: Theory and Practice, 21,* 434–441.

Miranda, A. O., & Umhoefer, D. L. (1998a). Acculturation, language use, and demographic variables as predictors of the career self-efficacy of Latino career counseling clients. *Journal of Multicultural Counseling and Development, 26,* 39–51.

Miranda, A. O., & Umhoefer, D. L. (1998b). Depression and social interest differences between Latinos in dissimilar acculturation stages. *Journal of Mental Health Counseling, 20,* 159–171.

Miville, M. L., Constantine, M. G., Baysden, M. F., & So-Lloyd, G. (2005). Chameleon changes: An exploration of racial identity themes of multiracial people. *Journal of Counseling Psychology, 52,* 507–516.

Miville, M. L., Darlington, P., Whitlock, B., & Mulligan, T. (2005). Integrating identities: The relationship of racial, gender, and ego identities among white college students. *Journal of College Student Development, 46,* 157–175.

Miville, M. L., Koonce, D., Darlington, P., & Whitlock, B. (2000). Exploring the relationship between racial/cultural identity and ego identity among African Americans and Mexican Americans. *Journal of Multicultural Counseling and Development, 28,* 208–224.

Mizock, L., & Fleming, M. Z. (2011). Transgender and gender variant populations with mental illness: Implications for clinical care. *Professional Psychology: Research and Practice, 42,* 208–213.

Modie, N. (2001, July 25). New hope for the immigrants in limbo. *Seattle Post-Intelligencer,* pp. A1, A6.

Moffitt, L. B., & Szymanski, D. M. (2011). Experiencing sexually objectifying environments: A qualitative study. *Counseling Psychologist, 39,* 67–106.

Mohr, J. J., Israel, T. & Sedlacek, W. E. (2001). Counselors' attitudes regarding bisexuality as predictors of counselors' clinical responses: An analogue study of a female bisexual client. *Journal of Counseling Psychology, 48,* 212–222.

Mohr, J. J., Weiner, J. L., Chopp, R. M., & Wong, S. J. (2009). Effects of client bisexuality on clinical judgment: When is bias most likely to occur? *Journal of Counseling Psychology, 56,* 164–175.

Molinari, V. (Ed.) (2011). *Specialty competencies in geropsychology.* New York, NY: Oxford University Press.

Mollen, D., Ridley, R., & Hill, C. L. (2003). Models of multicultural competence: A critical evaluation. In D. B. Pope-Davis, H.L.K. Coleman, W. M. Liu, & R. L. Toporek (Eds.), *Handbook of multicultural competencies: In counseling & psychology* (pp. 21–37). Thousand Oaks, CA: Sage.

Mollica, R. F., Wyshak, G., & Lavelle, J. (1987). The psychosocial impact of war trauma and torture on Southeast Asian refugees. *American Journal of Psychiatry, 144,* 1567–1572.

Monroe, C. R. (2005). Why are "Bad Boys" always Black? Causes of disproportionality in school discipline and recommendations for change. *Clearing House, 79,* 45–50.

Montague, J. (1996). Counseling families from diverse cultures. A nondeficit approach. *Journal of Multicultural Counseling and Development, 24,* 37–41.

Moodley, R. (2005). Shamanic performances: Healing through magic and the supernatural. In R. Moodley & W. West (Eds.), *Integrating traditional healing practices into counseling and psychotherapy* (pp. 2–14). Thousand Oaks, CA: Sage.

Moodley, R., & West, W. (Eds.). (2005). *Integrating traditional healing practices into counseling and psychotherapy.* Thousand Oaks, CA: Sage.

Moos, R. H., Mertens, J. R., & Brennan, P. L. (1995). Program characteristics and readmission among older substance abuse patients: Comparisons with middle-aged and younger patients. *Journal of Mental Health Administration, 22,* 332–346.

Moradi, B., & Hasan, N. T. (2004). Arab American persons' reported experiences of discrimination and mental health: The mediating role of personal control. *Journal of Counseling Psychology, 51,* 418–428.

Morales, E. & Norcross, J. C. (2010). Evidence-based practices with ethnic minorities: Strange bedfellows no more. *Journal of Clinical Psychology: In Session, 66,* 821–829.

Morrissey, M. (1997, October). The invisible minority: Counseling Asian Americans. *Counseling Today, 1,* 21–22.

Morrison, M. A., & Morrison, T. G. (2002). Development and validation of a scale measuring prejudice toward gay men and lesbian women. *Journal of Homosexuality, 43,* 15–37.

Morrison, T. G., Kenny, P., & Harrington, A. (2005). Modern prejudice toward gay men and lesbian women: Assessing the viability of a measure of modern homonegative attitudes within an Irish context. *Genetic, Social, and General Psychology Monographs, 131,* 219–250.

Mosqueda, L., & Dong, X. (2011). Elder abuse and self-neglect: "I don't care anything about going to the doctor, to be honest. . . . " *Journal of the American Medical Association, 306,* 532–540.

Moss, R. C., & Davis, D. (2008). Counseling biracial students: A review of issues and interventions. *Journal of Multicultural Counseling and Development, 36,* 219–230.

Moynihan, D. P. (1965). Employment, income and the ordeal of the Negro family. *Daedalus,* pp. 745–770.

Mulady, K. (2011). Behind bars: For African-American girls acting out is a crime. Retrieved from http://www.equalvoiceforfamilies.org/?p=430

Mullavey-O'Byrne, C. (1994). Intercultural communication for health care professionals. In R. W. Brislin & T. Yoshida (Eds.), *Improving intercultural interactions* (pp. 171–196). Thousand Oaks, CA: Sage.

Mulvaney-Day, N. E., Earl, T. R., Diaz-Linhart, Y., & Alegria, M. (2011). Preferences for relational style with mental health clinicians: A qualitative comparison of African American, Latino and Non-Latino White patients. *Journal of Clinical Psychology, 67,* 31–44.

Murashko, A. (2011). President Obama supports bill to repeal federal gay marriage ban. Retrieved from http://www.christianpost.com/news/president-obama-endorses-feinsteins-repeal-of-doma-bill-52536/

Muroff, J. (2007). Cultural diversity and cognitive behavior therapy. In T. Ronen & A. Freeman (Eds.), *Cognitive behavior therapy in clinical social work practice* (pp. 109–146). New York, NY: Springer.

Murphy, A. J. (2005). Life stories of black male and female professionals: An inquiry into the salience of race and sports. *Journal of Men's Studies, 13,* 313–319.

Murphy-Shigematsu, S. (2010). Microaggressions by supervisors of color. *Training and Education in Professional Psychology, 4,* 16–18.

Murray, M. (2010). Poll: On immigration, racial divide runs deep. Retrieved from http://www.msnbc.msn.com/id/37344303/ns/us_news-immigarion_a_nation_divided/

Muscatell, K. A., Slavich, G. M., Monroe, S. M., & Gotlib, I. H. (2009). Stressful life events, chronic difficulties, and the symptoms of clinical depression. *Journal of Nervous and Mental Disease, 197,* 154–160.

Myers, E. R. (2001). African-American perceptions of Asian-American merchants: An exploratory study. In Myers, Ernest R. (Ed.), *Challenges of a changing America:*

Perspectives on immigration and multiculturalism in the United States (2nd ed., pp. 171–179). San Francisco, CA: Caddo Gap Press.

Myers, J. E., & Harper, M. C. (2004). Evidence-based effective practices with older adults. *Journal of Counseling and Development, 82,* 207–218.

Nadal, K. L. (2004). Pilipino American identity development model. *Journal of Multicultural Counseling and Development, 32*(1), 44–61.

Nadal, K. L. (2011). *Filipino American psychology.* Hoboken, NJ: Wiley.

Nadal, K. L., Issa, M., Griffin, K. E., Hamit, S., & Lyons, O. B. (2010). Religious microaggressions in the United States. In D. W. Sue (Ed.), *Microaggressions and marginality* (pp. 287–310). Hoboken, NJ: Wiley.

Nadal, K. L., Rivera, D. P., & Corpus, J. H. (2010). Sexual orientation and transgender microaggressions. In D. W. Sue (Ed.), *Microaggressions and marginality* (pp. 217–240). Hoboken, NJ: Wiley.

Nagamatsu, L. A., Voss, M., Neider, M. B., Gaspar, J. G., Handy, T. C., . . . Liu-Ambrose, T. Y. L. (2011). Increased cognitive load leads to impaired mobility decisions in seniors at risk for fall. *Psychology and Aging, 26,* 253–259.

Nagayama-Hall, G. (2001). Psychotherapy research with ethnic minorities: Empirical, ethical, and conceptual issues. *Journal of Consulting and Clinical Psychology, 69,* 502–510.

Nassar-McMillan, S. C., & Hakim-Larson, J. (2003). Counseling considerations among Arab Americans. *Journal of Counseling and Development, 81,* 150–158.

Nassar-McMillan, S. C., Lambert, R. G., & Hakim-Larson, J. (2011). Discrimination history, backlash fear, and ethnic identity among Arab Americans: Post-9/11 snapshots. *Journal of Multicultural Counseling and Development, 39,* 38–47.

National Academies. (2006). *Beyond bias and barriers: Fulfilling the potential of women in academic science and engineering.* Washington, DC: National Academies Press.

National Alliance for Caregiving. (2009). Caregiving in the U.S. Retrieved from http://www.caregiving.org/data/Caregiving_in_the_US_2009_full_report.pdf

National Child Traumatic Stress Network. (2008). TF-CBT: Trauma focused cognitive behavioral therapy. Retrieved from http://www.nctsnet.org/nctsn_assets/pdfs/promising_practices/TFCBT_General.pdf

National Coalition for the Homeless. (2005). *Who is homeless? NCH Fact Sheet #3.* Retrieved from http://www.ncchca.org/files/Homeless/NCH_Who%20is%20Homeless_07.pdf

National Coalition for Women and Girls in Education. (2008). Report from the National Coalition for Women and Girls in Education: Title IX at 35: Beyond the headlines. Retrieved from http://www.ncwge.org/pubs-reports.html

National Conference of Christians and Jews. (1994). *Taking America's pulse: A summary report of the national survey report of intergroup relations.* New York, NY: Author.

National Council on Interpreting in Health Care. (2005). *National standards of practice for interpreters in health care.* Santa Rosa, CA: Author.

National Immigration Law Center. (2006). Fact about immigrants' low use of health services and public benefits. Retrieved from http://www.nilc.org

National Institute on Aging. (2007). One in seven Americans age 71 and older has some type of dementia, NIH-Funded Study Estimates. Retrieved from http://www.nia.nih.gov/NewsAndEvents/PressReleases/PR20071030ADAMS.htm

National Law Center on Homelessness and Poverty and the National Coalition for the Homeless. (2009). Homes not handcuffs. Retrieved from http://nlchp.org/content/pubs/2009HomesNotHandcuffs1.pdf

Navarrette, R., Jr. (2011). Brewer's "birther" veto was the right call. Retrieved from http://www.cnn.com/2011/OPINION/04/20/navarette.brewer.birther/_1_birther-bill-brewer-arizona-secretary?_s=PM:OPINION

Negy, C., Schwartz, S., & Reig-Ferrer, A. (2009). Violated expectations and acculturative stress among U.S. Hispanic immigrants. *Cultural Diversity and Ethnic Minority Psychology, 15,* 255–264.

Negy, C., & Woods, D. J. (1992). The importance of acculturation in understanding research with Hispanic-Americans. *Hispanic Journal of Behavioral Sciences, 14,* 224–247.

Neider, M. B., Gaspar, J. G., McCarley, J. S., Crowell, J. A., Kaczmarski, H., & Kramer, A. F. (2011). Walking and talking: Dual-task effects on street crossing behavior in older adults. *Psychology and Aging, 26,* 260–268.

Neighbors, H. W., Caldwell, C. H., Thompson, E. & Jackson, J. S. (1994). Help-seeking behavior and unmet need. In Sriedman (Ed.). *Disorders in African Americans* (pp. 26–39). New York, NY: Springer.

Nelson, G., & Prilleltensky, I. (Eds.). (2005). *Community psychology: In pursuit of liberation and well-being.* New York, NY: Palgrave Macmillan.

Neville, H. A., Worthington, R. L., & Spanierman, L. B. (2001). Race, power, and multicultural counseling psychology: Understanding White privilege and color-blind racial attitudes. In J. Ponterotto, J. M. Casas, L. A. Suzuki, & C. M. Alexander (Eds.), *Handbook of multicultural counseling* (pp. 257–288). Thousand Oaks, CA: Sage.

New Journalism on Latino Children. (2010). The cultural strengths of Latino families. Retrieved from http://www.ewa.org/site/DocServer/NJLC_CulturalStrengths_WEB.pdf?docID=641

Newport, F. (2011). For first time, majority of Americans favor legal gay marriage. Retrieved from http://gallup.com/poll/147662/First-Time-Majority-Americans-Favor-Legal-Gay-Marriage.asp

Ngo-Metzger, Q., Massagli, M. P., Clarridge, B. R., Manocchia, M., Davis, R. B., Iezzoni, L. I., & Phillips R. S. (2003). Linguistic and cultural barriers to care: Perspectives of Chinese and Vietnamese immigrants. *Journal of General Internal Medicine, 18,* 44–52.

Nguyen, S. D. (1985). Mental health services for refugees and immigrants in Canada. In T. C. Owen (Ed.), *Southeast Asian mental health: Treatment, prevention, services, training, and research* (pp. 261–282). Washington, DC: National Institute of Mental Health.

Nicolas, G., Arntz, D. L., Hirsch, B., & Schmiedigen, A. (2011). Cultural adaptation of a group treatment for Haitian American adolescents. *Professional Psychology: Research and Practice, 40,* 378–384.

Nichols, M. P., & Schwartz, R. C. (2002). *The essentials of family therapy.* Boston, MA: Allyn & Bacon.

Nickerson, A., Bryant, R. A., Silove, D., & Steel, Z. (2010). A critical review of psychological treatments of posttraumatic stress disorder in refugees. *Clinical Psychology Review.* doi: 10:1016/j.cpr.2010.10.004

Nicolaidis, C., Timmons, V., Thomas, M. J., Waters, A. S., Wahab, S., . . . Mitchell, R. (2010). "You don't go tell white people nothing": African American women's perspectives on the influence of violence and race on depression and depression care. *American Journal of Public Health, 100,* 1470–1476.

Nishihara, D. P. (1978). Culture, counseling, and ho'oponopono: An ancient model in a modem context. *Personnel and Guidance Journal, 56,* 562–566.

Nittle, N. K. (2010). Flurry of racist incidents on school campuses raises concerns. Retrieved from http://racerelations.about.com/b/2010/03/05/flurry-of-racist-incidents-on-school-campuses-raises-concerns.htm

Nittle, N. K. (2011). Five myths about multiracial people in the U.S. Retrieved from http://racerelations.about.com/od/understandingrac1/a/Five-Myths-About-Multiracial-People-In-The-U-S.htm

Nobles, A. Y., & Sciarra, D. T. (2000). Cultural determinants in the treatment of Arab Americans: A primer for mainstream therapists. *American Journal of Orthopsychiatry, 70,* 182–191.

Noh, S., Beiser, M., Kaspar, V., Hou, F., & Rummens, J. (1999). Perceived racial discrimination, depression, and coping: A study of Southeast Asian refugees in Canada. *Journal of Health and Social Behavior, 40,* 193–207.

Noonan, B. M., Gallor, S. M., Hensler-McGinnis, N. F., Fassinger, R. E., Wang, S., & Goodman, J. (2004). Challenge and success: A qualitative study of the career development of highly achieving women with physical and sensory disabilities. *Journal of Counseling Psychology, 51,* 68–80.

Nosek, M. A., & Hughes, R. B. (2001). Psychospiritual aspects of sense of self in women with physical disabilities. *Journal of Rehabilitation, 67,* 20–25.

Nwachuku, U., & Ivey, A. (1991). Culture specific counseling: An alternative approach. *Journal of Counseling and Development, 70,* 106–111.

Nydell, M. K. (1996). *Understanding Arabs: A guide for westerners.* Yarmouth, ME: Intercultural Press.

Obasi, E. M., & Leong, F. T. L. (2009). Psychological distress, acculturation, and mental health-seeking attitudes among people of African descent in the United States: A preliminary investigation. *Journal of Counseling Psychology, 56,* 227–238.

Offman, A., & Kleinplatz, P. J. (2004). Does PMDD belong in the DSM? Challenging the medicalization of women's bodies. *Canadian Journal of Human Sexuality, 13.* Retrieved from http://findarticles.com/p/articles/mi_go1966/is_1_13/ai_n7459081/

Olkin, R. (1999). *What psychotherapists should know about disability.* New York, NY: Guilford Press.

Olsen, C. S. (1996). African-American adolescent women: Perceptions of gender, race, and class. *Marriage and Family Review, 24,* 105–121.

Ong, M. (2005). Body projects of young women of color in physics: Intersections of gender, race, and science. *Social Problems, 52,* 593–617.

O'Reilly, J. P., Tokuno, K. A., & Ebata, A. T. (1986). Cultural differences between Americans of Japanese and European ancestry in parental valuing of social competence. *Journal of Comparative Family Studies, 17,* 87–97.

Organista, K. C. (2000). Latinos. In J. R. White & A. S. Freeman (Eds.), *Cognitive-behavioral group therapy: For specific problems and populations* (pp. 281–303). Washington, DC: American Psychological Association.

Osmo, R., & Rosen, A. (2002). Social workers' strategies for treatment hypothesis testing. *Social Work Research, 26,* 9–18.

Owen, J., Tao, K., & Rodolfa, E. (2010). Microaggressions and women in short term therapy: Initial evidence. *Counseling Psychologist, 38*(7), 923–946.

Pack-Brown, S. P., & Williams, C. B. (2003). *Ethics in a multicultural context.* Thousand Oaks, CA: Sage.

Paiva, N. D. (2008). South Asian parents' constructions of praising their children. *Clinical Child Psychology and Psychiatry, 13,* 191–207.

Pajor, C. (2005). White trash: Manifesting the bisexual. *Feminist Studies, 31,* 570–575.

Palmore, E. (2005). Three decades of research on ageism. *Generations, 29,* 87–90.

Paniagua, F. A. (1994). *Assessing and treating culturally diverse clients.* Thousand Oaks, CA: Sage.

Paniagua, F. A. (1998). *Assessing and treating culturally diverse clients* (2nd ed.). Thousand Oaks, CA: Sage.

Paniagua, F. A. (2005). *Assessing and treating culturally diverse clients: A practical guide* (3rd ed.). Thousand Oaks, CA: Sage.

Pankhania, J. (2005). Yoga and its practice in psychological healing. In R. Moodley & W. West (Eds.), *Integrating traditional healing practices into counseling and psychotherapy* (pp. 246–256). Thousand Oaks, CA: Sage.

Paras, M. L., Murad, M. H., Chen, L. P., Goranson, E. N., Sattler, A. L., . . . Zirakzadeh, A. (2009). Sexual abuse and lifetime diagnosis of somatic disorders: A systematic review and meta-analysis. *Journal of the American Medical Association, 302*(5), 550–561.

Parham, T. A. (1997). An African-centered view of dual relationships. In B. Herlihy & G. Corey (Eds.), *Boundary issues in counseling* (pp. 109–112). Alexandria, VA: American Counseling Association.

Parham, T. A. (2002). *Counseling persons of African descent.* Thousand Oaks, CA: Sage.

Parham, T. A. (2011). Derald Wing Sue: From all of the places we've been. *Counseling Psychologist, 39*, 1–41.

Parham, T. A., Ajamu, A., & White, J. L. (2011). *The psychology of Blacks. Centering our perspectives in the African consciousness.* Boston, MA: Prentice Hall.

Parham, T. A., & Helms, J. E. (1981). The influence of black students' racial attitudes on preferences for counselor's race. *Journal of Counseling Psychology, 28*, 250–257.

Parham, T. A., White, J. L., & Ajamu, A. (1999). *The psychology of Blacks: An African-centered perspective* (3rd ed.). Englewood Cliffs, NJ: Prentice Hall.

Parker, S., & Thompson, T. (1990). Gay and bisexual men: Developing a healthy identity. In D. Moore & F. Leafgren (Eds.), *Men in conflict* (pp. 113–121). Alexandria, VA: American Counseling Association.

Pascoe, P. (1991). Race, gender, and intercultural relations: The case of interracial marriage. *Frontiers: A Journal of Women Studies, 12*, 5–18.

Passel, J. S., & Cohn, D. (2009). *A portrait of unauthorized immigrants in the United States.* Washington, DC: Pew Research Center.

Patrick, E. (2004). The U.S. refugee resettlement program. Retrieved from http://www.migrationinformation.org/USFocus/print.cfm?ID=229

Patrinos, H. A. (2000). The cost of discrimination in Latin America. *Studies in Comparative International Development, 35*(2), 3–17.

Pavkov, T. W., Lewis, D. A., & Lyons, J. S. (1989). Psychiatric diagnosis and racial bias: An empirical investigation. *Professional Psychology: Research & Practice, 20*, 364–368.

Pearlman, L. (2006). Golden years. Retrieved from http://www.bohemian.com/bohemian/02.22.06/fountaingrove-0608.html

Pearson, J. C. (1985). *Gender and communication.* Dubuque, IA: W. C. Brown.

Pedersen, P. B., & Pope, M. (2010). Inclusive cultural empathy for successful global leadership. *American Psychologist, 65*, 841–854.

Pedrotti, J. T., Edwards, L. M., & Lopez, S. J. (2008). Working with multicultural clients in therapy: Bridging theory, research, and practice. *Professional Psychology: Research and Practice, 39*, 192–201.

Pennington, D. (2004, July). Until the 'sunset': Helping persons who are older and their caregivers to cope with Alzheimer's, other forms of dementia. *Counseling Today*, 22–23.

Perkins, J. (2011, September 30). Transgenders say they too should be allowed military service. Retrieved from http://www.christianpost.com/news/transgenders-say-they-too-should-be-allowed-military-service-56895/

Pew Hispanic Center. (2007). *2007 National Survey of Latinos: As illegal immigration issue heats up, Hispanics feel a chill*. Retrieved from http://pewhispanic.org/reports/report.php?ReportID=84

Pew Hispanic Center. (2011). *Featured research*. Retrieved from http://pewhispanic.org/

Pew Report. (2010). *Obama's ratings little affected by recent turmoil*. Retrieved from http://people-press.org/2010/06/24/section-3-opinions-about-immigration/

Pew Research Center. (2007). *Blacks see growing values gap between poor and middle class*. Washington, DC: Author.

Pew Research Center. (2009). *Between two worlds: How young Latinos come of age in America*. Retrieved from http://pewresearch.org/pubs/1438/young-latinos-coming-of-age-in-america

Pew Research Center. (2010a). *A year after Obama's election: Blacks upbeat about Black progress, prospects*. Retrieved from http://pewresearch.org/pubs/1459/year-after-obama-election-black-public-opinion

Pew Research Center. (2010b). *Obama's ratings little affected by recent turmoil*. Retrieved from http://people-press.org/2010/06/24/section-3-opinions-about-immigration

Pew Research Center. (2011a). *The future of the global Muslim population*. Retrieved from http://stage.pewforum.org/uploadedFiles/Topics/Religious_Affiliation/Muslim/Future-GlobalMuslimPopulation-WebPDF-Feb10.pdf

Pew Research Center (2011b). *Wealth Gaps Rise to Record Highs Between Whites, Blacks and Hispanics*. Retrieved from http://pewresearch.org/pubs/2069/housing-bubble-subprime-mortgages-hispanics-blacks-household-wealth-disparity

Peyser, M., & Lorch, D. (2000). High school controversial. *Newsweek*, pp. 54–56.

Pfeffer, R. (2011). *Growing incarceration of young African-American women a cause for concern*. Retrieved from http://oaklandlocal.com/posts/2011/05/growing-incarceration-young-african-american-women-cause-concern

Phelps, R. E., Taylor, J. D., & Gerard, P. A. (2001). Cultural mistrust, ethnic identity, racial identity, and self-esteem among ethnically diverse Black university students. *Journal of Counseling and Development, 79*, 209–216.

Pierce, C. (1995). Stress analogs of racism and sexism: Terrorism, torture, and disaster. In C. Willie, P. Rieker, B. Kramer, & B. Brown (Eds.), *Mental heath, racism, and sexism* (pp. 277–293). Pittsburgh, PA: University of Pittsburgh Press.

Pierce, C., Carew, J., Pierce-Gonzalez, D., & Willis, D. (1978). An experiment in racism: TV commercials. In C. Pierce (Ed.), *Television and education* (pp. 62–88). Beverly Hills, CA: Sage.

Pierre, M. R., & Mahilik, J. R. (2005). Examining African self-consciousness and Black racial identity as predictors of Black men's psychological well-being. *Cultural Diversity and Ethnic Minority Psychology, 11*, 28–40.

Pieterse, A. I., Evans, S. A., Risner-Butner, A., Collins, N. M., & Mason, L. B. (2009). Multicultural competence and social justice training in counseling psychology and counselor education: A review and analysis of a sample of multicultural course syllabi. *Counseling Psychologist, 37*, 93–115.

Pinderhughes, E. E., Dodge, K. A., Bates, J. E., Pettit, G. S., & Zelli, A. (2000). Discipline responses influences of parents' socioeconomic status, ethnicity, beliefs about parenting, stress, and cognitive-emotional processes. *Journal of Family Psychology, 14*, 380–400.

Plous, S., & Williams, T. (1995). Racial stereotypes from the days of American slavery: A continuing legacy. *Journal of Applied social Psychology, 25*, 795–817.

Plummer, D. C. (2001). The quest for modern manhood: Masculine stereotypes, peer culture and the social significance of homophobia. *Journal of Adolescence, 24*, 15–23.

Pomales, J., Claiborn, C. D., & LaFromboise, T. D. (1986). Effects of Black students' racial identity on perceptions of White counselors varying in cultural sensitivity. *Journal of Counseling Psychology, 34,* 123–131.

Ponterotto, J. G. (1988). Racial consciousness development among white counselors' trainees: A stage model. *Journal of Multicultural Counseling and Development, 16,* 146–156.

Ponterotto, J. G., & Austin, R. (2005). Emerging approaches to training psychologists to be culturally competent. In R. T. Carter (Ed.), *Handbook of racial-cultural psychology and counseling.* Hoboken, NJ: Wiley.

Ponterotto, J. G., & Mallinckrodt, B. (2007). Introduction to the special issue on racial and ethnic identity in counseling psychology: Conceptual and methodological challenges and proposed solutions. *Journal of Counseling Psychology, 54,* 210–223.

Ponterotto, J. G., Utsey, S. O., & Pedersen, P. B. (2006). *Preventing prejudice: A guide for counselors, educators, and parents.* Thousand Oaks, CA: Sage.

Pop Culture Information Society (2002). Stars that have really aged. Retrieved from http://www.inthe00s.com/archive/inthe80s/1035844983.shtml

Pope-Davis, D. B., & Ottavi, T. M. (1994). Examining the association between self-reported multicultural counseling competencies and demographic and educational variables among counselors. *Journal of Counseling and Development, 72,* 651–654.

Porterfield, E. (1982). *African American-American intermarriages in the United States.* New York, NY: Haworth.

Poston, W. S. (1990). The biracial identity development model: A needed addition. *Journal of Counseling and Development, 69,* 152–155.

President's Commission on Mental Health. (1978). *Report from the President's Commission on Mental Health.* Washington, DC: U.S. Government Printing Office.

President's Initiative on Race. (1998). *One America in the twenty-first centry.* Washington, DC: U.S. Government Printing Office.

President's Initiative on Race. (1999). *Pathways to one America in the 21st century.* Washington, DC: U.S. Government Printing Office.

Priester, P. E., Jones, J. E., Jackson-Bailey, C. M., Jordan, E. X., Jana-Masri, A., & Metz, A. J. (2008). An analysis of content and instructional strategies in multicultural counseling courses. *Journal of Multicultural Counseling and Development, 36,* 29–39.

Purdie-Vaughns, V., Davis, P. G., Steele, C. M., & Ditlmann, R. (2008). Social identity contingencies: How diversity cues signal threat or safety for African Americans in mainstream institutions. *Journal of Personality and Social Psychology, 94,* 615–630.

Queener, J. E., & Martin, J. K. (2001). Providing culturally relevant mental health services: Collaboration between psychology and the African American church. *Journal of Black Psychology, 27,* 112–122.

Quiroga, S. S., & Flores-Ortiz, Y. G. (2000). Barriers to health care for abused Latina and Asian immigrant women. *Journal of Health Care for the Poor and Underserved, 11,* 33–44.

Rabasca, L. (1999). Guidelines for spinal cord injuries don't go far enough. *APA Monitor, 30,* 1–2.

Raffaelli, M., Crocket, L. J., & Shen, Y. (2005). Developmental stability and change in self regulation from childhood to adolescence. *Journal of Genetic Psychology, 166,* 54–75.

Ramirez, D. A. (1996). Multiracial identity in a color-conscious world. In M. P. P. Root (Ed.), *The multiracial experience: Racial borders as the new frontier* (pp. 49–62). Newbury Park, CA: Sage.

Ramsey, S., & Birk, J. (1983). Preparation of North Americans for interaction with Japanese: Considerations of language and communication style. In D. Landis & R. W. Brislin (Eds.), *Handbook of intercultural training: Volume III* (pp. 227–259). New York, NY: Pergamon Press.

Rankin, S., Weber, G., Blumenfeld, W., & Frazer, S. (2010). *2010 state of higher education for lesbian, gay, bisexual & transgender people*. Retrieved from http://www.campuspride.org/Campus%20Pride%202010%20LGBT%20Report%20Summary.pdf

Rash of Indian suicides. (1998, February 8). *Bellingham Herald*, p. A5.

Ratts, M. J. (2010). Multiculturalism and social justice: Two sides of the same coin. *Journal of Multicultural Counseling and Development*, *39*, 24–37.

Ratts, M. J., & Hutchins, A. M. (2009). ACA advocacy competencies: Social justice advocacy at the client/student level. *Journal of Counseling and Development*, *87*, 269–275.

Red Horse, J. G., Lewis, R., Feit, M., & Decker, J. (1981). Family structure and value orientation in American Indians. In R. H. Dana (Ed.), *Human services for cultural minorities*. Baltimore, MD: University Park Press.

Reeves, J. (2011). *Alabama immigration law cutting Latinos in schools*. Retrieved from http://www.sfgate.com/cgi-bin/article.cgi?f=/c/a/2011/09/30/MNVJ1LBST8.DTL

Reiman, J. (2007). *The rich get richer and the poor get prison*. New York, NY: Pearson.

Resch, J. A., Mireles, G., Benz, M. R., Grenwelge, C., Peterson, R., & Zhang, D. (2010). Giving parents a voice: A qualitative study of the challenges experienced by parents of children with disabilities. *Rehabilitation Psychology*, *55*, 139–150.

Reyhner, J. (2002). American Indian/Alaska Native education: An overview. Retrieved from http://jan.ucc.nau.edu/~jar/AIE/Ind_Ed.html

Rezentes, W. C., III, (2006). Hawaiian psychology. In L. T. Hoshmand (Ed.), *Culture, psychotherapy and counseling* (pp. 113–133). Thousand Oaks, CA: Sage.

Rhode, D. (2004). Access to justice. *Georgetown Journal of Legal Ethics*, *17* (3), 369–422.

Ribner, D. S., & Knei-Paz, C. (2002). Client's view of a successful helping relationship. *Social Work*, *47*, 379–387.

Rich, T. R. (2004). Judaism 101. Retrieved from http://www.jewfaq.org/

Richardson, S. M., & Paxton, S. J. (2010). An evaluation of a body image intervention based on risk factors for body dissatisfaction: A controlled study with adolescent girls. *International Journal of Eating Disorders*, *43*, 112–122.

Ridley, C. R. (1995). *Overcoming unintentional racism in counseling and therapy*. Thousand Oaks, CA: Sage.

Ridley, C. R. (2005). *Overcoming unintentional racism in counseling and therapy* (2nd ed.). Thousand Oaks, CA: Sage.

Ridley, C. R., & Mollen, D. (2011). Training in counseling psychology: An introduction to the major contribution. *Counseling Psychologist*, *39*, 793–799.

Ridley, C. R., Mollen, D., & Kelly, S. M. (2011). Beyond microskills: Toward a model of counseling competence. *Counseling Psychologist*, *39*, 825–864.

Rieckmann, T. R., Wadsworth, M. E., & Deyhle, D. (2004). Cultural identity, explanatory style, and depression in Navajo adolescents. *Cultural Diversity and Ethnic Minority Psychology*, *10*, 365–382.

Rienzo, B. A., Button, J. W., Sheu, J-J., & Li, Y. (2006). The politics of sexual orientation issues in American schools. *Journal of School Health*, *76*, 93–97.

Riessman, F. (1962). *The culturally deprived child*. New York, NY: Harper & Row.

Riggle, E. D. B., Whitman, J. S., Olson, A., Rostosky, S. S., & Strong, S. (2008). The positive aspects of being a lesbian or gay man. *Professional Psychology: Research and Practice*, *39*, 210–217.

Rivas-Vazquez, R. A., Blais, M. A., Rey, G. J., & Rivas-Vazquez, A. A. (2001). A brief reminder about documenting the psychological consultation. *Professional Psychology: Research and Practice, 32*, 194–199.

Rivera, D. P., Forquer, E. E., & Rangel, R. (2010). Microaggressions and the life experience of Latina/o Americans. In D. W. Sue (Ed.), *Microaggressions and marginality* (pp. 59–83). Hoboken, NJ: Wiley.

Ro, M. (2002). Moving forward: Addressing the health of Asian American and Pacific Islander women. *American Journal of Public Health, 92*, 516–519.

Robbins, M. S., & Szapocznik, J. (2000). *Brief strategic family therapy*. Retrieved from https://www.ncjrs.gov/pdffiles1/ojjdp/179285.pdf

Robinson, T. L., & Howard-Hamilton, M. F. (2000). *The convergence of race, ethnicity, and gender*. Columbus, OH: Merrill.

Robinson-Whelen, S., Hughes, R. B., Powers, L. E., Oschwald, M., Renker, P., & Curry, M. A. (2010). Efficacy of a computerized abuse and safety assessment intervention for women with disabilities: A randomized controlled study. *Rehabilitation Psychology, 55*, 97–107.

Rockymore, M. (2008). *A practice guide for working with African American families in the child welfare system: The role of the caseworker in identifying, developing and supporting strengths in African American families involved in child protection services*. (DHS-4702-ENG 8–06). St. Paul, MN: Minnesota Department of Human Services, Child Safety and Permanency Division.

Roettger, M. E., Swisher, R. R., Kuhl, D. C., & Chavez, J. (2011). Paternal incarceration and trajectories of marijuana and other illegal drug use from adolescence into young adulthood: Evidence from longitudinal panels of males and females in the United States. *Addiction, 106*, 121–132.

Rogers, C. R. (1957). The necessary and sufficient conditionings of therapeutic personality change. *Journal of Consulting Psychology, 21*, 95–103.

Rogers, C. R. (1961). *On becoming a person*. Boston, MA: Houghton Mifflin.

Rohmer, O., & Louvet, E. (2009). Describing persons with disability: Salience of disability, gender, and ethnicity. *Rehabilitation Psychology, 54*, 76–82.

Root, M. P. P. (1990). Resolving "other" status: Identity development of biracial individuals. In L. S. Brown & M. P. P. Root (Eds.), *Diversity and complexity in feminist therapy* (pp. 185–205). New York, NY: Haworth Press.

Root, M. P. P. (Ed.). (1992a). *Racially mixed people in America*. Thousand Oaks, CA: Sage.

Root, M. P. P. (1992b). Reconstructing the impact of trauma on personality. In M. Ballou & L. Brown (Eds.), *Theories of personality and psychopathology: Feminist reappraisal* (pp. 229–265). New York, NY: Guilford Press.

Root, M. P. P. (Ed.). (1996). *The multiracial experience*. Thousand Oaks, CA: Sage.

Root, M. P. P. (1998). Facilitating psychotherapy with Asian American clients. In D. R. Atkinson, G. Morten, & D. W. Sue (Eds.), *Counseling American minorities: A cross-cultural perspective* (pp. 214–234). Boston, MA: McGraw-Hill.

Root, M. P. P. (2001). Negotiating the margins. In J. G. Ponterotto, J. M. Casas, L. A. Suzuki, & C. M. Alexander (Eds.), *Handbook of multicultural counseling*. Thousand Oaks, CA: Sage.

Rosario, M., Schrimshaw, E. W., & Hunter, J. (2004). Ethnic/racial differences in the coming out process of lesbian, gay, and bisexual youths: A comparison of sexual identity development over time. *Cultural Diversity and Ethnic Minority Psychology, 10*, 215–228.

Rosario, M., Schrimshaw, E. W., Hunter, J., & Braun, L. (2006). Sexual identity development among lesbian, gay, and bisexual youths: Consistency and change over time. *Journal of Sex Research, 43*, 46–58.

Rose, T. (2008). *The hip-hop wars*. New York, NY: Basic Books.

Rosenbaum, P. (2010). *Amazing success fueled by act of discrimination*. Retrieved from http://www.cnn.com/2010/LIVING/07/26/ada.talbot/?hpt=Sbin

Rosenblatt, P. C., Karis, T. A., & Powell, R. D. (1995). *Multiracial couples*. Thousand Oaks, CA: Sage.

Rosenfarb, I. S., Bellack, A. S., & Aziz, N. (2006). Family interactions and the course of schizophrenia in African American and White patients. *Journal of Abnormal Psychology, 115*, 112–120.

Rosenfeld, B. (2004). *Assisted suicide and the right to die*. New York, NY: Guilford Press.

Rosenthal, R., & Jacobson, L. (1968). *Pygmalion in the classroom*. New York, NY: Holt, Rinehart & Winston.

Rosette, A. S., & Tost, L. P. (2010). Agentic women and communal leadership: How role prescriptions confer advantage to top women leaders. *Journal of Applied Psychology, 95*, 221–235.

Rosmarin, D. H., Pirutinsky, S., Pargament, K. I., & Krumrei, E. J. (2009). Are religious beliefs relevant to mental health among Jews? *Psychology of Religion and Spirituality, 1*, 180–190.

Rothbaum, F., Morelli, G., Pott, M., & Liu-Constant, Y. (2000). Immigrant-Chinese and Euro-American parents' physical closeness with young children: Themes of family relatedness. *Journal of Family Psychology, 14*, 334–348.

Rotter, J. (1966). Generalized expectancies for internal versus external control of reinforcement. *Psychological Monographs, 80*, 1–28.

Rotter, J. (1975). Some problems and misconceptions related to the construct of internal versus external control of reinforcement. *Journal of Consulting and Clinical Psychology, 43*, 56–67.

Rouse, B. A., Carter, J. H., & Rodriguez-Andrew, S. (1995). Race/ethnicity and other sociocultural influences on alcoholism treatment for women. *Recent Developments in Alcoholism, 12*, 343–367.

Rowatt, W. C., Franklin, L. M., & Cotton, M. (2005). Patterns and personality correlates of implicit and explicit attitudes toward Christians and Muslims. *Journal for the Scientific Study of Religion, 44*(1), 29–43.

Rowe, W. (2006). White racial identity: Science, faith and pseudoscience. *Journal of Multicultural Counseling and Development. 34*, 235–243.

Rowe, W., Bennett, S., & Atkinson, D. R. (1994). White racial identity models: A critique and alternative proposal. *Counseling Psychologist, 22*, 120–146.

Rudman, L. A. (1998). Self-promotion as a risk factor for women: The costs and benefits of counter-stereotypical impression management. *Journal of Personality and Social Psychology, 74*, 629–645.

Rudolph, K. D., Flynn, M., Abaied, J. L., Groot, A. G., & Thompson, R. D. (2009). Why is past depression the best predictor of future depression? Stress generation as a mechanism of depression continuity in girls. *Journal of Clinical Child and Adolescent Psychology, 38*, 473–485.

Ruiz, A. (1981). Cultural and historical perspectives in counseling Hispanics. In D. W. Sue (Ed.), *Counseling the culturally different: Theory & practice* (pp. 186–215). New York, NY: Wiley.

Ruiz, A. S. (1990). Ethnic identity: Crisis and resolution. *Journal of Multicultural Counseling and Development, 18*, 29–40.

Ruiz, P. (1995). Assessing, diagnosing and treating culturally diverse individuals: A Hispanic perspective. *Psychiatric Quarterly, 66*, 329–341.

Ryan, W. (1971). *Blaming the victim*. New York, NY: Pantheon.

Ryder, A. G., Yang, J., & Heini, S. (2002). Somatization vs. psychologization of emotional distress: A paradigmatic example for cultural psychopathology. In W. J. Lonner, D. L. Dinnel, S. A. Hayes, & D. N. Sattler (Eds.), *Online readings in psychology and culture* (unit 9, chap. 3). Center for Cross-Cultural Research, Western Washington University, Bellingham, Washington. Retrieved from http://www.wwu.edu/_culture

Rytina, N. F. (2004). *Refugee applicants and admissions to the United States*. Washington, DC: Department of Homeland Security.

Sabnani, H. B., Ponterotto, J. G., & Borodovsky, L. G. (1991). White racial identity development and cross-cultural counselor training. *Counselor Psychologist, 19*, 76–102.

Sage, G. P. (1997). Counseling American Indian adults. In C. C. Lee (Ed.), *Multicultural issues in counseling* (2nd ed., pp. 35–52). Alexandria, VA: American Counseling Association.

Sahagun, L. (2006, September 8). A post-9/11 identity shift. *Seattle Post-Intelligencer*, pp. A1, 22.

Salvatore, J., & Shelton, J. N. (2007). Cognitive costs of exposure to racial prejudice. *Psychological Science, 18*, 810–815.

Samad, L., Tate, A. R., Dezateaux, C., Peckham, C., Butler, N., & Bedford, H. (2006). Differences in risk factors for partial and no immunisation in the first year of life: Prospective cohort study. *British Medical Journal, 332*, 1312–1313.

Samuda, R. J. (1998). *Psychological testing of American minorities*. Thousand Oaks, CA: Sage.

Sanchez, D. T., Shih, M., & Garcia, J. A. (2009). Juggling multiple racial identities: Malleable racial identification and psychological well-being. *Cultural Diversity and Ethnic Minority Psychology, 15*, 243–254.

Sandhu, D. S. (1997). Psychocultural profiles of Asian and Pacific Islander Americans: Implications for counseling and psychotherapy. *Journal of Multicultural Counseling and Development, 25*, 7–22.

Sandhu, D. S., Leung, A. S., & Tang, M. (2003). Counseling approaches with Asian Americans and Pacific Islander Americans. In F. D. Harper & J. McFadden (Eds.), *Culture and counseling* (pp. 99–114). Boston, MA: Allyn & Bacon.

Santiago-Rivera, A., Arredondo, P., & Gallardo-Cooper, M. (2002). *Counseling Latinos and la familia: A guide for practitioners*. Thousand Oaks, CA: Sage.

Santiago-Rivera, A., Kanter, J., Benson, G., Derose, T., Illes, R., & Reyes, W. (2008). Behavioral activation as an alternative treatment approach for Latinos with depression. *Psychotherapy: Theory, Research, Practice, Training, 45*, 173–185.

Saulny, S. (2011a). *Black? White? Asian? More young Americans choose all of the above*. Retrieved from http://www.amren.com/mtnews/archives/2011/01/black_white_asi.php

Savin-Williams, R. C. (2001). *Mom, Dad. I'm gay*. Washington, DC: American Psychological Association.

Scharlin, C., & Villanueva, L. V. (1994). *Philip Vera Cruz: A personal history of Filipino immigrants and the farmworkers movement*. Seattle, WA: University of Washington Press.

Scheibe, S., & Carstensen, L. L. (2010). Emotional aging: Recent findings and future trends. *Journal of Gerontology: Psychological Sciences, 65*, 135–144

Scheetz, L. T., Martin, P. & Poon, L. W. (2012). Do Centenarians Have Higher Levels of Depression? Findings from the Georgia Centenarian Study. *Journal of the American Geriatrics Society, 60*, 238–242.

Schindler-Rainman, E. (1967). The poor and the PTA. *PTA Magazine, 61*(8), 4–5.

Schlosser, L. Z. (2006). Affirmative psychotherapy for American Jews. Psychotherapy: *Theory, Research, Practice, Training, 43*, 424–435.

Schlosser, L. Z. (2009a). *Microagressions in everyday life: The American Jewish experience.* Retrieved from http://bjpa.org/Publications/downloadPublication.cfm?PublicationID=5615

Schlosser, L. Z. (2009b). *A multidimensional model of American Jewish identity.* Retrieved from http://bjpa.org/Publications/downloadPublication.cfm?PublicationID=5620

Schnitzer, P. K. (1996). "They don't come in!" Stories told, lessons taught about poor families in therapy. *American Journal of Orthopsychiatry, 66,* 572–582.

Schofield, W. (1964). *Psychotherapy: The purchase of friendship.* Englewood Cliffs, NJ: Prentice Hall.

Schulz, A. J., Gravlee, C. C., Williams, D. R., Israel, B. A., Mentz, G., & Rowe, Z. (2006). Discrimination, symptoms of depression, and self-rated health among African American women in Detroit: Results from a longitudinal analysis. *American Journal of Public Health, 96,* 1265–1270.

Schwartz, A., Rodriguez, M. M., Santiago-Rivera, A. L., Arredondo, P., & Field, L. D. (2010). Cultural and linguistic competence: Welcome challenges from successful diversification. *Professional Psychology: Research and Practice, 41,* 210–220.

Schwartz, S., Hoyte, J., James, T., Conoscenti, L., Johnson, R., & Liebschutz, J. (2010). Challenges to engaging Black male victims of community violence in healthcare research: Lessons learned from two studies. *Psychological Trauma: Theory, Research, Practice, and Policy, 2,* 54–62.

Scott, D. (2011). Coming out: Intrapersonal loss in the acquisition of a stigmatized identity. Retrieved from www.yourtherapist.org/www/wp-content/uploads/coming_out.pdf

Scott, J. (2005). Life at the top in America isn't just better, it's longer. In Correspondents of the New York Times, *Class matters* (pp. 27–50). New York, NY: Times Books.

Searight, H. R., & Searight, B. K. (2009). Working with foreign language interpreters: Recommendations for psychological practice. *Professional Psychology: Research and Practice, 40,* 444–451.

Seaton, E. K., Caldwell, C. H., Sellers, R. M., & Jackson, J. S. (2011). An intersectional approach for understanding perceived discrimination and psychological well-being among African American and Caribbean Black youth. *Developmental Psychology, 46,* 1372–1379.

Seeley, K. M. (2004). Short-term intercultural psychotherapy: Ethnographic. *Social Work, 49,* 121–131.

Seem, S. R., & Johnson, E. (1998). Gender bias among counseling trainees: A study of case conceptualization. *Counselor Education and Supervision, 37,* 257–268.

Seligman, M. E. P. (1982). *Helplessness: On depression, development and death.* San Francisco, CA: Freeman.

Seligman, M. E. P., & Csikszentmihalyi, M. (2001). Reply to comments. *American Psychologist, 56,* 89–90.

Shade, B. J., & New, C. A. (1993). Cultural influences on learning: Teaching implications. In J. A. Banks & C. A. McGee Banks (Eds.), *Multicultural education* (pp. 317–331). Boston, MA: Allyn & Bacon.

Shallcross, L. (2011). Seeing potential, not disability. *Counseling Today, 54,* 28–35.

Shapiro, D. H. (1982). Overview: Clinical and physiological comparison of meditation with other self control strategies. *American Journal of Psychiatry, 139,* 267–274.

Shapiro, E. (2006). Civil rights and wrongs. Retrieved from http://www.myjewishlearning.com/history_community/Modern

Shelton, K., & Delgado-Romero, E. A. (2011). Sexual orientation microaggressions: The experience of lesbian, gay, bisexual, and queer clients in psychotherapy. *Journal of Counseling Psychology, 58*(2), 210–221.

Sherry, A., Adelman, A., Whilde, M. R., & Quick, D. (2010). Competing selves: Negotiating the intersection of spiritual and sexual identities. *Professional Psychology: Research and Practice, 41*, 112–119.

Shih, M., & Sanchez, D. T. (2005). Perspectives and research on the positive and negative implications of having multiple racial identities. *Psychological Bulletin, 131*, 569–591.

Shih, R. A., Miles, J. N., Tucker, J. S., Zhou, A. J. & D'Amico, E. J. (2010). Racial/ethnic differences in adolescent substance use: mediation by individual, family, and school factors. *Journal of the Study of Alcohol and Drugs, 71*, 640–651.

Shockley, W. (1972). Determination of human intelligence. *Journal of Criminal Law and Criminology, 7*, 530–543.

Shorter-Gooden, K., & Washington, N. C. (1996). Young, Black, and female: The challenge of weaving an identity. *Journal of Adolescence, 19*, 465–475.

Shostrom, E. L. (Producer). (1966). *Three approaches to psychotherapy*. [Motion picutre]. Santa Ana, CA: Psychological Films.

Shostrom, E. L. (Producer). (1977). *Three approaches to psychotherapy: II* [Motion picture]. Corona Del Mar, CA: Psychological and Educational Films.

Shukovsky, P. (2001, March 29). "Urban Indians" are going home. *Seattle Post-Intelligencer*, pp. A1, A13.

Shullman, S. L., Celeste, B. L., & Strickland, T. (2006). Extending the Parsons legacy: Applications of counseling psychology in pursuit of social justice. In R. L. Toporek, L. H. Gerstein, N. A. Fouad, G. Roysircar, & T. Israel (Eds.), *Handbook for social justice in counseling psychology* (pp. 499–513). Thousand Oaks, CA: Sage.

Silvertsen, B., Omvik, S., Pallesen, S., Bjorvatn, B., Havik, O. E., . . . Nordhus, I. H. (2006). Cognitive behavioral therapy vs Zopiclone for treatment of chronic primary insomnia in older adults. *JAMA, 295*, 2851–2858.

Sinclair, S. L. (2006). Object lessons: A theoretical and empirical study of objectified body consciousness in women. *Journal of Mental Health Counseling, 28*, 48–68.

Singelis, T. (1994). Nonverbal communication in intercultural interactions. In R. W. Brislin & T. Yoshida (Eds.), *Improving intercultural interactions* (pp. 268–294). Thousand Oaks, CA: Sage.

Singer, D. (2002). *American Jewish Yearbook*, 2002. New York, NY: American Jewish Committee.

Singh, A. A., & Chun, K. S. Y. (2010). From "margins to the center": Moving towards a resilience based model of supervision with queer people of color. *Training and Education in Professional Psychology, 4*, 36–46.

Slavich, G. M., Way, B. M., Eisenberger, N. I., & Taylor, S. E. (2010). Neural sensitivity to social rejection is associated with inflammatory responses to social stress. *Proceedings of the National Academy of Sciences, 107*, 14817–14822.

Sleek, S. (1998, July). Mental disabilities no barrier to smooth and efficient work. *Monitor*, p. 15.

Smith, D. P. (2005). The sweat lodge as psychotherapy. In R. Moodley & W. West (Eds.), *Integrating traditional healing practices into counseling and psychotherapy* (pp. 196–209). Thousand Oaks, CA: Sage.

Smith, E. J. (1981). Cultural and historical perspectives in counseling Blacks. In D. W. Sue (Ed.), *Counseling the culturally different: Theory and practice* (pp. 141–185). New York, NY: Wiley.

Smith, J. M. (2003). *A potent spell: Mother love and the power of fear.* Boston, MA: Houghton Mifflin.

Smith, L. (2005). Psychotherapy, classism, and the poor: Conspicuous by their absence. *American Psychologist, 60,* 687–696.

Smith, L. (2009). Enhancing training and practice in the context of poverty. *Training and Education in Professional Psychology, 3,* 84–93.

Smith, L. (2010). *Psychology, poverty, and the end of social exclusion.* New York, NY: Teachers College Press.

Smith, L., Chambers, D. A., & Bratini, L. (2009). When oppression is the pathogen: The participatory development of socially-just mental health practice. *American Journal of Orthopsychiatry, 79,* 159–168.

Smith, L., & Redington, R. (2010). Class dismissed: Making the case for the study of classist microaggressions. In D. W. Sue (Ed.), *Microaggressions and marginalized groups in society: Race, gender, sexual orientation, class and religious manifestations.* New York, NY: Wiley.

Smith, L., & Romero, L. (2010). Psychological interventions in the context of poverty: Participatory action research as practice. *American Journal of Orthopsychiatry, 80,* 12–25.

Smith, L. C., Shin, R. Q., & Officer, L. M. (2011). Moving counseling forward on LGB and transgender issues: Speaking queerly on discourses and microaggressions. *Counseling Psychologist,* first published on June 27, 2011. doi: 10.1177/0011000011403165

Smith, M. E. (1957). Progress in the use of English after twenty-two years by children of Chinese ancestry in Honolulu. *Journal of Genetic Psychology, 90,* 255–258.

Smith, M. E., & Kasdon, L. M. (1961). Progress in the use of English after twenty years by children of Filipino and Japanese ancestry in Hawaii. *Journal of Genetic Psychology, 99,* 129–138.

Smith, S. L., & Choueiti, M. (2011). *Gender inequality in cinematic content? A look at females on screen & behind the camera in top-grossing 2008 films.* Retrieved from http://annenberg.usc.edu/News%20and%20Events/News/~/media/PDFs/smith_rpt_apr11.ashx

Smith, T. B., Rodriguez, M. D., & Bernal, G. (2011). Culture. *Journal of Clinical Psychology: In Session, 67,* 166–175.

Smokowski, P. R., Rose, R. A., & Bacallao, M. (2010). Influence of risk factors and cultural assets on Latino adolescents' trajectories of self-esteem and internalizing symptoms. *Child Psychiatry and Human Development, 41,* 133–155.

Snowden, L. R., & Cheung, F. H. (1990). Use of inpatient mental health services by members of ethnic minority groups. *American Psychologist, 45,* 347–355.

So, J. K. (2005). Traditional and cultural healing among the Chinese. In R. Moodley & W. West (Eds.), *Integrating traditional healing practices into counseling and psychotherapy* (pp. 100–111). Thousand Oaks, CA: Sage.

Society of Clinical Psychology (2011). Psychological treatments. Retrieved from http://bpd.about.com/gi/o.htm?zi=1/XJ&zTi=1&sdn=bpd&cdn=health&tm=6&f=00&tt=8&bt=1&bts=1&zu=http%3A//www.div12.org/PsychologicalTreatments/treatments.html

Sodowsky, G. R., Kwan, K. K., & Pannu, R. (1995). Ethnic identity of Asians in the United States. In J. G. Ponterotto, J. M. Casas, L. A. Suzuki, & C. M. Alexander (Eds.), *Handbook of multicultural counseling* (pp. 123–154). Thousand Oaks, CA: Sage.

Solomon, A., & Wane, J. N. (2005). Indigenous healers and healing in a modern world. In R. Moodley & W. West (Eds.), *Integrating traditional healing practices into counseling and psychotherapy* (pp. 52–60). Thousand Oaks, CA: Sage.

Solórzano, D., Ceja, M., & Yosso, T. (2000). Critical race theory, racial microaggressions, and campus racial climate: The experiences of African American college students. *Journal of Negro Education, 69*(1/2), 60–73.

Southern Poverty Law Center. (2010). *Injustice on our plates: Immigrant women in the U.S. food industry.* Retrieved from http://www.splcenter.org/sites/default/files/downloads/publication/Injustice_on_Our_Plates.pdf

Spanierman, L. B., Poteat, V. V., Beer, A. M., & Armstrong, P. I. (2006). Psychosocial costs of racism to Whites: Exploring patterns through cluster analysis. *Journal of Counseling Psychology, 17,* 81–87.

Speight, S. L. (2007). Internalized racism: One more piece of the puzzle. *Counseling Psychologist, 35,* 126–134. doi: 10.1177/0011000006295119

Speight, S. L., Myers, L. J., Cox, C. I., & Highlen, P. S. (1991). A redefinition of multicultural counseling. *Journal of Counseling & Development, 70,* 29–36.

Spengler, P. M., Strohmer, D. C., Dixon, D. N., & Shivy, V. A. (1995). A scientist-practitioner model of psychological assessment: Implications for training, practice, and research. *Counseling Psychologist, 23,* 506–534.

Spradlin, I. K., & Parsons, R. D. (2008). *Diversity matters.* Belmont, CA: Thompson Wadsworth.

Srivastava, S. (2009). *Nobody's model minority.* Retrieved from http://www.theroot.com/Home/Nobody's Model Minority

St. John, P. D., & Montgomery, P. R. (2009). Marital status, partner satisfaction, and depressive symptoms in older men and women. *Canadian Journal of Psychiatry, 54,* 487–492.

Stader, S. R., & Hokanson, J. E. (1998). Psychosocial antecedents of depressive symptoms: An evaluation using daily experiences methodology. *Journal of Abnormal Psychology, 107,* 17–26.

Stanback, M. H., & Pearce, W. B. (1985). Talking to "the man": Some communication strategies used by members of "subordinate" social groups. In L. A. Samovar & R. E. Porter (Eds.), *Intercultural communication: A reader* (pp. 236–253). Belmont, CA: Wadsworth.

Steele, C. M. (1997). A threat in the air: How stereotypes shape intellectual identity and performance. *American Psychologist, 52,* 613–629.

Steele, C. M. (2003). Race and the schooling of Black Americans. In S. Plous (Ed.), *Understanding prejudice and discrimination* (pp. 98–107). New York, NY: McGraw-Hill.

Steele, C. M., Spencer, S. J., & Aronson, J. (2002). Contending with group image: The psychology of stereotype and social identity threat. In M. Zanna (Ed.), *Advances in experimental social psychology* (Vol. 23, pp. 379–440). New York, NY: Academic Press.

Steiger, H., Richardson, J., Schmitz, N., Israel, M., Bruce, M. I., & Gauvin, L. (2010). Trait-defined eating-disorder subtypes and history of childhood abuse. *International Journal of Eating Disorders, 43,* 428–432.

Steinfeldt, J. A., Foltz, B. D., Kaladow, J., Carlson, T. N., Pagano, L. A., Benton, E., & Steinfeldt, M. C. (2010). Racism in the electronic age: Role of online forums in expressing racial attitudes about American Indians. *Cultural Diversity and Ethnic Minority Psychology, 16,* 362–371.

Stevens, L. (2003, November 20). Improving screening of women for violence: Basic guidelines for physicians. *Medscape.*

Stewart, A. E. (2004). Can knowledge of client birth order bias clinical judgment? *Journal of Counseling and Development, 82,* 167–176.

Stiffman, A. R., Brown, E., Freedenthal, S., House, L., Ostmann, E., & Yu, M. S. (2007). American Indian youth: Personal, familial, and environmental strengths. *Journal of Child and Family Studies, 16*, 331–346.

Stone, A. (2006, February 20). Drives to ban gay adoption heat up in 16 states. Retrieved from http://www.comcast.net/news/usatoday/index.jsp?fn=/2006/02/20/241702.html

Stonequist, E. V. (1937). *The marginal man.* New York, NY: Scribner's.

Stracuzzi, T. I., Mohr, J. J., & Fuertes, J. N. (2011). Gay and bisexual male clients' perceptions of counseling: The role of perceived sexual orientation similarity and counselor universal-diverse orientation. *Journal of Counseling Psychology, 58*, 299–309.

Strawbridge, W. J., Cohen, R. D., Shema, S. J., & Kaplan, G. A. (1997). Frequent attendance at religious services and mortality over 28 years. *American Journal of Public Health, 87*, 957–961.

Street, A. E., Vogt, D., & Dutra, L. (2009). A new generation of women veterans: Stressors faced by women deployed to Iraq and Afghanistan. *Clinical Psychology Review, 29*, 685–694.

Stricker, G. (2010). *Psychotherapy integration.* Washington, DC: American Psychological Association.

Strong, S. R. (1969). Counseling: An interpersonal influence process. *Journal of Counseling Psychology, 15*, 215–224.

Substance Abuse and Mental Health Services Administration. (2010). New nationwide study shows a dramatic rise in the proportion of older Americans admitted for substance abuse treatment from 1992 to 2008. Retrieved from http://www.samhsa.gov/newsroom/advisories/1006153959.aspx

Sue, D. (1990). Culture in transition: Counseling Asian-American men. In D. Moore & F. Leafgren (Eds.), *Men in conflict* (pp. 53–165). Alexandria, VA: American Association for Counseling and Development.

Sue, D. (2005). Asian American masculinity and therapy: The concept of masculinity in Asian American males. In G. R. Brooks & G. E. Good (Eds.), *The new handbook of psychotherapy and counseling with men: A comprehensive guide to settings, problems, and treatment approaches* (pp. 357–368). Hoboken, NJ: Wiley.

Sue, D., & Sue, D. M. (2008). *Foundations of counseling and psychotherapy.* Hoboken, NJ: Wiley.

Sue, D., Sue, D. W., Sue, D. M., & Sue, S. (in press). *Understanding abnormal behavior.* Boston, MA: Cengage.

Sue, D. W. (1978). Eliminating cultural oppression in counseling. Toward a general theory. *Journal of Counseling Psychology, 25*, 419–428.

Sue, D. W. (1981). *Counseling the culturally different.* Hoboken, NJ: Wiley.

Sue, D. W. (1990). Culture specific techniques in counseling: A conceptual framework. *Professional Psychology, 21*, 424–433.

Sue, D. W. (1993). Confronting ourselves: The White and racial/ethnic minority researcher. *Counseling Psychologist, 21*, 244–249.

Sue, D. W. (1995a). Toward a theory of multicultural counseling and therapy. In J. Banks & C. Banks (Eds.), *Handbook of research on multicultural education*, pp. 647–659. New York, NY: Macmillan.

Sue, D. W. (1995b). Multicultural organizational development: Implications for the counseling profession. In J. G. Ponterotto, J. M. Casas, L. A. Suzuki, & C. M. Alexander (Eds.), *Handbook of multicultural counseling* (pp. 474–492). Thousand Oaks, CA: Sage.

Sue, D. W. (2001). Multidimensional facets of cultural competence. *Counseling Psychologist, 29*, 790–821.

Sue, D. W. (2003). *Overcoming our racism: The journey to liberation.* San Francisco, CA: Jossey-Bass.

Sue, D. W. (2004). Whiteness and ethnocentric monoculturalism: Making the invisible visible. *American Psychologist, 59,* 761–769.

Sue, D. W. (2005a). The continuing journey to multicultural competence. In R. K. Conyne & F. Bemak (Eds.). *Journeys to professional excellence: Lessons from leading counselor educators and practitioners* (pp. 73–84). Alexandria, VA: American Counseling Association.

Sue, D. W. (2005b). Racism and the conspiracy of silence. *Counseling Psychologist, 33,* 100–114.

Sue, D. W. (2010a). *Microaggressions in everyday life: Race, gender, and sexual orientation.* Hoboken, NJ: Wiley.

Sue, D. W. (2010b). *Microaggressions and marginality: Manifestations, dynamics, and impact.* Hoboken, NJ: Wiley.

Sue, D. W. (2011). The challenge of White dialectics: Making the "invisible" visible. *Counseling Psychologist, 39,* 414–423.

Sue, D. W., Arredondo, P., & McDavis, R. J. (1992). Multicultural competencies/standards: A call to the profession. *Journal of Counseling and Development, 70*(4), 477–486.

Sue, D. W., Bernier, J. B., Durran, M., Feinberg, L., Pedersen, P., Smith, E., & Vasquez-Nuttall, E. (1982). Position paper: Cross-cultural counseling competencies. *Counseling Psychologist, 10,* 45–52.

Sue, D. W., Bucceri, J., Lin, A. I., Nadal, K. L., & Torino, G. C. (2007). Racial microaggressions and the Asian American experience. *Cultural Diversity and Ethnic Minority Psychology, 13,* 72–81. doi: 10.1037/1948-1985.S.1.88

Sue, D. W., Bucceri, J., Lin, A. I., Nadal, K. L., & Torino, G. C. (2009). Racial microaggressions and the Asian American Experience. *Asian American Journal of Psychology, S(1),* 88–101. doi: 10.1037/1948-1985. S.1.88

Sue, D. W., Capodilupo, C. M., & Holder, A. M. B. (2008). Racial microaggressions in the life experience of Black Americans. *Professional Psychology: Research and Practice, 39,* 329–336. doi: 10.1037/0735-7028. 39.3.329

Sue, D. W., Capodilupo, C. M., Nadal, K. L., & Torino, G. C. (2008). Racial microaggressions and the power to define reality. *American Psychologist, 63,* 277–279.

Sue, D. W., Capodilupo, C. M., Torino, G. C., Bucceri, J. M., Holder, A. M. B., Nadal, K. L., & Esquilin, M. (2007). Racial microaggressions in everyday life: Implications for clinical practice. *American Psychologist, 62,* 271–286. doi: 10.1037/0003066X.62.4.271

Sue, D. W., Carter, R. T., Casas, J. M., Fouad, N. A., Ivey, A. E., Jensen, M., . . . Vazquez-Nutall, E. (1998). *Multicultural counseling competencies: Individual and organizational development.* Thousand Oaks, CA: Sage.

Sue, D. W., & Constantine, M. G. (2003). Optimal human functioning in people of color in the United States. In W. B. Walsh (Ed.), *Counseling psychology and optimal human functioning* (pp. 151–169). Mahwah, NJ: Erlbaum.

Sue, D. W., & Constantine, M. G. (2005). Effective multicultural consultation and organizational development. In M. G. Constantine & D. W. Sue (Eds.), *Strategies for building multicultural competencies in mental health and educational settings* (pp. 212–226). Hoboken, NJ: Wiley.

Sue, D. W., & Frank, A. C. (1973). A topological approach to the study of Chinese- and Japanese-American college males. *Journal of Social Issues, 29,* 129–148.

Sue, D. W., Ivey, A. E., & Pedersen, P. B. (1996). *A theory of multicultural counseling and therapy.* Pacific Grove, CA: Brooks/Cole.

Sue, D. W., Lin, A. I., Torino, G. C., Capodilupo, C. M., & Rivera, D. P. (2009). Racial microaggressions and difficult dialogues on race in the classroom. *Cultural Diversity and Ethnic Minority Psychology, 15*, 183–190.

Sue, D. W., Rivera, D. P., Capodilupo, C. M., Lin, A. I., & Torino, G. C. (2010). Racial dialogues and White trainee fears: Implications for education and training. *Cultural Diversity and Ethnic Minority Psychology, 16*, 206–214.

Sue, D. W., Rivera, D. P., Watkins, N. L., Kim, R. H., Kim, S., & Williams, C. D. (2011). Racial dialogues: Challenges faculty of color face in the classroom. *Cultural Diversity and Ethnic Minority Psychology, 17*(3), 331–340.

Sue, D. W., & Sue, D. (1990). *Counseling the culturally different: Theory and practice.* New York, NY: Wiley.

Sue, D. W., & Sue, D. (1999). *Counseling the culturally different: Theory and practice* (3rd ed.). New York, NY: Wiley.

Sue, D. W., & Torino, G. C. (2005). Racial cultural competence: Awareness, knowledge and skills. In R. T. Carter (Ed.), *Handbook of multicultural psychology and counseling* (pp. 3–18). Hoboken, NJ: Wiley.

Sue, D. W., Torino, G. C., Capodilupo, C. M., Rivera, D. P., & Lin, A. I. (2009). How White faculty perceive and react to classroom dialogues on race: Implications for education and training. *Counseling Psychologist, 37*, 1090–1115.

Sue, S. (1999). Science, ethnicity and bias: Where have we gone wrong? *American Psychologist, 54*, 1070–1077.

Sue, S., Allen, D., & Conaway, L. (1975). The responsiveness and equality of mental health care to Chicanos and Native Americans. *American Journal of Community Psychology, 45*, 111–118.

Sue, S., Fujino, D. C., Hu, L., Takeuchi, D. T., & Zane, N. W. S. (1991). Community mental health services for ethnic minority groups: A test of the cultural responsiveness hypothesis. *Journal of Consulting and Clinical Psychology, 59*, 533–540.

Sue, S., & McKinney, H. (1974). Delivery of community health services to black and white clients. *Journal of Consulting and Clinical Psychology, 42*, 794–801.

Sue, S., McKinney, H., Allen, D., & Hall, J. (1974). Delivery of community health services to Black & White clients. *Journal of Consulting Psychology, 42*, 794–801.

Sue, S., & Sue, D. W. (1971a). Chinese-American personality and mental health. *Amerasian Journal, 1*, 36–49.

Sue, S., & Sue, D. W. (1971b). Chinese-American personality and mental health. *Amerasian Journal, 2*, 39–49.

Sue, S., Zane, N., Levant, R. F., Silverstein, L. B., Brown, L. S., Olkin, R. (2006). How well do both evidence-based practices *and* treatment as usual satisfactorily address the various dimensions of diversity? In J. C. Norcross, L. F. Beutler, & R. F. Levant (Eds.), *Evidence-based practice in mental health: Debate and dialogue on the fundamental questions* (pp. 329–337). Washington, DC: American Psychological Association.

Sue, S., Zane, N., Nagayama-Hall, G. C., & Berger, L. K. (2009). The case for cultural competency in psychotherapeutic interventions. *Annual Review of Psychology, 60*, 525–548.

Suleiman, M. W. (1999). *The Arab immigrant experience.* Philadelphia, PA: Temple University Press.

Sullivan, K. R., & Mahalik, J. R. (2000). Increasing career self-efficacy for women: Evaluating a group intervention. *Journal of Counseling and Development, 78*, 54–62.

Sullivan, P. M. (2009). Violence exposure among children with disabilities. *Clinical Child and Family Psychological Review, 12*, 196–216.

Sundberg, N. D. (1981). Cross-cultural counseling and psychotherapy: A research overview. In A. J. Mansella & P. B. Pedersen (Eds.), *Crosscultural counseling and psychotherapy* (pp. 29–38). New York, NY: Pergamon Press.

Suro, R., & Escobar, G. (2006). 2006 National survey of Latinos: The immigration debate. Retrieved from http://pewhispanic.org/reports/report.php?

Susman, N. M., & Rosenfeld, H. M. (1982). Influence of culture, language and sex on conversation distance. *Journal of Personality and Social Psychology*, *42*, 66–74.

Sutton, C. T., & Broken Nose, M. A. (2005). American Indian families: An overview. In M. Mc-Goldrick, J. Giordano, & N. Garcia-Preto (Eds.), *Ethnicity and family therapy* (pp. 43–54). New York, NY: Guilford Press.

Suyemoto, K. L. (2004). Racial/ethnic identities and related attributed experiences of multiracial Japanese European Americans. *Journal of Multicultural Counseling and Development*, *32*, 206–221.

Suzuki, L. A., Kugler, J. F., & Aguiar, L. J. (2005). Assessment practices in racial-cultural psychology. In R. T. Carter (Ed.), *Handbook of racialcultural psychology and counseling* (pp. 297–315). Hoboken, NJ: Wiley.

Suzuki-Crumly, J., & Hyers, L. L. (2004). The relationship among ethnic identity, psychological well-being, and intergroup competence: An investigation of two biracial groups. *Cultural Diversity and Ethnic Minority Psychology*, *10*, 137–150.

Swim, J. K., & Cohen, L. L. (1997). Overt, covert, and subtle sexism. *Psychology of Women Quarterly*, *21*, 103–118.

Swim, J. K., Hyers, L. L., Cohen, L. L., & Ferguson, M. J. (2001). Everyday sexism: Evidence for its incidence, nature, and psychological impact from three daily diary studies. *Journal of Social Issues*, *57*, 31–53.

Swim, J. K., Mallett, R., & Stangor, C. (2004). Understanding subtle sexism: Detection and use of sexist language. *Sex Roles*, *51*, 117–128.

Swinomish Tribal Mental Health Project. (1991). *A gathering of wisdoms*. LaConner, WA: Swinomish Tribal Community.

Szapocznik, J., & Kurtines, W. M. (1993). Family psychology and cultural diversity: Opportunities for theory, research, and application. *American Psychologist*, *48*, 400–407.

Szapocznik, J., Santisteban, D., Kurtines, W. M., Hervis, O. E., & Spencer, F. (1982). Life enhancements counseling: A psychosocial model of services for Cuban elders. In E. E. Jones & S. J. Korchin (Eds.), *Minority mental health* (pp. 296–329). New York, NY: Praeger.

Szasz, T. S. (1970). The crime of commitment. In *Readings in clinical psychology today* (pp. 167–169). Del Mar, CA: CRM Books.

Szasz, T. S. (1971). *The myth of mental illness*. New York, NY: Hoeber.

Szasz, T. S. (1987). The case against suicide prevention. *American Psychologist*, *41*, 806–812.

Szasz, T. S. (1999). *Fatal freedom: The ethics and politics of suicide*. Westport, CT: Praeger.

Szymanski, D. M., Carr, E. R., & Moffitt, L. B. (2011). Sexual objectification of women: Clinical implications and training considerations. *Counseling Psychologist*, *39*, 107–126.

Szymanski, D. M., & Gupta, A. (2009). Examining the relationship between multiple oppressions and African American lesbian, gay, bisexual, and questioning persons' self-esteem and psychological distress. *Journal of Counseling Psychology*, *56*, 110–118.

Takaki, R. (1998). *Strangers from a different shore: A history of Asian Americans*. Boston, MA: Bay Back.

Talleyrand, R. M. (2010). Eating disorders in African American girls: Implications for counselors. *Journal of Counseling and Development*, *88*, 319–324.

Taylor, M. J. (2000). The influence of self-efficacy on alcohol use among American Indians. *Cultural Diversity and Ethnic Minority Psychology, 6,* 152–167.

Taylor, R. D. (2010). Risk and resilience in low-income African American families: moderating effects of kinship social support. *Cultural Diversity and Ethnic minority Psychology, 16,* 344–351.

Taylor, Z. E., Larsen-Rife, D., Conger, R. D., Widaman, K. F., & Cutrona, C. E. (2010). Life stress, maternal optimism, and adolescent competence in single mother, African American families. *Journal of Family Counseling, 24,* 468–477.

Terman, L. M. (1916). *The measurement of intelligence.* Boston, MA: Houghton Mifflin.

Terrio, H. P., Nelson, L. A., Betthauser, L. M., Harwood, J. E., & Brenner, L. A. (2011). Postdeployment traumatic brain injury screening questions: Sensitivity, specificity, and predictive values in returning solders. *Rehabilitation Psychology, 56,* 26–31.

Thomas, A., & Sillen, S. (1972). *Racism and psychiatry.* New York, NY: Brunner/Mazel.

Thomas, C. W. (1970). Different strokes for different folks. *Psychology Today, 4,* 49–53, 80.

Thomas, C. W. (1971). *Boys no more.* Beverly Hills, CA: Glencoe Press.

Thomas, M. B., & Dansby, P. G. (1985). Black clients: Family structures, therapeutic issues, and strengths. *Psychotherapy, 22,* 398–407.

Thomason, T. C. (2000). Issues in the treatment of native americans with alcohol problems. *Journal of Multicultural Counseling and Development, 28,* 243–252.

Thoresen, C. E. (1998). Spirituality, health and science: The coming revival? In S. R. Roemer, S. R. Kurpius, & C. Carmin (Eds.), *The emerging role of counseling psychology in health care* (pp. 409–431). New York, NY: Norton.

Thurlow, C. (2001). Naming the "outsider within": Homophobic perjoratives and the verbal abuse of lesbian, gay and bisexual high school pupils. *Journal of Adolescence, 24,* 25–38.

Thurston, I. B., & Phares, V. (2008). Mental health utilization among African American and Caucasian mothers and fathers. *Journal of Consulting and Clinical Psychology, 76,* 1058–1067.

Ting, J., & Hwang, W.-C. (2009). Cultural influences on help-seeking attitudes in Asian American students. *American Journal of Orthopsychiatry, 79,* 125–132.

Ting, L., & Panchanadeswaran, S. (2009). Barriers to help-seeking among immigrant African American women survivors of partner abuse: Listening to women's own voices. *Journal of Aggression, Maltreatment & Trauma, 18,* 817–838.

Tobin, J. J., & Friedman, J. (1983). Spirits, shamans, and nightmare death: Survivor stress in a Hmong refugee. *American Journal of Orthopsychiatry, 53,* 439–448.

Todd, N. R., & Abrams, E. M. (2011). White dialectics: A new framework for theory, research and practice with White students. *Counseling Psychologist, 39,* 353–395.

Toldson, I. A., Braithwaite, R. L., & Rentie, R. J. (2009). Promoting college aspirations among school-aged Black American males. *Diversity in Higher Education, 7,* 117–137.

Toporek, R. L., Gerstein, L. H., Fouad, N. A., Roysircar, G., & Israel, T. (2006). Future directions for counseling psychology: Enhancing leadership, vision, and action in social justice. In R. L. Toporek, L. H. Gerstein, N. A. Fouad, G. Roysircar, & T. Israel (Eds.), *Handbook for social justice in counseling psychology* (pp. 533–552). Thousand Oaks, CA: Sage.

Toporek, R. L., Lewis, J. A., & Crethar, H. C. (2009). Promoting systemic change through the ACA advocacy competencies. *Journal of Counseling and Development, 87,* 260–268.

Toporek, R. L., & McNally, C. J. (2006). Social justice training in counseling psychology: Needs and innovations. In R. L. Toporek, L. H. Gerstein, N. A. Fouad, G. Roysircar, &

T. Israel (Eds.), *Handbook for social justice in counseling psychology* (pp. 37–43). Thousand Oaks, CA: Sage.

Torres, M. M. (1998). *Understanding the multiracial experience through children's literature: A protocol.* (Unpublished doctoral dissertation). California School of Professional Psychology, Alameda.

Townes, D. L., Chavez-Korell, S., & Cunningham, N. J. (2009). Reexamining the relationships between racial identity, cultural mistrust, help-seeking attitudes, and preference for a Black counselor. *Journal of Counseling Psychology, 56*, 330–336.

Triandis, H. C. (2000). Cultural syndromes and subjective well-being. In E. Diener & E. M. Suh (Eds.), *Culture and subjective well-being* (pp. 13–36). London, United Kingdom: MIT Press.

Triffleman, E. G., & Pole, N. (2010). Future directions in studies of trauma among ethnoracial and sexual minority samples: Commentary. *Journal of Consulting and Clinical Psychology, 78*, 490–497.

Trimble, J. E. (2010). The virtues of cultural resonance, competence, and relational collaboration with Native American Indian communities: A synthesis of the counseling and psychotherapy literature. *Counseling Psychologist, 38*, 243–256.

Trimble, J. E., Fleming, C. M., Beauvais, F., & Jumper-Thurman, P. (1996). Essential cultural and social strategies for counseling Native American Indians. In P. B. Pedersen, J. G. Draguns, W. J. Lonner, & J. E. Trimble (Eds.), *Counseling across cultures* (4th ed., pp. 177–209). Thousand Oaks, CA: Sage.

Tsui, P., & Schultz, G. L. (1985). Failure of rapport: When psychotherapeutic engagement fails in the treatment of Asian clients. *American Journal of Orthopsychiatry, 55*, 561–569.

Tully, E. C., Iacono, W. G., & McGue, M. (2008). An adoption study of parental depression as an environmental liability for adolescent depression and childhood disruptive disorders. *American Journal of Psychiatry, 165*, 1148–1154.

Turner, C. S. V., Gonzalez, J. C., & Wood, J. L. (2008). Faculty of color in academe: What 20 years of literature tells us. *Journal of Diversity in Higher Education, 1*, 139–168.

Turner, R. J., Lloyd, D. A., & Taylor, J. (2006). Physical disability and mental health: An epidemiology of psychiatric and substance disorders. *Rehabilitation Psychology, 51*, 214–223.

U.S. Census Bureau (2005a). *The American Community—Pacific Islanders: 2004.* Retrieved from: http://www.census.gov/prod/2007pubs/acs-06.pdf

U.S. Census Bureau. (2005b). *65+ in the United States: 2005.* Washington, DC: U.S. Government Printing Office.

U.S. Census Bureau. (2005c). *Statistical abstract of the United States: 2004–2005. The national data book.* American Indian, Alaska Native tables. Retrieved from http://www.census.gov/statab/www/sa04aian.pdf

U.S. Census Bureau. (2006). *U.S. Hispanic population: 2006.* Retrieved from http://www.census.gov/population/socdemo/hispanic/cps2006/CPS_Powerpoint_2006.pdf

U.S. Census Bureau. (2010a). *20th anniversary of Americans with Disabilities Act: July 26.* Retrieved from http://www.census.gov/newsroom/releases/archives/facts_for_features_special_editions/cb10-ff13.html

U.S. Census Bureau. (2010b). *2009 American community survey.* Retrieved from http://www.census.gov/prod/2011pubs/acsbr10–01.pdf

U.S. Census Bureau. (2010c). *About poverty.* Retrieved from http://www.census.gov/hhes/www/poverty/about/overview/index.html

U.S. Census Bureau. (2010d). Aging boomers will increase dependency ratio. Retrieved from: http://www.census.gov/newsroom/releases/archives/aging_population/cb10–72.html

U.S. Census Bureau. (2010e). *America's families and living arrangements: 2010*. Retrieved from http://www.census.gov/population/www/socdemo/hh-fam/cps2010.html

U.S. Census Bureau. (2010f). *Facts for features: Asian American heritage month*. Retrieved from http://www.census.gov/newsroom/releases/archives/facts_for_features_special_editions/cb10-ff07.html

U.S. Census Bureau. (2010g). *Income, poverty, and health insurance coverage in the United States: 2009, current population reports, consumer income*. Retrieved from http://www.census.gov/prod/2010pubs/p60–238.pdf

U.S. Census Bureau. (2010h). *United States Profile*. Retrieved from http://www.census.gov/

U.S. Census Bureau. (2011a). *Age and sex composition: 2010*. Retrieved from http://www.census.gov/prod/cen2010/briefs/c2010br-03.pdf

U.S. Census Bureau. (2011b). *Women's history month: March 2011*. U.S. Department of Commerce, Washington, DC: U.S. Government Printing Office.

U.S. Census Bureau. (2011c). *Current population survey, annual social and economic supplement, 2010*. Retrieved from http://www.census.gov/population/www.sodemo/race/ppl-aa10.html

U.S. Census Bureau. (2011d). Hispanic Heritage Month. Retrieved from: http://www.census.gov/newsroom/releases/archives/facts_for_features_special_editions/cb11-ff18.html

U.S. Census Bureau. (2011e). *Income, poverty, and health insurance coverage in the United States: 2010*. Retrieved from http://www.census.gov/prod/2011pubs/p60–239.pdf

U.S. Census Bureau. (2011f). *The 2011 statistical abstract*. Retrieved from http://www.census.gov/compendia/statab/cats/education/educational_attainment.html

U.S. Department of Commerce. (2011). *Women in America*. U.S. Department of Commerce, Washington, DC: U.S. Government Printing Office.

U.S. Department of Health and Human Services. (1998). *The national elder abuse incidence study*. Washington, DC: Government Printing Office.

U. S. Department of Health and Human Services. (2001). *Mental health: Culture, race, and ethnicity—a supplement to mental health: A report of the Surgeon General*. Rockville, MD: U.S. Department of Health and Human Services, Substance Abuse and Mental Health Service Administration, Center for Mental Health Services.

U.S. Department of Health and Human Services. (2007). Obesity and American Indians/Alaska Natives. Retrieved from http://aspe.hhs.gov/hsp/07/AI-AN-obesity/report.pdf

U.S. Department of Labor. (2012). Employment status of the civilian population by race, sex, and age. Retrieved from http://www.bls.gov/news.release/empsit.t02.htm

U.S. Department of State. (2002). Muslim life in America. Retrieved from http://usinfo.state.gov/products/pubs/muslimlife

U.S. Public Health Service. (2001). *A report of the Surgeon General on minority mental health*. Rockville, MD: U.S. Department of Health and Human Services.

Uba, L. (1994). *Asian Americans: Personality patterns, identity, and mental health*. New York, NY: Guilford Press.

United Cerebral Palsy. (2001). *Etiquette tips for people with physical disabilities*. Portland, OR: Author.

Urdaneta, M. L., Saldana, D. H., & Winkler, A. (1995). Mexican-American perceptions of severe mental illness. *Human Organization, 54*, 70–77.

Utsey, S. O., Gernat, C. A., & Hammar, L. (2005). Examining white counselor trainees' reactions to racial issues in counseling and supervision dyads. *Counseling Psychologist. 33*, 449–478.

Utsey, S. O., Giesbrecht, N., Hook, J., & Stanard, P. M. (2008). Cultural, sociofamilial, and psychological resources that inhibit psychological distress in African Americans exposed to stressful life events and race related stress. *Journal of Counseling Psychology, 55*, 49–62.

Utsey, S. O., Grange, C., & Allyne, R. (2006). Guidelines for evaluating the racial and cultural environment of graduate training programs in professional psychology. In M. G. Constantine & D. W. Sue (Eds.), *Addressing racism* (pp. 213–232). Hoboken, NJ: Wiley.

Utsey, S. O., Walker, R. L., & Kwate, N. O. A. (2005). Conducting quantitative research in a cultural context. In M. G. Constantine & D. W. Sue (Eds.), *Strategies for building multicultural competence in mental health and educational settings* (pp. 247–268). Hoboken, NJ: Wiley.

Vacc, N. A., & Clifford, K. (1995). Individuals with a physical disability. In N. A. Vacc, S. B. DeVaney, & J. Wittmer (Eds.), *Experiencing and counseling multicultural and diverse populations* (3rd ed., pp. 251–272). Bristol, PA: Accelerated Development.

Vakalahi, H. F. O. (2009). Pacific Islander American students: Caught between a rock and a hard place? *Children and Youth Services Review, 31*, 1258–1263.

Vandiver, B. J. (2001). Psychological nigrescence revisited: Introduction and overview. *Journal of Multicultural Counseling and Development, 29*, 165–173.

Vandiver, B. J., Fhagen-Smith, P. E., Cokley, K. O., Cross, W. E., & Worrell, F. C. (2001). Cross's nigrescence model: From theory to scale to theory. *Journal of Multicultural Counseling and Development, 29*, 174–200.

Vasquez, J. A. (1997). Distinctive traits of Hispanic students. *Prevention Researcher, 5*, 1–4.

Vazquez, L. A., & Garcia-Vazquez, E. (2003). Teaching multicultural competence in the counseling curriculum. In D. B. Pope-Davis, H. L. K. Coleman, W. M. Liu, & R. L. Toporek (Eds.), *Handbook of multicultural competencies in counseling and psychology* (pp. 546–561). Thousand Oaks, CA: Sage.

Vedantam, S. (2005, June 6). Patients' diversity is often discounted. *Washington Post*, p. A01.

Vega, W. A., Rodriguez, M. A., & Ang, A. (2010). Addressing stigma of depression in Latino primary care patients. *General Hospital Psychiatry, 32*, 182–191.

Velasquez, R. J., Gonzales, M., Butcher, J. N., Castillo-Canez, I., Apodaca, J. X., & Chavira, D. (1997). Use of the MMPI-2 with Chicanos: Strategies for counselors. *Journal of Multicultural Counseling and Development, 25*, 107–120.

Vera, E. M., Buhin, L., & Shin, R. Q. (2006). The pursuit of social justice and the elimination of racism. In M. G. Constantine & D. W. Sue (Eds.), *Addressing racism* (pp. 271–287). Hoboken, NJ: Wiley.

Vera, E. M., & Speight, S. L. (2003). Multicultural competence, social justice, and counseling psychology: Expanding our roles. *Counseling Psychologist, 31*, 253–272.

Verboom, C. E., Sentse, M., Sijtsema, J. J., Nolen, W. A., Ormel, J. & Penninx, B. W. (2011). Explaining heterogeneity in disability with major depressive disorder: Effects of personal and environmental characteristics. *Journal of Affective Disorders, 132*, 71–81.

Viglione, J., Hannon, L., & DeFina, R. (2011). The impact of light skin on prison time for Black female offenders. *Social Science Journal, 48*, 250–258.

Vigod, S. N., & Stewart, D. (2009). Emergent research in the cause of mental illness in women across the lifespan. *Current Opinion in Psychiatry, 22*, 396–400.

Villalba, J. A. (2009). Addressing immigrant and refugee issues in multicultural counselor education. *Journal of Professional Counseling: Practice, Theory, and Research, 37*, 1–10.

Vinkenburg, C. J., van Engen, M. L., Eagly, A. H., & Johannesen-Schmidt, M. C. (2011). An exploration of stereotypical beliefs about leadership styles: Is transformational leadership a route to women's promotion? *Leadership Quarterly, 22*, 10–21.

Vinson, T., & Neimeyer, G. J. (2000). The relationship between racial identity development and multicultural counseling competence. *Journal of Multicultural Counseling and Development, 28*, 177–192.

Vinson, T., & Neimeyer, G. J. (2003). The relationship between racial identity development and multicultural counseling competence: A second look. *Journal of Multicultural Counseling and Development, 31*, 262–277.

Vontress, C. E. (1971). Racial differences: Impediments to rapport. *Journal of Counseling Psychology, 18*, 7–13.

Vontress, C. E., & Epp, L. R. (1997). Historical hostility in the African American client: Implications for counseling. *Journal of Multicultural Counseling and Development, 25*, 170–184.

Vontress, C. E., & Jackson, M. L. (2004). Reactions to the multicultural counseling competencies debate. *Journal of Mental Health Counseling, 26*, 74–80.

Wagner, J., & Abbott, G. (2007). Depression and depression care in diabetes: Relationship to perceived discrimination in African Americans. *Diabetes Care, 30*, 364–366.

Waldron-Perrine, B., Rapport, L. J., Hanks, R. A., Lumley, M., Meachen, S.-J., & Hubbarth, P. (2011). Religion and spirituality in rehabilitation outcomes among individuals with traumatic brain injury. *Rehabilitation Psychology, 56*, 107–116.

Wallhagen, M. I., Pettengill, E., & Whiteside, M. (2006). Sensory impairment in older adults, Part 1: Hearing loss. *American Journal of Nursing, 106*, 40–48.

Walls, N. E. (2008). Toward a multidimensional understanding of heterosexism: The changing nature of prejudice. *Journal of Homosexuality, 55*(1), 1–51.

Walsh, R., & Shapiro, S. L. (2006). The meeting of meditative disciplines and Western psychology. *American Psychologist, 61*, 227–239.

Walsh, R., & Vaughan, F. (Eds.). (1993). *Paths beyond ego. The transpersonal vision* (pp. 387–398). Los Angeles, CA: J. P. Tarcher.

Wampold, B. E. (2001). *The great psychotherapy debate: Models, methods, and findings.* Mahwah, NJ: Erlbaum.

Wang, J., Leu, J., & Shoda, Y. (2011). When the seemingly innocuous "stings": Racial microaggressions and their emotional consequences. *Social Psychology and Psychological Bulletin*, 1–13.

Wang, K., Barron, L. G., & Hebl, M. R. (2010). Making those who cannot see look best: Effects of visual resume formatting on ratings of job applicants with blindness. *Rehabilitation Psychology, 55*, 68–73.

Wang, S., & Kim, B. S. K. (2010). Therapist multicultural competence, Asian American participants' cultural values, and counseling process. *Journal of Counseling Psychology, 57*, 394–401.

Wang, Y., Davidson, M. M., Yakushko, O. F., Savoy, H. B., Tan, J. A., & Bleier, J. K. (2003). The scale of ethnocutural empathy: Development, validation, and reliability. *Journal of counseling Psychology, 50*, 221–234.

Want, V., Parham, T. A., Baker, R. C. & Sherman, M. (2004). African American students' ratings of Caucasian and African American counselors varying in racial consciousness. *Cultural Diversity and Ethnic Minority Psychology, 10*, 123–136.

Ward, E. C. (2005). Keeping it real: A grounded theory study of African American clients engaging in counseling at a community mental health agency. *Journal of Counseling Psychology*, 52(4), 471–481.

Warren, A. K., & Constantine, M. G. (2007). Social justice issues. In M. G. Constantine (Ed.), *Clinical practice with people of color* (pp. 231–242). New York, NY: Teachers College Press.

Washington, A. T. (2005, September 6). Timidity no answer to racism in Katrina debacle. *Washington Times*, p. B2.

Washington, J. (2005). Katrina riles, rallies black America. *Bellingham Herald*, p. A3.

Watkins, N. L., Labarrie, T. L., & Appio, L. M. (2010). Black undergraduates' experiences with perceived racial microaggressions in predominately White colleges and universities. In D. W. Sue (Ed.), *Microaggressions and marginality* (pp. 25–51). Hoboken, NJ: Wiley.

Watkins, T. (2010). Aging issues can be tougher on gays. Retrieved from http://articles.cnn.com/2010-03-17/living/gays.aging.problems_1_couples-heterosexual-peers-social-security?_s=PM:LIVING

Way, N., Becker, B. E., & Greene, M. L. (2006). Friendships among Black, Latino, and Asian American adolescents in an urban context. In L. Balter & C. S. Tamis-LeMonda (Eds.), *Child psychology: A handbook of contemporary issues* (2nd ed., pp. 415–443). New York, NY: Psychology Press.

Weber, S. N. (1985). The need to be: The sociocultural significance of Black language. In L. A. Samovar & R. E. Porter (Eds.), *Intercultural communication: A reader* (pp. 244–253). Belmont, CA: Wadsworth.

Webster, S. C. (2011). Shock Poll: 46% of Mississippi Republicans think interracial marriage should be illegal. Retrieved from http://www.rawstory.com/rs/2011/04/07/shock-poll-46-of-mississippi-republicans-think-interracial-marriage-should-be-illegal

Wehrly, B., Kenney, K. R., & Kenney, M. E. (1999). *Counseling multiracial families*. Thousand Oaks, CA: Sage.

Weinberger, J. (2002). Short paper, large impact: Rosenzweig's influence on the common factor movement. *Journal of Psychotherapy Integration*, 12, 67–76

Weine, S., Feetham, S., Kulauzovic, Y., Knafl, K., Besic, S., Klebic, A., . . . Pavkovic, I. (2006). A family beliefs framework for socially and culturally specific preventive interventions with refugee youth and families. *American Journal of Orthopsychiatry*, 76, 1–9.

Weinrach, S. G. (1987). Ellis and Gloria: Positive or negative model? *Psychotherapy*, 23, 642–647.

Weinrach, S. G. (2002). The counseling profession's relationship to Jews and the issues that concern them: More than a case of selective awareness. *Journal of Counseling and Development*, 80, 300–314.

Weinrach, S. G., & Thomas, K. R. (2004). The AMCD multicultural counseling competencies: A critically-flawed initiative. *Journal of Mental Health Counseling*, 26, 81–93.

Weisman, A., Feldman, G., Gruman, C., Rosenberg, R., Chamorro, R., & Belozersky, I. (2005). Improving mental health services for Latino and Asian immigrant elders. *Professional Psychology: Research and Practice*, 36, 642–648.

Weiss, I. (2005). Interest in working with the elderly: A cross-national study of graduating social work students. *Journal of Social Work Education*, 41, 379–391.

Werner-Wilson, R. J., Price, S. J., Zimmerman, T. S., & Murphy, M. J. (1997). Client gender as a process variable in marriage and family therapy: Are women clients interrupted more than men clients? *Journal of Family Psychology*, 11, 373–377.

Werth, J. L., Jr., & Crow, L. (2009). End-of-life care: An overview for professional counselors. *Journal of Counseling and Development, 87*, 194–201.

West, M. (1987). *The psychology of meditation*. Oxford, United Kingdom: Clarendon Press.

Wester, S. R., McDonough, T. A., White, M., Vogel, D. L., & Taylor, L. (2010). Using gender role conflict theory in counseling male-to-female transgender individuals. *Journal of Counseling and Development, 88*, 214–219.

West-Olatunji, C. A., & Conwill, W. (2011). *Counseling African Americans*. Belmont, CA: Cengage.

Whaley, A. L. (2001). Cultural mistrust and mental health services for African Americans: A review and meta-analysis. *Counseling Psychologist, 29*, 513–521.

Wherly, B. (1995). *Pathways to multicultural counseling competence*. Pacific Grove, CA: Brooks/Cole.

White, R. W. (1963). Ego and reality in psychoanalytic theory: A proposal regarding independent ego energies. *Psychological Issues, 3*, 1–210.

Whitesell, N. R., Mitchell, C. M., Spicer, P., & The Voices of Indian Teens Project Team. (2009). A longitudinal study of self-esteem, cultural identity, and academic success among American Indian adolescents. *Cultural Diversity and Ethnic Minority Psychology, 15*, 38–50.

Wight, V. R., Chau, M., & Aratani, Y. (2011). Who are America's poor children? Retrieved from http://www.nccp.org/publications/pub_1001.html

Wight, V. R., Thampi, K., & Chau, M. (2011). Poor children by parents' nativity. National Center for Children in Poverty. Retrieved from http://www.nccp.org/publications/pdf/text_1006.pdf

Williams, K., Kemper, S., & Hummert, M. L. (2005). Enhancing communication with older adults: Overcoming elderspeak. *Journal of Psychosocial Nursing and Mental Health Services, 43*, 12–16.

Willie, C. V. (1981). *A new look at Black families*. Bayside, NY: General Hall.

Wilper, A. P., Woolhandler, S., Lasser, K. E., McCormick, D., Bor, D. H., & Himmelstein, D. U. (2009). Health insurance and mortality in U.S. adults. *American Journal of Public Health, 9*, 1–7.

Winerman, L. (2006). Reaching out to Muslim and Arab Americans. *APA Monitor, 37*, 54.

Wingert, P., & Kantrowitz, B. (2000, March 20). Two kids and two moms. *Newsweek*, pp. 50–52.

Winn, N. N., & Priest, R. (1993). Counseling biracial children: A forgotten component of multicultural counseling. *Family Therapy, 20*, 29–36.

Winter, S. (1977). Rooting out racism. *Issues in Radical Therapy, 17*, 24–30.

Wolfgang, A. (1985). The function and importance of nonverbal behavior in intercultural counseling. In P. B. Pedersen (Ed.), *Handbook of cross-cultural counseling and therapy* (pp. 99–105). Westport, CT: Greenwood Press.

Wong, Y. J., Tran, K. K., Kim, S.-H., Kerne, V. V. H., & Calfa, N. A. (2010). Asian Americans' lay beliefs about depression and professional help seeking. *Journal of Clinical Psychology, 66*, 317–332.

Wood, D. B. (2006, May 25). Rising black-Latino clash on jobs. *Christian Science Monitor*. Retrieved from http://www.csmonitor.com/2006/0525/p01s03-ussc.html

Wood, P. B., & Clay, W. C. (1996). Perceived structural barriers and academic performance among American Indian high school students. *Youth and Society, 28*, 40–46.

Wood, P. S., & Mallinckrodt, B. (1990). Culturally sensitive assertiveness training for ethnic minority clients. *Professional Psychology: Research & Practice, 21*, 5–11.

Woods, N. F., Mitchell, E. S., Percival, D. B., & Smith-DiJulio, K. (2009). Is the menopausal transition stressful? Observations of perceived stress from the Seattle Midlife Women's Health Study. *Menopause, 16*, 90–97.

Worrell, F. C., Cross, W. E., & Vandiver, B. J. (2001). Nigrescence theory: Current status and challenges for the future. *Journal of Multicultural Counseling and Development, 29*, 201–211.

Wren, C. S. (1998, June 5). Many women 60 and older abuse alcohol and prescribed drugs, study says. *New York Times*, p. 12.

Wrenn, C. G. (1962). The culturally-encapsulated counselor. *Harvard Educational Review, 32*, 444–449.

Wrenn, C. G. (1985). Afterward: The culturally encapsulated counselor revisited. In P. B. Pedersen (Ed.), *Handbook of cross-cultural counseling and therapy* (pp. 323–329). Westport, CT: Greenwood Press.

Wright, K. (2001). To be poor and transgender. *Progressive, 65*, 21–24.

Yabusaki, A. S. (2010). Reflections on the importance of place. *Training and Education in Professional Psychology, 4*, 3–6.

Yakushko, O. (2010). Clinical work with limited English proficiency clients: A phenomenological exploration. *Professional Psychology: Research and Practice, 41*, 449–455.

Yancey, G. (2002). Who interracially dates: An examination of the characteristics of those who have interracially dated. *Journal of Comparative Family Studies, 33*(2), 179–190.

Yao, T. Y., Sue, D., & Hayden, D. (1992). Counseling style preference of international students. *Journal of Counseling Psychology, 39*, 100–104.

Yeater, E. A., Treat, T. A., Viken, R. J., & McFall, R. M. (2010). Cognitive processes underlying women's risk judgments: Associations with sexual victimization history and rape myth acceptance. *Journal of Counseling and Clinical Psychology, 78*, 375–386.

Yedidia, T. (2005). Immigrant therapists' unresolved identity problems and countertransference. *Clinical Social Work Journal, 33*, 159–171.

Yee, B. W. K., Castro, F. G., Hammond, W. R., John, R., Wyatt, G. E., & Yung, B. R. (1995). Risk-taking and abusive behavior among ethnic minorities. *Health Psychology, 14*, 622–631.

Yeh, C. J., Kim, A. B., Pituc, S. T., & Atkins, M. (2008). Poverty, loss, and resilience: The story of Chinese immigrant youth. *Journal of Counseling Psychology, 55*, 34–48.

Yen, H. (2011). Census: Many gay couples say they're married—even if they technically aren't. Retrieved from http://www.msnbc.msn.com/id/44690992/ns/us_news-life/#

Yeung, A., Chang, D., Gresham, R. L., Nierenberg, A. A., & Fava, M. (2004). Illness beliefs of depressed Chinese American patients in primary care. *Journal of Nervous and Mental Disease, 192*, 324–327.

Yin, X.-H. (2000, May 7). Asian Americans: The two sides of America's "model minority." *Los Angeles Times*, p. M1.

Ying, Y.-W., Coombs, M., & Lee, P. A. (1999). Family intergenerational relationship of Asian American adolescents. *Cultural Diversity and Ethnic Minority Psychology, 5*, 350–363.

Yoon, E. (2011). Measuring ethnic identity in the ethnic identity scale and the multigroup ethnic identity measure-revised. *Cultural Diversity and Ethnic Minority Psychology, 17*, 144–155.

Yoon, I. (1997). *On my own: Korean business and race relations in America*. Chicago, IL: University of Chicago Press.

Young, G., & Davis-Russell, E. (2002). The vicissitudes of cultural competence: Dealing with difficult classroom dialogue. In E. Davis-Russell (Ed.), *The California School of*

Professional Psychology handbook of multicultural education, research, intervention, and training (pp. 37–53). San Francisco, CA: Jossey-Bass.

Younis, M. (2009). Muslim Americans exemplify diversity, potential. Retrieved from http://www.gallup.com/poll/116260/Muslim-Americans-Exemplify-Diversity-Potential.aspx

Zahnd, E., Aydin, M., Grant, D., & Holtby, S. (2011). The link between intimate partner violence, substance abuse and mental health in California. *UCLA Center for Health Policy Research* (PB2011–10), 1–8.

Zaki, M. (2011). Life for Arab and Muslim Americans a decade after 9/11. Retrieved from http://www.kuow.org/program.php?id=24539

Zanipatin, J., Welch, S. S., Yi, J., & Bardina, P. (2005). Immigrant women and domestic violence. In K. H. Barrett & W. H. George (Eds.), *Race, culture, psychology, and law* (pp. 375–389). Thousand Oaks, CA: Sage.

Zeiss, A. M. (2001). *Aging and human sexuality resource guide*. Washington, DC: American Psychological Association.

Zeranski, L., & Halgin, R. P. (2011). Ethical issues in elder abuse reporting: A professional psychologist's guide. *Professional Psychology: Research and Practice, 42*, 294–300.

Zetzer, H. A. (2011). White out: Privilege and its problems. In S. H. Anderson & V. A. Middleton (Eds.), *Explorations in diversity: Examining privilege and oppression in a multicultural society* (pp. 11–24). Belmont, CA: Cengage.

Zhang, W. (1994). American counseling in the mind of a Chinese counselor. *Journal of Multicultural Counseling and Development, 22*, 79–85.

Zilboorg, G., & Henry, G. W. (1941). *A history of medical psychology*. New York, NY: Norton.

Zlotnick, C., Capezza, N. M., & Parker, D. (2011). An interpersonally based intervention for low income pregnant women with intimate partner violence: a pilot study. *Archives of Women's Mental Health, 14*, 55–65.

Zogby, J. J. (2001a, March). National survey: American teen-agers and stereotyping. Retrieved from http://www.niaf.org/research/report_zogby.asp

Zogby, J. J. (2001b, October). Arab American attitudes and the September 11 attacks. Retrieved from http://www.aaiusa.org/PDF/attitudes.pdf

Zollman, J. W. (2006). Three waves of immigration. Retrieved from http://www.myjewish-learning.com/history_community/Modern

Zucker, K. J., & Cohen-Ketteris, P. T. (2008). Gender identity disorder in children and adolescents. In D. Rowland & L. Incrocci (Eds.), *Handbook of sexual and gender identity disorders* (pp. 376–422). Hoboken, NJ: Wiley.

Zuniga, M. E. (1997). Counseling Mexican American seniors: An overview. *Journal of Multicultural Counseling and Development, 25*, 142–155.

Zuroff, D. C., & Blatt, S. J. (2006). The therapeutic relationship in the brief treatment of depression: Contributions to clinical improvement and enhanced adaptive capacities. *Journal of Consulting and Clinical Psychology, 74*, 130–140.

Zuroff, D. C., Kelly, A. C., & Leybman, M. J. (2010). Between-therapist and within-therapist differences in the quality of the therapeutic relationship: effects on maladjustment and self-critical perfectionism. *Journal of Clinical Psychology, 66*, 681–697.

Author Index

Subject Index

621